RACE AND RACISM
IN THE UNITED STATES

RACE AND RACISM IN THE UNITED STATES

An Encyclopedia of the American Mosaic

VOLUME 3: N–T

Charles A. Gallagher and Cameron D. Lippard,

Editors

 GREENWOOD

AN IMPRINT OF ABC-CLIO, LLC
Santa Barbara, California • Denver, Colorado • Oxford, England

Library of Congress Cataloging-in-Publication Data

Race and racism in the United States : an encyclopedia of the American mosaic / Charles A. Gallagher and Cameron D. Lippard, editors.
    pages   cm
   ISBN 978-1-4408-0345-1 (hardback) — ISBN 978-1-4408-0346-8 (ebook)   1. United States—Race relations—Encyclopedias.
2. United States—Ethnic relations—Encyclopedias.   3. Racism—United States—Encyclopedias.   I. Gallagher, Charles A.
(Charles Andrew), 1962– editor.   II. Lippard, Cameron D., editor.
   E184.A1R254   2014
   305.800973—dc23   2013024041

ISBN: 978-1-4408-0345-1
EISBN: 978-1-4408-0346-8

18 17 16 15 14   1 2 3 4 5

This book is also available on the World Wide Web as an eBook.
Visit www.abc-clio.com for details.

Greenwood
An Imprint of ABC-CLIO, LLC

ABC-CLIO, LLC
130 Cremona Drive, P.O. Box 1911
Santa Barbara, California 93116-1911

This book is printed on acid-free paper ∞
Manufactured in the United States of America

Contents

Alphabetical List of Entries

Topical List of Entries

Health and Science

Identity

Work and Labor

List of Primary Documents

N

NAACP Legal Defense and Education Fund

The NAACP Legal Defense and Education Fund, Inc. (LDF) was officially chartered in 1940. Yet, the focus of the organization—legally challenging issues of education, voter protection, economic justice, and criminal justice—were central to the NAACP's initial legal campaign, following its founding in 1909. The inception of the LDF and the strategies that were devised are central to understanding how the LDF became the force behind a number of landmark decisions, including *Brown v. Board of Education* (1954) and how it continues to advocate for justice, equality, and fairness.

Beginning in the mid-1920s, the NAACP sought funding from the Garland Fund, a foundation dedicated to radical social reform. Having already supported the NAACP's anti-lynching campaign, the Garland Fund began supporting legal services offered by the NAACP, including its initial plan to oppose segregation. To begin its challenge on "separate but equal," the NAACP published the results of studies that focused on the inequities between white and black schools in Georgia, Mississippi, North Carolina, South Carolina, and Oklahoma. By 1930, the NAACP litigation campaign's efforts included suits against residential segregation and exclusion of blacks. Additionally, the NAACP offered support to cases filed by taxpayers in the Deep South and suits that challenged the inequalities, in particular financial disparities, between white and black schools.

Under Walter White's leadership as executive secretary, and with financial support from the Garland Fund, the NAACP hired Nathan Margold, a former assistant U.S. attorney for the Southern District of New York. Margold was responsible for coordinating the NAACP legal campaign and producing a study on the injustices facing black Americans. When the *Margold Report* was submitted on May 13, 1931, about half focused on school segregation, in part because education was a relatively new area of focus for the NAACP litigation campaign, and the other half discussed residential segregation. The report clearly showed the vast differences between the allocated monies for black and white schools, and the NAACP legal team focused on devising a legal strategy that would confront "separate but equal," as established by *Plessy v. Ferguson* (1896).

Prior to the 1930s, the NAACP legal team had primarily consisted of white attorneys because of the very few black lawyers available and the need for the NAACP to establish credibility in the courts. Yet in the 1930s, the NAACP sought to retain more black lawyers. Black attorneys Charles Hamilton Houston, Louis Redding, and Homer Brown joined the NAACP legal team helping to expand the group from seven in 1931 to 16 in 1933. In 1934, Houston was hired as special counsel for the NAACP; his credentials for coordinating the NAACP efforts were evident.

Born on September 3, 1895, Houston was the son of William and Mary Hamilton Houston, a general practice lawyer and hairdresser, respectively. Houston attended M Street High School in Washington, D.C., the first black high school in the United States. At M Street, Houston was taught by some of the leading black teachers in the country, and his coursework followed a liberal arts curriculum. Following high school, Houston attended Amherst College in Massachusetts, and graduated in 1915 as a newly inducted member of Phi Beta Kappa. After serving in World War I and returning home during the tumultuous Red Summer of 1919, Houston decided that the best way for him to attack inequalities in the United States was through the law.

In turn, Houston earned his law degree from Harvard University and was the first black elected to the *Harvard Law Review*. In 1924, Houston left the law practice he shared with his father in Washington, D.C., to become vice-dean of Howard University Law School. Under Houston's leadership, Howard became known as a leading law school after it received full accreditation. At Howard, Houston trained black men who would become leading civil rights attorneys including Edward P. Lovett, James G. Tyson, Oliver W. Hill, Coyness L. Ennix, and Leslie S. Perry. Houston also helped to craft two new fields of law: civil rights law and public interest law. Outside of Howard, Houston participated in a number of cases involving civil liberties, civil rights, and antidiscrimination activities, including serving as defense attorney for the Scottsboro Nine. Thus in 1934, Houston, considered the "most influential black lawyer in the United States," was the ideal choice to lead the NAACP's legal campaign.

Houston conceived his role as a lawyer as one of a social engineer charged with overturning the ways in which the law had been used to defend and maintain racial discrimination. Trained by Roscoe Pound and Felix Frankfurter at Harvard, Houston also adhered to the philosophy of legal realism. With these principles guiding Houston and those he trained, the NAACP legal campaign launched its attack on segregated education because according to Houston, "discrimination in education is symbolic of all the more drastic discriminations."

Between 1933 and 1950, the NAACP enjoyed considerable success in a revitalized campaign that defeated segregation by challenging the notion of "separate but equal." As the leader of the campaign, Houston stated, "I am primarily the administrator of the campaign, and my ideal of administration is to make the movement self-perpetuating . . . the best administration is self-executing." In developing the movement, Houston recruited his most well-known student, Thurgood Marshall, a 1933 graduate of Howard Law School.

Upon graduation, Marshall devoted his energies to both the NAACP legal campaign and to his own private practice in Maryland, his home state. When it became too difficult for Marshall to manage both commitments, Marshall joined the NAACP legal staff in October 1946. Thus with Houston's vision and Marshall's attention to detail, the NAACP legal team moved forward with its campaign to attack segregation legally and to help increase the influence of the NAACP in the black community, for the NAACP had begun to feel threatened by the Communist Party and the International Labor Defense.

The strategy of the NAACP legal campaign included pursuing higher education cases in state courts seeking mandamus relief, while fighting salary equalization cases in federal court seeking injunctive relief. In 1935, this strategy was first put into action in a case involving Donald Murray, a black graduate of Amherst College and applicant to the University of Maryland Law School, who had been denied admission. After two failed cases involving higher education in North Carolina and Tennessee, the coordination between national and local legal counsels became vitally important to NAACP victories. *Murray v. Maryland* (1935) provided an opportunity whereby national and local knowledge easily merged because of Marshall's familiarity with Maryland.

Together with Marshall, Houston argued against the feasibility of practicing law in Maryland if one was not educated in Maryland and the fact that out-of-state scholarships were instituted only after Murray's case had been filed. Based on these arguments, Judge Eugene O'Dunne ruled that Murray had been denied admission to the state law school because of race, and he ordered the immediate admission of Murray. Three years later in 1938, Murray became the first black graduate of the University of Maryland Law School. In addition to the Murray case, Marshall argued salary equalization cases in Maryland, and by 1941, the state legislature mandated equal salaries.

Asian Americans for Equality (AAFE)

Although the civil rights movement, which emerged in the 1950s, was primarily fueled by African Americans and their supporters, it was responsible for prompting political awareness in other communities of color as well. One of the first organized efforts toward Asian American empowerment was initiated when the community members in New York City were angered by a construction firm publicly expressing its intention not to hire Asian American workers for a federally funded project in Chinatown in 1974. In response to the firm's argument that Asian Americans lacked physical strength for construction work, a group of Asian American community members founded a volunteer organization, which later became Asian Americans for Equality (AAFE), to protest against the construction firm's hiring policy. This prompted the firm to establish a policy not to discriminate against workers of color. Inspired by this success, the AAFE has devoted much of its energy to protesting against housing discrimination faced by Asian Americans.

Today, the AAFE has grown to serve as an advocate for the rights of Asian Americans and other people of color and immigrants throughout the city of New York. On the one hand, the AAFE has expanded its campaigns against injustice, and it now deals not only with housing and employment discrimination but also with discriminatory public policies and practices, such as racial biases in criminal justice and immigration procedures. On the other hand, the organization provides hands-on financial, legal, and educational support for households of color and businesses owned by people of color, to facilitate their efforts toward realizing their American dreams.

DAISUKE AKIBA

Together, the Maryland cases and a second higher education case in Missouri began setting precedent for overturning the doctrine of separate but equal. Lloyd Lionel Gaines, a graduate of Lincoln University, applied for admission to the University of Missouri Law School in June 1935, because Lincoln did not have a law school. At first, the Missouri Supreme Court ruled against Gaines, concluding, "Gaines would not be deprived of any constitutional rights as long as the educational opportunities provided by the state [tuition for schools out of state] were 'substantially equal to those furnished to white citizens of the State.'" Two years later, however, in *Missouri ex rel Gaines v. Canada* (1938), the Supreme Court ruled that Missouri's offer of out-of-state tuition to in-state blacks was beside the point. The Court in effect concluded that Missouri did not offer legal education to blacks, and states were required to provide equal educational opportunities. Upon its decision, the Missouri Supreme Court was forced to reconsider its decision. Gaines, however, could not be found, and subsequently the case was dismissed. Despite the dismissal, the case attracted public and scholarly attention and provided a warning to segregated educational institutions.

As more cases formalized, the NAACP legal campaign became a new entity. By 1940, Houston had returned to Washington and was carrying less of the daily responsibilities. Marshall had assumed duties as special counsel to the NAACP and would now also direct the LDF. As the LDF developed, Marshall continued to be assisted by such lawyers as William Henry Hastie and hired additional lawyers including Robert Carter, Jack Greenberg, Constance Baker Motley, Franklin Williams, Spottswood Robinson Milton Konvitz, Edward Dudley, and Marian Wynn Perry.

The LDF continued its legal attack on separate but equal through the 1940s, with their efforts to set precedent culminating in 1950. Aiding the LDF's efforts was a 1944 publication by Swedish economist and politician Gunnar Myrdal entitled *An American Dilemma: The Negro Problem and Modern Democracy*. Myrdal illuminated how the United States' ideals of equality, freedom, and justice had not been reality for black Americans. His findings were evident in the following 1945 statistics: the South spent two to one in favor of whites and four to one on white facilities. White teachers on average earned 30 percent more than black teachers, and transportation for black students attending schools in rural areas was completely ignored. Following the publication of *An American Dilemma*, which raised consciousness about the existence of discrimination, the LDF also began using a sociological argument. Additionally in the 1940s, the LDF won significant cases regarding voting rights, public transportation, and housing.

The U.S. Supreme Court in effect abolished the "white primary" with its ruling in *Smith v. Allwright* (1944). The judges stated that denying African Americans the opportunity to vote in the Texas primary election violated the Fifteenth Amendment. In *Morgan v. Virginia* (1946), the Court ruled unconstitutional segregation on interstate transportation. Additionally in *Patton v. Mississippi* (1947), the Court delivered another victory to the LDF by finding unconstitutional all-white juries. The last significant decision in the 1940s occurred when the Court, in *Shelley v. Kraemer* (1948), found that housing covenants designed to keep African Americans out of all-white neighborhoods were unconstitutional, since the covenants denied blacks equal protection under the law. With these victories, increased NAACP membership, and stronger challenges to Jim Crow by black Americans after World War II, the LDF moved forward in fully confronting segregated education with two additional higher education suits.

In 1948, George McLaurin, a 68-year-old man, was denied admission to the University of Oklahoma Graduate School of Education. Despite his ordered admission by the court, McLaurin was separated from his white classmates. McLaurin sat in a desk outside of the regular classrooms, studied in a separate section of the library, and ate his lunch at a different time than the other students. Because of these conditions, Marshall and McLaurin petitioned the court's decision. By the time the case reached the Supreme Court, McLaurin had been allowed to sit in classes with other students. Yet his desk had been labeled "colored," and his separate designations remained in the library and cafeteria. In *McLaurin v. Oklahoma State Regents for Higher Education* (1950), the Supreme Court ruled that setting students apart by race, as the University of Oklahoma Law School had, immediately labeled one race the superior race and the other the inferior.

In February 1946, Herman Marion Sweatt, a postman, sought a legal education by applying to the University of Texas Law School. After his application was rejected, Sweatt filed a lawsuit against the University of Texas. Following the initial hearing, the state of Texas established a makeshift law school in connection with Prairie View University, a historically black institution, by locating the school in Houston,

40 miles away from Prairie View, renting a few rooms and hiring two black lawyers as instructors. With its acquisition of funds to construct a "real" separate law school, Texas tried to persuade Sweatt to stop his legal actions, but Sweatt and Marshall continued.

Although the district court ruled against Sweatt in 1947, the argument Marshall presented became the center of testimony for the eventual Supreme Court victory in 1950. Marshall attacked separate schools on the grounds that racial separation was scientifically unjustifiable and socially destructive. Earl Harrison, dean of the University Pennsylvania Law School, testified about the environment students enjoyed by attending majority institutions and the psychological detriments of segregation. In his 1949 brief to the Supreme Court, Marshall also used the words of law professors: "By sending Sweatt to a raw, new law school without alumni or prestige, Texas deprives him of economic opportunity which its white students have." For the first time, the LDF argued in *Sweatt v. Painter* (1950) that attending separate but equal institutions was unconstitutional because of the inequality in facilities, resources, prestige, and indirect benefits later utilized by white students. The Supreme Court agreed, for Chief Justice Fred Vinson declared that "the University of Texas Law School possesses to a far greater degree those qualities which are incapable of objective measurement but which make for greatness in a law school." Subsequently, Sweatt was admitted to the University of Texas Law School. Precedent had now been established for a challenge to segregation in elementary and secondary schools. However, the LDF would have to move forward without Houston, who died on April 22, 1950.

By the fall of 1953, the five collective cases known as *Brown v. Board of Education* (1954) were argued before the Supreme Court by team of LDF lawyers including Marshall, Louis Redding, Robert Carter, James M. Nabrit Jr., Oliver Hill, and Spottswood Robinson. In 1954, *Brown* overturned *Plessy v. Ferguson* and fundamentally challenged the inherent inequalities of "separate but equal." With *Brown* II in effect allowing for the desegregation of public schools to move with "all deliberate speed," the LDF continued to battle the legacy of legal segregation and subsequent resistance to change. LDF lawyers assisted with cases involving the desegregation of public schools, including institutions of higher education, the desegregation of public facilities, and individual rights to health care, voting, and equal protection. The LDF also represented such leaders as Martin Luther King, Jr.

As the LDF legal team continued to wage legal battles, a major change occurred in 1957, with the LDF becoming independent of the NAACP. Marshall no longer served the NAACP, and he assumed the position of director-counsel. Despite the change, the LDF retained the NAACP name. Also, during the height of the civil rights movement, such lawyers as James M. Nabrit III and Marian Wright Edleman joined the LDF. In 1961, Jack Greenberg became director-counsel upon Marshall's appointment by President John F. Kennedy to the U.S. Court of Appeals for the Second Circuit. Upon Greenberg's resignation from the LDF, Julius Chambers became director-counsel in 1984. Within 10 years, Elaine R. Jones became the first female director-counsel of the LDF, and currently Theodore M. Shaw serves as the fifth director-counsel. Throughout the last few decades, the LDF has remained committed to legal cases involving education, voter protection, economic justice, and criminal justice that will advance racial justice and equality.

MICHELLE A. PURDY

See also

National Association for the Advancement of Colored People (NAACP)

Further Reading:

Greenberg, Jack. *Crusaders in the Courts: How a Dedicated Band of Lawyers Fought for Civil Rights Revolution.* New York: Basic Books, 1994.

Kluger, Richard. *Simple Justice: The History of* Brown v. Board of Education *and Black America's Struggle for Equality.* New York: Vintage Books, 2004.

Martin, Waldo E. Brown v. Board of Education: *A Brief History with Documents.* Boston: Bedford/St. Martin's, 1998.

Meier, August. "Negro Protest Movements and Organizations." *Journal of Negro Education* 32 (August 1963): 437–50.

NAACP Legal Defense and Educational Fund, Inc., Web site. http://www.naacpldf.org/ (accessed May 27, 2008).

Tushnet, Mark V. *The NAACP's Legal Strategy against Segregated Education, 1925–1950.* Chapel Hill: University of North Carolina Press, 1987.

Ware, Gilbert. "The NAACP-Inc. Fund Alliance: Its Strategy, Power, and Destruction." *Journal of Negro Education* 63 (Summer 1994): 323–35.

"'With an Even Hand': *Brown v. Board* at Fifty." Library of Congress exhibition. http://www.loc.gov/exhibits/brown (accessed May 27, 2008).

Nadir of the Negro, The

The Nadir of the Negro is the era from 1890 to the 1930s. In these years, African Americans lost many of the rights they had won during Reconstruction. In the South, whites forced blacks back into noncitizenship, no longer allowed to vote or serve on juries, and cut funding for black schools by as much as two thirds. In the North, organizations ranging from restaurants to organized baseball to the dormitories of Harvard University that had previously admitted African Americans now rejected them.

Historian Rayford Logan, who earned his doctorate from Harvard in 1936 and chaired Howard University's history department in the 1940s and 1950s, established the term in his 1954 book, The *Negro in American Life and Thought: The Nadir.* The same year, C. Vann Woodward gave a series of lectures, reprinted later as *The Strange Career of Jim Crow,* telling how African Americans lost citizenship and social rights in the South not right after Reconstruction, but after 1890. Since then, the idea that race relations grew worse around 1890 has become well accepted in American history.

Three events in 1890 signaled the new era. Mississippi passed a new constitution, stripping voting rights from African Americans, and although the new law clearly violated the Fourteenth and Fifteenth Amendments, the federal government did nothing. The U.S. Senate failed to pass the Federal Elections Bill, which would have helped African Americans (and white Republicans) to vote freely across the South. Worse, after the defeat, when tagged as usual by Democrats as "nigger-lovers," Republicans this time denied the charge and largely abandoned the cause of civil rights. Since the Democrats already labeled themselves "the white man's party," African Americans now found themselves with no political allies. Finally, the Massacre at Wounded Knee, South Dakota, ended the last vestige of Native sovereignty, sending American Indians into their nadir period as well.

What caused the Nadir? The antislavery idealism spawned by the Civil War faded as memories of the war dimmed. By 1890, only one American in three was old enough to have been alive when it ended. Fewer still were old enough to have any memory of the war. Among older Americans, millions had immigrated to the United States long after the war's end and had played no role in it.

Three developments having nothing directly to do with black rights further eroded the position of African

Americans. The first was the Indian wars. Although the federal government had guaranteed their land to the Plains Indians "forever," after whites discovered gold in Colorado, Dakota Territory, and elsewhere, they took it anyway. If it was all right to take Indians' land because they were not white, was not it all right to deny rights to African Americans, who were not white either?

Second, immigrants from Europe persisted in voting Democratic, partly because they saw that it was in their interest to differentiate themselves from blacks, still at the bottom of the social hierarchy. Also, Republicans were moving toward Prohibition, hardly a preferred position among Italian, Greek, and Russian newcomers among others. Frustrated politically by the new arrivals from Southern and Eastern Europe, Senator Henry Cabot Lodge helped found the Immigration Restriction League to keep out "inferior" racial strains. This further sapped Republican commitment to the idea "that all men are created equal."

Third, the ideology of imperialism washed over the United States from Europe. Imperialism both depended upon and in turn reinforced the ideology of white supremacy. The growing clamor to annex Hawai'i included the claim that Americans could govern those brown people better than they could govern themselves. After winning the Spanish-American War, the administration of President William McKinley used the same rationale to defend making war upon our allies, the Filipinos. William Howard Taft, who was made U.S. commissioner over the Philippines in 1900, called the Filipinos "our little brown brothers" and said they would need "fifty or one hundred years" of close supervision "to develop anything resembling Anglo-Saxon political principles and skills." Democrats drew the obvious parallel, "What about our little black brothers in the South?" and Republicans could make no cogent reply.

Seeing that the United States did nothing to stop Mississippi's usurpation of black rights, whites in other Southern states and states as distant as Oklahoma followed suit by 1907. In 1894, Democrats in Congress repealed the remaining federal election statutes, leaving the Fifteenth Amendment lifeless, with no extant laws to enforce it. In 1896, in *Plessy v. Ferguson*, the U.S. Supreme Court declared de jure racial segregation legal. Schools were segregated statewide in Delaware, Maryland, West Virginia, Kentucky, Missouri, Arkansas, Oklahoma, Texas, and Arizona, as well as much of

Ohio, Indiana, Illinois, Kansas, New Mexico, and California. The South already had segregated schools, of course.

The new Mississippi constitution required prospective voters to "be able to read any section of the constitution of this State . . . or he shall be able to understand the same when read to him, or give a reasonable interpretation thereof." Other states incorporated similar measures in their new laws. In practice, black would-be voters were required to be able to read a section and interpret it. Local folklore has it that a professor at Tuskegee Institute with a doctorate in political science could not interpret the constitution to the satisfaction of the Macon County, Alabama, registrar, who was a high school dropout. Certainly even jurisdictions like Macon County—84 percent black, and home to two important black institutions, Tuskegee Institute and a large VA hospital—had white voting majorities until the civil rights movement.

Not only did these clauses remove African Americans from voting, and hence from juries, they also linked literacy and education as the mechanism. In their wake, every Southern state cut back on black schooling. Their new constitutions commanded racially segregated schools de jure, so it was easy to set up shorter sessions for black schools, require lower qualifications of black teachers, and pay them a fraction of white salaries.

In 1898, Democrats rioted in Wilmington, North Carolina, driving out all Republican officeholders and killing at least 12 African Americans. Astonishingly, the McKinley administration allowed this coup d'état to stand. Congress became resegregated in 1901 when Congressman George H. White of North Carolina could not win reelection owing to the disfranchisement of black voters. No African American served in Congress again until 1929, and none from the South until 1973. The so-called Progressive Movement was for whites only. In many Northern cities, its "reforms" removed the last local black leaders from city councils in favor of commissioners elected citywide.

Coinciding with the Nadir and helping to justify it was the ideology of social Darwinism—the notion that the fittest rise to the top in society. It provided a potent rationale not only for white supremacy, but also for America's increasing class hierarchy. Its "scientific" handmaidens, eugenics and psychometrics, flourished. Madison Grant, author of the 1916 eugenics tract *The Passing of the Great Race*, helped write the 1924 law that drastically cut immigration to the United States from Asia and Southern and Eastern Europe. Carl Brigham, concerned that "American intelligence is declining . . . as the racial admixture becomes more and more extensive," developed the Scholastic Aptitude Test in 1926 to select the brightest students for elite colleges. Popular culture also justified the Nadir. In this era, minstrel shows came to dominate our popular culture. They had begun before the Civil War but flourished after 1890 minstrel shows both caused and reflected the increased racism of the period. As author, politician, and activist James Weldon Johnson put it, minstrel shows "fixed the tradition of the Negro as only an irresponsible, happy-go-lucky, wide-grinning, loud-laughing, shuffling, banjo-playing, singing, dancing sort of being." In small towns across the North, where few blacks existed to correct this impression, these stereotypes provided the bulk of white "knowledge" about what African Americans were like. The first epic motion picture, *The Birth of a Nation*, glorified the Ku Klux Klan as the savior of white Southern civilization from the menace of black upstarts during Reconstruction. In 1936, near the end of the Nadir, the Margaret Mitchell novel *Gone with the Wind* sold a million hardbound books in its first month. The book and the resulting film, the highest-grossing movie of all time, further convinced whites that noncitizenship was appropriate for African Americans.

During the Nadir, lynchings rose to their height, and not just in the South, although the main "national" database has never included Northern lynchings. Segregation swept through public accommodations, North as well as South. In 1908, touring the North for an article, "The Color Line in the North," Ray Stannard Baker noted the deterioration even in Boston, the old citadel of abolitionism: "A few years ago no hotel or restaurant in Boston refused Negro guests. [N]ow several hotels, restaurants, and especially confectionery stores, will not serve Negroes, even the best of them." Writing of the day-to-day interactions of whites and blacks in the Midwest, Frank Quillen observed in 1913 that race prejudice "is increasing steadily, especially during the last twenty years." In the 1920s, Harvard barred an African American student from the very dormitory where his father had lived decades earlier when attending the university. Whites ousted African Americans from occupations ranging from major league baseball player and Kentucky Derby jockey to postal carrier, mason, firefighter, and carpenter. Even jobs like department store salesclerk and factory worker were closed to African Americans, and not just in Dixie.

Across the North and throughout the Appalachian South and the Ozarks, whites forced African Americans to make a Great Retreat from hundreds of communities. These then became all-white "sundown" towns for decades. Communities that had voted Democratic in the 1860s were especially likely to bar African Americans decades later, during the Nadir. Even some previously interracial Republican towns, like Hermann, Missouri, where African Americans had celebrated Emancipation Day in the 1870s, went sundown after 1890.

African Americans thrashed about, trying to cope with their increasingly desperate situation. Early in the Nadir, some left the Deep South for new homes in Kansas and Oklahoma (the Exodus), but Oklahoma entered the Union in 1907 with a constitution modeled after Mississippi's, while Kansas lost its abolitionist edge and developed many sundown towns. Booker T. Washington suggested blacks relinquish claims to social equality, concentrating on hard work and education, but this proved difficult because hostile Southern whites often targeted successful black farmers and businessmen.

W.E.B. Du Bois disputed with Washington, but his refusal to condone loss of black rights proved no more workable. Forming black towns like Boley, Oklahoma, and Mound Bayou, Mississippi, gave no relief, because these communities were ultimately under the white thumbs of county and state governments. The Back to Africa movements organized by Chief Sam and Marcus Garvey also provided no solution.

In this context, the Great Migration provided African Americans with environments in which they could vote freely, and hence could bargain for at least some municipal services and other basic rights. However, cities North and South became much more residentially segregated during the Nadir, and many suburbs formed on an all-white basis. Still, African Americans were able to establish small majority-black settlements on Long Island, New York; west of Detroit; south of Chicago; and on the outskirts of other Northern cities.

During the Woodrow Wilson administration, the Nadir intensified. Wilson segregated the navy, which had not been segregated before. He also replaced blacks who held appointed offices with whites. Responding to his leadership, whites rioted against black communities in Chicago, East St. Louis, Omaha, Washington, and other cities in what James Weldon Johnson called the Red Summer of 1919. The release of *The Birth of a Nation* led to a rebirth of the Ku Klux Klan, this time as a national organization that displayed astonishing if short-lived clout in Georgia, Indiana, Oklahoma, Oregon, and other states during the 1920s. The Klan prompted the expulsion of African Americans from additional Northern towns and counties. The Great Depression of the next decade spurred whites to drive African Americans from additional jobs like elevator operator and railroad fireman.

Anti-Semitism increased as well in the Nadir. Early in the Civil War, people of various religions—including Jews—had founded the Union League Club to combat the pro-secession sentiment that dominated New York City. When white segregationists removed the widow of an African American soldier from a streetcar, the Union League Club came to her defense. Joseph Seligman, a Jew, leading banker, and friend of Ulysses S. Grant, had been a founder of the club. His son Jesse became a member in 1868. Then, during the 1890s, members refused to admit Jews, as well as Italians, Catholics, and others of "incorrect background." In 1893, after 25 years of membership, 14 of them as a vice president, Jesse Seligman had to resign. Members blackballed his own son Theodore because he was a Jew. During World War I, the U.S. Army for the first time considered Jews "a special problem whose loyalty to the U.S. was open to question." Along with other government agencies (and the Ku Klux Klan), the Military Intelligence Department mounted a campaign against Jewish immigrants that helped convince Congress to pass a restrictive immigration bill in 1924.

The Nadir manifested itself in many ways, including treatment of African Americans in Iowa newspapers. During the 1870s, they covered the activities and individual happenings within the African American population. By the 1890s, however, most stories about blacks appeared on the crime page. Even the appointment of an Iowan as ambassador to Liberia, one of the highest posts available to African Americans during the Nadir, drew no notice in the Iowa press. African American intellectuals despaired of the Nadir. In 1900, African American poet Paul Laurence Dunbar wrote "Robert Gould Shaw," a bitter ode to the white colonel who led the 54th Massachusetts Colored Regiment in its charge at Fort Wagner during the Civil War. The poem ended by suggesting that Shaw's "cold endurance of the final pain" had been pointless. Only with the rise of the CIO unions and some important symbolic gestures by First Lady Eleanor Roosevelt did the Nadir begin to crack. The Great Migration itself helped end it. Coupled with the Great Retreat, it concentrated African Americans into a few large cities. This enabled blacks to win seats in Northern state legislatures and the U.S. House of Representatives, which in turn prompted white political leaders to moderate their racist rhetoric so as not to alienate urban black voters and political leaders. A second crack in the wall of white supremacy came from the crumbling of imperialism. In a Cold War context, America could not afford to offend the non-white leaders of newly independent nations in Asia and Africa. Most important of all was the role played by World War II. Germany gave white supremacy a bad name. It is always in victors' interests to demonize the vanquished, and Nazism made this task easy. Americans saw in the German death camps the logical result of eugenics and segregation, and it appalled them. As they sought to differentiate themselves from Hitler's discredited racial policies, the overt racism of the Nadir now made them uneasy. Swedish social scientist Gunnar Myrdal called this conflict our "American dilemma" and predicted in 1944, "Equality is slowly winning."

Although the Nadir has eased since 1940, it left the United States with two progeny: sundown towns and warped history. Near the end of the period, in 1935, W.E.B. Du Bois lamented the distorted account of Reconstruction to which it gave rise: "We have got to the place where we cannot use our experiences during and after the Civil War for the uplift and enlightenment of mankind."

JAMES W. LOEWEN

See also
Back to Africa Movement; Du Bois, W.E.B.; Great Retreat; Lynching; *Passing of the Great Race, The*; Reconstruction Era

Further Reading:
Baker, Ray Stannard. "The Color Line in the North." *American Magazine* 65 (1908). Reprinted in *The Negro Question: From Slavery to Caste, 1863–1910*, edited by Otto Olsen. New York: Pitman, 1971.

Bassett, John Spencer. *A Short History of the United States*. New York: Macmillan, 1923.

Bergmann, Leola. "The Negro in Iowa." *Iowa Journal of History and Politics* (1969 [1948]): 44–45.

DeVries, James. *Race and Kinship in a Midwestern Town*. Urbana: University of Illinois Press, 1984.

Du Bois, W.E.B. *Black Reconstruction*. Cleveland, OH: World Meridian, 1964 (1935), 722.

Johnson, James Weldon. *Black Manhattan*. New York: Knopf, 1930.

Loewen, James W. "Teaching Race Relations through Feature Films." *Teaching Sociology* 19 (January 1991): 82.

Loewen, James W. *Lies across America*. New York: New Press, 1999.

Loewen, James W. *Sundown Towns*. New York: New Press, 2005.

Logan, Rayford. *The Negro in American Life and Thought: The Nadir*. New York: Dial, 1954.

Myrdal, Gunnar. *An American Dilemma*. New York: Harper & Row, 1944.

Quillen, Frank. *The Color Line in Ohio*. Ann Arbor, MI: Wahr, 1913.

Upchurch, Thomas Adams. *Legislating Racism: The Billion Dollar Congress and the Birth of Jim Crow*. Lexington: University Press of Kentucky, 2004.

Narrowcasting

Narrowcasting is the strategy used in the media to target specific or smaller audiences, like urban women in their 40s and 50s, Latino girls under 20, or college-educated, middle-aged, white males. Narrowcasting creates profits for the cable TV, radio, and Internet companies by appealing to the supposed interests of the targeted groups. Cable television, satellite television and broadband-delivered cable orient their material (e.g., news, movies, drama, and cartoons) towards a fragmented and narrow audience.

In the 1980s, the boom of racial and ethnic diversity on television channels made for a segmented consumer audience. One of the common tactics of narrowcasting is the appeal to specific age, educational level, religion, sexual orientation, economic status, and most importantly, race and ethnicity. Sometimes these divisions are combined to create more specific targeted groups. One example of a narrowcasting by race in the United States is the creation of the television network called Black Entertainment Television (BET). BET was the first national cable channel devoted to a specific racial group. Founded by Robert Johnson, the television channel airs public affairs programs, music shows, comedies, and drama shows that focus on black themes and characters. In 2000, blacks controlled 20 out of 1,243 television stations.

Most cable networks practice narrowcasting. This practice also serves as an economic benefit for the cable networks. Television channels like MTV, HBO, Fox, and Lifetime were at the forefront of narrowcasting. Niches are being continually created into smaller groups. Gender and age are often intersected with ethnicity and other social categories that serve as nuanced, and often specific, consumers. Narrowcasting reproduces exclusionary patterns and ideologies, while also creating smaller groups that are exclusionary. Some scholars maintain that the information disseminated through media will enhance the social standing of the group in question and their awareness amongst the general public. Moreover, some assert that narrowcasting makes media programming more representative of the racial and ethnic differences in society, as well as more accessible and relatable to most people. On the other hand, some scholars believe that narrowcasting labors to maintain an asymmetrical status quo. In this light, the narrowcasting strategy is essentially hegemonic and hierarchical, recreating a marginalized and objectified "other," whose value is only that of a consumable and entertaining object.

BIANCA GONZALEZ SOBRINO AND MATTHEW W. HUGHEY

Further Reading:

Kuipers, Giselinde. "South Park Boys and Sex and the City Women: Television Trade, Narrowcasting and the Export of Gender Categories." *Interactions: Studies in Communication & Culture* 2, no. 3 (2010): 179–96.

Meyrowitz, Joshua, and John Maguire. "Media, Place, and Multiculturalism." *Society* 30, no. 5 (1993): 41–48.

Overby, L. Marvin, and Jay Barth. "Radio Advertising in American Political Campaigns: The Persistence, Importance, and Effects of Narrowcasting." *American Politics Research* 34, no. 4 (2006): 451–78.

Smith-Shamode, Berretta E. "Narrowcasting in the New World Information Order: A Space for the Audience?" *Television & New Media* 5, no. 69 (2004): 69–81.

Wible, Scott. "Media Advocates, Latino Citizens and Niche Cable: The Limits of 'No Limits' TV." *Cultural Studies* 18, no. 1 (2004) : 34–66.

Young, Greg. "From Broadcasting to Narrowcasting to 'Mycasting': A Newfound Celebrity in Queer Internet Communities." *Continuum: Journal of Media & Cultural Studies* 18, no. 1 (2004): 43–62.

Nation of Islam (NOI)

The Nation of Islam (NOI) is a religious Black Nationalist movement that emerged in the 1930s, just after the "Golden Age" of Black Nationalism. The NOI is one of the few remaining Black Nationalist movements that has survived from the Jim Crow era to the present, and that continues to thrive.

The Nation of Islam was founded in Detroit in 1930, not by an African American, but by Wallace Dodd, an immigrant from New Zealand. From Dodd's appearance, researchers have speculated that he may have descended from a "mixed" heritage that combined European and either Polynesian or Punjabi ancestry. Dodd's ambiguous racial appearance permitted him to switch his racial identity during his sojourn in the United States, variously claiming to be white, black, or Arab.

During the 1920s, Dodd served a prison sentence in California on a narcotics charge. Upon his release in 1929, Dodd traveled to Chicago and became involved in the Moorish Science Temple (MST), a group that combined new religious teachings with black nationalism. The MST's founder was Timothy Drew (aka Noble Drew Ali, the Prophet). Drew taught that African Americans are descended from "the Moors," and were originally of the Islamic faith. Drew published a book of his teachings that he entitled the *Koran* (not to be confused with the Islamic holy book of the same name). Drew plagiarized most of his *Koran* from previously published esoteric sources. Drew taught that "Moors" (African Americans) were "Asiatics," one of the world's two major races along with Europeans. While Drew's teachings sometimes advocated racial tolerance and equality, he also taught that "Europeans" represent a lower order of humanity who had been banished from Mecca by the Asiatic "Moslems." Thus Drew's theology reversed the logic of Jim Crow–era racism, holding that African Americans are racially superior to white Americans. Drew's religion also espoused Black Nationalist ideals.

Upon entering the MST, Wallace Dodd took the name "David Ford-el." The group quickly degenerated into internal squabbles. After one of Drew's rivals was stabbed, Drew himself died shortly thereafter, under mysterious circumstances. In the wake of Drew's death, Dodd became a contender for control of the organization. Dodd even claimed to be the reincarnation of "Noble Drew Ali." Because the MST's factional rivalries had devolved into kidnappings, shootouts, and assassinations, Dodd became of interest to Chicago law enforcement, and so he moved to Detroit.

In Detroit, Dodd found work peddling cloth and needles in black neighborhoods. He changed his name to "Wallace Fard," "Wallace Fard Muhammed," "W. D. Muhammed," and similar variations. Taking Timothy Drew as a role model, Fard/Dodd presented himself to residents of the city's black ghetto as a prophet of a new religion that was based on MST. However, Fard's new religion added many elements of his own devising. Fard eventually settled on the name "Nation of Islam" for his organization. While Fard told his followers that he was teaching Islam, his religion bears little resemblance to any orthodox version of Islam, and appears to be mostly of Fard's own invention.

Fard's new religion began to experience conflict with Detroit law enforcement as it had in Chicago. In 1932, one of Fard's followers committed a ritualistic murder. The murderer quoted a passage from a pamphlet Fard had published: "The unbeliever must be stabbed through the heart." He also told police: "Every son of Islam must gain a victory from the devil. Four victories and the son will attain his reward."

Detroit police saw Fard as complicit in the murder. He was not charged, but the police department encouraged him to shut down his religion and to leave town if he wanted to evade charges related to the murder. Fard complied, but snuck back into the city in early 1933 and began preaching again. The police again arrested Fard. In this police interview, Fard described his religion as "strictly a racket," and admitted that he was "getting all the money out of it he could." Fard returned to Chicago. There, Fard was arrested again, for disturbing the peace. Fard then disappeared from the historical record. Fard's common-law wife stated several decades later that Fard had returned to New Zealand. Neither the FBI nor any other researcher has been able to conclusively document Fard's whereabouts after his last arrest in Chicago. After Fard's departure, the NOI broke down in another series of violent internecine struggles. Elijah Poole, better known as Elijah Muhammad, emerged as the NOI's new leader, and retained that position until his death in 1975.

Elijah Muhammad did not substantially deviate from Fard's religion, but did add a few modifications. Most notably, Muhammad taught that Fard was not just a prophet, but the human incarnation of Allah himself. The NOI's creation

Nation of Islam members (also known as Black Muslims) applaud Elijah Muhammad during the delivery of his annual Savior's Day Message in Chicago during the 1970s. The Nation of Islam is a predominantly Black Nationalist religious organization. It advocates black self-sufficiency and family responsibility as well as adherence to a strict Islamic behavioral code. (National Archives)

myth held that the black race is 78 trillion years old. For most of that time, they were gods enjoying a utopian life. About 6,600 years ago, a deviant black named Yakub, also known as "the big head scientist," created the white race of devils, who would rule over blacks for six millennia. NOI theology thus contains a strong millenarian strain, by prophesizing that white rule is near its end. Fard originally taught that the world would be rid of evil by 1934, but that doctrine has subsequently been modified, with the expected day of reckoning being pushed back several times over the course of NOI's history. Fard taught that when the day comes, planes will be sent to Earth from "The Wheel," a plane made like a wheel. The planes would destroy the Earth, and carry black people away, possibly back to Mars, where people are living already even today. Elijah Muhammad retained this doctrine, as did subsequent NOI preachers such as Malcolm X

and Louis Farrakhan. Occasionally in later years, the plane was updated to a spaceship.

The primary theme of NOI's millenarian teachings is that black people are destined to regain their status as gods. NOI theology thus explains white malfeasance and black powerlessness in the United States, while also motivating blacks to prepare to seize power from whites. The theology accomplishes this by marrying black racial supremacism with millenarian prophecy.

NOI theology bears a few superficial resemblances to mainstream Islam: separation of the sexes, avoidance of pork, and a vague interest in the Arabic language. However, the core of NOI theology directly contradicts core Islamic beliefs: specifically, the NOI's racial supremacism, its identification of Allah with a specific human being (Fard), its derogation of the Koran, and its belief in a prophet other than

---

Million-Man March on Washington

On October 16, 1995, more than a million black men from across the United States participated in a march on Washington in support of blacks and their families. The march, sponsored by Minister Louis Farrakhan of the Nation of Islam, was seen as controversial by some feminists and liberals because the Nation of Islam had asked black women to stay home and pray with their children on that day. Minister Farrakhan did not invite black women to the march because the main objective of the day was to ask black men to atone for their treatment of black women and their lack of support of the black family. Furthermore, since Farrakhan is a controversial public figure because of his radical position on political and racial issues, many people thought that the march was going to be another opportunity for him to criticize other groups in the country. However, to the surprise of the media and his critics, more than a million black men attended the march, and it attracted several prominent speakers, including Maya Angelou, Benjamin Davis (the head of the National Association for the Advancement of Colored People at that time), and civil rights icon Rosa Parks.

The million-man march on Washington made Farrakhan a major national figure in the African American community and the United States. The march was important because it proved the mobilizing power of the black community in the United States. This was the first time that more than a million African Americans congregated in Washington, the center of political power in the United States, to protest the conditions of African Americans in society. This march took place at a time when Congress was creating policy to dismantle the welfare state.

FRANCOIS PIERRE-LOUIS

Muhammad. NOI theology not only bears little resemblance with mainstream Islam, it probably has more Christian overtones than it does Muslim.

At the core of NOI theology is the argument that black people are gods, and that white people are devils who were created by a demented black scientist. Thus Fard retained Drew's inversion of Jim Crow racial ideology, turning white supremacism on its head. NOI preached overt contempt for the white race.

Elijah Muhammad fled Detroit in the wake of the NOI's internal wars over Fard's succession. Muhammad traveled under a variety of aliases to evade the other NOI ministers who challenged his claim to Fard's legacy, and who intended to kill him. Muhammad's own brother had already been killed in the NOI's internecine warfare. NOI members had also engaged in street fights with police in several cities, and so Muhammad was also on the run from disgruntled and vengeful cops. Muhammad wandered from city to city, evangelizing and setting up new "temples." While Muhammad did attract followers in his circumspect travels, they were few in number.

During World War II, the Federal Bureau of Investigation (FBI) investigated Muhammad's contacts with Japanese agents. A federal court cleared Muhammad of sedition, but imprisoned him on charges of draft evasion. Upon Muhammad's release in 1946, the NOI had fewer than 400 members. But while incarcerated, Muhammad realized that prisoners were a population ripe for conversion. Black prisoners during the Jim Crow era often had strong motivation to be attracted to the NOI's racist, antiwhite teachings. The NOI's prisoner membership began to grow during the postwar period.

Among the new prison converts was Malcolm Little. He had sold drugs, burgled, pimped, been a numbers runner, and worked as a homosexual prostitute. Elijah Muhammad renamed him "Malcolm X." Malcolm was an unusually accomplished orator. He ascended rapidly in the NOI due to his ability to recruit and organize new converts. During the 1950s, NOI grew by leaps and bounds, eventually gaining several hundred thousand members and sympathizers.

Malcolm X was the NOI's major public representative after Muhammad, and his rhetoric was no less incendiary. Malcolm X advocated lynching random white people in retaliation for black lynchings. He advocated attacking white men who court black women. He recited all of the "black god/white devil" rhetoric he had learned from Muhammad.

In 1962, Malcolm learned that Muhammad had engaged in many adulterous affairs with his teenaged "secretaries," impregnating a number of them. (FBI surveillance tapes recorded Muhammad seducing his teenage secretaries by bragging about his "divine seed.") Muhammad had even impregnated a member of his own family in an incestuous affair. Furthermore, Muhammad and his family were spending lavish sums on their luxurious lifestyle, using funds appropriated from NOI temples. Malcolm became disaffected with Muhammad's teaching. He publicly criticized Muhammad, and was forced out of NOI in 1964. Malcolm now turned to mainstream Islam, formed his own church, and began to successfully recruit many NOI followers.

For decades, NOI members who publicly disagreed with Elijah Muhammad had often been attacked or killed. When Malcolm went public with his criticism of Muhammad, NOI members turned on him with equal ferocity. Malcolm told *Ebony* magazine that NOI "got to kill me. They can't afford to let me live . . . I know where the bodies are buried. And if they press me, I'll exhume some."

Louis X (aka Louis Farrakhan) wrote ominously in the NOI newspaper: "Only those who wish to be led to hell, or to their doom, will follow Malcolm. The die is set, and Malcolm shall not escape, especially after such evil, foolish talk about his benefactor. Such a man is worthy of death and would have been met with death if it had not been for Muhammad's confidence in Allah for victory over his enemies." Several attempts were made on the lives of Malcolm X, his wife, and his children. NOI assassins finally succeeded in gunning Malcolm X down while he gave a public address in February 1965.

After Elijah Muhammad died in 1975, his son dismantled much of NOI's business side, abandoned most of the Fard/Muhammad theology, renamed the organization, and began to transform it into a mainstream Islamic church. Several years later, a faction led by Louis Farrakhan splintered off. Farrakhan, whose birth name was Louis Wolcott, eventually announced the restoration of NOI. Farrakhan continues to preach the Fard/Muhammad religion. Farrakhan's NOI still emphasizes the NOI's traditional antiwhite racism. However, under Farrakhan's leadership, NOI rhetoric has become rabidly anti-Semitic. NOI published an anti-Semitic book that blames Jews for oppressions and injuries experienced by American blacks. Farrakhan teaches that Judaism is a "gutter religion," that Jews were responsible for black slavery, and that Jews continue to prey on black people today. Farrakhan

began to ally with white supremacist activists when their shared anti-Semitic interests overlapped. Farrakhan and his deputies began to threaten violence against Jews and whites. Catholics and homosexuals are also new NOI targets. NOI rhetoric has become increasingly homophobic.

Violence and crime have been endemic to NOI around the country for much of the organization's history. Within the NOI structure, the most feared group is the "Fruit of Islam." This is a paramilitary corps, which functions as bodyguards and enforcers. Furthermore, NOI prison gangs can be found in the correctional facilities in many states.

The Philadelphia NOI has the best documented links to organized crime. In Philadelphia, the NOI developed an extortionist offshoot, who described themselves as the "Black Mafia." This group became notorious for its involvement with a number of spectacularly violent crimes. For example, in 1971, a murderer associated with the Black Mafia was taken in by Elijah Muhammad and made one of Muhammad's personal "Fruit of Islam" bodyguards.

In 1973, an NOI minister from Philadelphia led a gang of assassins to Washington, D.C. Their target was a former NOI member who had converted to orthodox Islam, and who had subsequently dared to criticize Elijah Muhammad. The gang invaded the heretic's home, but he was not home. So instead, the assassins murdered everyone who was in the house, including two women and five children. One of the murder victims was a baby only nine days old. Then, the Black Mafia went to Cherry Hill, New Jersey, and murdered a black mayoral candidate with underworld connections, apparently because he had refused to broker a heroin deal for the Philadelphia gang.

The Black Mafia gang routinely kicked back part of its illicit profits to the local NOI temple in Philadelphia. The head of NOI's Temple 12 was Jeremiah Shabazz, also known as "Godfather of the Black Mafia." Local law enforcement overlooked the gang's activities as long as they restricted themselves to extorting black businesses and various other petty, ghetto-based hustles. However, once they transitioned into a large-scale drug trafficking enterprise, a series of arrests followed, in the late 1970s and early 1980s. Since then, the Nation of Islam have constituted one of the largest and most feared prison gangs in the Pennsylvania correctional system. More recently, in 2005, a NOI minister was convicted for racketeering and fraud for his role in misappropriating

Louis Farrakhan (1933–)

Louis (Abdul Haleem) Farrakhan is a controversial minister and the current leader of the Nation of Islam, a national religious organization in the United States that embraces elements of Islam, Black Nationalism, and separatism. Although he has detractors, Farrakhan has developed a reputation as a critic of racism and discrimination and is considered by some to be an influential leader in the black community. Farrakhan was born Louis Eugene Walcott, May 11, 1933, in New York City and grew up in Boston. After attending Winston-Salem Teachers' College in North Carolina, Farrakhan worked as a musician and singer. In 1955, while in Chicago to perform, he attended an American Muslim Mission convention, subsequently joined the movement, and changed his name to Minister Louis X and later to Minister Louis Farrakhan. He served as minister of the Muhammad Temple No. 11 in Boston. Although initially he was recruited and mentored by Malcolm X, Farrakhan would later renounce Malcolm X and, after Malcolm's death, replace him as the minister of Temple No. 7 in New York City in May 1965. After the death of Elijah Muhammad in 1975, and due to ideological differences with Wallace Muhammad, his successor, Farrakhan formed his own sect, the Nation of Islam. Known for his charismatic and sometimes controversial speeches, Farrakhan emphasizes black economic development, self-help, black solidarity, and personal responsibility for black men. In 1979, he developed the internationally circulated newspaper *The Final Call*. Farrakhan most recently gained recognition for his involvement in organizing the Million-Man March in Washington, D.C., in 1995. Farrakhan is married to Betsy Farrakhan and is the father of nine children.

SANDRA L. BARNES

minority-certified business contracts from the Philadelphia city government.

John Allen Muhammad committed a racist serial murder spree in the Washington, D.C., area in 2002. Muhammad and a younger partner killed 10 people in sniper attacks there, and another six or seven in other regions around the country. Muhammad had planned to recruit disaffected black youth all over the United States and Canada, and start up killing sprees in other cities as well. His goal was to spread chaos that would cause society to collapse. While the NOI leadership distanced itself from the killer and his plan, it is clear from trial testimony that Muhammad was motivated by the antiwhite rhetoric and the millenarianism that he had learned within the NOI.

The violence that follows in the NOI's wake represents the shadow image of Jim Crow. NOI theology teaches an inverted version of Jim Crow racial ideology. The difference is that NOI substitutes black supremacism for white supremacism. NOI's separatist Black Nationalism is another reflection of Jim Crow. NOI agrees with white supremacists that the races should live separately.

In 1959, CBS produced and aired a television documentary on the NOI entitled *The Hate That Hate Produced*. It features an excerpt from a NOI-sponsored play entitled *The Trial*, written by Louis Farrakhan. In the play, "the white man" is found guilty of a multitude of sins against African Americans, and is sentenced to death.

Thus, the racial hate engendered by the white supremacism of the Jim Crow era persists into the present. Racial hate is seen in its original, unaltered form in the rhetoric of the KKK and other white supremacist groups. But in the NOI, there is also the hateful legacy of Jim Crow in its mirror image. Just as white supremacism led to extremist violence in the form of lynchings, so does the NOI's racial extremism lead to violence.

THOMAS BROWN

See also

Black Nationalism; Malcolm X; Muslim Brotherhood; Sharia Law

Further Reading:

Beynon, Erdmann Doane. "The Voodoo Cult among Negro Migrants in Detroit." *American Journal of Sociology* 43, no. 6 (May 1938): 894–907.

Clegg, Claude Andrew. *An Original Man: The Life and Times of Elijah Muhammad*. New York: St. Martin's Press, 1998.

Essien-Udom, E. U. *Black Nationalism: The Search for an Identity*. Chicago: University of Chicago Press, 1995.

Evanzz, Karl. *The Messenger: The Rise and Fall of Elijah Muhammad*. New York: Pantheon Books, 1999.

Federal Bureau of Investigation, U.S. "Elijah Muhammad: File 105-24822." http://foia.fbi.gov/muhammad/muhammad1.pdf (accessed August 2007).

Gardell, Mattias. *In the Name of Elijah Muhammad: Louis Farrakhan and The Nation of Islam*. Durham, NC: Duke University Press, 1996.

Griffin, Sean Patrick. *Philadelphia's "Black Mafia": A Social and Political History*. Dordrecht, Netherlands: Kluwer Academic, 2003.

Griffin, Sean Patrick. *Black Brothers, Inc.: The Violent Rise and Fall of the Philadelphia Black Mafia*. Lancashire, UK: Milo Books, 2005.

Lincoln, C. Eric. *The Black Muslims in America*, 3rd ed. Grand Rapids, MI: Wm. B. Eerdmans, 1994.

Magida, Arthur J. *Prophet of Rage: A Life of Louis Farrakhan and His Nation*. Reprint edition. New York: HarperCollins, 1997.

McGarvey, Brendan. "Allah Behind Bars: Even La Cosa Nostra Members Fear the Nation of Islam in Jail." *City Paper*, November 7–13, 2002.

Tsoukalas, Steven. *The Nation of Islam: Understanding the "Black Muslims."* Phillipsburg, NJ: P & R Publishing, 2001.

National Association for the Advancement of Colored People (NAACP)

The National Association for the Advancement of Colored People (NAACP) is a sociopolitical body dedicated to ensuring social equity and justice for blacks in the United States. Although its current incarnation is a well-respected and influential organization with a widespread membership and board of governors whose members currently represent 29 U.S. states, earlier forms of the NAACP were marginalized by the political mainstream and, in some states, local offices were the site of race hatred and violence.

The beginnings of the NAACP are to be found in a three-day conference held from July 11–13 in Fort Erie, Canada, in 1904. The 29 attendees, all black intellectuals, were gathered together there by activist W.E.B. Du Bois to organize what would be known as the "Niagara movement." Its purpose was the complete abolition of all forms of racial discrimination and, somewhat ironically, the segregation of schools. Race separation was, at that time, desired by some black intelligentsia who felt that integration was antithetical to their left-wing social and cultural ambitions. Fearing that integration would result in children who assimilated and thereby valued American capitalism and Judeo-Christian moral dominance, some members of the Niagara movement, Du Bois in particular, argued strongly for educational segregation. This point became too contentious for many more moderate attendees and for any real progress to be made by the movement on a large scale; subsequent efforts by members would thereby forego segregation of education, and the long-term wisdom of this decision has been supported by both legislation and the formal mission of what would become the NAACP, which "is to ensure the political, educational, social and economic equality of rights of all persons and to eliminate racial hatred and racial discrimination" (NAACP Mission Statement).

In addition to educational segregation, the increased election of blacks into political office and the enforcement of black voting rights in the United States were crucial agenda items of the Niagara movement. Among the notable blacks present at the conference who would become part of its five-year membership as an activist body were John Hope, J. Max Barber, and William Monroe Trotter. Although initially a very concentrated and organized effort, the Niagara movement gained little momentum and no popular acceptance, and so its membership and their goals dissolved and revived in the new movement for black rights that would become the NAACP.

The NAACP was founded in New York City on February 12, 1909, heralded by the publication of "The Call." This announcement urged all leaders to abolish racially biased legislation and to take up the black cause in the United States by enforcing the Thirteenth, Fourteenth, and Fifteenth Amendments. Published in black newspapers across the United States, "The Call" successfully recruited members into the new social and political body whose national office was located in New York City. The initial board of directors for the NAACP was entirely composed of whites, including the organization's first president, Moorfield Storey, a white attorney. W.E.B. Du Bois, the only black initially named to an important position in the organization, was made publicity director and, by extension, editor of the NAACP's official journal, *The Crisis*. After the initial call for other progressives to join the racial struggle, the NAACP held its first official conference in New York on May 31, 1909, with more than 300 blacks and whites in attendance. Once the NAACP became relatively established, its board of directors became increasingly composed of blacks; by 1934, most board members were black, and this trend has continued to the present time.

Among the most notable successes of the new social body was its highly organized protest against Woodrow Wilson's segregation of the federal government (1913) and also against D. W. Griffith's film, *The Birth of a Nation* (1915), in which blacks were portrayed as lazy, violent, and ignorant. Many scenes in the film depicted blacks as rapists, thugs, or watermelon-eating field hands, thus portraying a series of horrible stereotypes to a widespread audience. Outraged by these intensely offensive and socially damaging images, the NAACP launched its earliest widespread antidefamation campaigns. Through the NAACP's rigorous advertising and lobbying, the racist film was banned or no longer shown in many cities around the country. This first use of organized protest against the film and the Ku Klux Klan it glorified set a precedence of success that inspired the organization to move quickly and loudly against any and all misrepresentations of black people and culture. These two protests forced NAACP organizers to recognize the body's growing power and so, in 1917, they chose to use this power as a lever to force the federal government to allow blacks to be commissioned as officers in World War I. This success led to the commission of 600 black officers and the registration of 700,000 blacks for the draft. Integral to the NAACP's protests of black misrepresentation and segregation was their persistent presentation of blacks as fully enfranchised American citizens whose rights were fundamentally protected in the U.S. Constitution. It would be this Constitutional argument that would finally result in the eradication of widespread lynching, arguably one of the early NAACP's most important battles.

Perhaps because of its early emphasis on local organizing practices and rigorous recruitment, the NAACP's membership grew quickly, as did its number of branch offices across the United States. By 1919, the NAACP had more than 300 branch offices and 90,000 members. The year 1919 was also a noteworthy year in the NAACP for its publication of its investigative report, *Thirty Years of Lynching in the United States: 1889–1918*. Although the organization had spoken out against lynching as early as 1917, with this report, the NAACP took up the anti-lynching cause first emphasized

in earnest by journalist Ida B. Wells-Barnett. Although the organization never successfully forced anti-lynching legislation to be passed on a federal or state level during this era touted by its chroniclers as the worst period of racism in American history, the NAACP's persistent protest against lynching is credited with its decrease and eventual cessation. Equipping all its branches with a flag hung outside each time "A Black Man Was Lynched Today," once again, the NAACP demonstrated the power of collective dissension as President Woodrow Wilson spoke out publicly against lynching. Associated as he was with the Ku Klux Klan prior to his presidency and given his elitist opinions regarding white supremacy, Wilson's public anti-lynching statements cannot be underestimated as an important NAACP achievement. Through the body's persistent pressure, Wilson was forced to speak out.

Even as the NAACP was still fighting lynch mobs and mob hostility against blacks on a more general level, they also began to turn their attention to the unequal access to education, housing, health care, and public transportation blacks had historically received. Fighting a series of court cases and legislation involving the unconstitutionality of discrimination in these areas so crucial to civil rights, the NAACP won a string of victories in state and federal court, as well as in Congress. Notable among these victories were *Buchanan v. Worley* (housing districts could not be forced on blacks, 1917); admission of a black student to the University of Maryland (1935); *Morgan v. Virginia* (Supreme Court recognizes that states cannot segregate interstate public transport by bus or train, 1946); discrimination in federal government offices banned (1948); *Brown v. Board of Education* (the doctrine of separate but equal struck down in favor of desegregation, 1954); and the Civil Rights Act of 1964.

After a series of race riots and conflicts rocked Arkansas throughout 1919, resulting in 67 blacks being imprisoned and 12 sentenced to death, the NAACP became involved in an ongoing battle on behalf of blacks' receipt of due process under constitutional law (*see* Red Summer Race Riots of 1919 entry). A nearly five-year engagement in these efforts to ensure fair trial and representation resulted in another landmark case and ultimate win in 1923's *Moore v. Dempsey*, in which the NAACP made large ground against unfair prosecution of blacks and secured the release of many of those imprisoned in the state of Arkansas and other states.

As the civil rights movement gathered momentum in the late 1950s and early 1960s, the NAACP discussed the role it would play in these important times. Resolute in their use of state and federal courtrooms to battle racism and discrimination, the body kept itself as a whole out of the often fractious and dangerous social battles being waged on the streets of the South. This, however, did not prevent individual members from engaging in nonviolent protests. In 1960, the NAACP's Youth Council began a series of lunch counter sit-ins around the South, resulting in the desegregation of more than 60 department store eateries. In addition to these nonviolent protests, NAACP members organized widespread civil rights rallies. Due to the rallies' success, the NAACP named its first field director to oversee the legal and safety concerns of these peaceful protests. Ironically, field director and highly successful organizer Medgar Evers was fatally shot outside his home in 1963 (just five months before the assassination of President John F. Kennedy).

As the civil rights movement evolved, the NAACP did as well, eventually turning its attention to black participation in self-government through voting. Lobbying for voting sites in high schools, the NAACP persuaded 24 states to set up such sites by 1979. Concentration on the black vote would continue through the 1980s, as the NAACP extended the Voting Rights Act (1981) and as they registered record numbers of black voters (500,000 in 1982 alone). In tandem with their persistent efforts in the 1980s to increase political participation among the black community, the NAACP also brought global attention to apartheid in South Africa by rallying in New York City (1989) and by encouraging a boycott of that nation by all people of color. By 1993, the antiapartheid movement was successful, and in 1994, South Africa held its first all-race elections.

Since then, the NAACP has focused on appointing racially sensitive Supreme Court justices, preventing economic hardship in the black community, promoting higher education among blacks and other people of color, and providing alternatives to gang affiliation and violent behavior for black youths. Still thriving, still with much work to do, the NAACP continues to be a viable social, economic, legal, and political force in, and for, the black community in the United States. Although the organization's earliest and most direct connections to American literature are certainly *Crisis* editor W.E.B. Du Bois (*The Souls of Black Folk*) and poet and lyricist James Weldon Johnson ("Lift Every Voice and Sing"), the NAACP is also closely linked to black arts and literature through its nearly 40-year distribution of the Image Awards to black cultural producers such as Nikki Giovanni (*Quilting the Black Eyed Pea*) in 2003.

DEIRDRE RAY

See also

Birth of a Nation, The; Civil Rights Movement; Du Bois, W.E.B.; Evers, Medgar; Jim Crow Laws; Lynching; Marshall, Thurgood; Niagara Movement

Further Reading:

Cortner, Richard. *A Mob Intent on Death: The NAACP and the Arkansas Race Riots*. Middletown, CT: Wesleyan University Press, 1988.

Janken, Kenneth. *White: The Biography of Walter White, Mr. NAACP*. New York: New Press, 2003.

Jonas, Gilbert, and Julian Bond. *Freedom's Sword: The NAACP and the Struggle against Racism in America, 1909–1969*. New York: Routledge, 2004.

Kellogg, Clint. *NAACP: A History of the National Association of Colored People*. New York: The Johns Hopkins University Press, 1967.

Ovington, Mary White. *Blacks and Whites Sat Down Together: The Reminiscences of an NAACP Founder*. New York: Feminist Press, 1996.

Ross, Barbara. *J. E. Spingarn and the Rise of the NAACP, 1911–1939*. New York: Scribner, 1972.

Smith, John David. *The Ticket to Freedom: The NAACP and the Struggle for Black Political Integration*. Gainesville: University Press of Florida, 2005.

Tushnet, Mark. *The NAACP's Legal Strategy against Segregated Education, 1925–1950*. Chapel Hill: University of North Carolina Press, 1987.

Wedin, Carolyn. *Inheritors of the Spirit: Mary Ovington and the Founding of the NAACP*. New York: John Wiley and Sons, 1997.

Zangrando, Robert. *The NAACP Crusade against Lynching, 1909–1950*. Philadelphia: Temple University Press, 1980.

National Association of Colored Women (NACW)

"Lifting as We Climb" was the motto adopted by the National Association of Colored Women (NACW) formed on July 21, 1896, in Washington, D.C. This organization was led by black activist women who had a long history of working toward equality and social justice for their people. The organization included Ida B. Wells-Barnett, Josephine St. Pierre Ruffin, Mary Church Terrell, Anna Julia Cooper, Harriett Tubman, and Mary McLeod Bethune. The NACW involved the merging of two key black women's organizations—the National Federation of Afro-American Women and the National League of Colored Women. This was a period during which black women's clubs were instrumental in sustaining the spirit and vitality of black communities throughout the United States. The NACW published the *National Association Notes* as a tool for disseminating information of interest to black club women.

The black women's club movement evolved out of women joining together to develop mutual aid societies where they could work to ameliorate some of the social problems plaguing their communities. Black women in such cities as Boston, Chicago, Philadelphia, and Washington, D.C., formed intercity clubs to combat particular social ills that they witnessed ravaging their communities. The club women understood that a history of discrimination, oppression, and racial violence was literally crippling thousands of their sisters, and they aimed to address these problems through collective social activism. They focused much of their energy on improving the living conditions and status of men, women, and children through educational opportunities, job training, and life skill assessments.

The benevolence of these black women's organizations also inspired them to honor those individuals who were actively engaged in what they deemed important race work on behalf of their people. Club women began to visualize how they might do more to contribute to their various community issues. Thus, the seed was planted for the NACW, a coalition of black women's organizations that would build on the history and legacy of the hundreds of black women's charitable organizations.

The formation of the NACW grew out of a specific meeting by various representatives of women's clubs who came together on that July day to protest a letter written by James Jacks, the white president of the Missouri Association. Jacks hoped to quell the activities of the anti-lynching campaign organized by Ida B. Wells-Barnett by labeling all black women as prostitutes and thieves in a news publication. In response to this brutal assault on the character and dignity

of black women, club women including Terrell and St. Pierre Ruffin held a meeting in Washington, D.C., to discuss how to best respond to Jacks's verbal assault.

At the meeting they rationalized that their response would require a mobilized effort to continue their work for racial and social uplift of their people as a coalition. They elected Mary Church Terrell as their first national president. Terrell, having worked tirelessly to end both racial and gender inequality in the United States, was a founder and natural leader of this organization. Understanding the need for black women's organizations to harness collective energy and individual and/or social activism was essential to her leadership of this organization. Terrell admonished the women in her organization to consider all that they were obligated to do as privileged members of their race who had received education and opportunities for self-improvement. She further acknowledged the dire need for black women to speak out against a heap of injustices across gender and racial lines.

Terrell saw the NACW as a vehicle for providing substantive, transformative change in the lives of individuals who were personally affected by the travesty of racial injustice. A gifted orator and leader, Terrell was both convincing and dogmatic in her ability to persuade people to participate in and support her efforts. She regularly gave speeches around the country to increase participation and maximize opportunities to get black women to work together.

Anti-lynching legislation was one of their primary platforms and, more importantly, the NACW women were instrumental in dismantling the oppressive system that allowed lynching to flourish in the United States. During the 50-year period between 1880 and 1930, there were at least 2,362 black men, women, and children lynched. These startling numbers necessitated action on the part of the NACW. The women of the NACW joined forces with the National Association for the Advancement of Colored People (NAACP) and worked within their various clubs to support initiatives to promote black advancement.

Specific NACW efforts included fundraising for education, training, and social service care for their people. The NACW worked with other organizations to form the National Urban League. They also raised funds to restore the home of activist Frederick Douglass. In addition, NACW member Ida B. Wells-Barnett encouraged women to participate in both the suffrage and anti-lynching movements. In 1912, the

NACW began a national scholarship fund for college-bound black women. In 1913, the Northeastern Federation of Women's Clubs worked with the NAACP to hold anti-lynching rallies. More specifically, women in these organizations worked as members of a group called the Anti-Lynching Crusaders to galvanize 1 million women to suppress lynching and to pass the Dyer Anti-Lynching Bill. Although the bill was not passed, the efforts of these women were later the model and inspiration for the Association of Southern Women for the Prevention of Lynching in 1930. Black women in clubs were influential in fighting racial and sexual oppression through their active involvement in numerous social service activities, and their work was instrumental in countering the hegemonic practices of the nation in which they lived.

KIJUA SANDERS-MCMURTRY

See also

Anti-Lynching Legislation; Black Women and Lynching; Lynching; National Association for the Advancement of Colored People; Terrell, Mary Church; Wells-Barnett, Ida B.

Further Reading:

Carson, Emmett, D. *A Hand Up: Black Philanthropy and Self-Help in America*. Washington, DC: Joint Center for Political and Economic Studies, 1993.

Giddings, Paula. *When and Where I Enter: The Impact of Black Women on Race and Sex in America*. New York: William Morrow, 1984.

Salem, Dorothy. "National Association of Colored Women." In *Black Women in America: An Historical Encyclopedia, Vol. II, M–Z*, edited by Darlene Clark Hine, Elsa Barkley Brown, and Rosalyn Terborg-Penn. Bloomington and Indianapolis: Indiana University Press, 1993.

White, Deborah Gray. *Too Heavy a Load: Black Women in Defense of Ourselves, 1894–1994*. New York and London: W. W. Norton, 1999.

National Chicano Moratorium

Led mainly by student activists and the Brown Berets, the National Chicano Moratorium arose out of widely held and deeply felt Mexican American grievances, especially long-suffered rebuffs from U.S. government officials. The immediate occasion was the rising concern about the country's military involvement in Vietnam and the high percentage of Mexican American casualties.

In December 1969, an antidraft conference in Denver began plans for a demonstration in Los Angeles, and the following March, final arrangements for the march were completed by the second Chicano Youth Conference in Denver. The Los Angeles march was to climax earlier demonstrations throughout the Southwest. In August 1970, the largest group of Chicano demonstrators ever assembled, more than 25,000, met in East Los Angeles to rally in protest against the Vietnam conflict. The war had politicized and polarized even conservative middle-class Mexican Americans, so the national moratorium march was supported by most community organizations.

To avoid possible problems, the rally was closely monitored. However, trouble in a liquor store on the march route precipitated massive police interference, which was immediately extended to Laguna Park where early marchers were enjoying lunch while listening to music and speakers like Corky Gonzales. Some 500 helmeted police and sheriff deputies began a sweep of the park. Tear gas canisters were fired. Panic ensued. Rock and bottle throwing in the park quickly escalated into rioting, vandalizing, and looting on the Whittier Boulevard route and led to the arrest of several hundred marchers and to three deaths. Among those killed was veteran journalist and TV station KMEX news director Rubén Salazar. The televised 13-day coroner's inquest into Salazar's death became an occasion for denouncing the marchers and condemning the moratorium march.

In the aftermath of the moratorium there were small outbreaks of confrontation and violence between demonstrators and police in the Southwest. These occurrences served to strengthen ethnic solidarity. They also served to attract Chicanos to the platform of the new La Raza Unida party, particularly in California.

MATT MEIER AND MARGO GUTIÉRREZ

See also

Chicano Movement

Further Reading:

Acuña, Rodolfo. *Occupied America: A History of Chicanos*, 4th ed. New York: Longman, 2000.

Gómez-Quiñones, Juan. *Chicano Politics: Reality and Promise, 1940–1990*. Albuquerque: University of New Mexico Press, 1990.

Muñoz, Carlos. *Youth, Identity, Power: The Chicano Movement*. New York: Verso, 1989.

National Origins Act of 1924

The National Origins Act of 1924 severely restricted the flow of immigrants to the United States and marked the culmination of 40 years of anti-immigrant legislation. Also known as the Immigration Act of 1924 or the National Origins Quota Act of 1924, the National Origins Act was designed to preserve the existing ethnic makeup of the population, which was dominated by Western and Northern Europeans.

Millions of new immigrants arrived in the United States between 1880 and 1924, dramatically changing the nation's demography. The vast majority of these newcomers hailed from Southern Europe, particularly Italy, and Eastern Europe, including a large number of Jews from Poland and Russia. At the same time, rising nativism in the United States began to find expression in a series of laws designed to limit and control the ethnic and racial composition of the U.S. population. The Chinese Exclusion Act of 1882 initiated the use of national origins to restrict immigration, barring Chinese laborers.

Later legislation expanded and extended this exclusion, which remained in place until 1943. The Immigration Act of 1907 doubled the head tax on immigrants from $2 to $4 and granted the president powers to block immigration. In 1911, the U.S. Immigration Commission, also known as the Dillingham Commission, embraced the pseudoscience of the eugenics movement. It argued that immigrants from Southern and Eastern Europe were inferior to other races and as such were degenerate and unassimilable, becoming the source of many social problems. The commission proposed a bill based on national origins to limit this immigration, though it was not enacted into law. World War I saw a decrease in immigration to the United States and a rise in out-migration, as many immigrants left the country in the face of intense Americanization crusades. At the conclusion of the war, the Immigration Act of 1917 continued the restriction trend by requiring language literacy for immigrants over the age of 16 and creating an Asian "barred zone" extending exclusion to India, Burma, Malaysia, Arabia, Afghanistan, and parts of Russia. Despite attempts to impose stricter limits, immigration rates began to rise again in the postwar period. In response, Congress passed the National Origins Act of 1921, establishing temporary immigration quotas of 3 percent of each foreign-born nationality living in the United States based on the 1910 census, with a ceiling of 350,000 European immigrants. Originally enacted for one year, in 1922 it was extended for two more. Also in 1922, Congress passed a punitive and discriminatory law removing citizenship from

Immigration Restriction League of 1894

During the 1890s, for the first time, more new immigrants came from Southern and Eastern Europe than from Northern and Western Europe. The most prominent group of newcomers at this time were Italians, followed by Jewish immigrants. During this second great immigrant wave, many "native" Americans thought that their American way of life, especially based on Protestantism, was threatened by these "undesirable immigrants." Under this perceived threat, the Immigration Restriction League was founded in 1894 by Charles Warren, Robert DeCourcy Ward, and Prescott Farnsworth Hall. It was founded in Boston but quickly spread to many other cities across the country. The constitution stated the following as the main objectives of the League:

To advocate and work for the further judicious restriction, or stricter regulation, of immigration, to issue documents and circulars, solicit fact and information, on that subject, hold public meetings, and to arouse public opinion to the necessity of a further exclusion of elements undesirable for citizenship or injurious to our national character. It is not an object of this league to advocate the exclusion of laborers or other immigrants of such character and standards as fit them to become citizens.

With such intention, the League proposed that all immigrants should pass a literacy test before entering the country. The League remained active for nearly 20 years and made a significant impact on the enactment of the so-called National Origins Act of 1924. After Hall's death, the league's influence waned, and it eventually disbanded.

HEON CHEOL LEE

any U.S.-born woman who married an alien ineligible for citizenship.

The National Origins Act of 1924 set a new temporary annual quota of 2 percent of the foreign-born members of each nationality living in the United States in 1890. Setting the bar at this historically low point intentionally excluded Southern and Eastern Europeans, who immigrated in much larger numbers after 1890. The act further placed a ceiling of 150,000 total immigrants from Eastern Hemisphere countries, placed no quotas on Western Hemisphere nations, and completely excluded Asian immigration (with the exception of the U.S. colony in the Philippines). Exempted from the quotas were nuclear family members, ministers, professors, students, and women who had lost their citizenship through marriage to an alien. Within the quotas, preferences were given to parents, spouses, and unmarried children under age 21, as well as to skilled agricultural workers and their families. The act also shifted the administration of the immigration process to U.S. consular officials abroad.

The temporary quotas of the 1924 act were made permanent in 1929, and the 1920 census was established as the basis for their calculation. The 1929 revisions also expanded the notion of national origins to a percentage of "national stock," incorporating native and foreign-born Americans. The National Origins Act and its 1929 revisions gave clear preference to immigrants from Northern and Western Europe, who in the ensuing years received 83 percent of all visas, compared to 15 percent for those from Southern and Eastern Europe and 2 percent from the rest of the world.

In 1921, then vice-president Calvin Coolidge stated, "America must be kept American." The National Origins Act of 1924 succeeded in codifying the nativist and anti-immigrant sentiments of the age, including a belief in Nordic superiority and a fear of race mixing. As a result, the United States enacted the most restrictive and comprehensive immigration laws in its history and provided the foundation of immigration policy until 1965.

Kenneth J. Guest

See also

287g Delegation of Immigration Authority; Anchor Baby; Anti-Immigrant Sentiment; Immigration Acts; Immigration and Customs Enforcement; Operation Wetback; Unauthorized Immigration

Further Reading:

Foner, Nancy. *From Ellis Island to JFK: New York's Two Great Waves of Immigration.* New Haven, CT: Yale University Press, 2002.

Salyer, Lucy E. *Laws Harsh as Tigers: Chinese Immigrants and the Shaping of Modern Immigration Law.* Chapel Hill: University of North Carolina Press, 1995.

National Urban League

The National Urban League was founded in 1911 to ameliorate the social conditions affecting urban American Negroes. Due to the oppressive forces of Jim Crow and segregation, many Southern blacks began to migrate to the North. On September 29, 1910, in New York City, to address the numerous challenges that these new Northerners faced, two important individuals were instrumental in creating an organization called the Committee on Urban Conditions among Negroes. Ruth Standish Baldwin, a widow and social activist, worked with Dr. George Edmund Haynes (the first black person to receive a doctorate from Columbia University) to form this organization.

The evolution of the National Urban League occurred when two organizations (the Committee on Urban Conditions among Negroes and the Committee for the Improvement of Industrial Conditions among Negroes) merged to form the National League on Urban Conditions among Negroes. The name was shortened to the National Urban League in 1920. The National Urban League originally served those Negroes who were migrating from the South to the North in search of jobs and improved social conditions. The primary purpose of the organization in its early days was to address social and economic issues facing Negroes who were in dire need of employment, job training, housing, and health services. The National Urban League worked to provide assistance through community centers, clinics, camps, and affiliated organizations. The league was led by Professor Edwin R. A. Seligman of Columbia University, Mrs. Baldwin, and Dr. Haynes during the early days between 1911 and 1918.

The organization began to strategically attack perceptions of the intellectual inferiority of Negroes during the 1920s and 1930s. Sociologist Charles S. Johnson became the director of research and investigation for the National Urban League in 1921. Johnson founded the league's first publication. Between 1923 and 1949, the organization published a journal, *Opportunity: A Journal of Negro Life*. The motto of the journal was "Not Aims, but Opportunity." As editor of the journal, Charles Johnson also worked hard to dispel myths about Negroes, and the journal published numerous sociological studies with scientific methods for this purpose. Also, under the editorship of Charles Johnson, *Opportunity* was a leading force in publishing the work of Negro literary writers of the time. *Opportunity* published works by Gwendolyn Bennett, Langston Hughes, James Weldon Johnson, and Countee Cullen. It was through this vehicle that Charles Johnson became a central figure in the Harlem Renaissance.

At the helm of the league from 1918 to 1941 was Eugene Kinckle Jones, who was instrumental in organizing boycotts against companies and employers that would not hire blacks. He consistently pushed schools to expand their vocational programs for young people, and pressured Washington, D.C., officials to include blacks in New Deal programs. He also began the work to get blacks included in previously segregated labor unions.

Lester B. Granger was appointed successor to Eugene Jones and continued to work diligently to integrate the racist trade unions that were in existence at that time. Granger's leadership was focused on increasing the number of job opportunities for blacks, and he was successful in developing the league's Industrial Relations Laboratory, which worked to integrate the numerous defense plants that were active during this period. Granger was also very supportive of the National Urban League Guild, which was led by Mollie Moon on behalf of the league.

One of the National Urban League's most famous leaders was social worker and civil rights activist Whitney M. Young Jr., who succeeded Granger as executive director in 1961. Prior to Young's leadership, the National Urban League was considered one of the more conservative civic organizations. Often referred to as the Urban League, the organization was frequently focused on providing direct social services to its target population. Whitney Young worked actively to move the National Urban League forward and align it with other civil rights organizations. Young worked jointly with other civil rights leaders to organize the March on Washington in 1963. The National Urban League also helped to organize the Poor People's Campaign of 1968. During the 10 years that Whitney Young was executive director of the National Urban League, there were significant improvements in the league. The number of local chapters of the Urban League increased from 60 to 98, the staff of the organization increased from 500 to 1,200, and there was an increased amount of monetary support to the league.

Whitney Young died unexpectedly in March 1971. After his death, Vernon Jordan became president of the organization. Jordan began to lead the organization in the direction of implementing programs that would focus on health, housing, education, and job training. The Urban League began to publish a journal called the *Urban League Review* in 1975. Jordan also promoted Ron Brown to general counsel of the Urban League. Vernon Jordan was shot in the back by a confessed white supremacist on May 29, 1980, in Fort Wayne, Indiana, after delivering an address to the Fort Wayne Urban League. Jordan was hospitalized for months after this attempt on his life. He decided to resign from the Urban League in 1981. Under his leadership, the National Urban League tripled its budget and was able to hire many additional employees due to Jordan's ability to obtain significant corporate funding for the organization.

John E. Jacob succeeded Jordan as the leader of the Urban League in 1982. In 1982, the organization began publishing *The State of Black America*. Jacob established a permanent development fund to secure the financial future of the league and also established awards and programs in honor of former leader, Whitney Young. The Urban League began to highlight important social justice issues affecting the lives of black Americans. The league focused on emphasizing the importance of implementing self-help programs that would address issues of teen pregnancy and single parenthood in the black community.

Hugh B. Price became leader of the National Urban League in 1994. Price established the Institute of Opportunity and Equality in Washington, D.C. This institute conducted a research and public policy analysis of urban issues. Price also focused on implementing scholarship programs and assessing ways to increase academic achievement among black youth. The current president of the National Urban League is Marc H. Morial, a former New Orleans, Louisiana, mayor, who has already contributed greatly to securing millions of dollars in funding for the league's future endeavors.

KIJUA SANDERS-MCMURTRY

See also
Jim Crow Laws; Segregation

Further Reading:
Estell, Kenneth. *African America: Portrait of a People.* Canton, OH: Visible Ink Press, 1994.

Gilpin, Patrick, and Marybeth Gasman. *Charles S. Johnson: Leadership Beyond the Veil in the Age of Jim Crow.* Albany: State University of New York Press, 2003.

Hughes, Langston, and Milton Meltzer. *African American History,* 6th ed. New York: Scholastic, 1990.

"Jordan, Vernon." In *African American Lives,* edited by Henry Louis Gates Jr. and Evelyn Brooks Higginbotham. New York: Oxford University Press, 2004. http://www.nul.org/history .html.

"Jordan, Vernon Eulion, Jr." In *Africana Civil Rights: An A-Z Reference of the Movement that Changed America,* edited by Kwame Anthony Appiah and Henry Louis Gates Jr. Philadelphia: Running Press, 2004.

"National Urban League." In *Africana Civil Rights: An A-Z Reference of the Movement that Changed America,* edited by Kwame Anthony Appiah and Henry Louis Gates Jr. Philadelphia: Running Press, 2004.

Native American Boarding Schools

The boarding school experiment began with the origins of eastern schools like Harvard University, the College of William and Mary, and Dartmouth College long ago as small institutions. These Ivy League schools included in their mission the boarding and education of Native American youth. They have since lost some of their original mission, although a small number of Native students have attended William and Mary. More have graduated from Harvard, and Dartmouth has recruited Native American students actively since the early 1970s.

The boarding school experiment on a broad scale happened when Captain Richard Pratt opened the doors of Carlisle Indian Industrial School in 1879 in Carlisle, Pennsylvania. The school would become famous through Pratt's efforts to promote it and for its play in sports. With Carlisle,

a second main era of boarding schools for Native Americans occurred. Others soon followed, such as Chilocco, Chemewa, Sherman Institute, and Rainy Mountain.

Church groups introduced mission boarding schools that also strove to convert Native souls to Christianity. Several, such as St. Labre Indian School, a Catholic school for the Cheyenne, and Santee Mission School for the Lakota, were operating prior to Carlisle. During the rest of the 1800s and early decades of the 1900s, boarding and mission schools competed for students. Catholic and Protestant missionaries competed against each other trying to find enough Native American children to start a school. Other Christian groups such as United Church of Christ, Lutherans, Mormons, and others began to open schools.

Pratt, a former military officer who once fought Native Americans in the West, became history's Indian educator during the late 19th century. All of this began when he founded Carlisle Indian Industrial School by receiving permission to use some old army barracks. Pratt officially opened the doors of Carlisle Indian Industrial School on November 1, 1879. No sooner had Pratt started Carlisle than criticism arose about his way of educating Native students. Pratt believed the students had to be completely assimilated into American society. They would no longer be Native American in their traditional manner.

The daily routine at Indian boarding schools like Carlisle and others included a half day in reading, writing, arithmetic, and spelling. The remaining half day involved vocational training in manual labor, which actually benefited the school. Carlisle and the other Indian schools tried to be as self-sufficient as possible. Students raised their food, which included dairy and poultry products, and the girls worked in the kitchen and learned homemaking.

Boarding school life was harsh for the children. At many schools like Carlisle, they wore cadet uniforms, marched to class when a bell rang and obeyed teachers' commands. A typical day's schedule began at 5:30 and every minute of the morning and afternoon was accounted for. The evening meal was scheduled at 5:30 and taps was played at 8:30, putting the students to bed to rise the next morning to start another day.

The teachers allowed only English to be spoken in the schools and punished the students if they spoke their native tongue. Forcing the ways of European American civilization on the youths, students were taught to love the American flag and call the United States their homeland. If the children misbehaved in school, they were denied permission to visit their families during holidays. In a letter dated January 1902, Indian affairs commissioner William Jones instructed Indian agents on controlling Indian students:

> You are . . . directed to induce your male Indians to cut their hair, and both sexes to stop painting [their faces]. With some of the Indians this will be an easy matter, with others it will require Considerable tact and perseverance . . . to successfully carry out these instructions. . . . The returned students who do not comply and if they become obstreperous about the matter a short confinement in the guardhouse at hard labor, with shorn locks, should furnish a cure. Certainly all the younger men should wear short hair, and it is believed that by tact, perseverance, firmness, and withdrawal of supplies can induce "all" to comply with this order . . . The wearing of citizen's clothing, instead of the Indian costume and blanket, should be encouraged . . . Indian dances and so-called Indian feasts should be prohibited. In many cases these dances and feasts are simply subterfuges to cover degrading acts and to disguise immoral purposes.

Stubborn objectives at reservation and boarding schools prevented young Native Americans from learning about their people's past. To overcome the criticism from parents, teachers applied propaganda, and taught that the traditional Native ways were useless. When these teachings failed, the teachers punished the youth frequently until they properly responded. Parents were helpless to do anything, as the government maintained that forced learning would be in the overall best interest of the youth.

Many native people who attended boarding schools in the early decades of the 20th century had their names changed by school officials from their original Native American names to Christian names. The new Christian names had little meaning to the children because they were in a foreign language. Their original names, according to their tribal languages, held a meaning or description of their personality, and often their Native name changed as they grew older and accomplished important deeds or had some extraordinary experiences.

School officials had more than one reason for the name changes. Too often, they could not pronounce indigenous names in Native languages and "only English" was spoken, thus students assumed European first and last names. For instance, the last name of Peter MacDonald, former chairperson of the Navajo Nation, comes from the nursery song "Old MacDonald Had a Farm."

After students completed training at Pratt's Carlisle Indian Industrial School, they were provided an applied education for three years. The program's so-called outing system involved placing the students with non-Native rural families near the school, and sometimes they were placed in nonagricultural settings farther away. The federal government paid the host family $50 a year for the student's medical care and clothing. For the student, he or she learned the agricultural lifestyle from the farmer and his family. Pratt wanted the students trained in vocations and prepared for jobs. Towards its end, Carlisle included the first two years of high school as a part of its curriculum, and some teaching training.

Irregular attendance was a frequent problem, and running away from school was a common practice. Upon reaching home, the students were caught and returned to school, and this pattern often reoccurred with the same child. High dropout rates were another serious concern. A lack of motivation existed among the students and a general feeling of defeatism was evident among the students and their parents. Even after they graduated, students returned to their old ways, but things had changed. The communities on reservations and values were changing with continuous contact with non-Natives. Rather than using their education to secure a job and integrating into the mainstream society, many Native youth felt caught between two cultures.

Another critical problem that school officials faced was coaxing Native children to enroll in schools. To meet school enrollment quotas, U.S. Army patrols visited reservations and literally kidnapped children. Indian police, who were supervised by Indian agents on reservations, had the same duty. At times, mothers had to choose which child to turn over to school authorities by hiding their other children.

Uncooperative parents were sometimes locked in jail, or rations and annuities were withheld by the Indian agent until consent was obtained to give up the children.

Finally, in about 1900, the Bureau of Indian Affairs (BIA) relaxed its rigid policy of separating indigenous children from families. Although the schools on some reservations had the same policy of separating families, the number of reservation schools increased and more children were enrolled in public schools near their families.

The almost 40-year, extraordinary history of Carlisle ended on September 1, 1918, when the facility became a hospital in World War I. Many male students were old enough to join the army and navy in the war, so the student population was severely depleted even though not all Native Americans were classified as U.S. citizens. Because the general citizenship act for all Native peoples would not be passed until 1924, the students at Carlisle were similar to foreign exchange students, as the Native nations on reservations still maintained a certain degree of sovereignty.

Native American education had undergone the start of an important transformation from boarding schools to day schools. By the end of the 19th century, more than 20,000 Indian students attended 148 boarding schools and 225 day schools. The federal tradition of educating Native children in boarding schools continued for the next 100 years and more. Many of the same problems persisted.

DONALD FIXICO

See also
Indian Claims Commissions; Indian Removal and the Creation of Indian Territory; Indian Reorganization Act (1934); Indian Reservations; Native Americans, Conquest of; Native Americans, Forced Relocation of

Further Reading:
Adams, David Wallace. *Education for Extinction: American Indians and the Boarding School Experience, 1875–1928.* Lawrence: University Press of Kansas, 1995.

Calloway, Colin G., ed. *Our Hearts Fell to the Ground: Plains Indian Views of How the West Was Lost.* Boston: Bedford, 1996.

Calloway, Colin G., ed. *First Peoples: A Documentary Survey of American Indian History,* 2nd ed. Boston: Bedford, 2004.

Prucha, Francis Paul. *The Great Father: The American Indian and the United States Government.* Lincoln: University of Nebraska Press, 1986.

Native American Graves Protection and Repatriation Act (1990)

The Native American Graves Protection and Repatriation Act (NAGPRA) is legislation signed by President George H. W. Bush in 1990. Focusing on human skeletal remains housed in federal agencies or any other institutions receiving federal funds, the law requires each institution to inventory its collection of human skeletal remains and to make a concerted attempt to identify their cultural affiliation. Each institution must then notify the responsible tribes or organizations and transfer the remains if so requested.

Since the 18th century, excavation of Native American mounds and burial sites has been an ongoing scientific practice. The remains of human beings and sacred artifacts have been collected and stored by the Smithsonian; in a variety of state, local, and private museums; and at historical societies and universities. By the mid-1980s, anthropologists and museologists estimated that the remains of more than 600,000 Native Americans were being stored in the United States. Red Power activists viewed the continued storage of the skeletons as an intolerable racist legacy. Native activists demanded the repatriation of the bodies and reinterment in tribal burial grounds.

In 1989, Congress passed the National Museum of the American Indian Act, which mandated establishment of a separate museum of American Indians within the Smithsonian Institution and required the Smithsonian to develop a comprehensive plan to repatriate the more than 18,500 skeletal remains of Native Americans it possessed. In 1990, Congress followed up that legislation with NAGPRA. Museums had until November 16, 1995, to inventory all their holdings; by May 1, 1996, they were required to notify Native groups of those holdings. Museums could have sought extensions in developing the descriptions of their holdings, and federal budget cuts to the Bureau of Indian Affairs and museums around the country had guaranteed that such extensions would occur. But eventually the museums were required to work out arrangements for the return of artifacts and skeletons to Native American groups requesting them.

In 2010, the Department of the Interior introduced new NAGPRA amendments that would allow for the repatriation of culturally unidentifiable Native American remains to a modern-day tribe on whose current or ancestral lands the remains were found. Before then, universities and institutions who held such remains had no clear direction on how to return them to tribes.

JAMES S. OLSON

See also

Bureau of Indian Affairs; Native Americans, Conquest of; Native Americans, Forced Relocation of

Further Reading:

Horse Capture, George P. *The Concept of Sacred Materials and Their Place in the World*. Cody, WY: Buffalo Bill Historical Center, 1989.

Mauch Messenger, Phyllis, ed. *The Ethics of Collecting Cultural Property: Whose Culture? Whose Property?* Albuquerque: University of New Mexico Press, 1989.

Price, H. Marcus. *Disputing the Dead: U.S. Law on Aboriginal Remains and Grave Goods*. Columbia: University of Missouri Press, 1991.

Zimmerman, Larry J. "Sharing Control of the Past." *Archaeology* 47 (November/December 1994): 65–68.

Native Americans, Conquest of

The continent of North America was a peaceable place where Native Americans lived in harmony with nature, before white settlers arrived there. Those first people had migrated from Asia across Beringia, a land that then connected Siberia to present-day Alaska, following the large animal herds at least 15,000 years ago. They spread over what is now the Americas, ranging from the Arctic to the southern tip of South America, and created hundreds of Indian nations with different languages and unique cultures. Italian explorer Christopher Columbus's arrival in the Bahamas in 1492 marked the European intrusion into the existence of these indigenous people. The Indian population in 1492 was at least 72 million in the Western Hemisphere, with more than 5 million of them living in what eventually became the United States. After the onset of European contacts and colonization, the Indian population of North America decreased tremendously, to 600,000 by 1800 and to 250,000 by the 1890s. European diseases, warfare, and the U.S. government's geographical removal and relocation caused the deaths of many Indians and the destruction of

their ways of life. The history of Indians in the United States has been a history of conquest.

After Columbus landed in the New World, European explorers, Jesuit priests, and slave hunters swarmed to the Americas in the 17th century. They were anxious to find gold, convert the "savages," and capture the natives and sell them as slaves. At first, the Indians helped Europeans settle down in the New World by providing food, shelter, and land and by teaching them how to grow crops and how to fish and catch wild animals. But European settlers treated Indians as "savages" and tried to exterminate them by using all kinds of methods, including spreading diseases through blankets contaminated with germs and killing them by swords and guns.

Hernando De Soto, Francisco Vasquez Coronado, and Hernando Cortez each explored Florida, New Mexico, and California respectively to find gold but could not find any. However, the Spanish government was successful in converting Indians to Catholicism. Unlike the Spaniards, whose goal was to find gold and other riches of the Indians, and the French, who concentrated on the fur trade, the British used every method to take away land from Indians. When English settlers landed in Jamestown, Virginia, in 1607, they were well received by Powhatans. But, as settlers started to take Indian land, as well as their crops and game, Indians became vigilant against the Europeans' greed and hostility. The tensions between the Europeans and Indians grew deeper, which made warfare unavoidable. Only 37 years after welcoming the first English settlers in Jamestown, the Powhatans were defeated by the English.

The pilgrims who arrived in Plymouth on the *Mayflower* in 1620 were well received by the Wampanoags, led by Massasoit. After Massasoit celebrated the first Thanksgiving with the pilgrims in 1621, more and more settlers came to the New England shore from England. From 1630 on, England sent more than 1,000 English settlers to Massachusetts with a slogan "to build a perfect Christian Society in the New World." They were eager to buy or take lands from the Indians because land meant commodity, wealth, and security for them. Indians, who had no concept of land ownership, considered land as a gift from God to be shared by everybody, so Massasoit signed the papers when the English wanted any land. Problems occurred when the English forbade Indians to hunt and fish in the land that Massasoit had allowed settlers to use. When Massasoit died and his second son, Metacomet (Europeans called him King Philip) became the chief, he prepared for war against the British as more and more settlers moved into Wampanoag territory and killed Indians. In 1675, Metacomet and his warriors destroyed 12 English colonies out of 52 with the help of other allied Indian tribes. But after several months of prolonged warfare, Metacomet's warriors were defeated and Metacomet was killed. Finally, the British soldiers defeated the Wampanoags.

In the early 18th century, the British colonists, who tried to expand their territory from the Atlantic coast to the West, came into contact with the French in the Mississippi area. After 10 years of warfare, the British defeated the French in 1763 by winning Montreal and occupied Canada and the vast Indian land from the Appalachians to the Mississippi River. After the war, the British Parliament started to collect money from the new colony to offset the financial deficit incurred by the war against France.

When the colonies became an independent nation in 1776, Indians hoped to maintain better relations with Anglos after the British, the French, and the Spanish left. However, Indians were forced to live under even more aggravated circumstances. The U.S. government signed treaties with Indian nations and then broke them to take Indian land and distribute it to white settlers. After frontiersman Daniel Boone invaded Indian land and built a village called Boone's Borough in the West, poor farmers and laborers who did not own any land wanted to go west. As tens of thousands of white settlers moved west of the Mississippi River, they killed Indians, destroyed their ways of life, and took their lands. For example, when the Shawnees tried to make the Ohio River the permanent boundary between the U.S. and Indian land, William Henry Harrison's troops destroyed Prophetstown founded by the Shawnee Chief Tecumseh in 1812. General Andrew Jackson and his army slaughtered more than 10,000 Creek Indians during the Creek War of 1813–1814 and took 14 million acres—two-thirds of their land.

When Andrew Jackson became the president of the United States in 1828, he started an aggressive policy toward Indians by using the power of the U.S. Army. With the Indian Removal Act passed by Congress, the U.S. government massively removed Indian tribes from their native lands and forcefully relocated them to unfamiliar and barren land in the West. In 1834, Indian Territory was created, including present-day Kansas, most of Oklahoma, and parts of Nebraska, Colorado, and Wyoming, which continued to be reduced until it eventually became the size of present-day Oklahoma. The U.S. government forced Indian tribes to move to Indian Territory, but the removal and relocation of the Cherokees from Northern Georgia to Oklahoma between 1838 and 1839 was especially tragic.

After gold was found in the Cherokee land in northern Georgia, the state of Georgia claimed jurisdiction over a part of the Cherokee land. The Cherokees resisted the pressures to cede their land and move west of the Mississippi River. After the Treaty of New Echota was signed between the U.S. government and some Cherokee people, Chief John Ross and other leaders protested. However, General Winfield Scott and his army invaded the Cherokee Nation and forced them to move out of their land. Chief John Ross and almost 17,000 Cherokees were held in stockades until they finally removed themselves into 13 groups and traveled north and west from Georgia to the Indian Territory in Oklahoma. They marched 1,000 miles, riding on horses or wagons or walking in freezing rains and blizzards for five months until they reached their destination. During this long march, approximately 4,000 Cherokee Indians were reported to have died from starvation and disease. Also, about 8,000 Navajos were forced to walk 300 miles from Arizona to a reservation in New Mexico by Kit Carson and his troops.

After removing Indians from their nations, the federal government started driving Indians into reservations. When the transcontinental railroad linking the East and West coasts was completed in 1869, the settlers took a lot of vast Indian hunting grounds and slaughtered a large number of buffalo. Plains Indians lost their supply of buffalo, which they needed for food, tents, and other necessities while those in the Indian Territories were forced onto smaller and smaller plots of poor lands unfit for cultivation. White settlers continued to demand more land, and the Indian reservations shrank rapidly.

Terminating the Identity and Culture of Indians through Military Campaigns

After the U.S. troops forcefully removed Indians from their native and sacred land to unfamiliar and barren Indian territories and relocated them on tiny reservations, the federal government made every effort to eradicate Indian identity and culture. With the Indian Appropriation Act of 1871, the U.S. government ceased recognizing Indian tribes as sovereign nations and forbade them to leave the reservations without permission.

When gold was discovered on the Cheyenne reservations in the Black Hills of South Dakota, General George Custer and his army attacked Sioux, Cheyenne, and Arapaho in the Little Big Horn Valley in his campaign to force them into reservations. The U.S. government drove the surviving Indians to reservations and took most of the Sioux land from the Indians. The U.S. Army also chased approximately 800 fleeing Nez Perce Indians and forced them onto a reservation and sent the survivors to Indian Territory in Oklahoma. The Black Hills in Dakota had been a sacred land for the Sioux Indians for many years. But, white miners invaded the Black Hills to find gold, with about 15,000 miners swarming to this area in 1875. The federal government asked the Sioux to sell the Black Hills, but they refused and decided to fight for the sacred land in late 1875 under the command of the great warrior Sitting Bull. In this battle, Indians had achieved their greatest victory yet, but after General Custer was killed in the battle, white people demanded harsh revenge against Indians. They redrew the boundary lines of the Black Hills, placing it outside the reservation and open to white settlement. Within a year, the Sioux nation was defeated and broken.

After losing the Black Hills as well as other lands, the Sioux people became dependent upon the U.S. government for food, clothing, and other things. Encountering starvation, fatal diseases, and reduced rations, they desperately needed hopes and dreams. The Ghost Dance Religion initiated by the prophet Wovoka was spreading among northern Plains Indians. Ghost dancers wore a spiritual shirt, believing that it would protect them from white people's bullets. They also believed that the Great Spirit would protect Indians from the white power and revive the Indians who were killed. In 1890, the Sioux people were totally enthralled to this religion. Even Sitting Bull learned this dance and taught it to other Sioux Indians. On the other hand, white settlers believed the rumor that Ghost Dance believers would kill the settlers. Upon receiving the petition from the settlers, the U.S. army marched through the Plains to arrest Sitting Bull. After Sitting Bull was shot during a violent fight between the Indian police and the

followers of Sitting Bull, some Sioux Indians joined Big Foot, the leader of the Miniconjou Sioux.

The military captured Big Foot, known as the Ghost Dance leader, and his followers, and took them to Wounded Knee Creek. There were 470 soldiers and around 350 Indians, including women, old men, and children. The military was going to disarm Big Foot's warriors before removing them by trains to the Cheyenne River Reservation. But when some warriors fired at the soldiers, they fired back and killed one half of the warriors in one volley. The combat between the soldiers and the warriors continued, and 31 soldiers and about 300 Indians were killed during this massacre. The troops had stripped the Ghost Dance shirts off the dead bodies and shoved the remaining bodies into the trench and buried them. This was the last resistance of the Sioux Indians, which completed the European conquest of Indians.

There are several indigenous peoples around the world, who make up about 5 percent of the total population of the globe, but no other indigenous group has been so cruelly massacred and terminated than Indians in the United States. During the colonial period, English settlers were more cruel to Native Americans than Spanish or French settlers had been. As noted, the U.S. government's changing policies toward Native Americans contributed to the extermination of Indians, appropriation of their vast land, and destruction of their culture and religion. The surviving Indians in the United States (approximately 2.4 million in 2000), whether living in reservations or cities, in general maintain a low standard of living and poor health conditions comparable to African Americans. But partly because of a relatively small population and partly because of Americans' amnesia regarding history, neither scholars nor policymakers have paid enough attention to "Indian issues."

ON KYUNG JOO

See also
Indian Claims Commissions; Indian Removal and the Creation of Indian Territory; Indian Reorganization Act (1934); Indian Reservations; Native American Boarding Schools; Native Americans, Forced Relocation of

Further Reading:
Bragdon, Kathleen Joan. *The Columbia Guide to American Indians of the Northeast.* New York: Columbia University Press, 2001.

"Cherokee Indians Forcibly Removed from North Georgia." http://ngeorgia.com/ history/hghisttt.html.

Cothran, Helen, ed. *The Conquest of the New World*. San Diego: Greenhaven Press, 2002.

Cothran, Helen, ed. *Early American Civilization and Exploration—1607*. San Diego: Greenhaven Press, 2003.

Jones, Constance. *The European Conquest of North America*. New York: Facts On File, 1995.

Sheppard, Donald E. NACC. (Native American Consulting Committee). "Native American Conquest. American History for Teens." http://e-student.net/inset32.html.

Thornton, Russell. *American Indian Holocaust and Survival: A Population History since 1492*. Norman: University of Oklahoma Press, 1987.

Native Americans, Forced Relocation of

Andrew Jackson, as the seventh president of the United States (1829–1837), introduced the Indian Removal bill, enacted in 1830, which made it possible to legally force all tribes remaining east of the Mississippi River to relocate west of the river. The Indian Removal bill, the first step toward the creation of a national reservation system, designated Indian Territory in the present-day states of Iowa, Kansas, Oklahoma, and Arkansas and required Native Americans to move there. The bill specified that tribes should be paid for their lands through negotiation. Resistance to the sale and relocation, however, was met with force to gain the tribes' compliance.

Jackson's removal policy was directed primarily against Native Americans who preferred to live in traditional ways under their own tribal government. The Indian Removal bill permitted members of these tribes to stay in the Southeast only if they agreed to live in the manner of white settlers. This meant that the tribe had to agree to divide the land into allotments to farm, become "civilized," and abide by the laws of the states they lived in.

By the time this bill was passed, the white population of the United States had increased to nearly 13 million. More land was needed to accommodate their needs. There was also growing animosity toward tribes as European settlement in the Southeast increased rapidly in the 1820s. At the same time, the government wanted to hold a buffer zone between United States and European holdings in the western part of the continent by moving eastern American Indians. This plan would allow for American expansion westward from the original colonies to the Mississippi River.

Five tribes of the Southeast—the Cherokees, Creeks, Chickasaws, Choctaws, and Seminoles—who already had begun assimilating, also had to sign treaties and move west to the Indian Territory under military escort. Under the terms of the treaties, the U.S. government promised that it would pay for tribal lands if the tribe gave up their eastern territory. It also promised to pay the cost of relocating and to support Native Americans for one year after relocation. After the treaties had been signed, some bands of the five "civilized" tribes decided to start for Indian Territory as soon as possible, hoping to obtain the best land. Other bands were determined to stay on in their ancestral homelands until the army forced them to leave.

In 1838, the last group of Cherokees began their journey on what became known as the Trail of Tears. Because most Cherokees had refused to abandon their land until the government demanded it, they did not have time to prepare for the trip. They suffered from disease and hunger, and out of 180,000 people who set out on the Trail of Tears, only about 140,000 (78 percent) reached the Indian Territory in Oklahoma. The figures do not measure the grief they felt about leaving their homes. This forced relocation also involved an eight-year war between the U.S. government and bands of Seminoles led by Chief Osceola. The Seminoles won the war, escaping into the Florida Everglades, out of reach of government troops. There they made a new life for their people.

Native Americans who survived the journey to Indian Territory found adapting to reservation life difficult. The main challenge, besides the unfamiliar environment, was frequent trouble with indigenous local tribes whose ways of life were quite different from theirs. The local tribes moved from place to place to hunt buffalo. As the buffalo population decreased and more Native Americans moved to Indian Territory, conflicts over hunting rights and dwelling resources increased among tribes. In addition, the U.S. government often failed to keep the promise that they would provide food, goods, and money and to protect them from attack by other tribes and white settlers. As more displaced Native Americans crowded into the Indian Territory, the government required them to live on smaller reservations. By the mid-1840s, most of the Native Americans who had lived east of the Mississippi River were gone. Between 1830 and 1850, the United States had forced at least 100,000 Native Americans to relocate to western reservations.

SOOKHEE OH

See also

Indian Claims Commissions; Indian Removal and the Creation of Indian Territory; Indian Reorganization Act (1934); Indian Reservations; Native American Boarding Schools; Native Americans, Conquest of

Further Reading:

Forman, Grant. *Indian Removal: The Emigration of the Five Civilized Tribes of Indians.* Norman: University of Oklahoma Press, 1953.

Sokolow, Gary. *Native Americans and the Law: A Dictionary.* Santa Barbara, CA: ABC-CLIO, 2000.

Nativism and the Anti-Immigrant Movements

The United States has been a nation of immigrants and for immigrants. From the earliest settlers to the latest newcomers, millions of immigrants have arrived, settled, and contributed to the building of the nation. And yet, it has also been a nation of anti-immigrant movements. Immigrants often have been reviled as sources of political, economic, and social problems. Discriminatory laws against immigrants have been enacted; their fundamental rights have been denied; and they have even been physically assaulted. The overall attitudes and actions toward immigrants have oscillated between welcoming new immigrants and restricting them.

This ambivalent attitude toward immigrants started after white Anglo-Saxon Protestants established themselves as a dominant host group and became the "native." Since then, the category of the native has expanded to white Protestants and then to all whites in contemporary America. As the category of the native has changed, the targets of anti-immigrant movements have also changed from non–Anglo-Saxons to non-Protestants and now to non-white immigrants.

The anti-immigrant movements have not been constant. They have surged and receded. What factors account for the rise of anti-immigrant movements? Despite the differences in different historical periods, some general patterns can be discerned. It seems obvious that when a large number of immigrants came to the United States, it created a conducive condition for the surge of nativism. When new waves of immigrants arrived on American shores during the periods of 1880–1924 and 1970–2003, anti-immigrant movements arose in America.

The volume of immigrants is just one condition. More importantly, nativist reactions have surged when a large number of new immigrants were physically and culturally different from the dominant native-born Americans. Such differences or perceived differences provided a fertile ground for anti-immigrant movements. During the 1880–1924 periods, Italian, Irish, Jewish, and Eastern European immigrants, as well as Asian immigrants, were thought to be significantly different from the dominant "native" Anglo-Saxon Americans. These latest immigrants from Southern and Eastern Europe differed from the previous immigrants, and it was widely claimed that they were much more difficult to assimilate. Some nativists believed that they were even "racially" different from and inferior to the native-born whites, who were said to be of "Nordic" racial stock.

Since the late 1960s, there has been similar concern about the different national origins of the newest immigrants. Immigrants from Latin America, Asia, and the Caribbean make up the vast majority of these new immigrant groups. To the natives, they are too different and too diverse to be assimilated into American culture and to become Americans. In this regard, it should be noted that, in the United States, nativism has often taken the form of racism.

The third condition that has contributed to the anti-immigrant movements is the existence of economic, political, and social problems in the United States. In other words, the anti-immigrant sentiments have surged not only because of the large number and characteristics of immigrants but because of when the existing social, political, and economic conditions of the United States were more severe. When the United States has been at war with other countries, its economy has been contracting and in recession, and/or it has been divided by controversial social issues such as slavery, anti-immigrant activities arose and strengthened. Such conditions often led to the targeting of immigrants as scapegoats for the hardships and fears of Americans.

Strangers in the Land: Patterns of American Nativism, 1860–1925

Historians Leonard Dinnerstein and David Reimers praise John Higham's 1955 publication, *Strangers in the Land*, as "the most sophisticated analysis of American nativist thought ever penned by an American historian." Although this book focuses only on the period from 1860 to 1925, it remains a classic and a must-read for anyone interested in American attitudes toward immigrants. In studying nativism, Higham analyzed a set of ethnocentric attitudes that united two ideas: (1) defining and celebrating as "American" only what was considered to be white, Protestant, Anglo-Saxon culture and its associated social, political, and economic institutions; and (2) depicting immigrants as dangerous threats to the nation because they were religiously different (Catholic or Jewish), alleged to be political radicals, or deemed to be racially inferior.

Strangers in the Land begins in a period of mass open immigration to the United States with no government regulation, and concludes in a time of very restrictive discriminatory nationality quotas imposed by Congress in 1917, 1921, and 1924. Higham analyzed the successes and failures of organizations that lobbied to reduce the number of immigrant "strangers" entering the United States, and described the actions of groups that tried to "Americanize" the newcomers. He shows fluctuations in the intensity, popularity, and content of Americans' beliefs and fears about foreigners by documenting opinions and attitudes of political, business, religious, scientific, editorial, and literary leaders as they shifted between an optimistic faith in the capacity of America to absorb large numbers of immigrants and create a better society, and a pessimistic belief that immigrants could not be absorbed and would weaken or destroy American society.

Strangers in the Land was one of the first books to delve into prejudice against immigrants. It was followed by many others and has been criticized for neglecting prejudiced attitudes toward Asians and Mexican "strangers," but it remains a monumental work of historical scholarship.

CHARLES JARET

Throughout U.S. history, nativism has been manifested in many different ways and taken a variety of forms. People organized themselves, creating anti-immigrant ideologies, publishing anti-immigrant materials, spreading anti-immigrant sentiment, and taking collective actions against immigrants, their descendants, and future immigrants. The Immigration Restriction League of 1894 and the Federation for American Immigration Reform of 1992 are two typical examples of such organizations. Nativists sometimes took violent actions against immigrants, as can be seen in the case of anti-Catholicism in the United States. Another extreme example of anti-immigrant sentiment was the Mexican Repatriation that was undertaken during the 1930s. In 1871, 62 Irish Catholics were killed and 100 others injured when they protested against the militantly anti-Catholic Orange Order.

However, the most effective anti-immigrant nativist strategy was to lobby politicians to enact laws to bar or restrict the immigration of "undesirable" people. The most notorious example of such restrictive immigration laws was the Immigration Act of 1924, better known as the National Origins Act or the National Origins Quota Act. Congress passed this law after many white supremacists, including influential scholars, such as Henry Goddard and Madison Grant, had emphasized the inferiority of non-Protestant immigrant groups. Beginning with the Chinese Exclusion Act of 1882, Congress passed a number of laws in the late 19th and early 20th centuries whose chief purpose was to exclude Asian immigrants. They include the Gentlemen's Agreement of 1907 and 1908 (which banned the immigration of Japanese laborers), the 1917 Immigration Act (which barred the immigration of laborers from the Asiatic Barred Zone), and the National Origin Quota Act of 1924 (which provided for the permanent exclusion of any alien ineligible for citizenship). Since a 1790 statute made only "Caucasians" eligible for citizenship, Asians and other people from non-European countries were ineligible for citizenship and could not immigrate to the United States. Thus, anti-immigration laws restricted immigration based on race or national origin.

In the post-1965 era too, many outspoken individuals and groups have emphasized the inassimilability of Third World immigrants and have lobbied for laws to reduce immigration generally and/or change the ethnic and racial composition

of immigrants. However, their efforts have not been successful. In fact, the Immigration Act of 1990 increased the
number of preference immigrants by 40 percent, to 675,000
per year. No individual or group can now persuasively argue
for the restriction of immigration from particular countries
or regions of the world, mainly because the Immigration Act
of 1965 abolished the discrimination in immigration based
on national origin or race. Instead, in the post-1965 era, the
general public and government of the United States are both
far more concerned about the flow of illegal aliens. Most
Americans think that the influx of illegal aliens has contributed to the increase in crime, welfare, job competition, and
housing difficulties. As a result, in 1994 California passed a
referendum that was to make illegal residents and their children ineligible for the benefits of free public education and
health care. The U.S. federal government, too, tried to restrict the flow of illegal immigration by reducing illegal entry
and visa overstay through more effective border patrol and
enforcement of the laws on the one hand and by sanctioning
employers who hire illegal residents on the other (the Immigration Reform and Control Act of 1986 and the Immigration
Act of 1990).

The nativists also reacted to the influx of immigrants by
lobbying for an assimilationist policy to make immigrants
and their children give up their cultural traditions as soon
as possible and acculturate to the American fabric along the
Anglo-Saxon line. However, the pursuit of assimilationist
policy also has been much less successful in the post-1965
era than in the beginning of the 20th century. In the first
two decades of the 20th century, federal and local governments, following the nativist, ethnocentric rhetoric, tried
to coerce immigrants to give up their old-world cultural
orientation and attachments to their homelands. The main
mission of public schools at that time was to Americanize the children of immigrants by replacing their language
and cultures with English and Anglo-Saxon customs, values, and habits. But similar arguments for the one-sided
assimilationist policy have not gained much support from
policymakers in the post-1965 era. African American and
other minority leaders and feminists had already started
the multicultural movement emphasizing cultural diversity
in the 1960s, concurrently with, or even before, the massive
immigration of Third World immigrants began. Since the
early 1970s, the U.S. government has gradually replaced the

policy of Anglo-conformity with that of cultural pluralism.
The change in the government's policy has been in its reaction to the multicultural movement and to the influx of new
immigrants who have entirely different cultural traditions.
Nativists have been successful in getting English-only laws
passed in several states, but these laws making English the
standard language have had little practical impact on the
lives of immigrants.

Nativists have provided various arguments as to why immigration should be restricted and/or immigrants should be
assimilated. Charles Jaret (2002) analyzed in detail the variety of claims on the negative impact of new immigrants. One
of the most persistent arguments has been that immigrants
pose a threat to the U.S. economy and place a burden on
government resources. Nativists have claimed that the immigrant workers take jobs away from native-born American
workers. Since immigrants are willing to accept lower wages
and work under worse conditions, nativists argue, they have
negative effects on American workers' ability to protect their
jobs, maintain wage levels, and ensure acceptable working
conditions. Thus, immigrant workers have been labeled
"wage-busters" or "wage-downers."

Nativist arguments by white workers about the negative
effects of immigrants on the American labor market were
typified by the anti-Chinese movement at the end of the 19th
century. The nativists repeatedly insisted that the Chinese
workers lowered wages and, consequently, the American
standard of living. Led by Denis Kearney, the Workingman's
Party argued that "the Chinese laborer is a curse to our land,
is degrading to our morals, is a menace to our liberties, and
should be restricted and forever abolished." Thus, the argument of white labor leaders about Chinese workers' "excessive competition," as well as anti-Chinese prejudice, was the
major factor that contributed to the passage of the Chinese
Exclusion Act by the U.S. Congress, the nation's first immigration restriction against a particular group on the basis of
national origin.

In the post-1965 era, proponents of immigration restriction have used the economic-burden argument more often
than the economic-threat argument. They have argued that
the newest immigrants pose a greater economic burden, especially because their skills and education levels are lower
than those of previous immigrants. Nativists argue that the
overall economic impact of immigrants has been negative

and that immigrants often aggravate the government's "fiscal crisis" because of the direct and indirect costs to the government. Under such circumstances, nativists assert that immigration is a drain on public resources and a drag on the economy. Especially in California, where large numbers of Mexican and other immigrants of generally lower economic status are settled, the economic-burden argument has gained popularity. In 1994, the anti-immigrant forces were mobilized and California voters approved Proposition 187, the enforcement of which would have deprived undocumented residents and their children of free education and medical treatment. Although it was eventually ruled unconstitutional, a few similar measures were incorporated in the Welfare Reform Law passed in 1996.

In the present era, "a new form of nativism" has emerged over the ownership of small business, which has always been the route for immigrants' upward mobility. Rooted in anger over economic disadvantage and exploitation, some native-born African Americans have targeted immigrants who own businesses in their neighborhoods, arguing that they are deprived of economic opportunities due to unfair competition from new immigrant entrepreneurs. Korean American merchants in Los Angeles have often been the victims of violent acts resulting in injuries and property damage caused by disgruntled blacks.

These arguments against immigration have been countered by the number of studies that conclude that immigration has a positive impact on the U.S. economy. Michael Fix and Jeffrey Passel (1994) reexamined the economic effects of recent immigrants and concluded that the cost of providing welfare benefits to legal immigrants is lower than has been claimed and that the impact of immigration on job displacement and wages is far more modest than it is widely perceived to be. Furthermore, immigrants contribute to economic growth by providing inexpensive labor, being willing to work hard, and taking risks as business entrepreneurs. Proponents of immigration argue that immigrants should not be blamed for problems such as the sluggish economy, when the source of the problem lies elsewhere.

Another common argument against immigrants has been that immigrants are threats to American identity and cultural unity. The nativists assert that certain types of immigrants undermine American identity and cultural unity—common values, a common language, and common

Uncle Sam and "Enemy Alien" sitting on a bench with a snake and a snail in "Liberty Park," 1918. "Enemy Alien" is monopolizing the bench, leaving little room for Uncle Sam. (Library of Congress)

political institutions. They are, culturally, too different from the "American mainstream" to be Americanized and too diverse among themselves to be culturally unified. The nativists assert that diverse immigrants are a direct threat to American identity and may lead U.S. society to cultural fragmentation. Such an argument has a long historical precedent. In the 1830s–1840s, when large numbers of Irish and German Catholic immigrants arrived, anti-Catholic activities surged in the United States to protect Protestant America from these "un-American" foreigners. Later, a similar argument was used to protect against the "unassimilable" Chinese. For the same reason, the alien land laws were passed in California in 1913 and 1920 to prevent "un-American" Japanese immigrants from owning American agricultural

Yellow Peril

The Yellow Peril is one of the most sinister stereotypes of Asians and Asian Americans. The Yellow Peril may have originated from a painting completed in 1895 by Kaiser Wilhelm II of Germany that depicted the menace to nations of Europe and their holiest possessions—civilizations and Christianity—by heathen of the Orient. But the origins of the idea of the Yellow Peril can be traced to the European imagination long before Wilhelm II's articulation, perhaps as early as the fifth century B.C., arising from the Greek-Persian conflict, or in the 13th century A.D., when Mongols devastated portions of Europe. The Yellow Peril was a means of defining European identity and a justification of European expansion and colonization.

In the American context, the notion of Yellow Peril suggests that Asians were seen as a threat to white-dominated society. Such a threat takes the material form of physical danger, economic competition with white labor, moral degeneracy, and sexual conquest. It signifies the irrational fear of Oriental conquest, with its racial and sex fantasy overtones. While not the first Yellow Peril character, the literary and cinematic character the diabolic Dr. Fu Manchu, created by British author "Sax Rohmer" (a.k.a. Arthur Sarsfield Ward) in *The Mystery of Fu Manchu* (1913; American title, *The Insidious Dr. Fu Manchu*), is the archetype of the Yellow Peril image. The Yellow Peril is created to demarcate racial lines, to reinforce white supremacy, and to alert against Asian invasion of white culture and society.

PHILIP YANG

land. The effort of keeping America as it was defined by nativists resulted in the enactment of anti-immigrant laws like the National Origins Quota Act of 1924.

The same argument—immigrants' threats to American identity and cultural unity—has been used again against recent immigrants. These recent waves of immigrants have been physically and culturally diverse among themselves and different from dominant white America, altering the nation's ethnic mix significantly. White Americans were again threatened by the influx of "different" people, mostly coming from Latin America and Asia. The nativists once again assert that America is going through an identity crisis and "disuniting of America" (Schlesinger 1991). They warn that these newest immigrants, in conjunction with the upsurge in ethnic awareness, may cause the fragmentation of American society and a national identity crisis.

Based on the fear of such cultural fragmentation, in the early 1980s, nativists launched a movement to restrict the language of government to English only. The campaign won broad support among Americans who believe that cultural unity is necessary to maintain the United States as a nation-state. Nativists also argued that immigrants needed to learn English for their own survival. But, in fact, the legislative means were often punitive, blocking essential services to immigrants and their children, such as driver's-license exams. For this purpose, nativists argue that the overall level of immigration should be reduced to "digest" the previous wave of immigrants and to assimilate them successfully into the American nation. Furthermore, in schools and elsewhere, they argue that diversity should be deemphasized and common values should be emphasized more.

Critics of the cultural-unity argument indicate that fears of excessive diversity amount to a new form of racism. They recall earlier episodes of xenophobia and racism in anti-immigrant movements. They believe that the key motif behind the resurgence of nativism in the contemporary United States is to keep America as the nativists define it: white. The American is tacitly understood to be of European descent. Among some whites, anxieties over losing their majority-race status have led them to anti-immigrant movements. Groups, such as the National Organization for European American Rights (NOFEAR), formed by former Klansman David Duke, and the Council of Conservative Citizens, overtly promote racial hatred, using vicious language to attack immigrants. As indicated before, critics argue that such anti-immigrant movements do nothing to address the root causes of social, economic, and political problems in the United States. Furthermore, critics argue that it would be a serious mistake to fix American identity without permitting the evolutionary change that additional diversity brings.

Another argument used against immigration has been that immigrants are threats to the political system and stability. During the early period of nation building, politically active immigrants from Europe were regarded as radical subversives threatening the stability of the new nation. They were portrayed as rabble-rousers threatening a stable republican form of government in the United States with revolutionary anarchy and mob violence. Their presence "was a menace to American institutions and American liberty" (Billington 1974: 45). The nativist Federalists succeeded in passing the Alien and Sedition Acts of 1798, giving the president arbitrary powers to exclude or deport foreigners deemed subversive and to prosecute anyone who criticized the government. The new Naturalization Act of 1790 sought to limit immigrants' political influence by extending the waiting period for citizenship to 14 years. The act dealt with the government's policy toward naturalization, but one can argue that one of the primary purposes of the act was to control immigration and that it was the beginning of the U.S. nativist, anti-immigrant movement to control immigration because of a perceived political threat.

Another example from history was the threat supposedly posed by Catholic immigrants who were alleged to be agents of a foreign power that wanted to conquer and seize political control of the United States. In the 1830s–1850s, the large wave of Irish and German immigrants who arrived were labeled "Papists" who followed the authoritarian leader. Catholic immigrants became scapegoats for economic insecurity and division on the slavery issue. Such charges against newcomers were common when there was an international conflict and political insecurity in America. Anti-German movements during World War I and anti-Japanese activities during World War II were notable cases of the fear and suspicion of various immigrant groups' loyalty to the United States.

Such suspicion of immigrants' loyalty to the United States and their threat to national security resurfaced again after the terrorist attacks of September 11, 2001. Arab and South Asian immigrants were stereotyped as potential terrorists as the violent acts of a few extremists were blamed on all Arab immigrants. Once again, the U.S. government resorted to legal means and enacted a law, the Patriot Act of 2001. The ensuing enforcement of the act led to the arrest and imprisonment of many innocent South Asian and Middle Eastern Muslims.

A new argument has emerged recently against immigration. The current nativists assert that immigrants are threats to the natural environment of the United States. They argue that population growth and new immigrants' different lifestyles will eventually create harmful effects on the natural environment of the United States. Some environmental organizations have urged a drastic reduction of immigrants on the basis of their concern over the long-term effect of overpopulation on the natural environment. This sentiment needs to be monitored in the future to track how it will affect U.S. immigration policy.

HEON CHEOL LEE

See also

Anti-Immigrant Sentiment

Further Reading:

Billington, R. A. *The Origins of Nativism in the United States, 1800–1844.* 1933. Reprint, New York: Arno Press, 1974.

Crawford, James. *Hold Your Tongue: Bilingualism and the Politics of "English Only."* Boston: Addison-Wesley, 1992.

Dinnerstein, Leonard, Roger L. Nichols, and David M. Reimers. *Natives and Strangers: A Multicultural History of Americans.* New York: Oxford University Press, 1996.

Feagin, Joe R. "Old Poison in New Bottles: The Deep Roots of Modern Nativism." In *Immigrants Out! The New Nativism and the Anti-immigrant Impulse in the United States*, edited by J. F. Perea, 13–43. New York: New York University Press, 1997.

Fix, Michael, and Jeffrey Passel. *Immigration Today: Myths and Realities.* Washington, DC: Urban Institute, 1994.

Higham, John. *Strangers in the Land: Patterns of American Nativism, 1860–1925*, 2nd ed. New Brunswick, NJ: Rutgers University Press, 1988.

Jaret, Charles. "Troubled by Newcomers: Anti-immigrant Attitudes and Actions during Two Eras of Mass Migration." In *Mass Migration to the United States: Classical and Contemporary Periods*, edited by Pyong Gap Min, 21–63. New York: AltaMira, 2002.

Jones, Maldwyn Allen. *American Immigration*, 2nd ed. Chicago: University of Chicago Press, 1992.

Schlesinger, Arthur M., Jr. *The Disuniting of America.* New York: Norton, 1991.

Naturalization and Citizenship Process

Naturalization is the process by which foreign-born noncitizens (also known as *foreign nationals*) become citizens of the United States. U.S. Citizenship is automatically conferred upon those born in the United States and U.S.

Naturalization and Citizenship Process

Naturalization Act of 1790

The Naturalization Act of 1790 was the first federal law concerning naturalization of immigrants. Based on the power given to Congress by the U.S. Constitution, the First Congress established a uniform rule of naturalization to be followed by all of the United States. It provided the first rules and procedures to be followed in granting U.S. citizenship to the foreign born. It stipulated that "any free white person" who had resided in the United States for two years could apply for citizenship. Thus, by that stipulation, slaves, Indians, and indentured servants were excluded as potential citizens. The act also ruled out applicants who were not of "good moral character."

The Naturalization Act of 1790 employed explicit racial criteria by limiting citizenship to free white persons. The act dealt with only the government's policy toward naturalization, but since immigration and naturalization are so closely linked, it had a significant impact on the immigration of non-white persons to the United States. One can argue that one of the primary purposes of the Naturalization Act of 1790 was to discourage the immigration of non-white persons to the United States.

The history of U.S. naturalization since that date has been the effort to realize uniformity in practice, procedure, and principle. It is from this structure of steps and requirements that U.S. naturalization laws evolved. While government policy still requires new naturalized citizens to be persons of "good moral character," limitations based on gender or race eventually disappeared and new requirements have been introduced by subsequent legislation.

HEON CHEOL LEE

---

territories due to the Fourteenth Amendment, and with limited restrictions upon those born abroad whose parents are U.S. citizens. However, all others must undergo the naturalization process in order to obtain U.S. citizenship. In the United States, the federal agency that oversees the naturalization process is the U.S. Citizenship and Immigration Services (USCIS), a division of the Department of Homeland Security.

To qualify for naturalization, foreign nationals must fulfill certain requirements established by the Immigration and Nationality Act (INA). In general, applicants must:

- Be 18 years of age or older;
- Be a permanent resident for at least five years (three years for spouses of U.S. citizens);
- Establish a physical presence and continuous residence in the United States;
- Demonstrate a basic understanding of U.S. history and government, including a general knowledge of the rights and responsibilities of U.S. citizens;
- Demonstrate basic proficiency in English, including the ability to read, write, and speak simple phrases.

Additionally, applicants must exhibit "good moral character" as outlined by the INA and determined by USCIS. Behaviors that might indicate a lack of good moral character

include: lying to USCIS, habitual drunkenness, polygamy, failure to pay court-ordered child support, or crimes such as prostitution, fraud, and illegal gambling. Those found guilty of certain crimes—including homicide, aggravated felonies, rape, sexual abuse of a child, or trafficking in drugs, weapons, or humans—are barred from naturalization.

Applicants must complete a naturalization interview, during which a USCIS official reviews their application and asks a series of questions related to their background and character. At this time, the USCIS official tests applicants on their knowledge of English, U.S. history, and U.S. government. Applicants must demonstrate the ability to read, write, and speak English and must answer correctly six out of 10 civics questions to receive a passing score. Some individuals are exempt from the English and civics requirements for naturalization based on age, disability, or length of residence in the United States.

Finally, applicants must swear an Oath of Allegiance to the United States. In this oath, applicants promise to renounce any allegiances to other countries, support and defend the U.S. Constitution, and serve the United States (through selective service in the armed forces or civilian service) when required by law.

Although most immigrants today are eligible to naturalize, provided they meet the requirements listed above, access to citizenship has historically been limited by race and national origin. Congress first established this process through the Naturalization Act of 1790, which restricted citizenship to free white persons. This act thus excluded from citizenship indentured servants, slaves, and Native Americans, and had far-reaching implications for Asian immigrants who were racialized as non-white.

The 1857 Supreme Court decision in *Dred Scott v. Sandford* affirmed the denial of citizenship to persons of African descent. Dred Scott, then a slave, sued for his freedom in 1847. After a decade of appeals, his case reached the Supreme Court; however, the Court determined that persons of African ancestry and descendants from slaves could not be citizens of the United States, regardless of whether they were enslaved or freed. Black Americans were not granted U.S. citizenship until after the abolition of slavery. The Fourteenth Amendment to the U.S. Constitution, adopted in 1868, granted automatic citizenship to those born in the United States, including the children of former slaves. Freed black Americans attained access to citizenship through the Naturalization Act of 1870.

Still, the 1870 Naturalization Act continued to exclude from citizenship others considered to be non-white, such as Asians and Native Americans. Though Native Americans were granted the right to naturalize in 1890, Asian immigrants were largely prohibited from the naturalization process for several decades more. In 1882, the Chinese Exclusion Act formally suspended Chinese immigration to the United States for a period of 10 years and specifically barred Chinese immigrants from applying for citizenship. This act was later extended in 1892 and again in 1902.

Race and national origin requirements for immigration and naturalization continued through much of the 20th century. The ban on Asian immigrants was prolonged through the Immigration Act of 1917, which established literacy requirements for entrants and specifically barred immigrants from Asia and the Pacific Islands. In 1923, the Supreme Court ruled in *United States v. Bhagat Singh Thind* that Indians were non-white, a decision that retroactively denied citizenship to Indians who had already completed the naturalization process. Next, the Immigration Act of 1924 (known as the Johnson-Reed Act) prohibited entry into the United States for anyone not eligible for citizenship, effectively excluding most Asian immigrants and others

---

Fourteenth Amendment

The Fourteenth Amendment, codified into law on July 9, 1868, confers automatic U.S. citizenship—known as birthright citizenship—to all persons born in the United States. This amendment also provides for due process and equal protection under the law for all U.S.-born and naturalized citizens. Originally, the Fourteenth Amendment was established in order to ensure citizenship rights for black Americans, who had been denied citizenship under the 1857 Supreme Court ruling in *Dred Scott v. Sandford*. In recent years, the Fourteenth Amendment has been the subject of heated debates regarding unauthorized immigration, since the amendment grants citizenship to all those born in the United States, regardless of the citizenship or immigration status of their parents. Legislators such as Sen. Jon Kyl of Arizona and Sen. Lindsey Graham of South Carolina, and organizations such as the Federation for American Immigration Reform and Numbers USA, have advocated the reinterpretation or outright repeal of the Fourteenth Amendment, arguing that it encourages unauthorized immigration.

---

considered to be non-white. The Johnson-Reed Act also established a national origins quota system, which allocated immigration visas to resemble the existing racial and ethnic composition of the nation. The Immigration and Nationality Act of 1952 eliminated race restrictions on naturalization and immigration but maintained the national origins quota system to restrict immigration from certain countries. The national origins quota was not abolished until 1965, when amendments to the Immigration and Nationality Act eliminated national origin as a basis for immigration to the United States.

In recent years, the rate of naturalization has risen dramatically, as a growing share of lawful permanent residents chooses to become citizens. By 2011, the share of immigrants who had naturalized rose to 56 percent of the total number of authorized immigrants living in the United States—the highest rate in three decades; in that year, the total number of naturalized U.S. citizens reached 15.5 million. Naturalization rates of authorized immigrants vary sharply by region and country of origin; immigrants from Asia and Europe are most likely to naturalize, while those from Latin America and the Caribbean are least likely to naturalize.

Meghan Conley

See also
Immigration Acts

Further Reading:
Batalova, Jeanne. "Spotlight on Naturalization Trends." *Migration Policy Institute.* http://www.migrationinformation.org/USfocus/display.cfm?id=737.
Harvard University Library Open Collections Program. *Immigration to the United States, 1790—1930: Key Dates and Landmarks in United States Immigration History.* http://ocp.hul.harvard.edu/immigration/timeline.html.
LeMay, Michael, and Robert Barkan Elliott, eds. *US Immigration and Naturalization Laws and Issues: A Documentary History.* Westport, CT: Greenwood Press, 1999.
U.S. Citizenship and Immigration Services. *A Guide to Naturalization.* http://www.uscis.gov/files/article/M-476.pdf.

Nature of Prejudice, The

First published in 1954, *The Nature of Prejudice* by Gordon Allport has influenced and guided the study of prejudice in many disciplines, particularly social psychology, for over 50 years. Allport's definition of prejudice has become the fundamental building block of the human-relations movement, better known today as the multiculturalism movement. *The Nature of Prejudice* was written during and for a turbulent period in U.S. history to address particular aspects and dimensions of prejudices brought about by economic, legal, political, and social inequality. Allport's book was monumental in that it was published just before the Supreme Court's historic decision overturning the legality of "separate but equal" public facilities: *Brown v. Board of Education.*

Allport defined prejudice as "an aversive or hostile attitude toward a person who belongs to a group, simply because he belongs to that group, and is therefore presumed to have the objectionable qualities ascribed to the group," and as "an antipathy based upon a faulty and inflexible generalization" (Allport 1979). Allport notes that human rivalries and hatreds are omnipresent.

The Nature of Prejudice explores racial, religious, ethnic, economic, and sexual prejudice while focusing on strategies for ameliorating the devastating effects of discrimination. Many of Allport's foundational concepts and theories for addressing social problems can now be found in the literature of various disciplines with new labels and more nuanced meanings. Allport was also one of the first scholars to substantively discuss anti-Semitism.

Among the book's most important theoretical contributions concerning the source of prejudice is the "frustration-aggression/scapegoat" hypothesis. Allport described how frustration over issues involving family, personal characteristics, and other social factors in the community can develop into "reactive aggression," which is then directed toward an out-group. This out-group becomes a scapegoat as the negative qualities that cause guilt in some prejudiced people are repressed and "displaced" onto the targeted population.

Khyati Joshi

See also
Prejudice; Prejudice Theory

Further Reading:
Allport, Gordon W. *The Nature of Prejudice.* Unabridged 25th anniversary ed. New York: Perseus Books Group, 1979.

Nazism

While never a formidable political force in the United States, advocates of National Socialism (Nazism) nonetheless attempted to broaden its racist ideology through astute recruiting efforts, public relations savvy, the repositioning of overt Nazi symbols with a broadened appeal to white unity, and by appealing to American religious and patriotic impulses.

In the early 1930s, before Adolf Hitler's rise to power in Germany, a constellation of small Nazi groups arose in the United States composed primarily of German citizens living abroad and disaffected German Americans. Hitler's political ascendance encouraged such organizations and their leaders to redouble their efforts to spread the Nazi vision of ethnic German solidarity and racial purity.

The most prominent Nazi group at this time, Friends of the New Germany (Bund der Freunde des neuen Deutschlands), began with support from high-level Nazi leaders

Rudolf Hess and Robert Ley. The leader, Heinz Spanknoebel, held the title "Führer of the Nazi Party in the United States." He sought to mobilize Nazi sympathizers in the United States within German American immigrant communities. *Das Neue Deutschland* (The New Germany), a weekly newspaper, was launched to support these efforts. The organization was short-lived. Public outcry over the activity of the *Friends* in New York City and the subsequent violent incidents invited scrutiny by both the German and American governments. German authorities called Spanknoebel home in late 1933 while he was under indictment for failing to register as a foreign government agent. The movement floundered in 1935 when Rudolf Hess ordered all German nationals out of Friends of the New Germany (well over half of its 10,000 members) out of concern that it was fueling anti-German sentiment.

Fritz Kuhn emerged from this disarray as the new American Führer, reforming and unifying the remnants of Friends of the New Germany and other like-minded groups into a new organization: the Amerika-Deutscher Volksbund or German-American Bund. Having become an American citizen himself in 1933, Kuhn sought to put an American face on the movement. However, he still kept the back door open for German nationals by setting up a Prospective Citizens League, accepting them into membership if they filed the initial paperwork for American citizenship and met the standard criteria of accepting Kuhn's leadership and had no black or Jewish ancestors.

The Bund attracted primarily urban lower-middle-class people, most of whom viewed the organization as a social outlet. A Youth Division was formed, in part, to counteract American anti-German sentiment that developed during World War I. It adapted features of the Hitler Youth including lessons on saluting the swastika, learning popular Nazi songs, listening to Hitler's speeches on shortwave radio, and wearing uniforms with Nazi symbols. Bund leaders understood the importance of recruiting and indoctrinating youth if the movement was to take root in American soil. Towards this end, a monthly magazine was produced that glorified the German American contribution to American history and the importance of Nordic-German racial identity to its future. American patriotism and strength was linked to racial purity. Anti-Semitic fiction linking Jews to communism and many other conspiratorial plots were regular features.

Bund camps were also established. Often first perceived by participants as inexpensive recreation in a socially comfortable German-American setting, leaders used them to openly propagandize for National Socialism.

Bund leaders supported other anti-Semitic organizations that experienced legal trouble and invited them to speak at Bund events. They also did not shy away from politics. They understood President Franklin D. Roosevelt to be sympathetic to both Jews and communists (often linked in their minds). One attack advertisement asserted that a Roosevelt victory would result in race mixing, a black republic and a black president. At their 1938 convention, "a socially just, white, Gentile-ruled United States," was at the top of their eight-point program to enliven the movement. Germanness was downplayed while being white and American was emphasized in order broaden the appeal and extend the reach of the movement. Still, Kuhn could not bring himself to eliminate the Nazi salute, though the swastika was thereafter displayed only on special occasions.

As with the Friends of the New Germany before them, the German-American Bund received close scrutiny from both the American and German governments in the wake of violence surrounding Bund rallies and the resulting counterdemonstrations. The German ambassador noted that the Bund was not even making inroads into the American-German community, much less America as a whole, and considered it to be a detriment to improving American perceptions of Germany.

In the end, Kuhn was indicted and found guilty of larceny and forgery, sentenced to a two and one-half years, and sent to Sing Sing prison in 1939. The National Committee expelled him from membership. Lacking strong recognized leadership, the organization fell into internal bickering and financial debt from which it did not recover. The executive committee voted to disband the Bund the day after the Pearl Harbor attack.

George Lincoln Rockwell picked up the post–World War II mantle of leadership for American National Socialism, founding the American Nazi Party in 1959 with the financial backing of Harold Noel Arrowsmith Jr., who had earlier contributed to the International Association for the Advancement of Ethnology and Eugenics—a group that gathered scientific evidence to support the segregationist position in *Brown v. Board of Education* case.

While Rockwell's primary target was the Jews, he also openly directed his hate speech towards African Americans, whom he wanted to return to Africa or be rounded up into remote relocation centers. Rockwell's strategy to gain power included recruiting and training a small but disciplined group of "stormtroopers," attracting media coverage through hate-speech and the overt use of Nazi symbols in order to bait the Jewish community into emotional overreaction. He would then mobilize the white population following the race riots he predicted for 1970 and the ensuing economic collapse. Finally, he believed he would be elected president of the United States in 1972 by white people seeking protection from the chaos and the prospects of a Jewish-led communist takeover.

Drawing on his background as a commercial artist, an advertising man, and the showmanship learned from his vaudeville performer father, Rockwell pulled off several publicity stunts to enrage the African American community, including a "Hate Bus" tour to New Orleans by his stormtroopers to mimic the Freedom Riders, hiring racist singers to perform at "Hate-o-nannies," and portraying himself as the white alternative to Martin Luther King, Jr. Even so, he was not beyond working with African Americans who advocated racial separation. Finding common cause with Nation of Islam leader Elijah Muhammad, whom he referred to as the "Adolf Hitler of the black man," Rockwell was invited to speak at their 1962 national convention at the Chicago Temple of Islam.

In order to combat this kind of publicity tactic designed to outrage and incite confrontation, drawing media attention, Solomon Andhil Fineberg of the American Jewish Committee worked hard to revive the countertactic of "quarantine," which he created and successfully used in the 1940s against the anti-Semite Gerald L. K. Smith. Originally called "dynamic silence," or the "silent treatment," Fineberg renamed it "quarantine" because it better described the strategy's two critical components: coordinating the major American Jewish community organizations to avoid or minimize public confrontations that draw media attention, and sensitize the news media to American Nazi Party tactics so they understand that lack of news coverage cuts off the publicity necessary for the growth of the movement.

The quarantine was effective and Rockwell increasingly looked abroad to spread his Nazi vision, playing a key role in forming and leading the World Union of National Socialists. One of his last media breakthroughs was his 1966 interview in *Playboy* magazine by Alex Haley who would go on to write *Roots*, a story of Haley's journey to discover his African ancestry. As with the pre–World War II National Socialist organizations, Rockwell came to realize that overt Nazi symbols were abhorrent to many Americans. He sought to broaden the appeal of the organization by denying Holocaust atrocities, by emphasizing "white power" in contradistinction to the "Black Power" movement, and by enfolding white supremacy within the garb of religion. Rockwell realized that the images of the Holocaust were too much to overcome in order to garner popular support. His Holocaust denial propaganda preceded Willis Carto, who is generally credited as the father of American Holocaust denial. While this strategy was designed to decrease the high negative perception of the American Nazi Party among white voters, Rockwell continued to incite racial opposition that he believed would result in publicity and his eventual election as governor of Virginia and later as president of the United States. He was not a factor in the Virginia election. Seizing upon Stokely Carmichael's 1966 "Black Power" slogan, Rockwell countered with a "White Power" campaign to feed the fears of white people. Deviating from Hitler's Nordic-German concept of racial purity, Rockwell created a white/black mythos pitting white people against dark people. This change of strategy is also reflected in renaming the American Nazi Party to the National Socialist White People's Party, consciously mirroring the National Association for the Advancement of Colored People. The final way in which Rockwell tried to make National Socialism more acceptable to whites at large was through the cloak of religion. Correspondence with some of his racist colleagues indicates that while he rejected the teachings of Jesus Christ, he found a Christian veneer useful in reaching the masses. In the racist teachings of the Christian Identity movement, which viewed white Anglos as the literal lost tribes of Israel who needed to wake up to their true identity, Rockwell found a home for Nazis with religious needs and many in Christian Identity churches found a political outlet consistent with their racist beliefs.

Some in his own party and some National Socialists abroad remained purists, considering this sort of "big tent" Nazism as a betrayal of Hitler's ideals. An angry National

Socialist Party veteran killed Rockwell on August 25, 1967. The already small and politically ineffective party splintered into additional fragments.

DOUGLAS MILFORD

See also

White Nationalism; White Supremacy

Further Reading:

Bell, Leland V. *In Hitler's Shadow: The Anatomy of American Nazism*. Port Washington, NY: Kennikat Press, 1973.

Simonelli, Frederick J. "The World Union of National Socialists and Postwar Transatlantic Nazi Revival." In *Nation and Race: The Developing Euro-American Racist Subculture*, edited by Jeffrey Kaplan and Tore Bjorgo, 34–57. Boston: Northeastern University Press, 1998.

Simonelli, Frederick J. *American Fuehrer: George Lincoln Rockwell and the American Nazi Party*. Urbana: University of Illinois Press, 1999.

Negro League Baseball

Segregation in baseball began in 1858 when the National Association of Baseball Players included in its constitution a clause excluding "persons of color" from playing. After a period of segregation from 1867 to 1871, the rules changed. In 1871, there were no formal rules against blacks in baseball in the newly organized National Association of Professional Baseball Players. African Americans, including Bud Fowler, Charlie Grant, George Stovey, and Moses Fleetwood Walker, played on professional integrated teams for a short time. In the 1880s, a "gentleman's agreement" shifted acceptance again, creating a color line in baseball. Owners forced the black players off teams and did not sign new ones.

After the reemergence of segregation in the last two decades of the 19th century, African Americans responded by creating their own teams and leagues. With no professional leagues from the late 1880s to 1920, blacks played on semi-pro teams. Attempts at organizing leagues proved unsuccessful. In 1886, the League of Colored Baseball included teams in Baltimore, Boston, Cincinnati, Louisville, New York, Philadelphia, Pittsburgh, and Washington, D.C. The league lasted for a week, with 13 games played. Other leagues included black teams in their schedule. In 1889, the Penn League included the Cuban Giants and New York Gothams,

but lasted only for one season. In 1898, the Acme Colored Giants played for a few months in the Iron and Oil League in Celeron, New York.

After 1898, no other teams of players of color participated in white leagues, and attempts at organizing separate independent leagues began. In 1890, black business owners tried to organize a league with teams in Chicago, Cincinnati, Cleveland, Indianapolis, Kansas City, and Louisville. Finances lacking, the teams never played any games. The International League of Independent Professional Baseball Clubs included teams of Cuban X Giants, Cuban Stars, Havana Stars, and Quaker Giants. In 1907, the league added two white teams, but financial difficulties again prevented implementation. Three years later, Chicago lawyer Beauregard Moseley led an effort to create the Negro National Baseball League. At an organizational meeting in December 1910, interested owners elected Moseley president and Felix Payne as secretary/treasurer. This attempt was the most successful in organizing, coming the closest to being a league, but it did not become a reality. Also in 1910, the United States League of Professional Ball Clubs organized, with teams in Baltimore, Brooklyn, Jersey City, New York, Newark, Philadelphia, and Trenton. Owners would include both black and white players. Financial reasons and the fact that this was an outlaw league hindered its development. In 1901, baseball teams had organized to create the National Association of Professional Baseball Leagues. Members of this organizational structure became "organized baseball" and those that were not members "outlaw." As different teams and leagues attempted to establish themselves, they also had to contend with a formalized structure that discouraged nonmembers. All of the attempts to establish leagues before 1920 and white teams playing against black teams helped establish a foundation for future successes. In the 19th century, approximately 70 blacks played on integrated professional teams, with several hundred playing on other kinds of teams.

During the first two decades of the 20th century, numerous independent black teams, including the long-lasting Baltimore Black Sox (1916–1934), Chicago American Giants (1911–1958), Hilldale Daisies (1910–1930s), Indianapolis ABCs (1902–1940), Homestead Grays (1911–1950), and Leland Giants (1905–1915), successfully kept African Americans playing baseball.

The Pittsburgh Crawfords, 1935 Negro National League Champions, are considered by many to be the greatest African American league team ever fielded. The team included five future Hall of Famers, from left: Oscar Charleston, first; Judy Johnson, fifth; Cool Papa Bell, 12th; Josh Gibson, 15th; and Satchel Paige, 17th. Others are not identified. (AP/Wide World Photos)

On February 13, 1920, leaders from eight cities met in Kansas City, Missouri, to establish the Negro National League (NNL). Andrew "Rube" Foster organized the business and sports writers. A former player and manager with the Leland Giants and Chicago American Giants, Foster essentially managed all the details of the new league to ensure its success. Born in 1879 in Calvert, Texas, Rube Foster pitched for semipro and independent teams. In 1908, Foster established his own team because he felt the owner of the team he played on did not respect the players. Foster's Chicago American Giants became part of the new Negro League. The National Association of Colored Professional Baseball came into being, with the team owners signing a constitution that placed Foster as president. Teams included the Chicago Giants, Detroit Stars, Indianapolis ABCs, Kansas City Monarchs, and St. Louis Giants. Owners paid an entrance fee and agreed to league rules. Most of the teams did not own stadiums but rented them from white teams. In addition to the regular league teams, other teams could play as associate teams, but the game would not count in league statistics.

In May 1920, the Negro Southern League played after two months of planning, but was not as organized as the NNL. Teams included the Atlanta Black Crackers, Birmingham Giants, Chattanooga Black Lookouts, Jacksonville Red Caps, Montgomery Grey Sox, Nashville Elite Giants, and New Orleans Black Pelicans. In 1921, the league dissolved due to conflicts among the teams. Other leagues including the Continental League (based in Boston), the Negro Western League (based in Kansas, Virginia, and Kentucky), and the Tandy League (based in St. Louis). As the National Negro League continued to develop, teams came into and out of the league. Rube Foster's Chicago American Giants was the only team to compete in all 12 seasons.

In 1923, Ed Bolden of the Hilldale Daisies organized the Eastern Colored League (ECL). To ease the distance in traveling to games and to exert control himself, Bolden's league included the Bacharach Giants, Baltimore Black Sox, Brooklyn Royal Giants, the Eastern Cuban Stars, Hilldale Daisies, and the New York Lincoln Giants. Teams played in the ECL from 1923 to 1928. In 1929, they reorganized as the Negro American League and played for one season.

In the Negro Leagues, contracts with players proved to be an ongoing struggle. Players would move to another team if the owner produced a better offer. Owners of Negro League teams were both white and black. Many team owners held businesses in the community. A handful of them participated in illegal activities. The community loved their local teams, and the team had a central role in the African American community. The community leaders would participate in the games. Games on Sunday would begin after church had ended, and fans would come to the ballpark dressed in their Sunday best.

Baseball teams in the Negro Leagues did not travel by train, but by bus. Play on teams in fluctuating leagues allowed players to play for many teams during the year. With the regular season from April to October, players could continue playing on traveling teams, winter ball teams, or barnstorming against white teams in warmer climates including the West Coast and Latin America. On average, players began their careers when they were 20 and played professionally for about five years. Some players were older or younger, and some played for two or more decades. Segregation made the extensive travel more difficult. Teams might not find hotels that would accept them or restaurants that would feed them. Members of the black community would regularly house the players in their own homes when a team came to town.

Until 1971, the National Baseball Hall of Fame did not consider Negro League players eligible for election. The initial plan was to place them in a separate wing, but, recognizing that it was the segregation of their time and not their ability as ball players, their achievements are now recognized in the same way as players from organized baseball. Some of the players in the Negro League now in the Baseball Hall of Fame include Satchel Paige, Josh Gibson, Cool Papa Bell, Oscar Charleston, Ray Dandridge, Leon Day, Monte Irvin, Judy Johnson, Buck Leonard, Alex Pompez, Bullet Rogan, and Willie Wells. Each of these players became a member of the Baseball Hall of Fame based on their career in the Negro Leagues.

The decline of the Negro League came with the integration of major and minor league baseball. After Jackie Robinson signed a contract with the Brooklyn Dodgers in October 1945, played for the minor league Montreal Royals in 1946, and played for the major league Dodgers in 1947, the death knell for Negro Leagues baseball sounded. Fans, players, and owners would choose integration over continued segregation. As more and more players went into major or minor league baseball, fewer top-quality players played into the Negro Leagues. One by one, the teams dissolved, and the end of the Negro Leagues is marked in 1960.

AMY ESSINGTON

See also
Sports and Racism

Further Reading:
Heaphy, Leslie A. *The Negro Leagues, 1869–1960*. Jefferson, NC: McFarland, 2003.
Holway, John. *The Complete Book of Baseball's Negro Leagues: The Other Half of Baseball History*. Fern Park, FL: Hastings House Publishers, 2001.
Lanctot, Neil. *Negro League Baseball: The Rise and Ruin of a Black Institution*. Philadelphia: University of Pennsylvania, 2004.
Peterson, Robert. *Only the Ball Was White*. New York: Gramercy, 1999.

Negroes with Guns

Negroes with Guns is a book written by Robert F. Williams in 1962, while he was living in exile in Cuba. The title refers to an armed group called the Black Guard, which was formed to defend the black community of Monroe, North Carolina. The book tells the story of a small black community's harrowing confrontation with the Ku Klux Klan and a racist Justice Department and law enforcement. It also explores the origins of Williams's controversial philosophy of black self-defense and subsequent opposition from the Federal Bureau of Investigation and civil rights organizations. Although less than 100 pages in length, *Negroes with Guns* inspired a host of black leaders, such as Stokely Carmichael, Huey P. Newton, H. Rap Brown, Eldridge Cleaver, and Malcolm X, thus helping to usher in the era of Black Power.

Black self-defense was not a new concept. After President Abraham Lincoln abolished slavery during the Civil War, antiblack violence ran rampant throughout the South. Free blacks threatened white supremacy. As a result, racist whites employed violence, as well as discriminatory laws, to maintain their social, economic, and political dominance. Whites freely threatened, harassed, and murdered individuals and rioted in black communities. In response to these attacks, some blacks fought bravely, though they were rarely successful. During the 20th century, numerous other black communities were destroyed, such as Greenwood, Oklahoma (*see* Greenwood Community entry) in 1921 and Rosewood, Florida (*see* Rosewood [Florida] Riot of 1923 entry), and only a few individuals in these communities survived despite attempts at collective self-defense.

In *Negroes with Guns*, Williams explains that he gained his first knowledge of racial violence and black protest through the stories of his grandmother, who had been a slave. Before her death, his grandmother gave him a rifle "that his grandfather had wielded against white terrorists at the turn of the century" (Williams 1998: xvii). After high school, Williams joined the U.S. Marines, where he learned how to handle and use arms.

After being dishonorably discharged from the Marines for challenging its discriminatory practices, Williams returned home to Monroe. Once home, Williams experienced firsthand the violence and threats directed at the small, local chapter of the National Association for the Advancement of Colored People (NAACP). Although many members quit the organization for fear of their lives, Williams stood firm and was elected president of the Monroe chapter of the NAACP in 1956. Over the next few years, Williams transformed the group. In general, the NAACP was composed of middle-class and professional blacks, and it strictly adhered to the philosophy of nonviolence. In contrast, Williams's chapter consisted largely of veterans, laborers, farmers, domestic workers, and the unemployed, and they subscribed to the concept of self-defense.

In *Negroes with Guns*, Williams describes the circumstances that led him to advocate self-defense. In addition to receiving frequent threats, Williams and other activists, while picketing in protest in 1961 for the right of black children to use a public swimming pool, were threatened and harassed by private individuals and police officers. Two black women, one of whom was pregnant, were assaulted by two white men on separate occasions. Both men were acquitted. After the court case involving the beating and attempted rape of the pregnant woman, Williams vowed publicly to meet violence with violence. Consequently, he was suspended from the NAACP for six months. Delegates at an NAACP convention later made a statement in support of self-defense, but Martin Luther King, Jr. was the only one to publicly side with Williams.

Williams felt that it was only natural and right for a people to protect themselves against brutality, especially in the absence of support from law enforcement and other authorities established to provide that protection. Williams did not disagree with the concept of nonviolence, and his branch of the NAACP engaged in many nonviolent demonstrations. Williams believed that within the movement, both nonviolence and self-defense were acceptable and essential. But he also argued that his philosophy was more effective than those of other civil rights organizations. Because the members of his group were willing to defend themselves, their demonstrations provoked less violence than activities such as the Freedom Rides.

Williams's self-defense group, formed in the 1960s and called the Black Guard, proved to be effective in subduing and averting Ku Klux Klan violence. Members of the Black Guard were trained by Williams and were charter members of the National Rifle Association. They received donations from various organizations, churches, and individuals—whites included—to purchase guns and rifles. On several occasions, they engaged in shoot-outs with white mobs and the Klan, without fatalities on either side. The Black Guard was even called on when the Freedom Riders, an interracial group of activists, arrived in Monroe to help the civil rights cause there. With Williams's support and assistance, the Freedom Riders found volunteers in Monroe, all of whom took an oath of nonviolence, which meant that they were not allowed to defend themselves if attacked. Williams even "stated that if they could show [him] any gains won from the racists by nonviolent methods, [he] too would become a pacifist" (Williams 1998: 41). However, the Freedom Riders were attacked, and shortly thereafter, whites drove into the black community and "fired out of their cars and threw objects at people on the streets" (Williams 1998: 47). Blacks armed themselves to defend their community, and a riot ensued.

During the riot, Williams helped protect a white couple he believed drove unintentionally into the community. When state troopers arrived to "restore law and order," Williams fled to New York, where he heard that the white couple he had protected had accused him of kidnapping them. Williams was forced to take refuge in Cuba. He moved to China in 1963. He was allowed to return to the United States in exchange for information President Richard Nixon wanted on China. Until his death in 1995, Williams continued to support the struggle for civil rights.

GLADYS L. KNIGHT

See also

American Literature and Racism

Further Reading:

Negroes with Guns: Rob Williams and Black Power. Directed by Sandra Dickerson and Churchill Roberts. Gainesville: University of Florida; The Digital Lighthouse, 2004.

Williams, Robert F. *Negroes with Guns.* New York: Marzani & Munsell, 1962.

Williams, Robert F. *Negroes with Guns.* Detroit, MI: Wayne State University Press, 1998.

Neighborhood Property Owners Associations

Neighborhood property owners associations were local organizations of home and business owners. Historically, they served to maintain patterns of residential segregation by enforcing racially restrictive covenants, battling blockbusting practices, and terrorizing black families who moved into white neighborhoods. These organizations were also known as neighborhood improvement associations, civic clubs, or homeowner associations.

In the late 19th century, neighborhood associations arose to provide services such as street paving for suburban areas that received little attention from city administration. By the early 20th century, though, the purpose of neighborhood associations began to change. Increasing migration of blacks from rural to urban areas and from the South to the North put pressure on available housing stock. Black residents were increasingly concentrated in particular sections of cities through a combination of government policy, real estate practices, and white resident resistance. Many black citizens resisted this confinement and bravely attempted to move into recently integrated or previously all-white neighborhoods. In response, neighborhood property owners associations now also functioned to protect white neighborhoods from black "invasion."

In newly constructed suburbs, property owners associations often formed in order to enforce racially restrictive covenants. Developers attached these covenants to deeds; they prohibited homeowners from selling their property to blacks, and sometimes Asian Americans, Jews, and Catholics as well. In the 1920s, the courts had tacitly upheld the use of such covenants because they were private agreements. Restrictive covenants had therefore taken the place of racial zoning, which the U.S. Supreme Court had struck down in *Buchanan v. Warley* in 1917.

In existing urban neighborhoods, particularly those bordering black neighborhoods, property owners associations took on a more defensive posture. They formed to combat blockbusting practices, in which real estate agents and speculators would acquire a property, move a black family in, and try to scare the remaining white property owners out of the area. Fleeing white families would often accept low prices in their panic, and the agents turned around and sold to black families at inflated amounts, reaping a huge profit. Property owners banded together to intimidate new black residents and boycott unscrupulous realtors. They held organizing meetings and sometimes introduced their own racially restrictive covenants, going door to door to obtain the necessary signatures.

At the same time, some associations built alliances with local realtors in order to defend the "color line" effectively. Neighborhood residents placed pressure on their neighbors to refrain from selling to minorities. Meanwhile, local real estate boards policed their own by threatening to revoke the license of any realtor who sold property in a white neighborhood to a black person. In other cases, neighborhood property owners associations cooperated with institutions such as local universities or prominent businesses, often procuring key funding for lawsuits.

The U.S. Supreme Court declared racially restrictive covenants unconstitutional in *Shelley v. Kraemer* in 1948. In some communities, they had already become unenforceable anyway, as enough black families managed to move into the neighborhood to render the restrictions hollow. The decline of racial covenants, however, did not pave the way for residential integration. Homeowners increasingly turned to overt acts of resistance. They planted bombs, vandalized property, and attacked their new black neighbors both physically and verbally. Neighborhood property owners' associations served organizing and dissemination purposes to draw community support.

Racial prejudice fueled all of these defensive strategies. That racial prejudice, though, was also fundamentally linked to ideas about property ownership. White homeowners resisted black incursion into their neighborhoods primarily because they believed that black neighbors would cause their property values to decline. They believed that a neighborhood containing "undesirable" neighbors would fetch much lower prices on the real estate market. For many of these families, their home represented their single largest investment and demanded protection at all costs. This same logic led neighborhood organizations to wage campaigns against the construction of public housing and nuisance businesses.

The success of the civil rights movement and the end of state-sanctioned segregation led neighborhood associations to broaden their agendas. A national neighborhood movement emerged in the late 1960s and early 1970s as residents demanded better city services and resisted urban renewal efforts and freeway construction. While these organizations were less likely to wage explicitly racial campaigns, their actions still had discriminatory effects. Support for neighborhood schools often translated into resistance against school integration. Critics charged that white residents demanded better city services because they felt black neighborhoods had received more than their fair share of government resources through Great Society programs and affirmative action initiatives. Meanwhile, white residents continued openly to harass new black neighbors late into the 20th century.

Neighborhood organizations have not disappeared. Homeowners' associations have remained particularly prevalent in condominiums and suburban, gated communities, where they try to maintain an air of exclusivity. These associations usually require property owners in a given subdivision to join and pay dues; they then provide services to the community, ranging from security to garbage collection.

These associations still employ deed restrictions that serve to limit diversity. Though these restrictions are no longer explicitly racial, they often prescribe minimum purchase prices, maximum occupancy levels, and strict guidelines for property maintenance. By defining a certain lifestyle for community residents, these regulations exclude potential neighbors who do not fit that mold.

ALYSSA RIBEIRO

See also

Fair Housing Audit; Gatekeeping; Housing Covenants; Reverse Redlining; Residential Segregation

Further Reading:

Gotham, Kevin Fox. "Urban Space, Restrictive Covenants and the Origins of Racial Residential Segregation in a US City, 1900–1950." *International Journal of Urban and Regional Research* 24, no. 3 (2000): 616–33.

Hirsch, Arnold. *Making the Second Ghetto: Race and Housing in Chicago 1940–1960*. Chicago: University of Chicago Press, 1998 (originally published in 1983).

McKenzie, Evan. *Privatopia: Homeowner Associations and the Rise of Residential Private Government*. New Haven, CT: Yale University Press, 1994.

Neo-Confederate Movement

The neo-Confederate movement consists of various individuals, groups, and organizations that aim to secede from the United States and rescue "Southern culture" from what they believe has been an ongoing attack on its symbols and monuments, as well as a distortion of its history and way of life. The ideological roots of this movement can be traced to the so-called Southern Agrarians, a group of 12 Southern poets, essayists, and novelists who wrote a manifesto published in 1930 titled *I'll Take My Stand*. In this work, the Southern Agrarians expressed dissatisfaction with the way industrialization and modernity was eroding "distinctive Southern traditions and lifestyles" (Hague and Sebesta 2008: 27–28). In response, these individuals called for a "traditional society that was religious, more rural than urban, and politically conservative—a society in which human needs were met by family, clanship, folkways, custom, and community" (Tindall 1962: 27). These basic ideals were later espoused by the so-called *Dixiecrats (*also known as the States' Rights Democratic Party*)*, a short-lived off-shoot of the Democratic Party that sought to "restore" the Southern way of life in the late 1940s.

A more recent ideological influence of the neo-Confederate movement is *paleoconservatism*, a variant of conservatism that emphasizes states' rights, local government, self-sufficiency, and a Christian-regional identity as a way to protect the Southern States from what is regarded as a "morally, culturally, and spiritually bankrupt country" that has strayed from the path laid out by the founding fathers. This deviant path, according to paleoconservatives, gained momentum during the civil rights era of the 1950s and 1960s. Drawing from these claims, neo-Confederates argue that issues such as federally mandated racial integration, women's rights, and gay and lesbian rights deviate not only from Southern culture but from the natural order of things. Restoring the "Southern way of life" is thus understood by neo-Confederates as an effort to reconnect with nature and the original vision of the founders. And while most neo-Confederates do not openly celebrate the legacy of slavery, they do emphasize how slavery was not exclusive to the U.S. South and instead practiced around the world throughout much of human history.

Important contemporary neo-Confederate organizations include the Council for Conservative Citizens (CCC) and the League of the South (LOS). The CCC started in 1985 in Atlanta, Georgia, but can be traced to the White Citizens' Council, which started in the 1950s as an organization opposing racial desegregation after the U.S. Supreme Court decision in *Brown vs. Board of Education*. The CCC has "publicly opposed interracial marriage, affirmative action, and [non-white] immigration into the US" (Hague 2012). The League of the South (originally named the Southern League) was founded in 1994 and calls for the secession of the Southern United States, which includes all the states that once constituted the Confederacy.

Some of the central tenets of the neo-Confederate movement were introduced for the first time to a mainstream audience in 1995, when the *Washington Post* published the *New Dixie Manifesto*. Widely considered "one of the most important articulations of Neo-Confederacy," the *New Dixie Manifesto* was written by two of the founding members of LOS, Thomas Fleming and J. Michael Hill. The authors of this document argue that a political, economic, and cultural elite in the United States has imposed a type of "national uniformity" that disregards regional identity, states' rights, and Christian traditions. The South, in effect, is being ruled by a network of elites that are foreign (and antithetical) to Southern culture. Accordingly, Fleming and Hill call "for the people of the Southern States to take control of their own governments, their own institutions, their own culture, their own communities, and their own lives."

Although a comprehensive description of the neo-Confederate worldview and version of U.S. history is beyond the scope of this entry, the following are some of the core beliefs associated with this movement. First, neo-Confederates believe that the U.S. Civil War was a war of aggression by Union forces on the Southern states, and regard Abraham Lincoln as a war criminal. Indeed, neo-Confederates believe that the "Civil War was a theological war over the future of [Christianity], pitting the heretical Union against the pious, devout Christians of the Confederacy" (Sebesta and Hague 2008: 50). Part of what motivates the neo-Confederate objective to secede from the United States, therefore, is a desire to establish an orthodox Christian nation in the Southern states.

Second, neo-Confederates reject ideals such as multiculturalism and egalitarianism as artificial objectives that stray from what they believe is a natural hierarchy among people and cultures. Claiming an "Anglo-Celtic" ethnicity that predisposes Southern whites to a "Southern way of life" (e.g., religious piety, commitment to family, etc.), the neo-Confederates understand race and culture in a way that is consistent with 19th-century theories such as social Darwinism. Specifically, neo-Confederates believe that "cultures and ethno-racial characteristics are inherited, that behaviors are innate and immutable, and that it is unnatural and thus impossible for two or more ethno-racial groups to co-exist in the same space on equal terms" (Hague and Sebesta 2008: 131). Therefore, in the neo-Confederate worldview, a free and natural society is hierarchical and hence all races and cultures (not to mention genders, social classes, etc.) must fit within that hierarchy.

Lastly, because of their hierarchical vision of the world, neo-Confederates reject the social-legal changes promoted by the civil rights movement. For example, policies or laws calling for diversity, gender and racial equality, racial integration, or affirmative action are understood as corrupt forms of "social engineering" that should be eradicated in a free society. The social order, according to neo-Confederates, should evolve organically, without political impositions. In doing so, societies become more harmonious and all groups ultimately benefit. It is precisely this quest to (re)build an "organic" order in the South that motivates neo-Confederates to oppose policies of "equality" and other "political intrusions" by the federal government and other authorities.

According to Euan Hague, neo-Confederates today are far from a "fringe group" and, in fact, have significant support among Whites in the South—most notably within the Republican Party and among Evangelical Protestants. In recent years, members of the neo-Confederate movement have aimed to fight not only against the intrusiveness of the U.S. federal government but also against what is often referred to as the New World Order, an alleged global network of elites (exemplified by the United Nations and NATO) who aim to create a tyrannical "global empire" rooted in principles of multiculturalism and relativism—both of which are antithetical to regional cultures and a Christian identity.

LUIGI ESPOSITO

See also

Confederate Flag Controversy; Ku Klux Klan (KKK); White Supremacy

Further Reading:

Hague, Euan. "The Neo-Confederate Movement." http://www .splcenter.org/get-informed/intelligence-files/ideology/ neo-confederate/the-neo-confederate-movement (accessed November 2012).

Hague, Euan, and Edward H. Sebesta. "Neo-Confederacy and Its Conservative Ancestry." In *Neo-Confederacy: A Critical Introduction*, edited by Euan Hague, Edward H. Sebesta, and Heidi Beirich, 23–49. Austin: University of Texas Press, 2008.

Hague, Euan, and Edward H. Sebesta. "Neo-Confederacy and the Understanding of Race." In *Neo-Confederacy: A Critical Introduction*, edited by Euan Hague, Edward H. Sebesta, and Heidi Beirich, 131–66. Austin: University of Texas Press, 2008.

Hague, Euan, Edward H. Sebesta, and Heidi Beirich. *Neo-Confederacy: A Critical Introduction*. Austin, TX: University of Texas Press, 2008.

Hill, Michael, and Thomas Fleming. "The New Dixie Manifesto: States' Rights Will Rise Again." http://dixienet.org/New%20 Site/newdixiemanifesto.shtml (accessed November 2012).

Sebesta, Edward, and Euan Hague. "The U.S. Civil War as a Theological War: Neo-Confederacy, Christian Nationalism, and Theology." In *Neo-Confederacy: A Critical Introduction*, edited by Euan Hague, Edward H. Sebesta, and Heidi Beirich, 50–75. Austin: University of Texas Press, 2008.

Tindall, George Brown. *Natives and Newcomers: Ethnic Southerners and Southern Ethics*. New York: Harper Torchbooks, 1962.

Webster, Gerald, and Jonathan I. Leib. "Fighting for the Lost Cause: The Confederate Battle Flag and Neo-Confederacy." *Neo-Confederacy: A Critical Introduction*, edited by Euan Hague, Edward H. Sebesta, and Heidi Beirich, 169–201. Austin: University of Texas Press, 2008.

New Bedford (Massachusetts) Riot of 1970

The New Bedford civil disorders of July 1970—sometimes called *the rebellion* by participants, sometimes simply called *the riots* by local residents—occurred during a summer of ghetto rioting in small cities, with upheavals in nearly a dozen communities in nine states, including Asbury Park, New Jersey; Fort Lauderdale, Florida; Lima, Ohio; and Mathis, Texas. By the definitions used in the Kerner Commission Report (1968), the New Bedford violence constituted a serious, even major civil disturbance. During the month, this city of just over 100,000 people, 60 miles south of Boston, witnessed extensive arson, intensive looting, dozens of sniper incidents, and sizeable street crowds confronting local, area, and state police. Although the use of National Guard forces was urged repeatedly by the city government, and a unit at the nearby Fall River armory was placed on alert several days into the events, those forces were never used.

The complaints among the aggrieved in New Bedford, heard from the pulpit, dais, and street corner for years, were similar to those that animated rioting in hundreds of communities between 1963 and 1968: high unemployment, inadequate educational facilities, poor housing, and a shortage of recreation space. The trigger was also familiar: the arrest of a young African American man in the early evening hours of July 8 in the predominantly black West End of town, near the main avenue in that section, Kempton Street. An increasing occurrence in the late 1960s that had generated a ritual inundation of the central police station by family and friends, activists, and community leaders, this time the lid seemed to come off a city long perceived as a backwater in an age of civil rights struggles. The city did have a long tradition of dissent. Religiously tolerant, racially diverse, and socially progressive from its earliest days, it was home to Quakers and Baptists, free people of color (including an especially large fugitive slave community), and a significant abolitionist presence. There were warm-weather youthful skirmishes with police in the 1960s, but only with Martin Luther King, Jr.'s assassination in April 1968, and the violence paled in comparison to what occurred elsewhere in the country. Generally, New Bedford lived in the shadow of big cities like Boston to the north.

July 8 changed that, at least for the moment. Although spontaneous and initially unorganized, by 1:00 A.M. on July 9, the city witnessed clashes between scores of youth and police and firefighters. There were injuries on both sides, the first of many that month. The young people in the West End built homemade barricades from overturned and burning cars, threw rocks and other debris, started numerous fires, and even began sniping at vehicles moving through the neighborhood, including police vehicles, though no one was shot. On more than one occasion, police drew their guns, though they did not discharge them. Most alarming to some was the common chant from the crowds: "Off the pig!" and "Pigs out of the community."

This was not merely a reflection of what had become common radical parlance; it indicated the presence of the group that had popularized such language, the Black Panther Party (BPP), which everywhere sought to organize and direct such rebellions. Begun in Oakland, California, in the fall of 1966 as the Black Panther Party for Self-Defense, by 1968 it had cropped the title to denote a political party and simultaneously went national. That summer, a chapter was established in Boston. Two years later, there was no organized Panther presence in New Bedford, but there was organizing activity, spearheaded by ex-gang member and radicalized Vietnam veteran Frank "Parky" Grace. For six months, he had been bringing from Boston newspapers, buttons, posters—and sometimes Panthers, who spoke to gatherings of young people at a teen hangout on Kempton Street they called The Club. Some in the audience would come to identify as Panthers and form the core of the future New Bedford National Committee to Combat Fascism (1970–1971), a Panther

front organization, and the New Bedford branch of the BPP (1971–1972).

But, that part of July 1970 was in the future on the night of July 8. By the time things had calmed in the wee hours of July 9, police had arrested three men in their early 20s, just the initial crop of hundreds arrested during the month. First was Warren Houtman, a militant black, perhaps for driving with a defective car light, perhaps for demonstrating the sound and speed of his souped-up car—eyewitness, police, and press reports conflict, as do memories. Next was Charlie Perry, known for his street fighting abilities and a good friend of Parky Grace; he would soon become a Panther, too. That night, he was taken in for helping a black girl escape the police in the troubled aftermath of Houtman's arrest. And, finally, there was Jimmy Magnett, arrested, apparently, just for being there. Well known as a fiery voice at local meetings and in the letters-to-the-editor column of the local paper, the *Standard Times*, Magnett was identified in press reports as the defense minister of a veterans group called the Black Brothers Political Party, a group to which Grace also belonged.

The next night, July 9, the violence escalated and spread to the South End of the city, which meant significant involvement of Puerto Ricans and the key element in New Bedford's ethnic and racial mix, the Cape Verdeans. The only substantial African migration to America that was not a forced migration of slaves, the Cape Verdeans came from an island archipelago off Senegal that had been colonized in the 15th century by the Portuguese as an outpost of the Atlantic slave trade. The islands soon became an entrepôt for trade and labor, attracting people from all over the world. Because of extensive intermixing, the islanders ranged in color from dark-skinned to fair-skinned, some with blue eyes and straight hair. The Cape Verdeans, then, were neither white nor black, Portuguese nor African. They came to New Bedford as early as the late 18th century—initially, as part of the whaling industry, later to work in the cranberry bogs and textile mills—and found themselves shunned by so-called white Portuguese as "colored," just as they sought to distance themselves from what they derisively called "Americans de couer" (Americans of color). But, in the context of the mid-1960s emergence of black consciousness in America's Negro communities, a younger generation of Cape Verdeans would become "black." And, in New Bedford, the

Cape Verdean capital of the United States, the Cape Verdeans outnumbered Negroes by two to one. They would be a significant constituency for those who sought to widen and deepen the rebellion, but especially for those local Cape Verdeans who identified as Panthers.

Parky Grace and Charlie Perry were both Cape Verdean, although they lived in the West End, which was predominantly West Indian, Southern black, and Afro-Indian. Another Cape Verdean and Black Panther, Dickie Duarte, would use a megaphone taken in the looting to proselytize young Cape Verdeans at Monte's Park in the South End. Meanwhile, all sought to build ties to the shrewd organizer who emerged among the Latino population farther south, Ramon "Tito" Morales. With a white man arrested carrying a loaded shotgun near the West End, union construction workers threatening to march on it, and three white radicals from Fall River nabbed for attempted arson in support of the rioters—all in the first couple of days—the mayor, city council, police, and press worried about maintaining control.

By Friday, July 10, a crew from Boston's public broadcasting station was in town filming interviews for the July 16 airing of, *Say, Brother!*, the first TV show in the country produced for and by black people. On tape, black men in the West End, where the anger on the screen seemed to rise like the steam from the city's sweltering streets, called the events "the awakening of a sleeping giant"; the mayor called the events a "revolt"; a young black called it a "revolution!" And all this before the incident of Saturday, July 11, which turned street violence into a true conflagration. Early that evening, as scores of mostly young people milled about in front of The Club where the Panthers had proselytized local youth earlier in the year, a gray-and-white 1957 Chevy containing three young whites from adjacent towns breached the barricades set up on the first night of trouble, and stopped in the middle of the street. The driver emerged from the car, laid a shotgun across the roof, and fired point-blank into the crowd. Dozens of shotgun pellets sprayed across the torso of 17-year-old Lester Lima, from his neck to his navel, riddling both arms and piercing his heart, liver, and intestines. A Cape Verdean from the South End, he was identified in the press as a black teenager. Whisked from the scene in a car by Magnett and others, Lima died shortly after arrival at the local hospital. Three others were seriously wounded by the scattered pellets.

By the first of the following week, in the wake of a dramatic escalation of violence after the shooting, two outside forces intervened. One, whose effect was largely ephemeral, came from the Massachusetts congressional delegation, most importantly in the person of Edward Brooke, the first black Republican U.S. senator since Reconstruction. After touring the riot areas, he appointed an ad hoc committee of local activists to negotiate with the mayor, city council, and police department. More significant for the course of events was the simultaneous arrival of several Boston Panthers, who set up shop—as a branch of the National Committee to Combat Facism—in the partially burned and looted remains of a local institution called Pieraccini's Variety on Kempton Street. For the mayor, the council, and the police, they were the quintessential outside agitators, the cause of the trouble.

During the month of July, this headquarters, as Parky Grace and others called it, became a kind of cross-generational community center; the Panthers ran it, but people of varying degrees of politicization came to talk, debate, discover. It also functioned as a kind of on-the-spot liberation school with outdoor classes; the text was usually *Quotations from Chairman Mao*. Pieraccini's was also a distribution center for Panther literature—leaflets, pamphlets, newspapers, posters. Most crucially, though, for the political and business establishment in New Bedford, the storefront was a fortress, complete with sandbags, gun slots, and a cache of weapons—thanks largely to the expertise of local radicalized Vietnam veterans.

When renewed rioting began in the South End during the week of July 27, after weeks of skirmishing, and especially when the violent winds blew back into the West End, rumors were rife that the city had had enough and intended to raid Pieraccini's to search for illegal weapons. At a press conference on July 30, the Panthers offered to open their doors, as long as their lawyers could be present. The officers came too late. At about 6:00 A.M. on the morning of July 31, a local resident named Stephen Botelho drove to police headquarters to report that he had been shot. While driving home from work on Kempton Street just after passing Pieraccini's, he claimed, a sniper had shot at his car, wounding him in the right ankle. Botelho's report would provide the catalyst for a massive raid by local police, with state police standing by and hovering overhead in helicopters.

Twenty-one people were arrested emerging from or standing outside Pieraccini's that morning, giving birth to what would be known, briefly, as the New Bedford 21. From the beginning and throughout, the group was associated with the Panthers, for Pieraccini's was essentially a Panther building, occupied by several people known to be members of the Boston Panther chapter. Still, some were merely community supporters, some unaffiliated activists, and some complete innocents. In any case, the charges against those arrested were serious: they included conspiracy to commit murder and anarchy, and to incite riot. Moreover, the original total bail was set at well over $1 million. The prisoners were questioned by the Federal Bureau of Investigation, which immediately opened a file on the NCCF and all associated with it.

Although the civil disorder itself was not the doing of the Panthers, Boston or local, it was clearly affected by them; moreover, the city establishment, especially the mayor, would see the entire affair as a product of outside agitators. And, although there were skirmishes in August and even, on occasion, the following fall, the July 31 raid did deflate the revolt. Organizing on behalf of the New Bedford 21 was the focus of local Panther activity that fall and winter; just before the trial was to begin in late March, all of the serious charges were dropped. As for the three whites charged in the July 11 killing of Lima and the wounding of the others, an all-white jury, after deliberating for 45 minutes, voted to acquit on all charges. A few fires were set, but New Bedford did not erupt at the verdict. And it never did again.

JAMA LAZEROW

See also
Black Self-Defense; Kerner Commission Report (1968); King, Martin Luther, Jr.; Police Brutality; Race Riots in America; World War I. Documents: The Report on the Memphis Riots of May 1866 (July 25, 1866); Account of the Riots in East St. Louis, Illinois (July 1917); The Cook County Coroner's Report Regarding the 1919 Chicago Race Riots (1919); A Southern Black Woman's Letter Regarding the Recent Riots in Chicago and Washington (November 1919); The Final Report of the Grand Jury on the Tulsa Race Riot (June 25, 1921); Testimony from *Laney v. United States* Describing Events during the Washington, D.C., Riot of July 1919 (December 3, 1923); The Governor's Commission Report on the Watts Riots (December 1965); Cyrus R. Vance's Report on the Riots in Detroit (July-August 1967); The Reports of the Oklahoma Commission to Study the Tulsa Race Riot of 1921 (2000-2001); The Draft Report of the 1898 Wilmington Race Riot Commission (December 2005)

Further Reading:
Feagin, Joe R., and Harlan Hahn. *Ghetto Revolts*. New York: Macmillan, 1973.
Fogelson, Robert M. *Violence as Protest: A Study of Riots and Ghettos*. Garden City, NY: Doubleday, 1971.
Gilje, Paul A. *Rioting in America*. Bloomington and Indianapolis: Indiana University Press, 1996.
Kerner, Otto, et al. *Report of the National Advisory Commission on Civil Disorders*. New York: Bantam Books, 1968.
Lazerow, Jama. "The Black Panthers at the Water's Edge: Oakland, Boston, and the New Bedford 'Riots' of 1970." In *The Black Panther Party in Historical Perspective*, edited by Jama Lazerow and Yohuru Williams. Durham, NC: Duke University Press, forthcoming.

New Deal
The New Deal was put into place by President Franklin D. Roosevelt during the Great Depression from 1933 to 1938. New Deal programs created a radical shift in the role of the federal government vis-à-vis the nation's economic sphere in an effort to reform the U.S. economy torn by the Depression. New Deal policies were guided by the "Three Rs": direct relief, economic recovery, and financial reform. However, New Deal initiatives extended well into the 1940s and 1950s, largely to support returning World War II veterans. During the New Deal, under the auspices of Roosevelt and largely controlled by the Jim Crow mentality of the South for whom most of the aid was geared toward, given the rampant rural poverty of both blacks and whites, the federal government transformed into an activist government that sought to advance human well-being and provide economic security to its citizens. The federal government tightened its grip on the nation's economic sector via New Deal programs. Of all the New Deal programs initiated during the course of this activist government's reign, three social initiatives particularly reveal the New Deal government's commitment to alleviating social ills, albeit in a fashion that is largely racist and indeed Jim Crowed (i.e., exclusionary or separate): welfare, work, and war. Aid to Dependent Children (ADC) was the largest social welfare initiative. In regard to the New Deal's

influence on labor laws, three laws are worth examining: the National Industrial Recovery Act, the National Labor Relation Act , and the Fair Labor Standards Act of 1938. In regard to war, the Selective Service Readjustment Act was the largest New Deal initiative, and its effects on the country were enormous. However, all of the New Deal initiatives, whether in the North or the South, were implemented in a race-based fashion that at best favored white Americans over African Americans, and at worst was a segregated system that could not escape the all-pervading influence of Jim Crow segregation and exclusion that divided the nation.

Aid to Dependent Children passed as one of 11 titles in the 1935 Social Security Act passed in Congress. The federal programs passed under the act, which was designed to provide 30 million Americans with a safety net by virtue of federal government support, in August during Roosevelt's term were Jim Crowed from the beginning. ADC was designed to offer grants to families in which one of the parents, usually the father, was absent. Aid often went to mothers who were divorced, never married, or abandoned, or whose husbands could not work. ADC, and other programs included within the Social Security Act, was funded by both the federal and state governments. However, the programs were governed at that state level, which ultimately made the programs decentralized from the federal government and subject to Jim Crow exclusion and segregation.

Black mothers were largely excluded from receiving such federal and state aid, often in the Jim Crow South where black population was the highest. The racial exclusionary policies of the landmark Social Security Act were employed in terms of labor performed. The act prohibited qualification for aid to those who toiled in the agricultural or domestic service sectors, jobs that were dominated by blacks and Mexicans. Black mothers often had to fight against locally state-controlled bureaucracies that were partially funded by the federal government. In the United States as a whole, 14 percent of children in the program were black. That the relief would be administered at the state level was detrimental to African Americans in the Jim Crow South. Thirty-seven percent of the children in Louisiana were African American, but only 26 percent were ADC recipients. Throughout the South, blacks were largely excluded.

During the New Deal era, the National Industrial Recovery Act, the National Labor Relations Act, and the Fair Labor Standard Act were passed to increase working conditions. These three very significant acts gave workers, among other things, the right to bargain collectively with unions, a maximum work week, better working conditions, and a minimum wage. These three acts were generally employed in a discriminatory fashion and ultimately harmed African American workers, both male and female.

The National Industrial Recovery Act (NIRA) passed during the famous first 100 days of Roosevelt's administration on June 16, 1933. One of the components of the bill was that it guaranteed workers the right to organize and bargain collectively with unions and other representatives without fear of employer coercion. Further, it put forth "codes of fair competition" that guaranteed a minimum wage and a maximum 40-hour work week. Although the act presented itself and had the potential to help African Americans, it ultimately had devastating consequences on African American workers.

The wage provisions guaranteed by the NIRA discriminated and harmed African Americans in a multiplicity of ways. After Southern legislators voiced concern over the consequences that increased wages would have on agricultural profits and easily affordable domestic workers, both industries that African Americans dominated, they agreed not to establish "fair labor codes" for agricultural and domestic labor. Wages in the agricultural and domestic fields remained stable, while wages in other sectors of labor, largely dominated by white workers, increased. The NIRA determined the minimum wage in relation to the category of work performed. Consequently, when the NIRA minimum wage codes happened to apply to occupations that African Americans dominated, the occupations received a lower classification than similar unskilled "white" occupations, and thus were granted a lower minimum wage. In short, the NIRA promoted and practiced separate wage differentials for white and African American workers. In the end, the minimum wage provisions dramatically harmed African American workers; it is estimated to have cost a half million African Americans their jobs.

The NIRA also attempted to raise wages through collective bargaining. When it came to collective bargaining with unions, blacks faced the same problems they met with wage provisions. The passage of NIRA, under Section 7a, gave racist unions, those that excluded and segregated African

Americans in their locals and federations, exclusive bargaining power on behalf of workers in various industries. Before the passage of the NIRA, American unions represented a small but significant, 2.25 million members, of whom 50,000 were black. Two months after the passage of the NIRA, union membership increased to a little less than 4 million. Ultimately, the exclusive right to bargain on behalf of workers granted to racist labor unions displaced many African American workers. When African Americans did complain about union discrimination to the National Labor Relations Board, the federal government failed to intrude on their behalf. In response, government officials attempted to pacify African American outrage by pointing out that the act had led to minimum wage laws, the elimination of child labor, and a maximum 40-hour work week, of which some, but by no means a vast majority, African Americans enjoyed.

On May 27, 1935, the Supreme Court declared that the NIRA was unconstitutional in *A.L.A. Schecter Poultry Corp. v. United States*. The National Labor Relation Act (NLRA), also known as the Wagner Act of 1935, replaced Section 7a of the NIRA. The NLRA guaranteed wage workers the right to organize and bargain collectively with unions, and made illegal "unfair labor practices" used by employers to avoid unionization. Moreover, the act prohibited employer discrimination on the basis of union activity and obliged employers to bargain with these organizations. Additionally, like the NIRA's Section 7a, the Wagner Act, through the National Labor Relations Board, made unions the only way to bargain collectively with employers. Union membership rose to 8 million by 1941, and by 1948, union membership surged to 14.2 million.

The Wagner Act, however, did not protect black workers. It was implemented in an exclusionary fashion, as it did not contain a clause that protected African American workers, as a result of racist labor unions, particularly the American Federation of Labor, that successfully lobbied to keep the clause from protecting African American workers. The Wagner Act also banned company unions, unions that were more racially egalitarian than affiliated unions, and made the hire of strikebreaking workers, usually African American, more difficult. The NLRA, in essence, gave unions governmental validation to exclude black workers from labor agreements.

The minimum wage provisions mandated by the NIRA, which were later found unconstitutional by the Supreme Court, were later smuggled in under the Fair Labor Standards Act of 1938 (FLSA). The FLSA guaranteed a minimum wage of 25 cents an hour for the first year of its passage, 30 cents for the second, and 40 cents an hour inside a six-year time period, overtime protections, maximum working hours at 44 hours a week in the first years of its passage, 42 in the second, and 40 hours henceforth, to many wage laborers. The act was designed to advance the cause of white workers. Again, like the New Deal labor laws passed before it, it was implemented in a Jim Crow fashion. Domestic and agricultural workers, an overwhelming majority of which were African or Mexican Americans, were not covered under the act. Further, FLSA cost many Africans Americans their jobs. The disemployment of workers was mostly felt by African American laborers in the South who often performed labor at a rate less than the minimum wage mandated by the government. Two weeks after the passage of the FLSA, it is estimated by the Labor Department that 30,000 to 50,000 workers, predominantly black in the South, had lost their jobs as a result of the minimum wage provisions. For example, the percentage of African Americans in the tobacco industry declined from about 68 percent in 1930 to about 55 percent in 1940.

Of all the bills passed during the progressive days of the New Deal, the Selective Service Readjustment Act, also known as the GI Bill, was implemented in the most discriminatory fashion, and it, more than any other bill, did more to increase the economic gap between African Americans and their white counterparts. The GI Bill, passed in 1944, marks the largest social benefit bill ever passed by the federal government in a single initiative. The bill was designed to (re)integrate 16 million returning veterans; it reached 8 of every 10 men born in the 1920s. In a 28-year span from 1944 to 1971, federal spending totaled over $90 billion, and by 1948, a massive 15 percent of the federal budget was geared toward funding the bill. The bill was designed to help returning veterans start a business, buy a home, or attend college. The bill is, no doubt, responsible for the making of the middle class.

The middle class it created was largely white. The GI Bill, like the New Deal bills it followed, was written under the patronage of Jim Crow and was prone to practice exclusionary policies that either rejected blacks outright or underfunded them dramatically in comparison to their white counterparts.

Upon returning from World War II, many black veterans, no doubt, reaped the fruits of the GI Bill and attended colleges, started business, and experienced some upward mobility. However, the entrenched racism in the Jim Crow South and throughout America put many obstacles in front of blacks who sought to secure the benefits of the GI Bill. The bill was drafted by the openly racist, antiblack, anti-Catholic, and anti-Jewish John Rankin of Mississippi, and had to pass by Southern members of Congress who insisted that the GI Bill be decentralized from the federal government. The GI Bill left the administrative responsibilities up to the states. Leaving administrative tasks in the hands of policy makers in Jim Crow South, who feared that blacks would use their new status to dismantle segregation, proved to have negative consequences on African Americans. Locals administering the program at the Mississippi Unemployment Compensation Committee, strongly encouraged blacks not to apply for social benefits. Two years after the GI Bill's implementation, the committee had received only 2,600 applications from African Americans, whereas it received 16,000 from white applicants. When black applicants were rewarded funding, they often had to overcome the discrimination of the institutions they wished to attend. Elite universities in the North were reluctant to admit blacks. The University of Pennsylvania, the most racially egalitarian university in 1946, boasted only 40 blacks out of an institutional enrollment of 9,000. Black enrollment in the North and the West never exceeded 5,000 African Americans in the 1940s. As a result, 95 percent of black veterans were forced to attend segregated, all-black colleges. However, because of Jim Crow policies that forced blacks to segregated, all-black institutions, and the failure of Southern states to fund black institutions, black colleges failed to keep up with the demand. Twenty thousand eligible blacks could not find an academic institution to attend in 1947, and as many as 50,000 might have sought admission if there would not have been such widespread Jim Crow policies.

JACK A. TAYLOR III

See also

Great Depression; Roosevelt, Franklin D.; Works Progress Administration (WPA)

Further Reading:

Bernstein, David E. *Only One Place of Redress: African Americans, Labor Regulations, and the Courts from Reconstruction to the New Deal.* Durham, NC: Duke University Press, 2001.

"The Depression, The New Deal, and World War II." African American Odyssey, Library of Congress. http://memory.loc .gov/ammem/aaohtml/exhibit/aopart8.html (accessed May 28, 2008).

Katznelson, Ira. *When Affirmative Action Was White: An Untold History of Racial Inequality in Twentieth-Century America.* New York: W. W. Norton, 2005.

Moreno, Paul. *Black Americans and Organized Labor: A New History.* Baton Rouge: Louisiana State University Press, 2006.

Roediger, David. *Working toward Whiteness: How America's Immigrants Became White: The Strange Journey from Ellis Island to the Suburbs.* New York: Basic Books, 2005.

Sullivan, Patricia. *Days of Hope: Race and Democracy in the New Deal Era.* Chapel Hill: University of North Carolina Press, 1996.

Zieger, Robert H. *For Jobs and Freedom: Race and Labor in America Since 1865.* Lexington: University Press of Kentucky, 2007.

New Jim Crow, The

Michelle Alexander's book *The New Jim Crow: Mass Incarceration in an Age of Colorblindness* explains how and why the U.S. criminal justice system has reinforced racial inequality and the consequences of such social repression. First appearing in 2010, a revised edition with a forward by Princeton University professor and social justice activist Cornell West was published in 2012. The critically acclaimed book was on the *New York Times* Best Seller List for 10 consecutive months and sold over 175,000 copies. Many Americans believe we live in a postracial society, with race making little difference in a person's life chances. Alexander, an Ohio State associate professor of law, provides substantial evidence that in spite of the few black individuals such as Barack Obama who have achieved positions of power and wealth, racism is still an active force in American life. According to Alexander, this system of racial discrimination is manifested in and reinforced by a criminal justice system in the United States that imprisons millions of people of color every year, effectively reinforcing long-standing systems of racial repression and discrimination. *The New Jim Crow* has been identified as giving a powerful voice to the racial inequity that continues to characterize American society despite the advancements of the civil

Michelle Alexander of the ACLU, holding sign, asks a California highway patrol officer, left, if she could give Gov. Gray Davis a report card giving him failing marks on his positions on racial justice, during a protest outside the governor's office in Sacramento, California, 2000. (Associated Press)

rights movement; it also offers astute research into the causes of such inequity.

In *The New Jim Crow*, Alexander compares the new system of racial discrimination in the United States to an older one known as "Jim Crow." The term, dating from the 1830s, originally referred to a dance. It became a shorthand expression for the racial inequalities that characterized the South following the end of Reconstruction in the 1870s and continued through the 20th century. Jim Crow laws and practices backed by terrorist organizations, most notably the Ku Klux Klan, were used to deprive blacks of the rights supposedly guaranteed to them by the Fourteenth and Fifteenth amendments. Passed in the aftermath of the Civil War, these amendments granted citizenship rights, including the right to vote, to all persons born in the United States. However, poll taxes, literacy tests, segregation, and violence were used to keep African Americans from exercising these rights. These Jim Crow laws and practices functioned as a way for white Southern elites to keep their economic and political control. According to Alexander, this old Jim Crow ended in the 1960s with the passage of civil rights legislation, but discrimination and the corresponding disenfranchisement of African Americans continues in the United States today, facilitated primarily by mass incarceration.

The primary statistic buttressing Alexander's argument in *The New Jim Crow* is that African Americans compose nearly 50 percent of the 2.3 million people now imprisoned in the United States, though they represent only 13 percent of the country's total population. In this way, mass incarceration can be seen as functioning as a system of racial control in a manner similar to the original Jim Crow laws of the late 19th century. Other progressive critics have joined Alexander in this assessment of the U.S. justice system, supporting her claim that the War on Drugs has functioned as the primary mechanism through which mass imprisonment has occurred. This "war," which began in the 1970s with then President Richard Nixon, was declared when drug use was actually declining. According to *The New Jim Crow*, the legislation created out of the War on Drugs has more to do with repressing and discriminating against blacks than about actually reducing drug use in the United States. For example, Alexander cites the statistic that black drug users are far more likely than whites to be imprisoned: 59 percent of prisoners in state facilities for drug offenses are African American, yet African Americans represent only 12 percent of drug users. Alexander also points out that African Americans typically receive longer sentences for drug-related offenses than do whites.

Out of the new Jim Crow system in the United States, Alexander believes that a new caste system has been created. The term "caste system" refers to a social hierarchy in which society is divided into rigid groups, each with their own social status. In traditional caste systems such as the one historically dominating India, a person is born into a specific social group, and that designation comes to determine much of what happens to them throughout their life. Alexander describes the millions of African Americans currently incarcerated in the United States as a "racial caste," drawing parallels between this system and earlier systems of racial discrimination such as slavery and 19th-century Jim Crow laws. However, unlike these earlier systems, the new Jim Crow is not as visible or blatant, making it even more insidious. Labeling someone a criminal or ex-prisoner allows for stigmatization and discrimination, restricting their rights and social opportunities. Prisoners and ex-felons cannot vote in many U.S. states, they can be barred from a number of professions, and they are not allowed access to public housing or driver's licenses. All of these consequences of incarceration signify that the new Jim Crow system is designed to exert racial social control, but in a more surreptitious way than the original Jim Crow laws.

The New Jim Crow has done much to realize Alexander's goal, which she says in her book "is to stimulate a much-needed conversation about the role of the criminal justice system in creating and perpetuating racial hierarchy in the United States." Alexander's book calls attention to facts about the reality of racial discrimination in the United States that have not received sufficient attention, even from major civil rights organizations. *The New Jim Crow* is a significant book because it points out how hard-won civil rights gains—including the right to vote—are being undermined in the United States today. Alexander argues that a new movement is needed to address the racial inequalities she describes in her book.

BARBARA CHASIN

See also

Jim Crow Laws; Racism

Further Reading:

Alexander, Michelle. *The New Jim Crow: Mass Incarceration in the Age of Colorblindness.* Rev. ed. New York: New Press, 2012.

Bill Moyers Journal. April 2, 2010.

NAACP. *Criminal Justice Fact Sheet.* 2012. http://www.naacp.org/pages/criminal-justice-fact-sheet (accessed December 27, 2012).

Schuessler, Jennifer. "Drug Policy as Race Policy: Best Seller Galvanizes the Debate." *New York Times.* March 7, 2012, C1.

Sentencing Times. "New Report Shows Record 5.85 Million Can't Vote." Sentencing Project: Washington, DC, 2012.

Woodward, C. Vann, *The Strange Career of Jim Crow*, 2nd rev. ed. New York: Oxford University Press, 1966.

New Negro Movement

The New Negro Movement was a collective political, artistic, and social response to the pressures of Jim Crow from the late 19th century until the mid-20th. It occurred in two phases: first in the post-Reconstruction era and, secondly, in the 1920s in its most recognizable form during the Harlem Renaissance. In both stages, the movement was led by black intellectuals and artists who were distinguished as "New Negroes" from previous generations of enslaved African Americans. To correspond with the changing times, the concept and figure of a "New Negro" were debated and reconceptualized when social conditions worsened for all African Americans. Black disenfranchisement, "peonage slavery," lynchings, race riots, and the creation of Black Codes to enforce systematic oppression marked the "nadir" of African American history in the last decades of the 19th century and ushered in a new modern age. Ultimately, the New Negro Movement was an opportunity to highlight African Americans' achievements in the arts and letters as possible solutions to the race problem.

New historicist scholars and literary critics trace the development of the movement to the 1890s, when black intellectuals were determined to reconstruct the public image of African Americans. Minstrel characters such as "mammies," "uncles," and "coons" were paraded before American audiences as a popular form of entertainment. These caricatures of "ole time Negroes" also saturated the consumer market in product advertisements. Such negative stereotypical images of black people were more common to white Americans than the educated, professional class that had emerged since slavery. The conditions of the post-Reconstruction era—the birth of Jim Crow culture—did not halt African Americans' racial progress. On the contrary, the period gave birth to the "New Negro," recognized by a difference in physical appearance, behavior, and attitude as a social equal. Such racial representatives were well-educated members of the black middle class. Their individual accomplishments in education, politics, the humanities, and sciences were taken as evidence of racial progress in general. Most importantly, these New Negroes would demand their political rights en masse.

It is more than mere coincidence then that the "nadir" of African American literature corresponds with the birth of Jim Crow. Public debates about the status of African Americans as second-class citizens ignited criticism from writers and poets alike. The corpus of protest literature produced during this first phase of the New Negro Movement address the deterioration of race relations. Crowned the "Poet Laureate of the Race," Paul Laurence Dunbar in "Sympathy" and "We Wear the Mask" evokes the pathos and frustration of African Americans. Frances E. W. Harper's political romance novel *Iola Leroy* (1892), Sutton E. Griggs's *Imperium in Imperio* (1899), and Pauline Hopkins's *Contending Forces* (1900) were among the earliest novels to appear as

a sign of a New Negro literary renaissance. This is a period that is also commonly referred to as "Post-Bellum, Pre-Harlem," a phrase coined by the Southern black writer Charles W. Chesnutt. His own contributions included short story collections *The Conjure Woman* (1899) and *The Wife of His Youth and Other Stories of the Color Line* (1899); race problem novels *The House Behind the Cedars* (1900), *The Marrow of Tradition* (1901), *The Colonel's Dream* (1905); and many political essays and speeches. In *A Voice From the South* (1892), renowned educator Anna Julia Cooper also contributed to this debate about race relations. Her text was essential to the development of black feminism as well as the New Negro Movement. Booker T. Washington's *Up From Slavery* (1901) and W.E.B. Du Bois's *The Souls of Black Folk* (1903) are also key works in the development of a literary tradition created by black writer-activists around the turn of the century.

Altogether, these New Negroes created a body of literature as a testament to the progress of the race. In 1895, Victoria Earle Matthews, noted clubwoman and writer, had issued a call for the collection of such "race literature," which were "all the writings emanating from a distinct class—not necessarily race matter; but a general collection of what has been written by the men and women of that Race: History, Biographies, Scientific Treatises, Sermons, Addresses, Novels, Poems, Books of Travel, miscellaneous essays and the contributions to magazines and newspapers." Matthews, as did many of her contemporaries, firmly believed that with race literature African Americans would take their place among the world's greatest civilizations. Poets like George Clinton Rowe and Josephine Delphine Henderson Heard captured the optimism of the age. The assimilationist images of African Americans "rising" to take their place in white society were common in the genteel traditions at the "nadir." While many of these early writers and poets have been dismissed as accommodationists, their collective works testify to the obstacles African Americans overcame as proof of racial survival for future generations.

In response to segregation, two major black political organizations appeared during the first phase of the New Negro Movement. The National Association for the Advancement of Colored People (NAACP) and the National Urban League (NUL) were established in 1909 and 1911, respectively. Du Bois, members of his "Talented Tenth," and liberal white activists worked to make the NAACP the leading advocate for black civil rights. The NUL was created to meet the needs of thousands of African Americans migrating from the South to Northern urban areas. Many black writers would participate in the activities and hold positions in both organizations. James Weldon Johnson's involvement in the NAACP, for instance, would continue well into the second phase of the New Negro Movement. His novel *The Autobiography of an Ex-Colored Man* (1912) is a transitional text, too. Initially published anonymously, the controversial work was later attributed to Johnson in 1927; by then, the author was already considered an architect of the Harlem Renaissance.

The outbreak of race riots after World War I stimulated the literary responses of the "new" Negro Movement of the 1920s. During the Red Summer of 1919, over 20 race riots exploded throughout the nation, especially in large cities like Chicago and Washington, D.C. with sizable populations of Southern black migrants. After returning from fighting for democracy abroad in Europe, African American soldiers arrived home to join the fight for social equality, too. The militant spirit of this generation, according to Gates, marks the evolution of the New Negro. Within the decade, this modern image and movement would be more political and place greater emphasis on literary aesthetics than the previous phase. Writings by Du Bois, A. Phillip Randolph, and Alain Locke signaled the reemergence of the New Negro as an educated, cultured, and, often, radical artist. Like Dunbar before him, Claude McKay became the new poetic voice of the New Negro Movement. His manifesto poem "If We Must Die" (1919) protests racial injustice as inspired by the violence of Red Summer. It introduced audiences to McKay's most important poetry collection, *Harlem Shadows* (1922), and to the black cultural renaissance in Harlem, New York.

For thousands of migrants, Harlem became the Black Mecca. Black Southerners believed it offered a chance to escape the harsh reality of Jim Crow segregation and racism in the South. With its nightclubs, theaters, literary societies, and businesses, the community's social, educational, and economic attractions catered to the black masses that congregated there. An exotic element was added with the arrival of black West Indians. Marcus Garvey's call for Black Nationalism, with his Universal Negro Improvement Association, appealed especially to thousands of his fellow foreign migrants from throughout the black diaspora. As Locke

described it, the "pulse of the Negro World [had] begun to beat in Harlem." White Americans also responded to this "beat" as they flocked to Harlem especially to witness the frenzy of the nightlife. For the black writers and artists, Harlem was a muse and cultural center. Langston Hughes, as a key figure of the Harlem Renaissance, helped to usher in this modern era of African American literature and culture that is defined by its creative mix of language and sound, rhythm and soul. He especially used the new American music, jazz and blues, to create poetry that could mimic the beat of jazz instruments, present the lamentations of a blues singer, or protest injustice, sometimes all in a single poem. Hughes's first poetry collection, *The Weary Blues* (1926), is among the most innovative works of the New Negro Movement. Jean Toomer's *Cane* (1923) and Jessie Redmon Fauset's *There Is Confusion* (1924) are also recognized as prolific novels of the new era. This younger generation of New Negro artists also includes poets Countee Cullen, Gwendolyn Bennett, Georgia Douglas Johnson, and Sterling Brown as well as a talented group of novelists like Nella Larsen, Rudolph Fisher, Wallace Thurman, and Zora Neale Hurston.

Political establishments and generous patrons sponsored most of the literature produced during the 1920s New Negro Movement. Both the NAACP and the NUL created awards for emerging writers and poets. Contests were announced in the pages of *The Crisis* and *Opportunity* magazines, the respective publications of the NAACP and the NUL. Banquets well attended by the cultural elite were held in honor of the award winners. Hughes, Fauset, Cullen, and Hurston, among others, were literary stars at these events. Their works attracted the attention of white patrons, whom Hurston nicknamed "Negrotarians." W.E.B. Du Bois and James Weldon Johnson were members of the old guard, or the "Talented Tenth," that formed alliances with these white patrons. By the middle of the movement, however, generational conflicts appeared between the civil rights establishment and members of the "Niggerati," Hurston's label for African American artists themselves. The publication of the infamous journal *Fire!!* (1926), edited by Thurman, led the charge against the older set and their artistic propaganda intentions for the New Negro Movement.

Thurman, Hughes, Hurston, and other younger rebels revolted in their more crude expressions of blackness that repulsed the refined tastes of the political guardians and financial backers of the renaissance. Du Boisian leadership had manipulated the arts and letters of the movement to improve race relations by insisting on aesthetic value as proof of racial progress just as his early contemporaries had envisioned around the turn of the 19th century. Hughes and his set were more interested in using their art to promote authentic blackness, images of the common folk, unfiltered for white audiences. As spokesman, Hughes proudly boasted: "We younger Negro artists who create now intend to express our individual dark-skinned selves without fear or shame. If white people are pleased we are glad. If they are not, it doesn't matter. We know we are beautiful. And ugly too. The tom-tom cries and the tom-tom laughs. If colored people are pleased we are glad. If they are not, their displeasure doesn't matter either." The "pure" black soul freely expressing itself was the ultimate goal of the New Negro artist by the end of the movement when the stock market crashed in 1929, leading to the start of the Great Depression of the 1930s.

SHERITA L. JOHNSON

See also

Great Depression; Roosevelt, Franklin D.

Further Reading:

Bruce, Dickson D. *Black American Writing from the Nadir: The Evolution of a Literary Tradition, 1877–1915.* Baton Rouge: Louisiana State University Press, 1992.

Gates, Henry Louis. "The Trope of a New Negro and the Reconstruction of the Image of the Black." *Representations* 24 (Fall 1988): 129–55.

Lewis, David Levering, ed. *The Portable Harlem Renaissance Reader.* New York: Penguin Books, 1995.

Matthews, Victoria Earle. "The Value of Race Literature" [1895]. *Massachusetts Review* 27 (Summer 1986): 169–91.

Wintz, Cary D., ed. *The Emergence of the Harlem Renaissance.* New York: Garland, 1996.

New Orleans (Louisiana) Riot of 1866

The New Orleans Riot of 1866 was one of the largest and most brutal events that occurred during the city's history. Although unique in its severity, the New Orleans riot was hardly a rare event. Race riots occurred in other cities that summer (Memphis in May and Charleston in June), and these related incidents are characteristic of the social, cultural, and racial unrest haunting this time period.

Many attribute the origin of the riot to the controversy surrounding the movement to reconvene the 1864 convention and implement the Civil Rights Act of 1866. This act attempted to grant citizenship to all native-born Americans regardless of race thus giving blacks equal rights and protection under the law. By 1866, some members, Republicans in particular, of the 1864 convention lost their power to conservative Democrats in the election of 1865. As a result, some Republicans deemed this situation as an opportunity to regain power in the state of Louisiana. The 1864 constitution provided two avenues for ratification. The conference could either make a request for the new state legislature to assemble a new convention, or they could ask the legislature to amend the constitution themselves and have it ratified by the people in the next state election. But many of the old members, also known as conventionalists, knew that they would have no power in making changes to the constitution because the Democrats would control a majority of the votes; and the second option would not be suitable to the conventionalists because the legislature would attempt to oppose their amendments to the Constitution. As a result, the conventionalists decided to reconvene without any of the newly elected members of the legislature.

The conventionalists' primary obstacle was getting the support they needed to reconvene the convention. The only person who had the power to reconvene the convention was its president, Judge E. H. Durell. Although he refused to assist the conventionalists and left the city, they issued a call to all of the former members of the convention and met on June 26, 1864. During this meeting, 39 of the original 96 members were in attendance. The conventionalists ousted Judge Durell as president and elected Judge R. K. Howell as president pro tem. Their second action was to assign June 30 as the date to reconvene the convention. This political maneuver set in motion the social and political basis for the riot a few days later.

The conventionalists' actions created a recipe for civil unrest in the city. The conventionalists' unlawful attempt to amend the Constitution unilaterally, without regard for their position, angered the legislative members who controlled the majority of the state's population. Additionally, members of the old planter and merchant aristocracy disliked the conventionalists because they were a threat to the social and political power base they initially established after the war. The larger white population was primarily angered that whites would lose their rights to vote, some former Confederate soldiers would lose jobs in government and, most importantly, that people of African descent might gain the right to vote. The days leading up to the riots were tense and filled with inflammatory speeches made by both supporters of the conventionalists and those who opposed them, which also created tension between the conventionalists and conservatives and blacks and whites.

On the morning of June 30, the city of New Orleans was tense. The first incident of racial violence occurred during a procession of 100 to 150 blacks marching to the Mechanics' Institute, the meeting hall for the convention. Violence erupted when a white boy made insulting remarks to a black participant and kicked him in the back. As the white crowd applauded and laughed, the black man knocked the young man down. A scuffle ensued, which ended in the black man's arrest. Additionally, a black man began to wave his flag in response to jeers from the white crowd. A policeman responded to this action by firing a shot at the flag bearer.

The riot broke out when another young white boy threw a rock into the black processional crowd of around 1,500 people in front of the Mechanics' Institute at about 1:00 P.M. As the blacks began to rush the boy, violence ensued as gunfire started. Initially, the blacks were able to repel the officers and the white crowd; however, the mob was better armed and eventually overtook them. As a result, many blacks dispersed throughout the city while others took refuge in the institute. Whites chased and harassed blacks within a one- to two-mile radius of the Mechanics' Institute, which led to the brutalization of many blacks who had not participated in the processional. Other members of the mob entered the Mechanics' Institute to take on conventionalists and the remaining blacks. Although some attempted to surrender to the mob, there was no sympathy for the trapped members. Anticipating the federal army would come to their rescue, they barricaded themselves in the hall. Due to either miscommunication or ambivalence on the part of the U.S. government, troops did not arrive until 4:00 P.M. By the end of the riot, over 130 blacks were injured and about 34 were killed; 3 whites associated with the conventionalists were killed and about 17 were wounded; 20 members of the police force were slightly wounded, and 1 person from the white mob was killed.

The New Orleans riot placed the social and political attitudes of Southerners after the Civil War in perspective for Northerners. The brutality of this riot gave the Republicans the ammunition they needed to make their campaign for Reconstruction a primary issue in the congressional elections of 1866. After gaining the majority in Congress, they were able to bring about radical Reconstruction and the passage of the Reconstruction Act of 1867.

CHRISTINA S. HAYNES

See also

Race Riots in America; Reconstruction Era. Documents: The Report on the Memphis Riots of May 1866 (July 25, 1866); Account of the Riots in East St. Louis, Illinois (July 1917); The Cook County Coroner's Report Regarding the 1919 Chicago Race Riots (1919); A Southern Black Woman's Letter Regarding the Recent Riots in Chicago and Washington (November 1919); The Final Report of the Grand Jury on the Tulsa Race Riot (June 25, 1921); Testimony from *Laney v. United States* Describing Events during the Washington, D.C., Riot of July 1919 (December 3, 1923); The Governor's Commission Report on the Watts Riots (December 1965); Cyrus R. Vance's Report on the Riots in Detroit (July-August 1967); The Reports of the Oklahoma Commission to Study the Tulsa Race Riot of 1921 (2000-2001); The Draft Report of the 1898 Wilmington Race Riot Commission (December 2005)

Further Reading:

Fogelson, Robert M., and Richard Rubenstein, eds. *Mass Violence in America: New Orleans Riots of July 30, 1866.* New York: Arno Press and New York Times, 1969.

Hollandsworth, James G. *An Absolute Massacre: The New Orleans Riot of July 30th, 1866.* Baton Rouge: Louisiana State University Press, 2001.

Vandal, Giles. *The New Orleans Riot of 1866: Anatomy of a Tragedy.* Lafayette: Center for Louisiana Studies, University of Southwestern Louisiana, 1983.

Vandal, Giles. "The Origins of the New Orleans Riot of 1866, Revised." In *African American Life in the Post–Emancipation South, 1861–1900,* edited by Donald G. Nieman. New York: Garland Publishing, 1994.

New York City Draft Riot of 1863

On Monday, July 13, 1863, the city of New York exploded into racial violence. For five days, the black community was ravaged by mob attacks as disgruntled white rioters expressed their outrage about black emancipation, the Civil War, and the mandatory proscription law President Abraham Lincoln had passed several months earlier. Although the first acts of violence were directed toward government agencies, within hours, the rioters focused on black people, neighborhoods, and symbols of black equality. Before the reign of terror subsided, 11 black men had been lynched, countless men, women, and children had been beaten and maimed, black homes and institutions had been torched, and thousands of black people had been driven from the city. The final death toll still remains unknown. Even after federal troops arrived to restore order, attacks persisted and were not fully quelled until the following Friday. In the months that followed, the devastated black community struggled to reclaim their lives and reassert their right to exist in American society as free and equal citizens.

The prelude to the New York City Draft Riot was deeply rooted in the larger context of American politics during the antebellum era. Not only was riot behavior a common form of political protest in the United States, but these outbursts routinely expressed distinctly antiblack consciousness. There was a particularly disturbing legacy of racial hostility in New York City, which peaked in 1834 with one of the most violent race riots in antebellum America. Racial tensions increased in 1861, when the United States dissolved into civil war over the issue of slavery, and tensions were exacerbated by the passage of the Emancipation Proclamation two years later. As a result, by early 1863, the specter of black emancipation created growing resentment in the North as the war seemingly dragged on interminably. In March 1863, Congress passed the stringent Conscription Act, which subjected eligible men between the ages of 20 to 35, and all unmarried men aged 35 to 45, to possible military service. According to the new law, the names of these men would be placed into a lottery and randomly selected to determine who would fight on behalf of the Union. Essentially, the government had effectively imposed a mandatory draft.

Although the federal government's actions may have appeared to be a necessary measure to bolster the war effort, there were powerful objections emanating from New York City that posed major challenges to Republican policies. City leaders had expressed consistent opposition to the war, most notably, beginning in 1860, Mayor Fernando Wood, who adamantly opposed the war and vocally criticized the Republican Party for waging a war against slavery. As Wood's antiwar rhetoric increased, he rekindled latent frustrations about black emancipation by directing his anger toward the black community, which he blamed for the conflict.

Wood's attitude toward black inequality, the necessity of Southern slavery, and his extreme opposition to the Civil War revealed deep-seated notions in New York City that inspired the draft riots. Although Wood was voted out of office in 1862 and replaced by Republican George Opdyke, Democrats in New York City formed a new organization in early 1863—the Society for the Diffusion of Political Knowledge (SDPK)—that was designed to articulate their frustrations and fears about black emancipation. Soon after its establishment, the SDPK blanketed New York City with pamphlets prophesying the horrors that would befall the United States if a Union victory destroyed Southern slavery; these noted, in particular, that full emancipation would destroy the social and economic fabric of the nation.

It was into this firestorm of antiblack thought and political agitation against the Civil War that the Conscription Act was thrust in March 1863. Unfortunately, the imposition of the new law served to exacerbate brewing tensions in the city over the war and over black emancipation. The mandate more severely impacted poor whites and their families who were dependent on them for economic survival, particularly because it was only possible to escape military service if one could afford to hire a replacement or pay $300 to the government. Even worse, it seemed that the law privileged black men, all of whom were exempt from the draft because they were not considered citizens. In general, most white New Yorkers felt they were being forced to fight in a war to free the black population, a community they already deeply feared and resented.

It was not long before President Lincoln, to the shock of most New Yorkers, authorized Republican officials to conduct the first draft lottery in New York City, which was held on Saturday, July 11. Although violence was not manifest at the draft headquarters during the day, there were definite rumblings of discontent in the city by that evening. Frustration mounted the following day, and by that night, reports began to pour in to police stations of dangerous and threatening activity. Soon, news arrived that several black men had been attacked and severely beaten, and an anonymous man declared that there would be a black man hanging from every lamppost in the city by the following day. City officials did little in response, evidently concluding that some mild disorder was to be expected and, with the coming workday, there would be no more substantial violence. They could not have been any more wrong.

On the morning of Monday, July 13, 1863, to the surprise of New York City officials, the grumbling among angry workers that had commenced over the weekend developed into an organized work stoppage. By 8:00 A.M., the streets were flooded with angry protesters marching through the city. The message was clear and strong—there would be no labor performed until politicians responded to their appeal. As the morning progressed, the mob began randomly attacking police officers, severely beating them in order to ensure that the campaign would not be silenced. Support for the movement increased as the hours passed, growing to over 12,000 people in the crowd.

Despite these early signs of discontent, the draft lottery proceeded at 10:30 A.M. at the Ninth District office. A crowd had already gathered there, prepared to bring the activities to a standstill. Soon, the protest swung into full action, as a pistol shot rang out and the mob descended on the draft headquarters. Rioters smashed the selection wheel, which was designed to draw the names of potential soldiers, and set the building ablaze. For the next several hours, the city was in chaos. Most economic endeavors had been brought to a screeching halt, and the streets were overwhelmed with angry mobs expressing their anger about the war, attacking various government agencies, and looting the buildings they destroyed. By the middle of that day, Republican officials had to admit that the lottery could not persist, and they called for a temporary cessation of their duties.

This decision was not enough to quell the mob. By that afternoon, what had begun as a political protest was clearly becoming a full-fledged riot, intent not just on ending the draft, but also intimidating and eliminating the free black population. In acts reminiscent of the protest against efforts to desegregate streetcars in the 1850s, black people were randomly snatched from the conveyances and savagely beaten. In addition, arson attacks reemerged that afternoon as the mob turned their attention to black homes on the West Side, which they looted and torched. One of the most egregious acts that day was the destruction of the Colored Orphan Asylum, which was methodically robbed, pillaged, and

subsequently burned to the ground. By Monday evening, the violence directed toward the black population accelerated. Innocent men and women trying to make their way home were subject to violent beatings and were chased through the streets of the city. Black workers were particularly in danger of assault, as mobs began patrolling the docks, determined to drive black economic competition out of the area. These actions were motivated, in particular, by the fact that black laborers had been brought onto the docks to work as strikebreakers a few months prior.

In addition, boardinghouses that catered to the black population were uniquely targeted, as the inhabitants were driven from their homes, stripped of their belongings, and tortured. As a result, when the first full day of rioting came to a close, black New Yorkers began to flee the city in large numbers, yet even this effort did not preclude them from attack. Those who could not manage to escape sought refuge at local police stations, but soon these sites were so overcrowded that many were turned away and sent back into the streets to fight for their lives. By Monday night, the city's police force was obviously overwhelmed by the size of the mob and had been rendered powerless to terminate the violence. Yet Mayor Opdyke refused to declare martial law and stood by as the carnage increased.

By Tuesday morning, July 14, it was clear that some sort of extreme action would be required to bring an end to the riot, but politicians were slow to enact an appropriate response. Gov. Seymour arrived on the scene and toured many wards in the city, but he did not immediately resort to the use of force to end the violence. Instead, he delivered a speech, hoping to appease the crowd with reassurances that he would do all in his power to declare the draft law unconstitutional and protect his citizens from enlistment. However, at this point, the riot was no longer just about the issue of the draft; it had become a ferocious, frenzied effort to eliminate the black community.

As a result, as the second day of the riot began, attacks on individual black people and institutions persisted. Many innocent black men were beaten by the mobs, and many more were murdered and lynched. As the day wore on, the crowd turned its attention to symbols of black success in the city, most notably a black church, which they set on fire and cheered as it burned to the ground. Finally, the angry mob headed into the heart of the black community, where they ravaged dance halls, taverns, and tenements that housed and served the black population. As the events on Tuesday made it clear that assistance was desperately needed to end the riot, Mayor Opdyke finally asked Secretary of War Henry Stanton to send troops to the city. Stanton complied and ordered five regiments from the Pennsylvania and Maryland battle lines to regain control of New York City. Despite the impending threat of military force, violence persisted on Wednesday, as rioters unleashed their rage on black men who had the courage to remain and defend their rights.

Thursday, July 16, brought new hope that the violence against black New Yorkers would eventually cease. Although rioters remained active, most black people had fled the city and there was little else to do beyond looting. More importantly, by the end of the day, the city was occupied by 4,000 federal soldiers who resolved that they would bring an end to the horrific pogrom that had devastated New York. Their efforts were quite effective. Soon, the city began to demonstrate the signs of resuming normal life: businesses opened and white people returned to their jobs. Yet all indications sent a clear message that black people would still not be safe if they showed their faces in the streets. Fortunately, by Saturday, July 18, there were 10,000 troops stationed in New York City, determined to impose order and maintain the peace.

In some ways, the immediate aftermath was almost as distressing for black New Yorkers as the actual events. Although some people trickled back into the city, many refused; in fact, the census of 1865 revealed that the black population had plummeted to its lowest point since 1820— less than 10,000. Indeed, nearly 20 percent of black people who had lived in New York City in 1860 absconded, never to return. Among the most famous refugees was black activist Albro Lyons, who was well known in his community for diligent work on behalf of fugitives from southern slavery. In the midst of the draft riots, Lyons took his family across the river into Brooklyn and vowed never to return.

Those black New Yorkers who returned were faced with the tireless and agonizing work of re-creating their lives. In the months that followed, they found that the racial hostility that had prompted the riot persisted. Most black men struggled to find employers who were willing to hire them, and streetcar operators regularly refused admittance to black passengers. Even worse was the painful fact that city

and state officials stubbornly refused to offer any substantial public assistance to ease their plight. Although the city had formed a Riots Claim Committee, most applications were dismissed.

Perhaps the most disturbing symbolic demonstration of city officials' indifference came when the black community realized that most rioters, even those arrested, would escape tangible punishment. Of the estimated 12,000 people who engaged in the riot, only 443 were arrested, and more than half of these had their cases dismissed before charges were even leveled against them. Only 81 men had a day in court, and most pled guilty to lesser charges and escaped with minor penalties. Ironically, the most severe punishments were enacted on those who had been caught looting; in the end, the men responsible for the beatings, tortures, and lynching of black people essentially emerged with no meaningful repercussions.

However, days after the conclusion of the riot, a benevolent organization, the Union League Club (ULC), devoted its energies to providing assistance to black survivors. Members of this association had been staunchly opposed to the riot and had pleaded with Mayor Opdyke to bring in federal troops to end the violence. Conscious that city officials were failing to make proper restitution, the ULC raised funds, eventually over $40,000, and employed a well-respected black leader, Rev. Henry Highland Garnet, to help blacks process claims. It was later reported that, under Garnet's careful guidance, financial aid was doled out to more than 6,300 people.

Perhaps most poignantly, black New Yorkers' resolve was revealed in December 1863 when, at the urging of the ULC, War Secretary Henry Stanton gave permission for a black regiment to be raised among New Yorkers to fight against Southern slavery. On March 5, 1864, an estimated 100,000 New Yorkers of all races poured into the streets to watch the 20th U.S. Colored Infantry march into battle on a mission to bring the Confederacy to its knees. The irony of this occasion was not lost on black New Yorkers; indeed, less than a year after the destructive pogrom, black activist James McCune Smith noted with pride that black Union soldiers were celebrated in the same streets where some of their people had been ravenously hunted by angry hordes.

For Smith, and likely other black New Yorkers, such triumphant moments signaled that all hope was not lost, that victory could still follow devastating assaults, and perhaps someday black people might be extended the rights of equality and citizenship. In August 1863, the draft quietly and unceremoniously recommenced, but the black community was forever altered.

LESLIE M. ALEXANDER

See also

New York City Riot of 1943; Race Riots in America; *Wages of Whiteness, The;* White Mobs. Documents: Report on the Memphis Riots of May 1866 (1866); Account of the Riots in East St. Louis, Illinois (1917); A Southern Black Woman's Letter Regarding the Recent Riots in Chicago and Washington (1919); The Cook County Coroner's Report Regarding the 1919 Chicago Race Riots (1920); The Final Report of the Grand Jury on the Tulsa Race Riot (June 25, 1921); Testimony from *Laney v. United States* (1923); The Governor's Commission Report on the Watts Riots (1965); Cyrus R. Vance's Report on the Riots in Detroit (1967); The Reports of the Oklahoma Commission to Study the Tulsa Race Riot of 1921 (2000–2001); Draft Report: 1898 Wilmington Race Riot Commission (2005)

Further Reading:

Bernstein, Iver. *The New York City Draft Riots: Their Significance for American Society and Politics in the Age of the Civil War.* New York: Oxford University Press, 1990.

Cook, Adrian. *The Armies of the Streets: The New York City Draft Riots of 1863.* Lexington: University Press of Kentucky, 1974.

Garnet, Henry Highland. *A Memorial Discourse Delivered in the Hall of the House of Representatives, Washington City, D.C., on Sabbath, February 12, 1865. With an Introduction by James McCune Smith, M.D.* Philadelphia: J. M. Wilson, 1865.

Harris, Leslie Maria. *In the Shadow of Slavery: African Americans in New York City, 1626–1863.* Chicago and London: University of Chicago Press, 2003.

McCague, James. *The Second Rebellion: The Story of the New York City Draft Riots of 1863.* New York: Dial Press, 1968.

Mushkat, Jerome. *Fernando Wood: A Political Biography.* Kent, OH: Kent State University Press, 1990.

New York City Riot of 1943

On August 1, 1943, a New York City police officer arrested an African American woman for disturbing the peace at the Braddock Hotel in Harlem. Robert Brady, a black soldier in the U.S. military, observed the fracas. He intervened by trying to get the police officer to release the woman. In the ensuing scuffle, the police officer was allegedly hit by the soldier. The police officer retaliated by shooting the soldier in the arm as he attempted to run from the scene. In the process of taking the serviceman away to a nearby hospital, a crowd of nearly 3,000 began to gather. It picked up momentum and fervor as the two, police officer and soldier, moved toward the hospital. Someone in the crowd shouted that a white cop had shot and killed a black soldier. It was not true, but the rumor ignited the crowd. Emotions escalated to mob proportions. The result was a full-fledged riot. The mostly black rioters set fires, broke windows and doors, turned over vehicles, and otherwise wreaked a wave of destruction, mainly against property. This led to looting. Most of the residents of Harlem at the time were black, while most of the businesses were under Jewish or white ownership. Black and white law enforcement officers moved in to restore order, but not before the rioters were beaten and bludgeoned.

Writer James Baldwin provided a firsthand account of the riot in an August 9, 1943, article in *Newsweek*. He wrote, "Windows of pawnshops and liquor stores and grocery stores were smashed and looted. Negroes began wielding knives and the police, their guns. Thousands of police reserves, many of them Negroes, were rushed to the district. . . . All traffic was rerouted around Harlem. It came down chiefly [to] a battle between the police and the Negro looters." Walter White, the head of the National Association for the Advancement of Colored People (NAACP), wrote in the *New York Times* on August 4, 1943, that Harlem boiled over. His article described the extent of the damage and great loss as a consequence of the riot.

The Negro press and especially the New York–based *Amsterdam News* published a detailed description of the riot; the details spread throughout the country. After all, the Harlem Renaissance had established Harlem as the cultural center of black Americans. It was also perceived by many as the political center of all black Americans. The mayor at the time was Fiorello LaGuardia. He took swift action to end the riot, appealing over the radio for calm. Afterward, he sent food to the residents of Harlem. This gesture endeared the mayor to many in the African American community. Depending on the source, 6 African Americans were killed, from 500 to 1,000 were arrested, and 40 law enforcement officers were injured. It took 6,600 city, military, and civil police officers;

8,000 state guardsmen; and 1,500 civilian volunteers to finally end the riot after nearly two days.

After it was all over, there was much speculation about the causes of the riot. Some advanced the notion that the riot occurred because there were no recreational facilities and parks for the residents of Harlem. Others said the reason was the high cost of food and price gouging by the merchants who owned stores, shops, and other businesses in Harlem. Still another reason given was the need for better housing. Police brutality and overall discrimination of Harlem's black population were also cited as reasons.

Those who have studied race riots have found that there are certain sociological and psychological commonalities among race riots. A rumor is one and an environment of mob violence is another. Accepting that observation, the New York City Riot of 1943, which is sometimes called the Harlem Riot of 1943, had these two key elements. According to others, it happened not only as a violent spontaneous response to a specific incident and rumor, but it was also a reaction to racism, poverty, segregation, and other related socioeconomic factors.

By 1920, Harlem had become predominantly black. The residents were blacks from the West Indies and other states in the United States, especially Virginia, North Carolina, South Carolina, and Georgia. As blacks arrived, whites fled. During the 1920s, 118,792 white people left Harlem, while 87,417 blacks replaced them there. Unrest in numerous towns and cities around the country was erupting. Some of these disorders, including the events in Detroit in 1943, rose to the level of a race riot. In 1944, the year after the Harlem Riot, there were 250 race riots in 47 cities and towns in the United States.

Lynchings, mostly in the South, were common. Blacks who served in World War II were stationed around the city, visited the city, or were moving there after returning home from the war. Many of those seeking a better life encountered segregation and other barriers to their successful attainment of the American Dream in Harlem. Although life for some blacks in Harlem at the time was vibrant, colorful, and intellectually stimulating, this was not the case for other blacks who were struggling. Even though it was the home of such luminaries as Langston Hughes, Countee Cullen, Zora Neale Hurston, Claude McKay, Congressman Adam Clayton Powell Jr., A. Phillip Randolph, James Weldon Johnson,

and a host of others, as well as the home of such established institutions as Small's Paradise, the Cotton Club, the Savoy Ballroom, the Apollo Theater, and the Abyssinian Baptist Church, prosperity existed parallel to poverty in Harlem. The residents of Harlem were ready for a change in the social order regardless of their station in life; the riot of 1943 was a sign of pent-up frustration. It only took a single incident to spark the riot.

Perhaps James Baldwin expressed the seething, underlying frustration best when he reflected on the riot years later by writing, "It would have been better to have left the plate glass as it had been and the goods lying in the store. Would have been better, but it would have also . . . been intolerable, for Harlem needed something to smash" (Baldwin 1943).

The Harlem Riot of 1943 has become an important part of history. It was an aftershock of the Harlem Riot of 1935, and a forerunner of the New York City Riot of 1964. All pioneered the way for the civil rights movement that swept the country in the 1950s and 1960s.

BETTY NYANGONI

See also

Harlem (New York) Riot of 1935; New York City Draft Riot of 1863; Race Riots in America. Documents: The Report on the Memphis Riots of May 1866 (July 25, 1866); Account of the Riots in East St. Louis, Illinois (July 1917); The Cook County Coroner's Report Regarding the 1919 Chicago Race Riots (1919); A Southern Black Woman's Letter Regarding the Recent Riots in Chicago and Washington (November 1919); The Final Report of the Grand Jury on the Tulsa Race Riot (June 25, 1921); Testimony from *Laney v. United States* Describing Events during the Washington, D.C., Riot of July 1919 (December 3, 1923); The Governor's Commission Report on the Watts Riots (December 1965); Cyrus R. Vance's Report on the Riots in Detroit (July-August 1967); The Reports of the Oklahoma Commission to Study the Tulsa Race Riot of 1921 (2000-2001); The Draft Report of the 1898 Wilmington Race Riot Commission (December 2005)

Further Reading:

Baldwin, James. "Harlem Hoodlums." *Newsweek*, August 9, 1943.

Brandt, Nat. *Harlem at War: The Black Experience in World War II*. Syracuse, NY: Syracuse University Press, 1996.

Capeci, Dominic. *Harlem Riot of 1943*. Philadelphia: Temple University Press, 1977.

Ellison, Ralph. *Invisible Man*. New York: Modern Library, 1994. Originally published in 1952.

Powell, Richard. *Homecoming: The Art and Life of William H. Johnson*. New York: Rizzoli International Publications, 1991.

Tate, Gayle. "The Harlem Riots of 1935 and 1943." In *Encyclopedia of African American Culture and History*. New York: Macmillan Publishing Company, 1996.

Newark (New Jersey) Riot of 1967

The Newark (New Jersey) Riot of 1967 pitted residents of the city's predominantly black neighborhoods against mostly white police and military forces. After five days of unrest, which ranged from July 12 through July 17, 1967, 23 people were dead, over 700 people were injured, and approximately 1,500 people were arrested. After the Los Angeles (California) Riot of 1965 (also known as the Watts riot) and Detroit (Michigan) Riot of 1967, the 1967 Newark riot was the most severe episode of urban unrest to take place in the United States during the 1960s (*see* Long Hot Summer Riots, 1965–1967). While a majority of white respondents and some African Americans label the Newark event a *riot*, some black and white political activists refer to it as a *rebellion* or *uprising*. Since the majority of victims were killed or injured by the police and military rather than by civilians of the opposite race, it might be a misnomer to call this event a *race riot*.

Underlying Structural Conditions

By July 1967, Newark was "ready to riot." After nearly three decades of black migration from the South and the flight of the white population to the surrounding suburbs, by 1967, Newark had become a majority black city. "Between 1960 and 1967, the city lost a net total of more than 70,000 residents. In six years the city switched from 65 percent white to 52 percent Negro and 10 percent Puerto Rican and Cuban" (National Advisory Commission on Civil Disorders 1968: 57). Yet, despite having attained a residential majority in Newark, black people held little formal political power—only two of nine city council seats. Of 1,512 Newark police officers on duty in 1966, only 145 (less than 10 percent) were black. In the schools, black teachers remained a minority, while the student body of several schools became largely black and Latino. In 1967, the local branch of the National Association for the Advancement of Colored People (NAACP) urged that Wilbur Parker, the first black

certified public accountant (CPA) in the state of New Jersey, be appointed to fill an anticipated vacancy on the Board of Education. Despite such pressure, Mayor Hugh Addonizio appointed an Irish high school graduate named James T. Callaghan to the prestigious post. This fueled resentment among black people in Newark who felt that even with the proper qualifications they could be denied commensurate employment.

For less-educated African Americans, particularly recent migrants from the South, the job situation in Newark was worsening. Drawn by the promise of steady factory employment, Southern blacks continued to move to Newark. At the same time, however, large employers like General Electric and Westinghouse were closing their manufacturing plants in Newark. As a result, unskilled and semiskilled industrial jobs were in short supply. Unemployment rose within the city of Newark. By 1967, unemployment among Newark's black population stood at 11.5 percent, roughly double that of the white population. In Newark's predominantly black neighborhoods, a sense of hopelessness set in.

These structural changes were most strongly felt in Newark's Central Ward, a previously mixed neighborhood of black migrants and Jewish immigrants that, by 1967, had been transformed into an almost exclusively black ghetto. During the 1950s and 1960s, the Central Ward became the site of numerous high-rise public housing projects. By 1967, Newark had the highest proportion of residents living in public housing of any city in the country, earning the nickname the Brick City. Then, in 1967, Newark's Central Ward became the target of a massive urban renewal campaign centered around the construction of a new campus for the University Medical and Dental School of New Jersey (UMDNJ), formerly located in Jersey City. Newark city officials believed that the medical school would be an anchor for the redevelopment of the Central Ward and began to draw up plans to declare parts of the Central Ward as dilapidated in preparation to clear land for the medical complex. The city's initial plan was to clear 20 to 30 acres of land, but the medical school asked for 150 acres. As a result, the area targeted for renewal was considerably enlarged, which in turn provoked a wave of protest among homeowners and tenants whose land and homes were slated to be taken by eminent domain. Public meetings regarding the medical school became especially contentious, in part due to the presence of militant activists who sought to disrupt the meetings and derail the construction of the medical complex.

Among these so-called militant activists were members of the Newark Community Union Project, an offshoot of Students for a Democratic Society (SDS), founded by Tom Hayden, as well as members of the Congress of Racial Equality (CORE), and representatives of the United Community Corporation (a local antipoverty organization). Along with the black nationalist poet/playwright Leroi Jones (now Amiri Baraka), these groups gave voice to the anger of the black community at the white political establishment. A National Conference on Black Power planned for July of that year raised fears among the politicians and police of the potential for racial unrest.

As with the 1967 Detroit riot, a major source of unrest in Newark involved the deterioration in police-community relations. In the years leading up to the riot, Newark police were involved in a series of high-profile incidents. In July 1965, 22-year-old Lester Long was shot and killed by police after a "routine" traffic stop. A few weeks later, Bernard Rich, a 26-year-old African American man, died in police custody under mysterious circumstances while locked in his jail cell. On Christmas Eve that year, Walter Mathis, age 17, was fatally wounded by an "accidental" weapons discharge while being searched for illegal contraband. Despite calls for the appointment of a civilian police review board and hiring of more African American policemen, such proposals went unheeded. On July 7, 1967, just five days before the riot began, Newark and East Orange police raided a house inhabited by a group of black Muslims. In a fruitless search for illegal weapons, they detained and interrogated the occupants of the house, allegedly beating them with their batons. This incident alone had the potential to spark unrest and certainly helped set that stage for the events that followed on July 12.

The Newark Riot of 1967 began on the evening of July 12 with the arrest of a cab driver named John Smith for an alleged traffic violation. After driving past a double-parked police car, Smith and an unnamed passenger were stopped by officers John Desimone and Vito Pontrelli and pulled over. As the passenger fled the scene, a scuffle ensued between Smith and the arresting officers. John Smith was reportedly beaten by the police officers en route to the Fourth Precinct's police headquarters on 17th Street and Belmont

Avenue (now Irvine Turner Boulevard). According to eyewitness accounts and the officer's testimony, John Smith was dragged into the Fourth Precinct house and placed in a jail cell. A crowd soon began to gather outside, and local civil rights leaders were contacted by residents of a public housing project that stood across the street from the Fourth Precinct building.

A group of civil rights leaders including Robert Curvin, representative of CORE, arrived at the Fourth Precinct at about the same time as Newark police inspector Kenneth Melchior. These civil rights leaders entered the building and were allowed to see the prisoner in his cell. Noting that Smith was injured, Curvin persuaded Inspector Melchior to have Smith transported to the hospital. Due to the crowd assembled at the front entrance, John Smith was taken out the back door to a police car and driven to Newark Beth Israel Hospital. Curvin volunteered to speak to the assembled crowd and was provided with a police bullhorn. By this time, rumors had circulated that John Smith had died in police custody. Curvin stood on top of a police car and sought to calm the crowd, but his speech had the opposite effect. He encouraged people to line up for a peaceful protest, but was soon shouted down. A hail of bottles, bricks, and a couple of Molotov cocktails hit the Fourth Precinct. Officers charged out of the building to disperse the crowd, but as the crowd dispersed, people started looting nearby stores. The looting did not spread very far beyond the Fourth Precinct.

By the following afternoon, Thursday, July 13, Mayor Addonizio proclaimed that the disturbance was over. However, some police officials worried that violence might resume at nightfall. A protest rally coordinated by CORE and the Newark Community Union Project (NCUP) was slated to be held at the Fourth Precinct later that evening. Based on his personal premonitions, Deputy Police Chief Redden ordered all of the men under his command to report for 12-hour shifts. By 7:30 P.M., a crowd of over 300 people stood in front of the Fourth Precinct. Mayor Addonizio sent his personal representative James Threat to inform the crowd that in deference to their demands, a well-known African American police lieutenant would be appointed to the rank of captain.

This promise failed to ameliorate the anger of the crowd, and soon thereafter, a volley of rocks and bottles was thrown at the police. The event at that time seemed like a replay of the previous evening. Once again, police charged into the crowd and dispersed the protesters, and once again looting spread to the nearby business thoroughfare. But unlike the previous evening, the looting spread in numerous directions, including the downtown.

Stores along Springfield Avenue, Prince Street, and downtown on Broad Street were looted and set on fire. By 9:00 P.M., Deputy Chief Redden told the mayor that they needed help, but was overruled by the mayor and Police Director Domenic Spina, who were reluctant to call for assistance from the state police. At 1:30 A.M., Spina called the state police and reminded them of their plan to provide assistance if necessary. At 2:30 A.M., Spina called Mayor Addonizio and said that state police help was needed immediately. Finally, just after 2:30 A.M., Mayor Addonizio called Governor Hughes and asked him to deploy both the New Jersey State Police and the National Guard. By 3:00 A.M., when Colonel Kelly of the New Jersey State Police arrived to meet with Mayor Addonizio, Addonizio proclaimed, "the whole town is gone" (Porambo 1971: 117).

Around 5:30 A.M., the first detachment of state troopers arrived in Newark, followed by the first National Guard units around 7:00 A.M. The National Guard and state police set up camp at the Roseville Armory in the city's North Ward. Their arrival was cheered by the mostly Italian residents of that community. A loose command structure was put in place with Colonel Kelly of the state police in nominal command of both the state police and National Guard troops. The Newark police remained under the command of Police Director Spina. But due to incompatible radio frequencies and a clash of egos among leaders of the three agencies, there was little actual coordination of police and military units. Indicative of the larger command problems, Colonel Kelly of the state police had to procure his own maps of the city. As troops fanned out across the city, they sought to establish a series of checkpoints, with three guardsmen manning each of 137 street blockades. Until Thursday night, there had been only 26 arrests and no reported deaths. By the end of the day on Friday, over 900 people had been arrested, and 10 people had been fatally shot (9 of the 10 by police).

As the Newark police, state police, and National Guard patrolled the city from Friday night through Saturday evening, gunfire erupted. Police and military officials claimed that gunfire was the result of snipers, but in a few well-documented cases, police and guardsmen were in fact firing on one another. On Saturday evening, believing that snipers were firing from the rooftops of public housing projects, national guardsmen and state police unleashed waves of machine-gun fire on those buildings, fatally wounding several apartment dwellers, including Eloise Spellman, a mother of 10 children who was shot in the neck while pulling her children away from the window. Also on Friday night, Fire Captain Michael Moran was killed while responding to a false alarm at a building on South Orange Avenue. While climbing a ladder to the second-floor window, he was struck in the back by an alleged sniper's bullet. Moran was one of only two whites to die during the entire five days of rioting. The other was Police Detective Fred Toto, who was also allegedly struck by a sniper's bullet the previous evening.

By Sunday morning, reports were arriving from residents and merchants who claimed that Newark police and state police officers were shooting into storefronts and looting merchandise. Some shopkeepers, whites included, had painted the words *Soul Brother* on their windows with the hope that their businesses would be left undisturbed, but according to testimony before the Governor's Commission on Civil Disorders, these stores became targets for retribution at the hands of the mostly white police forces. Nonetheless, despite these isolated incidents, the riot was winding down. National guardsmen began distributing food, and Governor Hughes offered clemency to any looters who could provide information leading to the arrest and conviction of a sniper. During this 24-hour period, from Sunday to Monday morning, three more people were killed: one a suspected looter, another a suspected car thief, and the third, a teenage boy struck by a police bullet while taking out the garbage outside his house. By Monday afternoon, the National Guard barricades had been lifted and the troops had begun their withdrawal from the city.

At the conclusion of five days of rioting, 23 people were dead and over 750 people were injured. Newark firefighters had responded to approximately 250 fires and 64 false alarms. According to an official count, state police and national guardsmen had expended 13,319 rounds of ammunition. Despite the relatively short duration of this episode of unrest, the riot has had a lasting impact on the city of Newark. For some political activists in the black community, the rebellion was empowering, promoting racial solidarity and paving the way for the election of Ken Gibson, the city's first black mayor. Others, both black and white, believe that the riot tore the community apart. After the riot, the pace of white flight accelerated. The last remaining segment of the city's Jewish population, located in the Weequahic section, left the city, as did whites who lived on the city's west side. Those whites who remained were largely from the Italian section in the North Ward and the Portuguese population of the East Ward/Ironbound. Both of these communities had been heavily defended during the riots by a combination of armed citizen patrols and National Guard troops. After the riot, racial polarization increased, manifested by clashes over schooling and housing between Italians and African Americans. Several large insurance companies decided to move their corporate headquarters out of Newark (Prudential Insurance Company was a notable exception). Heavy and light industry continued to decline and unemployment continued to increase. The municipal tax base eroded and city services were cut. The 1970s and 1980s were characterized by poverty, crime, and fiscal crisis. As with Detroit, it is quite possible that this situation would have existed anyway, independent of the riots. Yet, Newark, like Detroit, has struggled with the stigma of being a riot city.

In recent years, beginning in the mid-1990s, Newark has made somewhat of a comeback, constructing a world-class performing arts center, renovating its downtown office buildings, and attracting capital investment from New York–based real estate entrepreneurs. With federal HOPE VI funds, the city has demolished much of its high-rise public housing and replaced it with low-rise townhouses available for low-income residents. Yet Newark continues to struggle with a high percentage of its residents on public assistance, an underperforming school system operating under state receivership, and a recent spate of gang-related homicides. Although the central business district has experienced a renaissance, it is unclear how long it will take for this renaissance to bear fruit in the city's more impoverished and neglected neighborhoods. The future of Newark, almost 40 years after the riots of July 1967, remains an open question.

MAX HERMAN

See also

Race Riots in America. Documents: Report on the Memphis Riots of May 1866 (1866); Account of the Riots in East St. Louis, Illinois (1917); A Southern Black Woman's Letter Regarding the Recent Riots in Chicago and Washington (1919); The Cook County Coroner's Report Regarding the 1919 Chicago Race Riots (1920); The Final Report of the Grand Jury on the Tulsa Race Riot (June 25, 1921); Testimony from *Laney v. United States* (1923); The Governor's Commission Report on the Watts Riots (1965); Cyrus R. Vance's Report on the Riots in Detroit (1967); The Reports of the Oklahoma Commission to Study the Tulsa Race Riot of 1921 (2000–2001); Draft Report: 1898 Wilmington Race Riot Commission (2005)

Further Reading:

Governor's Select Commission on Civil Disorders in the State of New Jersey. *Report for Action: An Investigation into the Causes and Events of the 1967 Newark Race Riots*. New York: Lemma Publishing Corporation, 1972.

Hayden, Tom. *Rebellion in Newark: Official Violence and Ghetto Response*. New York: Vintage Books, 1967.

Herman, Max. *The Newark and Detroit "Riots" of 1967*. http://www.67riots.rutgers.edu.

National Advisory Commission on Civil Disorders. *Report of the National Advisory Commission on Civil Disorders*. New York: Bantam Books, 1968.

Porambo, Ron. *No Cause for Indictment: An Autopsy of Newark*. New York: Holt, Rinehart and Winston, 1971.

Winters, Stanley B., ed. *From Riot to Recovery: Newark after Ten Years*. Washington, DC: University Press of America, 1979.

Wright, Nathan, Jr. *Ready to Riot*. New York: Holt, Rinehart and Winston, 1968.

Newton, Huey P. (1942–1989)

Dr. Huey Percy Newton is best known for his cofounding, on October 15, 1966, of the Black Panther Party (BPP) for Self-Defense. He was an avid activist, intellectual, and political candidate, emphasizing the right to African American self-determinism and the primacy of critical thought.

Newton was born in Monroe, Louisiana, on February 17, 1942, the seventh and youngest child in his family, from Armelia and Walter Newton, a sharecropper and Baptist minister. He was named after Louisiana's governor Huey Long. When he was one year old, his family moved to Oakland, California, where he would grow up in poverty and later graduate functionally illiterate from Oakland Technical High School. He later learned how to read using a combination of audio records of Vincent Price narrating poetry and the corresponding written poems to correlate how the words

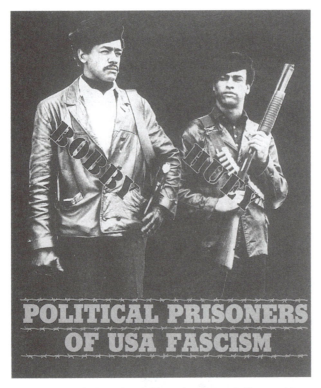

Poster showing Black Panthers Bobby Seale and Huey P. Newton with guns: "Political Prisoners of USA Fascism." (Library of Congress)

appeared. Soon, Newton found himself attending Merritt College intermittently, ultimately earning an Associate of Arts degree, as well as studying law at Oakland City College and San Francisco Law School. He eventually earned his PhD in 1980 in the history of consciousness from the University of California at Santa Cruz.

It was largely due to police brutality that the Black Panther Party (BPP) was formed. In response to events like the August 11, 1965, harassment of motorist Marquette Frye, his mother, and brother by the LAPD, which sparked what is now known as the Watts riots (*see* Los Angeles (California) Riot of 1965), Newton's philosophy of race and democracy solidified. As race riots spread across the United States in the summers of 1965, 1966, and 1967 (*see* Long Hot Summer Riots, 1965–1967), the BPP mobilized local chapters to politicize the actions as urban rebellions. Grassroots responses included the development of "legal first aid" by Newton—small books that included statutes and constitutional rights that informed readers of their rights when confronted by police. Additionally, Newton developed Panther Patrols—carloads of BPP members that would follow and

monitor police behavior, often informing black citizens of their rights. Because of police discrimination and brutality, coupled with the BPP decision to counter this repression, Newton and other BPP members were involved in an October 28, 1967, shoot-out with the Oakland police whereby he was wounded and subsequently accused of murdering Officer John Frey. While in jail, several of Newton's BPP members were charged with inciting riots during the Democratic National Convention of 1968.

Few can deny that Newton's life was strewn with incidents of violence. Critics such as Tom Orloff of the *San Francisco Chronicle*, Stanley Crouch, and author Hugh Pearson have labeled Newton a "thug," "criminal," and "hoodlum," respectively. Several tried to frame Newton in such a reductionist manner.

First, his association with both the Black Nationalist tradition of Malcolm X and the Leninist tradition of Marxism reduced him, in the eyes of many, to that of a radical extremist. Second, Newton's affiliation with communism and socialism coded him as a central figure in the McCarthy-era culture of fear. Third, Newton is often perceived as simply an outlaw and criminal due to his committed or provisional support of the civil disobedience and race riots of the 1960s and 1970s.

While the aforementioned vilification of Newton arrests the perception of his complexity, so does an overly simplistic heroification. During a rally for Newton on February 17, 1968, a reporter present at the rally remarked, "It was almost as though Huey P. Newton were already dead. . . . We usually require of those among us who would be immortal that they first cease to breathe and be buried before claiming the exalted status" (Moore 1971: 113). The fervor resulted in a cult-like worship of Newton, on which 1960s activist Donald Cox wrote as follows:

For some of us, Huey represented the equivalent of the Messiah. Since we didn't want to see any more of our leaders eliminated, we launched a massive campaign to assure that Huey would not be condemned to the death penalty. A cult of his personality was created. Huey was elevated to the status of the gods, and his every word became gospel. (2001: 121)

Like many activists, Newton was a complex figure. His radical activism prompted both conservatives and liberals alike to paint Newton as either savior or devil, concentrating on his misdeeds or romanticizing his revolutionary rhetoric. Tragically, in the last years of his life, he developed an addiction to crack cocaine and was fatally shot on August 22, 1989, by Tyrone Robinson, a local drug dealer who, ironically, as a child was fed by the Newton-led BPP breakfast program.

MATTHEW W. HUGHEY

See also

Black Nationalism; Black Panther Party (BPP); Cleaver, Eldridge

Further Reading:

Cox, Donald. "A Split in the Party." In *Liberation, Imagination, and the Black Panther Party: A New Look at the Panthers and Their Legacy*, edited by Kathleen Cleaver and George Katsiaficas. New York: Routledge Press, 2001.

Jeffries, Judson L. *Huey P. Newton: The Radical Theorist.* Jackson: University Press of Mississippi, 2002.

Moore, Gilbert S. *A Special Rage.* New York: Harper and Row, 1971.

Newton, Huey P. *Revolutionary Suicide.* New York: Writers and Readers Publishing, 1995 (1973).

Newton, Huey P. *War against the Panthers: A Study of Repression in America.* New York: Harlem River Press, 1996. (Published version of Newton's PhD dissertation, University of California at Santa Cruz, 1980, History of Consciousness.)

Newton, Huey P. *To Die for the People.* Edited by Toni Morrison. New York: Writers and Readers Publishing, 1999 (1973).

Newton, Huey P., and Erik H. Erikson. *In Search of Common Ground.* New York: W. W. Norton, 1973.

Newton, Huey P., and Ericka Huggins. *Insights and Poems.* San Francisco: City Lights Books, 1975.

Niagara Movement

The Niagara Movement was a short-lived association of mostly college-educated and professional black men in the North who held a series of annual conferences between 1905 and 1909 to call for an end to racial discrimination and to protest racial injustice. The movement, led by W.E.B. Du Bois and William Monroe Trotter, carried on its work independent of Booker T. Washington and despite his determined opposition. The annual meetings of the association called for full and equal civil rights for black people and rejected Washington's policies of accommodation and compromise. The Niagara Movement is regarded as a forerunner to the National Association for the Advancement of Colored People (NAACP), which was established in 1909.

By 1905, Booker T. Washington had consolidated his position as the leader of the Negro race in the United States with both black and white audiences. Washington was the founder and president of Tuskegee Institute (today Tuskegee University) and controlled a network of black newspapers, friends, supporters, and improvement associations—such as the Afro-American Council and the National Negro Business League—referred to collectively as the "Tuskegee Machine." His policies relied on the favor of white philanthropists, postponed black claims to civil rights, accepted racial segregation, and rejected protest as an instrument for black advancement. Du Bois and Trotter, among others, were critics of this approach.

Du Bois's classic volume *The Souls of Black Folk*, published in 1903, included a full chapter entitled "Of Mr. Booker T. Washington and Others" in which he dismissed Washington's approach to racial advancement as deeply flawed and contradictory. Nonetheless, Washington continued to seek Du Bois's cooperation and allegiance, inviting him late in 1903 to join a conference of African American leaders in New York, financed by Andrew Carnegie. There, Du Bois helped form the Committee of Twelve, dominated by Washington loyalists. Finding himself surrounded and outvoted, Du Bois again denounced Washington's policies in print and resigned from the committee in July 1904, parting ways with the Tuskegee Machine.

Du Bois and Trotter, together with Charles E. Bentley, a leading Chicago physician, and Frederick McGhee, a prominent lawyer in St. Paul, Minnesota—all opponents of Washington's accommodationism—agreed to arrange for a meeting of like-minded men in Buffalo, New York. Du Bois circulated a statement of intentions that was signed by some 50 prominent African American men. Twenty-nine of them (and one boy) gathered from July 10–14, 1905, in Fort Erie, Ontario, on the Canadian side of Niagara Falls. Racial barriers at the Buffalo hotel had forced a last-minute change of venue.

Those who gathered at the Niagara meeting represented the elite of the Talented Tenth—lawyers, newspaper owners, physicians, ministers, educators, and businessmen—mostly from the North and Midwest, although six were from the South. (The Far West was not represented.) Du Bois was elected general secretary of the association.

The "Declaration of Principles" issued by the first meeting of the Niagara Movement defined the goals of the group. Using the defiant language of protest, the declaration demanded full civil rights for all black people in the United States. One article states:

> Any discrimination based simply on race or color is barbarous, we care not how hallowed it be by custom, expediency or prejudice . . . [D]iscriminations based simply and solely on physical peculiarities, place of birth, color of skin, are relics of that unreasoning human savagery of which the world is and ought to be thoroughly ashamed.

Although Booker T. Washington was not mentioned by name, it was made clear that the participants, who were later to be known as the Niagarites, were unanimous in their opposition to his policies. One article of the Declaration reads:

> PROTEST: We refuse to allow the impression to remain that the Negro-American assents to inferiority, is submissive under oppression and apologetic before insults. Through helplessness we may submit, but the voice of protest of ten million Americans must never cease to assail the ears of their fellows, so long as America is unjust.

There was no question that the Niagara Movement rejected compromise and accommodation in favor of agitation and protest. Again:

> Of the above grievances we do not hesitate to complain, and to complain loudly and insistently. To ignore, overlook, or apologize for these wrongs is to prove ourselves unworthy of freedom. Persistent manly agitation is the way to liberty, and toward this goal the Niagara Movement has started and asks the cooperation of all men of all races.

The agent whom Washington had sent to spy on the conclave in Buffalo was foiled by the unexpected change of venue. Afterwards however, with a flurry of letters, his public denunciation of the "Declaration of Principles," orders to black newspapers to ignore the event, and favors of cash to reinforce his opinions, Washington was able to ensure that the Niagara Movement went almost unmentioned in the black press.

The second annual meeting of the Niagara Movement was held in August 1906, at Harper's Ferry, West Virginia, the site of John Brown's famous attempted insurrection. Women were not admitted to the conference, primarily due to the opposition of Trotter. But the assembly voted to allow women to attend the following year. Those who gathered heard reports of racial injustice and rousing speeches calling for Negro rights. Du Bois's "Address to the Country" at the end of the conference summed up: "We claim for ourselves every single right that belongs to a freeborn American, political, civil, and social; and until we get these rights we will never cease to protest and to assail the ears of America." But the movement was almost without financial resources.

By the time of the 1907 meeting in Boston, the Niagara Movement had 34 state chapters, although only one in the South. The Boston conference was the largest ever, attended by some 800 delegates. But neither Du Bois nor Trotter attended the conference in 1908, in Oberlin, Ohio, due to Trotter's personal disputes with Du Bois and with other Niagarites. That year, Trotter broke away to form his own group, the Negro-American Political League.

The last annual meeting was held in August 1909, at Sea Isle City, New Jersey, with members divided and discouraged. Constant opposition from the Tuskegee Machine, financial troubles, and personal disputes had all but destroyed the organization. In 1911, Du Bois sent a circular letter to all members of the Niagara Movement canceling plans for future meetings and disbanding the group. He urged all Niagarites to join the NAACP. Most did.

In terms of concrete political achievements, the Niagara Movement accomplished nothing. However, in the context of Booker T. Washington's near monopoly of power within the black community, his veto over white philanthropy, and his policies of silence in the face of racial injustice, the movement kept alive the tradition of black protest during a conservative era. Fiery sermons on racial equality at the Niagara meetings mostly preached to radical, educated black elites who were already converted. But the movement paved the way for its successor, the NAACP, and for the future civil rights movement, which would carry forward the same cause.

ANTHONY A. LEE

See also
Du Bois, W.E.B.; Washington, Booker T.

Further Reading:

Fox, Stephen R. *The Guardian of Boston: William Monroe Trotter.* New York: Antheneum, 1970.

Lewis, David Levering. *W.E.B. Du Bois: Biography of a Race, 1868–1919.* New York: Henry Holt, 1993.

Niagara's Declaration of Principles. 1905. http://www.yale.edu/glc/archive/1152.htm (accessed May 28, 2008).

Non-white Racism

Racism is a belief system designed to entrench inequalities on the basis of race. In the United States, it has usually been seen as a tool of the majority white population to be wielded against various minority groups. However, non-white racism—racism perpetuated by persons who do not identify themselves as white—has also had a significant and complex effect on American race relations and politics.

There are a couple of possible explanations for the development of non-white racism in the American context. The first lies in the complexity of social stratification itself. Minority groups are not evenly distributed across the economic or social ladder, and thus their relation to whites, and to each other, may be profoundly different based on where they are positioned. For example, Native Americans in the late 18th and early 19th centuries were known to have held racist views against black slaves. Scholars argue that some Native American groups developed a racist ideology to distinguish themselves from blacks, at a time when whites were increasingly eroding away Native American livelihoods. Thus, non-white racism in this instance may have been a way of protecting their marginally better status vis-à-vis slavery.

Non-white racism can also be a consequence of the "middleman" syndrome. Middleman minorities usually occupy an intermediate place in the ethnic hierarchy and take on intermediary occupational roles, such as shopkeepers, moneylenders, or traders. In the United States at varying times, Jews, Koreans, Asian Indians, and Pakistanis have been part of the middleman group. Because of their intermediate position, middleman groups can sometimes find themselves the target of racial hostility by either the dominant or subordinate groups. Subordinate groups may feel that middleman minorities perpetuate their own kind of racism, through their exploitative labor and business practices, and their cultural insularity. Such anger can coalesce in times of severe social stress, such as after the infamous Rodney King trial in 1992. In the riots that ensued in Los Angeles, Korean stores were targeted by angry black mobs, exposing ethnic tension, stereotyping, and discrimination that could not be explained simply by a black-white dynamic.

A recent manifestation of non-white racism that has bearing on contemporary racial politics is anti-Semitism. This can, on the one hand, be seen as an attempt to subvert traditional racial hierarchies, in that it is directed against people who in some measure have been associated with the "white" majority group. However, others have considered anti-Semitism to have its roots in the middleman syndrome, because Jews in America had historically played a middleman role, particularly in urban centers that have a large black underclass. Intellectuals such as Leonard Jeffries and Tony Martin have been accused of anti-Semitism, in part because of their contentious views regarding Jewish involvement in the African slave trade. Louis Farrakhan and the Nation of Islam have also been charged with fanning the flames of anti-Semitism among blacks.

Non-white racism should be seen as both similar to and separate from the historic American pattern of white racism against non-white groups. Like white racism, non-white racism can inflict tremendous psychological, social, and material damage. Non-white racism is also similarly built on a foundation of internalized racial hierarchy and privilege and can be encouraged through stereotypical portrayal of certain groups in media and popular culture. However, certain distinctions from "traditional" racism need to be emphasized. In some respects, non-white racism serves the interests of the dominant group because it is often enacted between subordinate groups, thereby preventing any economic or ideological alliance. Also, because minority groups do not have the same access to institutional and ideological power structures in America as the dominant group, one can argue that non-white racism has a less pernicious and widespread effect. So, although it can be said that white racism historically became manifested, and entrenched, in the system of slavery and segregation, little parallel exists with non-white racism, at least on the level of scale. However, the implications of non-white racism should not be underestimated.

As minority groups increasingly take center stage in a more multicultural political and economic environment, such racist beliefs may wield considerable power in the future.

REBEKAH LEE

See also

Modern Racism; Racism; Reverse Racism; Symbolic Racism; Systemic Racism

Further Reading

Blalock, Hubert M., Jr. *Toward a Theory of Minority-Group Relations*. New York: John Wiley, 1967.

Bonacich, Edna. "A Theory of Middleman Minorities." *American Sociological Review* 35 (1973): 583–94.

Marger, Martin. *Race and Ethnic Relations: American and Global Perspectives*, 6th ed. Belmont, CA: Wadsworth, 2003.

Noose Incidents

The noose is a symbolically violent representation of the systematic lynching of African Americans in the Southern and border states of the United States from the Reconstruction era to the mid-20th century. Though the word "lynching"

Washburn High School (2012)

On January 11, 2012, at Washburn High School in Minneapolis, four white students hung a dark-skinned doll in a stairwell, posed for pictures with the doll, and posted those pictures on social networking websites. Three of the students involved were disciplined with suspension while the fourth was expelled. There were a range of reactions to both the incident and the punishment. For instance, some students claimed that the intensions of their classmates were not racially motivated and the punishment was overly harsh. School administrators said that they would update the social studies curriculum in order to educate students about the historical implications of the noose. While some parents felt that the entire school was being penalized for the acts of a small number of individuals, other parents demanded more details about the incident and punishment and requested cultural training for all faculty and staff members at Washburn.

---

and statistics gathered on the practice denote a variety of methods of murder such as shooting, flogging, and drowning, in American society there exists an association of lynching specifically with hanging, and in particular, a white mob executing blacks with a rope. The expression, "strange fruit" has also been utilized as a reference to lynching, popularized by Billy Holiday's 1939 performance of the song of the same name. Race scholars explain that there is no misconstruing what the noose denotes; the historical dehumanization of blacks, the affirmation of white racial superiority and thus black inferiority, and an accoutrement of terror.

Still prevalent in American society, noose incidents, usually involving the public display of a rope that is knotted in such a way as to hang an individual, continue to depict the threat of physical violence and invoke fear. In the year 2000, the Federal Equal Employment Opportunity Commission handled dozens of allegations of workplace discrimination cases involving nooses. In 2006, the controversial noose incident in Jena, Louisiana, surrounding the beating of a white student by six black teenagers received national attention concerning racial injustice; however it also inspired an estimated 80 copycat noose hangings in locations around the country.

When discussing noose incidents, scholars usually point to two issues; the space in which the noose was hung and the different perceptions of the noose incident according to race. Most noose incidents occur in educational settings and the workplace, two areas of historical political struggle between blacks and whites. Thus it can be argued that noose incidents serve as an attempt to keep African Americans out of these structures of opportunity. Furthermore the areas in which noose incidents do not appear are similarly important, where a lack of noose incidents in athletic, comedy, rap, and hip-hop arenas demonstrate that these are traditionally accepted spaces for blacks, unlike settings of higher learning or professional mobility.

In terms of perceptions of noose incidents, research suggests that whites are more likely to view the placement of a noose as a prank or joke and claim that there are no racial connotations surrounding the incident whereas blacks are more likely to view noose incidents as genuine threats of violence. Goidel, Parent, and Mann (2011) in their research on the Jena Six incident found that race was an important predictor of public perception of racially charged incidents. This makes sense given the difference of experience with

Professor Madonna Constantine speaks at a protest rally at Teachers College at Columbia University, October 10, 2007, in New York, one day after a hangman's noose was discovered on her office door at the college. Authorities were looking into whether a noose hanging from the door of a black professor at Columbia University was the work of disgruntled students or even a fellow professor, an incident the university's president described as an assault on everyone at the prestigious school. (AP Photo/Diane Bondareff)

racial privilege and disadvantage between whites and blacks, where the lack of experience of personal racial discrimination leads whites not to grasp the seriousness of the physical threat of violence that a noose depicts since they have not likely been targeted for violence because of their race. Simultaneously, the experience of being a potential target of abuse or violence because of their race leads blacks to feel a serious threat when confronted by a noose. This effect can also be understood in terms of gender. Whereas males usually do not view sexually charged comments as harassment, females often feel genuinely threatened by these sorts of remarks because as women, they are targeted for sexual assault, rape, and domestic violence unlike their male counterparts who have never experienced the threat of violence due to sexism.

Although blatant acts of terror such as a mob lynching seem unthinkable nowadays, noose incidents as symbolic threats of terror occur frequently. A mere search of recent news stories serves to substantiate this claim. In 2007, at Columbia University Teachers College a noose was found outside the door of a black professor's office. A student at UC San Diego hung a noose from a bookcase in the school library and claimed that her actions were not racially motivated in 2010. In West Palm Beach, Florida, on Halloween 2011, officials investigated an envelope that was left on the city's television truck that contained photos of lynchings. The names of five black and Hispanic employees were attached to these photos of people hanging with ropes around their necks. Not too far from West Palm Beach, in November 2011,

Noose Hate Crime Act of 2011

In January 2011, H.R. 221: Noose Hate Crime Act of 2011 was introduced to Congress. This act proposed an amendment to Title 18 of United States Code to impose a fine and/or prison term for up to two years on anyone who, with intent to harass or intimidate any person, displays a noose in public because of that person's race, color, religion, or national origin. Rep. Sheila Jackson Lee (D-Texas) was responsible for sponsoring the bill, which was only estimated at a 2 percent chance of getting past the congressional committee before possibly being sent to the House or Senate as a whole for review.

three Palm Beach County employees hung a noose by a time clock in their workplace. Recently at UC San Francisco Medical Center, a noose was hung in an office out in the open. In Southern Maryland in February 2012, a student fashioned a noose out of a rope at his high school and held it up to taunt a group of black students. Similarly, in Battle Creek, Michigan, in February 2012, a white student also reportedly taunted a group of black students at a career center with a shoestring fashioned into a noose. In Wynne, Arkansas, in October 2012, white football players put a noose around the neck of a black ninth grader and dragged him through the school locker room.

Taken together, these recent incidents of nooses hung in educational and employment settings demonstrate the lasting symbolism of the noose as a violent representation of the oppression of blacks throughout American history.

ADRIENNE N. MILNER

See also
Hate Crimes in America; Jena Six

Further Reading:

ABC News. "Noose Hung in UCSF Warehouse." http://abclocal.go.com/kgo/story?section=news/iteam&id=8742679.

Barger, Allison. "Changing State Laws to Prohibit the Display of Hangman's Nooses: Tightening the Knot around the First Amendment?" *William and Mary Bill of Rights Journal* 17 (2008): 263–92.

Battle Creek Enquirer. "Taunting Incident Ignited Debate: Student Expelled Over Use of Noose." http://www.battlecreekenquirer.com/article/20120301/NEWS01/303010046/Taunting-incident-ignites-debate. March 1, 2012.

Bell, Jeannine. "The Hangman's Noose and the Lynch Mob: Hate Speech and the Jena Six." *Harvard Civil Rights-Civil Liberties Law Review* 44 (2009): 329–59.

Goidel, Kirby, Parent, Wayne, and Bob Mann. "Race, Racial Resentment, Attentiveness to the News Media, and Public Opinion Toward the Jena Six." *Social Science Quarterly* 92 (2011): 20–34.

Gootman, Elissa, and Al Baker. "Noose on Door at Columbia Prompts Campus Protest." *New York Times.* http://www.nytimes.com/2007/10/11/education/11columbia.html. October 11, 2007.

Huffington Post. "Washburn High School Students Hung Dark-Skinned Baby Doll, Posted Pictures Online." http://www.huffingtonpost.com/2013/01/18/washburn-high-school-stud_n_2500906.html. January 18, 2013.

Los Angeles Times. "Noose Ignited More Protests at UC San Diego." http://articles.latimes.com/2010/feb/27/local/la-me-uc-protests27-2010feb27. February 27, 2010.

NBC News. "African-American High School Students Allegedly Hazed with a Noose by White Teammates." http://thegrio.com/2012/10/03/african-american-high-school-student-hazed-with-a-noose-by-white-teammates/. October 3, 2012.

Oriola, Temitope, and Charles Adeyanju. "Haunted: The Symbolism of the Noose." *African Identities* 7 (2009): 89–103.

Palm Beach Post. "Should Noose Incident be Investigated as a Hate Crime." http://blogs.palmbeachpost.com/opinionzone/2012/01/12/should-noose-incident-be-investigated-as-a-hate-crime/. January 12, 2012.

Palm Beach Post. "Three Schools Employees Suspended Over Noose Hung by Time Clock." http://www.palmbeachpost.com/news/news/education/three-schools-employees-suspended-over-noose-hun-1/nLh3D/.

Southern Maryland Newspapers. "Noose Incident at LHS Condemned: Some Call for School Officials to Do More about Racism." http://www.somdnews.com/article/20120302/NEWS/703029759/1074/noose-incident-at-lhs-condemned&template=southernMaryland. March 2, 2012.

O

Obama, Barack (b. 1961)

Barack Hussein Obama is the 44th president of the United States, yet he is the first black president. In 2007, Obama, then the senator from Illinois, announced his candidacy for the Democratic Party's nomination in the 2008 presidential election. He went on to outlast Senator (and former First Lady) Hillary Clinton of New York in an extended Democratic primary to become the first person of color to win the nomination of a major political party in the United States. With a campaign based on the themes of hope and change, he went on to beat Senator John McCain of Arizona for the presidency on November 4, 2008.

A native of Honolulu, Hawaii, Obama grew up in the United States as well as abroad, spending time in Indonesia as a child. When his mother returned to Indonesia to conduct research, Obama remained in Hawaii with his grandparents. Upon completing high school in 1979, Obama attended Occidental College in Los Angeles before transferring to Columbia University. In 1983, he graduated with a degree in political science.

Prior to entering politics, Obama served as director of the Developing Communities Project (DCP) in Chicago where he worked as a community organizer from 1985 through 1988. After his organizing career, Obama attended Harvard Law School where he became the first black president of the *Harvard Law Review*. After law school he taught as

Obama's Opposition

The election of Barack Obama engendered opposition from groups such as the Tea Party and Birthers that contain racial components. Research examining each group has identified racial resentment as a component of their disapproval. This type of antagonism runs contrary to the notion of a postracial society that some suspected the Obama presidency would usher into the United States. In fact, surveys show that after Barack Obama's first term in office, white racial resentment actually increased in the United States.

a constitutional law professor at the University of Chicago Law School and practiced civil rights law from 1992 through 1994. Based on the recognition garnered as the president of the *Harvard Law Review*, Obama got a book deal that led to the publication of his memoir *Dreams of my Father: A Story of Race and Inheritance* in 1995.

Obama's political career began in the Illinois state Senate where he represented the South Side of Chicago in the 13th district from 1997 through 2004. In 2005 he resigned to become the junior U.S. senator from Illinois. In 2000, Obama lost a bid to become a member of the U.S. House of Representatives. In the Illinois state house, Obama took the lead

---

Mitt Romney's Welfare Claims

In the 2012 presidential campaign, Republican nominee Mitt Romney accused President Obama of eliminating the work requirement for welfare recipients that was instituted in the 1990s under President Bill Clinton. Obama refuted the claim, as did many independent fact checkers. Romney's critics accused him of subtly appealing to racial prejudice and long-standing associations between welfare and "undeserving" African Americans in white Americans' minds and contributed to the racial polarization of the electorate in the 2012 presidential race.

---

on issues pertaining to child healthcare, payday loan and predatory lending regulation, monitoring of racial profiling, as well as police interrogation and death penalty reform. In 2004, Obama easily won the race for the U.S. Senate in Illinois over Alan Keyes after the winner of the Republican primary, Jack Ryan, withdrew from the race in June of the same year. He became a rising star in Democratic national politics after delivering a well-received keynote address at the presidential nominating convention of John Kerry.

After less than a full term in the Senate, Obama pursued the Democratic Party's nomination for president in the 2008 election cycle. In a crowded field, his chief opponent was Senator Hillary Clinton from New York. Thanks to his campaign's money-raising capacity, turnout operations,

---

Racial Polarization in the 2012 Presidential Election

The 2012 presidential election produced the most racially polarized electorate in more than 20 years. President Obama carried racial minorities by wide margins, yet he lost the white vote by large amounts. Obama carried African Americans with 93 percent of the vote. Latino voters broke for the president by 40 points. Obama garnered only 39 percent of the white vote, a four-point drop from his 2008 totals. Obama won the election because these groups made up a larger portion of the electorate than they had in previous election cycles.

---

and ability to take advantage of the party's system for distributing delegates, Obama beat Clinton who conceded the nomination on June 7, 2008. Both Senator Clinton and her husband, former President Bill Clinton, endorsed candidate Obama and spoke on his behalf at the Democratic National Convention in Denver, Colorado. Obama accepted the nomination, with vice-presidential candidate Joe Biden, a senator from Delaware on August 28, 2008. On November 4, 2008, Obama won the presidency with 365 electoral votes.

Obama's first term in office was defined by an economic downturn that started under his predecessor, George W. Bush. His efforts to remedy the U.S. economy along with the reform of health insurance proved to be contentious legislation that engendered intense backlash from his political opponents. The two most controversial pieces of legislation were the Patient Protection and Affordable Care Act, also known as Obamacare, and the American Recovery and Reinvestment Act of 2009, referred to as the stimulus bill. Other legislation that proved to be contentious were the Troubled Assets Relief Program (TARP) that secured major banks and the intervention into the automobile industry that allowed General Motors and Chrysler to stay in business. The latter two initiatives began under President Bush but were implemented and carried out under Obama. These divisive policies are widely credited as being catalysts for the Tea Party movement that energized opposition to the new president and voted his Republican rivals back into the majority in the U.S. House of Representatives in 2010.

The War on Terrorism that began under Bush took a different form under Obama. The war that Bush initiated in Iraq was deemphasized and more resources were invested in the war in Afghanistan. On May 1, 2011, an operation was conducted inside Pakistan that led to the killing of Osama bin Laden, who had orchestrated the attacks of September 11, 2001 that engendered the War on Terrorism.

In 2012, Obama and Biden were again nominated for the presidency and vice presidency by the Democratic Party. They campaigned against the Republican challenger Willard Mitt Romney, the former governor of Massachusetts and CEO of Bain Capital. Against a backdrop of high unemployment and slow economic growth, Obama won reelection on November 6, 2012, with 332 electoral votes. He won by garnering the overwhelming support of black, Latino, and women voters, even as Romney carried the white vote. This coalition is regarded as signaling a demographic shift in the U.S. towards a more multicultural population.

Deeb Paul Kitchen

Further Reading:

Goldman, Seth K. "Effects of the 2008 Obama Presidential Campaign on White Racial Prejudice." *Public Opinion Quarterly* 76 (2012): 663–87.

Levenson, Michael, and Jonathan Saltzman. "At Harvard Law, A Unifying Voice: Classmates Recall Obama as Even-Handed Leader." *Boston Globe.* January 28, 2007. http://www.boston .com/news/local/articles/2007/01/28/at_harvard_law_a_ unifying_voice/?page=full (accessed November 13, 2012).

Maraniss, David. *Barack Obama: The Story.* New York: Simon and Schuster, 2012.

Melber, Ari. "Race Polarizes 2012 Electorate." *MSNBC.* November 6, 2012. http://tv.msnbc.com/2012/11/06/2012-electorate -polarized-along-racial-lines/ (accessed November 17, 2012).

Parker, Christopher. *2010 Multi-State Survey of Race and Politics: Attitudes Towards Black, Immigrants, and Gay Rights, by Tea Party Approval.* University of Washington Institute for the Study of Ethnicity, Race, and Sexuality, 2010.

Scott, Janny. "In Illinois, Obama Proved Pragmatic and Shrewd." *New York Times.* July 30, 2007. http://liveweb.archive.org/ http://www.nytimes.com/2007/07/30/us/politics/30obama .html?_r=5&oref=slogin&oref=slogin&oref=slogin&oref=slo gin& (accessed November 13, 2012).

Scott, Janny. "The Long Run: The Story of Obama, Written by Obama." *New York Times.* May 18, 2008. http://www.nytimes .com/2008/05/18/us/politics/18memoirs.html?pagewanted =all (accessed November 13, 2012).

Sides, John. "The Racializing Influence of Romney's Welfare Ad." *The Monkey Cage.* August 20, 2012. http://themonkeycage .org/blog/2012/08/20/the-racializing-influence-of-romneys -welfare-ad/ (accessed November 17, 2012).

Occupation of Alcatraz Island

On November 9, 1969, Mohawk Richard Oakes and a group of other young Native American college students sailed into San Francisco Bay on a chartered boat, *The Monte Cristo.* Their aim was to circle Alcatraz Island and claim the island for Native American people. This full-scale occupation lasted until June 11, 1971, and focused the attention of the American people on the government treatment of American Indians. The newly formed supratribal organization, Indians of All Tribes, kept their situation and demands before the public by starting their own radio program, "Radio Free Alcatraz," which was broadcast daily. As a result, letters and telegrams inundated government officials, including President Richard Nixon.

Legislators entered statements into the *Congressional Record* emphasizing the need for a review of the federal government's Native American policies. More to the point was the appeal made by California representative George E. Brown on December 23, 1969, when he called on President Nixon to negotiate with the Native American people to grant them title to the island to be used as a cultural center and an educational complex. It was in the midst of growing American Indian activism and public awareness of the plight of Native American people that President Nixon faced the task of formulating his Indian policy. He stated in his message to Congress: "The time has come to break decisively with the past and to create the conditions for a new era in which the Indian future is determined by Indian acts and Indian decisions."

The U.S. policy of termination of the recognition of American Indian tribes, in force roughly from the early 1950s through the 1960s, was the ultimate extension of assimilationist policy under which the Native American future was created by government acts and government decisions. Termination supporters argued for tribes to become subject to state laws in all respects. Since the trust status of tribal lands would end, that land would become taxable and transferable without Bureau of Indian Affairs (BIA) approval. All federal health, education, and other benefits to individuals would cease. Native Americans across the nation began to voice disapproval of the termination policy once it became evident that the end result would be a loss of federal protection and the further loss of Native American lands. During this period, 109 tribal groups, including the Menominees, the Klamaths, the Ottawas, and 36 California rancherias were terminated. Some groups attempted joint suits to recover lost lands and rights. Some, such as the Menominees, were partially successful. Others regained nothing at all. Native American people, however, were taking note of the success of national movements such as Black Power and La Raza, and leaders began to emerge from different tribal backgrounds to assert Native American nationalism.

The list of participants reads like a who's who of Native American leaders: Richard Delaware Dior McKenzie from the Rosebud Reservation; Allen Cottier, president of the American Indian Council, Inc.; Martin Martinez; Garfield Spotted Elk; Walter Means, father of the well-known Native American activist Russell Means; and Dennis Banks and George Mitchell, founders of the American Indian Movement. Richard Oakes, the founder of Indians of All Tribes, led the main occupation of Alcatraz Island. These young American Indians formed the nucleus of the first Indian supratribal organizations.

Alcatraz Island soon materialized as a place with which all Indians could identify. In a proclamation presented to T. E. Hannon, director of the California division of the General Services Administration (GSA), the occupiers stated that "it [Alcatraz Island] was isolated from modern facilities and without adequate means of transportation, it had no fresh running water, inadequate sanitation facilities, no oil or mineral rights, no industry, and no health care facilities. . . . There were no educational facilities, the population exceeded the land base, and the population had always been held as prisoners and kept dependent upon others. The Island was therefore equivalent to reservations set aside by the federal government for Indian people." The occupiers' intent was to claim unused federal land based on the provisions of the Sioux Treaty of 1868 (which allowed the Sioux to occupy any abandoned military base but did not specify where those bases had to be, although later court action found that the treaty applied only to unused federal land adjacent to the Sioux Reservation in South Dakota) and to construct a university for Native Americans as well as an Indian cultural center.

After the start of the occupation, Indians began to arrive from all across the United States, Canada, Mexico, and South America. At one point, the number of Indians living on the island grew to approximately 250. In November 1969, some 13,000 Indians visited the island. For the vast majority of Indian visitors, it was the first interaction they had had with Indians from other tribes, the first time they had felt a supratribal unity with other Indians.

Non-Indian citizens, particularly the Asian American community of San Francisco, responded to the needs of the occupiers. They provided clothing, food, water, medical supplies, and school supplies for the children, despite a U.S. Coast Guard blockade of the island. Celebrities such as Jane Fonda, Robert Redford, and Marlon Brando visited the island and encouraged private parties to support the effort not only by donating usable items but by contacting politicians as well.

The occupation originated as an idea during a discussion at the Native American Studies Program at San Francisco State College in February 1969. Members of the program were discussing the proposals being made for disposition of Alcatraz, and Richard Oakes announced to the students that taking Alcatraz would "be a good thing." Initially received with laughter, the idea remained in the minds of many students. Several months later, at a meeting in the American Indian Center in San Francisco, Oakes found a more receptive audience. Initial plans were made for a symbolic occupation in the summer of 1970.

The symbolic intent of the occupation was overcome by the political and social pressures and frustration felt by the American Indian youth. Embodying the activist, Richard Oakes and his supporters set out in their chartered boat. Suddenly, Oakes and four others jumped from the boat and swam to the island, claimed it "by right of discovery" in the name of Indians of All Tribes. Later that same day Oakes and his followers were removed from the island by the U.S. Coast Guard. However, LaNada Boyer, a Shoshone/Bannock woman, urged Oakes and his group to return to the island that night and after nightfall they did so, unopposed.

It was this night, November 9, 1969, that they spent their first night on Alcatraz. The following day, GSA Regional Director T. E. Hannon asked the Native activists to leave, which they agreed to do. Prior to leaving, however, they read a proclamation, claiming the island in the name of Indians of All Tribes by "right of discovery." In a prepared statement, Oakes claimed that the Indians had a right to Alcatraz under an 1868 treaty. Oakes then proceeded to offer to purchase the island for 24 dollars in glass beads and red cloth. Oakes and his followers then left the island for the second time. Later the same day in San Francisco, a spokesperson for the group said that the Indians planned to use Alcatraz as an Indian cultural and education center.

After the removal from the Island on November 10, Oakes went to the campus of the University of California at Los Angeles (UCLA) to think, plan, and gather supporters for a more organized occupation. Oakes appealed for support and as a result recruited 80 supporters from the UCLA campus. Oakes and his supporters then began plans for a November 20th occupation.

On the night of November 20, the most famous of the Indian occupations of Alcatraz began. Traveling by boat from Sausalito, the Indians were met by a blockade set up by the U.S. Coast Guard. The blockade proved unsuccessful, and the landing party put ashore.

On the day following the landing, Oakes and an attorney representing Indians of All Tribes presented a list of demands to the regional coordinator of the Department of Interior. Among the demands was the expectation that the federal government would give the Indians full title to the island within two weeks and provide ongoing funds for a major university and cultural center to be built on the island, to be administered by the Indian people.

On the island, however, the occupation force began to lose cohesiveness as time passed. Jealousy developed as the press identified Oakes as the leader of the occupation. Oakes's 12-year-old stepdaughter, Yvonne, was killed accidentally on January 7, 1970, when she fell three stories through an open stairwell in one of the island's apartment buildings. For some, including Oakes, this accident seemed to foretell the end of the occupation. A few days later, having left the island for his daughter's funeral, Oakes announced that he would not return to Alcatraz. Factions had already begun to form among the seven-member elected council on the island.

As the occupation wore on, boredom also increased, and the more militant Indians began to seize control of the Indian occupation force. Daily life on Alcatraz began to deteriorate sharply. Hygiene on the island was extremely poor, from sewage disposal to the preparation of food. Reports also began to surface that the sale and use of drugs was very much in evidence. In May 1970, San Francisco newspapers carried reports of Indian plans to begin destroying some of the buildings on the island. On June 1, three buildings were destroyed by fire. In November, some 90 Indians remained on Alcatraz, only three of whom were from the original landing party. Fewer than 30 Indians remained on the island by spring. On June 11, 1971, federal marshals removed the last 15 Indians from Alcatraz Island without incident.

The occupation of Alcatraz Island produced lasting and important changes on the policy of the U.S. government toward Indian people. In response to President Nixon's call for a thorough evaluation of Indian policy, the historian Alvin M. Josephy Jr. produced a document that established what many Indian experts already knew: the BIA and Indian policy were in need of a new direction. Although influenced by the Josephy recommendations, the cornerstone of the Nixon Indian policy was taken from the new voice of the Indian people and from the public concern about the treatment of Indian people. With this in mind, President Nixon laid the foundation for a federal policy of Indian self-determination. He acknowledged that the condition of Native Americans was the heritage of centuries of injustice, from the time of first contact with European settlers to the demeaning termination programs of the 1950s and 1960s. In this spirit, he also moved to honor some treaty provisions that had been ignored. This new respect for treaties and self-determination resulted in part in the return of significant land to various tribes, including 48,000 acres containing the sacred Blue Lake to the Taos people; 40 million acres to the Dine (Navajo) nation; 21,000 acres to the Yakima nation; and 60,000 acres to the Warm Springs nation.

The occupation of Alcatraz Island was only the beginning of collective action by supratribal organizations, most notably the American Indian Movement (AIM). The large increase in such events in the early 1970s marked a shift from specifically tribal issues, such as land usage or fishing rights, to issues involving Indians generally, and the events were engaged in primarily by urban Indians and Indian nationalist organizations. The occupation of Alcatraz Island was followed by a number of attempted and successful takeovers and occupations by supratribal urban groups: Fort Lewis and Fort Lawton in Washington; Ellis Island in New York; abandoned missile sites and military installations in Davis and Richmond, California, Minneapolis, Milwaukee, and Chicago; and Mount Rushmore and the Badlands National Monuments. Actions such as the 1972 Trail of Broken Treaties, the occupation of the BIA offices in Washington, D.C., and the 1973 occupation of the village at Wounded Knee, South Dakota, had direct antecedents in the Alcatraz occupation.

ABC-CLIO

See also

American Indian Movement (AIM); Black Power; Bureau of
Indian Affairs; Chicano Movement; La Raza Unida Party;
Means, Russell

Further Reading:

Cornell, Stephen. *The Return of the Native: American Indian
Political Resurgence*. New York: Oxford University Press, 1988.

Johnson, Troy R. *The Occupation of Alcatraz Island: Indian
Self-Determination and the Rise of Indian Activism*. Urbana:
University of Illinois Press, 1996.

Johnson, Troy, et al. *American Indian Activism: Alcatraz to the
Longest Walk*. Urbana: University of Illinois Press, 1997.

Josephy, Alvin M., Jr., et al. *Red Power: The American Indians'
Fight for Freedom*. Lincoln: University of Nebraska Press, 1999.

Smith, Paul Chatt, and Robert Allen Warrior. *Like a Hurricane:
The Indian Movement from Alcatraz to Wounded Knee*. New
York: New Press, 1996.

Operation Wetback

In July 1954, the United States Immigration and Naturalization Service (INS) launched the controversial paramilitary repatriation program "Operation Wetback," which, as
implied by the racist title, targeted Mexicans working illegally in the agricultural industry in the Southwest region of

A group of undocumented Mexican laborers from the northern Indiana and Illinois region walk to board a train in Chicago, to be deported to their native
Mexico, July 27, 1951. (AP/Wide World Photos)

the United States. *Wetback* is a racial slur, first used in the United States to describe immigrants who cross the border illegally, usually by crossing rivers or streams. The term *wetback* for Mexican Americans is as offensive as the term *nigger* is for Americans of African descent. The officially stated purpose of the operation was border patrol, but it became a paramilitary operation as armed officers implemented racial profiling and surprise raids, which in many cases violated with impunity the civil rights of legal immigrants and Mexican American citizens.

Before Operation Wetback, in 1942, the U.S. and Mexican governments had implemented the Bracero Program, which was designed to bring a large number of Mexicans to the United States as temporary workers. To have Mexicans working in the U.S. agricultural industry was viewed by both countries as mutually beneficial. The Bracero Program was successful and popular throughout the 1940s, but by the early 1950s, a backlash against Mexican immigrants emerged and Operation Wetback was the result. The anti-Mexican hysteria that swept across the Southwest in the early 1950s was a reaction to what was to become known as the "decade of the Wetback," the years between 1942 and 1954, when the number of illegal Mexican immigrants approached one million.

During the summer of 1954, INS officials swarmed Mexican neighborhoods all over the Southwest, capturing and deporting some 80,000 allegedly illegal immigrants. In some cases, children of immigrants who were born in the United States, and therefore citizens, were sent back to Mexico with their parents. The paramilitary practices of Operation Wetback outraged U.S. citizens who were of Mexican descent. They complained that American growers in the agricultural industry benefited from the influx of inexpensive labor from Mexico and that all immigrants deserved protection regardless of their legal status. It was not until the early 1980s that illegal immigrants from Mexico were given certain rights protected by the courts, so that now, BCIS officials are subject to litigation if they violate the rights of illegal immigrants. On the other hand, anti-Mexican sentiment is alive and well in the American Southwest as many, including radio talk show host Rush Limbaugh, have called for Operation Wetback II. In certain parts of Texas, rogue vigilantes loosely organized as the group "Ranch Rescue" roam privately held lands in search of illegal immigrants.

MICHAEL ROBERTS

See also

287g Delegation of Immigration Authority; Anchor Baby; Anti-Immigrant Sentiment; Immigration Acts; Immigration and Customs Enforcement (ICE); National Origins Act of 1924; Unauthorized Immigration; United States Border Patrol

Opportunity Hoarding

Charles Tilly, a renowned sociologist, coined *opportunity hoarding* to describe a mechanism of exclusion in society. Tilly theorized that the high-status group creates boundaries between themselves and others, excludes those on the other side of the boundary from value-producing resources, gains the resources, then uses some of the returns of the resources to reproduce the boundary. It consists of confining the use of a value-producing resource to members of an exclusionary group.

The people concentrated at the top of the socioeconomic hierarchy are able to gain control more of society's coveted resources. As a result, they are also most capable of hoarding resources for themselves and excluding others. However, opportunity hoarding does not only take place among those at the top; those with relative advantage over others also hoard opportunities to their advantage over the relatively less advantaged. Some empirical examples of this are blue-collar whites excluding blacks from their social networks, the black middle class excluding the poor, and upper-middle-class blacks excluding lower-status members of the black middle class. Despite being racial minorities, upper-middle-class people of color have access to valuable resources that are off-limits to the lower middle classes. These resources include the ability to afford to send children to private schools, or at minimum buy homes in affluent school districts in order to generate advantage for their children.

Advantaged groups in two key social institutions have exacerbated racial differences in achievement and well-being, education, and housing. The two are intricately linked as a result of the property-tax-based educational funding system in the United States. Homeownership and education are key factors in social inequality in general. Better schools have been among the reasons that families have left central cities for suburbs, and a key reason young

Cumulative Advantage

Cumulative advantage was originally developed by Robert Merton in 1942 to explain how advancement happens in scientific careers. The term came to be used widely in the social sciences, broadening to describe the mechanism by which a position of advantage becomes a resource that produces further advantage over time. In 1962, Blau and Duncan added the concept of cumulative disadvantage, which, conversely, describes the process by which a status can directly and indirectly contribute to cumulative or additive disadvantage over time. They argued that African American men suffered from cumulative disadvantage relative to whites in the occupational structure. Cumulative advantage and disadvantage have both been widely used in the social sciences to understand the creation and maintenance of social inequality.

urban families tend to move to the suburbs once their children reach school-age. Metropolitan areas are segregated by income, ethnicity, and other demographic characteristics, and of the segregated groups, higher-income, white suburbanites have enjoyed access to better education and social networks for their children than other groups. Recent scholarship has demonstrated that suburbanization and the resulting segregation are forms of opportunity hoarding, whereby the children in the advantaged suburban communities gain advantage over groups that have been excluded from suburban communities.

In their analysis of educational attainment using U.S. Census data from 1940 to 1980, Rury and Saatcioglu (2011) found results consistent with the suburban communities engaging in systematic hoarding of educational opportunities, which resulted in a growing social, economic, and educational divide over the four decades they examined. Jeffrey Henig (2009) has pointed out that spatial inequality of this nature can be thought of as a function of boundaries created to allow benefits to accrue to certain social groups while excluding others, demonstrating that once residents move into suburban areas they are able to use local government to protect their privilege through zoning and code enforcement, local tax policies, and other exclusionary policy making.

The process of acquiring, then furthering advantage Henig describes is consistent with Tilly's concept of opportunity hoarding. Suburban school districts, deliberately distinct from their urban counterparts, exclude children without social and economic resources by virtue of their location in relatively affluent districts based affluent neighborhoods. They create the conditions for educational inequality by neighborhood. Mainly poor and minority central city residents are generally excluded from suburban schools unless they can gain entry to these communities through a residential move or special program such as a school bussing program that allows their children to be bussed into higher-quality suburban schools. Gaining entry is extremely difficult in many suburbs because of prohibitive housing prices associated with better school districts, along with zoning requirements designed to restrict certain home sizes and family types, redlining, and other measures designed to limit access to community resources.

In addition to residential advantages, differences in intangible resources like cultural capital facilitate opportunity hoarding. Prudence Carter (2005) highlights the differences between poor and middle-class parents' cultural capital, demonstrating the way middle-class parents tend to use cultural capital to get their children into more prestigious academic tracks and to obtain other educational benefits. They are able to do so because of a familiarity with navigating institutions and leveraging their advantages to create more advantage. Poor and working-class parents are not generally unable to advocate for their children in this way because of a lack of knowledge and resources, like time and the ability to afford extracurricular tutoring. Although middle-class whites are most likely to have and spend this kind of cultural capital, middle-class African Americans also jockey for educational advantage for their children and are more likely to "customize" their child's school experience, despite race exhibiting an independent and negative effect on. Karyn Lacy (2007) confirms their findings in her study of three middle-class black communities where parents often would go to great lengths to secure the best possible education for their children, enabling them to have an advantage over other children.

RENEE S. ALSTON

See also

Black Middle Class; Intergenerational Social Mobility; Reverse Redlining

Further Reading:

Carter, Prudence L. *Keepin' It Real: School Success beyond Black and White*. New York: Oxford University Press, 2005.

DiPrete, Thomas A., and Gregory M Eirich. "Cumulative Advantage as a Mechanism for Inequality: A Review of Theoretical and Empirical Developments." *Annual Review of Sociology* 32 (2006): 271–97.

Henig, Jeffrey R. *Spin Cycle: How Research Is Used in Policy Debates*. Thousand Oaks, CA: Sage, 2009.

Lacy, Karyn R. *Blue-Chip Black: Race, Class, and Status in the New Black Middle Class*. Berkeley, CA: University of California Press, 2007.

Royster, Deirdre A. *Race and the Invisible Hand: How White Networks Exclude Black Men from Blue-Collar Jobs*. Berkeley: University of California Press, 2003.

Rury, John L., and Argun Saatcioglu. "Suburban Advantage: Opportunity Hoarding and Secondary Attainment in the Postwar Metropolitan North." *American Journal of Education* 117, no. 3 (2011): 307–42.

Tilly, Charles. "Relational Studies of Inequality." *Contemporary Sociology* 29, no. 6 (2000): 782–85.

Oppositional Culture

A prominent cultural explanation regarding educational differences among racial groups is John Ogbu's theory of oppositional culture (1978). An important distinction of oppositional culture lies in the difference between "immigrant minorities"—minorities who freely migrated from their country, and "involuntary minorities"—groups who were captured, enslaved, and conquered. Immigrant minorities tend to embrace societal institutions; they do not fear or mistrust the American system. However, due to the job ceiling experienced by many caste-like (involuntary) minorities, specifically blacks, members of caste-like minorities are not permitted to compete for jobs that they are qualified for or they are denied the most desirable positions because of their caste membership. Black children learn about the job ceiling by observing what happens to their parents, siblings, and other relatives. As black children grow older, they begin to see that all black Americans experience the inconsistency between educational credentials and job availability, not just those who are close to them. Therefore, the job ceiling creates ambivalent attitudes towards school, which hinders academic success.

However, if a black student does academically succeed, their peers may label them as "acting white"; therefore, even if the potential for success exists, the fear of ridicule may supersede educational aspirations. Further, by succeeding in school and "acting white," black students may be perceived as giving up their ethnic identity. Oppositional and ambivalent attitudes, once instilled, explain the poor school performance of black children.

While there are many sociologists who find this explanation relevant and powerful, others contend that there are a number of variables that influence the academic success of black students, and oppositional culture is not a powerful explanatory variable. For example, in Mickelson's (1990) study of black high school students, she found that a gap existed between students' attitudes and their performance. Although black students believed in success and hard work, their personal experiences of discrimination, which can hinder academic and occupational mobility, often become dominant. Thus, although black students espoused beliefs consistent with the American Dream, their reality is not consistent with these ideals, and their academic achievement was hindered. However, the "paradox" between bad grades and optimistic educational attitudes for blacks disappeared when attitudes are reflective of unrestricted opportunity. For example, middle-class black women had the lowest discrepancy score

John Ogbu (1939–2003)

John Ogbu was born in 1939 in Nigeria, Africa. He moved to New Jersey to attend Princeton University Theological Seminary. While attending Princeton, he became attracted to the study of anthropology, which he believed would empower him to better serve the people. He moved to Berkeley, California, in 1961 to purse his education. He received his bachelor's and master's degrees and PhD in anthropology from the University of California at Berkeley. Before completion of his PhD in 1971, he started teaching at UC Berkeley, where he taught throughout his whole career. At the center of Ogbu's work was his focus on collective identity and educational success. While his work was often controversial, he has extensively published and is the recipient of a number of awards/honors. He passed away in 2003.

between concrete (lived experience) and abstract attitudes (American Dream ideology); however, they are also the most likely to receive higher educational returns than blacks of any other group. Therefore, while Mickelson and Ogbu have similar findings when it comes to educational attitudes, Mickelson's study sheds light on how the intersection of social class, gender, and race affects attitudes about education.

Similar to Mickelson (1990), Ainsworth-Darnell and Downey (1998) challenge the oppositional cultural explanation. In their study concerning student achievement, black students did not have lower educational expectations compared to their white counterparts. Further, black students were more likely to have pro-school attitudes and be considered popular for earning good grades when compared to whites. Contrary to Ogbu's theory of oppositional culture, Ainsworth-Darnell and Downey argue that the poor performance among blacks is tied to a lack of material conditions (e.g., high unemployment and poverty rates, high rate of single-parent households) within the black family, conditions that lead to negative school outcomes.

According to Massey and Denton (1993), it is not an oppositional culture framework that explains educational differences. Instead, it is a culture of segregation that hinders economic and educational success in mainstream society. Due to residential isolation and concentrated poverty, joblessness thrives, and the adherence to mainstream norms is not strictly abided by. Living in the ghetto, separated from mainstream society, Black English Vernacular is commonly spoken, which creates one more barrier to educational success. Since the materials in the classroom (books and learning activities) are written in Standard English, the learning process becomes frustrating. In the end, the consequences of residential isolation (e.g., poor schools and racial isolation) experienced by blacks inhibit their ability to academically succeed.

Although oppositional culture, as well as other cultural explanations for the lack of educational success among blacks have been popular, many liberal sociologists adamantly disagree with this framework. Instead of critically examining how the structure of U.S. society creates opportunity for some while inhibiting it for others, cultural explanations often blame the victim. However, since the dominant ideology in America still rests upon the notions of equal opportunity and meritocracy, for those who do not succeed in society, their lack of hard work, ambivalent attitudes, or culture are often blamed.

BOBETTE OTTO

Self-Fulfilling Prophecy

The self-fulfilling prophecy refers to a process by which a person or group internalizes and then exhibits those qualities that others maintain that person or group has. It can have an especially destructive impact on minority groups, particularly when dominant groups create stereotypes (inaccurate generalizations regarding an entire group) about the minority group. This can happen in at least two ways. First, a dominant group may generalize that all members of a certain group lack the ability to perform a certain task. Eventually, from repeated exposure to the idea, and, subsequently, internalization of the idea that they cannot perform the task (even though the group actually has the ability to perform the task), the group develops an inability to perform the task.

Another way in which the self-fulfilling prophecy can hurt minorities is through the reaction by those in power to the stereotype. Dominant groups will emphasize the false stereotypical image. They will attempt to foster that image in the minority group by denying them opportunities that do not fit the stereotype. For example, the stereotypical image of black athletic superiority can hurt blacks in at least two ways. First, repeated exposure to this stereotype may prevent blacks themselves from developing intellectual skills in favor of athletics. Second, blacks will be denied opportunities by dominant groups, such as entrance into advanced learning programs.

However, the impact of the self-fulfilling prophecy is more complicated than this short essay may suggest. Sociologist Edwin Schur, for example, suggests that those who are stigmatized can overcome it. Indeed, there have been attempts by minority groups to overcome stereotypes. An example in the 1960s and 1970s is the popular euphemism "Black is beautiful."

JOHN ETERNO

Further Reading

Ainsworth-Darnell, James W., and Douglas B. Downey. "Assessing the Oppositional Culture Explanation for Racial/Ethnic Differences in School Performance." *American Sociological Review* 63 (1998): 536–53.

Anderson, Elijah. *Code of the Streets: Decency, Violence, and the Moral Life of the Inner City*. New York: W.W. Norton, 1999.

Fordham, Signithia, and John Ogbu. "Black Students' School Success: Coping With the 'Burden of "Acting White."'" *Urban Review* 18 (1986): 176–206.

Gibson, Margaret A., and John U. Ogbu, eds. *Minority Status and Schooling: A Comparative Study of Immigrant and Involuntary Minorities*. New York: Garland Publishing, 1991.

Massey, Douglas S. and Nancy A. Denton. *The American Apartheid*. Cambridge, MA: Harvard University Press, 1993.

Mickelson, Roslyn Arlin. "The Attitude-Achievement Paradox Among Black Adolescents." *Sociology of Education* 63 (1990): 44–61.

Ogbu, John. *Minority Education and Caste*. New York: Academic Press, 1978.

Ogbu, John. "Low Performance as an Adaption: The Case of Blacks in Stockton, California." In *Minority Status and Schooling*, edited by Margaret A. Gibson and John U. Ogbu, 249–85. New York: Grand Publishing, 1991.

Wilson, William J. *The Truly Disadvantaged: The Inner City, the Underclass, and Public Policy*. Chicago: University of Chicago Press, 1987.

Orangeburg (South Carolina) Massacre of 1968

The Orangeburg Massacre, an incident in which three African American students were killed and 27 others were wounded in a confrontation with police, occurred in February 1968 on the adjoining campuses of South Carolina State College (now South Carolina State University) and Claflin College (now Claflin University), two historically black colleges in Orangeburg, South Carolina. Although a great deal of violence occurred during antiwar and civil rights movement demonstrations of the 1960s, the Orangeburg Massacre was unprecedented because it was the first time in U.S. history that students were killed on an American college campus. Another aspect of the Orangeburg Massacre that makes it an unparalleled event in the annals of American history is that even though the deaths of the students at South Carolina State and Claflin Colleges occurred two years before the Kent State shootings in which four students were killed and nine others were wounded on May 4, 1970, the Orangeburg Massacre received negligible media coverage. In fact, compared to the national and international media coverage that the tragedy at Kent State received, it was almost as if the Orangeburg Massacre did not happen at all, or, at the very least, was not important enough to report. Perhaps the only event of its kind that received even less media attention was the deaths of two students during an incident at Jackson State University in Mississippi on May 14, 1970. Ironically, the 150 African American students at Jackson State were protesting the incident at Kent State when the National Guard fired into the crowd, leaving two students dead.

There are many possible reasons why the Orangeburg Massacre was neglected by the press. Even in death and injury it seemed that the students of South Carolina State and Claflin Colleges had fallen prey to the racial discrimination they spent their lives trying to overcome. However, an equally plausible reason is that less than two months after the Orangeburg Massacre, while the incident was still under investigation, the nation, particularly the individuals in the civil rights movement who had committed their lives to ending discrimination in this country, were shocked and angered by the assassination of Dr. Martin Luther King, Jr. on April 8, 1968.

Whatever the reason for the neglect of the topic, the fact is that on Thursday night, February 8, 1968, members of the South Carolina Sheriff's Office, the South Carolina Police Department, and the South Carolina Army National Guard shot 30 African American college students who had organized what was intended to be a peaceful protest. Approximately 200 students gathered on the adjoining campuses of South Carolina State and Claflin Colleges to protest the continued segregation of the All Star Bowling Lane, a bowling alley on Russell Street, within walking distance of the two colleges. The bowling alley was owned by Harry Floyd, a local businessman. Students were frustrated after a week's attempt to persuade the owner of the bowling alley to comply with the Civil Rights Act of 1964, which, in part, authorized the national government to abolish segregation and discrimination based on race, color, religion, national origin, and, in the case of employment, sex. The students organized a peaceful demonstration on the college campuses where they attended school. The act was signed into law on July 2, 1964, by

Two African American demonstrators killed in the Orangeburg Massacre lie on the ground at the edge of South Carolina State College in Orangeburg, South Carolina, February 8, 1968. Following three days of protests, which began when African Americans were barred from entering a bowling alley by the proprietor, state police and National Guardsmen confronted the demonstrators. Three students were killed and 27 wounded. (AP Photo)

President Lyndon Baines Johnson and, even though the law stressed voluntary compliance, it also included a stipulation that encouraged resolution of problems by local and state authorities.

During the days leading up to February 8, several representatives from South Carolina State and Claflin Colleges met with the mayor of Orangeburg, the chief of police, and the city manager. The students requested but were denied a permit to march through the streets of Orangeburg or to demonstrate in front of the All Star Bowling Lane.

On Monday, February 5, 1968, a group of students from Claflin and South Carolina State Colleges attempted to desegregate the only bowling alley in town, but they were denied entrance and the police were summoned by the proprietor. After a brief stand-off, the majority of the students returned to their respective campuses.

This effort to abolish segregation was not something new for students of Claflin and South Carolina State Colleges. They, along with black and white citizens in South Carolina, played an active role in the civil rights movement. In July 1955, 57 African Americans petitioned the school board to desegregate the public schools in Orangeburg. A year later, students from South Carolina State and Claflin Colleges organized a nonviolent protest march through the streets of Orangeburg. During February and March, students from Claflin, Morris, and Friendship Colleges conducted sit-ins to desegregate the lunch counter at S. H. Kress, a novelty store or "five and dime," founded by Samuel Henry Kress (1863–1955). On March 15, 1960, demonstrators were drenched with fire hoses and tear-gassed as they marched to protest the segregated lunch counter. In September 1963, over 1,000 protesters were arrested for picketing local merchants. A review of this brief history suggests that the events that took place in Orangeburg during February 1968 were not an aberration but part of the long struggle to abolish segregation and racial discrimination, which was a fundamental goal of the civil rights movement.

On Tuesday night, the local police were waiting when students arrived. The door of the bowling alley was locked, but the students refused to move. Chief of Police Roger Poston was called. When he arrived, the door was unlocked to allow him entrance. Several students rushed the door. They were asked to leave. When they refused, 15 were arrested for trespassing.

When rumors of the arrests reached the campuses, over 300 students gathered outside the bowling alley. They were met by the Orangeburg Police Department, state police, state highway patrol, deputies from the sheriff's office, and the state law enforcement division. A city fire truck arrived. The students chose that moment to rush the bowling alley. Someone smashed a plate glass window. The police beat back the crowd with nightsticks. Eight students and one officer were injured.

On Wednesday morning, student representatives from both colleges attended a meeting with city officials to discuss the events of the past couple of days and prevent any potential escalation. The students were again denied a permit to hold a demonstration but were able to submit a list of grievances; their list included: (a) closing of the All Star Bowling Lane until it changed its policy toward segregation;

(b) establishment of a biracial Human Relations Committee; (c) service from the Orangeburg Medical Association for all persons, regardless of race, color, creed, religion, or national origin; and (d) compliance of local and state officials with the Civil Rights Act of 1964.

On Thursday, February 8, 1968, another meeting was convened on campus and was organized by the Black Awareness Coordinating Committee (BACC), a student organizations that included members of the Student Nonviolent Coordinating Committee, the National Association for the Advancement of Colored People, and the Southern Christian Leadership Conference. Some members of BACC felt that they had been defeated by compromise when the group was denied another permit. The meetings lasted until evening without reaching a solution. The students were denied their permit to demonstrate, and the bowling alley remained segregated. The only concession was that Harry Floyd agreed to close his place of business at 5:00 P.M., several hours earlier than usual. But still, the stalemate continued. Exhausted, frustrated, and disappointed about their lack of progress, dozens of students conversed in small groups. Others wandered aimlessly around the campuses. After the meeting, instead of going straight back to their dorms, over 100 students walked around the campuses, talked in small groups, and wondered what tomorrow would bring.

Because it was a cold winter night, someone suggested a bonfire. It was not long before the blaze became a beacon for other students. It also attracted the attention of the police. Once the authorities arrived they built a barricade on Watson Street separating themselves from the students and the bonfire. There was a sudden tension and a sense of foreboding in the air—the sense that something was going to happen that night.

A fire truck arrived followed by an ambulance, which elicited an angry response from the students. As the firemen extinguished the already dying embers of the bonfire someone out of the darkness yelled, "I'm hit."

The police immediately opened fire. Students, stunned by the sudden assault, ran, screamed, fell to their knees, or dove for shelter. From start to finish, the terror lasted only seconds, but in that terrifying interval, 27 students were wounded and three young men were killed.

Samuel Ephesians Hammond Jr. (1949–1968), Henry Ezekial Smith (1948–1968), and Delano Herman Middleton

(1950–1968) were killed. Samuel Hammond, a freshman from Fort Lauderdale, Florida, was shot in the upper back. Henry Smith, a sophomore from Marion, South Carolina, was shot in the right and left sides and in the neck. Delano Middleton, a 17-year-old high school student from Orangeburg, was shot in the spine, thigh, wrist, and forearm. His mother worked on campus and he was there visiting friends. This was an unexpected culmination of events that began with so much hope and promise.

Even after an investigation, it was difficult to state exactly what triggered the confrontation. The police claimed that they fired in self-defense. Students claimed that the only shots fired were by the police, that they fired without warning into a defenseless crowd with no means of protecting themselves. The controversy over what actually ignited the Orangeburg Massacre has never been resolved. However, during the 112th Session of the South Carolina General Assembly in 1997–1998, the following resolution was passed (Bill 4576):

> To express profound gratitude for the supreme sacrifice made on February 8, 1968, by three young students, Samuel Hammond, Jr., Delano Herman Middleton, and Henry Ezekial Smith, and to recognize their courageous effort by declaring February 8, as Smith-Hammond-Middleton Memorial Day.
>
> Be it further resolved that we pray the governor of our great state immediately issue posthumously to those three brave young men The Order of the Palmetto, and pray also that these awards be presented to South Carolina State University on February 8, 1998, and that South Carolina State University display them in positions of honor and prominence in its Smith-Hammond-Middleton Memorial Center.

Every year, friends, family, and survivors gather on the campuses of Claflin and South Carolina State Universities to commemorate the Orangeburg Massacre.

JOHN G. HALL

See also

Historically Black Colleges and Universities; Police Brutality; Race Riots in America; Sellers, Cleveland. Documents: The Report on the Memphis Riots of May 1866 (July 25, 1866); Account of the Riots in East St. Louis, Illinois (July 1917); The Cook County Coroner's Report Regarding the 1919 Chicago Race Riots (1919); A Southern Black Woman's Letter Regarding the Recent Riots in Chicago and Washington (November 1919); The Final Report of the Grand Jury on the Tulsa Race Riot (June 25, 1921); Testimony from *Laney v. United States* Describing Events during the Washington, D.C., Riot of July 1919 (December 3, 1923); The Governor's Commission Report on the Watts Riots (December 1965); Cyrus R. Vance's Report on the Riots in Detroit (July-August 1967); The Reports of the Oklahoma Commission to Study the Tulsa Race Riot of 1921 (2000-2001); The Draft Report of the 1898 Wilmington Race Riot Commission (December 2005)

Further Reading:

Bass, Jack, and Jack Nelson. *The Orangeburg Massacre*. Macon, GA: Mercer University Press, 1996.

Brown, Linda Meggett. "Remembering the Orangeburg Massacre (South Carolina State University)." *Black Issues in Higher Education*, March 1, 2001.

Watters, Pat, and Weldon Rougeau. *Events at Orangeburg: A Report Based on Study and Interviews in Orangeburg, South Carolina, in the Aftermath of Tragedy*. Southern Regional Council, South Carolina, February 25, 1968.

Williams, Cecil J. "Selected Movement Photographs of Cecil J. Williams." http://www.crmvet.org/images/pwilliam.htm.

Orientalism

Orientalism is the long-held Western ideological bias that views Eastern societies and cultures as inferior, exotic, and erotic. Noted intellectual Edward W. Said first introduced the term in his classic book, *Orientalism*, published in 1979. He used this term to conceptualize in the framework of traditional scholarly thinking the relationship of power and knowledge between the "Occidental" colonizer and the "Oriental" colonized.

According to Said, the Orientalist scholars sharply divided the "Occident" as the West—in particular, England, France, and the United States—and the "Orient" as the romantic, imaginative, and exotic Middle East and Far East. By making a comparative review of European colonial arts and literature on the peoples of the Middle East, Said argued that Occidental scholarship had conflated a myriad of cultures of the East into a single, cohesive whole of the "Orient" or subjugated "Others." In this discourse, the Orientalist scholars used dominating and sexual terms to describe Eastern cultures; by doing so, the West and the East were dichotomously identified from a viewpoint of the Occidental.

The concept of Orientalism has greatly contributed to various academic areas by transforming scholarly views toward the East. Through the late 20th century, the postmodernist critique of Orientalism highlighted that the Orient is not a single, monolithic region but rather a broad area encompassing multiple civilizations. This intellectual discourse has encouraged academic institutions in North America to replace "Oriental" studies with "Asian" studies. This transformation has included a scholarly acknowledgment of the diversity of Eastern cultures and a localization of focus to specific regions, such as the Middle East, South Asia, and East Asia, in the postcolonial studies of the East.

The idea of Orientalism has also revolutionized scholarly thinking among postmodernists and conflict theorists of race. Referring to Said's work, many scholars now contend that the West's idea of itself during the colonial period was constructed largely by saying what others were not. The Orientalist studies imposed a homogenous image of a prototypical Oriental on the East by considering it biologically inferior and culturally backward, peculiar and static. In this way, the Occidentals enabled themselves to define the West as powerful, civilized, and superior, in striking contrast to the East in its image, idea, personality, and experience. This ideological framework by Orientalists helped to justify the political imperialism of Europe in the East during the colonial period. Scholars in this area also highlight that this historical discourse has led to Western dominance over other parts of the world in international politics and economics through the contemporary global age.

Social scientists in Asian American studies have pointed out that Orientalism has conceptualized the negative cliché fantasies of Asians and the stereotypical imagery of Asian immigrants and Asian Americans by European Americans. Orientalist novelists and filmmakers, especially in the early 20th century, portrayed Oriental men as feminine, weak, cunning, ugly, and dangerous villains, as characterized by "Yellow Perils/Hordes" and "Fu Manchu." Likewise, women in non-Western cultures were typically depicted as erotic, mysterious, and objects for conquest, as illustrated by the images of the "harem" in Arab society and the "geisha" in Japan. Taking a more recent example, the Broadway musical *Miss Saigon* and such Disney films as *Pocahontas* and

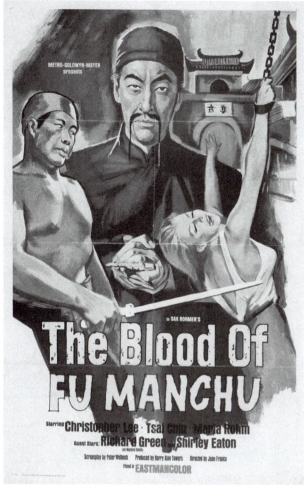

Movie Poster: *The Blood of Fu Manchu* (1968) also known as *Kiss and Kill*. Directed by Jesus Franco. (Commonwealth United Entertainment/Photofest)

Aladdin are often criticized for their Orientalist stereotypes and assumptions about non-Western women and cultures as a whole. Scholars in Asian American Studies claim that these negative images of Asians are inseparably tied to discrimination and prejudice that Asian immigrants and Asian Americans have experienced in reality.

In addition, it is important to note that although the concept of Orientalism originated as a critique of Western views of the Orient, recent studies of Asians and Asian Americans have revealed that Orientalism is prevalent even among postmodern Asian and Asian American writers. On close examination, popular fictions by such writers as Maxine Hong Kingston, Amy Tan, and Frank Chin have used the Orientalist views of Eastern histories and minority cultures.

It reflects the writers' unconscious deployment of the Orientalist stereotypes that have been built upon the enduring Western cultural hegemony.

ETSUKO MARUOKA-NG

See also

Discrimination; Prejudice; Racial Essentialism; Stereotype

Further Reading:

Lee, Robert G. *Orientals: Asian Americans in Popular Culture.* Philadelphia: Temple University Press, 2000.

Ma, Sheng-Mei. *The Deathly Embrace: Orientalism and Asian American Identity.* Minneapolis: University of Minnesota Press, 2000.

Macfie, Alexander Lyon. *Orientalism: A Reader.* New York: New York University Press, 2001.

Said, Edward W. *Orientalism.* New York: Vintage Books, 1979.

Said, Edward W. *Culture and Imperialism.* New York: Vintage Books, 1994.

Tchen, John Kuo Wei. *New York before Chinatown: Orientalism and the Shaping of American Culture, 1776–1882.* Baltimore: Johns Hopkins University Press, 1999.

Yu, Henry. *Thinking Orientals: Migration, Contact, and Exoticism in Modern America.* New York: Oxford University Press, 2002.

Owens, Jesse (1913–1980)

James Cleveland Owens was born September 12, 1913, in Oakville, Alabama, and died March 31, 1980, in Tucson, Arizona. As the youngest of 10 children growing up in rural Alabama, Owens went by the nickname "J.C." When he was nine years old, his family moved to Cleveland, Ohio. While attending public school in an inner-city school, a teacher taking attendance for class misunderstood Owens's heavy Southern accent mistaking his reply "J.C." for "Jesse," and his new nickname stuck.

Owens attended Ohio State University after he graduated from high school in Cleveland. Despite his impressive record-setting performances (he tied the international record for the 100-yard dash and the long jump), he was not awarded a scholarship from the Columbus school. Owens lived off campus and worked a number of jobs including elevator operator and janitor to pay his way through school in Ohio. His performances in the Big Ten championships in 1935 caught the attention of U.S. Olympic officials as he set three world records and tied a fourth all in the span of 45 minutes.

The story of Jesse Owens's victories in the 1936 Olympic Games in Berlin in front of Nazi leader Adolf Hitler is arguably one of the best known in the annals of African American sports. Hitler and Nazi Germany Olympic organizers had chastised U.S. Olympic officials for including African Americans and Jews on the U.S. team. For Owens, the matter was moot: in his autobiography he wrote that he was largely apolitical; he just wanted to compete on the international stage.

There also is an enduring myth that Hitler refused to greet Owens after the American sprinter had won the 100-meter dash. Owens debunked that rumor in an interview: "Hitler had a certain time to come to the stadium and a certain time to leave. It happened that he had to leave before the victory ceremony for the 100 meters," Owens told journalists when he returned to the United States after the Berlin Games. "But before he left I was on my way to a broadcast and passed near his box. He waved at me and I waved back."

Undoubtedly the myth endures because Hitler did, in fact, meet with and congratulate a group of German athletes after an earlier event. International Olympic officials told the German leader that he would be required to meet with all winning athletes from all participating countries or none at all. Hitler chose to forego meeting with any group of champion athletes after that incident.

In addition, as Owens would later say, "Hitler didn't snub me—it was [FDR] who snubbed me. The president didn't even send me a telegram" (Schaap 2007).

Far from being scorned by Germans in general, Owens was celebrated by those Germans who appreciated his athletic prowess. In fact, before he ran his first race, athletic shoe maker Adolf (Adi) Dassler (founder of Adidas) persuaded Owens to wear his specially designed track shoes, making Owens the first African American to have a corporate sponsor.

Owens later pointed out that it was German long jump champion Luz Long who suggested a change in Owens's jumping technique, which allowed Owens to qualify for the long jump finals. The two remained close friends for the rest of their lives. Owens's leap of 26 feet, five and one-half inches stood as the Olympic record for more than 25 years.

German athletes were not necessarily Owens's main concern when he lined up for his first event, the 100-meter dash. His main rival was not a German athlete but rather fellow U.S. Olympian Mathew "Mack" Robinson, older brother of Jackie Robinson. Jackie Robinson, of course, would break the color barrier a decade later in Major League baseball. Owens edged out the elder Robinson in a time of 10.3 to set the first of three individual Olympic records; he also won gold in the 200 meter and the long jump. His fourth gold medal was in the 400 meter relay, where he and Robinson were last-minute replacements after German officials objected to two American Jews who were scheduled to run the relay.

Owens's athletic success did not pan out after he returned to the United States and the ticker-tape parades became distant memories. Movie deals, athletic equipment endorsements, and special appearances did not appear for him, and he filed for bankruptcy. Owens struggled to find financial success after the Olympics and owned a dry cleaning business and worked several odd jobs to earn a living.

Owens married his high school sweetheart, Minnie Ruth Solomon, with whom he had three daughters. A pack-a-day smoker for 35 years, Owens died of lung cancer in Tucson on March 31, 1980.

KEN MUIR

See also

Sports and Racism

Further Reading:

Baker, William. *Jesse Owens—An American Life*. Urbana: University of Illinois Press, 2006.

Litsky, Frank. "Jesse Owens Dies of Cancer at 66; Hero of the 1936 Berlin Olympics." *New York Times*, April 1, 1980. http://www .nytimes.com/learning/general/onthisday/bday/0912.html.

Owens, Jesse, with Paul Neimark. *Jesse: The Man Who Outran Hitler*. New York: Random House, 1985.

Pittsburgh Press. "Owens Arrives with Kind Words for All Officials." http://news.google.co.uk/newspapers?id=zsoaAAA AIBAJ&sjid=IkwEAAAAIBAJ&pg=1814,6536771&dq=jesse -owens hitler&hl=en (accessed February 13, 2013).

Rose, Lacey. "The Single Greatest Athletic Achievement." *Forbes*, November 18, 2005. http://www.forbes.com/2005/11/18/ athletic_performance_olympics_cx_lr_1118experts.html (accessed February 4, 2013).

Schaap, Jeremy. *Triumph: The Untold Story of Jesse Owens and Hitler's Olympics*. Boston: Houghton Mifflin, 2007.

Shenkman, Rick. *Legends, Lies and Cherished Myths of American History*. New York: William and Morrow Company, 1988.

Ozawa v. United States (1922)

Ozawa v. United States was a U.S. Supreme Court case in the fall of 1922 that addressed the question of whether a Japanese person was eligible for citizenship in the United States in light of the 1906 Naturalization Act, which specified that its provisions apply to free white persons and those of African descent. The point on which this case turned was the fact that this act had been edited extensively since its passage to make it quite clear that only free white persons, those of African descent, and other individuals who had served three years or more in the U.S. armed forces were eligible for citizenship. The Court then turned to examining what the definition of a "free white person" is, and came to the conclusion that making clear boundaries for this term is very difficult, but that a Japanese person certainly is not white. Therefore, the Court concluded, Japanese individuals are ineligible for citizenship. They were careful to mention that this case has nothing to say about racial superiority or individual worthiness, particularly in light of the improved state of diplomatic relations with Japan at the time and the numerous briefs describing the accomplishments of Japanese art and culture submitted to the court.

This case paved the way for *United States v. Thind*, which aimed to determine just what the limits of whiteness were. It also established Japanese Americans as an ethnic group entirely unable to become citizens and thus subject to many forms of discrimination, particularly in terms of ownership laws and employment practices.

MIKAILA MARIEL LEMONIK ARTHUR

See also

Asian American Legal Defense and Education Fund (AALDEF); National Origins Act of 1924; Naturalization and Citizenship Process

P

Paine, Thomas (1737–1809)

Thomas Paine, known as a Founding Father of the United States and a prominent pamphleteer in the age of the American Revolution, denounced the slavery system in America to be the most monstrous crime against humanity and conscience. He was born in England, had been raised among commoners, and had received little formal education. But he belonged to a debating club called the Headstrong Club. Upon immigrating to America in 1774, he began publicly expressing his thoughts on religion, politics, and social issues in accessible language. He believed that the age of myth and superstition had gone and a new age of reason had come. Reason was something bestowed to every human being without distinctions by the Creator of the Universe. Justice based on common sense—reason and conscience—would abolish all conventional privileges, including monarchy and hereditary aristocracy. People would govern themselves in a representative government. His *Common Sense*, published in 1776, inspired thousands of Americans, including Thomas Jefferson and George Washington, and helped to shape the Declaration of Independence. He is also the one who conceived the name the United States of America. In the second part of *Rights of Man*, Paine proposed progressive taxation, funds for social protection of the poor, family allowances, publicly funded

The author of the extremely popular pamphlet *Common Sense*, Thomas Paine probably did more to inspire Americans to seek their independence from Britain and to endeavor to spread the principles of the American Revolution to Europe than any other writer. (Library of Congress)

general education, and old-age pensions, "not as a matter of grace and favor, but of right."

It is no surprise that such an egalitarian spirit debunked the evil of slavery in his tract "African Slavery in America." To Paine, it was unnatural that human beings were sold as commodities, and he called slave traders "men-stealers." Africans had been industrious farmers, peace-loving people inhabiting fertile lands, "before the Europeans debauched them with liquors, and bribed them against one another; and that these inoffensive people are brought into slavery, by stealing them, tempting Kings to sell subjects, which they can have right to do, and hiring one tribe to war against another, to catch prisoners." Buying slaves is no less criminal than selling them, insofar as they are ill-gotten goods. Slaves themselves are true owners of their freedom. For the already enslaved, Paine proposed, besides emancipation, humane treatment of aging slaves, granting land at reasonable rent, paying reasonable wages, helping all build up some property, having families living together, and settling on the frontiers. He thought these measures would lead them to active participation in public affairs.

DONG-HO CHO

See also
Abolitionist Movement

Further Reading:
Fruchtman, Jack, Jr. *Thomas Paine: Apostle of Freedom.* New York: Four Walls Eight Windows, 1994.

Panethnic Identity (Panethnicity)

A panethnic group denotes an inclusive ethnic category made up of several distinct ethnic groups, lumped together due to certain commonalities. In the North American context, it is an aggregated group such as the "Asian American," "Native Americans," "Hispanic, "Latino," and "black," based on the grounds of the subgroups' racial similarities as well as closeness of regional origins, common language and/or religion of subgroups, or shared experience of discrimination as minority groups in the host society. Espiritu refers to panethnic group as "a politico-cultural collectivity made up of people of several, hitherto distinct, tribal, or national

origins" (1992: 2). Panethnicity is "the development of bridging organizations and the generalization of solidarity among ethnic subgroups" (Lopez and Espiritu 1990).

There are various elements that can facilitate or inhibit panethnicity. Racial categorization and hierarchical racial relations play a crucial role in the United States that often promotes panethnicity. Although closely overlapping in terms of significance, race and panethnic identity connote different dimensions of similar phenomena related to racialization. Race describes a category imposed externally upon groups deemed to bear related features by those with the power to draw racial lines. A panethnic identity, on the other hand, is embraced by the groups themselves as a way of uniting across lines of ethnic or national origins, often in response to challenges from the dominant group. Although in many cases the two may seem to overlap in North America, race may be understood as a society's attempt to distance itself from minority/immigrant groups by imposing a sense of otherness upon groups, whereas panethnic identity represents deliberate efforts by those groups to unite, forging a shared identity in response to a shared experience.

For instance, immigrants from different Asian countries, such as Chinese, Filipinos, Japanese, Koreans, Taiwanese, and Vietnamese found similarities amongst themselves in part owing to the racialization that they experienced vis-à-vis white Americans. These subethnic or subnational groups, despite the linguistic, religious, and other cultural diversity among them, forge panethnicities such as Asian American. Lopez and Espiritu argue that a shared culture among subgroups is not a necessary condition of formation of a panethnic group (1990). Using data from the Children of Immigrants Longitudinal Study, Portes and Rumbaut found ethnic self-definitions of children of immigrants, as they grew up in the United States, shifted toward more panethnic identity rather than toward the direction to American or hyphenated-identity based on parents' ethnic/national origins. The increasing adaptation of panethnic identification among the second generation over time strongly suggests the impact of racial categories imposed by—and racism in—the host society to the identity formation of racialized groups (2001).

Political benefits can also facilitate panethnicity. Pan-Asian organization emerged in part due to the rising use of census data that employed ethnic categories. These categories led to potential economic benefits such as government funds, which in turn led to the rise of political action to acquire such funds. Civil rights legislation, grants-in-aid programs, and other political processes led to the increasing aggregation of diverse ethnic minority groups into a broader umbrella categorization. Thus, the political factor in the construction of panethnicity works both from above and from below: government policies as well as grassroots mobilization to acquire benefits simultaneously generate an impetus to form panethnic identities.

Another important element in the formation of panethnicity is reactive solidarity. In a host society where there is incidence of reaction against ethnic, racial, and cultural differences, hostile reception of newcomers can lead to friction or violence. Hate crimes against minority groups is sometimes a result of mistaken identity, as with the Vincent Chin case of 1982: a Chinese American man who was thought to be Japanese was killed by white men. As a result of this incident, Asian immigrants of diverse origins came together to fight against anti-Asian violence. Cross-cutting class, cultural, and generational divisions can be bridged when counterorganizational efforts are made to prevent violent discrimination. Negative stereotypes can also lead to aggregation: In December 2012, a woman pushed an Indian man to his death under a subway train in New York City because she lumped together Hindus and Muslims, accusing them of causing the events of 9/11.

Panethnicity goes beyond national or ethnic boundaries to bring together disparate groups, often in response to social attempts to impose a single category of race upon them. These groupings function as a means to mobilize groups facing similar marginalization or discrimination for social and even political change. Quite opposite to the once-held belief among immigration scholars that post-1965 immigrants would assimilate into the mainstream in a similar way to that of European immigrants who came to the United States at the turn of the century, newcomers responded to racialization by combining forces of those oppressed by racial divisions. Panethnic identities are alive to the power of agency of ethnic groups but also to the way racial categorization shapes shared meanings. Thus, they are products of a dialectical process in which ascriptions by others in the broader social sphere interact with groups' own assertions about a shared experience.

Latino Identity

Latino identity in the United States represents another expression of panethnicity. It unites groups from across Latin America, including those from Spanish-speaking countries as well as Brazil, where Portuguese is spoken. In the wake of the 1992 Los Angeles riots, for example, leaders from different Latin American communities came together for a Latino Unity Forum, to pool resources to address the different community needs and also to work against the perception of the role Latinos played in the looting that followed the riots. Groups brought together by the event were as diverse as Mexican Americans who have lived on the U.S. side of the border for more multiple generations as well as recent immigrants from Central American countries, particularly El Salvador. Leaders pointed to the success of the Asian American community, in which the various groups represent a large array of languages, as evidence of the possibility of uniting the Latino community.

One such example in the United States is the pan-Indian movement. Beginning in the mid-20th century, members of different tribes came together emphasizing those traits shared by tribal groups across the continent as a foundation for a shared identity: supratribal American Indian collective identity. The supratribal, or pan-tribal identity underscores similarities, excluding the uniqueness of the cultural and ethnic diversity of each tribe within the umbrella category. It has been a target of some critics, but it functions with the aim of improving the welfare of the disparate groups facing similar challenges. Beyond cultural similarities, such groups share experiences that make their alignment strategic, regarding, for example, past discrimination and relations with the American federal government, similar experiences of displacement from native territory, and the threat of the loss of culture from modernization and the increase of urban lifestyles of its members.

In short, the concept of panethnicity in the North American context provides a critique of the immanent volitional nature of ethnic identity that is shared by both instrumentalist and primordialist accounts. It underscores not the choice that individuals have in belonging to an integrated culture but rather the coercive aspect of ethnic identity. Euro-Americans, according to Espiritu, can decide whether to enact their ethnicity or not. Nonwhite groups, on the contrary, do not have this privilege because ethnic identification is often imposed upon them. Panethnicity emerges from simplifications carried out by white Americans who do not distinguish the problematic boundaries that exist among ethnic minorities. However, the term also entails a protective dimension of proactive solidarity despite—and because of—the racial lumping.

KAZUKO SUZUKI

See also

Ethnicity; Hate Crimes in America; Model Minority Thesis; Native American; Race

Further Reading:

Cornell, Stephen. *The Return of the Native: American Indian Political Resurgence.* New York: Oxford University Press, 1988.

DiPietro, Stephanie M., and Robert J. Bursik Jr. "Studies of the New Immigration: The Dangers of Pan-Ethnic Classifications." *Annals of the American Academy of Political and Social Science* 641, no. 1 (2012): 247–67.

Espiritu, Yen Le. *Asian American Panethnicity: Bridging Institutions and Identities.* Philadelphia: Temple University Press, 1992.

Foner, Nancy, and George M. Fredrickson, eds. *Not Just Black and White: Historical and Contemporary Perspectives on Immigration, Race, and Ethnicity in the United States.* New York: Russell Sage, 2004.

Itzigsohn, Jose, and Carlow Dore-Cabral. "Competing Identities? Race, Ethnicity and Panethnicity among Dominicans in the United States." *Sociological Forum* 15, no. 2 (2000): 225–47.

Knoll, Benjamin R. "¿Compañero o Extranjero? Anti-Immigrant Nativism among Latino Americans." *Social Science Quarterly* 93, no. 4 (2012): 911–31.

Lopez, David, and Yen Espiritu. "Panethnicity in the United States: A Theoretical Framework." *Ethnic and Racial Studies* 13, no. 2 (1990): 198–224.

Nagel, Joane. *American Indian Ethnic Revival: Red Power and the Resurgence of Identity and Culture.* Oxford: Oxford University Press, 1996.

Okamoto, Dina G. "Toward a Theory of Panethnicity: Explaining Asian American Collective Action." *American Sociological Review* 68, no. 6 (2003): 811–42.

Palida, Felix M. *Latino Ethnic Consciousness: The Case of Mexican Americans and Puerto Ricans in Chicago.* Notre Dame, IN: Notre Dame University Press, 1985.

Pew Research Center. "When Labels Don't Fit." http://www.pewhispanic.org/2012/04/04/when-labels-dont-fit-hispanics-and-their-views-of-identity/ (accessed January 1, 2013).

Portes, Alejandro, and Rubén G. Rumbaut. *Legacies: The Story of the Immigrant Second Generation.* Berkeley: University of California Press, 2001.

Waters, Mary. *Black Identities: West Indian Immigrant Dreams and American Realities.* Cambridge, MA: Harvard University Press, 1999.

Panethnic Movements

Panethnicity is a created ethnic identity that draws together diverse groups of people who differ in their language, national origin, religion, culture, immigration history, and other facets of identity but who nonetheless view themselves as part of the same group. In many cases, this identity is first a categorization developed externally; for example, by the U.S. Census Bureau. At other times, the identity is created by groups of individuals themselves as they search for those with whom they identify. Examples of panethnic identities are Asian American, Latino/a, South Asian, or Caribbean. As is evidenced by these types of names, the groups that make up a panethnic identity can come from an area as broad as a continent or as small as a group of islands. They can speak many different languages or just a few. The most important point is that they belong to different specific ethnicities but have come together to form a common identity.

The creation of a panethnic identity involves the following elements: the construction of a common history and of a unified symbolic culture (often involving elements common across the participant ethnicities, such as food, religion, or language); the development of a political ideology that mobilizes participants; the organization of groups and organizations that represent the panethnic identity to the outside world (such as political action committees and campus student groups); and the recognition of the panethnic identity by the outside world (in many cases, this is an easy task, since the outside world is often the force to first apply the panethnic label). In many cases, it was necessary for particular descent groups to live in the United States for multiple generations before their members could reach beyond national memories of conflict with their new "partner" groups to panethnic identities. Of course, panethnic groups still face internal divisions over specific aspects of ethnic identity, histories of national conflict, gender, social class, and other factors.

Panethnic identities are largely political in nature, and this means that they are likely to act in a political way and to develop social movements around their identity. These movements are, in the broad sense, civil rights movements. They fight for political representation of their constituents, educational policies that help their constituents succeed, employment practices that do not discriminate against them, and public awareness of the issues and problems that they face. Choosing to employ panethnic definitions and identities in these movements has been helpful as it allows them to present, in their activism, a unified front and a face consistent with outsider definitions. The development of panethnic identities and panethnic movements was also an important precursor to the establishment of ethnic studies departments and student centers on campuses, as these departments and centers speak to wide groups of students rather than those descended from particular nations and backgrounds.

The particular demands and outcomes of different panethnic movements have, of course, varied. In addition, there are constant struggles within movements over how they will define themselves and who counts as a part of the movement. (For instance, should there be an Asian Pacific American movement and identity, an Asian American one, or an East Asian American and South Asian American duality?) Movements also struggle with one another over the limited resources provided by the wider society for dealing with their needs and the demands that they press. Finally, the gains that movements do make are not guaranteed to be permanent, as the continued reorganization and reassessment of various affirmative action programs can demonstrate.

MIKAILA MARIEL LEMONIK ARTHUR

Further Reading:

Ackah, William B. *Pan-Africanism: Exploring the Contradictions: Politics, Identity, and Development in Africa and the African Diaspora.* Brookfield, VT: Ashgate, 1999.

Espiritu, Yen Le. *Asian American Panethnicity: Bridging Institutions and Identities.* Philadelphia: Temple University Press, 1992.

Hertzberg, Hazel W. *The Search for an American Indian Identity: Modern Pan-Indian Movements.* Syracuse, NY: Syracuse University Press, 1971.

Morales, Ed. *Living in Spanglish: The Search for a New Latino Identity in America.* New York: St. Martin's Press, 2002.

Parks, Rosa (1913–2005)

Known as the "mother of the civil rights movement," Rosa Louise McCauley Parks is one of the most famous historical figures in American history. By refusing to surrender her seat to a white passenger on a segregated bus, Parks violated one of the many Jim Crow laws. Her actions and arrest served as the impetus for the Montgomery Bus Boycott.

On February 4, 1913, Rosa was born in Tuskegee, Alabama, to James and Leona McCauley. Reared and educated in rural Pine Level, Alabama, Rosa was known as a soft-spoken, intelligent student. She continued her education at Montgomery Industrial School for girls and Alabama State Teacher's College High School. However, due to several illnesses in the family, Rosa postponed graduation to help out at home. In 1932, she married local barber Raymond Parks and received her high school diploma two years later. In Montgomery, the couple worked together in the National Association for the Advancement of Colored People (NAACP). Parks served as the branch secretary and youth leader of the NAACP and worked as a seamstress in a downtown department store.

On December 1, 1955, the 43-year-old Parks boarded the city bus after work. Since all of the seats in the back were taken, Parks sat in the first row of the black section. At the next stop a white male passenger asked for Parks's seat. She refused to move. The bus driver ordered Parks to move and threatened to call the cops. Again, she refused to move and was arrested. Parks never thought she would make history that day; her only desire was "to know once and for all what rights I had as a human being."

Parks became the symbol of hundreds of thousands of African Americans who had suffered as second-class citizens. Her actions served as the spark for the Montgomery Bus Boycott. The NAACP and Women's Political Council had organized long before this incident but had waited for such an event to rally their cause around. Only days after Parks's arrest, the boycott of the Montgomery bus system began.

Shortly after her arrest, Parks lost her job in the department store, and two years later, Parks and her husband moved to Detroit, Michigan. For more than 20 years, Parks worked as an assistant to Michigan's U.S. congressman John Conyers. In 1987, Parks cofounded the Rosa & Raymond Parks Institute for Self Development, which focuses its efforts on encouraging and leading children to reach their fullest potential.

As an activist, lecturer, and writer, Parks continued to inspire thousands of Americans. In addition to the 43 honorary doctorate degrees, Parks also received the NAACP Spingarn Medal, UAW's Social Justice Award, the Martin Luther King Jr. Non-Violent Peace Prize, the Medal of Freedom, and the Congressional Gold Medal, to name a few. The strong, soft-spoken woman whose courage changed the nation died at the age of 92.

EMILY HESS

See also

Montgomery Bus Boycott

Further Reading:

Brinkley, Douglas. *Rosa Parks*. New York: Viking, 2000.
Crawford, Vicki L., Jacqueline Anne Rouse, and Barbara Woods, eds. *Women in the Civil Rights Movement: Trailblazers and Torchbearers, 1941–1965*. Brooklyn, NY: Carlson Publishing, 1990.
Hine, Darlene Clark, Elsa Barkley Brown, and Rosalyn Terborg-Penn, eds. *Black Women in America: An Historical Encyclopedia*. Brooklyn, NY: Carlson Publishing, 1992.
Parks, Rosa, with Gregory Reed. *Rosa Parks: The Faith, the Hope, and the Heart of a Woman Who Changed a Nation*. Grand Rapids, MI: Zondervan, 1994.

Passing

The common perception of passing is of a light-complexioned African American assuming the identity of a white person. Under the conditions of Jim Crow, passing was an opportunity to gain social, political, and economic benefits afforded by white supremacist ideology. This phenomenon occurred regularly during slavery when mulatto slaves wanted to escape or prevent capture once free. In 1848, for instance, William and Ellen Craft devised an elaborate passing scheme when they ran away from a Georgia plantation.

Ellen was light enough to pass as a white man; she wore the disguise of a sickly gentleman, accompanied by "his" male slave (her husband William) traveling to the North. They figured that it would be more believable for Ellen to appear as a white man rather than face the impropriety of a Southern white woman accompanied by a black man. The Crafts arrived in Philadelphia undetected, and their story was later documented in *Running a Thousand Miles for Freedom* (1860). In places like New Orleans with large populations of free mulattos, many of them could or did easily assimilate into white society throughout the 19th century. Such accounts of racial passing were less frequent during the Reconstruction era (1863–1877), when more liberal circumstances provided less motivation for passing throughout the South. African Americans, for the first time in American history, enjoyed greater political freedom than ever before. However, Reconstruction ended when Southern states that were readmitted to the Union sought revenge for losing the Civil War and the radical Republican policies that destroyed and made amends for slavery. Segregation was codified and enforced as a systematic form of racial oppression, hence the birth of Jim Crow. Many African Americans who passed for white then did so to avoid the hardships of racial discrimination, prejudice, and often violence. Essentially, they could live as free people in a democratic society. Their choices for education, housing, shopping, employment, transportation, and even entertainment would not be limited by their black racial identity. On the contrary, the chance to acquire equal rights and social privileges then reserved for whites only seemed worth the risk.

Passing required life-altering changes based on the kind and length of the experience. Some individuals might have passed involuntarily if their mixed-race heritage was unknown; they could have been born under such pretenses if their family kept the secret of passing (which they often did). This is the sort of racial tragedy dramatized in fiction, though it occurred often in real life. Others severed ties completely from their black family to live a solitary white life. This separation of family or loss of communal relationships could have been devastating consequences for passing. The disconnection from familiar environments and people could symbolize "passing" as the death of a former life. While investigating race relations in the deep South during the 1930s, sociologists explained this kind of passing as social death and rebirth. When the truth was revealed or while passing, an individual could likely have experienced psychological conflicts about identifying with either race. Those who fully assimilated, however, may not have suffered emotional distress. Some even married "pure" whites to further dilute their bloodline. The fear of producing "black" offspring could then prevent the passer from having any children at all. So having a white complexion alone did not guarantee the passer success.

The discovery of an individual's true identity was a foremost concern when the "one drop rule" was used to define blackness. Having a traceable black ancestry (or any "black blood") was enough to classify a mixed-race person "black" despite the dominant white racial traits inherited. Descriptions of biracial individuals as "near-white" or "white Negroes" suggest racial impurities or an invisible blackness that many whites feared. Black-to-white passers were therefore complicit in their attempts to assimilate under white surveillance, especially in the Jim Crow South. Racial ambiguity threatened segregation and sensitized white Southerners to maintain the status quo. They proclaimed an ability to detect any passers with visible or invisible signs of blackness. If the average African American developed a double consciousness as theorized by W.E.B. Du Bois in *The Souls of Black Folk* (1903), passers were even more sensitive to racism. The "peculiar sensation" of "always looking at one's self through the eyes of others" was fundamental to their concealment. Du Bois challenged segregationists' reliance on ocular proof of black inferiority with his American Negro Exhibit at the 1900 Paris Exposition. Many of the photographs on display featured African Americans of questionable racial origins: pale complexions, light eyes, thin noses, and various hair textures. These images of exceptional blacks proved that they could "pass" as model citizens and undermine white peoples' perception of blackness.

Despite close racial scrutiny, the "great age of passing" occurred at the height of Jim Crow during the late 19th and early 20th centuries. Thousands crossed the color line to defy legal segregation, social restrictions, and geographical boundaries. Since the majority of African Americans lived in the South, those wanting to pass would migrate to the North, where they could become "new people" without the burden of race. Or, they could take advantage of the opportunity to live a double life. Alex Manly, a mulatto journalist

from North Carolina, fled the South during a race riot in 1898. When he relocated to Philadelphia, he divided his time working as a white man during the day and returned home to his black family in the evening. He eventually decided to live as a black man permanently, though he could not find suitable employment to support his family as such. When passing proved to be a costly venture, other alternatives became attractive options for circumventing the race problem. Some African Americans passed for European immigrants, who would often receive better treatment upon arrival to this country than black people in America. French, Italian, Spanish, and other foreign ethnicities were ideal covers used to explain the variations of colored complexions among African Americans resulting from generations of miscegenation. To appear more convincing, passers adopting a foreign ethnicity would even speak in a native tongue when approached by suspicious whites. Mary Church Terrell, a leading civil rights activist and black feminist, would often pass for white inadvertently or on purpose as she traveled through the South on lecture tours during the late 19th and early 20th centuries. Terrell spoke several languages and easily passed for a European native as well as a cultured, white Southern belle when necessary to avoid traveling in filthy Jim Crow railway cars.

Whether passing on a temporary or permanent basis, an individual who passed for white during the Jim Crow era risked their personal safety. There were (or could have been) violent repercussions after discovery. "Separate but equal" policies of segregation tried to determine the limits of interracial mixing in public spaces. Yet, the culture of segregation depended on the "myth" of absolute racial differences, and passing violated the metaphorical and legal limits of segregation. Cases of mistaken identity did occur when African Americans with Caucasian features did not appear "black." Such individuals were often treated with dignity and respect by whites who were unaware of the racial stigma that defined the passer's blackness. Charles Chesnutt was a popular light-skinned African American novelist who experienced life on the color line in this way. He withheld his racial identity with the release of early works to avoid racial censure and received critical reviews on the basis of his artistry alone and not his ancestry. When done as a conscious or deliberate act, however, others lived as a spy crossing racial boundaries. These African Americans sat or ate in the "white-only" sections of trains, theaters, and restaurants without detection. Walter White, for example, was an investigative reporter for the National Association for the Advancement of Colored People (NAACP) during the 1920s. With light skin, blue eyes, and wavy blond hair, the natural disguise White wore to investigate lynchings throughout the South protected him. His subversive act of passing could have easily made him a victim of the same crimes that he witnessed and reported on in *The Crisis*. Years earlier as a young boy, White and his father survived the 1906 Atlanta race riots also by passing as white men until they reached the safety of their home.

African American writers have often fictionalized passing narratives to depict Jim Crow race relations. In her 1892 novel *Iola Leroy*, Frances Harper's mulatto protagonist passes as a white woman until her black heritage is revealed after the death of her parents. The novel unfolds as Iola learns to survive as a "black" woman facing racial discrimination and prejudice. She decides not to pass as a white woman because of her familial relations and racial obligations. Both her and her brother devote their lives to "uplifting the race" as they identify with all African Americans in the struggle for civil equality. Their commitment to become race leaders instead of "race traitors" is a decision made by real mulattos like Walter White with his NAACP activism. Charles Chesnutt's novels often depict mixed-race or "tragic mulatto" characters that experience biological and social conflicts due to their "warring blood" or inherited racial traits. Those that do not succumb to a tragic end (death, desertion, exile, etc.) cross the color line and disappear into white society. As art imitates life, Chesnutt's stories explore the options for passing presented to light-skinned African Americans who seek the benefits of the privileged class. In *The Autobiography of an Ex-Colored Man* (1912), James Weldon Johnson examines the racial paradox in America through an anonymous protagonist who passes for both white and black: "I know that I am playing with fire, and I feel the thrill which accompanies that most fascinating pastime; and, back of it all, I think I find a sort of savage and diabolical desire to gather up all the little tragedies of my life, and turn them into a practical joke on society." Using social realism to captivate his readers, Johnson's novel was a successful literary hoax initially since many people believed the autobiography was a truthful account of passing. The

republication of the novel with Johnson's authorship finally acknowledged appeared in 1927.

Like Johnson, Nella Larsen, Jessie Redmon Fauset, and George Schuyler were other African American novelists that continued to develop the theme of passing during the Harlem Renaissance. Works by Larsen and Fauset are populated by characters with mixed-race ancestries and thus the burden of race. Larsen presents the psychological trauma of mulatto women in her 1929 novel about complex racial, class, and gender identities. Aptly titled *Passing*, the work explores the motivations and consequences of Irene Redfield and Clare Kendry passing as socialites on both sides of the color line. Schuyler's *Black No More* (1931) provides a satirical solution to America's race problem by interrogating the power of whiteness. The plot dramatizes racism when black people are transformed into white people via a commercially successful whitening process invented by a black scientist.

White writers like William Faulkner also experimented with the passing theme. He created mulatto characters in works like *Absalom, Absalom* (1936) and *Intruder in the Dust* (1948) that challenged white Southerners' abilities to sense race under segregation. His Mississippi settings were ideal to dramatize many white Southerners' racial paranoia. Not only were light-skinned blacks the target of bigots, but liberal whites sympathetic to blacks' civil rights were also labeled "white niggers" like those in Faulkner's fiction.

Reverse passing of "mulattos" with white skin and black behavior made for controversial headlines in 20th-century divorce cases. The scandalous Rhinelander trial of 1924, as detailed in *Love on Trial: An American Scandal in Black and White* (2002), captured the nation's obsession with racial purity and segregation culture. The marriage of a white New York socialite, Leonard Rhinelander, to a working-class domestic, Alice Jones, was annulled when the husband accused his wife of not being completely white. Jones did have mysterious racial origins, though her family did not try to pass for white. Ultimately, her class status proved more of a moral transgression than the scandalous interracial affair staged for the public. Other examples of white-to-black passers' moral failures were not uncommon in multiracial families. "Pure" white siblings would identify as "black" to keep their family relations with black half-siblings intact. Illegitimate whites would also identify as "black" to avoid the stigma of being born a bastard.

Recently, genealogical research has proven how generations of "white" Americans are actually descendants of light-skinned African Americans who passed for various reasons. Attempts to untangle ancestral roots have resulted in revised historical accounts of slavery, fractured memoirs, and emotional family reunions. Edward Ball, a white descendant of prominent South Carolina slaveowners, documents his tedious research into family records in two books, *Slaves in the Family* (1998) and *The Sweet Hell Inside: The Rise of an Elite Black Family in the Segregated South* (2002). In *Life on the Color Line: The True Story of a White Boy Who Discovered He Was Black* (1996), Gregory Howard Williams recalls his coming-of-age during segregation. Shirley Taylor Haizlip likewise reconstructs the difficult past relations of her multiracial family in *The Sweeter the Juice: A Family Memoir in Black and White* (1995); it chronicles the lives of two sisters who were separated for nearly 70 years as each lived in different worlds. The publication of these works and numerous others signals a sort of revival of passing narratives since the demise of Jim Crow.

While the authors present intriguing exposés of passing, first-hand accounts of passing rarely exist because of the fear of discovery. Anonymous testimonies were published only when necessary as political propaganda. Many "post-passing" narratives are only now being studied as evidence of the pressures to adapt to racist society; these stories and similar reports about the "past" trend of passing were published in popular black periodicals like *Ebony* and *Jet* during the 1950s. A notable example is John Howard Griffin's *Black Like Me* (1960), his autobiography of becoming a "black" man within the last decade of Jim Crow. Like Walter White, Griffin's mission as a white "spy" was to investigate black life in the Deep South and report his findings to promote racial understanding. His white-to-black passing appealed to American racism by dissecting America's own "white" consciousness. Griffin's timely publication appeared on the cusp of a new era in the history of passing. After all, black-to-white passing at least had become "passé" as the civil rights and Black Power movements redefined blackness in positive ways. The racial pride anthem "Black is beautiful," for instance, proclaimed a new generation of African Americans' acceptance of darker skin complexion and validated black culture in general.

Sherita L. Johnson

See also
"Acting White"; Cosmetics; Skin Lightening

Further Reading:
"The Adventures of a Near-White." *Independent* 75 (1913): 373–76.

Ginsberg, Elaine K. *Passing and the Fictions of Identity*. Durham, NC: Duke University Press, 1996.

Hale, Grace Elizabeth. *Making Whiteness: The Culture of Segregation in the South, 1890–1940*. New York: Vintage, 1998.

Sollors, Werner. *Neither Black nor White, Yet Both: Thematic Explorations of Interracial Literature*. Cambridge, MA: Harvard University Press, 1997.

Wald, Gayle. *Crossing the Line: Racial Passing in Twentieth-Century U.S. Literature and Culture*. Durham, NC: Duke University Press, 2000.

Williamson, Joel. *New People: Miscegenation and Mulattoes in the United States*. Baton Rouge: Louisiana State University Press, 1995.

Passing of the Great Race, The

Madison Grant's *The Passing of the Great Race* (1916), was a best-selling book claiming to trace the origins of the United States to the deeds of a heroic Nordic race. Despite the wave of antiblack riots that swept the nation following World War I, many white academics and intellectuals nevertheless believed that the white race was in danger of being overwhelmed by the darker races of the globe. Grant's book argued that only a stringent application of eugenics (forced sterilization and imprisonment of those whose genes were deemed defective) and immigration restriction would preserve what he termed the "Great Race." Historians have long disagreed about whether Grant's book represents the last gasp of 19th-century racial "science," or is best seen as an adaptation of racist ideology to the changing conditions of the 20th century.

The Passing of the Great Race became a best-seller because it both vastly simplified racist science and applied that science ruthlessly and viciously. In the late 19th century, white European and American intellectuals had argued for the existence of literally hundreds of races, based on a conception of race that combined physical appearance, language, history, heredity, behavior, intellectual ability, and so on.

European whites, they claimed, were at the apex of a vast racial and developmental hierarchy. Antiracist critics of this science, like pioneering anthropologist Franz Boas, had proved that the physical markers of race were notoriously inaccurate as scientific tools, and argued that the critical elements of perceived race difference—language, history, and culture—were not related at all to biology or heredity. Grant's *Passing of the Great Race* attacked these arguments by inverting them. In place of the myriad white races of Europe, however, Grant insisted that there were three: Nordics, or Northern and Western Europeans, including the English, Dutch, and German forebears of Grant's own illustrious family; Alpines, most prevalent in southeastern Europe and Russia; and Mediterraneans, who ringed the coast of the Mediterranean Sea. But culture, far from being the essence of race, was instead merely an effect of racial heredity. Grant asserted that qualities such as intellectual ability, cunning, honor, and virtue were inescapably biological characteristics, imprinted in the genes and passed down from parents to children. These most important racial characteristics were merely manifested in physical appearance, history, and individual behavior. Nordics were the Great Race in Grant's title who had wrested America from Native Americans and extended their imperial dominions across the world in an inevitable working-out of their innate superiority. Since, Grant argued, race was first and foremost biological and inherited, only racially pure offspring would retain the characteristics of their exalted forebears. Based on a common, but distorted, version of Gregor Mendel's experiments with hybridization of pea plants, Grant claimed that racially hybrid people reverted to the inferior type. Thus, he famously asserted, "the cross between a white man and a Negro is a Negro" (1916). The United States, he believed, suffered from a tragic lack of race consciousness, that is, an acknowledgement that Americans' Nordic heritage was primarily responsible for the conquest, settlement, and creation of the republic. As a result, "race suicide" threatened the "Great Race" and the nation it created. Degeneration of racial stock through unregulated immigration and cross-breeding had to be met, Grant argued, with a stringent program of immigration restrictions and eugenics—forced sterilization of individuals deemed by Grant and his allies as possessing defective racial characteristics, and breeding of the remaining members of the Great Race.

As ridiculous as Grant's ideas are, their influence on, for example, the concepts of race found in Nazi party ideology is chilling. In the American context, Grant's arguments can be seen to some extent as an elaboration and extension of the typical arguments used to rationalize racial violence: that lynching, for example, was necessary to protect the virtue of white women. But, at the time *The Passing of the Great Race* was published, only the beginnings of the massive migration of African Americans to northern cities could be observed. Grant himself was far more concerned with restricting the immigration and reproduction of Alpines and Mediterraneans in the North. However, Grant's intellectual scheme, which ultimately concluded that class differences in America were merely an effect of racial differences, provided an important transition for concepts of race challenged by black migration and the 1919 race riots that accompanied the Great Migration. Scholars have long seen the period around the 1919 riots as one of critical changes in academic and popular racial thought, but have disagreed about what changed and why the changes are important. Some writers have argued that Grant's assertion of race as primarily biological was already out of step with ascendant academic claims of race as primarily cultural. In their view, in 1916 academics were already rejecting the vicious conclusions and policies Grant and his allies advocated, and arguing for a new, tolerant view of racial difference that would ultimately dominate the 20th century. Other scholars have pointed to Grant's continuing role in both public life and academia as a sign that his beliefs were still important justifications for racial violence, and which continued to influence violent groups like the Ku Klux Klan well into the 20th century.

Jonathan S. Coit

See also

American Literature and Racism; *Birth of a Nation, The*; White Supremacy

Further Reading:

Grant, Madison. *The Passing of the Great Race; or, The Racial Basis of European History.* New York: C. Scribner, 1916.

Guterl, Matthew Pratt. *The Color of Race in America, 1900–1940.* Cambridge, MA: Harvard University Press, 2001.

Higham, John. *Strangers in the Land: Patterns of American Nativism, 1860–1925.* Rutgers, NJ: Rutgers University Press, 1984.

Patriot Act of 2001

The approval and passage of the USA Patriot Act on October 26, 2001, a wide-ranging piece of legislation centered upon national security, had a tremendous impact upon the structure and relations of the United States government, substantially expanding numerous law-enforcement practices pertaining to surveillance, interrogation, detection, and prosecution, among others. It likewise carried significant consequences in the areas of higher education, scientific research, library usage, immigration, and finance and banking. The initial drafting of the bill stemmed from a wave of executive actions on the part of President George W. Bush, for whom the catastrophic happenings of September 11, 2011, demanded a resolute and appropriately far-reaching national security strategy. On September 12, 2001, the President initiated the war on terrorism, promising that the "United States of America will use all our resources to conquer this enemy." By September 20, Bush had urged Congress for war powers to invade Iraq and thus engage promptly in the fight against terror and had also declared war on Afghanistan. In just a few weeks, on October 7, 2001, the opening military offensive of the global war on terror was executed. By October 26, the first domestic piece of antiterrorism legislation had been signed into law. This legislation, officially titled, "Uniting and Strengthening America by Providing Appropriate Tools Required to Intercept and Obstruct Terrorism Act of 2001" (hereafter, "The Patriot Act") was set forth to pursue this purpose: "To deter and punish terrorist acts in the United States and around the world, to enhance law enforcement investigatory tools, and for other purposes." This legislation was part of a larger, six-pronged, national security strategy that included the following provisions for action: (1) the execution of preemptive strikes against terrorist targets; (2) the identification and development of cooperative relationships with other nations that may serve as allies in antiterrorist efforts; (3) the sanctioning of states that serve as safe havens for terrorist organizations (e.g., Libya) and use of measures to freeze the economic assets of terrorist organizations (e.g., Hamas); (4) the large-scale cultural project of emphasizing a democratic civil society as a matter of choice in order to neutralize the circulation of Islamic fundamentalist extremism; (5) the establishment of a superordinary national security body, the Homeland Security Department, which may coordinate counterterrorist and homeland security functions

President George W. Bush signs the USA Patriot Act during a ceremony in the White House on October 26, 2001. The law was passed in response to the terrorist attacks of September 11, 2001, and gives intelligence and law enforcement agencies unprecedented authority to conduct terror investigations. (White House)

as single, yet multidimensional, unit; and finally, (6) to expand the powers of homeland security officials and law enforcement agents with little oversight from Congress and the court system (Wong 2007: 3). To many observers, such strategy and tactics evoked memories of other sweeping governmental interventions that resulted in the unethical surveillance and even attack of key African American civil rights leaders, including Malcolm X. Both a lack of governmental protection and racially motivated investigations have been associated with the deaths of Medgar Evers and Martin Luther King, Jr.

Easier Said Than Done: A Failed Patriot Act Program

The massive institutional upheaval that the Patriot Act sought to achieve placed considerable demand for producing adequately trained personnel and smooth institutional relations, two elements that could hardly be taken for granted. For instance, consider the consequences of the Patriot Act's call for renewed efforts at tracking foreign visitors. The Patriot Act mandated the formation of the Student and Exchange Visitor Information System (SEVIS) by January 30, 2003. SEVIS was configured to electronically track and monitor international students in the United States in a real-time, paperless, and relatively inexpensive fashion. However, the level of administrative training, both on the side of the Department of Homeland Security and colleges or universities, turned out to be quite time consuming to both plan and execute. Moreover, many administrators and academics thought it was antithetical to the spirit of the democratic, open-university culture to embrace an extensive student tracking system. As a result of a lack of institutional fit, the program never came to fruition.

Given the sheer scale of institutional resources required to implement this strategy, it is not surprising to discover that many challenges and difficulties attend the work of homeland security at every stage, from simple personnel training and organizational relations to the actual carrying out of local law enforcement tactics. More localized security tactics and practices have stirred fiery debate and grassroots protest. The impact on Muslims and Arabs, along with other persons who may be found "guilty by association" due to certain physical features, has been substantial since the passage of the Patriot Act. Many Muslims were compelled to submit to foreign registration, airport profiling, and immigration detention (Wong 2007: 190). The Patriot Act allows for the monitoring, detention, investigation, and deportation of Muslims without due process of law and hence in violation of fundamental rights. These unjust actions, unfortunately, have been rather disproportionately focused on Arabs and Muslims. As Cainkar notes, "[o]f the roughly twenty policies and initiatives implemented in the first twelve months after

9/11, fifteen explicitly targeted Arabs and Muslims" (2004: 245–48). The strategy constructed to target these persons was not, by any standard, light or lax in its capacities. Attorney General John Ashcroft, relying upon the Patriot Act, sought for technological development that would allow for total information control (which aimed to hide government actions from public disclosure) and total information awareness about "the enemy's position," which enabled the gathering of intelligence about individuals and groups by means of invasive techniques without a warrant (Wong 2007: 206–9). In a move that surely fed upon existing racial and ethnic tensions, Ashcroft also initiated a local counterterrorism system that called upon citizens and informants to closely observe neighbors and report them. Fortunately this system never materialized. Nevertheless, the FBI "special interest" dragnet of terrorism suspects and the "special registration" system directed at nonimmigrants carried out many secret operations that prosecuted persons from numerous Near Eastern and Middle Eastern nations without proper charges, evidence processing, or legal representation. The passage of the Patriot Act introduced and amplified the increasingly thorny matter of distinguishing between very reasonable concerns for safety and the undermining of democratic freedoms, along with the perpetuation of racism or prejudice regarding specific minority communities in a country with too many experiences of racial and ethnic conflict.

GABRIEL SANTOS

See also

Ideological Racism; Islamic Fundamentalism; Islamophobia

Further Reading:

Cainkar, Louise. "Post 9/11 Domestic Policies Affecting U.S. Arabs and Muslims: A Brief Review." *Comparative Studies of South Asia, Africa, & the Middle East* 24 (2004): 245–48.

Collins, Dan. "Bush To Congress: Give Me Force." *CBS News*, September 20, 2002. http://www.cbsnews.com/stories/2002/09/20/world/main522673.shtml.

"Remarks by the President in Photo Opportunity with the National Security Team." The White House. September 12, 2001. http://georgewbush-whitehouse.archives.gov/news/releases/2001/09/20010912-4.html.

Sales, Nathan Alexander. "Mending Walls: Information Sharing after the USA Patriot Act." *Texas Law Review* 88 (2010): 1795–854.

Sinnar, Shirin. "Patriotic or Unconstitutional? The Mandatory Detention of Aliens under the USA Patriot Act." *Stanford Law Review* 55 (2003): 1419–56.

Transcript of President Bush's Address. *CNN*, September 21, 2001. http://archives.cnn.com/2001/US/09/20/gen.bush .transcript/.

Wong, Kam C. *Impact of USA Patriot Act on American Society: An Evidence-Based Assessment.* Happauge, NY: Nova Science Publishers, 2007.

Peltier, Leonard (b. 1944)

Leonard Peltier is an American Indian Movement (AIM) activist who has served three decades of two consecutive life sentences in the federal prison system following his conviction for killing Federal Bureau of Investigation agents Jack Coler and Ronald Williams on the Pine Ridge Reservation during a shoot-out in June 1975. Many people believe that Peltier was wrongly convicted on falsified evidence, and he is widely considered a symbol of aboriginal peoples' political struggles worldwide, especially in the United States and Canada. Peltier also has become an artist and author while in prison. Peltier is considered a political prisoner by Amnesty International and other human-rights advocates around the world. The United Nations High Commissioner on Human Rights, the Dalai Lama, and the European Parliament, among others, have all called for his release.

A Lakota and Anishinabe, Peltier was born on September 12, 1944. His struggles began early, growing up in poverty on the Turtle Mountain Reservation in North Dakota. He witnessed U.S. government policies that forced Native families off their reservations and into cities and that caused the withdrawal of essential services from those who chose to remain. In this climate, Peltier became active in organizing and protesting for the rights of his people. By the early 1970s, he was strongly involved with AIM.

In 1972, Peltier took part in the Trail of Broken Treaties, a demonstration requesting the U.S. government to investigate treaty violations over the last 100 years. When met with a negative response from the Bureau of Indian Affairs (BIA), the demonstrators occupied the BIA Washington, D.C., headquarters for a week. The result was the promise of a hearing on AIM-initiated grievances. Another result was intense FBI scrutiny of the occupation's leaders, including Russell Means, Dennis Banks, and Peltier.

Through AIM's activities, Peltier came to the Pine Ridge Indian Reservation in South Dakota, where the 1975 shoot-out occurred. By the time AIM activists arrived, circumstances on the Pine Ridge Reservation included extreme poverty, violence, and fear.

Richard Wilson had been elected tribal chairman on the Pine Ridge Reservation in 1972 and had since been in conflict with the traditional Oglala people. Wilson represented big business, and he ignored demands and rights of traditional people on the reservation. Wilson's policies reduced the people to extreme poverty and fear. He enforced his regime and economic policies by misusing federal money to employ a personal police force, which he trained, armed, and deployed to control the residents of the Pine Ridge Reservation. This force called itself Guardians of the Oglala Nation, or the GOON squad. This squad committed violent acts of intimidation, violence, and outright murder against the traditional Indian people on the reservation. Despite the presence of FBI agents on the reservation at that time, the murders went largely uninvestigated. Appeals to the BIA also were ignored. In fact, the U.S. federal government provided funding for the GOON squad.

In 1973, traditional people at Pine Ridge asked AIM for help, and approximately 300 traditionals, AIM members, and supporters occupied the village of Wounded Knee, South Dakota, in protest of Wilson and his GOON squad. The background to this occupation included the historical relevance of the site, where in 1890 the U.S. Cavalry massacred 300 people, including many women and children. Under siege by the FBI and BIA, the occupiers of Wounded Knee in 1973 lasted 71 days, until U.S. government officials agreed to investigate conditions on the Pine Ridge Reservation. The investigation never occurred, but many AIM members were charged with various legal offenses related to the occupation.

Between 1973 and 1976, at least 66 people died violently at Pine Ridge (other deaths may not have been documented). The FBI is charged with investigating major crimes on U.S. Indian reservations, but these deaths were only lightly investigated, if at all. The majority of victims were members or supporters of AIM and the traditional Oglala people. During this time, the murder rate on the Pine Ridge Reservation was the highest in the country.

In 1974, Means ran for tribal chairman against Wilson. In a climate of stress and fear, with allegations of rampant fraud, Wilson narrowly won the election. The BIA refused to oversee the election or to investigate it for irregularities and fraud.

In this context, the traditional council of chiefs asked AIM to provide protection, alleging a lack of legal protection from Wilson and the GOON squad. A small group of AIM members responded, including Peltier, who arrived in March 1975. The AIM activists and local traditionalists set up a spiritual camp on the property of Cecilia and Harry Jumping Bull, who had been constantly under threat from the GOONs.

A month before the shoot-out occurred at Jumping Bull's, the FBI, aware of AIM's presence, increased its own presence in and around the reservation. On June 26, 1975, FBI Agents Williams and Coler entered the Jumping Bull compound following a red pickup truck, and gunfire erupted. During the firefight, the agents were killed. A Native American man, Joe Stuntz, also died that day; his murder was never investigated. By the end of the day, FBI and other law enforcement agencies had occupied the reservation and the AIM members involved, including Peltier, had fled the area.

Two months later, a car carrying Michael Anderson, Rob Robideau, Norman Charles, and others exploded. The FBI found a gun in the wreckage that it claimed was the murder weapon used against Coler and Williams. In November 1975, Dino Butler, Rob Robideau, Peltier, and a youth, Jimmy Eagle, were indicted for the murders of Williams and Coler. At this time Peltier was in Canada fighting extradition. Butler and Robideau were tried together and acquitted. The jury concluded Butler and Robideau acted in self-defense against the paramilitary assault on Pine Ridge by the FBI. Charges against Jimmy Eagle were dropped, and the full force of governmental prosecution was then directed at Peltier, who was later extradited from Canada, to stand trial before an all-white jury in U.S. District Court, Fargo, North Dakota, in April of 1977.

Preparing its case against Peltier, the FBI coerced Myrtle Poor Bear into signing three false affidavits that directly implicated him in the killing of the two agents. Later, the FBI admitted that Poor Bear was not even on the scene the day of the killings.

Peltier was found guilty of two counts of murder and sentenced to two consecutive life sentences. The trial, presided over by Judge Paul Benson, was based on false evidence in the Poor Bear affidavits, on a bullet that was incorrectly connected to the alleged murder weapon, and on testimony given by other witnesses under coercion from the FBI.

At the trial, the prosecution presented 15 days of evidence, and the defense was limited to six days. Peltier's defense team had the same evidence as was presented in the Bulter and Robideau trial indicating FBI misconduct but was not permitted to present most of it to the jury. Peltier also was not allowed to assert self-defense. Peltier's appeals to the Eighth Circuit Court and the U.S. Supreme Court were both denied. In 1993, even in the face of evidence of FBI misconduct and the admission of one of the prosecutors that the government does not know who killed the agents, the Eighth Circuit Court denied Peltier's appeal a second time.

With the assistance of Bobby Garcia, Dallas Thundershield, and Roque Dueñas, Peltier escaped from Lompoc federal prison in July of 1979. Thundershield was killed during the escape, and Garcia and Peltier were captured six days later. At his escape trial, Judge Lawrence Lydick prohibited Peltier from presenting evidence of his reasons for fleeing prison, and Peltier was sentenced for the maximum of seven years for escape and possession of a weapon. Garcia was sentenced to five years. Garcia was found dead in his cell a year later, and Roque Dueñas disappeared in a fishing accident.

Many who have studied the Peltier case claim to this day that Peltier was wrongly convicted and is thus a political prisoner. In 2000, former President Bill Clinton was rumored to have considered granting clemency that sparked protest outside the White House; he did not grant or deny clemency. In 2009, former President George W. Bush denied Peltier's plea for clemency. He is considered an important American Indian leader who fought to protect the rights of his people, as well as a symbol of the ongoing oppression of American Indian people at the hands of the U.S. federal government. Peltier continues to serve a prison sentence at Leavenworth Prison in Kansas.

BARRY M. PRITZKER

See also

American Indian Movement (AIM); Bureau of Indian Affairs; Red Power Movement

Further Reading:

Johansen, Bruce, and Roberto Maestas. *Wasi'chu: The Continuing Indian Wars*. New York: Monthly Review Press, 1979.

Matthiessen, Peter. *In the Spirit of Crazy Horse: The Story of Leonard Peltier and the FBI's War on the American Indian Movement*. New York: Penguin, 1992.

Messerschmidt, Jim. *The Trial of Leonard Peltier*. Boston: South End Press, 1983.

Peltier, Leonard. *Prison Writings: My Life Is My Sundance*. New York: St. Martin's Press, 1999.

Philadelphia (Pennsylvania) Riot of 1964

Two weeks after President Lyndon Johnson signed the Civil Rights Act of 1964 in the presence of Dr. Martin Luther King, Jr., racially motivated riots exploded in several northeastern cities, including New York City (July 18–23); Rochester, New York (July 24–25); Jersey City (August 2–4); Paterson (August 11–13); Elizabeth, New Jersey (August 11–13); and Chicago, Illinois (August 16–17). From August 28–30, 1964, Philadelphia erupted in violence and looting in response to the arrest and rumored death of Odessa Bradford in the predominantly black ghetto of North Philadelphia, marking a downturn in Philadelphia's population size, economic development efforts, and national reputation.

On the evening of August 28, 1964, Odessa Bradford's car stalled at 23rd Street and Cecil B. Moore, formerly Columbia Avenue. Two police officers urged her to move the vehicle out of the way of traffic; however, unable to comply because the car was disabled, an argument began between Bradford and police officers, one white and one black. The officers attempted to remove her from the vehicle as a crowd gathered. One man, whose identity is unknown, attempted to help Bradford, but was also arrested with her. Rumors that Bradford and her would-be protector had been killed proliferated throughout the surrounding neighborhood and a riot ensued. Blacks, in a reversal, threw rocks from inside their apartments and, on the street, physically challenged police officers outright. Outnumbered, the Philadelphia Police Department was forced to retreat. Over the next two days, the North Philadelphia neighborhood surrounding Temple University was battered and looted by thousands of people. When the riot officially ended, more than 300 people were injured, close to 800 had been arrested, and over 220 stores and businesses were damaged or permanently devastated. In addition to demonstrating the level of racial unrest in Philadelphia, the Bradford incident and the riot that followed mark the beginning of significant demographic, economic, political, and social changes in Philadelphia.

By 1970, in North Philadelphia, which extends to the Olney, East and West Oak Lane, and Mount Airy sections of the city, a considerable change in population had begun. The city's overall population dropped below 2 million as the city lost over 53,000 residents, most of them white. Blacks, who migrated from other parts of the city, suburban slums, and Southern states, such as Virginia, Maryland, and Delaware, moved into homes sold, abandoned, or rented by whites in the North Philadelphia area. Whites moved to nearby and budding Bucks, Chester, and Montgomery counties, and as their employers followed, the city suffered an economic recession from which it has yet to recover. Although the 1964 race riots in North Philadelphia are not solely blamed for the shifts in population or the economic downturn of the city, the incident is historically noted for encouraging white majority voters to support Police Commissioner Frank L. Rizzo in his first run for mayor in 1971. Rizzo was known for not only leading Philadelphia politics with an iron hand, but also for being quick to use force when confronting blacks in the city. It was under his leadership as police commissioner that Bradford was arrested and the 1964 riot ensued, and it was under his mayoral administration that reported incidents of police brutality against Philadelphia's black residents dramatically increased.

By 2004, blacks were not only the racial majority of Philadelphia, but John F. Street, a black man, was in his second term as mayor. In the North Philadelphia neighborhood in which Bradford and residents confronted police in what was argued to be black self-defense, Temple University has spearheaded a new growth of businesses, and a large portion of housing in the area has been rebuilt.

ELLESIA ANN BLAQUE

See also

Civil Rights Act of 1964; Race Riots in America. Documents: The Report on the Memphis Riots of May 1866 (July 25, 1866); Account of the Riots in East St. Louis, Illinois (July 1917); The Cook County Coroner's Report Regarding the 1919 Chicago Race Riots (1919); A Southern Black Woman's Letter Regarding the Recent Riots in Chicago and Washington (November 1919); The Final Report of the Grand Jury on the Tulsa Race Riot (June 25, 1921); Testimony from *Laney v. United States* Describing Events during the Washington, D.C., Riot of July 1919 (December 3, 1923); The Governor's Commission Report on the Watts Riots (December 1965); Cyrus R. Vance's Report on the Riots in Detroit (July-August 1967); The Reports of the Oklahoma Commission to Study the Tulsa Race Riot of 1921 (2000-2001); The Draft Report of the 1898 Wilmington Race Riot Commission (December 2005)

Further Reading:

Boger, John Charles, and Judith Welch Wegner. *Race, Poverty, and American Cities.* Chapel Hill: University of North Carolina Press, 1996.

Katz, Michael B., and Thomas J. Sugrue, eds. *W.E.B. Du Bois, Race, and the City: The Philadelphia Negro and Its Legacy.* Philadelphia: University of Pennsylvania Press, 1998.

Weigley, Russell. *Philadelphia: A 300-Year History.* New York: W. W. Norton, 1982.

Pimps and Hoes Parties

"Pimps and Hoes" parties refer to collective, celebratory rituals generally involving white middle- to upper-class, college-aged males and females, who dress up in outlandish costumes (and occasionally in blackface) to spend the better part of an evening drinking, dancing, and more or less caricaturing stereotypical icons associated with the African American community. Although their exact date of origin is unknown, Pimps and Hoes parties were well established in U.S. popular culture by the late 1990s. They involve male participants dressing up as stereotypical "pimps" (i.e., ringleaders or bosses behind the sex trade) and female participants playing the part as "hoes" (i.e., prostitutes or sex workers). More often than not, both the male and female partygoers identify as racially white, but during the celebration dress in attire and affect mannerisms that are considered to be stereotypically black or African American. Huge hats, sunglasses, heavy gold chains, leopard skin vests, colorful zoot-suits, and platform shoes are common costumes for the "pimps," while "hoes" typically adorn in garish makeup, quite revealing skirts or shorts, fishnet stockings, and high-heeled shoes. The parties are common in cities and towns across the United States and have even been recently found in the United Kingdom. They are often hosted by radio stations, night clubs, and other corporate entities.

From a sociological perspective, the question arises whether or not such parties are just harmless get-togethers or if they are racist and/or misogynistic in orientation. The icon or figure of the pimp has been a staple in the African American community since at least the early 1970s, and may even be dated to the Harlem Renaissance. The pimp or the hustler represented an alternative to the civil rights–oriented or black power radicals of the mid-to late 1960s, as well as working-class blacks who were thought to have sold out to "the Man." The pimp or the hustler is too busy making money to worry about such mundane things as a job and sees political action as beside the point. He is a significant role model for African Americans since he signifies an individual who has attained success without playing by the rules of the game. The pimp or hustler is a variant of the trickster figure in American folklore and is respected because he has money and status but does not engage in normal forms of wage labor to attain them.

Of course, the money that the pimp does earn comes at the expense of his stable of prostitutes who are more or less viciously exploited. Yet the realities of the prostitute's world of violence, abuse, disease, poverty, and so on are ignored and prostitutes are assumed to be simply sex-starved seductresses who like to party and who enjoy nothing better than to spend their time having sex with strangers. These images are reinforced through a consumer culture that sexualizes and commodifies the (black) female body and are reinforced and glamorized through hip-hop and rap music.

Since the late 1980s and early 1990s, such has been popular among white as well as black consumers and in part explains the appeal of Pimps and Hoes parties among white twentysomethings. Pimps and Hoes parties represent an instance of liminality where typical social roles and situations are suspended and individuals have an opportunity to act out subversive personalities. Normally well-behaved, middle- to upper-class young men who would otherwise be considered rather conformist are allowed to try on a persona characterized by violence, power, and bravado. If only for a short period of time, they get to experience what it feels like to act "black," to use slang, and to speak in derogative terms to the women in their company.

For their part, young white women partygoers, socialized to repress their sexuality, are given an opportunity to identify with the eroticism of the black female, which is normally held at bay due to its threatening nature. As "hoes," these women are afforded an opportunity to dress and act as provocatively as possible and experience a moment of unbridled sexuality.

Both male and female attendees at pimps and hoes parties take part in a collective, time-bounded fantasy about race, sex, and class. Whether or not these events present genuine instances of racism and are founded on an ideology of hate towards the Other is largely a matter of speculation. Certainly the parties have their supporters, especially nightclubs and radio stations who make considerable profits off expensive cover charges and overpriced shots of Courvoisier. Pimps and Hoes parties do appear to reinforce certain patriarchal gender attitudes and practices. Some feminist observers find the parties highly objectionable (though more on sex than on racial grounds) for reasons discussed above and seek to have the events banned. Others find the parties about as offensive as Halloween or other fancy dress events and don't see what the fuss is all about.

DANIEL M. HARRISON

See also

Film and Racial Stereotypes; Stereotype

Further Reading:

McCall, Nathan. *Makes Me Wanna Holler*. New York: Vintage, 1995.

Quinn, Eithne. "'Who's the Mack?' The Performativity and Politics of the Pimp Figure in Gangsta Rap." *Journal of American Studies* 34 (2000): 115–36.

Sherriff, Lucy. "Carnage Cardiff's Pimps and Hoes." *Huffington Post*. August 10, 2012. http://www.huffingtonpost.co.uk/ 2012/10/08/carnage-cardiffs-pimps-and-hoes-theme-angry -feminist-petition_n_1947599.html (cited December 28, 2012).

Plantation System

The plantation system was a system of capitalist agriculture that developed in the Americas in the late 17th and early 18th centuries. It was based on the acquisition of large plots of land, an organized pool of labor, and technological investment. The plantation system of agriculture represented a significant shift from the traditional yeoman style of farming that existed in the colonies of the New World previously. The development of plantation economies had a significant impact on the course of slavery in America.

Plantation economies were cash-crop economies, dependent in large part on single commodities that required intensive labor to produce: tobacco, cotton, rice, hemp, and sugar. Plantation economies were dependent on the subordination of a consistent, cheap, and large supply of labor to maximize profits. Slavery provided a convenient solution to this dilemma. In the balmy climates of the South (particularly the Deep South), where cash crops had the best chance for success, plantation slavery reached its zenith. Though debate exists as to the extent of the shift from small agricultural units to large plantations, it is clear that by 1860, most slaves were concentrated among plantations of varying sizes in the South.

Plantations operated in a highly organized and coercive manner. Plantations needed to run efficiently, thus slaves operated under a hierarchical system designed to train and discipline them. At the top of the hierarchy was the slave owner and his family. If the owner had a large number of slaves and a sizable plantation, he often hired an overseer to look after the day-to-day management of the plantation and to ensure that slaves were obedient and productive. Overseers were a diverse group. They were sometimes familial relations of the owners, or sometimes semiprofessional overseers who expected to oversee as a career for life, or in hopes of eventually buying land of their own.

"Field" slaves usually worked under the supervision of a slave "driver," normally a slave appointed to act as foreman of field labor and supervisor of living quarters. Drivers helped manage slave training and supervised agricultural activities, from planting to cotton-ginning, curing tobacco, and boiling sugar. "House" slaves tended to the maintenance of the owner's domestic quarters and gardens and were usually under the supervision of the slave owner's wife. In a large plantation, slaves were also employed as blacksmiths, carpenters, and other craftsmen.

Considerable scholarship has helped debunk the myth of the plantation system as a benign, paternalistic institution. The image of the "genteel" Southern plantation, where planter-owners leisurely pursued a "civilized" existence had little resemblance to slaves' experience of plantation life. Though significant variations existed in the level of coercion experienced by slaves, there is little doubt that slaves survived through a regimented, and often brutal, existence. Plantation owners in the South lived in perpetual fear of slave revolts and required maximum productivity, and thus maximum obedience, from their slaves. Thus, every aspect of a slave's life was regulated. Slaves toiled year-round, with precious little time for leisure or their own personal lives. Overseers often brutally beat their slaves into submission, with little fear of punishment because of the protection the slave codes provided. These coercive features gave the plantation system the characteristics of a "total institution."

Some scholars argue that slaves ultimately suffered because of the shift to a plantation style of agriculture in the South. They argue that slaves led a less-regulated existence under yeoman farming, because farms' smaller size and diversified agricultural output meant that a hierarchical division of labor could not become entrenched. There was less social distance between slaves and their owners, and sometimes owners participated in farming activities alongside their slaves. However, the importance of this distinction should not be overstated. Plantation slavery certainly introduced new mechanisms for the coercion and oppression of slaves. But conversely, because plantation slaves were able to live together in large numbers in slave quarters, away from the eyes of their masters, slave culture found room to flourish in ways not possible under yeoman farming.

REBEKAH LEE

See also

Slave Codes; Slave Families; Slave Revolts and White Attacks on Black Slaves; Slave Trade; Slavery in the Antebellum South

Further Reading:

Blassingame, John. *The Slave Community: Plantation Life in the Antebellum South.* New York: Oxford University Press, 1979.

Genovese, Eugene. *Roll, Jordan, Roll: The World the Slaves Made.* New York: Pantheon, 1974.

Stampp, Kenneth. *The Peculiar Institution: Slavery in the Ante-Bellum South.* New York: Vintage Books, 1956.

Plessy, Homer (1862–1925)

Homer Adolph Plessy was an African American artisan, activist, and the plaintiff in the defining U.S. Supreme Court case *Plessy v. Ferguson* (1896). Born on March 17, 1863, Plessy grew up in the city of New Orleans. In the pre–Civil War era, his parents, Homer Adolph Plessy and Rosa Debergue, belonged to a sizeable community of free people of color, many of mixed-race descent. These individuals, often known as Creoles (mixed-race people), spoke French, practiced Catholicism, could legally own property, and had access to education and other opportunities that slaves did not. Plessy married Louise Bordenave in 1889 and moved to the New Orleans neighborhood of Faubourg Tremé where he worked as a shoemaker, a craft he learned from his family. When he was 30 years old, Plessy challenged the newly passed Louisiana law mandating racial segregation on streetcars and trains. Law enforcement arrested him for sitting in the white section of a streetcar. Plessy appealed his conviction all the way to the Supreme Court, where he lost when the court declared that "separate but equal" was constitutional.

Until passage of the 1890 Separate Car Act in Louisiana, streetcars and train stations remained integrated. The new law required that railway companies segregate blacks and whites into separate coaches. A civil rights organization based in New Orleans, Comité des Citoyens (Committee of Citizens), decided to make a test case against the law. Plessy was one of the youngest members of this group of activists and professionals, many of whom came from the free people of color caste. The Comité des Citoyens viewed themselves as full American citizens and believed it was their duty to defend their constitutional rights against prejudice. They chose Plessy to challenge the intrastate law because he was light-skinned. In part, the group hoped that in selecting someone who could pass as white, they might be able to draw attention to the arbitrariness of conductors assigning seats based on race. Ironically, in the brief of *Plessy v. Ferguson*, Plessy was listed as "seven-eighths white," even though he was legally considered black in Louisiana.

On June 7, 1892, Plessy purchased a first class ticket to travel from New Orleans to Covington on the East Louisiana Railroad. When he boarded the train, he sat in the first-class coach, which was designated for whites only. The conductor asked him if he was colored. Plessy replied in the affirmative but refused to move to the "colored car" when ordered to do so. The Comité des Citoyens made arrangements with the conductor to confront Plessy and hired a private detective to arrest him to ensure that he would be taken into custody. The railroad company supported Plessy's challenge to the law because of the financial burden involved with providing separate cars. The East Louisiana Railroad also did not want its conductors to be responsible for making on-the-spot decisions about an individual's racial background. Plessy was tried before Justice John Howard Ferguson of the Orleans Parish Criminal Court and found guilty of violating the Separate Car Act.

Plessy appealed Justice Ferguson's decision to the Louisiana State Supreme Court and eventually the U.S. Supreme Court. One of Plessy's lawyers, Albion Tourgée, argued that the Separate Car Act had deprived Plessy of his rights to due process and equal protection under the law as outlined by the Thirteenth and Fourteenth Amendments. Tourgée asserted that Louisiana had imposed a "badge of servitude" on Plessy because the legal definition of a slave was a person with no rights. He reasoned that the Louisiana law made artificial distinctions between blacks and whites simply for the benefit and comfort of the whites. In short, the state had treated Plessy as a second-class citizen. In a seven-to-one decision, the U.S. Supreme Court ruled against Plessy. The Court's majority opinion, delivered on May 18, 1896, stated that the Separate Car Act's distinction between black and white was purely a legal one and did not intrinsically imply the inferiority of any one race. If an African American, such as Plessy, chose to view it as a mark of second-class citizenship, that was essentially a fiction created in the individual's mind. The Court also held that the law was reasonable since it followed the community's standards and traditions designed to keep public order.

As a result of the decision, Plessy appeared once more before the New Orleans court to pay a $25 fine for violation of the law. At the turn of the century, the rise of industrial manufacturing pushed Plessy out of the shoemaking business, and subsequently he worked as a laborer and a life insurance collector. Plessy died in 1925 and is buried in St. Louis Cemetery #1 in New Orleans.

NATALIE J. RING

See also

Plessy v. Ferguson (1896). Document: *Plessy v. Ferguson* (1896)

Further Reading:

Medly, Keith Weldon. *We as Freemen:* Plessy v. Ferguson. Gretna, LA: Pelican Publishing Company, 2003.

St. Augustine Catholic Church of New Orleans. "Famous Parishioner: Homer Plessy." http://www.staugustine catholicchurch-neworleans.org/plessy.htm (accessed May 28, 2008).

Thomas, Brook, ed. Plessy v. Ferguson: *A Brief History with Documents*. New York: Bedford Books, 1997.

Plessy v. Ferguson (1896)

Plessy v. Ferguson was a landmark decision of the U.S. Supreme Court in 1896 that upheld the constitutionality of state laws requiring racial segregation in public accommodations (particularly railroad passenger cars) and that established the doctrine of "separate but equal" as the constitutional standard for such laws. The Supreme Court held that neither the Thirteenth nor the Fourteenth Amendment to the Constitution could be used to challenge intrastate segregation laws. The decision resulted in a proliferation of laws mandating racial segregation in public spaces throughout the South, providing constitutional justification for hardening the de facto separation of the races established by custom into state law. This decision stood for nearly 60 years until the Court reversed itself, beginning in 1954 with *Brown v. Board of Education* and other cases that followed. The Court specifically outlawed segregation in all public transportation in 1956 in *Gayle v. Browder*.

With the end of the Civil War, Southern states were occupied by federal troops during the period known as Reconstruction (1865–1877). Military occupation could, at first, guarantee that former slaves could fully exercise their voting rights and their civil rights on an equal basis with whites. However, when Reconstruction ended and federal troops were withdrawn, newly won black rights came under attack. Even before the end of Reconstruction, a pattern of racial separation had developed that, while not compelled by statute, pervaded Southern life. By the 1880s, states began to give these patterns the sanction of law.

In 1890 the Louisiana state legislature passed a law that required "equal but separate accommodations for the white and colored races" on all passenger railroads within the state. An exception was provided for nurses attending children of another race. Almost immediately, the black and French-speaking Creole citizens of New Orleans organized to oppose the law. The Citizen's Committee to Test the Constitutionality of the Separate Car Law, known as Comité des Citoyens, resolved to establish in court that the law violated the Thirteenth and Fourteenth Amendments to the Constitution. The committee, which included prominent whites in New Orleans, agreed that a 30-year-old shoemaker, Homer Plessy, should test the law. Plessy was a French-speaking resident of New Orleans chosen specifically because he was only one-eighth black (an octoroon in the parlance of the

The Supreme Court opinion for which Henry Billings Brown is most remembered today is *Plessy v. Ferguson* (1896), the case that validated state laws legalizing segregation. (Collection of the Supreme Court of the United States)

time) and, according to his lawyer, "the mixture [was] not discernible." In this way, the committee hoped to expose the arbitrariness of the law.

Clearly, Plessy could have occupied the white car of any train in Louisiana without trouble. But on June 7, 1892, by prearrangement with the railroad company, he sat in a railway car reserved for whites only and refused to leave when asked. The railroad conductor and a private detective hired by the Comité des Citoyens then removed him to the police station, where he was booked and released on $500 bond. The railroad company officials seem to have lent some silent support to the committee's court challenge because they were unhappy about the extra expense of providing separate cars for blacks and whites mandated by the law.

At Plessy's first trial, the presiding judge was John H. Ferguson, a native of Massachusetts. He had earlier struck down as unconstitutional another Louisiana law that had mandated segregated accommodations for travel between states. This time, however, the law was restricted to travel only within Louisiana. Ferguson ruled that the state could impose such restrictions within its borders without violating the Constitution. The decision was appealed to the Louisiana State Supreme Court, which upheld the ruling. The decision at the state level cited other court decisions that had relied for support on the "natural, legal, and customary differences between the black and white races."

Plessy's case was argued before the U.S. Supreme Court by the white, activist New York lawyer Albion W. Tourgée, who had protested against racial segregation earlier in newspaper columns. He prepared a case that presented a variety of arguments to the court against the Louisiana law. He argued for a broad interpretation of the Thirteenth Amendment to the Constitution, which had abolished slavery. That amendment, his argument suggested, affirmatively established in law the equality of all citizens. Segregation, therefore, violated the Constitution by perpetuating one of the essential features of slavery.

The case also argued that the Louisiana law deprived Plessy of his right to equal protection of law guaranteed by the Fourteenth Amendment. The purpose of the law was not to promote the public good, but rather to ensure the comfort of whites at the expense of blacks. "The exemption of nurses," Plessy's lawyer argued, "shows that the real evil lies not in the color of the skin but in the relation the colored person sustains to the white. If he is a dependent it may be endured; if he is not, his presence is insufferable." This could not be called equal protection.

Tourgée also pointed out the arbitrariness of racial classifications, since Plessy had only one-eighth African ancestry and could be taken to be white. Indeed, the definition of who was black and who was white differed from state to state. By granting to railroad conductors (whom the law exempted from civil liability) the power to publicly declare racial designations, the state had deprived Plessy of his reputation (as a white man) without due process of law.

In addition, the arguments for Plessy had to take into account that schools were legally segregated, even in Boston and in Washington, D.C., and that interracial marriage was forbidden by law in most states (such laws would eventually be found unconstitutional by the Supreme Court in the following century). Those laws might be acceptable, but the matter of seating on railway coaches was different, Plessy's lawyer argued, being much less serious an issue than education or marriage and not affecting future generations. Therefore, the state had no interest in regulating it.

However, the Supreme Court ruled against Plessy on May 18, 1896. The judges voted seven to one to uphold the Louisiana law. Justice Brewer did not participate in the case. Justice Henry Billings Brown, a native of Massachusetts and a resident of Michigan, wrote the majority opinion. Justice John Marshall Harlan, a Southerner, wrote a ferocious but solitary dissent.

In the years prior to the *Plessy v. Ferguson* case, this same Court had handed down a number of decisions that limited the scope and effect of constitutional restraints on states' rights. These precedents made the Court's 1896 decision almost inevitable. In 1873, the Supreme Court had rejected a broad interpretation of the Thirteenth Amendment in a collection of suits that became known as the *Slaughter-House Cases*. In that decision, the Court held that the sole purpose of the amendment was to abolish slavery, and perhaps other forms of involuntary servitude. It had nothing to do with equal rights. Furthermore, the decision held that the Fourteenth Amendment was not intended to establish the federal government as the "perpetual censor upon all the legislation of the States." That amendment only forbade state infringement on the rights of United States citizenship, which the court took to be narrow in scope.

In 1876 the Supreme Court had decided (*U.S. v. Cruikshank*) that the Fourteenth Amendment could not provide federal protection against actions committed by private parties, but could only protect against the actions of states. Then, in 1883, the court had held in five cases collected together as the *Civil Rights Cases* that most of the provisions of the federal Civil Rights Act of 1875 were unconstitutional. The court again ruled that Congress had authority only to prohibit racial discrimination perpetrated by states, not by private citizens. Such precedents made the legal outlook for Plessy's Supreme Court challenge seem bleak indeed. His lawyer deliberately delayed bringing the case to the Court in hopes of finding a more favorable political climate.

Finally, the Supreme Court ruled against Plessy, citing the above precedents. Plessy's appeal to the Thirteenth Amendment was dismissed in favor of a narrow interpretation of the law. The court found, as well, that the Louisiana law did not violate the Fourteenth Amendment to the Constitution. Justice Brown wrote:

> The object of the [Fourteenth] amendment was undoubtedly to enforce the absolute equality of the two races before the law, but in the nature of things it could not have been intended to abolish distinctions based upon color, or to enforce social, as distinguished from political equality, or a commingling of the two races upon terms unsatisfactory to either. Laws permitting, and even requiring, their separation in places where they are liable to be brought into contact do not necessarily imply the inferiority of either race to the other.

The majority opinion noted that the Louisiana law had mandated "equal" accommodations be provided for blacks and whites. Therefore, the separation of the races by law was not an issue of equality, since it was just as illegal for whites to sit in the black areas of railway cars as it was for blacks to sit in the white areas. The court held that the "assumption that the enforced separation of the two races stamps the colored race with the badge of inferiority" was a false one. "If this be so, it is not by reason of anything found in the act, but solely because the colored race chooses to put that construction upon it." The ruling explicitly rejected the idea that racial prejudice could be overcome by legislation and denied that equal rights could only be achieved for blacks by enforcing "commingling" of the races. The Court's majority opinion simply assumed that racial separation was "in the nature of things."

Justice Harlan, who wrote the lone dissent to the majority opinion, was a native of Kentucky and a former slave owner, although he had fought for the Union in the Civil War and freed his slaves before it ended. Harlan argued forcefully that the Louisiana law was unconstitutional and should be struck down by the courts. He objected that:

> The arbitrary separation of citizens, on the basis of race, while they are on a public highway, is a badge of servitude wholly inconsistent with the civil freedom and the equality before the law established by

the Constitution. It cannot be justified upon any legal grounds.

Harlan's dissent specifically accepted a broad interpretation of the Thirteenth Amendment that would exclude laws requiring racial segregation. He states explicitly:

The Thirteenth Amendment does not permit the withholding or the deprivation of any right necessarily inhering in freedom. It not only struck down the institution of slavery as previously existing in the United States, but it prevents the imposition of any burdens or disabilities that constitute badges of slavery or servitude. It decreed universal civil freedom in this country.

Harlan's dissent was emphatic. He insisted that the Fourteenth Amendment should bar states from any abridgment, on the basis of race, of civil rights or "personal liberty":

In respect of civil rights, common to all citizens, the Constitution of the United States does not, I think, permit any public authority to know the race of those entitled to be protected in the enjoyment of such rights. . . . I deny that any legislative body or judicial tribunal may have regard to the race of citizens when the civil rights of those citizens are involved. Indeed, such legislation, as that here in question, is inconsistent not only with that equality of rights which pertains to citizenship, National and State, but with the personal liberty enjoyed by every one within the United States.

Harlan rejected the majority's argument that laws of racial segregation did not discriminate against blacks in language that came close to contempt:

It was said in argument that the statute of Louisiana does not discriminate against either race, but prescribes a rule applicable alike to white and colored citizens. But this argument does not meet the difficulty. Every one knows that the statute in question had its origin in the purpose, not so much to exclude white persons from railroad cars occupied by blacks, as to exclude colored people from coaches occupied by or assigned to white persons. Railroad corporations of Louisiana did not make discrimination among whites in the matter of accommodation for travellers. The

thing to accomplish was, under the guise of giving equal accommodation for whites and blacks, to compel the latter to keep to themselves while travelling in railroad passenger coaches. No one would be so wanting in candor as to assert the contrary.

He went on to say, "The thin disguise of 'equal' accommodations for passengers in railroad coaches will not mislead any one, nor atone for the wrong this day done."

Harlan insisted that the majority's decision would, in time, "prove to be quite as pernicious as the decision made by [the Supreme Court] in the *Dred Scott* case." At the conclusion of his dissent, he waxed prophetic:

I am of the opinion that the statute of Louisiana is inconsistent with the personal liberty of citizens, white and black, in that State, and hostile to both the spirit and the letter of the Constitution of the United States. If laws of like character should be enacted in the several States of the Union, the effect would be in the highest degree mischievous. Slavery, as an institution tolerated by law would, it is true, have disappeared from our country, but there would remain a power in the States, by sinister legislation, to interfere with the full enjoyment of the blessings of freedom; to regulate civil rights, common to all citizens, upon the basis of race; and to place in a condition of legal inferiority a large body of American citizens.

Of course, laws "of like character" that enforced racial segregation were eventually enacted in all Southern states, and in some Northern states as well. Such laws relegated African Americans to the status of second-class citizens, excluded from public spaces and vulnerable to public humiliation. Segregated public facilities for blacks were always separate, but very rarely equal to those provided for whites. Nonetheless, the Supreme Court's decision in *Plessy v. Ferguson* protected the constitutionality of such laws and provided them with a legal foundation.

Eventually, the Southern states passed laws that enforced a rigidly segregated society. Every restaurant, every school, every train or public conveyance was segregated by law. Separate facilities for blacks and whites were legislated for hotels, elevators, libraries, colleges and universities, swimming pools, drinking fountains, cemeteries, and prisons. An

Excerpts from *Plessy v. Ferguson* (1890)

That petitioner was a citizen of the United States and a resident of the state of Louisiana, of mixed descent, in the proportion of seven-eighths Caucasian and one-eighth African blood; that the mixture of colored blood was not discernible in him, and that he was entitled to every recognition, right, privilege, and immunity secured to the citizens of the United States of the white race by its constitution and laws; that on June 7, 1892, he engaged and paid for a first-class passage on the East Louisiana Railway, from New Orleans to Covington, in the same state, and thereupon entered a passenger train, and took possession of a vacant seat in a coach where passengers of the white race were accommodated; that such railroad company was incorporated by the laws of Louisiana as a common carrier, and was not authorized to distinguish between citizens according to their race, but, notwithstanding this, petitioner was required by the conductor, under penalty of ejection from said train and imprisonment, to vacate said coach, and occupy another seat, in a coach assigned by said company for persons not of the white race, and for no other reason than that petitioner was of the colored race; that, upon petitioner's refusal to comply with such order, he was, with the aid of a police officer, forcibly ejected from said coach, and hurried off to, and imprisoned in, the parish jail of New Orleans, and there held to answer a charge made by such officer to the effect that he was guilty of having criminally violated an act of the general assembly of the state, approved July 10, 1890, in such case made and provided. . . .

We consider the underlying fallacy of the plaintiff's argument to consist in the assumption that the enforced separation of the two races stamps the colored race with a badge of inferiority. If this be so, it is not by reason of anything found in the act, but solely because the colored race chooses to put that construction upon it. The argument necessarily assumes that if, as has been more than once the case, and is not unlikely to be so again, the colored race should become the dominant power in the state legislature, and should enact a law in precisely similar terms, it would thereby relegate the white race to an inferior position. We imagine that the white race, at least, would not acquiesce in this assumption. The argument also assumes that social prejudices may be overcome by legislation, and that equal rights cannot be secured to the negro except by an enforced commingling of the two races. We cannot accept this proposition. If the two races are to meet upon terms of social equality, it must be the result of natural affinities, a mutual appreciation of each other's merits, and a voluntary consent of individuals. [. . .]

Mr. Justice HARLAN dissenting [excerpt]

In respect of civil rights, common to all citizens, the constitution of the United States does not, I think, permit any public authority to know the race of those entitled to be protected in the enjoyment of such rights. Every true man has pride of race, and under appropriate circumstances, when the rights of others, his equals before the law, are not to be affected, it is his privilege to express such pride and to take such action based upon it as to him seems proper. But I deny that any legislative body or judicial tribunal may have regard to the race of citizens when the civil rights of those citizens are involved. Indeed, such legislation as that here in question is inconsistent not only with that equality of rights which pertains to citizenship, national and state, but with the personal liberty enjoyed by every one within the United States. [. . .]

Oklahoma law segregated telephone booths. Louisiana required separate entryways to circuses for blacks and whites. A Florida law demanded that schoolbooks for white schools be stored separately from schoolbooks used in black schools. Such laws rested on the Supreme Court's standard of "separate but equal" established in *Plessy v. Ferguson.*

This standard was finally repudiated by the Supreme Court in 1954, at least with regard to the legal segregation of public schools, in the famous case of *Brown v. Board of Education.* Other cases would follow quickly that found laws of segregation to be unconstitutional in all circumstances. However, the 1896 *Plessy v. Ferguson* decision found its defenders right up until the end. In 1952, William Rehnquist (then a law clerk and later chief justice of the Supreme Court) composed a memo for the Court during early deliberations that led to the *Brown* case. He wrote: "I realize that it is an unpopular and unhumanitarian position, for which I have been excoriated by 'liberal' colleagues but I think *Plessy v. Ferguson* was right and should be reaffirmed." The Supreme Court disagreed unanimously, and *Brown v. Board of Education* marked the beginning of the end of de jure racial segregation in the United States.

ANTHONY A. LEE

See also

Brown v. Board of Education (1954); School Segregation. Document: *Plessy v. Ferguson* (1896)

Further Reading:

Lofgren, Charles A. *The "Plessy" Case: A Legal-Historical Interpretation*. New York: Oxford University Press, 1987.

Olsen, Otto H. *The Thin Disguise:* "*Plessy v. Ferguson.*" New York: Humanities Press, 1967.

Plessy v. Ferguson, 163 U.S. 537 (1896). http://www.law.cornell.edu/supct/html/historics/USSC_CR_0163_0537_ZS.html (accessed May 28, 2008).

Thomas, Brook, ed. Plessy v. Ferguson: *A Brief History with Documents*. Boston: Bedford Books, 1997.

Pluralism

Pluralism, or more often in discussions of race and ethnicity, cultural pluralism, is a state of society in which there is social parity or equality among racial and ethnic minorities and the dominant group in a society. Groups of people are allowed to be culturally different, but they still share the basic resources and identity of the society as a whole. The value of the different ethnic or racial subcultures in making up the society as a whole is recognized and allowed to co-exist. This differs from the two other main forms of racial and ethnic relations currently found in the United States, assimilation and the melting pot (Gordon 1978). In classic assimilation, ethnic or racial groups adapt themselves to the traditions and culture of the dominant host culture they move into. In contrast, with the melting pot model, the traditions and cultures of host and immigrant populations are blended to form a new cultural pattern taking on aspects of both groups.

Classic assimilation had not been easy for all immigrants to the United States. More recent immigrants tend to be from Latin America and Asia and are considered nonwhite by the host society. The sociologists Alejandro Portes and Min Zhou note that this makes them more likely to have to live in urban areas of the country where assimilation and upward mobility are less likely (1993).

The melting pot model also has its difficulties. In the 1940s, sociologist Ruby Jo Reeves Kennedy noted that intermarriage was taking place across ethnic and national boundaries, just as would be expected in a melting pot situation. But at the same time, marriage was staying strictly within three general religious groups: Protestant, Catholic, and Jewish. This created what she referred to as the "triple melting pot." With a separate pot for each of the religious cultures, this can be considered a type of cultural pluralism. In cultural pluralism, the overall society provides a large sociocultural framework with a number of diverse cultures functioning within it.

The most common example used of a truly culturally pluralist country is Switzerland, which has three major cultural groups—French, German, and Italian. The Swiss recognize the languages and cultural traditions of all three groups, though they tend to use English as a common language. Despite differences between the groups, none of them dominate Switzerland's politics or economy. Notably, the Swiss are maintaining this cultural pluralism in an environment that does not have the multiracial aspects of the United States.

Since the late 20th century, many in the United States have striven to create a multicultural America where there is tolerance and acceptance of the many ethnic traditions that make national life. There has been limited success in bringing this about. American society provides universal education and social programs to all groups of people counted as citizens despite any differences in race, ethnicity, or religion. They are promised equality before the law and equal opportunities for advancement. However, while the United States is advancing toward pluralism, it has not achieved it.

Many people do not want to remain in cultural or ethnic enclaves. They wish to assimilate or meld with the host society. Furthermore, not all of those in the host society wish for cultural pluralism either, as evidenced by the many movements to make English the official language of the United States.

The United States may need to have a broader definition of pluralism than what is used in Switzerland. In terms of not having a single ethnic majority group, America will be statistically pluralist by 2050. Will this be the same as cultural pluralism? Possibly not, but it will be a step closer.

DONALD P. WOOLLEY

See also
Assimilation; Melting Pot; Segmented Assimilation

Further Reading:
Gordon, Milton. *Human Nature, Class, and Ethnicity.* New York: Oxford University Press, 1978.

Kennedy, Ruby Jo Reeves. "Single or Triple Melting-Pot? Intermarriage Trends in New Haven, 1870–1940." *American Journal of Sociology* 49 (1944): 331–39.

Portes, Alejandro, and Min Zhou. "The New Second Generation: Segmented Assimilation and Its Variants." *Annals of the American Academy of Political and Social Sciences* 530 (1993): 74–96.

Warren, Jonathan W., and France Winddance Twine. "White Americans, the New Minority? Non-Blacks and the Ever-Expanding Boundaries of Whiteness." *Journal of Black Studies* 28 (1997): 200–218.

Poitier, Sidney (b. 1927)

American actor, director, and activist Sidney Poitier was the first African American to win an Academy Award for best actor. He began in theater and moved to film and television. Confronted with racism and discrimination, Poitier became active in the civil rights movement in the 1960s. He also wrote, directed, and produced films during the latter portion of his career. Poitier became an icon for many African Americans as he garnered popularity and critical success at a time when few African Americans found roles in Hollywood.

Poitier was born while his parents were en route to the United States from the Caribbean. His father was of Haitian descent, while his mother was from the Bahamas. He spent his childhood in Miami, Florida, in a segregated section of the city known as Colored Town. By 1920, Miami had one of

In 1958 Sidney Poitier became the first African American to be nominated as best actor by the Academy of Motion Pictures Arts and Sciences for his costarring role in the Hollywood film *The Defiant Ones.* In 1963, he became only the second African American actor ever to win an Oscar, for his performance in the film *Lilies of the Field.* He is credited with paving the way for public acceptance of African American men in American films, and such contemporary film figures as Eddie Murphy and Spike Lee have him partially to thank for their huge success.

the highest degrees of residential segregation in the United States. Poitier confronted Jim Crow laws as a child, including an incident in which police officers stopped him at gunpoint and ordered him to walk back to the African American section of the city, which was several miles away. Hoping to escape the Jim Crow South, he moved to New York City in spring 1943. Upon arriving, Poitier moved from job to job working as a butcher's assistant, drug store clerk, porter, and dishwasher. He joined the U.S. Army later that year and served in the 1267th Medical Detachment at the Veterans

Administration Hospital in Northport, Long Island. The army released him the following December.

Poitier's first acting experience was at an apprentice program with the American Negro Theater in 1945. His first role was in a production of *You Can't Take It with You* in 1946. He then accepted a part in the all–African American cast of the Broadway production of the Classical Greek play *Lysistrata*. Poitier moved to California in 1949 and was cast in his first film role in *No Way Out*. The film explicitly portrays racial hatred, and Poitier's role as town doctor Luther Brooks broke many common African American stereotypes. Although the film and Poitier's performance received strong reviews, many Southern theaters banned the film for its racial content. His reputation grew as he garnered further accolades for his performance as a rebellious African American high school student in the 1955 film *Blackboard Jungle*.

By the late 1950s, Poitier found steady work in Hollywood but continued to face hardships as an African American in the predominantly white film industry. He faced strict enforcement of Jim Crow laws while filming in Louisiana for *Band of Angels* (1957). While lead actor Clark Gable and the rest of the white cast and crew ate dinner upon their arrival at the airport restaurant, Poitier and the African American cast and crew ate hidden from other patrons behind a makeshift screen in the rear of the building. They were also forced to stay in separate lodging at Southern University, at the time an all–African American college, and to use segregated transportation and bathroom facilities. Poitier continued to receive roles but found these parts to be limited in content, as many of the films were written, directed, and produced solely by whites. He and his friends and fellow actors Paul Robeson and Harry Belafonte fought to secure prominent parts for African Americans that were not stereotypical. Poitier received his first Academy Award nomination for best supporting actor for his role as an escaped convict in *The Defiant Ones* (1958). Like his previous films, many Southern theaters refused to run the film despite good reviews, due to the close friendship that develops between Poitier's character and a white convict played by Tony Curtis. Many Southern critics also viewed the film as anti-South, pro-integration, and as communist propaganda.

Poitier balanced his career as both actor and activist at the height of the civil rights movement in the 1960s. In an attempt to help dismantle discrimination and racism in the film industry, Poitier testified before New York Congressman Adam Clayton Powell's Labor Committee about racial discrimination in the entertainment industry in October 1962. He was part of a delegation of actors, including Sammy Davis Jr., Josephine Baker, and Marlon Brando, to take part in the March on Washington of 1963. Poitier went on to make history in 1964 by becoming the first African American to win an Academy Award for best actor for his performance in *Lilies in the Field*.

Later that year he appeared at the White House to congratulate President Lyndon B. Johnson for the signing of the Civil Rights Act of 1964. By March 1965, Poitier ranked as one of the busiest Hollywood actors and was the only African American to appear on the list. He starred in *A Patch of Blue* (1965), highlighting an interracial romance that sparked protests throughout the South, including bomb threats made to a theater in Concord, North Carolina.

In 1967, a hotel refused to lodge Poitier while residents protested daily during the filming of *In the Heat of the Night* in Tennessee. The film portrays an African American detective from the North investigating a murder alongside a white police officer in a racist Southern town. White Southern reviewers condemned the film for Poitier's performance as an aggressive African American police officer from the North who physically confronts whites. Later that year, he played actress Katharine Haughton's fiancé in *Look Who's Coming to Dinner*. The interracial romance made the film one of Poitier's most famous and successful productions. However, the film set off protests throughout the United States, including widespread picketing by the Ku Klux Klan. Poitier continued to make gains in Hollywood as he made his directorial debut in 1972 with *Buck and the Preacher*, which starred himself and Belafonte.

Poitier continues to make appearances in film and television. In 2000 Poitier received the Screen Actors Guild Life Achievement Award. He also received an honorary Academy Award for Lifetime Achievement in 2002.

FRANK CHA

See also

Films and Racial Stereotypes

Further Reading:

Goudsouzian, Aram. *Sidney Poitier: Man, Actor, Icon*. Chapel Hill: University of North Carolina Press, 2004.

Poitier, Sidney. *The Measure of a Man: A Spiritual Autobiography*.
San Francisco: HarperSanFrancisco, 2000.

Public Broadcasting Service. "American Master: Sidney Poitier."
American Masters Exhibition. http://www.pbs.org/wnet/
americanmasters/database/poitier_s.html (accessed May 28,
2008).

Police Brutality

Formal policing began in the United States in the major urban areas such as New York, Boston, and Philadelphia when these municipalities paid officials for crime control in the mid-19th century, primarily in response to riots by newly arriving immigrants. Prior to this time, policing was mostly carried out through the "night watch" system, an idea borrowed from Europe in which local citizens were required to observe and report criminal behavior to authorities.

Southern cities such as New Orleans, Louisiana, also began to develop professional police forces in the 19th century although Southern slave patrols and vigilante committees continued to be the primary means of controlling slave escapes and revolts, which became increasingly common during the early and mid-19th century. Racial conflicts did not end with the emancipation of slaves; the lynching of blacks continued at a startling rate, with the newly emerging police forces often ignoring the practice or even actively participating.

As an abuse of authority and power, agents of social control express police brutality through physical, emotional, or legal exploitation of those under their control. More than any other type of police misconduct, this type of violent behavior by police has resulted in calls for reforms by the public. In fact, local and national commissions have chronicled police excesses of force, including a report from the National Commission on Law Observance and Enforcement (1931), which resulted in a book titled *Our Lawless Police*.

In addition, reports have been drawn up by the mayoral commission on police actions during the Harlem riots (1935), the President's Commission on Civil Rights (1947), the U.S. Civil Rights Commission (1961), the McCone Commission (1965), the Crime Commission (1967), the National Commission on Civil Disorders (commonly known as the Kerner Commission Report of 1968), the Knapp Commission (1972), and the Christopher Commission, which reported on the Rodney King beating (1991). Police brutality has occurred throughout police history and has been especially prominent, or at least visible, during race riots.

American policing as we know it today traces back primarily to England and the London Metropolitan Police. In the early years of the American police, the early 1800s, the departments were not as well organized as those of their British predecessors. Boston experienced a riot at the inception of its police department in 1837 when a mob of Protestants attacked the homes of the newly arrived Irish immigrants. In 1845, New York City formed its first police department. On July 12 and 13, 1863, the New York police had to quash the New York City Draft Riot of 1863, which occurred when a large group of whites rose in opposition to being drafted to fight in the Civil War.

One of the earliest documented accounts of unnecessary police force at the dawning of the 20th century occurred in New York City in 1900 when a confrontation between a white officer and a black citizen erupted in mob activity that involved police and a large number of Irish immigrants, who together attacked blacks in the area. Riots at the beginning of the century also occurred in Springfield, Ohio (1904); Greensburg, Indiana (1906); and Springfield, Illinois (1908).

In 1917, a riot occurred in Houston, Texas, when a group formed to protest the practices of the city police department after an incident in which white police officers refused to turn over a suspect in compliance with the instructions of a black military officer. They placed another military officer in custody, beat him, and later shot at him when he attempted to escape. As word of the incident got out, several black citizens armed themselves and shot two white police officers. A firefight between the two groups resulted in the deaths of 11 to 17 white officers and four black soldiers. The surviving black soldiers were either executed or given life sentences in prison.

The National Commission on Law Enforcement and Observance, which is more commonly known as the Wickersham Commission, released its well-known report in 1931. This document noted the use of excessive police force and intimidation by officials, commonly referred to as "the third

---

Amadou Diallo (1975–1999)

Amadou Diallo was a 23-year-old African immigrant to the United States whose controversial death at the hands of four New York City police officers on February 4, 1999, prompted outrage throughout the country. News that Diallo was unarmed and was believed to have done nothing to threaten the officers led to charges of police brutality and demands for an end to racial profiling.

Diallo was born in 1975 in Liberia. He was the first of four children to Saikou and Kodiatou Diallo. His father is a businessman. The family moved around a lot because of his father's business. Diallo arrived in the United States in 1996 with the hope of one day attending an American university and studying computer science. Diallo worked as a street vendor selling clothes and took General Education Development classes. In the early morning hours of February 4, 1999, he was standing in the vestibule of his Bronx apartment building when he was approached by four white officers. The officers say they were in his neighborhood searching for a serial rapist who had raped 40 women in the minority communities in the Bronx. The officers say they thought Diallo was reaching for a gun and they fired 41 shots, 19 of which hit Diallo, killing him instantly. He was found to be unarmed and was reaching for his wallet.

The white officers went to trial in Albany, where they were acquitted by a predominantly white jury. Rev. Al Sharpton, president of the National Action Network, and other black leaders, including former New York City mayor David Dinkins, staged daily demonstrations. A demonstration took place outside the Bronx courthouse where a grand jury investigated the conduct of the police. Other acts of civil disobedience included a demonstration at City Hall, protests at a Wall Street firm, and a sit-in that blocked the entrance to New York City's central police headquarters. Diallo's death sparked several weeks of unrest and civil disobedience over the treatment of minorities by the police.

CATHERINE ANYASO

---

degree" and suggested that it was widespread by the time of the report's release. Despite recommendations from the national commission report, police brutality continued.

In 1935, riots in Harlem, New York, broke out after rumors spread that a black youth had stolen a knife and was beaten to death by police. The effects of the Depression are often blamed as an underlying cause of the incident, but conditions of police brutality as a common way of life in the area are also cited as a factor. The Harlem Riot Commission Report was very condemning in its description of the police responses during the disruption.

In the 1940s, excessive police force was a common theme in the race riots of that decade. A major exodus of African Americans from the South to Northern factories set the stage for confrontation. Serious complaints of police brutality occurred during the riots in Detroit in 1943 when a fight erupted between young black and white men in a predominantly recreational area of the city. Looting followed by rioting occurred and was so extensive that federal troops had to be called in to suppress the activity that left 34 people dead and over 1,000 injured. Thurgood Marshall, a young civil

rights lawyer who later became a U.S. Supreme Court justice, rebuked the police actions during this riot by claiming that the police used undue force. Measures taken by the police to control white and black citizens in the riot were unequally represented, according to Marshall, as blacks were dealt with in an unnecessarily harsh manner while the violent actions of whites were ignored or condoned. A governor's commission report, however, stated that the actions of the police to contain the situation were appropriate.

The inner-city disturbances that occurred during the 1960s also brought many complaints of police brutality. A series of so-called ghetto riots occurred in several U.S. cities. In the 1960s, race riots erupted in large and small cities across the nation, such as Chicago, Illinois; Philadelphia, Pennsylvania; Savannah, Georgia; and Cambridge, Maryland.

However, the most visible example of police brutality took place in Birmingham, Alabama, where officers under the supervision of city Police Commissioner T. Eugene "Bull" Connor attacked a group of young children and adolescents who were peacefully marching in the city. Dogs were unleashed on the crowd and high-pressure water hoses and cattle prods were used against the protesters even though they were not directly attacking anyone. This event is responsible for furthering public attention and outrage at police abuse of power.

In the Los Angeles area known as Watts, another example that is commonly cited as excessive and unnecessary police force occurred in 1965. Like the 1943 encounter in Detroit, the riot, which in this case lasted almost a week, claimed the lives of 34 people and left over 1,000 injured. Police made approximately 4,000 arrests, and rioters caused nearly $40 million in property damage. Many of the injured were police officers, firefighters, National Guard soldiers, and other government agents. Several sources reported that police brutality was used in the Watts riot. Although the McCone Commission cited the area's poor social and economic conditions as a cause of the event, the most salient factor leading to the riot involved a growing rupture in the relations between the black citizens and mostly white police. There was a particular dislike and distrust of Police Chief William H. Parker, who was viewed by black Watts residents as an advocate of police brutality due to police tactics and his insistence on his officers possessing a paramilitary presence in the community.

The Long Hot Summer Riots of 1965–1967 involved over several hundred race riots in a number of cities and rural areas. It was reported that small events ignited the riots, and one of the primary causes was poor police–community relations. The resulting police responses were seen by many as excessively violent or as possible contributors to already volatile conditions. Detroit, the home of the disastrous riots of 1945, had one of the worst riots of this period as well.

Newark, New Jersey, also saw major rioting during the summer of 1967. When an African American cab driver named John Smith was arrested and subsequently beaten by police on the way to the precinct, a crowd rioted after an inaccurate report that the officers had killed him.

The 1970s did not see the same level of riotous behavior as the previous decades, but police misconduct was still at center stage, especially in regard to corruption, due in large part to the attention given Frank Serpico, the New York Police Department detective who exposed the high level of corruption that went on in that agency. One incident that occurred at the very end of the decade did, however, bring charges of police brutality. On December 17, 1979, police in Miami, Florida, gave chase to an African American man who supposedly was engaged in traffic violations on his motorcycle. Six white officers attacked Arthur McDuffie and proceeded to beat him until he was unconscious. He died a few days later. Three days of rioting followed his death; 18 people were killed, and much property was damaged.

Although there were not many serious race riots in the 1980s, an event in the early 1990s made an indelible mark on the issue of police violence. Perhaps the case most commonly connected with police brutality occurred on March 3, 1991, in Los Angeles when an African American named Rodney King was traveling at a high rate of speed in his car with two other men and was stopped after a chase by officers of the California Highway Patrol. King later claimed that he had refused to stop because he was on probation for robbery. Officers from the Los Angeles Police Department (LAPD) and from the Los Angeles Unified School District Police joined the chase. By the time King's vehicle was stopped, a host of officers, including 23 from the LAPD, had congregated on the scene, including officers hovering overhead in a police helicopter. King failed to exit the vehicle when ordered to do so by officers, although his passengers quickly complied. It is reported that King, acting in an erratic manner, ran at police. The officers believed that King was high on drugs and shocked him with a Taser. Four officers began beating him with nightsticks and kicking him as he lay on the ground. King ended up with fractures to his skull, broken teeth, a broken ankle, internal organ damage, and brain damage as a result of the 56 blows that were dealt by the four officers.

A white amateur video camera operator who was watching from his apartment captured the King beating on film. The camera operator, George Holliday, attempted to provide this film to the LAPD the next day; a sergeant at the station was not interested in the tape, so Holliday went to local television stations that broadcast the video that night. The victim's brother, Paul King, also attempted to complain to the LAPD, but was turned away. By the next day, the 90-second tape was shown on national television, and interest in the case began to grow. When LAPD chief of police Daryl Gates and L.A. mayor Tom Bradley, a former police officer, saw the video, they both displayed disgust over the brutal treatment of King.

The four officers who were directly involved in the beating—Stacey Koon, Laurence W. Powell, Timothy Wind, and Theodore J. Briseno—were indicted for assault. Due to the intense media exposure surrounding the case, a trial was scheduled in a new venue in Ventura County. A jury of ten whites, one Asian American, and one Latin American acquitted the four officers of the charges against them. Within a few hours of the verdict, explosive rioting and looting broke out in Los Angeles, followed by disturbances in Atlanta, Georgia; Seattle, Washington; and Madison, Wisconsin. The violence in Los Angeles became extreme, and the LAPD enlisted the assistance of county, state, and federal law enforcement to stop the riots (*see* Los Angeles [California] Riots of 1992 entry). President George H. W. Bush intervened and ordered the military to establish order in the main hot spots of civil disruption. The massive violence, arson, and looting that accompanied the rioting resulted in over 54 deaths, 2,000 injuries, and great property loss, making it the largest outbreak of riot violence in the United States in the 20th century.

The four officers were then charged with civil rights violations and were found guilty in federal court. A special commission to investigate the L.A. riots was assembled and attorney Warren Christopher was called on to lead the investigation. Many have surmised that the LAPD, headed by Chief Daryl Gates, who was a young officer at the time of the 1965 riots, had an overly aggressive tone and a pervasive racist ethos.

Theorists have long speculated the potential causes of police brutality; however, the issue is complex and multifaceted. In many of the riot situations discussed above, the precipitating factors were essentially minor issues that were worsened by underlying social conditions. The cities where the violent activity occurred all have their own unique qualities that added fuel to the fire, or perhaps made conditions more amenable to compromise. Some cities saw more than their share of riots and police violence, including Harlem, which experienced major race riots in 1935, 1943, and 1964. Economic problems due to periods of depression, occupational competition, and poor housing, were often factors. And, of course, America's unique history of race relations, brought about by slavery, played a major part in all of the race riots. Regarding police brutality in relation to these riots, several factors also appear to present themselves and involve personal characteristics of the officers, agency philosophy, and police–community relations. Again, the issue of racism due to the nation's distinctive past is a recurring issue in police brutality in the United States.

Although excessive police force and intimidation has marred the history of American law enforcement, it should be noted that not all those who have been called to serve and protect have been guilty of this type of misbehavior. Most police officers believe in the law that they are required to uphold, and most understand that excessive force is unacceptable. It is important to note that commissions have always been formed to produce reports that not only describe the riot behavior and resulting police action, but also make recommendations for improvement. Greater police professionalism, through an increase in education and training programs, will hopefully reduce the amount of excessive force that is used by officers to control riots.

LEONARD A. STEVERSON

See also

Connor, "Bull"; Detroit (Michigan) Riot of 1967; Harlem (New York) Riot of 1935; Houston (Texas) Mutiny of 1917; Long Hot Summer Riots, 1965–1967; Los Angeles (California) Riots of 1992

Further Reading:

Amadou Diallo Foundation. http://www.amadoudiallo foundationinc.com.

Barlow, David E., and Melissa Hickman Barlow. *Police in a Multicultural Society: An American Story*. Prospect Heights, IL: Waveland Press, 2000.

Cannon, Lou. *Official Negligence: How Rodney King and the Riots Changed Los Angeles and the LAPD*. Boulder, CO: Westview Press, 1999.

Hays, Tom. "Diallo Officers Innocent of All Charges, Says Jury." *Birmingham Post* (England), February 26, 2000.

Kappeler, Victor E., Richard D. Skuder, and Geoffrey Alpert. *Forces of Deviance: Understanding the Dark Side of Policing*, 2nd ed. Prospect Heights, IL: Waveland Press, 1998.

Platt, Anthony, ed. *The Politics of Riot Commissions 1917–1979: A Collection of Official Reports and Critical Essays*. New York: Collier Books, 1971.

Puddington, Arch. "The War on the War on Crime." *Commentary* 107 (May 1999).

Skolnick, Jerome H., and James J. Fyfe. *Above the Law: Police and the Excessive Use of Force*. New York: Free Press, 1993.

Stark, Rodney. *Police Riots: Collective Violence and Law Enforcement*. Belmont, CA: Wadsworth, 1972.

Waskow, Arthur I. *From Race Riot to Sit-In, 1919 and the 1960s: A Study in the Connections between Conflict and Violence*. Garden City, NY: Doubleday, 1966.

Political Correctness (P.C.)

The term *political correctness* is most often used as a negative description of attempts to change the way issues are talked about, particularly issues of race and gender, and to avoid stereotyping. It gained prominence in the late 1980s and 1990s in response to social movements that sought to change the language used to discuss politically important and often controversial issues. A central assumption of those who advocated such changes is that everyday language can bring with it power dynamics that work against particular groups, particularly those that are already marginalized.

For example, some activists argued that labeling people "disabled" implied that they were less able than others and that the term *disability* was purely negative. In place of that term, some activists suggested that *physically challenged* or *differently abled* be used because they lack the negative connotations of *disabled* and, it was argued, more accurately reflect the experience of individuals being described and do not imply a deficit. Many of the terms called into question are related to race. For example, some terms such as *Negro* and *Oriental* are outdated and carry with them strongly negative connotations and stereotypes. Similarly, the use of the term *Indian* to refer to people indigenous to the Americas is incorrect and reflects historical inaccuracies. Activists promoted the use of more neutral terms, such as *African American*, *Asian*, and *Native American*.

Critics of so-called political correctness argue that being forced to use the new terms amounts to censorship and mangles the English language by replacing commonly accepted terms, such as *disabled*, with more cumbersome terms, such as *differently abled*. But the most cumbersome of the new terms will most likely fall out of use and others may simply appear cumbersome as we adjust to them. Therefore, in some cases, concerns about verbal censorship and mangling of the English language may be misplaced. The language may simply be catching up to new social realities.

Concerns about free speech and censorship, however, are more valid. Arguments over language can be used to stifle the voices of groups who voice unpopular or dissenting views. Ironically, this argument against political correctness draws on the fundamental insight of many of its early proponents: Language is powerful, and the privileging of some terms over others has political consequences. Battles over supposedly politically correct terms are often battles to define the nature of a situation. Although most charges of political correctness are made by the political right against the political left, Christian fundamentalists have also faced charges that they are stifling debate—particularly in school textbooks—by being politically correct. Left-wing critics have also convincingly argued that the term *politically correct* is itself used to stifle debate and to discredit the arguments of those who wish to challenge the power assumptions implicit in everyday language.

Although the argument over political correctness cooled in the late 1990s, the fundamental issues remain. How is a language that accurately describes the experience of all groups in a multicultural society created? How is civil debate encouraged without encroaching on free speech? When, if ever, does one person's right to his or her opinion infringe on another person's right not to live or work in a hostile environment? How should government and educational institutions weigh the rights of various groups when they come into conflict? How should this translate into the language used within these institutions? Perhaps one of the most dangerous aspects of the arguments over political correctness in the 1990s was that these vital and complex issues were trivialized.

ROBIN ROGER-DILLON

See also
Stereotype

Further Reading:
D'Souza, Dinesh. *Illiberal Education: The Politics of Race and Sex on Campus*. New York: Free Press, 1998.
Wilson, John K. *The Myth of Political Correctness: The Conservative Attack on Higher Education*. Durham, NC: Duke University Press, 1995.

Poll Taxes

A levy placed on the right to vote, poll taxes were first established in the years following the American Revolution as a substitute for the traditional requirement that only property owners could cast ballots. Initially, the poll tax expanded the number of eligible voters, but was abandoned as states established unrestricted suffrage for most white males. However, when most male citizens were guaranteed the right to vote as a result of the ratification of the Fifteenth Amendment in 1870, the poll tax was resurrected for a more ignoble purpose. Many whites, alarmed at the sight of former slaves voting and holding elective office, were determined to restrict or even eliminate black political influence in the South. Between 1871 and 1902, the states of Alabama, Arkansas, Florida, Georgia, Louisiana, Mississippi, North Carolina, South Carolina, Texas, and Virginia adopted the poll tax specifically to deny African Americans the right to vote. Georgia was the first state to adopt a poll tax, in 1871. Citizens were required to pay between one and two dollars to their local election commissions several months before a scheduled primary and general election. On Election Day, voters then had to show proof that the tax was paid in order to cast their ballots. If a voter in Alabama, Georgia, Mississippi, and Virginia failed to pay the levy, then his poll tax bill would double for each subsequent election. This cumulative tax erected an additional barrier between economically disadvantaged Southerners and their constitutional rights.

The poll tax was chiefly designed to prevent African Americans from exercising their franchise, but in this regard, it was unsuccessful. It did make it more difficult for citizens to vote and undoubtedly prevented many from casting ballots especially in the states where the levy was cumulative. However, it fell far short of its goal of entirely disenfranchising black Southerners. Many were able to pay the tax; for example, in Shelby County, Tennessee, 24,086 African Americans registered to vote in 1931. In addition, the poll tax often disenfranchised more white citizens than black. Largely because it restricted white voting, North Carolina repealed the poll tax in 1920, and Louisiana and Florida followed suit in 1934 and 1937, respectively. Around the same time, reformers in the South began to focus a great deal of attention on the inequities of the poll tax. In November 1938, the Southern Conference for Human Welfare was founded by a group of African American and white reformers to address the economic and political inequality that existed in the American South. The conference's Civil Rights Committee investigated the poll tax, and in 1941, it formed the National Committee to Abolish the Poll Tax. Petitioning Congress to abolish the tax in federal elections, the committee played a large role in convincing several Southern states to abolish the excise. Georgia, the first state to enact a poll tax, repealed the law in 1945. South Carolina abolished the poll tax in 1951, and Tennessee did the same in 1953.

Despite the success of the National Committee to Abolish the Poll Tax, Alabama, Arkansas, Texas, and Virginia refused to abandon the levy. As the civil rights movement spread across the South, increased pressure was directed at Congress to abolish the restrictive tax. As a result of this pressure, a constitutional amendment was introduced that would eliminate the use of poll taxes in federal elections. After fierce debate, the amendment passed the House and Senate, and in 1964, the required number of states ratified the Twenty-fourth Amendment to the Constitution. The ability to charge voters to cast ballots in state and local elections came to an end in 1966 when the U.S. Supreme Court ruled that Virginia's poll tax violated a citizen's right to equal protection under the law as guaranteed by the Fourteenth Amendment to the Constitution. Although it did not accomplish its primary goal of stripping all African Americans of their right to vote, poll taxes were an important tool in preventing blacks from achieving full equality in the segregated South.

Wayne Dowdy

See also

Racial Gerrymandering; Voter ID Requirements; Voting and Race; Voting Rights Act of 1965

Further Reading:

Key, V. O. *Southern Politics in State and Nation*. New York: Knopf, 1949.

Martin, Waldo E., Jr., and Patricia Sullivan, eds. *Civil Rights in the United States*. New York: Macmillan, 2000.

Roller, David C., and Robert W. Twyman, eds. *The Encyclopedia of Southern History*. Baton Rouge: Louisiana State University Press, 1979.

Poor People's Campaign

The Poor People's Campaign was a movement organized and led by the Southern Christian Leadership Conference (SCLC) and its director, Dr. Martin Luther King, Jr. It was intended to dramatize the plight of the nation's poor and address economic injustice. The plan was to bring thousands of poor

Poor People's March in Washington, D.C., on June 18, 1968. (Library of Congress)

people of all races to Washington, D.C., where they would engage in radical nonviolent direct action to convince Congress and President Lyndon B. Johnson to make eliminating poverty the number one goal of the nation.

Most African Americans appeared to be untouched by the Civil Rights Act of 1964—the most sweeping legislation guaranteeing civil rights since Reconstruction. In 1965, almost one-third of African Americans lived below the poverty line, and half of all black households lived in substandard dwellings. Indeed, the percentage of poor blacks had actually increased between 1959 and 1965. The unemployment rate for blacks was almost double that of whites; for black teenagers, it was more than twice that for white teens. The crumbling infrastructure of inner-city neighborhoods was further eroded by so-called urban renewal, and the employment situation was exacerbated by the movement of jobs to the suburbs. The high school dropout rate soared, drug abuse became rampant, and fragile families were further strained.

Northern urban communities with thousands of poor, black residents were also fertile ground for the nascent Black Power movement. Nonviolent direct action that had been so successful in the past held no appeal for the hundreds of thousands of blacks who were trapped there with little to no opportunity for improvement. Nor had the War on Poverty, developed by the administration of President Lyndon B. Johnson to eradicate poverty in America, been much help. Although noble, its efforts were too little, and it was opposed by powerful politicians at the local level and whites who felt Johnson was giving handouts to the undeserving poor. The poor, their hopes raised by community action programs and maximum feasible participation, again found their hopes unanswered. As such, the cities became simmering cauldrons of frustration, alienation, and hopelessness that exploded in 1965.

Every summer from 1965 through 1969, Northern cities were visited by urban rebellions, sometimes referred to as race riots. The Los Angeles neighborhood of Watts was the first of these on August 11, 1965. Six days of rioting reduced Watts to rubble, claimed 34 lives, and recorded property damage of $35 million. Urban rebellions also occurred in 1966, but arguably the worst year of the phenomenon was 1967. A total of 59 riots occurred, the deadliest being in Newark, New Jersey, and Detroit, Michigan. The Newark rebellion left 27 dead, including children, a police officer, and a firefighter, and caused millions of dollars in damage. Conditions in Detroit were so bad that 43 blacks were killed. Not even 800 state and city police and the National Guard could restore order. President Lyndon Johnson was forced to send in the Army's 82nd and 101st Airborne divisions to restore order.

After the Newark and Detroit riots, Johnson established the National Advisory Commission on Civil Disorders, commonly known as the Kerner Commission, after its leader, Gov. Otto Kerner of Illinois. Johnson recognized that the only way to end the despair of the masses of blacks was a sustained government program designed to end joblessness, substandard housing, poverty, and disease. The Kerner Commission report surprisingly blamed white racism as the chief cause of the riots and warned that America was once again becoming a dual society, one black and one white.

King and the SCLC were keenly aware that the times called for bold measures. He recognized that the Poor People's Campaign would be different from those implemented during the civil rights movement; it was demanding nothing less than a wholesale transformation of American capitalism. Moreover, King intended to force the nation to choose between eliminating poverty, which he saw as a moral issue, and continuing an increasingly unpopular Vietnam War, against which he had become a vocal critic. To him, the two were inextricably linked.

The Poor People's Campaign had three stages. First, it would crisscross the nation putting together a group of several thousand black, Latino, Native American, and white Appalachian poor people who would travel to Washington to live in a shantytown much like that erected by the Bonus Army of the early 20th century. They would participate in daily demonstrations in the capital and be joined by parallel demonstrations in cities across the country. These would be crowned by a mass march echoing the 1963 March on Washington. Second, the demonstrations would engender mass arrests as they had in the South, further dramatizing the plight of the poor. Finally, there would be an economic boycott of the most powerful businesses in America. The Poor People's Campaign would show that all the gains of the civil rights movement were hollow without economic parity and opportunity. It would either be a brilliant success or a humiliating failure.

King and the SCLC were instantly attacked by the media, the political Left, and white Americans who were weary of the struggle for equality. Leaders of the other civil rights organizations also criticized King, not only for the campaign, but for his stinging and public rebuke of the Vietnam War. In addition, most of organized labor refused to support the effort. Finally, President Johnson turned against King, too, and he lost the warm working relationship they had developed. However, King pressed on.

In 1968, King's empathy for and support of the poor took him to Memphis, Tennessee, where he marched in solidarity with city garbage collectors who were seeking a living wage and better working conditions. On April 4, he was assassinated. Coretta Scott King, his widow, and the SCLC decided to continue the Poor People's Campaign under the leadership of the Rev. Ralph Abernathy, a close friend and confidant of King. From May 14 to June 24, more than 2,500 poor people lived in a Washington, D.C., shantytown they had erected and named Resurrection City. The camp boasted a city hall, cultural capital, a medical facility, dining hall, psychiatrist, a university, and a ZIP code. It fanned out across the Reflecting Pool to the base of the Lincoln Memorial. Residents policed themselves and provided a model for interracial cooperation. Thousands of them fanned out daily across locations in the capital to shame the U.S. government into significant action against poverty.

Unfortunately, conditions in the camp quickly turned miserable. Washington was unusually cool that year in May and June, and it rained 28 of the 42 days of the operation. Residents were soon knee-deep in mud, trash, and rotting food. Then, on June 4, Sen. Robert F. Kennedy, who had become a champion of the poor and was running for the Democratic nomination for president, was assassinated. Finally, it was clear that Dr. King's leadership was sorely missed. Abernathy lacked the charisma and contacts of King, and he spent little time at the camp, appearing to prefer the comfort of the black-owned Pitts Hotel to the muddy squalor of Resurrection City. By the middle of June, fewer than 300 people remained in the camp.

Fighting and near-riots broke out in the camp on June 22. Police were called in, but police dogs and more than 1,000 tear gas grenades failed to stem the trouble. On June 24, about 1,000 police closed Resurrection City, arresting Abernathy and 175 people. Charges of assault against police officers, disorderly conduct, curfew violations, and public drunkenness were levied against those arrested. The Poor People's Campaign had not persuaded public officials to pour more resources into eliminating poverty, and it was deemed a failure and the end of the civil rights movement.

Recent scholarship, however, has reevaluated the campaign and somewhat redeemed its reputation. The Poor People's Campaign ignited the third wave of the civil rights movement: economic empowerment. The interracial structure of the effort showed that a strong alliance based on class was not only important but necessary. Indeed, Rev. Jesse Jackson would bring this alliance to fruition with his emphasis on a Rainbow Coalition during his 1988 presidential campaign. The Poor People's Campaign highlighted the weaknesses of runaway capitalism and consumerism in a manner not seen since the Great Depression.

MARILYN K. HOWARD

See also

Black Power Movement; Civil Rights Act of 1964; King, Martin Luther, Jr.; Southern Christian Leadership Council (SCLC). Document: The Kerner Commission Report (1968)

Further Reading:

Freeman, Roland L. *Mule Train: A Journey of Hope Remembered.* Nashville, TN: Thomas Nelson, 1998.

Honey, Michael. *Going Down Jericho Road: The Memphis Strike, Martin Luther King's Last Campaign.* New York: W. W. Norton, 2007

McKnight, Gerald. *The Last Crusade: Martin Luther King, Jr., the FBI and the Poor People's Campaign.* New York: Westview Press, 1998.

Post-Racialism

Many people today describe U.S. society as "postracial," espousing the belief that race is no longer a key organizing feature of society. Post-racialism refers to an environment in which a society is devoid of racial discrimination and prejudice. In contrast to the history of racism in the United States where blacks and other minority citizens have been discriminated against, many claim that today's United States is devoid of racial preference and prejudice and is instead a "color-blind" society. Many Americans today choose to believe that racism and race privilege no longer exist in the United States and that every citizen is treated equally, regardless of race. Post-racialism and race blindness are concepts typically supported and embraced by whites, who choose to believe they live in a color-blind society but nevertheless still occupy positions of privilege and power in relation to racial minorities.

Post-racialism is more than just a singular concept. It is a post–civil rights belief system that consists of five interrelated ideas. These ideas include the notion that race-based exclusion is a thing of the past; that there is no need for race-conscious identities, decision making, or political mobilization; that racial minorities who struggle today lack motivation, self-discipline, and self-reliance and therefore have no one to blame but themselves; and that racism is a two-way street. The final idea underwriting the postracial belief system is that whites and ethnoracial minorities are equally capable of being racist or being victims of racism. For supporters of postracial thinking, there is a need to distinguish oneself, practices, and organizations from the past. Despite the persistence of ethnoracial inequality in American society, the interrelated ideas making up post-racialism attempt to explain this inequality by factors not having to do with race.

The idea of post-racialism has become so popular that it is easy to forget that *postracial* is a relatively new term, first gaining prominence during the historic 2008 U.S. presidential election campaign. At the core of the public discussion of post-racialism during the campaign was an aspiration held by many pundits and voters that the election of the first black U.S. president, Barack Obama, would be an indicator that we had finally transcended race. For instance, following the election, Bill Schneider, a CNN senior political analyst, speculated in a *National Journal Magazine* article that "it was as if race didn't matter" after showing that President Obama did as well as other recent Democratic presidential candidates among white voters.

Nevertheless, many scholars have dismissed the notion of post-racialism, calling its description of contemporary racial dynamics inaccurate. However, post-racialism as a belief system continues to grow, appearing to be on its way to becoming an orthodoxy as more and more individuals declare themselves believers. For instance, in 2000, blacks and whites were asked in a nationwide survey, "Do you think that blacks have achieved racial equality, will soon achieve racial equality, will not achieve racial equality in your lifetime, or will never achieve racial equality?" Their responses indicated that fully one-third of whites (34 percent) and a mere 6 percent of blacks believed that we had already achieved racial equality. In 2009, in the aftermath of the 2008 presidential election, this question was asked again of blacks and whites nationally. The results revealed a significant rise in both groups endorsing the view that we have achieved racial equality with almost two-thirds of whites (61 percent), and almost one in five blacks (17 percent) affirming this belief. These survey results were published by sociologist Lawrence Bobo in his 2004 book and 2011 article. Of course it is no surprise that black Americans and white Americans disagree about the actual degree of racial equality in U.S. society, but what is noteworthy is the similar trend among both groups with now a majority of whites and a significant minority of blacks believing the postracial moment is already here. Postracialism is clearly a growing sentiment in the United States in the 21st century.

A major concept that underwrites the postracial belief system is the notion of color blindness. Also referred to as *race blindness*, *color blindness* is a sociological term that refers to a disregard of race when interacting with another person. Color-blind practices make no distinctions or classifications based upon race, upholding the postracial belief that racism and racial bias are a thing of the past. Color blindness and post-racialism disregard the history of institutional discrimination and prejudicial practices that have led to the ethnoracial inequality that still exists in American society today. Nevertheless, a large number of Americans today are subscribers to the postracial logic. In 2010, the National Opinion Research Center's General Social Survey asked a nationwide sample of blacks and whites about their opinions on post-racialism. Five out of 10 whites surveyed (52 percent) and three out of 10 blacks (31 percent) agreed that "African Americans do not need any special consideration because racism is a thing of the past." 94 percent of whites and 86 percent of blacks agreed with the statement, "For the most part, I'm colorblind; that is, I don't care about what race people are." Finally, a little more than eight in 10 whites (84 percent) and two-thirds of blacks (65 percent) agreed with the view that "for African Americans to succeed they need to stop using racism and slavery as excuses." These survey results make it clear that post-racialism is gaining traction in U.S. society as a powerful interpretive framework for understanding ethnoracial inequity, even though scholars and historians agree it is precisely a history of racism that accounts for this inequity.

While post-racialism is becoming more popular, social science research over the past few years has called into question almost every underlying assumptions of this belief system. In fact, the real danger of post-racialism is that it blinds its adherents both to realities of entrenched ethnoracial inequality and to the more subtle forms of prejudice and discrimination that remain in place today. The power of this emergent post–civil rights racial ideology is not necessarily in the direct harm it inflicts on individual ethnoracial minorities, as was the case with Jim Crow racism. Its power instead lies in its indirect impact on ethnoracial minorities' life chances through its creation of a social climate that prevents growing numbers of Americans from recognizing and taking actions to redress persistent ethnoracial inequity.

T. A. Forman

See also
Discrimination; Prejudice; Racism

Further Reading:
Bobo, Lawrence. "Inequalities that endure? Racial ideology, American politics, and the peculiar role of the social sciences." In *The Changing Terrain of Race and Ethnicity*, edited by Maria Krysan and Amanda Lewis. New York: Russell Sage Foundation, 2004.
Bobo, Lawrence. "Somewhere between Jim Crow & Post-Racialism: Reflections on the Racial Divide Today." *Daedalus* 140, no. 2 (2011): 11–36.
Cho, Sumi. "Post-Racialism." *Iowa Law Review* 94 (2009): 1589–649.

Crenshaw, Kimberle. "Twenty Years of Critical Race Theory: Looking Back To Move Forward." *Connecticut Law Review* 43. no. 5 (2011): 1253–352.

Dawson, Michael. *Not in My Lifetime: The Future of Black Politics.* Chicago: University of Chicago Press, 2011.

Logan, Enid. *"At This Defining Moment": Barack Obama's Presidential Candidacy and the New Politics of Race.* New York: New York University Press, 2011.

Rossing, Jonathan. "Deconstructing Post-racialism: Humor as a Critical, Cultural Project." *Journal of Communication Inquiry* 36, no. 1 (2012): 44–61.

Schneider, William. "What Racial Divide?" *National Journal Magazine*, November 8, 2008.

Sugrue, Thomas. *Not Even Past: Barack Obama and the Burden of Race.* Princeton, NJ: Princeton University Press, 2010.

Powell v. Alabama (1932)

Powell v. Alabama was one of the U.S. Supreme Court's early opinions that expanded the scope of the Fifth Amendment. In this case, for the first time it was suggested that the right to counsel was a national right, if only in capital cases and that aspect of the Bill of Rights was applied to the states. The case resulted in more trials, convictions, reversals, appeals, and retrials than any crime in American history.

The case revolved around nine black teenagers who were accused of raping two white girls on a train traveling through the South in 1931. The group became commonly known as the Scottsboro Boys (*see* Scottsboro Boys Case). The incident stemmed from a fight that broke out on the train between the nine black youths and several whites. The confrontation ignited when a white youth crossing on top of the train stepped on the hand of Haywood Patterson, one of the black youths, who were hanging on to the side to the train. A stone-throwing fight then erupted between Patterson and his friends and the white youths. The result was that almost all of the whites were forced off the train, with the exception of one, Orville Gilley, whom Patterson saved. Some of the whites who were forced off the train complained to the stationmaster that they had been attacked by a gang of blacks. The next town was notified, and when the train arrived in Paint Rock, Alabama, an armed posse surrounded, tied up, and hauled the nine black youths off to jail in Scottsboro, Alabama.

However, it would turn out that the key element of that stop in Paint Rock was not the fight that had broken out, but the complaint of two white girls—Victoria Price and Ruby Bates—who had also been on the train. The girls claimed they had been raped by a gang of 12 blacks at pistol and knife point. Price positively identified six of the nine Scottsboro Boys.

The others were assumed guilty by association. Attempts by the boys to deny the accusations were met with violence, and the threat of a lynching materialized as the nine sat in jail. Several hundred local citizens gathered around the Scottsboro jail looking for quick justice on the night of their arrest. However, courage on the part of the local sheriff, and the order by Alabama's governor B. M. Miller to send the National Guard, quieted the crowd, which eventually dispersed.

Amidst this fear of potential violence and lynching, local officials in Alabama hurried through the legal proceedings. All but one of the trials was held and concluded in one day. The counsel afforded to the defendants was suspect at best, with one having no experience in criminal law at all. The lawyers and defendants met only right before the trials began, giving them no time to plan a defense, and both lawyers acted minimally in their appearance in court. The nine were quickly convicted and sentenced to death. The ruling was appealed to the Alabama Supreme Court, which ruled 6–1 that the trial was fair, and subsequently appealed to the U.S. Supreme Court. What was an obvious perversion of due process to many outside the Deep South, and even some within, became a national cause, hailed by diverse organizations from the National Association for the Advancement of Colored People to the Communist Party.

The Supreme Court agreed to hear the appeal combining *Weems v. Alabama* and *Patterson v. Alabama* into the case of *Powell*. Justice Sutherland explained that, in his opinion, the trial had been unfair. He concluded that the lack of effective counsel had violated the defendant's right to due process as required by the Fourteenth Amendment, and to counsel as guaranteed in the Fifth Amendment.

The decision overruled an earlier decision from 1884, *Hurtado v. California*, in which the Court ruled that the specific dictates of the Fifth Amendment did not apply to the states via the Fourteenth Amendment. *Powell* rejected that reasoning and represented a major step in extending the Bill of Rights to the states, which had begun not even a decade earlier in a series of cases referring to the First Amendment. This was the first time that, with the exception of free-speech guarantees, the Bill of Rights was impressed on state governments.

Justice Sutherland's opinion noted that the atmosphere around the case was unfriendly, unsettling, and downright hostile. With the threat of mob violence hanging over the proceedings, the defendants were escorted to and from the jail under armed guard. The judge made no effort to afford the defendants any help, including never asking them if they wanted counsel. The counsel that was eventually procured (with no help from the court) and paid for by concerned citizens was useless. One lawyer, from out of state, had no knowledge of Alabama law and was not even a member of the local bar. The other was so drunk he could barely stand. The Supreme Court noted that the trial court could have granted a delay to give the eventual counsel some time to prepare, or even find some effective counsel. In the end, the trial court did not even consider the issue of counsel as a vital and important component to the proceedings.

Sutherland made it clear that the counsel in this case was vital for justice to be achieved. The failure of the trial court to secure lawyers that were not in the least bit effective, or capable of being so, denied the defendants due process under the Fourteenth Amendment. However, Sutherland was careful to limit the ruling to capital cases, noting that whether there was such a need in other criminal cases was not at issue in this case. (That decision would take 30 more years; in *Gideon v. Wainwright*, the Court did extend the right to counsel to noncapital cases.) But the Court noted very specifically that in any capital case, when the defendant was not able to hire a lawyer and was incapable of making a proper defense because of a variety of circumstances, the demands of due process of law made it the duty of the Court, whether it was asked or not, to assign counsel. Any contrary decision would deny the basic "immutable principles of justice which inhere in the very idea of free government" (*Holden v. Hardy*, 169 U.S. 366, 389).

GARY GERSHMAN

See also

Masculinity, Black and White; Rape and Racism; Scottsboro Boys Case (1931)

Further Reading:

Carter, Dan T. *Scottsboro: A Tragedy of the American South*. Baton Rouge: Louisiana State University Press, 1979.

Goodman, James E. *Stories of Scottsboro*. New York: Pantheon Books, 1994.

Linder, Douglas O. *Famous American Trials: The Scottsboro Boys 1931–1937*. http://www.law.umkc.edu/faculty/projects/FTrials/scottsboro/scottsb.htm.

Preachers

As sources of moral authority, preachers could either advocate or condemn various Jim Crow practices and have a wide-reaching influence through the attitudes of their audiences. Among African Americans, preachers were able to challenge Jim Crow more directly because their livelihood depended upon the support of an African American congregation, not on white employers. Among whites, preachers might join the Ku Klux Klan or condemn it. Some white preachers actively worked to eliminate Jim Crowism, while others encouraged support. The high level of involvement on the part of preachers allowed opposing arguments to take on religious tones and justifications. Other preachers, however, attempted to avoid racially charged issues as much as possible.

African American Preachers

In the early days of Jim Crow, many African American preachers told their congregations that it was best to submit to the laws and codes to try to avoid conflict. As conditions in the South worsened and economic opportunities in the North opened up, many preachers saw streams of their congregants leaving the South. Preachers in the North did their best to receive and care for this incoming population, although at times, the huge wave of migrants made the task difficult.

Both Northern and Southern African American churches served as not only a spiritual but also a social center for members. Historically, African Americans had been excluded from leadership roles in other social institutions, but the churches were an exception. In African American churches, members exerted a level of control and authority that they did not find in other social settings. In many estimations, the church was the nerve center of African American life well into the 20th century. The space of the church allowed African Americans to develop leadership skills and provided a safe forum for social concerns. In addition to the religious services provided, other groups might be organized within the space of the church. The preacher, as the leader of this spiritual and social center, fulfilled many roles. Preachers might be responsible for providing financial assistance to members, helping them find employment or housing, in addition to serving as a spiritual leader. Due to its central position in the lives of many African Americans, the church was well respected and lent the civil rights movement increased credibility.

African American preachers, who were already seen as leaders of the community, were more readily available to take on leadership positions against Jim Crow injustices. Other adult African Americans often worked for a white employer or rented their housing from a white landlord. These adults were discouraged from speaking out against Jim Crow laws and codes because they feared losing their jobs or homes. African American preachers were supported by their congregations, which were made up almost entirely of African Americans. These preachers had greater freedom to challenge Jim Crow, as long as the members of their congregations supported them. In areas where white reactions to such a challenge might be violent, African American preachers were constrained by fear of being attacked. Even in those situations though, African American preachers typically had greater freedom to advocate for civil rights advancements because their livelihood depended on the support of other African Americans, not on a white employer.

One of the most widely known organizations of the civil rights movement was the Southern Christian Leadership Conference (SCLC). Founded in 1957, the SCLC was initially led by African American pastor Martin Luther King, Jr. Its ranks were filled disproportionately with African American pastors who wanted to see advancements made against Jim Crow. The executive staff and governing board were composed almost entirely of preachers, primarily Baptist. African American preachers who were SCLC members typically continued to have ties to their congregation, who then provided the grassroots support the SCLC needed to carry out its vision. Organizationally, the SCLC patterned its structure, meetings, and language after the church. They framed the discussion over Jim Crow laws in terms of religious as well as social injustices, adding to their moral legitimacy.

As preachers rose to leadership positions in the battle against Jim Crow, they found language familiar to their religious vocation worked well to motivate others for the civil rights cause. Religious imagery was familiar to African Americans, and preachers used that imagery to encourage a sort of religious fervor towards the push against Jim Crow inequalities. The exodus was a poignant image used during the days of slavery and the Underground Railroad to depict enslaved African Americans as a new "chosen" people whom God would redeem. This notion of chosen-ness was invoked long after the legal abolition of slavery. Religious songs were also appropriated or developed by participants of the civil rights movement, further invoking a sense of sacred purpose, religious fervor, and devout commitment. Preachers, who drew on biblical passages, stories, and imagery, lent the movement religious legitimation and fervor.

Some critics accused African American preachers of being "in it" for the money, and some may have been dishonest. Because many African American congregants struggled financially, some resented the monetary pleas of preachers. For those preachers who became involved in politics, it was commonplace to be accused of corruption. While some preachers with large constituencies tried to use the voting power of their congregation to garner alliances and promises from politicians, other preachers entered politics themselves. Whether this was in hopes of improving the plight of their fellow African Americans or with an eye towards personal benefits can be evaluated on a case-by-case basis, as there were certainly instances of both.

Regardless of political involvement, a preacher's role in cities with an influx of African Americans was widely seen as helping people adjust to life in their new surroundings. Preachers might help congregants find housing, jobs, or financial relief agencies. The church itself sometimes provided financial relief, support networks, child care, and other services. Churches were places for migrants to come into contact with other African Americans who had been living in the cities for a longer period of time. This contact helped newcomers learn the ways of the city and adapt to their new surroundings.

White preachers were also involved in the battle that raged over Jim Crow. Their responses ranged a full spectrum. Many supported Jim Crow laws. Some tried to stay neutral. Others became heavily involved, even serving jail time and risking personal injury for their involvement. Although white preachers did not become involved in a social movement advancing or denouncing Jim Crow laws to the extent that African American preachers became involved in the civil rights movement, they were involved in the moral confrontation.

The Ku Klux Klan was perhaps the closest white preachers came to being leaders of an organized movement advancing Jim Crow laws. A significant number of Klan leaders were drawn from the ranks of white preachers. Just as African American preachers were drawing on biblical passages, their white counterparts advocating for Jim Crowism also mined the Bible for passages supporting slavery or the social subordination of some groups of people to others. Due to the covert nature of the Klan, preachers' involvement in the group was not explicit, although often implicitly recognized by both African Americans and whites. Other white preachers actively resisted identification with the Klan and said Klansmen were unchristian. Klan members did not leave such denunciations unnoticed, and those who openly condemned the Klan risked retaliation.

White pastors who were sympathetic towards the plight of African Americans were often a point of contact between the civil rights movement and whites in the community. These preachers were able to communicate with African American civil rights leaders, who were often also preachers. The white pastor could then mediate the message of those leaders to his white congregation. Such sympathetic white pastors sometimes engaged in demonstrations against Jim Crow laws with African Americans, sometimes bearing the brunt of violence inflicted by opposing whites.

Preachers were involved in the struggle over Jim Crow laws, but their positions were not defined simply by their position. African American pastors, while cautious about opposition in some contexts, were largely involved in the fight against Jim Crow and the battle for civil rights. Their impact is immeasurable. Without the freedoms they had from white employers, countless pastor leaders would never have emerged. They strengthened the civil rights movement from all corners. White preachers also had an impact on the fate of Jim Crow laws. Some viscously defended the codes through the Ku Klux Klan or simply through the power of their pulpit to reinforce ideas of white supremacy among their congregants. Other white preachers just as vehemently opposed the laws, although in a less violent manner than their Klansman opponents. These civil rights supporters tried to sway the hearts of their audiences to sympathize with African Americans, and in some cases these pastors joined movement demonstrations. Overall, regardless of their position on Jim Crow laws, pastors had wide-reaching effects on the battle over Jim Crow.

SHAWNTEL ENSMINGER

See also

Black Church Arsons; Black Churches

Further Reading:

Chappell, David. *A Stone of Hope: Prophetic Religion and the Death of Jim Crow.* Chapel Hill: University of North Carolina Press, 2004.

Fairclough, Adam. *To Redeem the Soul of America: The Southern Christian Leadership Conference & Martin Luther King, Jr.* Athens: University of Georgia Press, 1987.

Packard, Jerome M. *American Nightmare: The History of Jim Crow.* New York: St. Martin's Press, 2002.

Sernett, Milton C. *Bound for the Promised Land: African American Religion and the Great Migration.* C. Eric Lincoln Series on the Black Experience. Durham, NC: Duke University Press, 1997.

Predatory Lending

Most Americans place a high value on homeownership. It is often difficult, however, for low-income and minority citizens to gain access into the housing market. Low-income citizens may not have the means to buy and maintain a home, and discrimination and segregation affect the prospects of minority home ownership. Predatory lenders know this and seek out groups that historically have had less access to homeownership to target them to receive subprime loans.

Although sometimes found in the prime market, predatory lending usually occurs in the subprime lending market where there is less competition. *Predatory lending* refers to the process of mortgage lenders systematically granting loans to low income and minorities at higher rates than similarly qualified white or higher income applicants, often using deceit to do so. Predatory lenders exploit low income or minority individuals by selling them properties that are worth less than the appraised value, lending money to borrowers knowing that they cannot afford the loan, charging higher

Protesters react during a news conference held by the Association of Community Organizations for Reform Now (ACORN), November 2001, in downtown Los Angeles, California. According to a report by the group, predatory lending has skyrocketed in the past decade and minorities are the main targets. (Associated Press/Nick Ut)

interest rates than necessary, convincing homeowners to refinance multiple times, pressuring homeowners to buy home improvements financed at high rates, or using fraud or other deceptive practices to entice individuals into borrowing money. In fact, many predatory lenders offer loans that have no benefit to the borrower.

Predatory lending burdens minorities, even those who are not low income, by charging them more money for the same services and loans offered to similarly well-off whites. Although often viewed as a reflection of historical segregation in neighborhoods, a recent study found that, regardless of income level, blacks are more likely than whites to be served by lenders that specialize in high priced credit and are less likely than whites to receive loans at all. The U.S. Department of Housing and Urban Development (HUD) has found

similar results. In a 2000 study they found that minorities and people who live in predominantly minority neighborhoods are becoming increasingly subject to predatory lending. In fact, the HUD study found that 51 percent of refinance loans in black neighborhoods were subprime, compared to 9 percent of loans in predominantly white neighborhoods even after income was taken into account.

One reason for this is that people who live in predominantly minority neighborhoods historically have had a difficult time receiving loans, so subprime loans are an attractive way to enter the mortgage market. Although these loans are initially viewed as positive by the applicants receiving them, they often serve to deny people with low incomes and minorities access to the same wealth acquisition that whites obtain through prime home loans.

Subprime Loans

Predatory lending is not the same thing as subprime lending, although it usually occurs in the subprime market. The prime market is available for people who do not pose a risk for non-repayment. These individuals have a good credit rating and means for repaying the loan. In contrast, the subprime loan market offers loans to people who may otherwise not be qualified to receive a loan. The subprime market focuses on offering loans to people who have more risk such as a large amount of debt or low credit scores. To counter the higher risk, subprime loans have higher interest rates than loans in the prime market. These loans are marketed as ways for high-risk individuals to build their credit rating or get out of debt.

Predatory lending often has far reaching consequences for the borrowers. Borrowers who are victims of predatory lending are more likely to become delinquent in their payments and have higher rates of foreclosure. The loss of a family's home not only devastates the individual, but has consequences for the neighborhood as well. Foreclosed homes often stay vacant for long periods of time, bringing down the value of the surrounding homes.

Due to the damage predatory lending has caused to low income and minority borrowers, some states and cities have implemented laws against these practices. The first statewide law against predatory lending was in North Carolina. Harvey and Nigro (2004) found that when restrictions were placed on predatory practices, the number of subprime lenders, many of which were nonbank lenders, declined. This was not due to banks refusing more loans, but rather there were fewer applications, likely due to lenders being less aggressive after the law was implemented.

In 2009 the federal government increased their oversight of lenders with the Secure and Fair Enforcement for Mortgage Licensing Act of 2008 ("SAFE Act"). Among other requirements, this act mandates that loan originators be licensed and supervised, have a criminal background check and continue education. The act also states that borrowers must show an ability to repay the loan and loan documents must be presented to the borrower along with potential risks

in writing. By 2010, all 50 states and the District of Columbia have legislation implementing the SAFE Act.

STEPHANIE SOUTHWORTH

Further Reading:

Beeman, Angie, Davita Silfen Glasberg, and Colleen Casey. "Whiteness as Property: Predatory Lending and the Reproduction of Racialized Inequality." *Critical Sociology* 37, no. 1 (2010): 27–45.

Caggiano, Julie R., Jennifer L. Dozier, and Therese G. Franzen. "Developments in State and Federal Mortgage Lending Laws: Predatory Lending and Beyond." *Business Lawyer* 16, no. 2 (2010).

Feinstein, Diane, "Mortgage Fraud and America's Foreclosure Crisis." http://www.feinstein.senate.gov/public/index .cfm?a=Files.Serve&File_id=3b152e79-bc45-48e3-8692-ad9 c80c21ca8&SK=0C8380A3AC716A7F84E1D44142357089 (accessed December 21, 2012).

Gans, Kale. "Anatomy of a Mortgage Meltdown: The Study of the Subprime Crisis, the Role of Fraud, and the Efficacy of the Idaho Safe Act." *Idaho Law Review* 147 (2012).

Harvey, Keith D., and Peter J. Nigro. "Do Predatory Lending Laws Influence Mortgage Lending? An Analysis of the North Carolina Predatory Lending Law." *Journal of Real Estate Finance and Economics* 29, no. 4 (2004): 445–56.

Office of the Federal Register. "Safe Mortgage Licensing Act (Regulations G & H)." https://www.federalregister.gov/ articles/2011/12/19/2011-31730/safe-mortgage-licensing-act -regulations-g-and-h#h-21 (accessed January 1, 2013).

U.S. Department of Housing and Urban Development a. "HUD-Treasury Report Recommendations to Curb Predatory Home Mortgage Lending." http://archives.hud.gov/reports/treasrpt .pdf (accessed December 12, 2012).

U.S Department of Housing and Urban Development b. "Title V. Safe Mortgage Licensing Act." http://portal.hud.gov/ hudportal/documents/huddoc?id=DOC_19673.pdf (accessed December 12, 2012).

U.S. Department of Housing and Urban Development c. "Don't be a Victim of Loan Fraud." http://portal.hud.gov/hudportal/ HUD?src=/program_offices/housing/sfh/buying/loanfraud (accessed December 12, 2012).

Prejudice

Prejudice is a form of bias or partiality that is informed by both irrationality and an affective component against a particular individual or group. In the spheres of human cognition and affect, the conception of prejudice is utilized to comprehend people's actions and sentiments on a foreign individual or group. The norm of rationality, which prompts people to search for accurate information, is stymied by prejudice, with overgeneralizations and prejudgments. From a position of limited understanding, prejudice is wielded to maintain power of a particular person or group while defending from the perceived threat of the oppositional person or group. Largely, prejudice can be thought of as an "irrationally based, negative attitude against certain ethnic groups and their members" with a faulty generalization.

First, in a cognitive framework, prejudice is conceived through an irrationality that is formed through an inadequate understanding and overgeneralization of a group to comprehend an individual's characteristics and persona. This is best shown in the example of Americans being prejudiced of Muslims by equating them with terrorists. Obviously, not all Muslims are terrorists, and these overgeneralizations stem from a prejudicial approach. Such overgeneralizations can be traced to the creation of stereotypes (*see* Stereotypes; Stereotype Threat).

With regards to the affective element, sentiments and feelings influence prejudice by creating distinct lines of emotion—"positive" and "negative" outlooks on a particular group and its members. A good example is racial profiling; a policeman who "negatively" views African Americans will be more prone to arrest them due to the connotation and stereotype that associates African Americans with criminality.

When prejudice is utilized against racial and ethnic groups, prejudice becomes a crucial component in the deployment of racism (*see* Racism). In the case of individual racism, prejudicial attitudes and discriminatory actions become the basis for the belief of an innate inferiority in a subordinate individual and group. On a macro level, institutional racism refers to the institutional organization of maintaining the racial privilege for a select few and the marginalization of the rest through a prejudicial justification.

JEFFREY YAMASHITA

See also

Ethnogenesis; *Nature of Prejudice, The*; Prejudice Theory; Racism; Stereotype; Xenophobia

Further Reading:

Omi, Michael, and Howard Winant. *Racial Formation in the United States: From the 1960s to the 1990s*. London: Routledge, 1994.

Pettigrew, Thomas F., George M. Fredrickson, Dale T. Knobel, Nathan Glazer, Reed Ueda. *Prejudice*. Cambridge, MA: Belknap Press of Harvard University Press, 1982.

Prejudice Theory

Herbert Blumer's racial prejudice theory (1958) illuminates a fundamental shift in examining racial prejudice through the focus of racial groups rather than the individual. By centering the importance of the racial group, Blumer argues that "race prejudice exists basically in a sense of group position rather than in a set of feelings which members of one racial group have toward the members of another racial group." The dominant racial group is defined and redefined in relation to the subordinate racial group. Racial group prejudice is in large part a mechanism of protection in order to defend against the challenges posed by a subordinate group. Blumer locates racial prejudice as a historical product, and that individuals conceive of racial prejudice in opposition of a representation of an entire group.

Blumer presents the fact that other scholars who locate the individual in racial prejudice trace these complex feelings to innate tendencies, oppressive personalities, and prejudice developed through social experience. In light of these ideas, Blumer illuminates the shortcomings of analyzing the individual in terms of racial prejudice by highlighting the fact that the racially prejudiced individual imagines himself/herself belonging to a distinct, racial group. Thus, the racial identification of the individual hinges upon the larger schema of the collective identification of the racial group.

Blumer documents four basic types of feelings that are present in a dominant group in relation to a subordinate group: (1) a feeling of superiority; (2) a feeling that the subordinate group is inherently different; (3) a feeling of the right to certain advantages and privileges not afforded to the subordinate group; (4) an incessant fear and suspicion that the subordinate group is conspiring against the dominant group. These four sentiments are important because it signals to the positional arrangements of the racial groups, and thus, the positional relation of the two racial groups (dominant and subordinate) is pivotal in race prejudice.

The collective identification of a particular racial, dominant group is created in opposition and relation to another group, which at times is the subordinate group. These collective identifications of the group inform and shape the individual in the group through the creation of an abstract image of the subordinate or other group. Blumer charts four critical implications in the development and maintenance of the abstract image of the subordinate group: (1) The collective image of the abstract group is created by assigning characteristics by a spokesperson or person with authority; (2) Definitions of a subordinate group is solidified not by the quotidian encounters between the dominant group and the subordinate group but through certain events that hold significance in shaping perspectives; (3) Key figures in the dominant group have the power to formulate and dictate the perceptions of the subordinate group; (4) Interest groups can manipulate and manufacture the assigned attributes of the subordinate group in order to retain certain privileges and advantages.

Although Blumer advocates for the racial prejudice of the group, Blumer does indicate the tension between racial prejudices of the group versus the individual. Blumer states that "there is likely to be considerable difference between the ways in which the individual members of the dominant group think and feel about the subordinate group." Even though individuals in a particular dominant racial group may have disparate attitudes and views on a subordinate group, Blumer elucidates that the common dimension among the individuals is their sense of social position as a group.

Blumer's group racial prejudice theory is a fundamental way of viewing racial prejudice from the standpoint of the group rather than the individual. However, Blumer's group racial prejudice theory falls short because it fails to incorporate the group dynamics of the subordinate group. Throughout Blumer's explanations, the analysis is devoted solely to the dominant racial group and its relationship with the subordinate group. Blumer does not shift the focus on the subordinate group and its deployment of group racial prejudice against the dominant racial group. Although the subordinate group's group racial prejudice is not fully developed, Blumer's theory is a major shift in the ways in which

scholars before him thought about racial prejudice. Bobo and Hutchings (1996) extended Blumer's prejudice theory to take into account group positioning in a multiracial context in order to show the formation of perceptions of group threat and competition.

JEFFREY YAMASHITA

See also
Nature of Prejudice, The; Prejudice; Racism; Scapegoat Theory of Racial Prejudice

Further Reading:
Blumer, Herbert. "Race Prejudice as a Sense of Group Position." *Pacific Sociological Review* 1, no. 1 (1958): 3–7.
Bobo, Lawrence, and Vincent L. Hutchings. "Perceptions of Racial Group Competition: Extending Blumer's Theory of Group Position to a Multiracial Social Context." *American Sociological Review* 61, no. 6 (1996): 951–72.

Prison Gangs

Gangs, social groups organized around geographical territory, race/ethnicity, and criminal activities, originate in prison or are imported into correctional systems. The functions of a gang are useful inside prison and outside in mainstream society. By providing security for their members, organizing criminal activities, and satisfying inmates' recreational and sexual needs, the gangs are an attractive option for newly incarcerated convicts. The gang structure and subsequent job titles vary, but most gangs form a pyramid-shaped hierarchy with a few individuals in top leadership positions and more people in lower levels. Potential recruits are identified by current members and, once admitted, they are taught the gang rules, expectations, and symbols like hand signs, phrases, and tattoos. Gangs value loyalty and require a life-long commitment, so admittance is a serious decision. Prison gang members must act on behalf of the gang inside prison walls and outside. "Blood in and blood out" means a long-term relationship based on violence during the criminal's career.

The most significant prison gangs are spread throughout mostly state facilities and they have a large membership. The correctional setting proves to be advantageous for gang enterprises. Gang members can plan and execute criminal activities while serving their sentences and they continue upon their release from prison. The "revolving door" of prison life provides a new set of recruits to replace the released members until they return. A prison bid enhances a gang member's reputation on the streets, and since crime is prevalent in prison, he contributes to the gang wherever he is.

Inmates participate in prison gangs to meet different inmate needs including being safe, remaining affiliated, getting sex, receiving privileges like extra food, and obtaining good prison jobs. Gang membership means people are willing to fight together when the inevitable conflicts occur. During the daily course of prison life, fights occur regularly and fellow gang members assist each other by providing weapons to arranging hits in and out of prison. The correctional facilities meet basic inmate needs, but the luxuries and security given to gang bangers means a better quality of life while inside. Prison gangs exist alongside prison administration as a separate form of governance, discipline, and service provision.

The Mexican Mafia, the first documented prison gang, began in 1957 at the Deuel Vocational Institution in Tracy, California. Original members banded together to survive threats from other prisoners. Long-time residents of California, people of Mexican descent were included in the prison population, too, and congregated together to protect themselves from other groups. "La Eme" is a common name for the gang, a shortened title based on the phonetic Spanish pronunciation of the letter M. One gang symbol shows a black hand-print with one finger representing each word in the five-word creed: vengeance, terror, death, valor, and silence. Other tattoos include the word "eme," an eagle with a snake in its mouth, the number 13 with the words "eme mexicana" or the word "sur" standing for southern.

While the Mexican Mafia work and recruit in Southern California, Nuestra Familia is its counterpart in Northern California. In the correctional system of the mid 1960s, the "Norteños" consisted of Hispanic people living north of Bakersfield. Once inside the prisons, they needed protection from the Mexican Mafia and formed their own gang. The similarities of the two groups continue with the "La Eñe" symbol and the number 14 representing the group. Tattoos show a sombrero with a bloody dagger or include the word "Norteño" or the initials NF. The commonalities between the Norteños and the Sureños did not bring the groups together as they still remain rivals and competing criminal enterprises. The continuing violence between the two prison gangs leads California prison administrators to locate known gang members in different facilities and keep them strictly separated.

Texas Syndicate completes the trio of Latino prison gangs. Although started at Folsom Prison in California, the members have Texas roots and joined together to stop other gangs from preying upon young men without ties to California gangs. Their crimes include human trafficking, drug sales, and murder for hire and, like other prison gangs, they continue their criminal activities while incarcerated. Their gang tattoos usually include the letters T and S incorporated into different designs in order to obscure the letters.

Another significant prison gang is Black Guerilla Disciples, which originated in the California prison system during the civil rights tumult of the 1960s. Doubling as a gang and a drug enterprise, the prison gang began as a set of loosely affiliated African American groups using "Black" in their titles like Black Vanguard and the Black Family; racial identity is an important component in the group's formation. The radical gang's beginning is attributed to Black Panther leader George Lester Jackson when he was incarcerated in San Quentin. His political agenda included the conditions facing black men in prison making him a popular figure among black felons and, when his death occurred in 1971 after an attempted prison escape, the group adopted the BGD title permanently. The gang celebrates him in their activities by having an outdoor celebration in his honor. Tattoos usually involve the initials BGD with a black dragon wrapped around a prison tower or a sword and rifle crossed into an X.

The 1960s brought the inception of the largest white prison gang, the Aryan Brotherhood. Born out of the same civil rights era, members of this gang were protecting white supremacy and racism. San Quentin and Folsom had prison inmates who bonded over maintaining dominance in the prison population. Their symbols include white cultural elements like the four-leaf clover in addition to Nazi imagery of the swastika and double lightning bolts. Like other prison gangs, membership is for life, but unlike the other gangs, the Aryan Brotherhood does not have a large presence outside of prison.

M. Kelly James

See also
Aryan Brotherhood; Mara Salvatrucha (MS 13)

Further Reading:
Hagedorn, John. 2008. *A World of Gangs: Armed Young Men and Gangsta Culture.* Minneapolis: University of Minnesota Press.
Santos, Michael. (2007) *Inside: Life Behind Bars in America.* New York: St. Martin's Press.
Skarbeck, David. "Prison Gangs, Norms, and Organizations." *Journal of Economic Behavior and Organizations* 82 (2012): 96–109.
Trulson, Chad, James W. Marquart, and Soraya K. Kawucha. "Gang Suppression and Institutional Control." *Corrections Today* (April 2006): 26–31.
Valdez, Alfonso. "Prison Gangs 101." *Corrections Today* (February 2009): 40–43.

Prison-Industrial Complex

The term *prison-industrial complex* (PIC) is based on a phrase in President Eisenhower's 1961 Farewell Address. Upon leaving office the president warned the American people to beware of the *military-industrial complex*, an alliance between corporations and the armed forces that were promoting high levels of military spending but harming the American people. The term has been adapted to refer to the private sector's influence on the criminal justice system, especially on incarceration policies. The growth of a prison industry, since the 1980s, is part of a corporate-sponsored move toward privatization of government provided services. The "wars" on crime and drugs helped create a burgeoning prison population with attendant opportunities for profit for the private sector if they could replace government-run penal institutions. In 1985, there were only 935 individuals in privately operated prisons. In 2000, private prisons held 87,360, about 6 percent of all prisoners. As of July 2009, they housed 127,688 or 8 percent of prisoners.

The American Legislative Exchange Council (ALEC), established in 1973, is a major promoter of business interests, including those profiting from prison contracts. ALEC writes model legislation that is then advocated by legislators who agree with the organization's goals and benefit from financial assistance from ALEC's member corporations. With a vested interest in having more prisoners, ALEC sponsored laws for getting tough on crime such as the "three strikes" policy and mandatory minimum sentences for drug offenders—even nonviolent ones. In 2002, American Public Radio reported "ALEC's corporate members include at least a dozen companies that do prison business. Like Dupont; the drug companies, Merck and Glaxo Smith-Klein; and the telephone companies that compete for lucrative prison contracts. And Corrections Corporation of America (CCA). [*sic*] It dominates the private prison business—building and running prisons and renting cells to governments." CCA vice-president Louise Green estimated that the corporation was running 65 facilities in 21 states and Puerto Rico with an inmate population of about 55,000.

ALEC's efforts helped CCA and the GEO Group (formerly Wackenhut) become the biggest of the private prison companies worth billions. Many companies, members of ALEC or not, gain from supplying the equipment to prisons and services. Banks, especially Wells Fargo, supply capital to the private prison corporations. A coalition of organizations, the National People's Action Campaign has been pressuring Wells Fargo to end its investments in private prison enterprises. It has had some success, but to date Wells Fargo continues to make these investments.

The Prison-Industrial Complex provides facilities for adult and juvenile prisoners and detained immigrants. Since the 1990s there has been an expansion of facilities to hold the latter with the companies involved investing millions in lobbying for these facilities. In addition prison labor is a source of a very inexpensive work force. ALEC has helped write immigration policies that have led to detention of thousands of undocumented migrants in privately run detention centers. Between 2001 and 2012, there was a 188 percent increase of immigrants in privately owned facilities compared to a 26 percent increase in government-run ones.

In the late 1970s, ALEC was instrumental in changing the rules that forbid prisoners working for private companies because of the difficulty of other businesses competing with such cheap labor. The outcome was the Prison Industries Enhancement (PIE) Certification Program. Among the major companies employing prison labor are Victoria's Secret, Starbucks, McDonalds, and Microsoft. This labor does provide benefits to inmates giving them something to do, helping them learn a skill, and an opportunity for some income. These workers, however, are competing with free labor. At the same time, Chinese goods made with prison labor are banned from importation to the United States. Since African American men are greatly overrepresented in the prison system, their labor is once again being exploited.

With strained state budgets spending less on prison populations is an attractive option for state governments. Privatizing incarceration helps achieve this goal. An agency of the Department of Justice, the Bureau of Justice Assistance report noted that while the private sector can be more efficient, "The profit motive will inhibit the proper performance of duties. Private prisons have financial incentives to cut corners." One way they do this is by hiring "non-union labor, allowing for the lowest benefit packages" (Austin and Coventry 2001: 14, 16). As a result the staff is likely to be overworked and underskilled. Corruption is also more likely since political figures can award contracts to their friends and political allies. There have been a number of reports of problems including very inadequate health care, violence toward inmates, sexual abuse, and lax oversight resulting in escapes.

Through lobbying, campaign contributions, and the hiring of former government officials, a few private companies are influencing public policies instead of there being open debates about these issues. Those benefitting economically and politically from incarceration as a solution to crime are unlikely to put forth alterative solutions which might better protect the public by lessening recidivism. While some of the private facilities do provide rehabilitation services, most do not, and there is no powerful constituency able to effectively advocate for these. This is especially hard on the communities that have the greatest proportion of their residents in prisons—communities of color.

BARBARA CHASIN

Further Reading:
American Corrections Association. 2012. http://www.aca.org/Advertise/exhibition.asp.
American Public Radio. "Tough-on-Crime Measures Increase Prison Population." 2002. http://americanradioworks.publicradio.org/features/corrections/laws4.html (accessed October 29, 2012).
Austin, James, and Gary Coventry. "Emerging Issues on Privatized Prisons." National Council on Crime and Delinquency, Bureau of Justice Assistance. February 2001.
Detention Watch Network. "The Influence of the Private Prison Industry in Immigration Detention." http//www.detentionwatchnetwork.org/privateprisons (accessed October 26, 2012).
Elk, Mike, and Bob Sloan. "The Hidden History of ALEC and Prison Labor." 2011. http://wwwthenation/com/print/article162478/hidden-history-alec-and prison-labor (accessed October 26, 2012).
Greene, Judith A. "Entrepreneurial Corrections." In *Invisible Punishment: The Collateral Consequence of Mass Imprisonment*, edited by Marc Mauer and Medea Chesney-Lind. New York: New Press, 2002.
Lee, Suevon. 2012. "By the Numbers: The Growing For-Profit Detention Industry." *Propublica*, June 20, 2012. http://www.propublica.org/article/by-the-numbers-the-u.s.s-growing-for-profit-detention-industry (accessed November 2, 2012).
National People's Action/Public Accountability Initiative. "Jails Fargo: Banking on Immigrant Detention, Wells Fargo's Ties to the Private Prison Industry." September 2012: 3. http://npa-us.org/files/wells_fargo_-_banking_on_immigrant_detention_0.pdf.
Schlosser, Eric. "The Prison-Industrial Complex," *The Atlantic*, December 1998. http://www.theatlantic.com/magazine/archive/1998/12/the-prison-industrial-complex/304669/ (accessed October 25, 2012).
Sloan, Bob. "The Prison Industries Enhancement Certification Program: Why Everyone Should be Concerned." *Prison Legal News*. https://www.prisonlegalnews.org/22190_displayArticle.aspx (accessed November 3, 2012).
West, Heather C. "Prison Inmates at Midyear 2009—Statistical Tables." Bureau of Justice Statistics. 2009.

Prison Riots

Prison administrators "rule with the inmates' consent" meaning the smaller number of staff must maintain control over the larger number of inmates, and this can only be done with their cooperation. The prison population is already divided into subgroups based on types of crime committed and race. The officers and other staff work among the antagonist groups while trying to maintain peace in their facilities. Although prison officials develop and implement procedures to combat violence, prisoners don't fear violence or administrative attempts at control. Surviving a prison bid usually requires gang affiliation or the prisoner uses violence to deter predatory behavior from other inmates. Violent behavior communicates dominance in prison and attracts other prisoners. When enough prisoners are involved, a riot occurs.

Inmates at Attica State Prison in Attica, New York, raise their hands in clenched fists in a show of unity, September 1971, during the Attica uprising, which took the lives of 43 people. (Associated Press)

The 1950s heralded a big wave of prison riots in the United States. The correctional facilities were deteriorating and conditions were harsh; prisoners had many grievances stacked up. In his 1955 *Atlantic Monthly* article, H. W. Hollister wrote of his eight-year prison stint. He likens riots at this time to inmates "pulling their homes down about their ears." Daily life of bad food, restrictive rules, gang fights, and boredom led prisoners to lash out at people and property. When inmates follow the prison code, they can usually avoid altercations, but if problems do occur, retribution is rapid and certain. Inmate frustrations led to conflict among prisoners and violence spreads like fire in the closed environment of a correctional facility. The officers and staff attempted to contain these situations, but the riots stemmed from random fights that are hard to control and frustrations that were not easily fixed. This decade heralded worse times to come.

Depending on the facility and the number of inmates, some riots are more challenging to quell than others. California prisons are the most overcrowded, and this problem typically correlates with bad living conditions. When the necessary services are strained or inadequate, riots can occur. The California Institute for Men in Chino witnessed a riot in August of 2009 that exemplifies this issue. Starting with a fight between Latino and African American inmates, prisoners made weapons from destroyed furniture and lockers and fought throughout the night. They burned down a dorm building, and over 300 inmates were injured with 55 of those taken to the hospital. No officers were harmed, and after 80 officers removed the barricaded prisoners, the prison went on lockdown to investigate and punish participants. Administrators were constrained by budgetary limits and unable to stop overcrowding in the state prison system, so the conditions that spawned the violence were not easily remedied.

Inmates want an opportunity to communicate grievances to administrators. When their voices are ignored, it upsets the balance of daily life. The Attica Prison Riot of 1971, one of the more significant events in corrections history, demonstrates the need for inmates and officials to keep the lines of communication open. African American inmates made charges of racism and unequal treatment against the predominantly white staff and the lack of response upset the already stressed community. One random event sparked the riot. An Attica officer stopped a fight and punished the offenders involved. The next day inmates attacked the officer in retaliation. They quickly got control of the prison and proceeded to attack each other and destroy property causing much damage. As negotiations between rioters and officials took place, the rioters held hostages to gain some leverage, but Governor John D. Rockefeller maintained his "tough on crime" stance and denied the rioters the amnesty they sought. The police finally gained control of the inmates by using tear gas and weapons on the group assembled in the Yard. The Attica Riot came to a bloody end with 10 dead hostages, 29 dead inmates, and 80 inmates with gunshot wounds. Once the prison officials were back in control, the rioters were harshly punished for their involvement. Many years later, the remaining rioters and their descendants received reparations for the administrative reaction. The length and intensity of the Attica riot inspired corrections administrators to revamp their anti-riot policies.

A second, equally significant event is the 1980 riot at New Mexico State Penitentiary in Santa Fe. Extreme overcrowding led to this riot when angry prisoners took advantage of a corrections officer's slip-up in security procedures. After taking the officer's keys, the inmates accessed the pharmacy for drugs and acquired weapons as they spread throughout the prison causing destruction. The rioters went on a three-day rampage after first torturing and murdering the segregated population of snitches and child molesters, the most unpopular prisoners in any facility. Although no staff died during the riot, they experienced brutal beatings and rapes. Some prisoners defied the rioters and helped the wounded, but the damage was widespread and harsh including 33 inmates killed during the riot and over 200 inmates with injuries. The New Mexico correctional staff hadn't adequately prepared for large-scale violence, although good did come out of the brutal rebellion. The state of New Mexico built more facilities to ease their overcrowding problem and to improve the living conditions of New Mexican inmates.

Any act of violence can lead to a riot as all situations are unique and unpredictable. Predicting and explaining riots is helpful, but prison staff will not be able to stop them all from occurring. Researching riots and studying history can lead administrators to circumvent or manage riots more effectively.

M. KELLY JAMES

See also

Prison-Industrial Complex; Prison Gangs; Race Riots in America. Documents: Report on the Memphis Riots of May 1866 (1866); Account of the Riots in East St. Louis, Illinois (1917); A Southern Black Woman's Letter Regarding the Recent Riots in Chicago and Washington (1919); The Cook County Coroner's Report Regarding the 1919 Chicago Race Riots (1920); The Final Report of the Grand Jury on the Tulsa Race Riot (June 25, 1921); Testimony from *Laney v. United States* (1923); The Governor's Commission Report on the Watts Riots (1965); Cyrus R. Vance's Report on the Riots in Detroit (1967); The Reports of the Oklahoma Commission to Study the Tulsa Race Riot of 1921 (2000–2001); Draft Report: 1898 Wilmington Race Riot Commission (2005)

Further Reading:

Hassine, Victor. *Life Without Parole: Living in Prison Today*. Oxford: Oxford University Press, 2008.

Hollister, H. W. "Why Prisoners Riot." *Atlantic Monthly*. 1955. http://www.the atlantic.com/past/docs/issues/95nov/prisons/whyriot.html (accessed January 28, 2012).

Mozingo, Joe, and Margot Roosevelt. "Dormitory Burns Down in Chino Riot." *Los Angeles Times*. August 10, 2009. http://articles.latimes.com/2009/aug/10/local/me-prison10 (accessed February 18, 2013).

Pollock, Joycelyn. *Prisons and Prison Life: Costs and Consequences*. New York: Oxford University Press, 2012.

Santos, Michael. *Inside: Life Behind Bars in America*. New York: St. Martin's Press, 2007.

Schmalleger, Frank, and John Ortiz Smykla. *Corrections in the 21st Century*. Boston: McGraw-Hill, 2009.

Store, Mary, and Anthony Walsh. *Corrections: The Essentials*. Los Angeles: Sage Press, 2012.

Trulson, Chad, James W. Marquart, and Soraya K. Kawucha. "Gang Suppression and Institutional Control." *Corrections Today* (April 2006): 26–31.

Useem, B., and P. A. Kimball. *States of Siege: U.S. Prison Riots 1971–1986*. New York: Oxford University Press, 1989.

Prisons

Southern prisons during the Jim Crow era earned the "dubious distinction" of "America's worst prisons." Jim Crow prisons in the South took various, yet equally brutal forms—a traditional penitentiary, a penal farm, a former slave plantation, brickyards, or temporary road camps. The prisons were erected in forests, swamps, mines, brickyards, or levees, and the convicts were housed in tents, log forts, and rolling cages. Jim Crow punishment existed in two phases, during the leasing era, which ran from 1890 to the 1920s, and then in the state control system, from the 1920s to 1965. Distinctive in the penal history of this era, the use of state prisons to control black population are deeply rooted in the South.

Immediately after the Civil War, Southern states turned to the criminal justice system in order to control the newly freed slave population. They also needed a labor force to repair Civil War damages. Although Southern states had built penitentiaries before the Civil War, most of them were so badly damaged during the war that they were unusable. By the early 1900s, blacks composed anywhere from 85 to 95 percent of the prison population, although they composed no more than half of the total population in the South. Black men, women, and children were summarily convicted and delivered by the local sheriffs to a road camp, penal farm, or, less likely, a penitentiary. Moreover, the penitentiary philosophy—to change prisoners and make them productive citizens—did not fit the Southern perception of their prisoners who were still seen as former slaves and not equipped for reformation and change. The terms "slave," "convict," and "Negro," were interchangeable in the white Southerner's perceptions of blacks after the Civil War.

On the surface, leasing appeared to address the issues of prisoner security and safety at a minimum cost to the state. Southern states, including Florida, Texas, Louisiana, Arkansas, Mississippi, Alabama, Georgia, and Tennessee, turned to a variety of leasing arrangements with private individuals and companies, wherein the state turned over the whole prison operation to a private entrepreneur. Virginia never leased its convicts, and the Carolinas did so tentatively and for a short time only. Some states expected the contractor to pay some amount to the state. Others literally gave away complete responsibility for the state prisoners without any monetary or state supervisory expectations; one state even paid the lessee to take the prisoners. Often states signed leases with one individual or organization.

Soon, the leasing of convicts became one of the most exploitative aspects of the prison system during Jim Crow. Prisoners were leased to build railroads, levees, and roads; to work in mines, brickyards, and turpentine camps; and to do agricultural work on former plantations. Conditions under the leasing system were particularly brutal and deadly. Since the lessees did not own the prisoners, they often did not care about their welfare. The life expectancy of convicts in the lease system ranged from seven to 10 years. Prisoners died of overwork or of violence from the guards or each other, and an ever-growing population of black convicts allowed for the quick replacement of prisoners.

Leasing came to an end by the 1920s for a variety of reasons. In some states, it was no longer economical. In others, railroad building subsided, and road building was generally designated to local governments. Some states had a penitentiary that they used. As it was purported that many companies who leased prisoners had made millions, other states resumed control hoping such large profits would ensue to the state. Still, the change was not fueled by humanitarian concern for the prisoners. Instead, Southern states switched from leasing to chain gangs and prisons in order to transfer manufactured goods via convict labor to the public sector.

After the 1920s, the two most common forms of punishment systems were the penal farms and the chain gangs. The penal farm is the most notorious type of prison system in the South. More than an agricultural production center, the penal farm followed the plantation model of imprisonment. It incorporated both a structure and philosophy of slave plantations, reinforcing black inferiority and subservience to white planters and prison guards. Though they emphasized economy and agricultural work, the penal farm used isolation and neglect of rehabilitation to break down the mostly black prisoners and inculcate convicts with a sense of worthlessness. The purest form of the plantation model of imprisonment emerged in Arkansas, Louisiana, Mississippi, and Texas. Louisiana and Mississippi eventually established one geographical location for its penal farms, while Arkansas used two and Texas used multiple sites. Angola, Louisiana, is now 18,000 acres, while Parchman, Mississippi, was once 20,000 acres. The two farms in Arkansas, Tucker for white convicts and Cummins for black women and men, were located on 4,500 acres and 16,600 acres, respectively.

Although the type of agricultural work has varied through the years, depending upon the economy, natural disasters, and technological developments, the majority of prisoners at these farms have worked in the fields. To this day, prisoners admitted to Angola must spend their first 90 days in the fields. The geographical isolation of these farms also served multiple functions. Largely kept out of the public eye, isolation of the prison led to the horrific conditions. On occasion, news reports would filter out and reach the national press. Investigating committees would visit and make recommendations, most often to no avail. No fewer than five recommendations, beginning in the 1930s, were made to move the women prisoners out of Angola. They were not moved until 1961, and not removed from Angola's administration until almost a decade later.

The prevailing belief about the limits of rehabilitation helped maintain bad conditions. Neither state nor federal courts interfered with prison business until the late 1960s. Furthermore, agricultural work was believed to be suited to the limited ability of the imprisoned classes, mostly African Americans and Mexican Americans. Such practices had the effect of perpetuating segregation, as black and Mexican American prisoners were then limited to agricultural work once they were released. The emphasis on maximizing product, coupled with the long-held beliefs about black inferiority, precluded the development of a reform movement or rehabilitation of prisoners.

Spurred by the "good road" movement of the 1920s, chain gangs and road gangs emerged all throughout the South. Generally, county criminal justice agencies oversaw the Southern road gangs, also known as chain gangs. For example, the state of Alabama ran the chain gang system. Alabama's road gang was initially all-black, and even when some white prisoners were introduced they were always a minority in both number and proportion of convicts, and they were maintained in separate camps. Conditions were hard and exploitative; discipline was often brutal, but not as deadly as under the lease system. Guards routinely whipped prisoners with a three-inch strap, until Alabama outlawed the practice in 1962. Initially, men were housed in portable wooden barracks and sometimes rolling cages. By the mid-1930s, road camps were standardized with wooden buildings that included dormitories, with showers, a mess hall kitchen, and hot and cold running water.

States immediately classified all inmates upon their entrance into the system. They were separated according to age, gender, and dangerousness of offense. These classification systems in the South were consistent with assumptions about race and echoed 19th-century notions about gendered divisions of labor. Usually, young black male prisoners were sent to do the most strenuous work tasks on the plantation prisons and road gangs, while white prisoners were sent to do industrial or clerical jobs. Both black and white women worked in gender-specific jobs such as washing and sewing uniforms. When needed, however, black women worked alongside the men in the fields, whereas white women usually did no fieldwork. Initially, Louisiana classified prisoners into four categories, beginning with first-class men (almost entirely black) who were assigned to the most arduous labor, and ending with fourth-class men, who were assigned to the hospital. Almost all white men and women were classified as fourth class, although some white men worked on the plantations and levee camps as clerks. When the crop demanded it, all classes of prisoners labored in fields, particularly during the sugar harvest.

Gendered divisions of labor were also segregated. Black women served as cooks, laundresses, and seamstresses exclusively. They also hoed sugar cane stumps and sorted tobacco leaves in the tobacco barn. During leasing in Alabama, black women worked alongside black men in lumber camps, mining camps, and rock quarries. White women sewed uniforms and bedding, or worked in the canneries. Mississippi employed both black and white women as trustees armed with rifles.

The system of Jim Crow in the prison system rationalized that African Americans and Mexican Americans had limited abilities and could do only physical labor. Since black and Mexican American convicts numbered in the majority of prisoners, Alabama, for example, not only used the bulk of the black male population to create the convict road labor force but designated the convicts on the road gangs to do the most strenuous maintenance work. Black convicts did the weed cutting, shoulder work on the paved roads, and the most arduous work of all—breaking and crushing rock in the quarries, while the free white laborers working alongside them operated the heavy equipment and the trucks. Although it was in use only from 1883 until 1917, one penitentiary in Texas held only white men, and the inmates worked entirely in factories. The Louisiana penitentiary in Baton Rouge housed mainly white men who made the prisoners' uniforms and sewed flags.

With a structure similar to an antebellum plantation, Southern prisons in Jim Crow amassed several thousand black workers supervised by a small group of rural lower-class whites, who, in turn, worked directly under the direction of sheriffs and wardens. Convicts worked from sunup to sundown, or as they said, from "can to can't." Plagued by boll weevils, floods, and other natural disasters, many Southern states had not made the anticipated profits since the state took over from the lease system. In a cost-saving measure, they turned to the "trusty" convict system. Paid guards were fired and convicts would guard other convicts.

The use of trustees also extended to the living quarters in the prison camp. On the Parchment, Mississippi, prison plantation, prisoners were housed in a number of camps. Each camp had one sergeant, and two assistant sergeants. The sergeant was equivalent to the slave plantation's overseer. He was in charge of the work schedules, disciplining the convicts, and setting the work routine. One assistant sergeant oversaw the fields and functioned as the driver. Called the "rider" in Arkansas, he determined the work quota for the men in the fields. The other assistant sergeant was responsible for the barracks. A number of trusty-shooters watched over the regular convicts, known as gunmen, (rankmen in Arkansas) who worked in the fields. In most circumstances, trusty-shooters and gunmen did not communicate with each other.

Guards and wardens heavily supervised male convicts working in the fields. A typical scenario called for two "highpowers" armed with carbines on horseback and at least three pairs of "shotguns" on foot accompanying the line at different intervals. Usually one pair of guards stood watch some distance from the rear in case of trouble. All these guards were prisoners, or what are commonly called convict-guards. The convict-guards had different ranks and concomitant levels of power, dependent upon the type of prison and work that they supervised. Convict-guards also may have had the ticket to their own release. Occasionally, a convict-guard who shot an escaping prisoner could be rewarded with his freedom. When the federal courts intervened in prison business in the early 1970s, the convict guard or trusty system was declared the worst abuse of power maintained in the Southern prisons.

Punishment in the penitentiaries, penal farms, and road gangs was brutal and occasionally deadly. Death rates were staggeringly high during leasing. For instance, 216 prisoners died during 1896 in Louisiana, nearly 20 percent of the 1,152 prisoners in the state. Yet in Louisiana State Penitentiary's Biennial Report of the Board of Control for the years 1896–1897, Warden W. H. Reynaud claimed no responsibility for the 1896 death rate but only the 6 percent death rate in 1897, maintaining that he was not appointed warden until August 1896. Since the majority of the prisoners were leased out, his argument that there were no deaths under his watch was correct only in abstract. Prisoners spoke of killings that happened in camps that were almost hidden away. Scandals of prisoners being beaten to death by sadistic whipping bosses emerged in the other Southern states. Although mortality rates generally fell after the states took control of their prisoners, stories continued about cruel treatment, torture, and beatings under state control, sometimes administered by convict guards and sometimes free guards. Although figures are not available for Alabama convict mortality rates, the convicts were susceptible to horrific mining disasters. One of the most famous, the Banner Coal Mine tragedy resulted in 122 convict deaths.

Corporal punishment was the most common penalty for infractions; it was also most often applied without concern for the welfare of the convict. Leather straps known as "Black Annie" in Mississippi and "Old Caesar" in Texas were used for the whippings. Mississippi's "Black Annie" was three feet long and six inches wide. In one year alone, there were 1,547 floggings at Angola, with a total of 23,889 blows. Generally, guards administered whippings on the convict's bare flesh. Men and women alike were required to remove their shirts and/or pull down their pants for the lashings. In order to strike fear or to maintain strict order, guards dispensed punishments in public, requiring convicts to count the number of stripes out loud and in unison.

Although they lived under conditions of extreme oppression, Southern prisoners did not always cooperate with the authorities. They used both covert and overt techniques to resist. Whether in penitentiaries, on the plantation prisons or road gangs, prisoners stole, committed arson, faked illness, engaged in sabotage, horribly mutilated themselves, participated in riots and work stoppages, and escaped. Escapes were exceptionally high under the leasing system, as opportunities in the camps and on the farms were greater than inside the penitentiary walls. For instance, from 1872 to 1874, 881 convicts entered the Tennessee prison system. During the same time, 95 escaped. Prisoners, primarily white prisoners, wrote memoirs and some wrote letters to the press revealing the horrible conditions under which they lived and worked. Other prisoners used collective action to start riots.

Although there were few incidents labeled as "riots" in the South, a series of incidents took place that forced authorities to reform conditions. In the "heel-slashing incident" of the early 1950s, 37 white prisoners at Angola, Louisiana, cut their Achilles tendons over two separate occasions to protest work conditions and fears that they would be beaten to death if they went out to the field. In 1935, a group of white Texas prisoners maimed themselves, two by chopping off a lower leg entirely. Self-mutilations became more common over the next decade or more in Texas. The Texas prisoners stated the same reasons that the Louisiana prisoners did—they were afraid of being beaten to death in the fields because they could not make it under the grueling work conditions.

Prisoners also resisted using covert techniques. On the plantation prisons and on the road gangs, convicts used work songs to accompany gang work. Work songs were used exclusively by African American male prisoners. Although black women sang prison songs, there is no record of them using the songs in the fields as the men did. Prison songs functioned to pass the time, pace the work, and provide safety while doing dangerous tasks and gave the men some control over their daily lives. Convicts could protest by singing things that could not be said in ordinary conversation. They expressed tension, frustration, and anger.

Work songs had a structure, the call-response pattern. The "caller," or work group leader, shouted a phrase and the gang responded. In this manner, the leader slowed down the pace when he noticed that some of the men were having trouble keeping up with the work. All the men had to keep up at the same rate, or they would be beaten. The songs regulated the pace of the teams and the strokes of the axes so that they would not cut each other's limbs. A good work song leader did not necessarily have to have a good voice, but he had to be loud. He also had to know the work and the ability of the men on his gang in order to guide them from sunup to sundown without being injured or beaten.

Even as separate women's facilities (reformatories) were being built for women up north, between 1870 and 1930, there were no women's reformatories in the Southern states. In Southern penitentiaries, women could be found anywhere from cells at the end of a male cell block, to a cell block of their own, to a building of their own, which sometimes was located close to the male buildings and sometimes farther away. Women remained under the administration of the men's institution well into the 1960s.

During the leasing era and under state control, women were sent to the plantations, mining camps, railroads, and road gangs. Sometimes they worked alongside the men. Other times, a small group of female convicts cooked and washed for the leased men. When sharing penal farms with men, the women were particularly vulnerable to physical brutality and sexual assault from prison guards and male convicts. On the plantation prisons, women were housed at a separate camp, situated some distance from the men's camps. However, the security was quite lax, and there was considerable unsupervised interaction between the men and women. Prisoners' memoirs report that men and women met each other in all kinds of secluded places on the prison grounds. At Angola, they met in the sugar cane fields when the cane was tall enough.

Although a married couple was often assigned to supervise the women's camps, the husband often had single, unsupervised control over the women. Men supervised women in their work places—the fields, the sewing rooms, and in the canneries. Angola's punishment reports reveal that men administered floggings to the female convicts on their bare backs and breasts. Finally, when women worked in the fields alongside men, they were required to answer the call of nature right there in the fields in front of the men.

MARIANNE FISHER-GIORLANDO

See also

New Jim Crow, The; Prison-Industrial Complex; Sentencing Disparities

Further Reading:

Ayers, Edward L. *Vengeance & Justice. Crime and Punishment in the 19th-Century American South.* New York: Oxford University Press, 1984.

Carleton, Mark T. *Politics and Punishment. The History of the Louisiana State Penal System.* Baton Rouge: Louisiana State University Press, 1971.

Mancini, Matthew. *One Dies, Get Another. Convict Leasing in the American South.* Columbia: University of South Carolina Press, 1996.

Oshinsky, David M. *"Worse Than Slavery": Parchman Farm and the Ordeal of Jim Crow Justice.* New York: Free Press. 1996.

Rafter, Nicole Hahn. *Partial Justice: Women, Prisons and Social Control.* New Brunswick, NJ: Transaction Press. 1990.

R

Race

The meaning of race varies across disciplines. According to traditional biological definitions, a race is group or population categorized on the basis of various sets of heritable characteristics from a common heritage, ancestor, or breed. Similarly, geneticists consider race a subgroup of people categorized by genetically transmitted physical characteristics and phenotypic traits. As a sociological concept, race is also viewed as a way to categorize people; however, it is rejected that race has natural, biological, or genetic basis. Rather, race represents a symbolic category used to mark differences among people, based on phenotype or ancestry, but is often misrecognized as a natural category. In addition to categorizing, race is believed to be a social construction, which has been used as a system of stratification within modern society, and although the meaning of the construct has transformed, it continues to have a significant impact on individuals' lives that deserves sociological attention.

Race, as a social construction, is an invention bound to social and historical contexts and signifies sociopolitical interests. Tracing the history of both race as a broad concept and specific racial categories reveals the socially constructed nature of race. Prior to the 17th century, human distinctions were based on location, religion, and language. The creation of a modern view of race surfaced during the Age of Enlightenment—a time in which scientists set out to create

ASA Task Force

The American Sociological Association created a 20-member task force, representing over 13,000 sociologists, to discuss the importance of collecting data and doing social scientific research on race. The task force took the position that failure to collect data on race would do more harm than good, by preserving the status quo. Although they believe racial categories do not necessarily reflect biological or genetic categories, race has a significant role in social institutions and remains a social reality. The report contends that race can have a consequence on race relations and social institutions in the following ways: (1) as a sorting mechanism for mating, marriage, and adoption; (2) as a stratifying practice; (3) as an organizing device for mobilization to maintain or challenge systems of racial stratification; (4) as a basis for the scientific investigation of proximate causes and critical interactions.

classification systems for all flora and fauna, including humans. Pseudoscience was used to support the categorization of humans into subspecies on the basis of geography, skin color, facial features, and bone structure. These categories were considered biologically real, natural and immutable. Thus, the first invention of race was a biological one.

Racial Formation in the United States: From the 1960s to the 1980s

Published in 1986 by sociologists Michael Omi of the University of California, Berkeley, and Howard Winant of the University of California, Santa Barbara, *Racial Formation in the United States: From the 1960s to the 1980s* is a groundbreaking work on racial theory. Recognizing the fact that race is a fundamental dimension of social organizations and cultural meaning in the United States, this book critiques three paradigmatic approaches to race and race relations that are based on ethnicity, class, and nation. It then develops an alternative racial-formation theory based on the idea that the concepts of race are always politically constructed and contested, and that the state is the preeminent site of racial contestation. Guided by the racial formation theory, the book analyzes postwar U.S. racial politics from the 1960s to the 1980s.

Since the publication of its first edition, this highly acclaimed book has become an instant classic in racial and ethnic studies and in the social sciences and humanities in general. Influenced by the racial-formation approach, the idea of the social construction of race has been widely accepted in the academy.

In 1994, Omi and Winant released the second edition of this book. The new edition further elaborates on the racial-formation theory by detailing the racial-formation processes. It also offers new materials on the historical development of race, racism, race-class-gender interrelations, everyday life, and hegemony. It updates the developments of racial formation in the United States to the early 1990s, covering such events as the 1992 presidential election, the Los Angeles riots, and the racial politics and policies of the Clinton administration.

PHILIP YANG

Sociopolitical interests were influential in the invention of race. Biological definitions of race were actually needed during this time characterized by European colonization and the transatlantic slave trade to justify the racial domination. For example, the invasion, capturing, and selling of African slaves by Europeans was believed to be legitimate on the scientific grounds that the African race was inferior and incapable of self-governance. An important factor of the creation of race was the simultaneous creation of the racial ideologies, such as white supremacy. White supremacy means that whiteness, however it was defined within a certain context, was constructed as superior and conferred advantage whereas darker skin signified inferiority. These ideologies perpetuated the biological understanding of race and, importantly, ranked races on a racial hierarchy—races situated at the top received the most advantage whereas races situated at the bottom received the most disadvantage. Thus, race and racial hierarchies were co-constructed.

The formation of modern nation-states coincided with biological and hierarchical constructions of race. For example, race was stipulated twice in the Constitution of the United States: Indians would not be taxed—therefore not citizens—and persons other than freedmen and Indians (i.e., black slaves) should be counted as three-fifths of a person—therefore subhuman. Both racial distinctions and hierarchies were a fundamental part of the formation of the United States. However, race as a stratifying agent extends pass the United States and is argued to be a part of the formation of modern society as a whole. Though race is a part of every society, the particular racial structure is variable.

Large-scale civil and human rights movements of the mid-20th century were important historical points in changing the construction of race in America and abroad. Decolonization, the downfall of Nazi Germany, passage of laws promoting equality (e.g., the Civil Rights Act of 1964), scientific refutations of a biological basis to race, and the deterioration of public acceptance towards overt racism highlighted the unjust aspects fabricated within the initial construction of race and led the transformation of race. During this period race became rejected as both a natural category determined by institutions and/or states and legitimate justification for domination. This shift weakened the detrimental and stratifying impacts of race and strengthened the view that race can be malleable and influenced by individuals. The slow transformation of race as a biological construct to a social construct further reveals how political and social factors influence the meanings and definitions of race.

The contemporary view that race is not biological or natural has accompanied a debate regarding whether it is necessary to continue racial discourse and enumeration. Whereas some believe that the refutation of "real" race should translate into the erasure of the construct altogether, most sociologists believe that race as a social fact is real and its significance in creating divisions in the social world have stuck. A large body of social science research documents the role and consequences of race in social institutions and environments, including the criminal justice, education and health systems, job markets, and where people live. These studies illustrate how racial hierarchies are embedded in daily life, from mass incarceration of racial minorities, to "red-lining" communities of color in residentially segregated neighborhoods, to sharp disparities in health. On the other hand, the social reality of race has also manifested as a positive factor in the lives of many individuals and groups; one's racial identity can be a significant part of the self-concept and membership within a racial category can elicit a sense of pride. For these reasons, social scientists believe that race is still an important construct that should be a part of public and academic discourse.

Although most administrations and social scientists agree that race should be enumerated, there is still disagreement in how to best capture race in general and specific racial categories. Social scientists have recently debated about inclusivity of racial measurements and methods of racial measurement because some groups are intentionally or unintentionally left out and also because people differ on how they define themselves. In terms of race in general, self-identified race, interviewer-identified race, skin color, and qualitative assessments of racial identities are examples of methods used to capture race. An example of debates around specific categories of race revolved around the U.S. Office of Management and Budget. This office has the task of deciding which racial categories should be included on government documents and has changed the inclusion standards twice in the last two decades. The fluctuations in the broad definition of race and the particular changes in racial categorizations provide further evidence of the social construction of race. Despite the transformations, race has remained a fundamental feature of modern society and although race can be resisted as a means of stratifying, the construct will forever be a part of social life.

WHITNEY LASTER

Racialism

The term *racialism*, as commonly used in the United States, refers to a preoccupation with racial issues and the constant filtering of events, experiences, and decisions through the lens of race. In other words, racialism gives race an important (if not paramount) role in making sense of life, classifying people into groups, and determining how to arrange the social world. Many social thinkers make the point that the United States is a particularly racialist society, as demonstrated by the fact that race is often the dominant characteristic that people use to differentiate each other and that racial categories are very rigid and hierarchical. Additionally, racialist thought makes it impossible to perceive alternatives to the essentialist and hierarchical system of racial categories in place in the particular racialist society. This can be compared with the situation in other societies such as in the Caribbean and Latin America, where distinctions between people and groups are based on more gradual color-based classifications as well as on nonracial identities such as social class. Racialism can be used as a derogatory term against African American groups when whites accuse African Americans of believing that all negative occurrences in their lives are racially motivated.

Racialism has an additional meaning, more common in the United Kingdom, which is synonymous with racism. This term has been picked up on by many white supremacist groups, who use it to describe their ideology. Since racialist is not a common word, these groups can use it to describe what they believe in without encountering the same angry responses that might emerge if a group described itself as actively racist.

MIKAILA MARIEL LEMONIK ARTHUR

See also

Ethnicity; History of U.S. Census Racial Categorizations; Racial Taxonomy; Social Construction of Race

Further Reading:

American Sociological Association. *The Importance of Collecting Data and Doing Social Scientific Research on Race.* Washington, DC: American Sociological Association, 2003.

Bonilla-Silva, Eduardo. "Rethinking Racism: Toward a Structural Interpretation." *American Sociological Review* 62, no. 3 (1997): 465–80.

Desmond, Mathew, and Mustafa Emirbayer. "What Is Racial Domination?" *Du Bois Review* 6, no. 2 (2009): 335–55.

Frederickson, George. *White Supremacy: A Comparative Study in American and South African History*. New York: Oxford University Press, 1997.

Omi, Michael, and Howard Winant. *Racial Formation in the United States: From the 1960s to the 1980s*, 2nd ed. New York: Routledge, 1994.

Pettit, Becky. *Mass Incarceration and the Myth of Black Progress*. New York: Russell Sage Foundation, 2012.

Snipp, Mathew C. "Racial Measurement in the American Census: Past Practices and Implications for the Future." *Annual Review of Sociology,* 29 (2003): 563–88.

Winant, Howard. *The World Is a Ghetto: Race and Democracy Since World War II*. New York: Basic Books, 2001.

Race Card

The race card is an idiom used in the American language. Often referenced in the accusation of "playing the race card," the purpose is to accuse a perpetrator of imposing race into a discourse or agenda for the purpose of directing the discourse or agenda in a desired way. The perpetrator takes many forms; it can be an individual, organization, policy, or ideology. Communication, psychology, and sociology scholars have studied the use and implications of the race card; however, political scientists have done the crux of the research in regards to campaign strategies or legislation.

The uses of the race card in American discourse can be split into two approaches. In the first approach, the perpetrator is accused of using the race card by triggering implicit racial stereotypes about a targeted group in order to intimidate or anger audiences. This is also called "race baiting." In this approach, the perpetrator is most often accused of acting in the interests of whites. In the second approach, the race card is used as a countercharge; it claims that the perpetrator is bringing race or racism into a discourse or agenda superfluously in efforts to charge the challenger of racism. This is also called "crying racism." In this approach, the perpetrator is most often accused of acting in the interests of racial minorities.

The race card surfaced in American discourse after the civil rights movement of the 1960s. Public acceptance of outright, explicit stereotypes and racist rhetoric has diminished since this time. This period marked a wave of political correctness that attempted to minimize racial offensive language but often results in censoring speech. The race card captures attempts to opine attitudes about race but in a covert manner.

Given the social context, successful use of the race card under the first approach is best received by employing racial appeals. Racial appeals, also referred to as "racial imagery" or "racial cues," have an implicit nature and are used to prime racial stereotypes, fears, and resentments while not appearing to do so. A key example is the Willie Horton advertisement used by the George H. W. Bush 1988 presidential campaign. The campaign broadcasted a mug shot of Horton, an African American male prisoner who, while released on a weekend leave under a program authorized by Bush's opponent, kidnapped a couple and raped the woman. The advertisement did not explicitly discuss race, but relied on implicit racial appeals to trigger stereotypes of black criminology and hypersexuality. According to Mendelberg (2001), the campaign's playing of the race card by using racial appeals was successful in helping Bush defeat his opponent.

Most recently there has been a decline in the general public's acceptance of any racial discourse (racist or nonracist). Scholars, such as Eduardo Bonilla-Silva (2010), argue that this attitude is a result of *colorblind racial ideology*: the belief that racism is no longer an issue in structuring life outcomes and, accordingly, race should no longer be an issue. It is in this current context that the second approach of the race card occurs. For instance, an individual who claims they did not get a job because of their racial group membership could be accused of playing the race card under the argument that race had no part in hiring selection. The challengers in this example often argue that lack of qualifications, or some other factor, is the reasoning behind the decision not to hire and not race.

The Scar of Racism, a book by Paul Sniderman and Thomas Piazza (1993), provides an example of the second approach to the race card. The authors use analyses of public opinion surveys to argue that prejudice is no longer prevalent in whites' attitudes, but despite these facts, they believe race has become tangled with politics. Thus, they claim that

Willie Horton Case

Michael Dukakis, governor of Massachusetts from 1983 to 1991, ran against George H. W. Bush in the 1988 presidential election. Dukakis supported the furlough program, which allowed prisoners weekend leave, during his governorship. Willie Horton was sentenced to life in prison for murder, but was allowed 10 temporary leaves on the furlough program. On one leave, he kidnapped an engaged couple, assaulted the man, and raped the female twice. Horton was caught and sentenced to prison in another state. The Bush campaign broadcasted an advertisement telling the Horton story and showing his mug shot while contrasting Bush's stance on crime to Dukakis's.

race is brought into political agendas when it shouldn't be. As such, they allude to the accusation of "crying racism" by asserting the charge of "new racism"—charges like that of Bonilla-Silva's colorblind racism—are unfounded.

Although the race card is approached in two different ways, the accusation is the same: race is superfluously incorporated into a discourse or agenda for a desired purpose. On the one hand, liberals and people of color typically lead the charge against conservatives and whites in the first "race baiting" approach to the race card. On the other hand, conservatives and whites typically lead the charge against liberals and people of color in the second "crying racism" approach to the race card. There are exceptions to each rule, and both sides have been able to produce research to support their claims, which means reconciliation between the two may be out of reach. However, in reviews of social scientific literature regarding the race card, the trend reveals that a slight majority of these social scientists call out the race card in the first approach and disagree with race card accusations in the second approach. These academics agree with the research that contends racism has been institutionalized and therefore still structures the lives of individuals and groups. Therefore, the argument follows that it remains important to study how race shapes public discourse and agendas.

WHITNEY LASTER

See also
Advertising; Affirmative Action; Color-Blind Racism; *Declining Significance of Race, The*

Further Reading:
Bonilla-Silva, Eduardo. *Racism without Racists: Color-Blind Racism and the Persistence of Racial Inequality in the United States.* New York: Rowman & Littlefield, 2010.
Ford, Richard T. *The Race Card: How Bluffing About Racial Bias Makes Race Relations Worse.* New York: Farrar, Straus and Giroux, 2008.
Mendelberg, Tali. *The Race Card: Campaign Strategy, Implicit Messages, and the Norm of Equality.* Princeton, NJ: Princeton University Press, 2001.
Neubeck, Kenneth, and Noel A. Cazenave. *Welfare Racism: Playing the Race Card Against America's Poor.* New York: Routledge, 2001.
Sniderman, Paul M., and Thomas Piazza. *The Scar of Race.* Cambridge, MA: Harvard University Press, 1993.
Wilson, William Julius. *The Declining Significance of Race: Blacks and Changing American Institutions.* Chicago: University of Chicago Press, 1989.
Wise, Tim. *Colorblind: The Rise of Post-Racial Politics and the Retreat from Racial Equity.* San Francisco, CA: City Lights Publishers, 2010.

Race Relations Cycle

In the 1920s, after a large number of new immigrants from Southern and Eastern European countries had arrived, settled, and formed their own ethnic communities in urban America, many social scientists were interested in their adjustment process in the new land. What happens when new immigrant groups come, meet, and interact with other groups? Are ethnic and racial conflicts inevitable? Will new immigrant groups assimilate to the Anglo-centered mainstream America? Robert Park was one of the first sociologists to be concerned with such questions.

Park proposed a theory of race relations cycle. According to him, immigrant groups would pass through a sequence of stages: contact, competition, accommodation, and eventual assimilation. Different groups of people first come into contact through migration. Once they are in contact, they compete for scarce resources, such as land, educational opportunities, and/or jobs, and competition often develops into conflict. But, as time passes, overt conflict is less frequent, and these groups gradually learn how to accommodate each other. Park argued that the members of minority groups,

Race Matters

Published in 1994, *Race Matters* is a social commentary on contemporary race relations in the United States written by Cornel West, scholar, theologian, author, minister, activist, and public intellectual. The author addressed the role of race in shaping the experiences of blacks in the United States, especially poor and disenfranchised inner-city residents. According to West, "race" continues to matter economically (government cutbacks of aid to the poor), spiritually (stereotypes and negative portrayals of black culture), and politically (black leaders coopting for profit and publicity). He acknowledges the importance of social policy to address poverty as well as individual initiative to reject controlling influences and counterproductive behavior. But he contends that liberal and conservative rhetoric have only minimized the complexity of racial issues and the long-term effects of racism in the United States that include poverty and growing nihilism and angst in black America. He is especially critical of black political and intellectual leaders who possess the socioeconomic status and resources to effectively serve as activists but who instead become co-opted by personal ambition. The current tenure of U.S. race relations that views blacks as the "problem" rather than as citizens who face problems has resulted in the collective inability of citizens to acknowledge common Americanness and humanness. *Race Matters* has achieved national acclaim because it has informed both academic and mainstream audiences about the negative effects of racism and strained race relations in the United States. West was formally trained at Harvard University and Union Theological Seminary. He is currently the Class of 1943 University Professor of Religion at Princeton University.

SANDRA L. BARNES

especially new immigrant groups, would gradually learn the language, customs, manners, and beliefs of the dominant group. Over several generations, such acculturation occurs, structural integration in schools and workplaces is complete, group boundaries break down, and the society becomes more blended. The cycle completes itself with "eventual assimilation." To Park, this cycle of race relations is inevitable, and "progressive and irreversible." Furthermore, the process of assimilation is also universal. He asserts that "the processes by which the integration of peoples and cultures has always and everywhere taken place." Since the term *race* was used much more broadly in Park's day than now, race may refer to both racial and ethnic groups.

Park's theory was popular until the 1960s, but it has been subject to severe criticism since the late 1960s. One major criticism is that his theory is not an explanation of historical reality on race relations but in fact an ideology advocating assimilation as a desirable end-state of American society. He seems to promote full assimilation and amalgamation as an ideal pattern of race relations when he asserts, "Because the tendencies to the assimilation and eventual amalgamation of races exist, they should not be resisted and, if possible, altogether inhibited." The theory, according to his critics, is an ideology justifying one particular model of assimilation in

the United States: the Anglo-conformity model. It is a tacit endorsement of assimilation to the dominant white Anglo-American culture and institutions. His theory of the race relations cycle might have represented the prevailing thought on race relations during the 1920s in the United States.

Furthermore, his race relations cycle may describe and explain fairly well the experiences of white European immigrants in the United States, especially those who settled in the Chicago area. But, his critics argue, his theory is not applicable to the experiences of racial minorities with distinctive physical markers such as Native Americans, African Americans, Hispanic Americans, and Asian Americans. Their experiences seemed to diverge from Park's cycle as they encountered relocation, genocide, exclusion, segregation, and continued conflict. Although African Americans have lived in the United States for many generations, they have never achieved the type of full assimilation Park envisioned. Moreover, his theory ignores the possibility of maintaining stable race relations with different arrangements, such as cultural pluralism, that do not lead to complete assimilation.

Another problem in his theory is that the hypothesis of an inevitable cycle is not empirically testable. If assimilation and eventual amalgamation do not occur, it would be explained as the result of obstacles or interference of the process. There is no way to prove or disprove the validity of his theory empirically. In fact, such race relations cycles are rarely complete.

Another problem in Park's race relations cycle is the universality of conflict in race relations. There are cases in history where conflict and competition did not occur when different groups came into contact. Brazil and Hawaii are two examples of ethnically diverse societies where relatively peaceful and harmonious interactions have existed between different groups of people.

The key problem in his theory is that he ignored several significant variables that could affect the assimilation processes of diverse groups differently. Some of these factors are the context of migration and contact (voluntary versus involuntary), the size and dispersion of a particular group, its cultural similarity to the dominant group, and its physical distinctiveness. The dominant group's willingness to accept the subordinate group also affects the assimilation process. Such situational variables affect the group's assimilation. Historically, racial minorities in the United Stated have been excluded, segregated, and prevented from full assimilation in the United States.

HEON CHEOL LEE

See also
Ethnic Enclaves; Race Relations in the Post–Civil Rights Era

Further Reading:

Park, Robert E. *Race and Culture*. New York: Free Press, 1964 [1950].

Shibutani, Tamotsu, and Kian M. Kwan. *Ethnic Stratification: A Comparative Approach*. New York: Macmillan, 1965.

West, Cornel. *Race Matters*. New York: Vintage Books, 1994.

Race Relations in the Post–Civil Rights Era

Racism has changed over time, as has the racial climate in the country. Though the dynamics of racism have become less overt, they have not been eliminated. Several recent surveys have found that many whites think blacks are as well off as or are better off than whites in regard to education, health care, and jobs. For example, Feagin points out several polls and surveys done recently that demonstrate that whites do not think that discrimination is a big obstacle for people of color. A recent Pew Research Center survey found that more than 80 percent of the black respondents reported widespread racial discrimination in at least one major society area. Of the African American respondents, two-thirds reported that they always or often face discrimination in jobs or in seeking housing. The survey results showed that a majority of whites once again denied the black views of significant societal discrimination.

Whites have an impression that people of color are doing as well or better than whites, when the reality is that they often lag behind whites in areas like income attainment, home ownership, and education. Whites are able to make the claim that racism is not a big problem anymore when they believe ideas like the one articulated above. Whites believe that legislation like affirmative action and the Civil Rights Acts (1964) have equalized the playing field or even tipped the scales to favor people of color. As Feagin points out, they tend to blame people of color for their plight. They forget the decades of racial oppression that preceded this time, as well as the continuing significance of race in shaping a person's life chances in a racist society; or are unaware of how racism has and continues to work to the detriment of people of color.

Contrary to this misperception by whites, many race scholars argue that racism in the post–Civil Rights era has been transformed, not eliminated. During the Jim Crow period and before, racism was blatant and overt. Blacks were restricted in a number of ways, for example in education, employment, voting rights, and much more. With the civil rights movement of the 1960s, legal barriers were eliminated. However, many of the structures that separated whites and blacks and perpetuated inequality continue to exist. For example, residential segregation is normative. School segregation persists. A study by the Civil Rights Project at UCLA found that although the suburbanization of nonwhite families has increased significantly, 80 percent of Latino students and 74 percent of black students attend majority nonwhite schools (50–100 percent minority), and 43 percent of Latinos and 38 percent of blacks attend intensely segregated schools (those with only 0–10 percent of whites students) across the nation. The racial gap regarding wealth has grown. People of color are underrepresented in the government. Additionally, many individuals of color still experience racism from

Pew Research Center Study on Impact of Race on American Wealth Today

Before the 2008 housing bust and economic downturn, whites had 8 times the wealth of African Americans. However, that gap has increased dramatically. According to a study by the Pew Research Center, "from 2005 to 2009, inflation-adjusted median wealth fell by 66% among Hispanic households and 53% among black households, compared with just 16% among white households" (Kochhar and Taylor 2011). This is one example of how race and racism (especially institutional racism) continue to be significant in the post–civil rights era.

whites. Despite this, there is still a perception among many whites that race is no longer an important factor in determining life chances for people of color. A study by the Greenlining Institute found that "just 16% of whites believe that there is a lot of discrimination in America today, while 56% of blacks and 26% of Latinos believe that there is a lot of discrimination in America today" (Byrd and Mirken 2011: 4).

Bonilla-Silva's research demonstrates how the racial structure has changed in the post–Civil Rights era. This new racial structure comprises the following elements:

1. the increasingly covert nature of racial discourse and practice;
2. the avoidance of racial terminology and the ever growing claim by whites that the experience "reverse racism";
3. the elaboration of a racial agenda over political matters that eschews direct racial references;
4. the invisibility of most mechanisms to reproduce racial inequality; and finally,
5. the rearticulation of some racial practices characteristic of the Jim Crow period of race relations.

In contrast to the pre–Civil Rights era, racism has become less overt, most embedded in institutions, and easily denied by whites.

In the color-blind transformation of society, institutional discrimination maintains boundaries without the need for overt racist practices. As it is no longer normative, nor legal, to blatantly discriminate against someone because of their race, society has adapted by utilizing institutional discrimination to exclude those deemed unworthy or undesirable. Blauner noted: "The processes that maintain domination—control of whites over nonwhites—are built into major social institutions. These institutions either exclude or restrict the participation of racial groups by procedures that have become conventional, part of the bureaucratic system of rules and regulations. Thus there is little need for prejudice as a motivating force" (2001: 20). The institutional aspects of discrimination and racism in today's society also make these practices invisible to most whites.

Few people now claim to be racists and the term is considered to be a socially unacceptable label. Bonilla-Silva points out that most whites claim to be color-blind to race, despite the fact that race is often a factor in how whites make decisions about schools, friendships, partners, housing, and so on. Additionally, whites tend to believe equality has already been achieved. According to Bonilla-Silva,

whites believe that the United States has de facto extended equal opportunities to all of its citizens and is, for the most part, a race-neutral society. Therefore, they exhibit little sympathy if not outright resentment for affirmative action, race-targeted government programs, or minorities' demands for their fair shares. . . . Furthermore, because whites believe that discrimination is no longer a salient factor in the United States, they believe that blacks' plight is the result of blacks' cultural deficiencies (e.g., laziness, lack of the proper values, and disorganized family life). (2001: 161–62)

Not only are we in a post–Civil Rights era, but with the election of President Barack Obama, there are those who believe that the United States is also postracial, meaning that race no longer matters and therefore should no longer be discussed. President Obama's election, to some, proves that race is no longer significant.

Kathrin A. Parks

See also

Bigotry; Color-Blind Racism; Racism; Racist Nativism; Reverse Racism; *Racism without Racists*

Further Reading:

Blauner, B. *Still the Big News: Racial Oppression in America.* Philadelphia: Temple University Press, 2001.

Bonilla-Silva, E. *White Supremacy and Racism in the Post-Civil Rights Era.* Boulder, CO: Lynne Rienner Publishers, 2001.

Byrd, D., and B. Mirken. *Post-Racial? Americans and Race in the Age of Obama.* Berkeley, CA: Greenlining Institute, 2011.

Feagin, J. R. *Racist America: Roots, Current Realities, and Future Reparations.* New York: Routledge, 2010.

Kochhar, R., R. Fry, and P. Taylor. *Twenty-to-One: Wealth Gaps Rise to Record Highs Between Whites, Blacks and Hispanics.* Washington, DC: Pew Research Center, 2011.

Orfield, G., J. Kucsera, and G. Siegel-Hawley. *E Pluribus... Separation: Deepening Double Segregation for More Students.* Los Angeles: Civil Rights Project, 2012.

Race Riots in America

Racial violence has a long, tragic, and ironic history in North America. The frequency of race riots defies any attempt to describe them as anomalies; their ferocity illuminates the savage inequalities present in the United States. Indeed, the very presence of race riots becomes one of the most vexing components of the American paradox. In some important ways, race riots reveal certain truths about American society. Sociologists, political scientists, and historians have been at the forefront in the study of race riots in the United States and have greatly broadened understanding of these phenomena. This topic has spawned an enormous amount of scholarly attention and has even been the focus of fictional treatments, both in print and on film. Federal, state, and local governments have formed commissions to analyze the origins of race riots. Churches, religious associations, and civil rights organizations have also voiced concerns about violent racial disturbances; few sectors of American society have been unaffected by racial violence. This pervasive influence may be due to the fact that many of the defining moments in North American history were shaped, in profound ways, by racial conflict. Thus, a closer study of these phenomena, with a particular focus on race riots, may deepen our collective understanding of the American past and present.

In the 20th century, race riots became the most frequently encountered form of race conflict in the United States. Highlighted by the Red Summer of 1919, the 1943 race riots, and the urban rebellions of the mid- to late 1960s, these examples of racial conflict demonstrate how race, white supremacy, urbanization, and various socioeconomic factors can contribute to violent race relations in the midst of a pluralistic society. The presence of frequent race riots has become one of many paradoxes in U.S. history. While heralded worldwide as the paragon of freedom, justice, tolerance, and opportunity, the United States has seen its history warped by such forces as racial slavery, racial injustice, violent intolerance, and prejudice.

Although the modern idea of race clearly was a creation of 18th-century Enlightenment, North American history was at its start (during the founding of Jamestown in 1607) defined by racial conflict and the elevation of whiteness as a status. The uniquely English notions of civilization prefigured the disastrous relations the early colonists established with the local Algonkians and other Native American groups. In addition to constrictive and ethnocentric definitions of civilization, the early English settlers in the Chesapeake brought a sense of religious superiority and an enormous thirst for acquiring more land. All these factors converged in 1676 with the first race war in North American history—Bacon's Rebellion.

Although he came to Virginia with a fair amount of wealth, Nathaniel Bacon created a doctrine that would inspire the thousands of poor and landless Englishmen, who had rapidly multiplied in the colony. In the decades before the rebellion, impoverished Englishmen were lured to the colony with the hope of gaining land and becoming yeomen farmers. In exchange for their passage across the Atlantic, however, they had to give their allotment of land and between four and seven years of labor as indentured servants to tobacco planters who financed their voyage. Once their term of indenture was finished, these former servants would receive freedom dues—a small allotment of land, tobacco seed, guns, livestock, and some currency. Because this system created a steady stream of competitors for the tobacco-planter elite, they conspired to eliminate the land allotment portion of the freedom dues, which allowed them to monopolize all arable land in the colony. As a direct result, Virginia had a growing population of landless, hopeless, but armed, young Englishmen in the decade leading up to 1676.

Although this growing group of landless poor could have vented their collective anger and frustration at the white landed elite, Nathaniel Bacon found a different solution—one that would doom American race relations from that time forward. Bacon's doctrine elevated the status of the landless poor by reinforcing the notion of white supremacy. His plan was to attack all Native Americans—friend and foe alike—and take their land. This diverted the anger of the English poor away from the English elite and toward a common racial enemy. His war, "against all Indians in general," allowed poor whites to rally around notions of white supremacy and racial scapegoating in an all too familiar pattern. This unique form of race consciousness worked against attempts to forge collaborative efforts across racial lines in the colonial and antebellum South. It may also explain why poor Southern whites supported, and even fought to protect, the system of racialized slavery, despite the fact that slavery's very existence guaranteed them a degraded socioeconomic status.

During the decade leading up to Bacon's Rebellion, another terrible transformation was underway. When the planter elite realized that indentured servitude would not be a permanent solution to their labor needs, they turned to a group that had recently been imported into the colony—Africans. Between 1619 and 1641, some 300 Africans had entered Virginia. Ironically, they were not legally defined as slaves. Instead, they were treated much like other indentured servants; once they gave four to 10 years of labor, they would be freed and given freedom dues. For a variety of complex reasons, the landed elite moved to legalize racialized slavery in 1667.

One of the most compelling reasons for this shift was Bacon's Rebellion, which provided the best rationale for the permanent substitution of black slaves for white servants. The legalization of racial slavery was not only the crowning moment in the creation of the American paradox, it also prefigured an enormous amount of racial violence in the 18th, 19th, and 20th centuries.

Although a number of 17th-, 18th-, and 19th-century conflicts had racial components—the First and Second Powhatan Wars, King Philip's War, the Seven Years' War—the two conflicts with the greatest potential impact on modern race relations were the American Revolution

and the American Civil War. Both wars began with the hope of inaugurating a new era of peace, prosperity, and justice. Both ended with bitter disappointment and continued racial strife. Fueled by classical liberal ideology, the American Revolution promised to bring liberty, justice, and prosperity for all. However, when Thomas Jefferson penned the famous words "all men are created equal," neither he nor other members of the American elite sought to extend this statement to Native Americans or African Americans. Instead, a war was fought to bring freedom to the country, but not to the half-million slaves whose labor helped generate revenue for the war effort. The American Revolution, therefore, added yet another dimension to the growing American paradox, and slavery would continue to have a firm base in the land of freedom.

Although it would be difficult to label slave rebellions as race riots, in many ways they became violent attempts to overthrow the white Southern aristocracy and to challenge white supremacy. Gabriel Prosser, Charles Deslondes, Denmark Vesey, and Nat Turner each led movements that sought—at the very least—to kill whites who directly benefited from the labor of the enslaved. Only two of these rebels—Charles Deslondes (1811) and Nat Turner (1831)—managed to carry out these plans. While abolitionists fought each other over the right of slaves to rebel against their masters, one particular abolitionist—John Brown—took matters into his own hands. His 1859 raid on the Harper's Ferry federal arsenal was a clear attempt to foment an antiwhite, antislavery revolt in Virginia. Although his attempt was ultimately unsuccessful, Brown did force the nation to address the central paradox in American society, and his raid was one of a series of events leading directly to the Civil War.

One of the worst race riots in U.S. history occurred in the midst of the Civil War. In July 1863, a mostly Irish mob engaged in an orgy of violence in New York City that left 18 dead (not including the more than 70 black men reported missing) and dozens injured, and caused more than $4 million in property damage. Convinced that the Civil War had become a crusade for the benefit of African Americans and angered at losing industrial jobs to black men because they were drafted into the Union army, thousands of unskilled Irish workers attacked draft offices and any African Americans they could find. Ironically, a number of Irish were convicted and hanged in 1741 after they had allegedly formed a conspiracy with slaves to destroy New York City and establish a biracial regime. A century later, there was no room for such collaborations and any appeals to the common ground between the black and immigrant poor fell on deaf ears. Again, a unique sense of racial consciousness allowed Irish workers to attack black workers, but not the wealthy whites in New York who could purchase exemptions from the draft. Nor would they think to attack white factory owners or other employers who actively hired African American men as cheap labor or used them as strikebreakers and scabs. Even as late as 1863, the doctrines of race consciousness, white supremacy, and racial scapegoating—promoted two centuries earlier by Nathaniel Bacon—continued to determine race relations in North America.

Like the American Revolution, the American Civil War was greatly anticipated as a force for positive change in the United States. With the coming of the Thirteenth Amendment, the paradox of racial slavery was finally brought to an end, although this did not mean an end to racial strife. Perhaps the epitome of this notion was the emergence, in 1866, of the Ku Klux Klan (KKK). Established as a social club for former Confederate soldiers, the KKK and other white supremacist organizations began a campaign of political terrorism using arson, rape, threats, intimidation, beatings, and murder to force newly freed slaves and their Republican Party allies into a subordinate position in the South. Groups like the KKK, the Knights of the White Camellia, the White Caps, and others violently upheld the tenets of white supremacy in their attempts to redeem the South after defeat during the Civil War. More importantly, these groups were responsible for the increasing number of antiblack riots and lynchings that convulsed the black South beginning in the 1870s.

With the premature end of Reconstruction in 1877, a new set of paradoxes emerged. The end of Reconstruction inaugurated a reversal of rights that African Americans and their Northern allies had fought for between 1865 and 1876. Democracy in the South was short-lived as Southern states assumed control over civil rights and the federal government seemingly supported this troubling reversal. For example, the 1896 *Plessy v. Ferguson* U.S. Supreme Court ruling gave federally sanctioned form to the substance of segregation and the nearly insurmountable color line that had long been a major component of American society. By

establishing the "separate but equal" doctrine, this pivotal decision essentially rendered two previous civil rights acts (those of 1866 and 1875) and the Fourteenth Amendment null and void. Without protection provided by the federal government, the collective fate of millions of African Americans hung in the balance.

Southern blacks were forced to suffer through what Rayford Logan refers to as the Black Nadir, as they faced the five-headed hydra of sharecropping, political disenfranchisement, social segregation, antiblack propaganda, and racial violence during the century following the Civil War. In 1903, when W.E.B. Du Bois prophetically announced that "the problem of the twentieth century is the problem of the color line," he, like many of his contemporaries, saw the 1896 ruling as the pinnacle of the movement by state and federal government officials to make white supremacy the official law of the country. Unprecedented amounts of racial violence were the most visible outcome of these various initiatives.

The oppressive weight of Southern racism became a major push factor, as thousands—then later, millions—of African Americans left the only homes they knew for new opportunities elsewhere. The growing tide of race riots and lynchings were key forces providing enormous impetus to these migrations. In the 1890s alone, lynching claimed the lives of 104 black men, women, and children annually. As historian Leon Litwack notes, between 1882 and 1959 "an estimated 4,742 blacks met their deaths at the hands of lynch mobs. As many, if not more blacks were victims of legal lynchings (speedy trials and executions), private white violence, and 'nigger hunts,' murdered by a variety of means in isolated rural sections and dumped into rivers and creeks" (Allen, Als, and Litwack 2000). Lacking the ability to serve on juries, hold political office, or even vote, African Americans throughout the South were virtually powerless in the face of violent antiblack repression of this sort.

Roughly 40,000 black Southerners were part of the Exoduster movement. Between 1879 and 1898, the Exodusters established independent, all-black communities in Kansas, Oklahoma, and Nebraska. More importantly, the largest internal migration in U.S. history witnessed close to 2 million African Americans leaving the South between 1910 and 1940. This massive wave of migrants concentrated primarily in the Midwest and North, although many made it as far as

California during the Great Migration. While the push of the Black Nadir explains much of this movement, the various socioeconomic pulls of better job opportunities, better housing, and higher living standards played important roles in the decision of African Americans to leave the South. Similar to the utopian views of the Midwest and North shared by many enslaved African Americans before 1850, these regions were envisioned as the "Promised Land" for millions of black migrants during the early portion of the 20th century. These dreams would soon be dashed as African American settlers realized there was no escape from the Black Nadir or the American paradox.

One set of responses to the influx of such large numbers of African Americans into the Midwest and North was an increasing number of race riots. Two riots in Illinois—Springfield (1908) and East St. Louis (1917)—proved that the Midwest would not necessarily be more hospitable for African Americans. Accusations of raping white women and intense labor competition led to the deaths of dozens of African Americans and hundreds being forced or displaced from their homes. Despite the intensity of these incidents, nothing matches the Red Summer of 1919 in which two dozen race riots occurred throughout the country. Pioneering historical and sociological assessments of this violent summer have explained it as the outcome of labor competition, antiblack propaganda in the media (especially the 1915 release of *The Birth of a Nation*), and the influx of white supremacist doctrines into Midwestern and northern states. Whatever the specific causes of the numerous race riots in 1919, they proved once again that the American paradox was alive and well in the 20th century. The irony of sending more than 300,000 young black men to fight to make the world "safe for democracy" during World War I was made more glaring by the number of antiblack race riots and overt attempts to deny these same men full citizenship.

Mirroring the anti-Jewish pogroms in Eastern Europe, the savage destruction of two black communities in the 1920s became additional proof that the United States had not found an effective way to negotiate the widening gulf between African Americans and whites. In 1921, the Greenwood section of Tulsa, Oklahoma, suffered through an all-out war, complete with death squads and incendiaries dropped from airplanes by whites. What was once a prosperous black community lay in ashes after days of uncontrolled rioting. In addition, more than 200 black residents were killed in what can be described as a massacre.

In 1923, the all-black community of Rosewood, Florida, suffered a similar fate. After a white woman in a neighboring community claimed that she had been raped—apparently to hide an extramarital affair she was having—hundreds of whites descended on Rosewood. After a week of rioting, the entire town was destroyed and as many as 300 African Americans were killed. Again, a prosperous black community was razed at the hands of a white mob. What both of these cases prove is that economic competition and white supremacy were not the only provocation for race riots in the United States. Jealousy and the fear of African Americans acquiring wealth and property were also significant factors.

During a renewed effort to make the world safe for democracy, the country witnessed another wave of race riots in 1943. Major disturbances occurred in Detroit, Harlem, and Mobile. Again, labor competition was among the principal causes in these examples. Although there would be a number of white-on-black murders, civil rights assassinations, and at least two more lynchings—Emmett Till (1956) and Mack Charles Parker (1959)—the tide of racial violence shifted dramatically in the aftermath of World War II. With a handful of exceptions, the vast majority of race riots in the postwar era were urban revolts that involved black mobs attacking white business owners and police officers. White flight, which resulted in the creation of impoverished black urban ghettos, created a volatile powder keg. It was the frequent examples of police brutality and "justifiable homicide" that often served as the spark. The result of these combined factors was massive and destructive riots in Los Angeles, California; Newark, New Jersey; and Detroit, Michigan, among others. These examples continue to epitomize race riots even in the 21st century.

The radicalism of the mid- to late 1960s reflected a growing acceptance of militancy in blacks. Leaders like Robert F. Williams, Malcolm X, Huey P. Newton, and Stokely Carmichael called for self-defense initiatives and economic self-help for the black urban poor. These endeavors reflected, perhaps, the notion that the civil rights movement had benefited the African American middle class but had done little to improve the condition of the black masses. This circumstance was compounded by specific sociological phenomena that convulsed black communities around the country. One of the most significant responses to successful civil rights legislation and court rulings by whites was urban flight. As the doctrine of social integration became more of a reality in the United States, white Americans began leaving major cities and created exclusive all-white suburbs. In the wake of this considerable white flight, jobs, services, and tax funding for local schools disappeared. In addition, banks, grocery stores, and restaurants left inner-city neighborhoods and relocated to the expanding white suburbs. This reshaping of the urban–suburban landscape across the country created what can be called the Doughnut Effect—essentially, once prosperous cities became impoverished, mostly black cores surrounded by affluent white suburban peripheries. Thus, the "black ghetto" was created.

As high school dropout rates, unemployment, underemployment, crime, and drug use began to soar in inner-city ghettos, the hope that once provided impetus for the civil rights movement began to fade. Martin Luther King, Jr., in the last year of his life, sought to reorient the movement to deal with the growing problem of poverty in the United States. His "Poor People's Campaign" was short-lived, and no relief for the spreading problem of urban poverty seemed to be in sight. Combined with worsening economic conditions in black inner cities, police brutality became a growing issue. In addition to alleged beatings, a number of unarmed black men had been killed by white police officers in incidents that were later deemed justifiable homicides. Without hope, lacking any support from federal, state, or local government institutions, black urbanites created their own solution to the enormous problems they faced—urban rebellions.

Beginning with the 1965 Watts riot in Los Angeles and continuing into the 21st century with the 2001 Cincinnati riot, a new pattern of racial strife emerged. In more than three dozen cases—including examples in Detroit, Michigan (1967); Augusta, Georgia (1970); Miami (1980) and Tampa, Florida (1987); Los Angeles, California (1992); and Cincinnati, Ohio (2001)—race riots or urban rebellions began in impoverished black communities typically after instances of police brutality. The only exception to this rule was the 1992 Los Angeles riot, which was sparked after three white police officers were initially found not guilty of various charges in relation to the videotaped beating of an African American, Rodney King. The ensuing riot was linked more

to the perception of injustice by an all-white jury than to the actual beating, which occurred several months prior to the controversial ruling. In every case, however, black urban residents looted and burned businesses owned by nonblacks who reportedly had long histories of either not hiring African Americans or of treating black customers with disrespect. In addition, white motorists were attacked and white police officers and firefighters became targets of black rage.

It was in the aftermath of the 1967 urban rebellions in Newark, New Jersey, and Detroit, Michigan, that President Lyndon B. Johnson established the National Advisory Commission on Civil Disorders, headed by Governor Otto Kerner of Illinois. In their final report, published in 1968, the eight-member commission concluded as follows:

> There was, typically, a complex relationship between the series of incidents and the underlying grievances. For example, grievances about allegedly abusive police practices, unemployment and underemployment, housing, and other conditions in the ghetto, were often aggravated in the minds of many Negroes by incidents involving the police, or the inaction of municipal authorities on Negro complaints about police action, unemployment, inadequate housing or other conditions.

In the estimation of the Kerner Commission, poverty, more than anything else, created the necessary conditions for the 23 urban riots that occurred between 1964 and 1967. In addition to poverty, the Kerner Commission cited white racism as a cause of urban rioting, noting that the United States was "moving toward two societies, one black, one white—separate and unequal." In fully implicating white Americans in the creation of black ghettos, the Kerner Commission created a long list of recommendations for government reform to address these issues. Although the Johnson administration did not enact any of the specific recommendations of the Kerner Commission, the concerns the report raised became a linchpin in Johnson's "War on Poverty" and his goal to create "the Great Society."

As watersheds and defining moments in American history, race riots represent one of many ways to track the continuation of various paradoxes in American society. From, quite literally, the opening act of American history to the dawn of the 21st century, racial strife has been a constant in a country known more for its various political liberties and economic opportunities. By assessing the nature of racial conflict in the American context, we not only expand our understanding of this country's nuanced history, but we can perhaps more accurately gauge the troubles and dynamics inherent in any pluralistic society.

WALTER RUCKER

See also

Asbury Park (New Jersey) Riot of 1970, Atlanta (Georgia) Riot of 1906, Atlanta (Georgia) Riot of 1967, Bellingham Riots (1907), Bensonhurst (New York) Incident (1989), Biloxi Beach (Mississippi) Riot of 1960; Black Church Arsons; Bloody Sunday; Boston (Massachusetts) Riots of 1975 and 1976; Brownsville (Texas) Incident of 1906; Charleston (South Carolina) Riot of 1919; Chattanooga (Tennessee) Riot of 1906; Chester and Philadelphia (Pennsylvania) Riots of 1918; Chicago Commission on Race Relations; Chicago (Illinois) Riot of 1919; Cincinnati (Ohio) Riots of 1967 and 1968; Cincinnati (Ohio) Riots of 2001; Cleveland (Ohio) Riot of 1966; Detroit (Michigan) Riot of 1943; Detroit (Michigan) Riot of 1967; East St. Louis (Illinois) Riot of 1917; Election Riots of the 1880s and 1890s; Greenburg (Indiana) Riot of 1906; Greenwood Community (Tulsa, Oklahoma); Harlem (New York) Riot of 1935; Houston (Texas) Mutiny of 1917; Howard Beach (New York) Incident (1986); Johnson-Jeffries Fight of 1910, Riots Following; Knoxville (Tennessee) Riot of 1919; Long Hot Summer Riots (1965–1967); Longview (Texas) Riot of 1919; Los Angeles (California) Riot of 1965; Los Angeles (California) Riots of 1992; Miami (Florida) Riot of 1982; New Bedford (Massachusetts) Riot of 1970; New Orleans (Louisiana) Riot of 1866; New York City Draft Riot of 1863; New York City Riot of 1943; Newark (New Jersey) Riot of 1967; Orangeburg (South Carolina) Massacre of 1968; Philadelphia (Pennsylvania) Riot of 1964; Prison Riots; Red Scare and Race Riots; Red Summer Race Riots of 1919; Rosewood (Florida) Riot of 1923; Saint Genevieve (Missouri) Riot of 1930; San Francisco (California) Riot of 1966; Springfield (Ohio) Riot of 1904; Tampa (Florida) Riots of 1987; Texas Southern University Riot of 1967; Tulsa (Oklahoma) Riot of 1921; Washington (D.C.) Riot of 1919; Washington (D.C.) Riots of 1968; Wilmington (North Carolina) Riot of 1898; Zoot Suit Riots. Documents: Report on the Memphis Riots of May 1866 (1866); Account of the Riots in East St. Louis, Illinois (1917); A Southern Black Woman's Letter Regarding the Recent Riots in Chicago and Washington (1919); The Cook County Coroner's Report Regarding the 1919 Chicago Race Riots (1920); The Final Report of the Grand Jury on the Tulsa Race Riot (June 25, 1921); Testimony from *Laney v. United States* (1923); The Governor's Commission Report on the Watts Riots (1965); Cyrus R. Vance's Report on the Riots in Detroit (1967); The Reports of the Oklahoma Commission to Study the Tulsa Race Riot of 1921 (2000–2001); Draft Report: 1898 Wilmington Race Riot Commission (2005)

Further Reading:

Allen, James, Hilton Als, and Leon Litwack. *Without Sanctuary: Lynching Photography in America*. Santa Fe: Twin Palms, 2000.

DuBois, W. E .B. *The Souls of Black Folk*. New York: New American Library, 1982[1903].

Graham, Hugh Davis, and Ted Robert Gurr. *The History of Violence in America: A Report to the National Commission on the Causes and Prevention of Violence*. New York: Bantam Books, 1969.

Grimshaw, Allen D., ed. *Racial Violence in the United States*. Chicago: Aldine, 1969.

Morgan, Edmund. *American Slavery, American Freedom: The Ordeal of Colonial Virginia*. New York: Norton & Norton, 1975.

Racial Customs and Etiquette

Racial customs and etiquette predated the period generally designated as the Jim Crow era. The forced physical separation of blacks and whites associated with the period began and ended in the North before the Civil War and pervaded the West and Midwest throughout the period of westward expansion in the United States. Jim Crow was legalized in the South by the U.S. Supreme Court in *Plessy v. Ferguson* (1896), which declared "separate but equal" to be constitutional and permitted the segregation of blacks and whites on railroads in Louisiana. The ruling provided a legal basis for the development of intricate rules of behavior that applied to all areas of life. Their collective design was to reinforce white supremacy and relegate blacks to second-class citizenship. Such customs varied according to gender, geography, hue, and social climate, and they were more rigidly followed in public situations than in private ones. But they were applied to all known African Americans regardless of their educational or social standing. Given the debilitating, even humiliating, nature of these rules, African Americans sought legal and creative ways to counter their negative social, political, and economic impact. They also made a sustained effort to curb, if not altogether neutralize, the psychological impact of such customs, especially on black children.

As Jim Crow laws were initiated with systems of transportation, many of the first rules of etiquette emerged in this area and quickly expanded to include other public spaces where blacks and whites encountered each other from day to day. Regardless of social position, identifiably black passengers were forced to ride in Jim Crow cars, which were often unclean and lacked the comforts of those carrying white passengers. When separate accommodations were not possible, as was sometimes the case with city buses, blacks were to sit at the back of the bus. They were also expected to relinquish their seats if whites exceeded the capacity of the section provided for them. In places of business, whites were served first even if black customers were the first to arrive. Black customers were not allowed to try on certain clothing items, particularly shoes, nor could they return such items once purchased because white store owners feared that whites would not buy products that had been worn by blacks.

In public hospitals, blacks and whites were cared for in separate wards. Black nurses were permitted to care for white patients, but never the reverse, although white doctors were permitted to treat black patients in the colored sections of segregated hospitals. Racial custom nonetheless dictated that white doctors refrain from showing compassion when treating black patients. Blacks in need of blood transfusions were never to be given blood from whites. The reverse was also true. Black writers of the era, and those who wrote fictional works set during the Jim Crow period, often believed this deleterious act captured the quintessence of racism. Lillian Bertha Horace's *Angie Brown* (1949) opens with the death of the protagonist's child, which occurred because the hospital refused to give blood that had been drawn from whites to a black child. Similarly, Toni Morrison's *Song of Solomon* (1978) opens with a black woman in labor in front of "No Mercy Hospital," the name members of the black community gave the hospital because of its treatment of blacks.

An elaborate set of customs governed intimate relations between blacks and whites during the Jim Crow era. Thomas Dixon's novel *The Clansman* (1905) and the subsequent movie based on it, *The Birth of a Nation* (1915), underscored and reinforced white men's profound fear of interracial mixing, namely between black men and white women, as many white men continued to maintain intimate relationships with black women after Emancipation. Rules on interracial relationships were never applied as strictly to white men as they were to black men during the Jim Crow era.

Black males, regardless of their age, were not to even look at white women, nor were they to touch them. Even an accidental brush was considered to be a serious offense. If a black man saw a white woman approaching on a sidewalk, he was to step off the sidewalk until the woman passed. Black men and boys were beaten, castrated, tarred, feathered, and lynched for purportedly not keeping out their place with white women. Black men had to stay on constant alert for their safety, especially if a white woman in the vicinity had purportedly been raped. White men, on the other hand, engaged in intimate relations with black women without prosecution or public controversy.

White women who maintained intimate relationships with black men were in danger of social ostracism or disinheritance. When pregnancy resulted, the babies were generally aborted or given up for adoption. Many white women whose affairs with black men were discovered cried rape to protect themselves from disgrace or public censure. Gwendolyn Brooks's "Ballad of Pearl May Lee" (1945) offers one of the most riveting presentations of the peril black men faced when they dared have an affair with white women.

Publicly, white men went to great lengths to protect white female purity, but privately, many continued to have intimate relationships with black women. Such relationships were often explored by black and white fiction writers of the period, with the story usually ending in tragedy. Real life examples also abounded, with one of the most famous cases involving Senator Strom Thurmond, a staunch segregationist, who fathered a daughter, Essie Mae Washington, by a black maid. Given the historic vulnerability of black women to sexual aggression, many black parents from emancipation onwards set out to educate their daughters to preclude their having to "work in a white woman's kitchen," where they were often targets of sexual aggression.

In the rural Jim Crow South, racial etiquette was highly articulated and localized. Because most rural black

"Members of the Race Find It Hard to Get Waited On," 1916

African American men and women found that race discrimination hindered good service at a prominent Chicago department store, Marshall Fields.

It has been well known that Marshall Field & Co., although considered as the world's greatest department store, had nothing for the Race man nor woman to do since the daughter of the founder of the store fell in love with his coachmen, and after the affair had been discouraged by the father, later gave birth to a child, it is alleged, and since then the family has been against our race. It will well be remembered that the son was supposed to have been shot in the red light district.

Many of their customers have been members of the race, however, but here of late they find it hard to be waited on and that the clerks are indifferent, complaints made to floor walkers have been ignored. The Defender sent two ladies down to investigate. One was so fair that they could not tell that any African blood was in her veins and the other was just the opposite. The first place visited was the main floor and the floorwalker told her that the articles would be found in the basement. Miss A. followed a moment later and asked for the same article and she was directed to the floors above. Getting out of the sight of the informer they both went to the basement. Standing there for several moments the Miss A. was waited upon. No one paid any attention to Miss B.

Finally, a floorwalker named Mr. Simpson, a little, insignificant, bald headed fellow came and asked all those who were standing around, "Are you being waited upon?" with the exception of Miss B. nor asked her what she wanted.

The same two ladies went to the other part of the store. Miss A. was again served, but Miss B. stood there, all the clerks ignoring her. Finally, having orders from this office to see how far a man whom the clerks called Mr. Waller or Wallace; he said he would find her someone to take care of her, but he disappeared and never returned for about thirty minutes. Seeing that she was getting provoked he said, "Have you been standing here all this time?" Miss A. was waiting and timing the affair. Mr. G. was sent to the glove counter; he was ignored. The clerks, going around on the other side, and there engaging in a conversation with other clerks. He went to the floorwalker and was informed that he could not expect the clerks to hurry as it was warm and they were working pretty hard. So noticeable has this state of affairs become that we print the following from a local white journal: Marshall Field's Draw Drastic "Color Line."

The Colored population of Chicago was handed a severe shock this week by an order issued from the management's office at Marshall Field's that this class of trade was to be treated with "indifference" whenever they made their appearance as prospective buyers on the main floor or above and were to be directed to the basement by all sales-persons as the most likely place where they could find the articles they desired to purchase.

Embodied in the same order were the directions to the help in the basement to show Colored patrons "inattention" and treat them in a manner indicative of the fact that their trade was not desired.

It is particularly noteworthy that the order was not put in the form of writing but was carried by a special messenger by word of mouth to each one of the department heads.

Source: *Chicago Defender*, June 10, 1916.

Southerners were farmers, sharecroppers, or tenants, the landlord-tenant relationship shaped most interactions. As a result, segregation, economic exploitation, and oppression were more pronounced in rural areas than in cities.

As the racial composition of towns ranged from predominantly white to predominantly black, variations on the theme existed. In predominantly black towns or predominantly black sections of predominantly white towns, racial etiquette was namely important when occasional white visitors came for various purposes or when blacks ventured outside a given predominantly black enclave. Writer and anthropologist Zora Neale Hurston often gave primacy to such places in her creative writings. Some predominantly white towns were off limits to blacks. Custom, if not the law, precluded blacks' entering them. Sometimes warning signs were posted on the outskirts of towns to discourage black visitors, such as "Niggers, read and run." Even though there were no laws insisting that blacks not enter, custom dictated as much. Blacks learned from experience and by word of mouth which places were off limits.

Boundaries were less rigid in other rural spaces. Country stores, rural roads, and cotton gins were usually not segregated. Certain recreational activities were also not segregated. Young black and white men sometimes drank and gambled together at cockfights, saloons, and card games. At mutual aid events, white landowners and black hired hands frequently worked together as white farm wives and black domestics prepared meals for the laborers. But in such cases, racial etiquette was decidedly pronounced. African Americans had limited access to most small-town retail shops, but some business, such as barbershops that served whites, were out of bounds. Different from cities, most rural towns had few buses, hotels, or restaurants, all of which provided distinct stages for blacks and whites to play their prescribed roles.

Whites in rural and urban areas generally withheld everyday courtesies from blacks. They did not invite blacks to their homes as guests. Black workers and domestics had to go to the back door of whites' houses, although this rule was not universally applied. Visits and courtesy were avoided because they implied equality, a concept contrary to the racial hierarchy that Jim Crow was designed to reinforce. Whites insisted that blacks use titles that showed deference or respect. Black men and women were to address white men and women as "Sir" and "Ma'am" respectively. In less formal situations, black men might also refer to white men of standing as "boss" or "cap'n" without fear of reprisal. Whites, on the other hand, were never to address black men respectfully. Black men regardless of social standing were addressed by their first names or called "boy," "nigger," or "niggra," a polite substitute for the aforementioned derogatory term. Black men were often called by any name a white interlocutor might conjure on a moment's notice, with the name "Jack" being one of the most common substitutes.

White women sometimes permitted their black servants and acquaintances to address them by their first names, but only if they prefaced the name with the title "Miss." Black women, on the other hand, were never addressed respectfully as "Miss" or "Mrs." The term "wench," which dated back to slavery, still appeared in some legal documents during the Jim Crow period. Although educated whites sometimes referred to black women collectively as "colored ladies," black women were generally referred to as "auntie," "girl," "gal," or by their first names, which black women generally resented. Texas native Lillian Bertha Horace, an educator and writer, noted in her diary that she felt "hurt, indignant, disgusted" when the greeting in a "long formal letter on definite business" opened "Dear Lilly."

White men were careful not to publicly perform any courteous act that hinted that they treated black women like "ladies," a category reserved for white women. They refrained from such polite habits as addressing black women respectfully as "Miss" or "Mrs.," carrying or lifting heavy packages for black women, helping them into street cars, holding doors open for black women and allowing them to enter ahead first, tipping or removing their hats in the presence of black women, or retrieving on their behalf an item that might have fallen to the floor or ground. The lack of courtesy often approached outright discourtesy.

Educational institutions were largely segregated in the Jim Crow South, but black and white educators and administrators still had occasion to interact with each other, particularly during summer certification periods and campus visitations by white supervisors. White officials visiting black schools were often strict, intimidating, and critical as opposed to helpful. Even beyond the South, black students and scholars were not spared the inconveniences of race. In educational institutions in which blacks were admitted, they were often not acknowledged by their professors. Some white professors summarily failed black students, while others never granted black students a grade above "C." The few black scholars who found semipermanent posts at universities outside the South often could not dine in university faculty clubs, nor could they find hotel accommodations when they traveled to professional meetings. Black students, particularly those involved in extracurricular activities such as debate and athletics, faced the same dilemma. Professor Thomas Freeman and members of the Texas Southern University's highly acclaimed debate team had to establish living accommodations with families and religious organizations whenever they had to travel to competitions in the United States. Students, including Barbara Jordan, eventually the first congresswoman in the United States, were coached to maintain their dignity despite the bias they faced.

Racist customs and etiquette also impacted blacks in the U.S. military, whose unique position as defenders of the nation and its democratic ideals made their sustained encounter with white supremacy particularly unsettling. Black men in uniform instilled pride in African Americans who appreciated the significance of their sacrifice but incited deep resentment in whites committed to white supremacy. One of the most famous photographs of the Jim Crow era captures in still frame the lynched body of an African American soldier in uniform hanging from a noose in the midst of a crowd of jeering, angry whites.

The deep-seated resentment of white civilians was also evident on military bases, where black men were never treated as equals to white soldiers. They were in segregated units, attended separate training schools, and lived in segregated facilities. They were generally limited to service and supply units and were not allowed to command white officers. They also had to bear with the indignities stemming from legalized subjugation. They were often called "nigger" and other derogatory names by their superiors, often mistreated, and generally subject to much harsher reprimand than their white counterparts. The Houston Riot of 1917 is perhaps the most historic event underscoring the tension that permeated such environments. The riot erupted on August 23, 1917, when black soldiers of the 24th Infantry, then stationed in Houston, Texas, armed themselves and challenged the beating of two fellow soldiers by local police. The event resulted in the largest court-martial held in the United States.

Black women in the U.S. military were denied equal treatment as well. They entered the U.S. military first as nurses, with Civil War nurse Susie King Taylor being among the first to record her experiences. During the Spanish American War, most of the 32 black women recruited as nurses were sent to Santiago, Cuba, in July and August 1898, where they rendered service during the worst years of a yellow fever epidemic. Some black nurses were contracted by the surgeon general to serve in the Spanish-American War. Five black graduate nurses joined the army, according to records at the Tuskegee Institute. Black women nurses were also recruited from various hospitals and training centers in Chicago, Illinois; New Orleans, Louisiana; and Washington, D.C.

During World War I, many black nurses hoped to increase their chances of serving in the Army or Naval Nurse Corps by joining the American Red Cross. Eighteen black Red Cross nurses were offered assignments in Illinois and Ohio not long after the Armistice, but the end of the war precluded the planned assignment of black nurses to other camps. Those who served were limited to caring for German prisoners of war and black soldiers. By August 1919, all were released from duty.

During World War II, black women were permitted to join the nurse course, but their number was limited to 56. On June 25, 1941, President Franklin D. Roosevelt's Executive Order 8802 established the Fair Employment Practices Commission, which initiated the eradication of racial discrimination in the U.S. military. In June 1943, Congresswoman Frances Payne of Ohio introduced an amendment to the Nurse Training Bill to eradicate racial bias. Black women's enrollment in the Cadet Nurse Corps quickly mushroomed to 2,000.

In July 1944, the quota for black army nurses was eliminated, and on January 24, 1945, the U.S. Navy opened its doors to black women. Black women were also enlisted in the Women's Army Auxiliary Corps (WAAC), eventually renamed the Women's Army Corps (WAC), which employed 6,520 black women during the war. Black women also joined the Navy WAVES (Women Accepted for Volunteer Emergency Service) and the Coast Guard SPARS (derived from the Coast Guard motto "Semper Paratus," Latin for "Always Ready"). Similar to black men, black women were assigned to segregated living quarters, ate at separate tables, received segregated training, and used separate recreational facilities. They were not allowed to serve white American soldiers until intervention from Eleanor Roosevelt.

Racial etiquette and customs impacted the lives of black children as well. They learned the rules governing black and white relations by observation and through conversations with their parents and others. For example, Helen Green, the first black woman admitted into Methodist Hospital of the Dallas School of Professional Nursing, as a child wondered why the white woman whom her mother helped with canning never came to their house, especially given that Green's family had at least more space in their front yard for her and the white woman's little girl to play. She also wondered why the little girl always insisted on naming the games, creating the rules, and changing them for her benefit. Green essentially did not enjoy visits to the white woman's house because she was under constant pressure to be careful. The lessons she and other black children learned directly and indirectly were never easy to receive and were often painfully applied. The often repeated statement "If I don't beat you, the white man will kill you" reflected the rationale some black parents living in Jim Crow cultures used to teach their children respect and even fear of authority, especially given that the ultimate face of authority was white.

Black parents nonetheless found creative ways to insist on a modicum of respect for their children by using titles as first names for their son and daughters, including "King," "Prince," "President," "Princess," "Queen," and "Duke." Others attempted to counter the psychological impact of sustained racism on their daughters by giving them black dolls to help them develop self-respect from their earliest days. Black parents, especially those of aspiring, middle and elite classes, attempted to instill racial pride and "race love" in their children by surrounding them with positive images of blacks, including pictures and Sunday school cards depicting black characters.

Many African Americans masked their displeasure with the racial etiquette and customs when in the company of whites. But they expressed their discontent in private, in their personal writings or via the black press. The tenor of such relationships continued to change over time. Black domestics of the early 20th century, for example, did not demonstrate the same deference to whites in public that their enslaved foremothers had shown, and subsequent generations of blacks found it increasingly difficult to respect the rules. Many even resorted to mocking them, sometimes with deadly results, as in the case of Emmett Till. With the help of early black activist scholars, professionals, professional organizations, fraternities, sororities, lodges, clubs, and churches, African Americans and their supporters eventually challenged the legal foundation of Jim Crow, the dismantling of which led to a gradual dissolution of the racial customs and etiquette that legalized discrimination had spawned.

KAREN KOSSIE-CHERNYSHEV

See also

African American Humor and Comic Traditions; Derogatory Terms; Minstrelsy

Further Reading:

Brooks, Gwendolyn. *A Street in Bronzeville*. New York: Harper and Row, 1945.

Delany, Sarah L., and A. Elizabeth Delany, with Amy Hill Hearth. *Having Our Say: Delany Sisters' First 100 Years*. New York: Dell, 1994.

Franklin, John Hope. *Mirror to America: The Autobiography of John Hope Franklin*. New York: Farrar, Straus and Giroux, 2005.

Green, Helen. *East Texas Daughter*. Fort Worth: Texas Christian University Press, 2003.

Haynes, Robert V. *A Night of Violence: The Houston Riot of 1917*. Baton Rouge: Louisiana State University Press, 1976.

Johnson, Kevin R. "The Legacy of Jim Crow: The Enduring Taboo of Black-White Romance." *Texas Law Review* 84, no. 3 (February 2006): 739–66. http://www.utexas.edu/law/journals/tlr/abstracts/84/84johnson.pdf (accessed September 2007).

Jones, Jacqueline. *Labor of Love, Labor of Sorrow: Black Women, Work and the Family from Slavery to the Present*. New York: Vintage Books, 1995.

Kossie-Chernyshev, Karen, ed. *Diary of Lillian B. Horace*. New York: Pearson Custom Publishing, 2007.

Kossie-Chernyshev, Karen, ed. *Angie Brown*. Acton, MA: Copley Custom Publishing, 2008.

Love, Spencie. *One Blood, The Death and Resurrection of Charles R. Drew*. Chapel Hill: University of North Carolina Press, 1996.

McGuire, Phillip, ed. *Taps for a Jim Crow Army: Letters from Black Soldiers in World War II*. Lexington: University of Kentucky Press, 1993.

Mitchell, Michele. *Righteous Propagation: African Americans and the Politics of Racial Destiny after Reconstruction*. Chapel Hill: University of North Carolina Press, 2004.

Patterson, Tiffany Ruby. *Zora Neale Hurston and a History of Southern Life*. Philadelphia: Temple University Press, 2005.

Sheldon, Kathryn S. "Brief History of Black Women in the Military." Women in Military Service for America Foundation. http://womensmemorial.org/Education/BBH1998.html#2 (accessed September 2007).

Walker, Melissa. "Shifting Boundaries: Race Relations in the Rural Jim Crow South." In *African American Life in the Rural South, 1900–1950*, edited by R. Douglas Hurt, 81–107. Columbia: University of Missouri Press, 2003.

Racial Disparities in Capital Punishment

The United States is the only Western democracy to retain executions as a form of criminal punishment today. The death penalty in the United States dates back to the early colonial era wherein public executions were held to deter others from crimes involving people and property, but also to spread a message of white dominance during the era of slavery. Throughout this time, there have been stark racial, ethnic, class, gender, and geographic disparities in death sentencing and executions. Despite decades of social and legal challenges to correct these disparities, the American death penalty today continues to reflect a racist administration of justice.

Since 1608, there have been nearly 16,000 recorded executions in the United States. This number does not reflect "unofficial executions"—lynchings—that numbered in the thousands and primarily targeted African Americans in the late 19th and early 20th century. From 1882 and 1930, white mobs killed over 3,100 black citizens in dramatic, terroristic displays of torture and death. While whites, Mexicans, American Indians, and Asians were also lynched in America during this time, black men, women, and children composed roughly 85 percent of lynching victims. Lynchings disproportionately involved crimes committed by blacks against whites, particularly white women. Yet, by all accounts, it was actually white on black violence that dominated in these communities. Exposing these stark racial and gendered disparities was at the heart of the anti-lynching movements in the early to mid-20th century. While lynching declined significantly during this time, racially disparate sentencing would continue to characterize the state-sanctioned executions that replaced them.

Between 1930 and 1972, states continued to sentence and execute African American men disproportionately for the crimes of homicide and rape, well beyond rates that could be explained by chance. The National Association for the

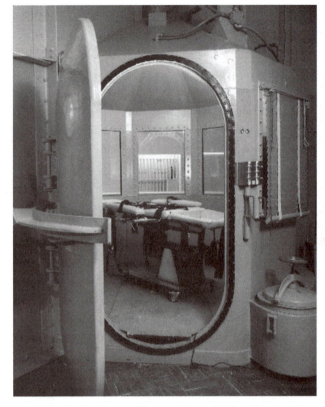

Lethal injection chamber used for executions at San Quentin State Prison in California. (California Department of Corrections)

Advancement of Colored People's Legal Defense and Education Fund prioritized the death penalty as a civil rights issue, waging a legal battle against glaring racial disparities and unequal treatment of black defendants. Their efforts culminated in the U.S. Supreme Court's finding that the death penalty, as practiced, was "capricious and arbitrary" and thus

Life without the Possibility of Parole

Today, 49 states and the federal judicial system offer "life without parole" (LWOP) as a sentencing alternative to the death penalty. Although an offender sentenced to LWOP will not technically be executed by the state (typically via lethal injection), scholars instead refer to this as "death by incarceration," as the individual will indeed die in prison. Similar to the death penalty, LWOP sentencing demonstrates racial disparities with an overrepresentation of persons of color being sentenced to LWOP. In July 2009, the Sentencing Project released a report that examined the burgeoning practice and the racial composition of life without parole sentencing. Primarily, their study revealed enormous racial disparities in life without parole sentencing: two-thirds (66.4 percent) of individuals serving life sentences are persons of color and African Americans make up 56.4 percent of the entire population. These disparities are more pronounced among juveniles serving life without the possibility of parole—77 percent are youth of color. Hailed as a solution to the death penalty among some abolitionists, LWOP sentencing continues a pattern of racially disparate sentencing.

unconstitutional, in the landmark *Furman v. Georgia* (1972) decision that invalidated all states' death penalty statutes.

Despite states' adoption of updated sentencing guidelines in the wake of *Furman*, racial disparities continued. Prior to *Furman*, scholars found that the defendant's race was the most significant predictor of a death sentence. Black defendants were overwhelmingly and disproportionately more likely to be sentenced to death, particularly in cases involving white defendants. In the post-*Furman* era, new studies demonstrate that the race of the victim still strongly predicted death sentencing. Defendants charged with killing whites, whether black or white, are significantly more likely to be sentenced to death, revealing a pattern that privileges white lives over black lives. One analysis by the U.S. General Accounting Office found that this pattern showed up in 82 percent of all studies examining death penalty sentencing disparities.

Today, there are nearly 3,200 people on death row in the United States. Of those, 98 percent are men. Since 1976, states within the Southern region of the United States have accounted for over 80 percent of the 1,320 executions during this time. America's death row is 43 percent white, 42 percent black, 12 percent Latino, and 3 percent "other." Despite the fact that roughly half of homicide victims in the United States are white each year, 77 percent of all executions since 1976 have involved cases involving white victims.

Several factors help to explain the continued existence of racial disparities in the American capital punishment system. First, nearly all criminal justice and legal actors in the capital punishment system are white, even in areas where citizens of color compose the majority. Scholars argue that this lack of representativeness routinely subjects defendants of color to the conscious or unconscious racial biases and prejudice of prosecutors, defense attorneys, judges, and jurors. Second, police devote much more time, energy, and resources to homicides involving white victims than any other group, meaning that a defendant is more likely to be found. Third, prosecutors are most likely to seek the death penalty in cases involving white victims and black defendants. Fourth, all-white juries, once thought to be a relic of the past, are common throughout the Southern region of the United States. All-white juries are 2.5 times more likely to sentence black defendants to death for cases involving white victims. Lastly, jurors who perceive black defendants as appearing more

Jury Bleaching and Capital Sentencing

A 2010 report by the Equal Justice Initiative (EJI) found that "jury bleaching"—a practice of striking black jurors by using "peremptory strikes," deemed unconstitutional by the U.S. Supreme Court's 1986 *Batson v. Kentucky*—continues today. In examining the jury selection process in eight Southern states—Alabama, Arkansas, Florida, Georgia, Louisiana, Mississippi, South Carolina, and Tennessee—the EJI found that over 80 percent of jury-qualified eligible black jurors had been struck from capital juries. Similar to the all-white juries that tried and convicted black defendants to death in the 19th century, black defendants today are tried by all-white juries, even in areas where the majority of the population is black. All-white juries are significantly more likely to sentence black defendants to death, particularly in cases involving a white victim. These practices continue despite the passage of the 1875 Civil Rights Act to end racially discriminatory jury selection and several U.S. Supreme Court cases to redress racially disparate capital sentencing.

"stereotypically black" are more likely to sentence them to death, demonstrating that racial stereotypes influence death sentencing. As these few examples demonstrate, the American death penalty involves a complex set of actors and decisions, and racial bias can taint each step of this system.

In the United States, the death penalty—sentences, executions, and public support—has declined by all metrics since the 1990s. Several states have abolished the death penalty and adopted life without parole as a sentencing alternative, citing costs and the risk of wrongful conviction. Legal attempts to address racial disparities since *Furman* have been weak at best, with the U.S. Supreme Court even referring to them as "inevitable." In the same way that racial bias permeated the practice of lynching throughout the United States, it continues today, demonstrating a profoundly flawed justice system.

EMMA ZACK AND DANIELLE DIRKS

See also

Crack versus Cocaine; Crime and Race; Criminal Justice System and Racial Discrimination; Disproportionality Index Scores; Implicit Bias. Document: *Furman v. Georgia* (1972)

Further Reading:

Baldus, D. C., and G. Woodworth. "Race Discrimination in the Administration of the Death Penalty: An Overview of the Empirical Evidence with Special Emphasis on the Post-1990 Research." *Criminal Law Bulletin* 39 (2003): 194–226.

Eberhardt, Jennifer L., Paul G. Davies, Valerie J. Purdie-Vaughns, and Sheri Lynn Johnson. "Looking Deathworthy: Stereotypicality of Black Defendants Predicts Capital-Sentencing Outcomes." *Psychological Science* 17 (2006): 383–86.

Sarat, Austin, and Charles J. Ogletree Jr., eds. *From Lynch Mobs to the Killing State: Race and the Death Penalty in America*. New York: New York University Press, 2006.

U.S. General Accounting Office. *Death Penalty Sentencing: Research Indicates Pattern of Racial Disparities*. Washington, DC: U.S. General Accounting Office, 1990.

Wolfgang, Marvin, and Marc Reidel. "Race, Judicial Discretion, and the Death Penalty." *ANNALS of the American Academy of Political and Social Science* 407 (1973): 119–33.

Racial Earnings Gap

There has been a large racial gap in earnings in the United States for some time. African American, Latino, and Native American workers have earned much less than white workers, and the racial gap has been much greater for men than for women. For example, according to 2001 census data, African American men earned on average approximately 78 percent ($30,409) of white men's earnings ($38,869), and Latino men earned only 63 percent ($24,638). The racial gap in earnings has been shrinking between African American and white men but growing between Latino and white men. Asian American men earned slightly more ($40,946) than white men on average.

In 2001, African American women earned on average about 90 percent ($25,117) of white women's earnings ($28,080), while Latino women earned 72 percent (20,527). Asian American women earned more than ($31,156) white women. To consider race and gender together, white women earned 72 percent of white men's earnings, while African American, Latino, and Asian American women earned 64 percent, 52 percent, and 80 percent, respectively.

What factors contribute to the big racial gap in earnings? One explanation for the racial differences in earnings is the racial gap in education. African American and Latino workers on average have attained substantially lower educational levels than white workers, while Asian American workers have attained a substantially higher educational level than whites. However, analyses of census data show that minority workers earn less than white workers with the same educational level. This means that minority workers receive a lower return for their educational investment than white workers because of racial discrimination.

The gender gap in earnings is narrower for African Americans than for white and for other minority groups. This can be explained partly by African American women's higher level of education than African American men and partly by their experience with lower levels of labor market discrimination than African American men. African American men may experience a higher level of discrimination in the labor market than African American women in part because white men consider African American men rather than African American women as a threat to their occupations. Although Asian American workers earn more than white workers, the rate of return for their educational credentials is not as great as that for white workers. This suggests that other minority workers, in addition to African American workers, are subject to racial discrimination in the labor market.

Still, it is necessary to analyze the discrimination that contributes to racial earnings gaps. First, past discrimination, which was more blatant in form, has lingering effects. Past instances of discrimination and labor-market segregation may result in creating a pool of minority workers who are less experienced and less skilled than white workers, because they have not had the same opportunities. Older minority workers will continue to experience significant wage gaps, since their base rate of pay may have been established when it was acceptable to pay racial minority workers less than white workers.

Second, the impact of nonmarket discrimination must be considered. Factors such as education, region, and residential segregation also influence wages. Minority workers are more likely to live in racially segregated neighborhoods with depressed economies and jobs that offer lower wages. Minority-dense communities were especially hard hit by job loss when manufacturing companies left central-city areas for more space and lower taxes in the suburbs. The industries that replaced the manufacturing industries are typically service oriented or white collar in nature and often do not match the skills of the residents in central-city areas.

Finally, instances of current discrimination must be examined. This form of discrimination must be subtle, given that laws have been established (Civil Rights Act of 1964) that make it illegal to discriminate in the labor market based on race, among other factors. These subtle practices include occupational segregation, quality of employment differences (fewer hours, lower wages, fewer benefits, less training, less prestige), higher rates of and longer periods of unemployment, and lower hire rates for racial minorities.

Recent evidence indicates that a dual labor market has emerged in the United States. Minorities have historically been excluded from certain occupations, and they continue to encounter barriers to entering many prestigious occupations. When minorities are able to break into these formerly "reserved" occupations, they frequently have difficulties accessing the better-caliber jobs within the field. Minorities with an immigrant background in particular are likely to work in the secondary, rather than the primary, labor market.

The greater earnings gap between whites and Latinos than that between whites and African Americans is due mainly to the heavily immigrant background of Latino workers. Minorities who are also immigrants may experience certain challenges or disadvantages in the labor market, because they are usually not proficient in English and may be unfamiliar with the social-network practices in the mainstream, or primary, labor market. Lacking knowledge about how social networks operate could prevent minority members with immigrant backgrounds from obtaining information about employment opportunities. Some immigrants are forced to reestablish their educational credentials, since degrees they have earned at institutions in their home countries are not always recognized in the United States. Finally, illegal immigrants are generally exploited by employers, who hire them to work cheaply (below market rates) in exchange for not reporting their illegal status.

ROMNEY S. NORWOOD

See also

Affirmative Action; Hiring Practices; Split-Labor Market Theory.
    Document: Glass Ceiling Commission (1995)

Further Reading:

Hacker, Andrew. *Two Nations: Black and White, Separate, Hostile, Unequal.* New York: Scribner, 2003.

National Committee on Pay Equity. "The Wage Gap by Education, Race and Gender." U.S. Census Bureau, Current Population Survey, March 2001.
Siegel, Paul. "The Cost of Being a Negro." *Sociological Inquiry* 35 (1965): 41–57.

Racial Essentialism

Essentialism is a philosophical view that the essential properties, or essences, of an object can be known and the object defined by them. Essentialists look at society and attempt to explain social phenomena such as race or gender solely in terms of natural phenomena. Using this biological determinism, essentialist thought would indicate that what a person does in the social world is a direct result of their biology. Racial essentialism is the concept that there are distinct biological traits among humans that determine racial membership much as there are distinct biological traits that determine species membership. Similarly to how it is generally believed that a plant or animal can only belong to one species, racial essentialism posits that a person can only belong to one race and this cannot be changed.

The anthropologist Lawrence Hirschfield once noted, "A three-legged, albino tiger is a tiger, despite the fact that tigers are typically striped quadrupeds." It is the tiger's essence that makes it a tiger, not its stripes. In the same way, a human's racial membership as seen in racial essentialism is not based solely on physical appearances such as skin color or eye shape. Instead it goes deeper to a presumed genetic level, i.e., the person's essence. Because of this, changing one's racial appearance does not change one's race and is only superficial. The racial essence of the person is still there—their race is fixed at birth.

The problem with this is that the concept of race itself is not fixed. Racial categories have had considerable variation from culture to culture and even between historic eras within a single culture. In some states in the pre–Civil War American South, a child who had a black and a white parent was considered to be a third, new race—a mulatto. Just a century later, the same child would be considered unquestionably black, as would all of their descendants. They would all be considered black on the basis of what was called the

---

Racialization

Racialization is the extension of racial meaning to a previously racially unclassified relationship, social practice, or group. Racialization has been characterized as an ideological process shaped by history, prejudice, and the human tendency to use conceptual categories to simplify their ascription of meaning to nonidentical experiences. Among other things, racialization involves the attribution of undifferentiated identities, cultures, and behaviors to individuals based on their membership in a racialized group. While the characteristics so attributed are not always negative per se—take, for example, the association of Asian Americans with academic success—they are pernicious in that they replace individual uniqueness with facile assumptions about motives, background, conduct, and interests.

Racial difference as such is not at the root of racialization. Within the unique context of their own time and place, human beings ascribe social meaning to certain biological characteristics to differentiate, to exclude, and to dominate. Reinventing the ideation of "race," individuals create a racialized other and simultaneously racialize themselves. This process occurs not in a vacuum but in the context of the historical moment; social values and political presumptions are connected to the racialized object. Racialization is most obvious when its effect is directed at groups that are visibly—phenotypically—different from others, but "invisible" minorities are equally vulnerable to being racialized. The racist imagination views these minorities' nonvisibility as the proof of their "essential" but concealed difference; this difference is then signified by a socially imposed mark. While the term *racialization* is most often used to describe this phenomenon, similar processes may be found to occur with respect to ethnicity, religion, gender, sexual orientation, political affiliation, and other characteristics.

KHYATI JOSHI

"one drop of blood rule." Under this rule, if a person had a single black person in their ancestry, then they were also black. That one drop of blood passed the essence of the black race on to them.

A problem with using the biological determinism of essentialism in dealing with race is that race is not a biological fact as much as it is a social construct. At the beginning of the 21st century, most modern surveys use four main racial categories (white, black, Asian, and Native American) along with possible options for multiple-race options and Hispanic ethnicity. However, Michael Jacobson notes that the United States government surveys and records from the beginning of the 20th century could list up to 75 possible race choices. The intervening 100 years has left less official need for so many categories. As the historian Imani Perry remarks, race "is produced by social arrangements and political decision making."

The previously mentioned one-drop rule shows some of the racist underpinnings of racial essentialism. In the early 20th century many parts of the United States made the one-drop rule into law and it was even used in court rulings as recently as the mid 1980s. The common assumption was that it was not possible for whites and blacks to mix without causing damage to the white race and the one-drop laws were a way of maintaining the white race.

Because of the ties that racial essentialism has had to racism, many social scientists dismiss racial essentialism out of hand. This may be a mistake. Race may be a social construction, but it is so deeply rooted in our culture that it is an important structure people use to organize their lives and their understanding of the world. The beliefs that different races possess different and possibly unequal traits have profound meanings in people's day-to-day lives. Our understanding of racial essentialism helps us to understand the social world of those who have believed in it.

DONALD P. WOOLLEY

See also

Social Construction of Race; Third Wave Whiteness

Further Reading:

Davis, Floyd James. *Who Is Black: One Nation's Definition.* University Park: Pennsylvania State University Press, 1991.
Hirschfield, Lawrence. "Natural Assumptions: Race, Essence, and the Taxonomies of Human Kinds." *Social Research* 65 (1998): 331–49.
Jacobson, Michael F. *Whiteness of a Different Color: European Immigrants and the Alchemy of Race.* Cambridge, MA: Harvard University Press, 1998.

Omi, Michael, and Howard Winant. *Racial Formation in the United States: From the 1960s to the 1980s*, 2nd ed. New York: Routledge, 1994.

Perry, Mani. *More Beautiful and More Terrible: The Embrace and Transcendence of Racial Inequality in the United States*. New York: New York University Press, 2011.

Racial Gerrymandering

In politics, *gerrymandering* refers to the practice of setting electoral districts in such a way that creates an advantage for a particular party. Gerrymandering can be used to garner a disproportionate amount of power for one political party over another. *Racial gerrymandering* refers to the deliberate distortion of district boundaries for racial purposes. In other words, racial gerrymandering may be used to limit the voting power of racial minorities by confining them to certain districts and excluding them from others.

Racial gerrymandering has historically been used to limit minority representation in U.S. government. For a century after the Civil War, the reapportionment of congressional districts that occurred every 10 years intentionally sought to limit minority government representation. The effect can clearly be seen in the number of African Americans serving in Congress during this time. From 1870 to 1901, a total of 22 blacks were elected to the national legislature. However, intimidation of black voters and Jim Crow laws combined to reduce the number of black legislators to zero between 1900 and 1929 and just seven between 1929 and 1966.

The civil rights movement in the United States began in the 1950s and produced a number of legal and legislative victories in the 1960s. Racial gerrymandering was a major issue addressed as part of this movement. In its ruling in *Gomillion v. Lightfoot* (1960), the U.S. Supreme Court applied the Fifteenth Amendment to overturn an Alabama law that changed the city boundaries of Tuskegee so as to exclude all but a handful of black voters. This case was significant because it found that gerrymandering was being used to disenfranchise black voters, essentially segregating black citizens out of a certain electoral district.

Probably the most significant law passed on the issue of minority representation was the Voting Rights Act of 1965.

Not only did the law remove a number of discriminatory procedures which inhibited voting, but it prohibited gerrymandering of districts on account of race or color. Although more blacks were being elected to Congress following the 1965 Act, the 1980 census revealed that the 17 U.S. House districts represented by blacks were shrinking. This led to a series of 1982 amendments to the Voting Rights Act of 1965, which were interpreted by many as requiring states to construct new districts with black majorities whenever possible.

After the number of congressional districts with a majority of African American residents rose to 32 following the 1990 census, it was clear that racial gerrymandering was being used to increase minority representation. Opponents to that practice filed suits in several states, contending that it violated the Equal Protection Clause of the Fourteenth Amendment. The initial constitutional challenge to reach the Supreme Court was *Shaw v. Reno* (1993), which set the tone for a series of decisions on racial gerrymandering.

Shaw v. Reno involved an effort by the state of North Carolina to satisfy U.S. Department of Justice demands to augment the number of congressional districts with a majority of African American residents. While the Court determined that the shape of the district in question had violated traditional district principles—including geographical and political considerations such as compactness, contiguity, and preservation of governmental boundaries—it nonetheless upheld the concept of minority-based districts provided that they met "strict scrutiny" standards. Such districts had to be based on a compelling state interest and the legislation that established them had to be narrowly tailored.

Shaw v. Reno was followed by a number of Supreme Court rulings on the same issue at different levels of government, including *Johnson v. DeGrandy* (1994), *Holder v. Hall* (1994), *Miller v. Johnson* (1995), *Bush v. Vera* (1996), *Shaw v. Hunt* (1996), *Meadows v. Moon* (1997), *Lawyer v. Department of Justice* (1997), and *Hunt v. Cromartie* (2001). All but the *Lawyer* and *Meadows* cases were decided by 5-to-4 votes, and all but the *Lawyer* and *Hunt v. Cromartie* cases rejected the minority districts proposed.

Despite the ongoing controversy over racial gerrymandering, the number of black members in Congress reached an all-time high of 42 in the 109th Congress, a number that

Shaw v. Hunt (1996)

Decided in 1996, *Shaw v. Hunt* was a U.S. Supreme Court case important in determining the constitutionality of the principle of redrawing congressional districts on the basis of race. When North Carolina gained an extra seat in the House of Representatives in 1990, it redrew district boundaries and created two irregularly shaped districts to include a majority of black voters. One of these was District 12, drawn with a distinctive "snake-like" shape to incorporate much of North Carolina's major urban centers. In essence, this redrawing created a "majority-minority" district in which historically underrepresented minorities became the majority constituency. In a series of cases between 1993 and 2001, including *Shaw v. Hunt*, the Supreme Court ruled on the constitutionality of such redrawings on the basis of race, also called "racial gerrymandering."

By a narrow 5–4 majority, the Supreme Court ruled in *Shaw v. Hunt* that the creation of District 12 was unconstitutional under the equal protection clause of the Fourteenth Amendment. This upheld their previous ruling in *Shaw v. Reno* (1993), which said that race could not be the sole factor in the redrawing of congressional districts. The *Shaw* decisions resulted in the invalidation of irregularly shaped congressional districts in several states that were drawn primarily to increase the representation of black and Hispanic voters. However, in *Easley v. Cromartie* (2001), the Supreme Court revisited this issue and ruled that the creation of majority-minority districts could be constitutional provided that states use the criteria of "voting behavior" rather than race to draw district boundaries. This signaled a shift to a more flexible attitude on the part of the Court toward racial gerrymandering.

Shaw v. Hunt is significant because it highlights the legal and political complexities involved in attempting to address minority underrepresentation. African Americans were subject to racially discriminatory measures related to voting after they received the right to vote in 1870. Before the Voting Rights Act of 1965, discriminatory district drawing, literacy tests, and property requirements, particularly in the South, prevented blacks from achieving equal representation under the law. Racial gerrymandering is a controversial way in which states have attempted to undo the legacy of these discriminatory practices.

REBEKAH LEE

---

has held through the 111th Congress elected in November 2008, which was also the year when the nation elected its first African American president, Barack Obama. Roland Burris of Illinois, who was appointed to fill the Senate seat that had been held since 2004 by Obama, is only the sixth African American in the history of the Senate.

SAMUEL HOFF

See also

Voter ID Requirements; Voting and Race; Voting Rights Act of 1965

Further Reading:

Burke, Christopher M. *The Appearance of Equality: Racial Gerrymandering, Redistricting, and the Supreme Court.* Westport, CT: Greenwood Press, 1999,

Clayton, Dewey M. *African Americans and the Politics of Congressional Redistricting.* New York: Garland Publishing Company, 1999,

O'Brien, David M. *Constitutional Law and Politics: Struggles for Power and Government Accountability.* New York: W. W. Norton, 2003.

Racial Profiling

Racial profiling occurs when law enforcement officers target individuals for stops based on their real or perceived membership in a racial or ethnic group, as opposed to probable cause or suspicion grounded in individual actions or behaviors believed to be criminal. Although initially applied to racial and ethnic minorities, the American Civil Liberties Union expanded the definition to include religious affiliation and national origin under the heading of racial profiling. Underlying the alleged practice is either a personal bias, a supposition by police officers that race/ethnicity constitutes a risk factor for criminal involvement, or organizational policies and procedures that either expressly or tacitly encourage racial profiling. Notwithstanding the problematic nature in determining the origins of racial profiling, the majority of research on racial profiling has traditionally focused on the higher risk of traffic stops experienced by minorities, a phenomenon popularly referred to as *Driving While Black or Driving While Brown*. But, more recently

Robert Wilkins listens as President Barack Obama speaks in the Rose Garden of the White House in Washington, June 3, 2013, where he announced his nomination of Wilkins, Patricia Ann Millet, and Cornelia Pillard to the U.S. Court of Appeals for the District of Columbia Circuit. Wilkins successfully sued the Maryland State Police for racial profiling after his family was pulled over and searched for drugs while driving back from a funeral. (AP Photo/ Manuel Balce Ceneta)

academicians have extended inquiry to include stops/frisks of pedestrians (especially in large urban areas), searches, seizures, detainment, and arrest. At any stage of the police-citizen encounter where officers can exercise discretion and make decisions, the potential exists for racial profiling.

At the federal level, racial profiling gained popularity in drug trafficking investigations during the 1970s and 1980s, offering law enforcement officials a rationale to stop and detain individuals in airports who matched the vague profile of a drug trafficker. Similarly, the Drug Enforcement Agency trained state and local police departments in the use of such profiles, and they soon appeared as a tactic for dealing with highway motorists believed to be trafficking drugs. However, by the 1980s, individuals began taking legal action for what they believed were unwarranted investigations and detentions by police. Citing the Fourth Amendment search and seizure protections and the absence of clear probable cause, along with the Fourteenth Amendment's equal protection clause, the legal remedies sought by complainants appeared to do little to curb the practice. The U.S. Supreme Court in *U.S. v. Sokolow* in 1989 upheld the right of police to engage in profiling in cases involving suspected drug couriers.

During the 1990s, a number of academic studies exposing the disproportionate traffic stops and searches experienced

Flying While Muslim

Following the September 11, 2001, attacks on the World Trade Center, the expression "driving while black" was adapted to create a label for the increased scrutiny of Muslim individuals suspected of terrorism. "Flying while Muslim" emerged as the new moniker used to describe the racial profiling of individuals believed to be Islamic terrorists simply because they display cultural and ethnic markers associated with Islam. During the decade following the terrorist attack, hate crimes, verbal harassment, and other forms of discrimination increased among individuals believed to be of Muslim faith.

by minorities in the United States received significant attention in mainstream media outlets, owing in part to the groundbreaking research of John Lamberth published in the *Washington Post*. Lamberth's study of Maryland traffic stops demonstrated that although less than 18 percent of the vehicle drivers violating traffic laws were black, 72 percent of the individuals stopped and searched were black (as cited in Harris 1999). A similar study in New Jersey showed even more marked disparity, with only 13.5 percent of cars containing black drivers or passengers constituting over 73 percent of those stopped and arrested. These studies, and others of their kind, including those examining Hispanics stopped and searched at rates significantly higher than whites, lent credence to what many minorities had reported anecdotally.

Political figures have publicly condemned racial profiling since the 1990s as well. President Bill Clinton spoke out against the practice, calling for additional civil rights legislation to effectively ban racial profiling and supporting initiatives that focused on the collection of demographic data on race/ethnicity for each police-motorist encounter. Similarly, President George W. Bush pledged to end the practice of racial profiling. President Bush contended that when racial profiling occurs, public confidence in police is undermined by the actions of a few, suggesting that racial profiling is the result of a few bad apples, rather than a more systemic problem. In 2001, the U.S. Department of Justice issued federal guidelines expressly prohibiting reliance on stereotypes regarding who commits crime, the use of skin color as a factor

in law enforcement activities and investigations unless it is part of specific suspect identification, and traffic and foot patrols that selectively stop citizens on the basis of their perceived race.

Contemporary scholarly work grapples with identifying and empirically demonstrating racial profiling, in part because other factors can contribute to the widespread racial and ethnic disparities visible in the limited data available. That is, patterns in police stops can be attributed to the demographics of drivers within a community, and other traffic patterns that make establishing a baseline problematic. Moreover, determining at which threshold unequal distribution becomes inequality challenges researchers. In addition, the case for racial profiling would insist that police are aware of the race of the driver prior to initiating a traffic stop, which may or may not be the case. While empirically demonstrating whether or not racial profiling exists within a department or community is of great consequence, the actual objective reality may not be as influential as public perception. In addition, in the 1990s, the Gallup Organization began collecting data on public sentiments regarding racial profiling, making data widely available for academic and public use and far more accessible than the traffic stop data researchers had been using.

Weitzer and Tuch (2002) were among some of the first researchers to make use of the Gallup data on racial profiling. According to their research, although sentiments about the problematic nature of racial profiling were widespread among the civilian population in the United States, their findings suggested significant variance in attitudes based on race and personal experience with police. Nonwhites were significantly more likely than whites to believe that racial profiling was widespread. Similarly, analyses of national-level data suggested that negative perceptions of police and beliefs that police routinely denigrate and target blacks were also a product of class, with middle-class blacks more likely to believe that racial profiling is a widespread practice. In contrast with public perception, the majority of officers and police chiefs do not believe that racial profiling is a significant problem in their departments, despite clear shifts in policy to curb potential discrimination against minority citizens.

Immediately prior to the September 11, 2001, terrorist attacks, racial profiling was largely condemned by

Arizona's SB 1070

In a controversial move in 2010, the state of Arizona passed legislation that allowed law enforcement officers to request verification of citizenship when performing a traffic stop. The bill, SB 1070, while prohibiting discrimination based on real or perceived nationality, race, or color, can be viewed as allowing for the de facto consideration of such factors when determining whether there was a need to verify immigration status. Although much of the bill was deemed unconstitutional, the U.S. Supreme Court upheld immigration status checks for individuals detained by law enforcement officers.

government officials, and public sentiment showed overall disapproval for the practice. However, following the terrorist attacks and the racialization of a new group, Muslims and Arabs, public sentiment and governmental policy on racial profiling shifted significantly. In the midst of the War on Terror, citizens were more likely to view the racial profiling of Arab and Muslim individuals as understandable, given mounting safety concerns. What had become a documented and significant social problem, denounced by members of the public, police, the media, and government officials, reemerged as a strategy for ensuring safety and security in a post 9/11 world. Although still prohibiting the stereotyping and profiling of racial groups through official guidelines, policy appeared to forego the creation of laws or penalties to ensure follow through. Despite the guidelines advanced by the Department of Justice, national security and border integrity were preserved as exceptions to the guidelines. In this way, racial profiling of Muslims, and in particular, the detention and interrogation of Muslims suspected of terrorist involvement, was allowable. The USA Patriot Act expanded the powers of the government to conduct surveillance and seize property of those believed to be connected to terrorism. As of 2012, the status of the End Racial Profiling Act, a countermeasure designed to legally prohibit racial profiling and provide effective training to law enforcement, was still undetermined.

DANIELLE LAVIN-LOUCKS

See also

Disproportionality Index Scores; Gates/Crowley Incident

Further Reading:
American Civil Liberties Union. "Racial Profiling: Definition." http://www.aclu.org/racial-justice/racial-profiling-definition.
Glover, Karen S. *Racial Profiling: Research, Racism, and Resistance.* Lanham, MD: Rowman & Littlefield, 2009.
Harris, David A. "The Stories, the Statistics, and the Law: Why 'Driving While Black' Matters." *Minnesota Law Review* 84 (1999): 265–326.
Johnson, Devon, Daniel Brazier, Katrina Forrest, Crispin Ketelhut, Darron Mason, and Marc Mitchell. "Attitudes toward the Use of Racial/Ethnic Profiling to Prevent Crime and Terrorism." *Criminal Justice Policy Review* 22, no. 4 (2011): 422–47.
Reitzel, John, and Alex R. Piquero. "Does It Exist? Studying Citizens' Attitudes of Racial Profiling." *Police Quarterly* 9, no. 2 (2006): 161–83.
United States v. Sokolow, 490 U.S. 1 (1989).
Weitzer, Ronald, and Steven Tuch. "Perceptions of Racial Profiling: Race, Class, and Personal Experience. *Criminology* 40, no. 2 (2002): 435–56.

Racial Projects

A racial project is a two-part enterprise that first identifies and signifies racial categories and then organizes resources according to the particular signification attached to the racial categories. The term was first described by Michael Omi and Howard Winant in their 1994 book, *Racial Formation in the United States: From the 1960s to the 1990s*. In this text, Omi and Winant articulate their theory of *racial formation*: the process in which social, economic and political forces determine the importance of racial categories, which, in turn, extends racial meaning to social, economic and political institutions. According to Omi and Winant (1994), racial projects are a series of initiatives employed throughout the overall process of racial formation.

It should be noted that racial formation theory operates under the assumption that race is a socially constructed concept. This means that the construction of race is a sociohistorical one; racial categories and racial meanings are formulated within specific social relations and historical contexts. By recognizing race as a construction, an analysis of racial projects makes it possible to examine how a society first determines racial categories and distributions of resources according to these categories, and how they change over time. Given the strong history of race as a system of stratification and domination, most analyses of racial projects reveal racist goals. However, not all racial projects are racist. A racial project is racist only if it creates or upholds structures of domination based on essential categories of race.

As a whole, racial projects are important to consider in any exploration of race or racial dynamics because they help pinpoint the particular law, codes, practices, and ideologies implemented to signify and stratify race within a certain context. Moreover, the analysis can explain the process in which race comes to be a central feature of an institution (e.g., schools), a particular society (e.g., the United States) or even the world system. Analyses focus on dynamics such as demographic change, racially based movements, alterations in state politics, and global context.

Hypodescent is an example of a noteworthy racial project in the racial formation of the United States. The rule of hypodescent, also known as the one-drop rule, reassigned anyone with any portion of black blood to be classified as black. The widespread belief that race was biological, fears of white impurity and political and economic interests to keep black slaves in bondage, promoted hypodescent during the mid- to late-1800s. Hypodescent is considered a racial project because it realigned racial categories and restricted the resources that people of mixed-parentage had received. Furthermore, hypodescent upheld the racial status quo; whiteness represented superiority, purity, and advantage whereas any nonwhite population represented inferiority, impurity, and disadvantage.

The civil rights movement represents the most antiracist racial project in the racial formation of the United States. The movement encapsulates individual acts of resistance, the rise of social justice organizations such as the National Urban League and the National Association for Advancement of Colored People, and a series of equal opportunity laws such as the Civil Rights Act of 1964 and Voting Rights Act of 1965. As a whole, it motivated a change in racial formation because it included a series of victories that demanded greater resources for Americans of color and sought for a redefinition of racial minorities that incorporated positive aspects (e.g., "Black is beautiful"), which included traditions and values.

Taking it a step further, global initiatives or ideologies can also be analyzed as racial projects. The first master racial project, according to Daniel (2007), was *eurocentrism*. Eurocentrism, which was fostered in the late fifteen century, created a worldview predicated on the supremacy of the white race and the justification of conquest of anything non-white—be it "others," land, or objects. Similarly, Winant (2001) argues that white supremacy acts as a racial project, one that has persisted through time. He opines that racism has become hegemonic. Racial hegemony means that those in power (i.e., whites) are in control even without having the consent of others (i.e., blacks) because of an ideology of normalcy. This racial project upholds white supremacist ideologies but does so under a guise; whites in power remain in power by making their norms seem common sense and universalistic. Therefore, whiteness still confers advantage and prestige while otherness confers disadvantage and stigmatization.

Racial projects, as an initiative to organize and distribute resources by racial lines, operate as the building blocks for racial formation. Examples of racial projects are numerous, because race remains a significant aspect of modern society. Detailed analyses of racial projects by social scientists will continue to serve as a useful and informative tool for understanding racial dynamics in changing contexts.

WHITNEY LASTER

See also

History of U.S. Census Racial Categorizations; Race; Social Construction of Race;

Further Reading:

Daniel, G. Reginald. *Race and Multiraciality in Brazil and the United States: Converging Paths*. University Park: Pennsylvania State Press, 2006.

Davis, F. James. *Who Is Black? One Nation's Definition*. University Park: Pennsylvania State University Press, 1991.

Omi, Michael, and Howard Winant. *Racial Formation in the United States: From the 1960s to the 1990s*. New York: Routledge, 1994.

Staiger, Annegret. 2004. "Whiteness as Giftedness: Racial Formation at an Urban High School." *Social Problems* 51 (2): 161–81.

Winant, Howard. *The World Is a Ghetto: Race and Democracy Since World War II*. New York: Basic Books, 2001.

Racial Segregation

Three hypotheses may explain the persistence of residential segregation between blacks and whites in the United States: economic differentials, discrimination in housing and lending markets, and neighborhood preferences. The view that economic differentials and institutional discrimination have attributed to residential segregation has been undeniable. But apparently, people choose where to live. The preference hypothesis posits that segregation results not so much from discriminatory practices or economic difference but mainly from blacks' and whites' own preferences. According to this view, both races desire to live in racially homogenous neighborhoods; with similar incomes and assets and without racial discrimination in the housing market, blacks and whites would live in different communities.

Scholars who investigate racial segregation differ significantly in their assumptions about what underlies these preferences. Some argue that racial preferences are derived from "neutral preference." These scholars believe that residential segregation is the consequence of a desire among whites and blacks to live "with their own kind." Such preferences could presumably arise from a widespread desire to preserve common family, church, and cultural ties. Others argue that racial preferences are largely an outcome of each group's concerns about possible hostility in neighborhoods where either group is the minority. These preferences reflect an unwillingness to confront the expected antagonism of the community. Preferences, then, are both a cause and an effect of racial discrimination and can thus be seen as a part of the web of simultaneous forces generating and maintaining residential segregation.

National surveys asking whites about their preferences for the principle of residential integration began in the early 1940s. Whites were asked about their preferred neighborhood racial composition; whether it would make a difference to them if a black family with income and education similar to theirs moved onto their block. In 1942, 65 percent said that it would make a difference, but by the 1970s, just 15 percent of whites said it would make a difference. Such survey of blacks' preferences began much later. One early effort was the 1976 Detroit Area Study, which assessed the preferences of blacks and whites. Findings from this study have frequently been cited as supporting the hypothesis that blacks' and whites' residential preferences do not overlap.

According to the study, 42 percent of whites said that they would feel uncomfortable if blacks constituted 20 percent of their neighborhood, and 25 percent said they would try to move away in such a circumstance. Whites were unwilling

Segregated drinking fountains labeled "white" and "colored" in the Dougherty County Courthouse in Albany, Georgia, ca. 1963. (Library of Congress)

to move into integrated neighborhoods. In contrast, Detroit-area blacks overwhelmingly preferred integrated neighborhoods, specifically, those in which there were roughly equal numbers of blacks and whites; 82 percent of black respondents said that they prefer neighborhoods containing equal numbers of blacks and whites. Findings from a second Detroit Area Study conducted in 1992 showed a considerable moderation of whites' preferences relative to 1976. Forty percent of white respondents, however, still indicated that they would not move into neighborhoods where blacks constitute 20 percent of the population.

The findings from the two Detroit studies suggested that "white preference" played a major role in segregation. Many whites resisted integration and indicated that they would move out of their neighborhood if it became integrated. The preference hypothesis, therefore, suggests that residential segregation should be determined not by the preferences of one population group but rather by the relationship of preferences across groups. Many scholars frequently use the original Detroit study to set the issues of preference within the context of avoidance rather than preference, emphasizing white avoidance as the central cause of persistent residential segregation.

Recently, Farley, Fielding, and Krysan (1997) addressed the danger of generalizing from the Detroit study and emphasized the idea that preferences differ significantly from one metropolitan area to another. Preferences clearly are relevant in generating and maintaining de facto residential segregation. But looking at preferences leaves many questions about racial segregation unanswered. Any consideration of residential segregation must also take into account other forces, such as the historical and spatial contexts, institutional practices, and governmental policies.

SOOKHEE OH

See also

Plessy v. Ferguson (1896). Document: *Plessy v. Ferguson* (1896)

Further Reading:

Bobo, Lawrence, and Camille Zubrinsky. "Attitudes on Residential Integration: Perceived Status Differences, Mere In-Group Preferences, or Racial Prejudice." *Social Forces* 74, no. 3 (1996): 883–909.

Farley, Reynolds, Elaine Fielding, and Maria Krysan. "The Residential Preferences of Blacks and Whites: A Four-Metropolis Analysis." *Housing Policy Debate* 8, no. 4 (1997): 763–800.

Schnare, Ann Burnet. *The Persistence of Racial Segregation in Housing*. New York: Urban Institute, 1978.

Racial Socialization

Racial minority children, especially African American children, in the United States can expect to experience different forms of racism in the contexts of school, neighborhood, workplace, and street. Therefore, parents and teachers need to provide racial socialization to prepare their children psychologically to resist and endure racial subordination. Racial socialization refers to race-related socialization that transmits knowledge about racial identity, racial discrimination, and race relations. Racial socialization serves to forewarn children about the nature of their racial reality and teach them what to expect and how to develop adaptive techniques to resist negative forces of racial devaluation.

Some upper-middle-class African Americans live in predominantly white neighborhoods and send their children to a predominantly white private school. They may never talk to their children about racial barriers and disadvantages encountered by African Americans. They emphasize that if their children have high motivations and work hard, they can achieve any goal. This kind of color-blind child socialization is naïve and unhealthy. It can leave children at a disadvantage when they grow up and encounter racism. Personal narratives by black college students reveal that when black students are not prepared for racial reality, they often have psychological problems and may experience an identity crisis.

Frustrated by experiences with racism over many years, some African American parents in lower socioeconomic groups go to the other extreme in their children's socialization by overemphasizing racial barriers encountered by African Americans. They blame racism for their failure. They again and again send the message that no matter how hard their children work, they cannot make it in this country because of racial discrimination. This kind of cynical racial socialization can destroy or at least weaken their children's motivation to work hard to resist racial adversity. Instead, it is seen that African American parents should emphasize that because of disadvantages, their children need to work much harder than white children to achieve the same goals. Moreover, they need to teach their children to develop their racial pride and strategies to resist and protect themselves from racially biased treatment.

PYONG GAP MIN

See also

Education and African Americans; Educational Achievement Gap

Further Reading:

Bowman, P. J., and C. Howard. "Race-Related Socialization, Motivation, and Academic Achievement: A Study of Black Youth in Three-Generation Families." *Journal of the American Academy of Child Psychiatry* 24: 134–41.

Garrod, Andrew, Janie Victoria Ward, Trancy Robinson, and Robert Kilkenny, eds. *Souls Looking Back: Life Stories of Growing up Black*. New York: Routledge, 1999.

Racial Steering

Racial steering is when real estate brokers and agents use race as a factor in showing homes, providing listings, giving advice, and setting requirements for real estate purchases. This practice is based on the institutional belief by realtors that introducing blacks into a white area disturbs white residents and will cause the area to deteriorate. Because of this belief, blacks are steered away from white areas and directed to integrated areas that are in transition. Racial steering is cited as at least partially responsible for hindering the process of resegregation. Furthermore, steering produces such negative consequences as generating feelings of shame in those who are discriminated against in the sale or rental of housing, limiting freedom of choice in housing, and perpetuating segregated neighborhoods.

There are three basic types of racial steering: information, segregation, and class steering. *Information steering* refers to the information a realtor shares with homebuyers, which is often limited depending on the buyer's race. Under information steering, patterns of home showings differ between minority and white homebuyers. *Segregation steering* refers to patterns of home showings in which areas shown to minority homebuyers have larger minority populations than areas shown on average to whites. Finally, *class steering* is when areas shown to minority homebuyers have lower socioeconomic status, including lower incomes and property values than areas shown, on average, to whites. Furthermore, there are three methods through which these types of steering can occur. These include inspecting, recommending, and editorializing.

For several decades, housing discrimination in the form of racial steering was a difficult issue to prove and an even more difficult issue to correct. In 1968, after decades of alleged housing discrimination and years of advocates calling for fair and equitable housing rights, the U.S. Congress passed and enacted the Fair Housing Act. This Act is part of the larger Civil Rights Act of 1968, which guarantees equal housing opportunities for all American citizens. The Fair Housing Act specifically prohibits both public and private discrimination on the basis of race, color, religion, and national origin in the sale and rental of housing. In 1974, the act was expanded to include gender and in 1988, people with disabilities. The Office of Fair Housing and Equal Opportunity within the U.S. Department of Housing and Urban Development (HUD) is responsible for enforcing this law.

One of the first landmark cases of alleged racial steering being prosecuted was *Gladstone Realtors v. Village of Bellwood*, which was heard before the Supreme Court in 1979. This case was brought by residents who accused two brokers of racial steering practices that impeded the homeowners' access to the perceived benefits of living in an integrated setting. The Supreme Court held that the neighborhood and homeowners in a racially changing area have the right to challenge steering practices as indirect victims of housing bias. Furthermore, the Court determined that a municipality could be injured when its racial composition is adversely affected by racial discrimination.

A second landmark case prosecuted under the Fair Housing Act was *Havens Realty Corp. v. Coleman* in 1982. In the case, Havens Realty Corp., an apartment complex owner in a suburb of Richmond, Virginia, was accused of engaging in racial steering in violation of the Fair Housing Act. The suit was brought by Housing Opportunities Made Equal (HOME), a nonprofit corporation devoted to supporting fair housing in the Richmond area. Before the suit, HOME employed two "testers," one black and one white, to apply for housing through the Havens Realty Corp. The black tester was told by Havens that there were no apartments available, while the white tester was told about vacancies. The Supreme Court held that the testers had standing to sue and validated their allegations that the neighborhood was damaged by the denial of interracial associations. Furthermore, the Supreme Court held that HOME had standing to sue because Havens's racial steering practices impaired the organization's ability to provide housing counseling and referral services. In this case, the Fair Housing Act was successfully used to support the plaintiffs and their accusations of racial steering.

Another important case in the history of racial steering and the Fair Housing Act was *HUD v. Blackwell* in 1989. HUD is responsible for administering the Fair Housing Act, and this was the first case to uphold their enforcement authority. In the *HUD v. Blackwell* case, the judge held that the defendants were practicing racial steering in violation of the Fair Housing Act and ordered the defendants to pay over $65,000 in damages.

In recent years, HUD has conducted studies to gauge levels of housing discrimination in major metropolitan housing markets. In these studies, HUD uses paired testers who are actually investigators posing as renters or homebuyers. Research findings based on the past 30 years of these HUD surveys show declines in obvious forms of discrimination, while overall levels of discrimination remain extremely high. Overall, the HUD studies show that the practice of racial steering in the United States continues to increase.

The practice of steering continues to occur in the 21st century despite the Fair Housing Act of 1968, which prohibits steering in the sale and rental of housing and allows for monetary compensation through lawsuits for those affected by steering. Steering occurs in many covert forms of discriminatory practices such as encouraging or discouraging members of major ethnic or racial groups to purchase homes in particular neighborhoods based on their race, or not showing particular homes because of the interested buyer's race. These practices are notoriously difficult to prove and prosecute. One possible reason for the prevalence of racial steering may have to do with the real estate organization's assumption that minorities prefer to reside in segregated neighborhoods. Additionally, racial steering may be pleasing for the neighborhood because it often allows the neighborhood to remain unchanged and less diverse. Racial steering is an unfair, discriminatory practice that perpetuates segregation and racial discrimination, with real estate brokers assumptions' often limiting buyers' choices and preventing them from having total control over their decision-making process.

Sonja V. Harry

See also

Fair Housing Act of 1968; Fair Housing Amendments Act of 1988; Fair Housing Audit

Further Reading:

"Benign Steering and Benign Quotas: The Validity of Race-Conscious Government Policies to Promote Residential Integration." *Harvard Law Review* 93 (1980) : 938–65.

Galster, George, and Erin Godfrey. "By Words and Deeds." *Journal of the American Planning Association* 71 (2005): 251–68.

Leadership Conference on Civil and Human Rights. "The Future of Fair Housing: Report of the National Commission on Fair Housing and Equal Opportunity." Washington, DC, 2008. http://www.civilrights.org/publications/reports/fairhousing/future_of_fair_housing_report.pdf

McGrew, Teron. "The History of Residential Segregation in the United States and Title VIII." *Black Scholar* 27 (1997): 22–30.

"Racial Steering: The Real Estate Broker and Title VIII." *Yale Law Journal* 85 (1976): 808–25.

U.S. Department of Housing and Urban Development. "39 Steps Toward Fair Housing." March 17, 2007. http://portal.hud.gov/hudportal/documents/huddoc?id=DOC_7377.pdf.

42 U.S.C. 3601–3606. Sec. 800–806.

Racial Stigmatization

A stigma is an attribute considered to be socially undesirable. The attribute itself may not be harmful or negative, but the social reaction to that attribute is negative. Racial stigmatization occurs when a racial group or groups are considered to be less desirable than other groups. This is not because of any fundamental difference between groups (in fact, there is considerable scientific debate over whether racial classifications are biologically meaningful), but rather because of the social reaction of others. The sociologist Erving Goffman separated stigmatized people into two categories, the *discredited* and the *discreditable*. The discredited are those whose stigma is immediately known to others; for example, someone in a wheelchair has a visible stigma and therefore is considered discredited. The discreditable refers to those whose stigma is not visible, such as ex-convicts. The terms *stigma*, *discredited*, and *discreditable* refer only to the negative social reaction; they do not represent personal judgments about the desirability of the attribute itself.

Racial stigmatization is for the most part visible; therefore, those in racially stigmatized groups often have to counter the negative assumptions that others make about them in everyday interactions. Young African Americans, for example, often find themselves watched more carefully in stores than are whites. Racial stigmatization makes others assume that they are more likely to shoplift than their white counterparts. Because racial stigmatization is based on social reaction, it varies from place to place. Members of particular racial groups may find themselves stigmatized in some countries, regions, or even neighborhoods, but not in others. Racial stigmatization can make it more difficult for some groups to advance socially or economically. Employers often prefer some racial and ethnic groups to others.

Similarly, at one point, banks routinely refused to make loans in neighborhoods dominated by blacks and Latinos. That practice has a name: redlining. Research now suggests that the stress of racial stigmatization can even result in physical health problems. Racial stigmatization can greatly affect many aspects of an individual's life.

ROBIN ROGER-DILLON

See also
Racial Essentialism; Racial Profiling; Whiteness Studies

Racial Taxonomy

The centuries-old scientific quest to create a consistent system of racial taxonomy is best understood as a manifestation of the widely held cultural assumption that human diversity can be described in terms of biologically distinct races. Taxonomy is a necessary condition for science because in order to understand nature it must first be named and organized so that it may be discussed and studied. During the 16th century, as some European powers explored and colonized the world, they encountered the tremendous diversity of humanity. Race was one way to account for the physical differences they saw, and arranging the races into a hierarchy was a way to reconcile that diversity with their own sense of cultural superiority. Despite the best efforts of some of the brightest minds in science, there is still no universally agreed-upon system of racial classification.

The scientific worldview perceives racial taxonomy as standing in contrast to cultural or folkloric models of understanding race. Taking a cross-cultural view of race reveals its socially constructed nature. The existence of racial categories is present even in written documents from Ancient Egypt and Greece. Colonial Spain had a veritable pantheon of more than 15 races and race mixtures, even constructing racial distinction between white Europeans born in Europe from white Europeans born in the Americas. By contrast, in contemporary Brazil, a person's race is defined by skin color but not heritage. Thus siblings of the same parents can be of different races if they exhibit different complexions. In the United States the emphasis is on a person's "blood," so that a person is the same race of their parents regardless of their complexion. In Japan there exists a race known as the Burakumin that has endured stigmatization since the feudal era. Membership in the group is inherited at birth, but there are no physical characteristics that distinguish it from the larger population—it is an "invisible race." All systems of racial categorization include the belief that social differences reflect biological difference, which is seen as natural, inherited, and fixed. But as the Burakumin example shows, the lack of observable physical differences does not prohibit the implementation of racial categories.

In opposition to cultural beliefs in races, scientific taxonomies offer the authority and certainty of fact. Starting with Linnaeus in the 18th century, biologists, doctors, and anthropologists have all offered definitions of race that they claim is based on evidence. Scientific discourses about race must be looked at critically, but this does not mean that science has nothing to say about human diversity particularly since the modern synthesis was formed from the merger of genetics and the theory of evolution by natural selection. From an evolutionary standpoint, no human population has ever been isolated long enough for it to become substantially different from the rest of the species. Because of gene flow, the constant interbreeding among populations, humans have remained a single species despite having dispersed to even the most remote corners of the globe. There are three main reasons why biological definitions of race have failed historically and in the present.

First, racial distinctions based on physically observable characteristics such as skin color are arbitrarily defined. The human body can be described in myriad ways, and both genetic and environmental factors influence the development of these physical characteristics. However, race gives disproportional importance to a small set of rather insignificant traits. There is no basis behind the weight given to these traits or why others should be considered less significant. Skin color is obvious, so people consider it important. If different traits were given emphasis, then a different set of races would result.

Second, race does not provide an adequate description of real genetic variation. All racially defined groups exhibit variation within the group, and, in fact, these variations can be quite dramatic. However a racialized worldview allows one to flatten these differences by lumping them into the same category. For instance, Congolese pygmies are some of the shortest humans in stature, while the Nilotic peoples of Sudan are some of the tallest, yet these biological differences are ignored by racial classifications that label both groups as "black." Contemporary scientists do study biological differences between populations by looking at the geographic distributions of gene frequencies known as clines. Some well-documented clinal distributions include ABO blood type, lactose intolerance, and the sickle-cell trait.

Third, race taxonomy is confounded by the fact that identical physical traits can be observed among unrelated populations. The traits that have been used to define racial categories are not exclusive to any one race. Nor do people who share similar racial characteristics necessarily share similar origins. For instance, not everyone with black skin comes from Africa. People with similar complexions live in New Guinea. But from a genetic perspective, Europeans are more closely related to Africans than they are to Melanesians.

MATTHEW D. THOMPSON

See also
Biological Determinism; Blumenbach, Johann; Linnaeus, Carolus

Further Reading:
Andrews, George Reid. "Racial Inequality in Brazil and the United States: A Statistical Comparison." *Journal of Social History* 2 (1992): 229–63.

De Vos, George A., and Hiroshi Wagatsuma. *Japan's Invisible Race: Case Studies in Culture and Personality*. Berkeley: University of California Press, 1966.

Haller, John S. *Outcasts from Evolution: Scientific Attitudes of Racial Inferiority, 1859–1900*. Chicago: University of Illinois Press, 1971.

Patterson, Thomas C., and Frank Spencer. "Racial Hierarchies and Buffer Races." *Transforming Anthropology* (1994): 20–27.

Templeton, Alan R. "Human Races: A Genetic and Evolutionary Perspective." *American Anthropologist* (1998): 632–50.

Harvard University psychologist Dr. Gordon W. Allport's *Nature of Prejudice* (1954) dealt with the topic of racial threat theory. (AP Photo/ Bill Ingraham)

Racial Threat Theory

Racial threat theory holds that dominant racial groups may perceive minority groups as economic and political threats to their dominant social status. The theory also explains that actions against the minority group may be taken to protect the racial order and diminish the perceived threat. In the United States, whites are the dominant racial group, and racial threat theorists hold that whites as a group may resort to discrimination and segregation to subordinate minority populations who appear to threaten their interests. Racial threat as a concept became popular in social science research during the mid-20th century with Gordon Allport's (1954) *Nature of Prejudice* and Herbert Blumer's (1958) *Prejudice as a Sense of Group Position*. Allport was first to distinguish between realistic threat and racial threat. He held that while direct competition is a realistic threat, competition can become a racial threat when prejudiced attitudes towards a racial group are upheld as a primary reason behind the threat. For instance, blacks may constitute a realistic threat to lower classes of white Americans for job opportunities, but this threat is between individuals—it becomes a racial threat when blacks as a group are targeted as the competitors for labor.

Blumer extended Allport's ideas about racial threat by arguing that competition and hostility between racial groups emerges from historically developed judgments about racial group positioning. According to Blumer, perceptions of racial threat can develop when members of an in-group, such as whites, believe they should rightfully occupy a position relative to members of an out-group, such as blacks. For example, members of the in-group might develop feelings of superiority, feelings that the subordinate race is intrinsically different and alien, a sense of ownership over resources and privilege, or a perception of threat from the subordinate group. Out of these beliefs, the in-group develops a sense of racial threat wherein the out-group appears to be putting these privileged positions at risk.

Sociologist Hubert Blalock further developed racial threat theory in his 1967 book, *Toward a Theory of Minority-Group Relations*. In it, Blalock explained his racial threat hypothesis. Using mathematical reasoning, Blalock generated his specific hypothesis of racial threat, which is: increasing the proportion of minorities in an area will be directly related to elevated levels of discrimination. Moreover, Blalock's racial threat hypothesis holds that whites perceive increased presence and visibility of minority groups as both an economic and political threat to their social positioning. Even more, whites respond to this threat by increasing discriminatory practices to hold on to social control. According to Blalock, the level of these discriminatory practices varies depending on whether the perceived threat is economic or political. He argued that discrimination levels increase more rapidly when the motivation is a product of political threat.

Most of the early empirical tests of the racial threat theory support Blalock's hypothesis. For example, research has revealed there is a significant relationship between the size of the black population and measures of social control like police force size, arrest rates, and segregation laws. In other words, things like police force strength increase in areas where there is a higher perceived racial threat. However, Blalock's hypothesis has also been criticized for not being regionally generalizable, and for incorrectly drawing conclusions from ecological data. In other words, there might be more explanations besides just racial threat for the increase in things like police force strength. For instance, one study found that prejudice, rather than threat of increased minority presence, was responsible for whites taking actions to protect their political position.

Despite the critiques, today racial threat is still a prominent sociological concept, especially because there is still much racial intergroup conflict in the United States. At its most basic level, racial threat emerges when a subordinate group gains power and presence and the dominant group comes to believe they might need to compete to protect their position in the racial hierarchy.

WHITNEY LASTER

See also
Crime and Race; Prejudice Theory

Further Reading:
Allport, Gordon W. *The Nature of Prejudice*. Cambridge, MA: Addison-Wesley, 1954.

Behrens, Angela, Christopher Uggen, and Jeff Manza. "Ballot Manipulation and the "Menace of Negro Domination": Racial Threat and Felon Disenfranchisement in the United States, 1850–2000." *American Journal of Sociology* 109, no. 3 (2003): 559–605.

Blalock, Hubert, Jr. *Toward a Theory of Minority-Group Relations*. New York: John Wiley, 1967.

Blumer, Herbert. "Race Prejudice as a Sense of Group Position." *Pacific Sociological Review* 1, no. 1 (1958): 3–7.

Bobo, Lawrence, and Vincent L. Hutchings. "Perceptions of Racial Group Competition: Extending Blumer's Theory of Group Position to a Multiracial Context." *American Sociological Review* 61, no. 6 (1996): 951–72.

Corzine, Jay, James Creech, and Lin Corzine. "Black Concentration and Lynchings in the South: Testing Blalock's Power-Threat Hypothesis." *Social Forces* 61, no. 3 (1983): 774–96.

Kinder, Donald R. and David O. Sears. "Prejudice and Politics: Symbolic Racism Versus Racial Threats to the Good Life." *Journal of Personality and Social Psychology* 40, no. 3 (1981): 414–31.

Stolzenberg, Lisa, Stewart J. D'Alessio, and David Eitle. "A Multilevel Test of Racial Threat Theory." *Criminology* 42, no. 3 (2006): 673–98.

Williams, Robin M. *The Reduction of Intergroup Tensions*. New York: Social Science Research Council, 1947.

Racialized Poverty

Racialization is a process that gives racial meanings to groups, relationships, and organizations that did not previously have racial meanings. To understand racial inequality in the United

Rural Poverty

The racialization of poverty has contributed to the invisibility of rural poverty, especially poverty among minorities in rural areas. Rural areas have a greater share of residents with incomes below the poverty level, but exhibit the same unequal distribution of poverty by race and ethnicity. Rural areas with high poverty rates are concentrated in the South. In 2010 rural blacks had the highest poverty rate at 32.9 percent, with Latinos close behind at 29.5 percent. There is some evidence that welfare reforms have a particularly devastating impact on the rural poor because factors such as local job markets, child care resources, and transportation are even less amenable to transitioning from welfare to work than in urban areas.

States it is important to understand this process. Cultural constructions of poverty are linked to political and economic shifts and to race/ethnic difference, as understandings about poverty translate into material outcomes in terms of jobs, social service provision, and government spending

Media coverage is central to the public impression of people living in poverty. For example, Americans, on average, believe that blacks make up 50 percent of all poor people, when in reality 27 percent of the poor were black. Media coverage from the 1960s tended to feature pictures of poor blacks in stories about welfare abuses, waste, and inefficiency, but would feature images of poor whites in more neutral stories about antipoverty programs. Gilens views 1965 as a clear turning point in the racialization of poverty, as the percentage of blacks featured in pictures of the poor increased dramatically from 27 percent in 1964 to 49 percent in 1965. The context surrounding this change was the beginning of the War on Poverty, the height of the civil rights movement, race riots, and increasing backlash against New Deal programs among the white electorate. The poverty rate actually declined for blacks between 1959 and 1972, but this was precisely the timeframe in which poverty became raced as black then as generally nonwhite, as fears about the rapid expansion of welfare dependency were stoked.

Public housing was, and remains, an important site for understanding racialized poverty. Like the image of the welfare queen, public housing is cemented in the minds of the American public as very poor and black, and inherently dysfunctional as a result. Racialized poverty is very much related to the racialization neighborhoods and spaces. Although racial segregation has always existed in some form in the United States, the racialization of urban and suburban spaces played an important role in racialized poverty. Federal public housing was implemented in the 1930s mainly as a solution to a shortage of appropriate housing in urban areas; therefore in its inception there was no specific stigma attached to residents.

Public housing was marketed and, largely, viewed as a temporary housing solution for hardworking (white, nuclear) families. Families applying for apartments who were too poor, too rich, too big, too small, too lazy, and too dirty were carefully screened out by interviewers. The perceived potential for upward mobility figured prominently in the selection of tenants. The screening process also explicitly excluded applicants based on race. Rather than places where structurally disadvantaged groups could be guaranteed safe, decent housing, housing projects were designed as places where white families with appropriate values could be helped gain or regain middle-class status. The distinction in intention is vital to understanding housing policy's changes over time, and the role of those changes in the racialization of poverty.

What had begun as respectable, temporary, low-rent apartment communities for white working- and lower-middle-class families quickly became large, run-down, crime-ridden complexes occupied predominantly by black, very-low-income, single-parent families. Mah (1999) observed that public housing's value as a means of upward mobility declined as home ownership opportunities expanded, and that the use of public housing as a measure of social uplift was abandoned for its current function as housing of last resort. The most devalued population in public housing is low-income blacks. Mah (1999) argues that the devaluation of public housing's use as a means for social uplift compounded the stigma attached to blacks in an era where they were believed to have a generally negative effect on property values. As a result of all of these processes, a racialized image of poverty that was also related to neighborhood and culture began to emerge. Housing projects and project life became synonymous with blackness in popular culture, and poverty associated with blackness.

Low-income blacks are not the only group to suffer from racialized poverty. Even higher-income blacks are associated with poverty such that whites exit neighborhoods once a tipping point of integration is reached for fear of eventual reduction of property values. Latinos are increasingly included in popular images and discourse about poverty, especially as underserving poor people in the case of illegal or undocumented immigrants. The idea of poor, migrant workers from Mexico who take advantage of government assistance and drain social resources like emergency room care is one that has gained traction in the last decade in discussions of immigration reform. Lawson, Jarosz and Bonds (2008) found that white residents in the rural northwest United States viewed Latinos as undeserving of social services and as draining public resources. Racialized poverty invariably includes the idea that deserving poverty is raced as white while undeserving poverty is raced as nonwhite, with specific characterizations varying by location and situation.

RENEE S. ALSTON

See also

Code of the Street; Underclass, The (Ghetto Poor); Welfare Queens

Further Reading:

Calmore, John O. "A Call to Context: The Professional Challenges of Cause Lawyering at the Intersection of Race, Space, and Poverty." *Fordham Law Review* 67 (1999): 5.

Clawson, Rosalee, and Rakuya Trice. "Poverty as We Know It: Media Portrayals of the Poor." *Public Opinion Quarterly* 64 (2000): 53–64.

Gilens, Martin. *Why Americans Hate Welfare: Race, Media, and the Politics of Antipoverty Policy*. University of Chicago Press, 2000.

Gilens, Martin. "How the Poor Became Black." In *Race and the Politics of Welfare Reform*, edited by S. F. Schram, J. Soss, and R. C. Fording, 101–30. Ann Arbor: University of Michigan Press, 2003.

Lawson, V., L. Jarosz, and A. Bonds. "Building Economies from the Bottom Up: (Mis) Representations of Poverty in the Rural American Northwest." *Social & Cultural Geography* 9 no. 7 (2008): 737–53.

Mah, Teresa. "Buying into the Middle Class: Racial Segregation and Racial Formation in the United States, 1920–1964." Dissertation. University of Chicago, 1999.

Wilson, D. "Introduction: Racialized Poverty in US Cities: Toward a Refined Racial Economy Perspective." *Professional Geographer* 61, no. 2 (2009): 139–49.

Wynn, Lyndelia B. "The Attitude of AFDC Recipients Towards Work." *Sociation Today* 1, no. 2 (2003) http://www.ncsociology.org/sociationtoday/v2/wynn.htm.

Racism

Racism is a consequence of an ideology and set of structural conditions that justify and rationalize the oppression of a group of people who are deemed biologically or culturally inferior. Race, as a biological phenomenon, centers on the idea that each race has innate, unalterable characteristics that determine individual culture, temperament, and biological quality. However, race is *not* biological; rather "race" is a *social construction* denoted by a common set of phenotypical characteristics that are assigned socially significant meanings. Thus, though race is not real in a biological sense, it still carries great social, economic, and political consequences in society.

Racism can be viewed in three primary ways: (1) old and new racism, (2) de jure and de facto racism, and (3) institutional and individual racism. Old racism is characterized by notions of biological inferiority and includes claims by scientists who measured skull size and analyzed genes to explain white superiority. In the 18th century, the theory of polygenesis was used to explain that the races were the descendants of biologically distinct humans, thereby arguing for white dominance. New racism, in contrast, stays away from biological conversations and instead uses ideas about equal opportunity and culture to defend white privilege and deny the persistence of racism. New theories of racism such as Kinder and Sears's (1981) and Sears and Henry's (2005) Symbolic Racism, Bobo, Kluegel and Smith's (1997) Laissez Faire Racism, Bonilla-Silva's (2003) Color-Blind Racism, and Feagin's (2006) Systemic Racism all articulate the aspects and causes of new racism in varied ways, yet all agree that the hallmark of "new racism" is that it operates in a complex and covert manner. De jure racism is discrimination "in law," or discrimination that is legally coded in the laws and system. An example of de jure racism is segregation that legally required that there be separate schools, shops, and water fountains for blacks and whites (among other things). De facto racism is "in fact," or discrimination

An African American man uses the "colored entrance" to a segregated cinema during the 1940s. The doctrine of segregation established by the Supreme Court case *Plessy v. Ferguson* (1896) determined the social landscape of separate facilities that persisted even after the landmark desegregation case of *Brown v. Board of Education* (1954). (Library of Congress)

that is a result of how racial logics are embedded into our institutions and beliefs. An example of de facto racism is less wealth and less home ownership, which is tied to poorer neighborhoods and low taxes, which is connected to failing schools, which is tied to less education and worse employment opportunities. Thus, while de facto discrimination is not racism written into law, it is equally (if not more) detrimental in its consequences. The third way to look at racism is institutionally or individually. Individual racism tends to be the type of racism that most people first think of and is typified by derogatory labels such as "nigger," "wetback," or "chink" and by racist beliefs such as "All Latinos are illegal aliens stealing American jobs" or "All black people are

lazy, have too many kids and take advantage of welfare." Institutional racism is discrimination that operates via the institutions of society such as government, schools and universities/colleges, the criminal system, and the media. For example, 1 in 3 black men will serve time in prison because of the ways in which police patrol black communities, prosecutors push plea bargains, judges enforce harsher punishments, and because of cultural perceptions of black men as criminals.

In today's post–civil rights movement, there is disagreement over whether racism is still predominant and what exactly constitutes racism. Conservative think tanks and media outlets tend to argue that racism is no longer a problem and the United States is an equal opportunity society where merit and hard work are the central components for success. These opinions are buttressed by the political successes of President Obama and Secretary of State Condoleezza Rice along with the athletic achievements of LeBron James and Tiger Woods or the television accomplishments of George Lopez and Ann Curry. On the other hand, liberal think tanks and media outlets emphasize the continuing importance of race and racism by pointing to national racial inequality statistics. Frequent numbers cited are the $20,000 gap in median household income between blacks/Latinos and whites or the 20 percent plus poverty rate for blacks and Latinos compared to the 10 percent poverty rate for whites.

For most people who understand that racism can operate on covert, de facto, and on the macro level it is clear that racism continues to plague contemporary society. Regardless of one's stance on whether racism persists, however, the race and racism question is not seemingly disappearing any time soon. News stations and media contributors continue to debate whether "the race card" is in play and if it is being used justifiably or not. Recent exit polls for the 2010 presidential election showed that people of color overwhelmingly voted for Obama while older white men voted for Romney, thus revealing people's concerns about how race and racism is addressed in the 21st century.

HEPHZIBAH STRMIC-PAWL

See also

Color-Blind Racism; Cultural Racism; Laissez-Faire Racism; Racial Threat Theory; Reverse Racism; Social Construction of Race; Symbolic Racism; Systemic Racism

Further Reading:

Alexander, Michelle. *The New Jim Crow: Mass Incarceration in the Age of Colorblindness*. New York: New Press, 2010.

Blauner, Robert. *Still the Big News*. Philadelphia: Temple University Press, 2001.

Bobo, Lawrence, James Kluegel, and Ryan Smith. "Laissez Faire Racism: The Crystallization of a 'Kinder, Gentler' Anti-Black Ideology." In *Racial Attitudes in the 1990s: Continuity and Change*, edited by Steven Tuch and Jack Martin, 15–44. Westport, CT: Praeger, 1997.

Bonilla-Silva, Eduardo. *Racism Without Racists: Color-Blind Racism and the Persistence of Racial Inequality in the United States*. Lanham, MD: Rowman and Littlefield, 2003.

Bonilla-Silva, Eduardo. *Racism Without Racists: Color-Blind Racism & Racial Inequality in Contemporary America*, 3rd ed. New York: Rowman & Littlefield, 2010.

Feagin, Joe. *Systemic Racism: A Theory of Oppression*. New York: Routledge, 2006.

Gold, Steven J. "From Jim Crow to Racial Hegemony: Evolving Explanations of Racial Hierarchy." *Ethnic and Racial Studies*. 27 (2004): 951–68.

Kinder, Donald, and David Sears. "Prejudice and Politics: Symbolic Racism Versus Racial Threats to the Good Life." *Journal of Personality and Social Psychology* 40 (1981): 414–31.

Lusane, Clarence. "The New Supermajority: Latinos and People of Color." *Huffington Post: Politics—The Blog*. November 9, 2012. http://www.huffingtonpost.com /clarence-lusane/ election-minority-voters_b_2101449.html.

Sears, David, and P.J. Henry. "Over Thirty Years Later: A Contemporary Look at Symbolic Racism." In *Advances in Experimental Social Psychology*, edited by M. P. Zanna, 95–150. San Diego: Academic Press, 2005.

Takaki, Ronald. *A Different Mirror: A History of Multicultural America*. Boston: Back Bay Books, 1993.

Racism and Athletic Coaching

The coaching profession, particularly college and professional football and basketball coaches, provides a unique puzzle for those interested in racial inequality. On one hand, these are professions that have a relatively large percentage of minorities (particularly African Americans) compared to other professional and managerial occupations. Yet when compared to the largest potential pool of coaches—former players—black and white coaches' access to and mobility within these coaching professions remains unequal. This is evident in data gathered by The Institute for Diversity and Ethics in Sport (TIDES) and the association of Black Coaches and Administrators (BCA) demonstrating that the minority representation of head coaches is less than their representation among assistant coaches which is less then their representation among current players at the same level.

At the beginning of the 2012 National Football League (NFL) season, minority coaches accounted for 19 percent of the head coaches (5 black and 1 Latino), down from an all-time high of 25 percent (7 black and 1 Latino) the prior season. In 2012, minorities accounted for 34 percent of assistant coaches (32 percent black, 1 percent Latino, and 1 percent Asian/Pacific Islander) and 71 percent of the players

The Rooney Rule (2003)

The "Rooney Rule" was implemented in the NFL in 2003 to address the lack of minorities in head coaching positions throughout the history of professional football. Named after Pittsburgh Steelers owner Dan Rooney, who was an early advocate of its passage, the Rooney Rule requires NFL franchises to interview at least one minority candidate before filling a head coaching vacancy. The Rooney Rule is the brainchild of two civil rights lawyers, Cyrus Mehri and Johnnie L. Cochran Jr., who also provided the impetus for the rule with a report they authored with the help of University of Pennsylvania economist Janice Fanning Madden. They found that the five black head coaches in the NFL's modern era were more successful than the average white coach from 1986–2001 in terms of both wins and playoff appearances, even though they inherited worse teams on average. Prior to the Rooney Rule's passage, there had been only 6 black head coaches in the NFL's 82-year history and only 5 since 1990. In the 10 seasons since its passage, 12 head coaches of color were hired in the NFL, 10 of which had not held head coaching jobs prior to the Rooney Rule.

(67 percent black, 1 percent Latino, 2 percent Asian/Pacific Islander, and 1 percent other). During the same season, at the highest level of college football—Football Bowl Subdivision (FBS)—minority coaches accounted for 15 percent of head coaches (14 African Americans, 2 Latino, and 2 Asian/Pacific Islanders), their largest representation in the history of major college football, 34 percent of assistant coaches (31 percent black, 1 percent Latino, 1 percent Asian/Pacific Islander, and 1 percent other), and 57 percent of FBS athletes (52 percent black, 2 percent Latino, 2 percent Asian/Pacific Islander, and 1 percent other).

The basketball coaching profession has a considerably larger representation of minorities. At the end of the 2011–2012 National Basketball Association (NBA) season, over half (53 percent) of the head coaches were minority (14 black, 1 Latino, and 1 Asian), minority assistants accounted for 44 percent of all assistants in the NBA (41 percent black, 1 percent Latino, 1 percent Asian, and 1 percent other), while NBA players were 81 percent minority (78 percent

black, 3 percent Latino, and less than 1 percent Latino and Asian). In the Women's National Basketball Association (WNBA), African Americans held four of the 12 head coaching positions within the league (33 percent) and made up 42 percent of the assistant coaches while minorities accounted for 75 percent of WNBA players (74 percent black, 1 percent other). At the highest level of college basketball—Division I—during the 2010–2011 season, minority coaches were in charge of 20 percent men's basketball programs (19 percent black, and less than 1 percent Latino and other), accounted for 41 percent of assistant coaches (39 percent black, 1 percent Latino, 2 percent other, and less than 1 percent Asian and Native American), and 63 percent of the athletes at the same level (57 percent black, 2 percent Latino, 2 percent multiracial, and less than 1 percent Native American and Asian). Among Division I women's programs, 17 percent of the basketball programs were led by coaches of color (15 percent black, 1 percent Latino, 1 percent other, and less than 1 percent Asian), and minorities accounted for 40 percent of assistant coaches (35 percent black, 1 percent Latino, 1 percent Asian, 3 percent other, and less than 1 percent native American) and 57 percent of the athletes at the same level (47 percent black, 2 percent Latino, 1 percent Asian/Pacific Islander, 3 percent multiracial, and less than 1 percent native American).

The academic research on the basketball and football coaching professions has confirmed that black coaches experience fewer promotions and are underrepresented in high status positions compared to white coaches. Furthermore, scholars have found that black coaches perceive more barriers to advancement and are less satisfied with their careers than their white counterparts (see Day and McDonald 2010 for a brief review). In explaining these disparities, scholars have focused on primarily on (1) job-level segregation and stereotyping, and (2) social capital and sponsorship from existing coaches.

Job-level segregation begins when coaches are players through a process referred to as "stacking" or the racial segregation of players into "central" or "noncentral" positions based on their responsibility for controlling the outcome of competition (Washington and Karen 2001). Just as black players are disproportionately represented in noncentral playing positions (e.g., center in basketball, running backs or wide receivers in football), research finds that black coaches are disproportionately overrepresented in noncentral coaching positions and that central position players and coaches are more likely to become head coaches than noncentral players and coaches. This segregation results from stereotypes coaches hold regarding the physical and mental abilities of black and white players as well as stereotypes regarding the mental and physical abilities associated with playing central and noncentral positions. Although research has not directly examined whether black and white coaches are evaluated differently, scholars have found that stacking among players is perpetuated in the coaching ranks.

Finding that black coaches are less likely to enter the profession and move up within the profession net of experience, education, and playing accomplishments has led scholars to also focus on the role of social connections and sponsorship from existing coaches (i.e., social capital) in the success of coaches within football and basketball coaching labor markets. Research finds that black coaches are often excluded from white networks and that these homophily processes have consequences for their career attainment as white coaches disproportionately occupying positions of authority within the profession. Furthermore, research demonstrates that black coaches receive worse returns compared to white coaches from similar types of social connections.

JACOB C. DAY

See also

Segregation; Stereotype; Sports and Racism; Sports Mascots

Further Reading:

Black Coaches and Administrators (BCA). *Hiring Report Cards.* 2012. http://www.bcasports.org/.

Cochran Jr., Johnnie L. and Cyrus Mehri. *Black Coaches in the National Football League.* Mehri and Skallet, PLLC, 2002. http://www.findjustice.com/special-projects/minority-coaches-in-the-nfl/materials/.

Cunningham, George B., and Michael Sagas. "Access Discrimination in Intercollegiate Athletics." *Journal of Sport & Social Issues* 29 (2005): 148–63.

Day, Jacob C., and Steve McDonald. "Not So Fast My Friend: Social Capital and the Race Disparity in Promotions among College Football Coaches." *Sociological Spectrum* 30 (2010): 138–58.

Duru, N. Jeremi. *Advancing the Ball: Race, Reformation, and the Quest for Equal Coaching Opportunity in the NFL.* New York: Oxford University Press, 2011.

Fritz Pollard Alliance. *Rooney Rule Fact Sheet.* 2013. http://fritzpollard.org/?p=802

The Institute for Diversity and Ethics in Sport (TIDES). *The Racial and Gender Report Card.* 2012. http://www.tidesport.org/racialgenderreportcard.html.

Washington, Robert E., and David Karen. "Sport and Society." *Annual Review of Sociology* 27 (2001): 187–212.

Racism without Racists

Racism without Racists: Color-Blind Racism & the Persistence of Racial Inequality in the United States by Eduardo Bonilla-Silva was first published in 2003. The book is an analysis of the paradox of changing racial attitudes that reflect greater acceptance of minorities and racial equality alongside significant evidence of racial inequities. In other words, the question is how can society continue to have racism when there are seemingly no racists. Bonilla-Silva critiques racial theorists who rely too much on analysis of psychological, individual attitudes, and instead uses a "materialist interpretation of racial matters and thus sees the views of actors as corresponding to their systemic location" (2010: 8). In other words, people who are at the top of the racial hierarchy, whites, have racialized views that support the power structure that is in their favor.

As the Jim Crow era (denoted by legalized segregation and related race-based policies) grows more distant in the past, contemporary racism, which is often covert and subtle, has become the dominant racial ideology, what Bonilla-Silva calls "color-blind racism." Color-blind racism is composed of four central "frames"; frames are set ways in which people filter issues in order to understand them. Bonilla-Silva outlines the four frames that whites use to explain away racial inequities as *abstract liberalism, naturalization, cultural racism,* and *minimization of racism.* Abstract liberalism is when whites use abstract ideas of equal opportunity and individualism to appear moral; for example, Affirmative Action should be banned because everyone should have a fair chance at employment. Naturalization is the idea that racial disparities are simply natural; for example, races segregate by neighborhoods and friends because people naturally associate with people like them. Cultural racism claims culture is the root of the problem. For instance, black people don't have good jobs because they don't work hard and prefer to live off of welfare. The minimization of racism frame allows whites to see that some racially motivated acts still occur but that overall race and racism are no longer a central barrier for people of color. Using this frame, whites might say that, yes, there are bigoted people, but if one works hard enough, then racism will not be a barrier to success. Through systematically analyzing in-depth interviews with white college students and older white and blacks adults, Bonilla-Silva shows how whites use a combination of the frames to explain away racial inequality and racial discrimination *without* appearing, or even realizing themselves, that they are utilizing racist ideologies. Moreover, whites develop a "white habitus," or "a racialized, uninterrupted socialization process that *conditions* and *creates* whites' racial taste, perceptions, feelings, and emotions and their views on racial matters" (2010: 104). This habitus leads to whites feeling they belong together while holding negative views about blacks.

Bonilla-Silva's book indicates that surveys on racial attitudes reveal white attitudes about blacks are moving in a positive, more lenient direction but that actions and ideologies are not. Specifically, some contemporary issues that color-blind racism can be used to understand are opposition to Affirmative Action and school busing; in both instances, whites oppose policies that are aimed at creating equal opportunities. Affirmative Action has come under attack several times since the 1990s with claims such as "reverse racism" and denial of equal opportunity as the overriding racial ideologies behind the lawsuits. This color-blind view of Affirmative Action ignores the historical legacy of racism and the structural conditions that maintain racial discrimination, both of which made Affirmative Action necessary in the first place. Bonilla-Silva argues that color-blind racism explains how whites can "deem almost all proposals to remedy racial inequality necessarily as illogical, undemocratic, and 'racist' (in reverse)" (263).

Racism Without Racists is widely acclaimed and now in its third edition. In the second edition, published in 2006, three sections were added: one on how the racial hierarchy of the United States may be changing towards a more color-conscious society wherein the racial hierarchy is composed of whites, honorary whites, and collective blacks (the Latin Americanization thesis); one that answers questions from readers; and one on how to fight post–civil rights racism. After President Obama's election in 2008, Bonilla-Silva's claims of a reinvigorated racism seemed faulty to many readers, so the third edition includes a chapter on Obama and "Obamerica." Rather than being symbols of postracialism, Obama and his election, Bonilla-Silva argues, align with new racism as Obama is resistant to address race and support race-related policies. To combat this "new racism," Bonilla-Silva puts forth several proposals: blacks and their allies should educate blacks about how color-blind racism operates so that they can understand contemporary oppression; antiracist whites need to be actively nurtured; the intricacies of whiteness need to be emphasized including highlighting white segregation; and a new militant civil rights movement wherein the struggle for equality is central should be fostered.

HEPHZIBAH STRMIC-PAWL

See also

Color-Blind Racism; Cultural Racism; Laissez-Faire Racism; Racism; Social Construction of Race; Symbolic Racism; Systemic Racism

Further Reading:

Bonilla-Silva, Eduardo. *Racism Without Racists: Color-Blind Racism and the Persistence of Racial Inequality in the United States.* Lanham, MD: Rowman and Littlefield, 2003.

Bonilla-Silva, Eduardo. *Racism Without Racists: Color-Blind Racism and the Persistence of Racial Inequality in the United States,* 2nd ed. Lanham, MD: Rowman and Littlefield, 2006.

Bonilla-Silva, Eduardo. *Racism Without Racists: Color-Blind Racism & Racial Inequality in Contemporary America,* 3rd ed. New York: Rowman & Littlefield, 2010.

NPR Staff. "Affirmative Action: Factious Past, Uncertain Future." December 9, 2012. http://www.npr.org/2012/12/09/166838575/the-end-of-affirmative-action-what- could-be -next.

Totenberg, Nina. "Justices Return to Affirmative Action In Higher Ed." October 10, 2012. http://www.npr.org/2012/10/10/162567137/justices-return-to-affirmative-action-in -higher-ed.

Racist Nativism

Racist Nativism is opposition to a group based on its foreign, un-American connections; that is, nativism is the preference for natives as opposed to immigrants. Racist nativism is discrimination against immigrants who are not part of the dominant Anglo-Saxon or white race. Nativism has a long history in the United States as this country is a land of immigrants: in the 1850s Irish Catholics were seen as savages; in World War I there was a strong anti-German sentiment; in World War II there were anti-Japanese campaigns; and today Mexicans and Central Americans are the target of racist nativist thought.

Anglo Protestants were the first immigrants to the future United States. These Anglo-Saxons created what they deemed a dominant, superior culture marked by white skin and the use of the English language—all others were deemed inferior and less than human. However, the burgeoning country needed many laborers, so immigration was a necessity; by the turn of the 20th century there was an influx of migrants from Southern and Eastern Europe and some from Asia. These immigrants were seen as immoral, and fears of being overrun by licentious characters were widely held. As a result, the 1924 Immigration Act enacted a quota system so that only a limited number of immigrants were allowed from undesirable countries. The quota system was eventually overturned in 1965, and immigrants from Asia, the Caribbean, and Africa began immigrating to the United States. All immigrants were expected to assimilate to whiteness; that is, they were to adopt the norms, values, and language of whites. Those who would not or could not assimilate were viewed with particular distaste and were systematically denied full participation in the social, economic, and political realms of society. Thus, it is throughout American history to the present that as long as immigration continues so does nativism. Feagin (1997) outlines four themes of nativism that are useful for understanding how undesired immigrants are universally perceived: (1) the races of immigrants are deemed as intellectually and culturally inferior; (2) certain races cannot attain complete assimilation; (3) immigrants take good jobs and disrupt economic success for native Americans; and (4) immigrants create government crises by corrupting the voting system, overloading school systems, and abusing the welfare system.

Three movements today dominate racist nativism, and they are not necessarily mutually exclusive: (1) the Official English movement, (2) the movement to eliminate benefits for undocumented immigrants, and (3) the birthright citizenship movement. The Official English movement is the effort to make English the official and only language. Between

---

Birthright Citizenship

One of the most fundamental citizenship rules of the United States is that those who are born in the United States (or its territories) are automatically citizens. Birthright citizenship is guaranteed under the Fourteenth Amendment, which states, "All persons born or naturalized in the United States, and subject to the jurisdiction thereof, are citizens of the United States and of the State wherein they reside." This type of citizenship has often been criticized; most recently Rep. King of Iowa (R) introduced a bill, which has 81 cosponsors, to redefine the "subject to the jurisdiction thereof" to exclude the children of undocumented immigrants. Other Republicans have spearheaded campaigns to end birthright citizenship, including a national campaign that coordinated with the beginning of the 2011 Congress. Critics of the campaign to end birthright citizenship point to the bureaucratic nightmare and costs that would result from the influx of children trying to attain or prove citizenship as well as those who would no longer be able to participate fully in society because they are no longer citizens.

1981–1990 alone, 13 states passed statutes mandating English as the official language, and today 31 states have some form of an Official English law on the books. This move to legislatively recognize English is rooted in anti-immigrant attitudes, particularly against those of Latino and Asian descent. The sentiment is rooted in an entrenched idea that all immigrants must assimilate and learn English and those who do not are un-American and become threats to America. Another significant nativist movement is one aimed at eliminating benefits for immigrants and can most clearly be seen in California's move to pass Proposition 187, the campaign slogan of which was "SOS" or "Save Our State." The campaign was implicitly targeted at Mexicans, who were seen as threats to the stability of California. The measure was never implemented, but it had lasting effects such as criminalizing Mexicans and extending the "invasion threat" to other immigrants, especially to Arabs post 9/11. The third movement, the birthright citizenship movement, attacks the Fourteenth Amendment guarantee that those born in the United States are automatically citizens and pushes to amend the Constitution to eliminate this right. Roberts (1997) argues that this movement sends a very important message about whose children are worthy enough to become citizens and be part of the U.S. community. Denying dark-skinned immigrants the constitutional right for their children to be citizens perpetuates the racist ideal of a white American identity.

Nativism is a fear of foreigners and a deeply held pride in being a native. In the 21st century, racist nativism is largely targeted at (perceived) undocumented, Latino immigrants. Most people overestimate the number of undocumented Latino immigrants; approximately one-third of non-Hispanics believe that over half of Hispanics are undocumented when in fact 18 percent of Hispanics are undocumented, and only 37 percent are immigrants. Nativism is theoretically discrimination against foreigners of any color, but there is a definite racial subtext wherein race and color exacerbate nativism; nonwhite immigrants are the targets of racist nativism. As white births are no longer the numerical majority in the United States, and it is likely whites will no longer be the majority of the population soon, it is uncertain whether racist nativism will get worse or better.

HEPHZIBAH STRMIC-PAWL

See also

Immigration Acts; Nativism and the Anti-Immigrant Movements

Further Reading:

Feagin, Joe. "Old Poison in New Bottles: The Deep Roots of Modern Nativism." In *Immigrants Out! The New Nativism and the Anti-Immigrant Impulse in the United States*, edited by Juan F. Perea, 12–43. New York: New York University Press, 1997.

Jacobson, Robin Dale. *The New Nativism: Proposition 187 and the Debate over Immigration*. Minneapolis: University of Minnesota Press, 2008.

Lilley, Sandra. "Poll: 1 Out of 3 Americans Inaccurately Think Most Hispanics are Undocumented." *NBC Latino* September 12, 2012. http://nbclatino.com/2012/09/12/poll-1-out-of-3 -americans-think-most-hispanics-are-undocumented/.

Perea, Juan F, ed. 1997. *Immigrants Out! The New Nativism and the Anti-Immigrant Impulse in the United States*. New York: New York University Press, 1997.

Roberts, Dorothy. "Who May Give Birth to Citizens? Reproduction, Eugenics, and Immigration." In *Immigrants Out! The New Nativism and the Anti-Immigrant Impulse in the United States*, edited by Juan F. Perea, 205–22. New York: New York University Press, 1997.

Tatalovich, Raymond. "Official English as Nativist Backlash." In *Immigrants Out! The New Nativism and the Anti-Immigrant Impulse in the United States*, edited by Juan F. Perea, 78–104. New York: New York University Press, 1997.

Tavernise, Sabrina. "Whites Account for Under Half of Births in the U.S." *New York Times*. May 17, 2012. http://www.nytimes .com/2012/05/17/us/whites-account-for-under-half-of-births -in-us.html?pagewanted=all&_r=0.

U.S. English. "About U.S. English." 2012. http://www.us-english .org/view/24.

Radio

Radio is a colorless medium. Even so, the color line was evident from the industry's earliest years. Race was a shifting, contested element, playing a central role in the production and the reception of radio content. Race is relevant in two distinct ways. First, from the earliest radio broadcasts of the 1920s until the civil rights revolution of the 1960s, the color line was a barrier, but a porous one, for African Americans in the production of radio content. As important were the complex ways that race was portrayed in radio. While de jure or de facto was the norm in public, African Americans entered the parlors of white American homes through the radio. Black Americans heard their own American culture portrayed as exotic and alien. And both races listened as minstrelsy reemerged with its white construction of black identity.

African Americans made appearances on radio from the earliest days of commercial broadcasting. Pianist Earl Hines appeared on pioneering station KDKA in Pittsburgh in 1921. The black vaudeville team of Flournoy Miller and Aubrey Lyles made their radio debut as early as 1922, as did comedian Bert Williams. Black musicians in particular benefited from the new medium. In 1922, the American Society of Composers, Authors and Publishers began demanding royalty payments from radio stations that broadcast recorded music. Over the next few years programmers adapted by broadcasting live performances. Kid Ory's Sunshine Orchestra's live performances at the Plantation Club in Los Angeles were broadcast locally. WHN in New York began broadcasting Duke Ellington's orchestra nightly from the Cotton Club in 1924. Ethel Waters and Fats Waller had regular shows, and dozens of other African Americans appeared across the radio spectrum.

Nevertheless, it was much more difficult for black musicians than white ones to find regular work in radio. Jazz and blues musicians faced criticism for their "primitive" styles, and much of what passed for jazz music on the radio by the decade of the 1930s were orchestral arrangements by white bandleaders who refused to hire black musicians. The house orchestras of the two major networks were not integrated until the end of the decade. In 1937, trumpeter and actor Louis Armstrong headlined a show featuring an all-black cast, but the show was cancelled after a six-week run when confronted with skittish sponsors, and in part because Armstrong refused to read his scripted lines in what the producers of the show intended as Negro dialect.

Fewer black performers appeared on the radio in the medium's second decade. The Great Depression fell hard on the black entertainment industry. The Theater Owners' Booking Association (TOBA), the organization that had provided employment for black artists on the vaudeville circuit, collapsed, and with it the opportunity for entertainers to find access to radio audiences. Cutbacks in the production of "race" records meant that fewer black artists were familiar to radio producers or audiences.

The development of radio networks diminished considerably the presence of African Americans on the air. Advertisers, who quickly became the dominant force in radio programming, feared that the association of their products with black consumers would discourage white customers. Advertisers and programmers developed content intended to appeal to Southern affiliates. Sponsor-affiliated dance orchestras, such as the Ipana Troubadours and the Lucky Strike Orchestra, replaced pioneer black jazz musicians, and many of the new orchestras would not hire African Americans. White singers covered songs originally recorded by black artists. Radio management was not the only barrier to African Americans. The American Federation of Radio Actors and the Radio Writers Guild was denied to African Americans and refused to accept black members until the 1940s.

Louis Armstrong's troubles highlight a dilemma faced by black performers in the early decades of radio. White listeners made up the great majority of the radio audience, and producers of radio content, who also were white, assumed that African Americans should conform to a familiar stereotype to engage a white audience. With few exceptions, black musicians came from blues, jazz, or gospel traditions. Black actors and comics portrayed only black characters, a peculiar restriction since the radio audience could not see the skin color of the actor. Moreover, the depiction of African Americans on the radio during the 1920s and 1930s conformed to racist stereotypes and to characterizations common to 19th-century minstrelsy and, later, vaudeville. As Armstrong discovered, an African American who spoke in too-standard English, who did not conform to the stereotype, might lose access to an audience. Female performers faced similar hurdles. Hattie McDaniel began her career in a family minstrel act as a singer. She moved to Los Angeles in the 1920s to find work in the film industry. Supporting herself working as a maid, she finally found work in radio playing a maid with all the characteristics of the black "mammy" on the *Optimistic Doughnut Hour* on KNX, a role she reprised on the radio show *Showboat*, and in film in *Gone With the Wind*.

Black male characters were expected to exhibit a narrow range of behavior. Most drew directly from the minstrel characters Jim Crow and Zip Coon. A Jim Crow character would satirize the rural African American. He would be slow-witted, ignorant, and servile. Zip Coon was a stereotype of the Northern black dandy. He would be ambitions and vain, but would demonstrate no real understanding of the "white" culture to which he aspired. Both characters spoke in stage "Negro dialect," a drawling mockery of standard English characterized by sustained malapropism. Black male actors would be cast as servants or as unemployed, shirking work for drinking, gambling, and womanizing.

The most successful black radio actor was Eddie Anderson, who was cast in the role of Rochester, the chauffeur and valet to Jack Benny on Benny's long-running radio program. Anderson's character spoke in a false-black dialect, worked as a servant to the show's star, and engaged in stereotypical bad behavior. Nevertheless, African American audiences had a wide range of responses to Anderson's portrayal of a member of their race. Particularly in the early years of the series, many black listeners were pleased that at least an African American, rather than a white actor, was cast in the part. Moreover, Anderson's character wielded considerable authority over Benny's. He was indispensable and often wiser than his clueless employer. Anderson himself was impatient with critics of his character and with critics of other stereotypical black characters in radio. He asserted that they were not intended to be representative of a race of people, but were simply singular comic characters. Certainly Anderson's success in radio may have influenced his judgment. Likely he would have seconded Hattie McDaniel's explanation that she would rather play a maid on the radio for $500 a week than work as a real maid for $50.

One radio pioneer who resisted the stereotyping and still overcame racial discrimination to pursue a successful and influential career was Jack Cooper. Cooper had begun his career in vaudeville on the TOBA circuit, and had worked for the *Chicago Defender*, the premier African American newspaper in the nation. In 1925 he was hired by radio station WCAP in Washington, D.C., to produce comedy sketches in black dialect for a variety show. That would be the last time that Cooper was heard on the radio speaking in "Negro dialect." He soon left that position and returned to Chicago, determined to develop radio content that would appeal to black audiences. Beginning with a modest effort on a low-power station in 1929, Cooper produced the *All-Negro Hour*, a variety show of comedy and music, and featuring many of the prominent black performers in the city. He soon added spirituals to the musical lineup, and then began broadcasting religious services from black churches on Chicago's South Side. In 1932, after a dispute with a pianist who was scheduled to play on *The All-Negro Hour*, Cooper began including recorded music on his broadcasts, an innovation that would lead to the rise of the disc jockey as a cultural icon. Cooper also developed news programs in partnership with the *Chicago Defender*, pioneered in sports broadcasting, and produced public affairs programs with discussions of issues affecting African Americans. This latter effort was particularly significant, since, apart from entertainment programming, most radio stations scrupulously avoided racial issues until the end of the 1930s. Cooper also was the rare pioneer African American radio personality who managed to make a comfortable living in the medium.

Even many of the stereotyped characters on the radio did not provide employment opportunities for African Americans. From the early 19th century, whites had portrayed African Americans in minstrel shows. The form developed first in the Northern states, drawing on traditions from the British music halls. After the Civil War, minstrelsy declined in popularity in the Northern states, but found an

unprecedented popularity in the former Confederacy. Revived again with the rise of vaudeville in the 1880s, minstrelsy moved easily into radio. Without the burnt cork makeup of the minstrel show, white performers drew on familiar characters, patter, stylized dialect, and song to create a radio version of a blackface performance. Indeed, white actors played most black roles on radio in the 1920s and 1930s. George Moran and Charlie Mack appeared regularly on the *Eveready Hour* as the Two Black Crows, a vaudeville-style comedy act. Tess Gardella, a white actress, was cast as Aunt Jemima, first as a blackfaced spokeswoman for Quaker Oats pancake flour, then as a featured performer in the Broadway musical *Showboat*. Eventually, she starred in a daily radio broadcast. Marlin Hurt, also white, played the black maid Beulah, first on stage, later appearing regularly on radio in *Showboat*, the *Fibber McGee and Molly Show*, and finally in her own show. Evidently, radio producers felt that white actors could best portray the white fantasy of a black character.

The most successfully white actors to portray black characters were Freeman Gosden and Charles Correll, creators of the long-running *Amos 'n' Andy* series. Drawing on their experiences in semiprofessional minstrelsy and with the Joe Bren theatrical company of Chicago, Gosden and Correll developed a radio show that drew an unprecedented audience from the earliest days of its broadcast. Executives at WGN in Chicago hired the two to develop a radio serial, a novel idea drawn from the successful comic strip serials in the *Chicago Tribune*. Gosden and Correll decided to play black characters, undoubtedly because of their experience in minstrelsy, but also because, as Freeman Gosden later reported, he believed that blackface was funnier than whiteface. Their earliest incarnations were the characters Sam and Henry, two rural Alabamians who began their radio journey from Birmingham to Chicago on January 12, 1926. The show broadcast for 10 minutes, six nights a week, and consisted solely of Gosden and Correll's scripted dialogue. The show was a hit locally and in other locations where WGN's broadcast could be received. The two men also recorded comic dialogue and songs on the Victor label as Sam and Henry, and these efforts provided them an even wider audience.

Like other blackface radio acts, *Sam and Henry* drew on the conventions of minstrelsy. Freeman Gosden's Sam was a Jim Crow character, sincere, deferential, and naïve. Charles

Correll's Henry was the Zip Coon, conniving and ambitious, but in the end as dimwitted and ignorant as his trusting partner. Nevertheless, Sam and Henry were more sympathetic and complex than similar minstrel pairs. The two creators avoided malicious characterizations and racist language. Indeed, they suppressed most racial issues altogether. Like many Southern African Americans in the early 20th century, the two characters migrate North to find employment in a Northern city; unlike their authentic counterparts, the two black characters confront little in the way of racism and poverty upon their arrival in Chicago.

After their contract with WGN expired in 1928, Gosden and Correll began a national tour, drawing considerable crowds and press. Upon their return to Chicago they accepted an offer from WMAQ, the radio broadcast affiliate of the *Chicago Daily News*. Since WGN owned the rights to *Sam and Henry*, the pair had to develop new names, even if the characters remained constant. After testing a few options, they settled on Amos and Andy, and as those characters Gosden and Correll remained on the air for years, first in Chicago and after 1929 on the national NBC Blue network.

In its early years, *Amos 'n' Andy* was the most popular show on radio. The serial format was in part responsible. Audiences tuned in night after night to hear the narrative unfold. Much of the popularity of the show also was due to the appeal and complexity of Gosden and Correll's creations. While based on the stereotypes from minstrelsy, Amos and Andy were appealing characters. Amos was portrayed as noble and hardworking, and Andy, while certainly more devious than his partner, was a likeable scoundrel. Difficult racial issues were ignored. Indeed, one of the remarkable features of the show was the fact there were no white characters in the series. Nevertheless, the fact that the two characters were part of the Great Migration to the Northern cities, gave it an authenticity to which even black audiences were drawn.

That is not to suggest that all African American audience members approved of a show in which white actors portrayed sympathetic, but hardly flattering, black characters. Amos and Andy were sympathetic characters, but the show's humor relied on their malapropism, their gullibility, and their unsuccessful efforts to understand business or politics. In short, the humor depended on the characters' inability to master the culture of their white audience.

Gosden and Correll made much of their attention to the authenticity of their creations. Freeman Gosden was a native of Virginia, and had close contact with black Virginians in his childhood. Both creators claimed to have done extensive research in the black communities where the show was set, first in south Chicago and later, when the show moved to network radio, in Harlem. The two made public appearances in the black community, and donated to charities that aided African Americans.

Even so, from the earliest days of the show, there were African Americans who were offended by *Amos 'n' Andy*. Jack Cooper was never a fan of his Chicago rivals, believing that they were inauthentic and degrading. At Howard University, Clarence LeRoy Mitchell criticized Gosden and Correll for leading white audiences to believe that Amos and Andy were typical of the African Americans who had migrated from the Southern states. Bishop W. J. Walls of the African Methodist Episcopal Zion Church was an early critic of the series. Robert Vann, editor of the *Pittsburgh Courier*, criticized the show for its effect on both white and black audiences. In 1931, he began a campaign to have the show removed from the airwaves. The *Courier* announced a campaign to collect a million signatures to petition NBC to abandon the show, and reported in October 1931 that 740,000 had been received. The petition drive was unsuccessful, and opposed by the *Chicago Defender*, the largest black newspaper in the nation, but it set the stage for later critics who saw little value in Gosden and Correll's blackface caricatures.

With the rise in Europe of fascism, critics of racial stereotyping in American radio found new reasons to press their case. The administration of President Franklin D. Roosevelt made effective use of radio from the earliest days of the New Deal to explain and promote its economic policies, but race issues were rarely aired. Industry leaders, except for the occasional African American innovator like Jack Cooper, carefully avoided race, except as an element of comedy or musical programming. Beginning in 1938, federal policy makers began tentative steps to address the racial divide in America, and to contrast America's pluralism with the racist regime in Germany.

That year, the Department of the Interior under Harold Ickes produced the first of 26 episodes of *American All, Immigrants All*, broadcast on the CBS network, celebrating the contributions of immigrant and minority Americans.

The series did not recall the struggle of various groups to find a place in America so much as it assured listeners that America was a nation that generously rewarded hard work from anyone regardless of origin, ethnicity, or color. Alain Locke and W.E.B. Du Bois served as unpaid consultants on the episode entitled "The Negro." Conflicts with the series' writer and production problems complicated the production, but the result was a more historically accurate portrayal of African Americans than radio listeners ever had heard before. For listeners, one obvious difference would have been the absence of "Negro dialect," even in the dramatic portrayal of antebellum slavery.

For African Americans, an even more significant federally sponsored series was *Freedom's People*, conceived by Ambrose Caliver in the Office of Education in the Interior Department. The first episode aired on the NBC radio network 10 days after the bombing of Pearl Harbor, and continued into the spring of 1942. Advisors to the series included a stellar group of black intellectuals, including Du Bois, Alain Locke, Mary McLeod Bethune, Roy Wilkins, Carter Woodson, and Charles Johnson. Paul Robeson appeared in the first episode, and music for the series was provided by such luminaries as W. C. Handy, Joshua White, and Noble Sissle. Joe Lewis, Cab Calloway, Jesse Owens, Count Basie, Fats Waller, A. Philip Randolph, and George Washington Carver made appearances. The series was a critical and popular success, winning rave reviews from professionals and from First Lady Eleanor Roosevelt, who helped to secure a promise from her husband to appear on the final broadcast, although it was a promise he failed to keep.

The development of a new consciousness on the part of radio programmers and executives led many African Americans to expect that the medium would be a part of the advancement of civil rights in postwar America. Public affairs shows like *Roundtable* and *America's Town Meeting of the Air* took up, if only hesitantly, issues of race that had been carefully avoided in the prewar years. In New York, WMCA began broadcasting *New World A'Coming* in 1944, a series that examined the challenges faced by African Americans and their expectations for the new era. In 1948, journalist and radio screenwriter Richard Durham began broadcasting *Destination Freedom* on WMAQ in Chicago, a series of biographical sketches of prominent African Americans in

history with commentary and analysis that had a clear political intent.

The advancement of a civil rights agenda suffered serious setbacks by the end of the 1940s. The onset of the Cold War and the ensuing red scare in America took a toll on black activists in particular. Paul Robeson, who had been both popular and effective as a spokesman for racial issues, was blacklisted and persecuted as a communist. He was unable to make public appearances for fear of the violence that often erupted. Canada Lee, one of the most successful African Americans in radio and stage, and a childhood friend of Fats Waller, also was blacklisted. Networks scaled back their overtly reformist content for fear of appearing sympathetic to leftist politics and losing sponsors. Nevertheless, overtly racist programming fell out of favor and black radio performers did make quiet advances. In 1951 NBC instituted a code of standards and practices that required that all groups represented on the radio be treated with dignity and respect, a requirement that regularly would be breached in the following decade. The next year the network implemented a policy of "integration without identification," allowing African Americans to appear on the radio without explicit reference to their race, and even clearing the way for black actors to portray white characters.

Meanwhile, the disc jockey format developed by Jack Cooper was gaining in popularity. In Chicago, Cooper's popularity was eclipsed by Arthur Lerner, who appeared after the war on WGES. Benson, a migrant from Mississippi, first hosted a religious program, featuring a sermon and gospel music, but after the station management refused to let him sell advertising for a religious broadcast, he transformed his show and himself. As Al "the Ole Swingmaster" Benson, Lerner abandoned Cooper's style of broadcasting in formal standard English and instead employed a black vernacular, adopting current slang terms and stressing his Southern, African American vocal style, and playing records by Chicago jazz and blues musicians. Moving away from the big-band swing music featured on network stations, Al Benson highlighted the emerging rhythm-and-blues music that developed from the synthesis of Southern Delta blues and urban jazz. By the end of the decade he was the most popular radio personality in the city, black or white.

The remarkable success of Al Benson in Chicago influenced African American broadcasters in other cities. The racial pride evident at the end of the war years raised the expectations of black audiences. And while *Amos 'n' Andy* remained on the air in a skeletal form until 1960, the decline of radio minstrelsy opened a space for authentic black voices on the airwaves. Jesse Burke in St. Louis, Ramon Bruce in Philadelphia, Lavada Durst in Austin, and Willie Bryant in New York each developed a stylized patter utilizing rhyme, slang, and rapid-fire delivery that, along with rhythm-and-blues musical format, appealed to a younger audience.

In Memphis, WDIA became the first major station in the nation to develop a full-time format for an African American audience. Struggling in a market in which the national networks were devoting more resources to television, and recognizing the untapped potential of the black consumer market, the white owners of the station began providing incrementally more airtime to programming for the city's black population. In 1948, they hired Nat D. Williams to host *Tan Town Jamboree*, and as "Nat D.," Williams quickly became the station's most valuable asset. Within a year, Williams had persuaded the station owners to complete the transition to an all-black format. The station relied heavily on recorded music, but also broadcast live performances, religious shows, and public affairs programs pitched directly to African Americans. In 1954 the station acquired a 50,000-watt transmitter, and overnight, the station acquired an audience throughout the region.

The decline of the national radio networks, the success of WDIA, and the realization on the part of independent station owners and sponsors that African Americans remained a mostly unexploited market for advertising led to a dramatic increase in the number of stations with programming targeted to a black audience. During the 1950s, hundreds of stations around the nation switched their format to "black appeal," hired black DJs and directed their advertising to black audiences. Despite these developments, ownership of these stations remained overwhelmingly in white hands. Radio provided a platform for African American broadcasters to reach African American audiences, but, except occasionally as local sponsors, the economic benefits remained out of reach.

As R&B music reached a wider audience, black DJs became significant celebrities in their own right. Through the 1950s listeners were entertained and schooled by the likes of Jack Gibson, who eventually left broadcasting to work for Berry Gordy at Motown Records, "Joltin'" Joe Howard, Tommy Smalls, and Jocko Henderson. Henderson, whose *Rocket Ship* show was syndicated in several markets, also worked as a concert promoter, continuing a tradition that still fuels and finances radio production today. With the advent of Top 40 radio and the payola scandals in the late 1950s, the power of radio programming shifted away from the DJs and into the hands of the management of radio stations, but as the civil rights struggle heated up in the 1960s, black DJs were well placed to report events, to contribute to the message, and provided the soundtrack for the movement. Significantly, when Martin Luther King, Jr. was assassinated in 1968, black DJs around the country acted quickly to get out the news and to discourage violent reaction.

While "urban contemporary" programming occupies a significant fraction of the broadcast spectrum in recent times, the color line is still evident in radio. After a significant increase in the number of black-owned radio stations between the mid-1970s and the mid-1990s, legislative and policy changes began to encourage the corporate consolidation of radio ownership. Jim Crow cannot be heard on the radio, but race is still a contested territory in the medium.

WILLIAM A. MORGAN

See also
Music Industry, Racism in

Further Reading:

Barlow, William. *Voice Over: The Making of Black Radio.* Philadelphia: Temple University Press, 1999.

Douglas, Susan J. *Listening In: Radio and the American Imagination.* Minneapolis: University of Minnesota Press, 1999.

Ely, Melvin Patrick. *The Adventures of Amos 'n' Andy: A Social History of an American Phenomenon.* New York: Free Press, 1991.

Hilmes, Michelle. *Radio Voices: American Broadcasting, 1922–1952.* Minneapolis: University of Minnesota Press, 1997.

MacDonald, J. Fred. *Don't Touch That Dial! Radio Programming in American Life from 1920–1960.* Chicago: Nelson-Hall, 1979.

Savage, Barbara. "Radio and the Political Discourse of Racial Equality." In *Radio Reader: Essays in the Cultural History of Radio,* edited by Michele Hilmes and Jason Loviglio. New York: Routlege, 2002.

Radio Free Dixie

Radio Free Dixie was a radio program broadcast from Havana, Cuba, on Friday evenings at 11:00 P.M. from 1962 to 1965. Robert F. Williams, helped by his wife, Mabel, was its conductor. The program's strong signal made it heard almost everywhere in the United States, although it was primarily aimed at African Americans living in the South because, as Williams put it, they did not have any voice. *Radio Free Dixie* called on African Americans to rise and free themselves. As Williams said, *Radio Free Dixie* was the first radio program on which black people could say whatever they wanted and did not have to worry about sponsors.

Although the program had its roots in African American cultural traditions, it was also highly innovative, for Williams was close to the Black Arts movement and the Black Panther Party (BPP). His choice of music included such African American artists as Leadbelly, Joe Turner, Abby Lincoln and Max Roach, Otis Redding, Nina Simone, The Impressions, and Josh White. Selections heard on *Radio Free Dixie* included not only jazz (dubbed "freedom jazz"), but also blues and soul music. Among the well-known listeners were Amiri Baraka, Richard Gibson, Conrad Lynn, and William Worthy. Listeners sent Williams hundreds of records to be played. The show highlighted the anthems of the Southern movement. Williams's use of jazz was intended as a new type of political propaganda. He saw *Radio Free Dixie* as much more than a radio program; for Williams, it was a political act meant to reassure African Americans and help them free themselves from an overly racist American society. Williams mixed music with news about racial violence or voter registration campaigns in the South. Music was intended to motivate people in their struggle.

"Dixie" was a familiar song composed in 1859 by Dan Emmett, a member of the Bryant's Minstrels troupe in New York. During the Civil War, the song reinforced and strengthened white identity in the South, which it pictured as a happy land. For a large number of Americans, the song retained its wartime and racial connotations in the 20th century. During the civil rights movement, "Dixie" served as an anthem for white Southerners and a reminder of racism and slavery for African Americans. Williams rejected the white Southerner vision of the South as a happy land and used the word *Dixie* in an attempt to free the South from cultural, as well as political, racism. In a press conference after a trial in which a white man was acquitted for the attempted rape of a black woman, Williams said, "If the United States Constitution cannot be enforced in this social jungle called Dixie, it is time that Negroes must defend themselves" (1959).

Williams was at odds with the civil rights movement. He called for black self-defense and published *Negroes with Guns*, although he also called for the continued pressure of nonviolent direct action. Williams believed in flexibility in the freedom struggle. For some time, he was leader of the local chapter of the National Association for the Advancement of Colored People and helped increase the membership from 6 to 200. He also formed the Black Guard, an armed group committed to the protection of the local black population, since calls of African Americans to law enforcement often went unanswered. He brought to the attention of national and international media the reality of Jim Crow.

Although Williams eventually went into exile, living in Cuba, the U.S.S.R., and China, he was neither a communist nor a black nationalist, but called himself an internationalist (see Black Nationalism). He realized that lack of freedom tainted communist regimes, and their view of the United States as imperialist distorted a political reality that was much more complex. Moreover, communist regimes did not understand the racism faced by African Americans, either because there were no important ethnic communities in their countries, or because such communities had already been marginalized and removed from the public consciousness.

Radio Free Dixie provided African Americans with a new way of grappling with racial stereotypes and lack of confidence. Williams was an influential figure in the struggle for civil rights, and his call for flexibility was followed by young black activists across the South who rejected the tactics of nonviolence. By broadcasting for the South, Williams intended to raise the level of confidence in African Americans. He gave new arguments to the Black Power movement and, although far from the United States for a number of years, he was an inspiration to, and a strong supporter of, the African American struggle for civil rights.

Eventually, CIA jamming and Cuban censorship ended *Radio Free Dixie*, but WBAI in New York and KPFA in Berkeley, California, often rebroadcast tapes of the shows. Bootleg tapes were also circulated in Watts and Harlem. The program ended in 1965 but Williams's influence has continued ever since.

SANTIAGO R. GUERRERO-STRACHAN

See also
Music Industry, Racism In; Radio

Further Reading:
Carmichael, S., and C. V. Hamilton. *Black Power: The Politics of Liberation in America.* London: Jonathan Cape, 1967.
Carson, C. *In Struggle: SNCC and the Black Awakening of the 1960s.* Cambridge, MA: Harvard University Press, 1981.
Tyson, Timothy B. *Radio Free Dixie: Robert F. Williams and the Roots of Black Power.* Chapel Hill: University of North Carolina Press, 1999.
Williams, Robert F. Press conference, Monroe, NC, 1959.

Randolph, A. Philip (1889–1979)

Asa Philip Randolph was an activist, union organizer, and civil rights leader. Born on April 15, 1889, in Crescent City, Florida, to Rev. James William and Elizabeth Robinson Randolph, he had one brother, James. When Randolph was two years old, the family moved to Jacksonville, Florida. He obtained his early education there and graduated from the Cookman Institute. He excelled academically. After graduating from high school, he decided that opportunities were limited for him in Jacksonville. Soon, he left for New York City and settled in Harlem. His initial ambition was to study acting. Before long, he entered the City College of New York, where he became a student of economics and philosophy. He taught at the Rand School of Social Science. It was during this time that he met well-known socialists Eugene Debs and Norman Thomas. Socialism appealed to him, which led him to join the Socialist Party. While living in New York City, Randolph met and married Lucille Green, a widow from Virginia. She was a teacher by training, but when they met she was the owner of a thriving hair salon. Using resources from the business, she was able to provide financial and other support to her husband's efforts. Lucille Green Randolph shared many of her husband's ideals, and they remained married until her death on April 12, 1963. There were no children born to the union.

To disseminate the vision that Randolph had regarding African Americans and the future of American society in

U.S. labor and civil rights leader A. Philip Randolph. (Bettmann/CORBIS)

general, he began publishing a new magazine. He cofounded and coedited it with his good friend Chandler Owen. First published in 1917, this new publication was called *The Messenger.* Later, the name was changed to *The Black Worker.* The publication mostly addressed issues surrounding socialism, integration, nonviolence, and unionism. Randolph believed that the condition of blacks in America at that time was not unlike that of other groups in the society. He believed that the source of the problem, which all poor and working-class people faced, was the uneven distribution of power, wealth, and resources. One issue of the magazine editorialized that "the employing class recognize no race lines. They will exploit a White . . . as readily as a Black" (Randolph 1919: 11). Profit was the motive, and it was more important than race. Thus, Randolph envisioned a critical role for unions to play. Unions could unite workers across the spectrum. Only then, he believed, would American society be changed.

On the throes of the United States entering World War I, Congress passed the Espionage Act. It called for a fine of $1,000 and 20 years in prison for interfering with military recruitment. It was during this time that Randolph's opponents often referred to him as "the most dangerous Negro in America" (Brinkley 1988: 83). *The Messenger* carried articles that were staunchly against the war. Randolph rejected the claim that the war was "to make the world safe for democracy" (Wilson 1917). This was particularly unbelievable to him when he saw blacks being lynched and subjected to outright discrimination in the United States, the bastion of democracy. He became embroiled in a public dispute over the war issue with W.E.B. Du Bois, who urged blacks to participate in the war.

During one of the many trips that Randolph took around the country lecturing, organizing, and espousing his war views, he and his friend Owen were arrested in Cleveland, Ohio. The charge was treason. Seymour Stedman, a socialist lawyer, successfully got the pair released in his custody. This did not deter Randolph and Owen. They continued their antiwar crusade. Soon, Randolph himself was drafted to serve in the war. Just one day before he was scheduled to report for duty, the war ended.

In 1925, the dream of forming a union for workers was fulfilled. The Brotherhood of Sleeping Car Porters was formed. Amid ugly and vicious attacks, a union was finally organized. It was a momentous occasion in the history of unionism within the United States. The new union prevailed over one of the most powerful and richest companies in the country—the Pullman Company. Most of the workers were black men. In 1935, the union officially became a part of the American Federation of Labor (AFL). After the AFL joined with the Council of Industrial Organization (CIO), Randolph was appointed to the executive council and became a vice-president in 1957. At many meetings, conferences, and conventions of the organization, Randolph often found himself out of step with many of the AFL-CIO leadership. His was the constant voice urging the unions to rid their ranks of discrimination. True to his earlier beliefs, he championed the rights of not only blacks, but poor whites, Puerto Ricans, Native Americans, Mexican Americans, and other minorities.

In 1940, just prior to World War II, Randolph embraced the problems of discrimination of blacks from wartime factory jobs. He was relentless in his efforts to change discriminatory practices in the industry. One strategy he proposed was a march on Washington. His hope was that the march would get the attention of the federal government and persuade Washington officials to abolish discrimination. Randolph's union had a natural constituency of black labor unionists and other sympathizers, and getting thousands of workers to descend on Pennsylvania Avenue in the nation's capital would send a powerful message. It is widely acknowledged that the prospect of a march of this magnitude weighed heavily on President Franklin D. Roosevelt's decision to sign Executive Order 8802, which banned discrimination in defense plant jobs. It was no small feat that the most powerful leader of the world responded to the demands of the Brotherhood of Sleeping Car Porters, essentially a black labor union. The march was called off as a result of the president's proactive measures. The mission was accomplished.

On July 26, 1948, Randolph pursued and won another battle against discrimination. He called on blacks to refuse to serve in the military because it was segregated. He pressed another U.S. president, Harry Truman, to sign an order to end discrimination in the armed forces as well as in federal civil service jobs. The order also provided for blacks to enter the Army and Navy service academies. Although other blacks and their supporters pushed for these changes, Randolph was clearly in the forefront. He founded and served as president of the Afro-American Labor Council from 1960–1966.

In 1964, Randolph served as a pivotal figure in the legendary March on Washington where Martin Luther King, Jr. delivered the "I Have a Dream" speech. Joining him in organizing labor unionists to participate in the march was a seasoned civil rights warrior, Bayard Rustin. He had been involved in planning the 1940 March on Washington that had been abandoned. The AFL declined to support the march, but Randolph successfully recruited a number of rank-and-file members of unions to participate. By the time of the 1963 March on Washington, Randolph was recognized as the elder statesman of the civil rights movement and was frequently referred to as such. After the March on Washington, which was held on August 28, 1963, he joined Dr. King, Whitney Young, Roy Wilkins, and other civil rights leaders in meeting with President John F. Kennedy. In 1964, President Lyndon B. Johnson presented Randolph with the Presidential Medal of Honor. The legacy of A. Philip Randolph is far reaching.

He was an indisputable pioneer in the American civil rights movement. He opened up unprecedented opportunities for blacks and other minorities in labor unions and other walks of life. One of his favorite quotes was, "A quitter never wins and a winner never quits."

On May 16, 1979, A. Philip Randolph died in New York City. He had risen from being viewed as the most dangerous Negro in America to one of the most influential and respected black leaders in the United States. It seemed altogether fitting that President Jimmy Carter would attend his funeral.

BETTY NYANGONI

See also
Civil Rights Movement; Lynching; March on Washington of 1963; Truman, Harry S.

Further Reading:
Brinkley, David. *Washington Goes to War*. New York: Alfred A. Knopf, 1988.
Cwiklik, Robert. *A. Philip Randolph and the Labor Movement*. Minneapolis: Lerner Publishing Group, 1993.
Harris, William. *Keeping the Faith: A. Philip Randolph, Milton P. Webster, and the Brotherhood of Sleeping Car Porters 1925–1937*. Blacks in the New World Series. Urbana: University of Illinois Press, 1991.
Miller, Calvin Craig. *A. Philip Randolph and the African American Labor Movement*. Greensboro, NC: Morgan Reynolds Publishing, 2005.
"Presidential Medal of Freedom Recipient A. Philip Randolph: 1889–1979." http://www.medaloffreedom.com/APhilipRandolph.htm.
Randolph, A. Philip. "Our Reason for Being." *The Messenger* (August 1919): 11–12.
Reef, Catherine. *A. Philip Randolph: Union Leader and Civil Rights Crusader*. Berkeley Heights, NJ: Enslow Publishers, 2001.
Tye, Larry. *Rising from the Rails: Pullman Porters and the Making of the Black Middle Class*. New York: Henry Holt, 2004.
Wilson, Woodrow. Speech, 65th Cong., 1st Sess., April 2, 1917, Senate Doc. 5.

Randolph, Benjamin Franklin (c. 1820–1868)

A state senator and Republican Party organizer in South Carolina, Benjamin Randolph was among the first African American political leaders to be murdered for speaking out against racial discrimination in the Reconstruction South.

Born free to mixed-race parents in Kentucky, Randolph grew up in Ohio, where he attended Oberlin College between 1857 and 1862. Having studied at the college's theological seminary, Randolph was ordained into the Methodist Episcopal Church shortly after graduation. Becoming chaplain with the 26th Colored Infantry Regiment, Randolph was posted to Hilton Head, South Carolina, in 1864. He returned to South Carolina in 1865 as an agent for the American Missionary Association. In 1866, he founded the Charleston *Journal* with Rev. E. J. Adams and, in 1867, became editor of the Charleston *Advocate*. In the latter year, Randolph also received a Freedmen's Bureau appointment, working first as a teacher and then becoming assistant superintendent of schools, a position he used to advocate complete integration of public education in South Carolina.

As a traveling minister who actively worked for the recently formed state Republican Party, Randolph encouraged political activism among the state's Methodist Episcopal congregations. In 1867, he was elected vice-president of the Republican state executive committee, and became committee chairman in the following year. In 1868, he became one of 226 African American delegates elected to the South Carolina Constitutional Convention, where his powerful speeches on behalf of African American civil rights aroused the ire of Democrats. Elected to the state senate from Orangeburg County in 1868, Randolph demanded that no African American in South Carolina be discriminated against on the basis of race.

On October 16, 1868, while canvassing for the Republican Party in the mostly white upland counties of the state, Randolph, who had been warned of the risks of openly campaigning on behalf of the freedmen, was shot and killed by three white men as he stepped from a train at Hodges Depot in Abbeville County. Committed in broad daylight, the murder was rumored to have been the work of the Ku Klux Klan. Although a mentally disturbed white man later confessed to involvement in the crime, he died, perhaps as a result of foul play, before he revealed who had paid him to kill Randolph. One of six black delegates to the South Carolina Constitutional Convention who were later slain by the Klan, Randolph was honored in 1871—a time when blacks were excluded from burial with whites—by the founding of

Randolph Cemetery, a burial place for African Americans in Columbia, South Carolina. Randolph is today remembered as one of the most radical and influential African American leaders of the Reconstruction period.

John A. Wagner

See also

Disenfranchisement

Further Reading:

Holt, Thomas C. *Black over White: Negro Political Leadership in South Carolina during Reconstruction.* Urbana: University of Illinois Press, 1977.

Litwack, Leon, and August Meier, eds. *Black Leaders of the Nineteenth Century.* Urbana: University of Illinois Press, 1988.

Rabinowitz, Howard N., ed. *Southern Black Leaders of the Reconstruction Era.* Urbana: University of Illinois Press, 1982.

Williamson, Joel. *After Slavery: The Negro in South Carolina during Reconstruction, 1865–1877.* Chapel Hill: University of North Carolina Press, 1965.

Rap Music

Rappers are individuals who perform rap music, a genre that emerged as a definitive form in New York in the 1970s. Rap music is defined as spoken words delivered in assorted styles at a variety of tempos, usually rapid and rhythmic, and accompanied to music. Since the 1970s, rap music has increasingly flourished, looming in the new millennium as one of the most popular music genres in African American popular culture.

Rap music is believed to have its roots in many different traditions. Among the earliest examples of rapping traditions include traditional West African oral storytelling. In West Africa, griots, or storytellers, frequently recounted historic narratives or folk stories with the accompaniment of drums or other instruments. An important element of this craft was the griot's ability to produce an effective and effortless delivery and captivate audiences. From this skill, the griot attained status and prestige. Dawn M. Norfleet contends that rap also incorporates "African-derived oral traditions [such as], 'boasting' (self-aggrandizement), 'toasting' (Long narrative poems that sometimes bestow praises) and 'playing the dozens' (competitive and recreational exchange of verbal insults)."

Rap music also resembles music genres and phenomenon that developed in America's early history. For example, blues musicians in the 1920s, like the Memphis Jug Band, incorporated rap-style lyrics in their songs. Swing and jazz musicians like Louis Jordan and Cab Calloway integrated lively repartee in popular songs. In the 1940s and 1950s, black radio show hosts regularly spoke "jive talk," a form of rapid, melodic, seamless jargon. Jamaican disc jockeys (DJs) emulated African American radio show hosts, speaking rhythmically over music playing in the background. In the 1960s, poets created an urbane genre referred to as spoken word. Spoken word poetry could be set to drums, jazz, or other music. Spoken word albums gained popularity throughout the 1960s and 1970s. Jive-talk was also a popular form of black speech, as reflected in blaxploitation films of the 1970s.

Kool DJ Herc, Afrika Bambaataa, and Grandmaster Flash, popular DJs that performed in the Bronx, New York, in the 1970s, played instrumental roles developing the sounds and culture that were essential to first generation rap music. These new sounds, as well as the street dances, including break dancing, which also originated in New York, would emerge as two prominent features of hip-hop culture. Kool Herc, Bambaataa, and Flash all hailed from the West Indies. Kool Herc was well known for his prowess at the turntable; Bambaataa encouraged black youth to express their frustrations through, among other things, dance, rather than participate in violent gang activity; and Flash is notable for creating the electronic beat-box sound. These DJs produced the sounds from which rap music was founded.

From this period in the early development of hip-hop music, rap music emerged. Early on, rapping was performed underground. In 1979, the Sugar Hill Gang produced "Rappers Delight," which was credited as the first commercial hit for rap music. Since then, rap music has evolved and metamorphosed. Norfleet classifies rap music in four phases, representing rap music's growth and development. Between 1979 and 1985, rap music increasingly emerged as a mainstream phenomenon, although it was still exclusively part of black popular music. Between 1979 and 1985, rappers signed on with major record labels with access to larger markets and budgets. Between 1988 and 2000, rap music fragmented into three distinct styles; East Coast rap (where rap originated), West Coast rap (which emerged in the late 1980s in California), and Southern rap (which appeared in the late 1990s, debuting rappers from a variety of Southern states such as Texas, Louisiana, and Alabama). Gangster rap, a subgenre within rap, was pioneered by West Coast rappers. Sir Mix-A-Lot, a Seattle, Washington native, representing the Pacific Northwest, a location not known for producing rappers, debuted during the nascent rise of California rappers in the late 1980s. Sir Mix-A-Lot, however, made a name for himself with hits, such as "Baby Got Back." Southern rap is differentiated from other regional rap subgenres largely by stylistic differences and the use of Southern slang and vernacular. Each phase saw the debut of new rappers, many of whom would become icons in the industry.

The pioneers of rap music brought forth what is now considered old-school fashion and sounds. Trademark sounds of this phase included, among other things: beatboxing, an array of vocally produced sounds and percussion beats, and scratching, a term used to describe the electronic "scratch" sound produced on turntables. Some of the most popular rappers were the Sugar Hill Gang, Kurtis Blow, Grandmaster Flash, Kool Moe Dee, Run-DMC, Whodini, the Fat Boys, Roxanne Shanté, and the Beastie Boys. Kurtis wore a jheri curl hair style, which was enormously popular in the 1980s. Born in New York, he was immersed in hip-hop culture early on in his youth, break dancing and performing as a DJ and an MC before beginning his rapping career in the late 1970s. He produced several hits, including "Christmas Rappin," "The Breaks," and "If I Ruled the World." He later became a record producer. Kool Moe Dee, another New York native, was born in 1962. He exhibited an urban, sophisticated style. He was rarely seen without a hat that matched his outfits and his trademark Porsche 5620 sunglasses. His second album, *How Ya Like Me Now*, was a sensation; the title would become a popular catchphrase.

Other stand-out rappers included Run-DMC, Roxanne Shanté, and the Beastie Boys. Run-DMC was a rap trio featuring Joseph "Run" Simmons, Darryl "D.M.C." McDaniels, and Jason "Jam-Master Jay" Mizell. Joseph Simmons is the brother of Russell Simmons, who pioneered one of the first black-owned hip-hop record labels, Def Jam, and produced *Def Poetry Jam*, a HBO television series. The rappers of Run-DMC were well-known for their trendsetting appearance. They wore fedora hats, over-sized gold chain necklaces, and Adidas without shoelaces. Like subsequent hip-hop styles that integrated street and prison-influenced styles, wearing

shoes with shoelaces was prohibited for prisoners, to prevent hangings. Run-DMC also popularized tough posturing, such as crossing the arms in front of the chest and bearing a stony-faced expression, which was emblematic of urban cool and dignity. A significant moment in Run-DMC's career was when they teamed up with Aerosmith rock legends Steven Tyler and Joe Perry for "Walk this Way." Simmons, who has since become a Reverend, currently appears in *Run's House*, an MTV reality show, featuring himself and his family.

While Run-DMC helped to define rap music in the 1980s, Roxanne Shanté and the Beastie Boys challenged the conventions of the genre. Rap music, in this decade, was dominated by African American males in their twenties or older. Shanté, however, was one of the first major female rappers in the industry, and she was only 14 when she debuted her first single, "Roxanne's Revenge." Shanté went on to produce two albums and several singles. The Beastie Boys, comprising three white artists, Michael "Mike D" McDonald, Adman "MCA" Yauch, and Adam "Ad-Rock" Horovitz, started out as a punk group and then, in the mid-1980s, experimented in rap music, producing several hits, including a best-selling album, *License to Ill*, which was released in 1986. The Beastie Boys were noteworthy not only for being the first successful white rappers in the industry but for exposing rap music to white audiences, who did not traditionally listen to black music in the 1980s.

The start of the next phase in rap music saw the release of the popular film, *Krush Groove* (1985), which featured many of the predominant rappers of the first generation. However, new rappers would proliferate in the ensuing years. Some of the most popular rappers, between 1985 and 1988, were Doug E. Fresh, Salt-N-Pepa, Ice-T, and Public Enemy. Salt-N-Pepa, a female rap group, featuring a female DJ that went by the name of Spinderella, generated an enormous fan base with their New York–accented and forcefully executed lyrics, synchronized dance moves, and up-to-date hairdos, including asymmetrical styles, blonde dyes, and bobs. Public Enemy produced songs loaded with political and racial themes and social criticism. The group consisted of Chuck D, Flavor Flav, Professor Griff, DJ Lord, and the S1W. Flavor Flav, adorned with an oversized clock as a necklace, had a unique and erratic rapping style that helped to modernize rap music's sound. Public Enemy's "Fight the Power" song appeared on the soundtrack of one of Spike Lee's most iconic films, *Do the Right Thing* (1989).

The number of rappers who have appeared since the late 1980s have increasingly proliferated, representing every region in America. DJ Jazzy Jeff and Fresh Prince, Queen Latifah, and MC Hammer were among the leading rappers to usher forth a new era in rap music. Will Smith and DJ Jazzy Jeff were clean-cut rappers from Philadelphia, Pennsylvania. During their rapping careers, they crossed over into television, where Will Smith became the star of the television series *The Fresh Prince of Bel-Air* and then, in the 1990s, became a successful movie celebrity. New Jersey native Queen Latifah, whose rap songs frequently incorporated critical analysis of sexism and racism, successfully transitioned from rap music to television and the movies. Hammer, who was born in New York, was one of the most influential mainstream rappers, popularizing trends such as male hair styles, the Hammer dance, and Hammer pants, in black communities during the apex of his career. He produced hits like "U Can't Touch This," which included song samples from Rick James's "Super Freak," and "Too Legit to Quit." With a clean image and sanitized lyrics, Hammer translated easily into mainstream media. This would not be the case for the majority of new rappers.

The emergence of West Coast rappers, like N.W.A and Snoop Dogg, beginning in the late 1980s, added a new dimension to rap music. Many of these rappers had had troubled pasts, coming from poor, crime-ridden, and violent neighborhoods and single-headed households. Several individuals had been in gangs, sold drugs, and served time in prison. These experiences would, in the rap industry, function as emblems of authenticity, masculinity, and status. The life experiences would also provide a plethora of material from which West Coast rappers crafted controversial rap songs, songs that were regarded by many critics as misogynistic, violent, materialistic, and debased. But the subgenre was popular with many black youth, and, in the 1990s, the music expanded into predominately white communities. In that same decade, East Coast rappers, like the groups Wu-Tang Clan, Onyx, and Notorious B.I.G., were also producing gangster rap. References to hardcore rap songs increasingly appeared in mainstream society and media.

Rappers, however, not only rapped about hard lives, many of them lived hard and fast lives. Entangled in the notorious phenomenon known as East Coast–West Coast hip-hop rivalry, Tupac Shakur and Notorious B.I.G both ended up mysteriously murdered. Several rappers, like T.I., one of the pioneers in Southern rap music, Shyne, DMX, Lil' Boosie, and Lil' Wayne have found themselves in trouble with the law over assorted charges for, among other things, violating drug and gun laws. However, T.I., for example, has used his experiences to motivate black youth to make better choices in life.

In the 2000s and 2010s, older rappers like Lil' Wayne, through his Young Money Entertainment label, have showcased such younger talent as Drake and Nicki Minaj. These artists offer a more popular genre of rap while still retaining a unique style. Drake, in particular, has been able to engage international audiences while continuing to build on a diverse domestic fanbase. Rappers with long careers, like Jay-Z, Ice Cube, and Eminem, have continued to produce albums, maintaining their provocative lyrics while also incorporating newer themes, such as fatherhood or dealing with substance abuse, based on their own experiences. The advent of social media networks, notably Facebook, Twitter, and MySpace, have also shaped how new rap music is received by its fanbase, thus influencing how record companies distribute new albums.

Despite what many regard as its negative side, rap music and the industry continue to thrive. Rap has inspired new forms and subgenres, like reggaetón, created by Latino youth, and Christian rap, and rap headliners like Jay-Z, Snoop Dogg, Missy Elliott, Common, and 50 Cent maintain sensational and productive careers.

GLADYS L. KNIGHT

See also

Hip-Hop; Rhythm and Blues; Rock and Roll

Further Reading:

Burnim, Mellonee V., and Portia K. Maultsby. *African American Music: An Introduction*. New York: Routledge, 2006.

Hess, Mickey. *Icons of Hip Hop: An Encyclopedia of the Movement, Music, and Culture*. Westport, CT: Greenwood Press, 2007.

Keyes, Cheryl. *Rap Music and Street Consciousness*. Urbana: University of Illinois Press, 2004.

Rose, Tricia. *Black Noise: Rap Music and Black Culture in Contemporary America*. Middletown, CT: Wesleyan University Press, 1994.

Rape and Racism

Rape is a violent crime. According to the FBI, 95,136 forcible rapes were reported in the United States in 2002, but federal crime-victimization surveys indicate that number to be nearly three times higher because only about one in three rapes is reported. Women are 91 percent of the victims and men are 99 percent of the offenders. The vast majority of rapes against women are perpetrated by offenders of the same race, with about 81 percent of the victims being white. Certainly gender stereotyping—the dominant male and the submissive female—plays a part in many cases of rape, but in cases of interracial rape, the addition of racial stereotypes born of racial prejudices creates a complex set of circumstances that affect both victims and offenders.

When the U.S. Constitution was hammered out by the white Founding Fathers, it institutionalized the racist ideology by counting black slaves as three-fifths of a person. The prevailing white belief that blacks were not just unequal to whites but somehow subhuman, led to stereotyping black males as animals with insatiable sex drives and black females as readily available for the pleasure of white men without consequence to the men. This gave rise to, among other things, the myth of the black rapist. Thus, before the Civil War, many Southern states punished rape offenders by race rather than by deed. A black man who raped a white woman would be sentenced to death, but a white man who raped a white woman might get two to 20 years in prison. Raping a black woman might get a fine or some jail time, but only if the court so decided.

The persistence of these stereotypes has led to countless travesties of justice. Charges of rape were used to prop up white supremacy and to provide a ready excuse to lynch black men. Black women victimized by rape were victimized again in judicial hearings. A violent crime against a black woman was not considered as something serious by judges or juries, just evidence of the way blacks lived everyday life. How could a subhuman be violated? Not surprisingly, many black women chose not to report the crime at all. One of the best-known examples of functional racism in rape cases was the case of the "Scottsboro Boys" in Alabama. Two young white women accused nine black teenagers who were removed from a Southern Railroad freight train of gang rape. All but one of the nine, a 12-year-old, were convicted of rape and sentenced to death in the course of a few weeks after their arrest, but only after the governor of Alabama called in the National Guard to save them from a lynch mob. It turned out that the rape had never occurred. It took 20 years, countless court battles, and intervention from national organizations like the National Association for the Advancement of Colored People to put an end to the injustice.

The fate of the Scottsboro Boys did not end racism in rape cases. Long after that, juries continued to convict black men alleged to have committed rape at higher rates than white men accused of rape. Black women who alleged rape, on the other hand, tended not to be believed, even after having suffered the incredulity of police and the skepticism of the medical establishment to pursue a case. And even then, prosecutors were less likely to take their case to court, a case they had a good chance of losing. Latino women, who like blacks were stereotyped as members of a culture that tolerated all kinds of violence, including rape, had similar experiences.

In more recent times, as women and minorities have found their rightful political power and voice, the old racial, sexual stereotypes are collapsing if not being reversed. Many social observers saw a larger message in the jury's innocent verdict that ended the 1995 murder trial of O. J. Simpson. A racially diverse jury seemed to be announcing to the nation that the days of racial discrimination in court proceedings were over, no matter how solid the physical evidence and no matter what the alleged crime. A sense of guilt on the part of whites for the documented mistreatment of blacks through American judicial history suggested a bias for innocence. This was the so-called race card. Too many black men had been victimized by the U.S. criminal justice and judicial systems for too many years. That was also the message of Kobe Bryant's attorneys when the basketball star was accused of rape by a white woman. There was nothing deviant and certainly nothing illegal about a black man and a white woman having consensual sex. Yet no matter what the Simpson jury's intentions were, there was an immediate backlash to it, notably among whites, who believed that justice had not been served. The evidence against Simpson was too clear and obvious.

For example, a 2002 study of college students found that racial factors determined victim blaming. Men's scores on the Modern Racism Scale were correlated positively with victim blaming in all rapes. The conclusion of the study was that racial stereotyping in rape cases persists and directly influences judicial outcomes.

BENJAMIN F. SHEARER

See also

Anti-Lynching Legislation; Black Women and Lynching; Lynching; Masculinity, Black and White; Rape as Provocation for Lynching; White Mobs

Further Reading:

Davis, Angela. "Rape, Racism, and the Myth of the Black Rapist." In *Feminism and "Race,"* edited by Kum-Kum Bhavnani, 50–64. New York: Oxford University Press, 2001.

George, William H., and Lorraine J. Martinez. "Victim Blaming in Rape Effects and Perpetrator Race, Type of Rape, and Participant Racism." *Psychology of Women Quarterly* 26 (June 2002): 110–19.

Hacker, Andrew. *Two Nations: Black and White, Separate, Hostile, Unequal.* New York: Scribner, 1992.

Rape as Provocation for Lynching

Lynching is the illegal killing of a person by mob action, which usually involved torture, mutilation, and hanging. It denotes mob action that takes place without due process of the law—no trial, no defense, no attorneys, no judge, no jury. The illegal action was particularly prevalent in the Southern states during the late 1800s and into the early 1900s. African Americans were most often the victims of this vigilante movement carried out by white mobs and often witnessed by inhabitants of an entire town. Vigilante organizations such as the Ku Klux Klan (KKK) frequently initiated and executed the deadly practice, complete with torture and maiming of the individual prior to the hanging.

A lynching would commonly be advertised in local newspapers, and great crowds would appear to witness the event. The stereotype of the hypersexuality of the black male was central to the number of lynchings that used rape of white women as justification for the mob's brutality and killing. Body parts of the victim, including ears, noses, fingers, and genitalia were often given to members of the attending crowd as souvenirs. Authorities of the law did not intervene on the victims' behalf, and there are only rare cases in which the perpetrators were ever tried and punished for their illegal

participation and actions in the execution of thousands of African Americans and supportive Caucasians.

Five hundred African Americans were lynched from the 1800s to 1955 in the state of Mississippi, while some nationwide estimates for the same time frame near 5,000 victims. Others report that between 1884 and the beginning of World War I, between 3,600 and 3,700 incidents of lynching occurred. The Tuskegee Institute reports that between the time when solid statistical data was available in 1882 to 1964, a total of 4,743 people died as a result of lynching, with 3,445 people being black and lynched by whites.

The term *lynch* was most likely derived from Colonel Charles Lynch (1736–1796) who fought in the American Revolution and was a torrid justice of the peace in the state of Virginia. Those Caucasians who publicly supported abolition or the eradication of the practice of lynching were also targeted by the mobs and lynched. Elijah Parish Lovejoy is an example of this form of Caucasian lynching. He, as a white man, wrote articles in 1837 expounding on the evils of slavery and calling for an end to lynching. He was, himself, lynched and killed for these actions.

Accusations of black men raping white women were but one of the many reasons given for lynching. It is commonly thought that rape constituted the most essential and popular provocation for lynching, but current research does not confirm this perspective. John Hope Franklin writes that "in the first fourteen years of the twentieth century only 315 lynch victims were accused of rape or attempted rape" (Franklin 1967). He notes that homicide, robbery, insulting whites, and other offenses constitute the bulk of justifications for lynching. The primary provocation for lynching was, instead, accusations of slave insubordination. The perception of an uppity attitude on the part of an African American person was sufficient mob justification for lynching. Black men were most often the victims, but many African American women were also lynched for allegedly displaying signs or attitudes of superiority—or the lack of humbleness, debasement, and subservience that was expected of blacks and desired by the dominant Caucasian population.

There are estimates that approximately one-fourth of the killings from 1880 to 1930 were motivated by accusations of rape (PBS Online). In 1933, Dr. Arthur Raper wrote a book titled *The Tragedy of Lynching* on the practice of lynching in the United States beginning in 1889. He reported that over four-fifths were of African American descent and less than one-sixth of the victims were accused of rape.

Concerns of rape across the black-white barrier remained an issue, regardless of the number or actual percentages of lynching provoked by accusations of rape. The threat of lynching was a horrific tool of the status quo used to maintain social dominance and control over emancipated or enslaved African Americans. White slave owners were known to rape black female slaves without reprisal or any sanctions. White men also feared the black man for his supposed virility, coupled with the stereotypical assumption that all black men possessed an intense desire and uncontrollable lust for white women. This fear was only intensified by the white man's perception of the white woman's returned attraction to African American men. Caucasian men of the time—especially in the South—would tolerate the image of the subservient, docile, unthreatening black man who happily expressed gratitude for the white man's paternalism. The counterimage of the virile, sexually superior black man seeking out white women for erotic pleasure or rape was an intolerable perception for the Caucasian slaveowner to endure, especially when he suspected reciprocity on the part of his Caucasian female partner. Some white women also falsely accused African American men of rape, and although some women later recanted and told the truth that a rape was not committed, their confession often did nothing to nullify the mob's original intent and execution of a lynching.

In her 2003 book *Race, Ethnicity, and Sexuality: Intimate Intersections, Forbidden Frontiers*, Joane Nagel describes the phenomenon in her chapter titled "Sex-Baiting and Race-Baiting: The Politics of Ethnosexuality":

I have argued that there is no more potent force than sexuality to stir the passions and fan the flames of racial tension. Sex-baiting can be as provocative as race-baiting in conjuring up a vision of ethno-sexual threat. In fact, sex-baiting is a mechanism of race-baiting when it taps into and amplifies racial fears and stereotypes, and when sexual dangerousness is employed as a strategy to create racial panic. Sex-baiting and race-baiting often are used together by defenders of particular ethnosexual orders to maintain the status quo. It is the sexualized nature of things

ethnic, racial, and national that heats up the discourse on the values, attributes, and moral worth of Us and Them, that arouses anger when there are violations of sexual contact rules, that raises doubts about loyalty and respectability when breaches of sexual demeanor occur, that provokes reactions when questions of sexual purity and propriety arise, and that sparks retaliation when threats to sexual boundaries are imagined or detected. (255)

The point of imagined actions driven by fear is also an important aspect of this phenomenon. Whether or not a black man really raped a white woman was often inconsequential and secondary to the fact that the action was considered reality by the lethal crowd. This accentuates the Thomas Theorem, which states that "If men define situations as real, they are real in their consequences" (Thomas and Thomas 1928). The alleged rapes did not have to be real to satisfy their function to the perpetrators of crimes such as lynching. They needed only be perceived as real in order for the consequences of lynching to become very real. Assigning hypersexuality to subordinate but threatening groups is not uncommonly used by the dominant society in order to justify horrendous behavior, including torture, bodily dismantlement, castration, and eradication of entire populations.

African American editor Ida B. Wells-Barnett, a strong social activist, found that consensual sex between black men and white women was prevalent at the time, even though it was forbidden. She also found that the accusations of rape used as rationale for lynching were but another form of the white male–dominant population seeking social control over the Caucasian female population. Historic legislation from 1870 to 1884 supports her finding, with 11 Southern states passing laws to ban miscegenation, or marriage across racial and ethnic lines.

Wells-Barnett, a graduate of Rust College in Memphis, Tennessee, and teacher in 1888, sparked an intense campaign against lynching in the United States. She traveled to England to promote her cause on the world stage and became the editor of a local black newspaper titled *The Free Speech and Headlight*. She found it necessary to write editorials under the pen name of Iola. In 1895, Wells-Barnett published *A Red Record*, her study of race and the practice of lynching in the United States. She was particularly focused on the men who were hung due to accusations of rape. She found that in her own town of Memphis, African American men were being lynched, not predominantly because of accusations of rape, but because they were financially and independently established members of their newly thriving African American communities.

Reconstruction had made African American affluence vibrant in many towns throughout the South. Wells-Barnett also joined forces with W.E.B. Du Bois in her fight for social justice and equality. She was forced to leave Memphis and took residency in Chicago.

For decades, strong opposition to lynching was not forthcoming from government or law enforcement agencies. Finally, in 1948, President Harry Truman supported legislation that posed a serious threat to the practice of lynching. The U.S. Senate—in particular, Southern representatives—blocked the passage of Truman's bills. The determined intent of the federal government, however, could not be dismissed. Truman developed the Civil Rights Commission as a long-standing facet of the federal government to monitor the cessation of the crimes of lynching.

Caucasian women, predominantly from the South, formed an anti-lynching movement through an association named the Association of Southern Women for the Prevention of Lynching. This organization protested the violent practice of lynching perpetrated in the name of protection of white women. It began in the 1920s and by the 1940s had impacted the end of this violent social action. In 1900, the African American congressman George White brought forward the first anti-lynching bill, which died in the House Judiciary Committee. Lillian Smith is considered one of the most literate Caucasian females who wrote with the hope of ending lynchings. In her 1944 novel *Strange Fruit* and an anthology titled *Killers of the Dream*, Smith examines lynching in terms of the racism and sexism that was prevalent in the South. Actions of these individuals and other anti-lynching organizations eventually brought about the end of lynching in the United States.

SHEILA BLUHM MORLEY

See also

Anti-Lynching Legislation; Black Women and Lynching; Lynching; Masculinity, Black and White; Rape and Racism; White Mobs

Further Reading:

Baker, Lee D. "Ida B. Wells-Barnett and Her Passion for Justice." In *Living Our Stories, Telling Our Truths: Autobiography and the Making of African American Intellectual Tradition*, edited by Vincent P. Franklin. New York: Scribner, 1995. http://www .duke.edu/~ldbaker/classes/AAIH/caaih/ibwells/ibwbkgrd .html.

Cardyn, Lisa. "Sexualized Racism/Gendered Violence: Outraging the Body Politic in the Reconstruction South." *Michigan Law Review* (2002).

Davis, Ronald L. F. "Creating Jim Crow: In-Depth Essay." *The History of Jim Crow*. http://www.jimcrowhistory.org/history/ creating2.htm.

Franklin, John Hope. *From Slavery to Freedom: A History of Negro Americans*, 3rd ed. New York: Knopf, 1967.

Gibson, Robert A. *The Negro Holocaust: Lynching and Race Riots in the United States, 1880–1950*. New Haven, CT: Yale-New Haven Teachers Institute. http://www.yale.edu/ynhti/ curriculum/units/1979/2/79.02.04.x.html.

LeMay, Michael C. *The Perennial Struggle: Race, Ethnicity, and Minority Group Relations in the United States*, 2nd ed. Upper Saddle River, NJ: Pearson, Prentice Hall, 2005.

Nagel, Joane. *Race, Ethnicity, and Sexuality: Intimate Intersections, Forbidden Frontiers*. New York: Oxford University Press, 2003.

PBS Online. "People & Events: Lynching in America." *American Experience: The Murder of Emmett Till*. http://www.pbs.org/ wgbh/amex/till/peopleevents/e_lynch.html.

Raper, Arthur F. *The Tragedy of Lynching*. Chapel Hill: University of North Carolina Press, 1933.

Steinhorn, L., and B. Diggs-Brown. *By the Color of Our Skin: The Illusion of Integration and the Reality of Race*. New York: Plume, 2000.

Thomas, William Isaac, and Dorothy Swaine Thomas. *The Child in America: Behavior Problems and Programs*. New York: A. A. Knopf, 1928.

Women in History. "Ida B. Wells-Barnett." http://www.lkwdpl .org/wihohio/barn-ida.htm.

Zangrando, Robert L. "About Lynching." *Modern American Poetry*. http://www.english.uiuc.edu/maps/poets/g_l/ lynching/lynching.htm.

Reconstruction Era

The Reconstruction Era is the period that followed the Civil War (1861–1865) and ended with the reintegration of the Confederate States into the Union. It also produced a legal framework allowing African Americans to live as citizens in

The Reconstruction period following the Civil War was a time of political empowerment for African Americans, although many of the gains were short-lived. This 1881 montage depicts many of the influential African American elected officials and leaders during this era. (Library of Congress)

a postslavery American society. This was done most notably through three amendments to the U.S. Constitution and several civil rights acts. The Thirteenth Amendment abolished all forms of slavery; the Fourteenth Amendment gave African Americans citizenship and promised them equal protection under the law; and the Fifteenth Amendment extended the right to vote to black men. On April 9, 1866, the Republican-dominated Congress overrode President Andrew Johnson's veto and passed the Civil Rights Act of 1866 (also known as the New Freedman Bureau Act), which gave citizenship to any person born in the United States, with rights and privileges such as voting; owning, selling, and inheriting property; and suing and giving evidence in court. President Johnson had questioned the qualification of former slaves to be citizens and had deemed the bill too

favorable to blacks and unfair to whites. The act was essentially ignored and was only enforceable after the ratification of the Fourteenth Amendment, which reaffirmed citizenship rights and privileges to former slaves and the "equal protection of the laws."

Because of the relentless racism and violence of vigilante organizations such as the Ku Klux Klan (KKK), and the continuous resentment of the South, which felt humiliated by defeat and by what it perceived as imposition by the Northern victors, African Americans could not fully enjoy the rights promised by the 1866 Civil Rights Act and the Fourteenth Amendment. From 1870 to 1871, Congress passed three acts known as enforcement acts (the Enforcement Act of 1870, also known as the Ku Klux Klan Act of 1870, and two enforcement acts in 1871), mainly targeting the KKK,

Emancipation Proclamation (1862)

The Emancipation Proclamation issued by President Abraham Lincoln in September 1862 freed slaves in Confederate-controlled areas effective January 1, 1863. Contrary to popular belief, the scope of the Emancipation Proclamation was limited to slaves residing in Confederate states, including Arkansas, Texas, Mississippi, Alabama, Florida, Georgia, South Carolina, North Carolina, and parts of Louisiana and Virginia. President Lincoln's Emancipation Proclamation declared that "all persons held as slaves within said designated States and parts of States are, and henceforward shall be, free." It was not until the passage of the Thirteenth Amendment in December 1865, after the end of the American Civil War, that slavery would eventually be abolished throughout the nation.

Few slaves were actually freed immediately after the 1862 Emancipation Proclamation, because Confederate states and controlled areas did not heed President Lincoln's orders. Moreover, the proclamation did not apply to slaves in border states or Southern areas that were under Union control. Despite its limited jurisdiction, the proclamation made the abolition of slavery a central issue in the Civil War. Recognizing the untapped resources of African American men, the proclamation also called upon freed slaves to enlist in the Union effort, emphasizing that they would be welcomed "into the armed service of the United States to garrison forts, positions, stations, and other places, and to man vessels of all sorts in said service." As a result, in the two and a half years following the 1862 Emancipation Proclamation, nearly 200,000 African Americans joined the Union Army.

TARRY HUM

who were using violence to prevent African Americans and some whites from voting, holding office, serving on juries, or attempting to get educated.

In 1870, Massachusetts congressmen Charles Sumner and Benjamin Butler introduced a bill to reaffirm equality and justice for all Americans as guaranteed by the Declaration of Independence and the Constitution. What became known, after years of negotiations, as the Civil Rights Act of 1875 sought to end discrimination and segregation against African Americans in the enjoyment of public places, facilities, and conveyances. In 1883, however, following Southern legislatures' reversal of the legal achievement of Reconstruction and the general violence against blacks in the South, the U.S. Supreme Court declared the 1875 Civil Rights Act unconstitutional on the grounds that discrimination in public facilities was not within the power of Congress to legislate, nor was it a federal offense against the Thirteenth or Fourteenth Amendments.

Other problems that newly freed African Americans had to face included laws that had been in place in the past, such as the so-called black codes, a set of local and state laws already in place in the North before the Civil War and put in place by former slave states in the South to limit the civil rights and privileges that African Americans acquired as a result of the amendments and the civil rights acts. The Fourteenth and Fifteenth Amendments offered protection but did not completely shield African Americans from the intimidation and violence of white supremacists, the frequent burning of newly established black schools, and the beating and murder of teachers in those schools.

The promise of Reconstruction was further shattered by the violence of post-Reconstruction, which started after the Union Army pulled out of the South. Previously humiliated by the defeat in the Civil War, the South embarked on a steady and unapologetic course to reverse the achievement of Reconstruction. Tactics including the grandfather clause, literary test, the poll tax, and sheer violence led to the legal disenfranchisement of African Americans. The triumph of Jim Crow laws was sealed by the landmark Supreme Court decision *Plessy v. Ferguson* of 1896 that legalized segregation and discrimination, thus crushing the promise of racial harmony generated by the idealism of Reconstruction.

In spite of legal wrangling, the reconfiguration of the plantation system through the practice of sharecropping, and the continuing racism and discrimination against African Americans, Reconstruction brought hope to newly freed African Americans. Thousands of black and white volunteers, missionaries, and churches in or from both the North and the South established thousands of new schools and/or labored to educate the black population of all ages whom the institution of slavery had, by and large, forbidden to learn to read and write. Within three years of the end of the Civil War, several institutions of higher education were also launched; they included Fisk University, Hampton University, Howard University, and Morehouse College.

Even in the face of many daunting challenges, the amendments to the Constitution and the civil rights acts that followed the end of the Civil War allowed African Americans to vote, seek political office, own personal and real property, own the fruit of their labor, and use public facilities. Unfortunately, all of these achievements were legally suppressed by the triumph of post-Reconstruction Jim Crow laws.

AIMABLE TWAGILIMANA

See also

Civil Rights Act of 1875; Jim Crow Laws; Lynching; Sharecropping; Slavery

Further Reading:

Du Bois, W. E. B. *Black Reconstruction in America 1860–1880*. Introduction by David Levering Lewis. New York: Free Press, 1998.

Foner, Eric. *Reconstruction: America's Unfinished Revolution, 1863–1877*. New York: HarperCollins, 1988.

Smith, John David. *Black Voices from Reconstruction 1865–1877*. Gainesville: University Press of Florida, 1997.

Red Power Movement

The term "Red Power" has been used to describe the Indian civil rights movement of the 1960s and 1970s, particularly the demands of Native American activists for equality, self-determination, and the restoration of the landed estate and traditional hunting, fishing, and movement privileges.

Some historians target the American Indian Chicago Conference of 1961 as the real beginning of the modern Red Power movement, when a younger, more urban generation of Indian leaders challenged older, more traditional tribal leaders in the National Congress of American Indians for control of the Indian rights movement. Young men like Clyde Warrior (Ponca), Melvin Thorn (Paiute), and Herbert Blatchford (Navajo) left the Chicago meeting unhappy about the slow pace of change. They reconvened in Gallup,

New Mexico, and formed the National Indian Youth Council, which demanded an end to racism, ethnocentrism, and paternalism in American Indian policy and greater influence of Native Americans in the decision-making process of the Bureau of Indian Affairs (BIA).

By the mid-1960s, Indian activists were inspired and galvanized into action by the Black Power Movement among African Americans. Between 1964 and 1966, activists staged "fish-ins" to proclaim Indian independence from state fish and game laws. Such groups as the Indian Land Rights Association, the Alaska Federation of Natives, and the American Indian Civil Rights Council demanded the restoration of tribal lands, denouncing the idea of monetary compensation for the loss of the Indian estate. The Pan-Indian movement, led by people like Lehman Brightman and his United Native Americans, worked to overcome tribal differences and construct a united, powerful Indian political constituency in the United States.

In 1969, a pan-Indian group known as Indians of All Tribes occupied Alcatraz Island in San Francisco Bay, demanding its return to Native peoples. Groups such as the American Indian Movement (AIM), in addition to insisting on the restoration of tribal lands, demanded complete Indian control over the BIA. In 1972, activists Hank Adams of the "fish-ins" and Dennis Banks of AIM organized the "Trail of Broken Treaties" caravan and traveled to Washington, D.C., to demand the complete revival of tribal sovereignty by repeal of the 1871 ban on future treaties, restoration of treaty-making status to individual tribes, provision of full government services to unrecognized eastern tribes, review of all past treaty violations, restitution for those violations, and elimination of all state court jurisdiction over American Indians. They also invaded and trashed the offices of the BIA in Washington, D.C., to dramatize their demands.

By the early 1970s, however, the Red Power movement had increasingly developed into a campaign for self-determination. Although self-determination meant different things to different people, several controlling principles emerged during the debate over its merits. First, self-determination revolved around Indian control of the government agencies dealing most directly with them. The idea of having non-Natives administering Indian health, educational, and economic programs was unacceptable to self-determinationists. Second, self-determination called for an end to assimilationist pressures and a restoration of tribal values and culture. Allotment, citizenship, compensation, termination, and relocation had all aimed at the annihilation of tribal cultures, and self-determinationists wanted to prevent the future reemergence of such programs. Third, self-determinationists insisted on maintaining the trust status of the tribes with the federal government.

Although many non-Natives saw self-determination and the continuance of the trust status as contradictory (a combination of paternalism and independence), self-determinationists were convinced that Native societies needed the trust status to protect them from non-Native majorities at the state and local levels. Finally, self-determinationists hoped to bring about the economic development of reservation resources so that Native peoples could enjoy improved standards of living without compromising their cultural integrity or tribal unity. Many of the demands of self-determinationists were achieved when Congress passed the Indian Education Act of 1972, the Indian Finance Act of 1974, the Indian Self-Determination and Education Assistance Act of 1975, and the Indian Child Welfare Act of 1978.

JAMES S. OLSON

See also

American Indian Movement (AIM); Bureau of Indian Affairs; Native Americans, Conquest of; Native Americans, Forced Relocation of

Further Reading:

Cornell, Stephen. *The Return of the Native: American Indian Political Resurgence.* Oxford: Oxford University Press, 1988.

Hauptman, Laurence M. *The Iroquois Struggle for Survival: World War II to Red Power.* Syracuse: Syracuse University Press, 1986.

Josephy, Alvin M., Jr., Joane Hagel, and Troy Johnson, eds. *Red Power: The American Indians' Fight for Freedom.* Lincoln: University of Nebraska Press, 1971.

Olson, James Stuart, and Raymond Wilson. *Native Americans in the Twentieth Century.* Chicago: University of Illinois, 1984.

Red Scare and Race Riots

The term *red scare* refers to two periods in U.S. history, both marked by widespread and intense nationalist and anti-radical sentiment. During the first Red Scare, 1917–1920,

the U.S. government, industry leaders, soldiers, and citizens attacked communists, socialists, anarchists, labor organizations, and recent immigrants, particularly German-Americans. The scare found U.S. blacks in the midst of both a regional and psychological shift, changes that served to further threaten a nation in the throws of hysteria. Blacks were both victims and actors in the events surrounding the Red Scare, as many of the blacks who sought to change the status quo by seeking economic opportunity in northern cities were included among accounts of the radicals who posed a threat to America. During the high tide of the scare, in 1919, there were 78 lynchings and 25 race riots, phenomena that caused James Weldon Johnson to dub the summer and autumn of 1919 the "Red Summer." The rise of the *New Negro* (a termed coined by black philosopher Alain Locke), or the change in black self-understanding, was also a source of anxiety for whites, as blacks fought back against the mobs that attacked them.

Wars often serve to bolster nationalist sentiment in a nation. When groups of people, divided by race, class, gender, and region, can come together against a common enemy, they are able to forget the problems they have with their fellow citizens. President Woodrow Wilson put this social tendency in overdrive in the United States as he took extraordinary steps to manufacture national cohesion before American entry into World War I in 1917. Wilson created the Committee on Public Information, led by journalist George Creel, which distributed an enormous amount of pro-America propaganda—more than enough, it turns out, than was necessary to sustain the war effort; after the Great War, a violently nationalist populace, aided by industrial leaders, journalists, and the U.S. government, still hungry for a foe, turned its attention away from foreign enemies and took steps to root out the enemy within.

Anarchists were responsible for a series of bombing attempts throughout the country. Many Americans were concerned that these attempts might succeed, especially in the wake of Russia's Bolshevik Revolution. During the scare, Congress broadened the Espionage Act to include the Sedition Act of 1918, an act that made it illegal to speak out against the government and gave the Postmaster General the power to intercept dissenter mail. In November 1919, and on New Year's Day 1920, Attorney General Palmer authorized the infamous Palmer Raids. On January 1, officials arrested over 10,000 communists, left-wingers, and people with foreign-sounding names. Among the lay population, anarchist plots seemed illogical to many, and were unpredictable and shrouded in secrecy; workers, on the other hand, presented visible targets. With each passing strike, citizens began to more closely associate labor unrest with the ongoing plot to overthrow the U.S. government.

In 1919, the United States was also in the midst of massive labor unrest, as factories switched to peacetime production and soldiers returned to strained domestic labor markets. According to reports, there were as many as 3,000 labor disputes, strikes, and lockouts, involving over 4 million workers, as workers whose salaries had been frozen to help out with the war effort began to organize for better conditions. The Seattle General Strike, which took place from January 21 through February 11, began in earnest when 25,000 workers joined 35,000 striking shipyard workers and succeeded in shutting down the city. The Cleveland May Day Riot was also a major event, as local unionists, socialists, communists, and anarchists met at the behest of socialist leader Charles Ruthenberg to protest the detention of Eugene Debs. The September Steelworkers Strike grew to include 365,000 workers around the nation.

The communist and striker became intertwined in the American mind; industrialists, journalists, and officials only served to help Americans conflate the two. In addition to journalists' accounts that condemned strikers as un-American, Industrialists fighting collective bargaining efforts were not afraid to exploit nationalist sentiment. Although involved in a noble battle for fair working conditions, workers were not immune to racism. Labor leaders and industrialists alike mobilized antiblack sentiment, often with violent consequences.

As stated above, blacks were both actors and objects of violence during the Red Scare. As the conventional belief in black inferiority met the newfound hatred of foreigners and anyone who might upset the status quo, both attitudes merged against black efforts to realize the benefits of American society. Many of the 450,000 blacks who relocated to urban centers met angry whites who were afraid of what the influx of black workers would do to their economic and social standing. Any survey of the mobs that attacked blacks during the Red Summer found frustrated white workers and soldiers without a war to fight among the participants.

A change in attitude accompanied the black migration. The argument that blacks should not seek political and social equality, championed by Booker T. Washington, fell out of favor among the black population, as postwar blacks had reason to believe that they deserved full citizenship. The president's efforts to create national pride did not bypass the black community. African Americans were soldiers in the Great War, bought Liberty Bonds, and followed rationing restrictions. The Harlem Renaissance, the most well known of the New Negro efforts, and Carter G. Woodson's Association for the Study of Negro Life and History, founded in 1915, stand as evidence of a move to celebrate black historical and cultural achievements and the decision to reject the conventional belief in white superiority. Black newspapers, including W.E.B. Du Bois's *The Crisis* and the *Chicago Defender*, encouraged blacks to hold their heads high as they relocated to cities across the country. Although many blacks lost their lives in the Red Summer, black people were no longer willing to believe that they deserved to die according to the whims of whites. Blacks heeded Claude McKay's Red Summer call, and mobs met them, "pressed to the wall, dying, but fighting back!" (McKay, "If We Must Die," line 14).

SHATEMA A. THREADCRAFT

See also

Chicago (Illinois) Riot of 1919; Communist Party; East St. Louis (Illinois) Riot of 1917; Race Riots in America. Documents: Report on the Memphis Riots of May 1866 (1866); Account of the Riots in East St. Louis, Illinois (1917); A Southern Black Woman's Letter Regarding the Recent Riots in Chicago and Washington (1919); The Cook County Coroner's Report Regarding the 1919 Chicago Race Riots (1920); The Final Report of the Grand Jury on the Tulsa Race Riot (June 25, 1921); Testimony from *Laney v. United States* (1923); The Governor's Commission Report on the Watts Riots (1965); Cyrus R. Vance's Report on the Riots in Detroit (1967); The Reports of the Oklahoma Commission to Study the Tulsa Race Riot of 1921 (2000–2001); Draft Report: 1898 Wilmington Race Riot Commission (2005)

Further Reading:

Hallgren, Mauritz A. "The Right to Strike." *The Nation* 137, no. 3566 (November 8, 1933): 530.

Rudwick, Elliott M. *Race Riot at East St. Louis, July 2, 1917.* Carbondale: Southern Illinois University Press, 1963.

Tuttle, William M., Jr. *Race Riot: Chicago in the Red Summer of 1919.* New York: Athenaeum, 1970.

Red Summer Race Riots of 1919

The race riots of the Red Summer represent the height of white mob riot activity in the United States, never surpassed in frequency, breadth, or severity. In addition to the 78 lynchings of black individuals by white mobs that year, white mobs also attacked entire black communities throughout the United States. The most well known of the Red Summer race riots are those that occurred in Charleston, South Carolina (May); Chicago, Illinois (July); Longview, Texas (July); Washington, D.C. (July); Knoxville, Tennessee (August); Omaha, Nebraska (September); and Elaine, Arkansas (October).

In May 1920, congressional Rep. Leonidas C. Dyer introduced an Anti-Lynching Bill in the House of Representatives. The bill contained a list of 26 riots, put together from the records of the National Association for the Advancement of Colored People (NAACP) and the Tuskegee Institute. The locations were Bisbee, Arizona; Elaine, Arkansas; New London, Connecticut; Wilmington, Delaware; Washington, D.C.; Blakely, Dublin, Millen, and Putnam counties, Georgia; Chicago and Bloomington, Illinois; Corbin, Kentucky; Homer and New Orleans, Louisiana; Annapolis and Baltimore, Maryland; Omaha, Nebraska; New York City and Syracuse, New York; Philadelphia, Pennsylvania; Charleston, South Carolina; Knoxville and Memphis, Tennessee; Longview and Port Arthur, Texas; and Norfolk, Virginia. Sen. Charles Curtis from Kansas introduced an anti-lynching bill to the Senate and used similar information.

Scholars have not yet determined the official total number of Red Summer riots, but the most often stated count is 26. Several factors make it difficult to establish an accurate number. At the time of the incidents, local officials sometimes suppressed information, invoking a code of silence. As time went on, many people wanted to forget the incidents; consequently, much information has been lost. Alternately, it was common practice for newspapers at the time, both white and black, to sensationalize any news whatsoever. Exaggerating, or in some cases even inventing, racial conflicts sold papers, so newspaper accounts cannot be taken at face value.

These local, national, and international newspaper accounts and other reports do suggest additional locations. The black press in both the United States and Great Britain devoted attention to the reporting of race riots, often in more graphic detail and with a political edge. Using these sources, an extended list of possible incidents in the United States contains 56 entries. A verification model in which an incident must appear on one of the NAACP, Tuskegee, or Dyer lists, in addition to a newspaper account, or be referred to in official government accounts, either local or federal, adds these riot locations to the ones on the Dyer list: Mulberry, Florida; Berkeley, Milan, and Cadwell, Georgia; Camp Zachary Taylor, Kentucky; Gary, Indiana; Bogalusa, Louisiana; Youngstown, Ohio; and Donora, Pennsylvania.

Another factor affecting the count is the definition of terms. Incidents such as those in Chicago and Omaha involved mobs of hundreds of whites rampaging through black neighborhoods, looting and burning property, and injuring people. These are clearly riots. In some incidents, however, such as those in Bisbee and New London, the mob comprised authorities of the law acting outside their official capacity while on duty. This type of situation requires interpretation as to whether, and at what point, the action became unlawful, thereby making it a riot. Other incidents involved smaller mobs, or the white mob was met with the resistance of an equal number of black people, and so these events may be considered by some sources or researchers to be fights or clashes, rather than riots.

The NAACP annual report from the years 1919 until 1923 uses the phrase *race riot* when reporting events in which white mobs targeted black communities. As the frequency of these events declined, the phrase fell out of common use, until, briefly, during the spate of riots after World War II. Then, during the riots in the 1960s, use of *race riot* was revived to describe events of destruction by mobs made up of black people. Such a transformation in meaning can generate confusion and can hide white responsibility for violence. Additionally, an alternate phrase, *white mob violence*, was used by many of the newspapers at that time as a euphemism for lynching.

In many ways, the Red Summer's antiblack riots were similar to lynchings. Both lynching mobs and rioting mobs used precipitating events as excuses to try to justify their violence, and in both cases these excuses were usually an alleged crime or social trespass of some sort by a black individual. Accusations of murder and rape were common, but sometimes it was an offense as minor as the failure to remove a hat. Both riots and lynchings were often inflamed by rumors, and were promoted and sensationalized in press coverage. The riots often included the murder of an accused person, and this murder was sometimes performed as a carefully enacted lynching ritual, with the riot preceding and/or following. Riots and lynchings produced a similar result—the targeted community was terrorized.

Yet the riots differed from lynchings in significant ways. Riot participation consistently crossed lines of age and gender. A riot targeted the entire community directly, while lynching targeted the community as a whole indirectly. Lynchings were highly ritualized, whereas riots, while conforming to a certain pattern, were less organized and more chaotic and random. Despite its popularity during the Red Summer, rioting never attained the level of societal approval that lynching did.

There was no one simple cause for this epidemic of white mob violence directed at black people. In some of the urban locations, there had been significant growth in the black population, resulting in overcrowding in the black neighborhoods and pressure on white neighborhoods to accommodate in various ways. World War I had just ended and many demobilized white troops returned home to find themselves competing with black workers for jobs and homes. Also, the war itself had acclimated people to the idea of using violence to solve problems, and had desensitized people to the horror of violence. Each of the Red Summer riots was a result of these overarching general factors combining with many other factors specific to each location.

The riots of the Red Summer can be sorted into four localized context categories. There were riots that occurred in relation to a labor dispute; involved military personnel as rioters or targets; related to local politics and a "boss" or political machine; and riots that rose out of a threatened, perceived, or actual rupture of the local racial caste system.

Lumber camps, textile mills, steel mills, mines, and waterfront docks were all sources of dangerous jobs requiring great numbers of strong laborers, and were places where black workers found employment during World War I. In 1919, unions were actively organizing in these industries, as they had been throughout the war. The racial composition of the unions varied. Many were all white; some were all black; some were biracial, with separate subdivisions by race; and a very few were beginning to be interracial, with membership recruitment from among both black and white workers. The high level of union activism heightened the tension among all parties in these industrial communities, adding yet another factor to the volatile postwar atmosphere, so it is no surprise that some of the Red Summer race riots occurred out of this context.

The labor-related riots took two forms. One pattern, by far the most common, was that of a mob of white strikers attacking black workers, regarding them as their enemy, competing for scarce jobs and status. During the Great Steel Strike, which affected much of the industrial Northeast for several months, as many as 40,000 black workers were brought in as strikebreakers. In Syracuse, New York, in July, striking iron molders attacked black workers at Globe Malleable Iron Works using clubs, stones, and firearms. Injuries to both workers and strikers occurred. Police made arrests and assigned all mounted officers, reserve patrolmen, and detectives to the area. Four white men were charged in the rioting.

In Gary, Indiana, the unions had excluded black workers who were already working in the mills. Once the steel strike began, they did try to get black workers to support it, but without success. U.S. Steel used local and nonlocal black strikebreakers, housing them in the plants or transporting them to and from work, for their safety. The riot in Gary occurred when several thousand strikers left a mass meeting and came on a streetcar bringing 40 strikebreakers, many black, into town. The strikers attacked the streetcar with stones and bricks, beating the workers and dragging them through the streets. Witnesses said that two of the black workers fought back with razors. The governor ordered in the state militia and finally requested federal troops. Gen. Leonard Wood, fresh from riot duty in Omaha, Nebraska, immediately declared martial law. The rioting in Gary broke the unions there.

For the *New York Times*, reporting the Great Steel Strike in Donora, Pennsylvania, the news was not that the strikers attacked the workers, or that most of those workers were black, but rather that the bulk of those attacked fought back. The first of two altercations occurred in the morning when black workers returned to work at the American Steel and Wire Company. They were attacked by strikers throwing bricks, and several of the workers were hurt. The workers then fired at the strikers with revolvers, wounding two men in the legs. State police broke up the incident. Then, that evening, strikers again threw bricks at the workers, injuring one woman and several men. Shots were fired without hitting anyone, and the workers fought back with fists and bricks.

In Youngstown, Ohio, also during the Great Steel Strike, black workers at Youngstown Sheet and Tube Company were attacked by strikers. Several workers were injured, one critically; one was killed. No injuries were reported among the strikers.

There were, on the other hand, industries and regions where black workers were union members. The other type of labor-related race riot took the form of a white mob, comprising company-hired assailants acting on behalf of an employer, attacking black union members out on strike. This type of riot was rare, and during the Red Summer happened only in Bogalusa, Louisiana, and Mulberry, Florida. In Bogalusa, the Great Southern Lumber Company, unhappy with unionizing in general, perceived the union of black lumber workers as a particular threat. A mob led by company men waged a violent campaign of fear and intimidation over a series of months, harassing the workers and their families, both white and black, in their homes. This campaign culminated in a riotous shoot-out in which four union men were killed.

In Mulberry, Florida, in what was probably an attempt to scare the black strikers back to work, a group of at least four white company guards from Prairie Pebble Mine fired directly into the black section of town, reportedly as many as 25 rounds, from high-powered rifles. At least three black people were hit; one, a two-year-old black boy, was killed, and the woman holding him, possibly his mother, was seriously wounded. Another black man was killed the same night when the guards continued to fire into Mulberry's black neighborhood.

The military subculture offered a particularly complex environment for interracial conflict to play out. While black troops had met with great success overseas during the war, and many had discovered a new definition of freedom, back in the United States during the Red Summer it was a different story. Many racist whites were threatened by the appearance of uniformed black men, and many white veterans were anxious to see any vestige of the temporarily esteemed status of their black compatriots restored to its prewar marginality. After the war, the government was closely studying the performance and role of black troops in order to determine the future attitude of the military toward its racial composition. Due in part to these complicated factors, the riots of the Red Summer display a full range of military involvement, with black soldiers in different roles in various circumstances, being alternately targets of violence, upholders of the law, and activists for change. White soldiers, as well, were variously stopping riots and starting them, and the target of the violence was sometimes black soldiers and sometimes black civilians.

Mobs of white sailors started riots in Charleston, South Carolina, and Washington, D.C., targeting black residents and their property indiscriminately. In Washington, D.C., the mob's excuse was an alleged assault by two black men of a white woman, following a barrage of newspaper sensationalism promoting fear of a black crime wave, and the rioting continued for days. In Charleston, the alleged offense was the pushing of a sailor off the sidewalk. In both cases, Marines were called in to stop the rioting.

In New London, Connecticut, tension between white sailors and black sailors erupted in violence. Each side had accused the other of lying in wait for them as they crossed Long Cove Bridge after dark. When two white "bluejackets" were arrested for a fight, their comrades were unable to make the police turn them loose. In frustration, the white sailors raided the Hotel Bristol, a popular congregating spot for black sailors. A group of hotel patrons was thrown into the street and severely beaten. Reinforcements arrived on both sides and the fighting continued. The town's police, even with the help of the fire department, were unable to stop the riot. Marines with rifles came and restored order.

In Bisbee, Arizona, local officials and off-duty white infantrymen harassed and assaulted with gunfire the black 10th U.S. Cavalry. Five people were shot. George Sullivan, a white military policeman with the 19th Infantry, passed by Brewery Gulch, a club popular with black soldiers, and there were words between him and five 10th Cavalrymen. The black soldiers went to the police station and reported the incident, and the police chief tried to confiscate their weapons. When they refused to give up their guns, the police went up to Brewery Gulch to disarm any black troops with weapons. Gunfire was exchanged, repeatedly, until 50 black soldiers were placed in custody. During the melee, bystanders were shot as well, including Teresa Leyvas, a Mexican resident of Bisbee who was struck in the head.

A celebration honoring the return of Norfolk, Virginia's black veterans was halted because of rioting in which six people were injured. The Norfolk City Council had planned a week-long celebration, but on the first day of the festivities, a black soldier was arrested and a riot followed. Soldiers and Marines were sent in from the naval base to help restore order.

At Camp Zachary Taylor, tension simmered for months between the black soldiers stationed there and the white residents of Louisville, Kentucky, as well as between the white soldiers stationed there and the black residents. Many fractious incidents occurred, but one in particular stood out, involving many black soldiers and a large crowd of whites, both military and civilian. The fracas developed when local white authorities arrested a black soldier, and his compatriots reacted with resistance. Violent confrontation followed.

Political players vying for power have exploited social turmoil to reach their goals since time immemorial, and such appears to be the case in at least three of the Red Summer riots. A relationship between a key player in the incident and the mayor of the locality or some other community leader is a red flag to identifying riots in this local context category.

In Milan, Georgia, Berry Washington was a venerable figure in the black community. When two white men, John Dowdy and Levi Evans, came into the black neighborhood and attacked two girls, Washington shot and killed one of the men. That the dead man was the son of a local minister is no doubt of some importance in the events that followed. A mob of 75 to 100 people lynched Washington and subsequently forced the entire black community out of their homes for two days.

Another example is the riot in Knoxville, Tennessee. Maurice Mays was a politically active man about town. It was rumored that his real father was the mayor of Knoxville, and son or not, on the day the trouble started, Mays had been distributing campaign literature for the mayor's reelection. Mays had his enemies among the police, and it was one of these enemies who arrested him for the murder of a white woman. The mob in Knoxville did not want to wait for the trial and was set on lynching him. He was successfully protected by the authorities, who moved him to another town, but when the mob was unable to obtain Mays, they raged through the black part of town, burning homes and shooting people. Seven people were killed, and 20 were injured.

In Omaha, Nebraska, Mayor Ed Smith was nearly killed when he attempted to stop a mob, numbering more than 1,000, from lynching a black man, Will Brown, accused of assaulting a white woman. After burning the courthouse, hanging and shooting Brown, and burning his body, the mob cut a path of destruction through Omaha's black neighborhoods. The mob's actions may have been motivated, defined, and even paid for, by the political machine of Tom Dennison. From 1897, Dennison had a mayor of his choice in place for 29 years, except for the 1918–1921 term, and he had a close relationship with the publisher of the *Omaha Bee*, which had been running sensationalized crime reports all summer. This, along with financial connections to certain leaders of the rioting mob, suggests that Dennison may have hoped to use the riot to discredit the local administration. In the next election, Smith was voted out of office, replaced with Dennison's man, James Dahlman.

The formal and informal structures of the binary black/white caste system, also known as the Jim Crow laws, were challenged in many ways after World War I, for the first time since Reconstruction. During the Red Summer, white mobs used these perceived caste ruptures as justification for violence.

One type of caste rupture, long at the heart of many racial conflicts, was demographic. The movement of black residents out of the neighborhoods allotted to them and into white neighborhoods heightened racial tension in many urban areas in the North. Demographic caste rupture was behind the rioting in Baltimore, Maryland, for example, where groups repeatedly clashed during the Red Summer as black residents moved into previously all-white neighborhoods. In one incident, white youths were harassing black residents with noise and taunts, and the residents complained to police many times without result. When the black residents confronted the youths, a mob of 50 whites, armed with bottles, bricks, and rocks, rioted. Police from two districts came to stop the disturbance.

The struggle of the black farmers in Phillips County, Arkansas, near the town of Elaine, represents economic caste rupture, as they began to try to break out of the peonage system by forming a Progressive Farmers and Household Union of America. The Southern agricultural system was structured in such a way that most blacks worked as farmhands or sharecroppers. The landlord provided supplies in advance, receiving in payment a share of the season's crop. The situation was rigged so that the sharecropper would remain perpetually in debt. The landlord rarely gave a written statement of account to the sharecropper, which many illiterate sharecroppers would not have been able to read, and the crop was just never enough to pay off what the sharecropper owed for supplies.

The whites in Phillips County were highly fearful of the Progressive Farmers and Household Union of America alliance, and rumors spread that an organized insurrection was imminent. On this pretext, white mobs, bolstered with people from nearby counties in Tennessee and Mississippi, hunted down, captured, and killed hundreds of black people, not only the farmers, but others as well. The highest profile deaths were those of the four Johnston brothers, among them a doctor and a dentist, who were killed while in custody of the authorities.

Other riots occurred out of a more general context of caste rupture in which whites were threatened by perceived differences in quality of life. In both Millen and Cadwell, Georgia, a fear that blacks were building a strong cultural alliance led whites to attack the symbols of the black community along with its leaders, burning a total of 11 church and lodge buildings and killing eight people. White locals in Corbin, Kentucky, ran black railroad workers out of town for challenging local social mores. Similarly, in Longview, Texas, whites were threatened by the economic success of the local black community and its increasingly expanded worldview inspired by the national black press. There, a mob of 1,000 white men, armed with rifles, pistols, and stolen ammunition, went to the black neighborhood, set several houses on fire, and shot several people.

Isolated incidents of caste rupture precipitated other riots. In Dublin, Georgia, black citizens fought against a mob to prevent a lynching. In New York City, a black man grabbed the straw hat of an off-duty white police officer. The officer retaliated by shooting his gun, and a racial melee ensued, involving large numbers of whites and blacks fighting one another.

Philadelphia, Pennsylvania, having had a huge race riot in 1918, suffered through the Red Summer with several racial clashes, one of which was reported as a riot. At a carnival, a crowd of whites fought a crowd of blacks, but most trouble was averted when 100 police officers showed up and made arrests.

In Wilmington, Delaware, a white mob formed in hopes of lynching two black men accused of killing a police officer, but the men had been moved to Philadelphia. Someone opened fire on the mob, which fired back and then proceeded to move through the black neighborhood vandalizing homes and other property.

The contagion theory of rioting has been applied to the Red Summer, the hypothesis being that many of these riots would not have happened without those that preceded, leading the way. This theory is practically impossible to test, but one riot was so lame in its triggering incident and weak in its execution that contagion is the most likely explanation. On a Port Arthur, Texas, streetcar, a black man was accused of smoking in the presence of a white woman. A white mob, estimated by witnesses as numbering 40, attacked him, and a group of black men, numbering about 20, fought back. Port Arthur is located between Houston, which had a serious race riot in 1918, and Longview, a location of one of the major Red Summer riots, which had occurred only a week or so prior to the Port Arthur incident.

The Red Summer rioting in Chicago crosses the categories, because labor issues, political maneuvering, as well as demographic caste rupture, were all present. The incident that triggered the rioting there was the stoning and subsequent drowning of teenager Eugene Williams. Williams had, while swimming, strayed into the white part of the lake, and white people started throwing rocks at him. Unable to keep his head out of the water because of the rocks, he drowned. When a police officer at the scene refused to arrest the rock throwers, black citizens became angry, and the officer arrested them instead. Whites throughout the city used this as an opportunity to vent their rage, stoked that summer by competition for jobs and housing. White gangs, such as Regan's Colts, sought out trouble as a way of asserting power. Some scholars argue that labor unions played a large role, particularly in the meatpacking industry, while other scholars counter that if labor had gotten involved, things would then have been much worse, given meatpackers' skill with knives.

Immediately after World War I, the entire world reeled with change. There had been the Bolshevik Revolution in Russia in 1917. In Peru, there were rebellions and a great climate of unrest as the indigenous people revolted in unprecedented numbers and uprisings were met with massacres and mob violence. There were labor strikes in Colombia; the British government killings of many protesters in the Amritsar province of India; and unrest in many Muslim populations.

In South Africa, defiant demonstrations led to skirmishes between protesters and police, and later to conflict between groups of whites and blacks.

During the five-year span of World War I and subsequent postwar adjustment, from 1917 to 1921, the tenor of the times reverberated with increased nativism, racism, fear, suspicion, and economic uncertainty. A key feature of the political climate was the Red Scare, promoted and driven by Attorney General A. Mitchell Palmer. Promoting the fear of a Red menace made up of anarchists, radicals, Bolshevik propagandists, and revolutionaries, Palmer suspected the American labor movement was being infiltrated and polluted. Palmer used labor unrest and a series of letter bombs as evidence that sinister organizing was taking place nationally.

Palmer and his believers thought this radical trade unionism was gearing up to destroy capitalism in the United States and establish a new social order, ruled by the workers. Race was a focus of this Red Scare fear. The federal government was convinced that American blacks as a group were vulnerable to the persuasions of the Bolsheviks, and much money and resources were allotted to monitoring and infiltrating radical black activity. The Department of Justice, the Federal Bureau of Investigation, the State Department, the General Intelligence Division, the Department of the Post Office, the Military Intelligence Division, and the Office of Naval Intelligence are all on record as being concerned with finding a link between Bolshevik propaganda and black militancy. Black publications, including the *Messenger*, the *Chicago Defender*, the *Whip*, the *Crusader*, and the *Emancipator* were carefully watched for what was referred to as "Negro subversion." Some of the weekly newspapers and monthly magazines were investigated and censured, and in some cases were withheld from distribution, or confiscated altogether. The Post Office sometimes revoked the second-class permit of a publication, forcing an underfunded publisher to pay first-class postage rates, effectively silencing the issue.

It was in this climate that race relations among the U.S. populace took on the volatility that allowed for the violence of the Red Summer. White violence increased and diversified. Black response became more active and focused. World War I had brought something new to the United States—that of the heroic return of the black soldier. One reaction was the revival of the Ku Klux Klan, and the Red Summer race riots

were akin to this spirit. This racism was not universal. Both the mayor of Knoxville and the governor of Tennessee, for example, went on record as repudiating the organization. The national black news magazine *The Crisis* summed up the situation by pointing out that the black soldier, after facing chemical warfare and artillery fire in the war, was not going to be intimidated by a bunch of cowards running around in bed linens. Rather, the article said, the war had taught black soldiers to face a danger and see it through.

The Red Summer race riots became a turning point in the history of race relations in the United States. White racists learned that the mob spirit methodology was not the powerful tool it may once have been, and that white mob violence would be met with both theoretical and practical resistance from black people, along with societal resistance, in the form of legislation and social policy lobbying and activism. Although ultimately the Dyer Anti-Lynching Bill was not enacted, the fight for its passage was part of a social and cultural force that laid the groundwork for the later rise of the civil rights movement.

JAN VOOGD

See also

Jim Crow Laws; Labor Unions; Lynching; World War I; Race Riots in America. Documents: Report on the Memphis Riots of May 1866 (1866); Account of the Riots in East St. Louis, Illinois (1917); A Southern Black Woman's Letter Regarding the Recent Riots in Chicago and Washington (1919); The Cook County Coroner's Report Regarding the 1919 Chicago Race Riots (1920); The Final Report of the Grand Jury on the Tulsa Race Riot (June 25, 1921); Testimony from *Laney v. United States* (1923); The Governor's Commission Report on the Watts Riots (1965); Cyrus R. Vance's Report on the Riots in Detroit (1967); The Reports of the Oklahoma Commission to Study the Tulsa Race Riot of 1921 (2000–2001); Draft Report: 1898 Wilmington Race Riot Commission (2005)

Further Reading:

Cortner, Richard C. *A Mob Intent on Death*. Middletown, CT: Wesleyan University Press, 1988.

Flynt, Wayne. "Florida Labor and Political 'Radicalism,' 1919–1920." *Labor History* 9 (1968).

Kitchens, John W., ed. *Tuskegee Institute News Clippings File*. Sanford, NC: Microfilming Corporation of America, 1981.

Kornweibel, Theodore. *"Seeing Red": Federal Campaigns against Black Militancy, 1919–1925*. Bloomington and Indianapolis: Indiana University Press, 1998.

Lakin, Matthew. "'A Dark Night': The Knoxville Race Riot of 1919." *Journal of East Tennessee History* 72 (2000): 1–29.

Meier, August, ed. *Papers of the NAACP*. Part 7, Series A. Frederick, MD: University Publications of America, 1981.

Murray, Robert K. *Red Scare: A Study of National Hysteria, 1919–1920*. Minneapolis: University of Minnesota Press, 1955.

Norwood, Stephen. "Bogalusa Burning: The War Against Biracial Unionism in the Deep South, 1919." *Journal of Southern History* 63 (1997): 591–628.

Palmer, A. Mitchell, Attorney General. *Investigation Activities of the Department of Justice*. 66th Congress, 1st Session, Senate Document 153, Vol. XII. 1919.

Schmidt, Regin. *Red Scare: FBI and the Origins of Anticommunism in the United States, 1919–1943*. Copenhagen, Denmark: Museum Tusculanum Press, 2000.

Stockley, Grif. *Blood in Their Eyes: The Elaine Race Massacres of 1919*. Fayetteville: University of Arkansas Press, 2001.

Tuttle, William. *Race Riot: Chicago in the Red Summer of 1919*. Urbana: University of Illinois Press, 1996.

Waskow, Arthur O. *From Race Riot to Sit-In, 1919 and the 1960s; A Study in the Connections between Conflict and Violence*. Garden City, NY: Anchor Books, 1966.

Reparations

Reparations are defined as the act or process of making amends through compensation or some other means. Efforts to allocate reparations to black slaves and their descendants in America have a long and thorny history. Early on, some whites made significant attempts to address the damage slavery had inflicted on freedmen and freedwomen, but they were thwarted at every turn. White mobs, particularly in the South, often used violence to suppress blacks, thus preventing them from seeking restitution. Significant black crusades for reparations did not occur until the 1950s. A number of individuals and organizations have since joined the movement, but they continue to face massive resistance. In 1994 and 2004, respectively, survivors of the Rosewood massacre and the Tulsa race riot received reparations.

During Reconstruction, several attempts were made to ameliorate the residual aftereffects of slavery on blacks. Congress established the Freedmen's Bureau to provide aid to former slaves. This aid focused on what the bureau believed to be their most urgent needs—food, medical care, education, and land. The bureau, with the help of numerous blacks, was able to accomplish this goal to a limited degree. Their greatest contribution was the establishment of new schools. For the first time ever, black politicians were elected into office. However, by 1877, Southern white Democrats had ousted all black politicians from office throughout the nation.

In 1865, Gen. William Tecumseh Sherman declared that the land confiscated during the war should be given to former slaves. Congress charged the Freedmen's Bureau to distribute that land. Word of the promise of "40 acres and a mule" spread quickly amongst blacks. However, President Andrew Johnson returned the land to the former slave owners instead. In 1866, opposition to Congress's Southern Homestead Act prevented all but 1,000 blacks from buying land at low cost. Thaddeus Stevens proposed a slave reparations bill, which would allot 40 acres of land and $100 to build a home for every recently freed male, but it did not pass. A few proponents of Black Nationalism, such as Henry McNeil Turner, also advocated reparations. Turner sought financial assistance from whites to support black migrations to Africa. He believed blacks were owed remuneration as a result of several hundred years of forced slavery and unpaid wages. He received support from the American Colonization Society. In 1915, blacks failed to win a lawsuit against the U.S. Treasury Department for labor rendered during slavery.

Blacks benefited little from Reconstruction, as systematic subjugation and violence kept blacks in check. Landless, penniless, and denied the freedoms and opportunities they had anticipated after Emancipation, blacks were disheartened. Nonetheless, with the exception of a few dauntless leaders, blacks did not openly demand retribution. White mobs squelched black opponents and white sympathizers through violence and intimidation. Following Reconstruction, race riots occurred throughout the nation. In these riots, whites often murdered and raped blacks, and burned down their homes, churches, and businesses. Among the decimated communities were Tulsa, Oklahoma, and Rosewood, Florida.

The Tulsa (Oklahoma) Riot of 1921 was one of the most horrendous assaults on a black community in the nation. A young white woman charged that she had been raped in an elevator in a public building by a black youth, who was put in jail. Armed black men, hearing rumors that a white mob had formed to lynch the youth, gathered to guard him. A mob confronted the black men and a riot ensued. By the

Survivor of the 1921 Tulsa race riots, Wess Young, 88, right, with fellow survivors, Dr. Olivia Hooker, 90, second right, and Otis Granville Clark, 102, third right, gives his personal account of the historic race riot before members of the Congressional Black Caucus and other leaders, on Capitol Hill, May 2005, in Washington. After being silenced for more than half a century, survivors of one of our nation's worst incidents of racial violence finally had a chance to tell their stories to America's lawmakers. (AP Photo/Manuel Balce Ceneta)

time the National Guard arrived, the community had been ravaged: white mobs killed several hundred blacks, looted their homes, and burned down more than 1,200 buildings. Fifty whites were killed, and no members of the mob were charged with crimes.

On New Year's Eve, 1923, a white mob invaded the thriving black community of Rosewood after a white woman named Fannie Taylor falsely accused a black man of attacking her. During the seven days the riot lasted, the mob burned Rosewood to the ground and murdered eight to 17 people (the actual numbers are not known). Many of the survivors narrowly escaped by hiding in nearby swamps. With help from local whites, they eventually managed to get out

of Rosewood. Local law enforcement did not provide protection, and the perpetrators were never punished. Out of fear, the survivors did not attempt to return to Rosewood to reclaim their property, nor did they speak out against the violence against them.

The modern reparations movement occurred simultaneously with the nonviolent activism of the 1950s and 1960s. In 1955, Queen Mother Audley Moore founded the Reparations Committee of Descendants of the United States Slaves. On a Sunday morning in 1962, the committee filed a claim in California, without results. Seven years later, James Forman, a member of the Student Nonviolent Coordinating Committee proclaimed his Black Manifesto at the Riverside Church in

Manhattan, New York. The manifesto demanded $500 million from the churches and synagogues and outlined how the money would be used to finance social programs, businesses, education, and other institutions to advance blacks. Surprisingly, the minister of the church was sympathetic. In a radio announcement, he acknowledged the abuses and degradations long suffered by blacks and defended Forman's demand for redress.

Reparations activism increased during the latter half of the 20th century. The 1980s brought forth critical wins in reparations for other racial groups. For example, in 1980, the Supreme Court ordered the federal government to pay eight Sioux Indian tribes $122 million to compensate for the illegal seizure of tribal lands (in 1877). In 1988, the United States issued an apology and paid out $1.25 billion to 60,000 Japanese-Americans who had been forcefully placed into internment camps during World War II. As blacks continued to grapple with state and federal governments for reparations, the wins experienced by other races helped support their cause.

In 1989, Rep. John Conyers introduced the Commission to Study Reparation Proposals for African Americans Act, the first of several reparations bills he proposed to the House of Representatives. None of these bills passed. Also in 1989, Detroit City Council member Ray Jenkins requested $40 billion in federal education monies to form a fund for black college and trade school students. In *Cato v. United States* (1995), blacks were denied $100 million in reparations and an apology for slavery. In 1997, President Bill Clinton spoke of the evils of slavery and the need to resolve the effects it had on blacks. In 2000, Rep. Tony Hall proposed bill H.R. 356, which would acknowledge and apologize for slavery. This bill did not pass. In 2002, a former law student filed a federal lawsuit against several American corporations for their involvement in slavery. None of the companies has yet to pay reparations to blacks, but Aetna did make a formal apology for having insured slaves. Compensation is sought for the profits the companies gained at the expense of enslaved blacks, and for wages not paid to slaves. Many other individuals and organizations, such as the Nation of Islam and the Race Relations Institute at Fisk University, have contributed to the struggle for reparations. These groups regularly sponsor conferences and engage in marches to rally support.

Despite the repeated refusal to grant reparations, victims of the Tulsa, Oklahoma riot (1921) and the Rosewood massacre (1923) achieved significant victories in 1994 and 2004. In both of these incidents, white mobs either destroyed or stole property that had belonged to blacks. White capping was a common occurrence, particularly in the South and between 1900 and 1929. The practice, which got its name from the white caps the participants wore, involved whites who terrorized and threatened blacks for the purpose of seizing their property. Between 1880 and the 1900s, there were at least 239 occurrences of white capping.

In 1997, the Oklahoma Legislature created the Tulsa Race Riot Commission to explore recommendations for reparations. In 2002, Tulsa race riot survivors received reparations payments totaling $28,000. After a two-year legal battle, Florida's governor Lawton Chiles approved the Rosewood Claims Bill, which provided more than $2 million in reparations for the survivors, as well as scholarships for their descendants. This win was an acknowledgement that the state was responsible for not protecting the lives and property of its constituents. Significantly, the Rosewood attorneys partially predicated the lawsuit on cases involving Japanese Americans and Jewish Holocaust survivors.

Blacks believe reparations, whether in the form of monetary compensation, stock, land, a formal apology, or other actions, are crucial to righting the wrongs committed against—and still affecting—blacks. They argue that some whites unlawfully deprived their ancestors of freedom, life, property, equality, as well as social, economic, and political power, and that atonement is necessary.

The arguments against reparations movements are numerous. Former president Bill Clinton, although he empathized with the horrific history of blacks in America and took on a race relations initiative, commented that too much time had elapsed since slavery, and that the persons culpable for the suffering of blacks no longer existed. In place of reparations, he recommended that the country must come up with remedies to fix the disproportionate hardships experienced by blacks. Other individuals opposed to reparations point to the innumerable programs to alleviate current social problems for blacks and other disadvantaged groups. Clinton also suggested that America should work toward creating a more diverse and racially inclusive democracy. On the other hand, many supporters of reparations are not looking for corrective programs. They argue that programs such as affirmative action have better assisted other groups—not blacks—and do not make amends for the monies owed their ancestors for their slave labor, the indignities and hostilities inflicted on them, or their lost property.

Another prominent opponent is David Horowitz, a conservative author and political commentator who wrote *Uncivil Wars: The Controversy over Reparations for Slavery* (2002). One of his arguments against reparations is that they are racist. Opponents also argue that blacks are better off in America than they would have been in Africa. They also believe that the impoverished and crime-ridden inner cities—not slavery—are the cause of the current plight of blacks and point to the many blacks who have done well in America. Other popular arguments include the point that a reparations plan would be too expensive, and that slavery, though horrendous, was sanctioned, and, therefore, amends cannot legally be made.

Reparations adherents believe that expiations are more than reasonable and justifiable. They assert that the concept is not racist, and that reparations will actually help relieve the disillusionment many blacks feel toward the United States, and the feeling that America exhibits enmity toward them. They also point to the conditions of slavery that caused the so-called modern-day ills, such as broken families and poverty. They believe that life under Jim Crow, where blacks were denied the access, opportunities, and resources to better themselves, continues to affect them today, and that successful blacks make up only a small percentage of the population. Although slavery was legal, reparations activists claim that since Reconstruction, many whites have violated federal ordinances, such as the Fourteenth Amendment, to secure control over blacks.

Reparations proponents look to other groups and their causes to strengthen their arguments. For example, Holocaust survivors received reparations despite laws that enforced discrimination against Jews, and tort laws permit individuals who have been harmed by toxic waste to seek out compensation for medical care costs, lost wages, and pain and suffering, even if the exposure originated from an incident that occurred over 100 years ago. The recent triumphs of the Rosewood and Tulsa race riot survivors are two poignant cases in point. Reparations activists celebrated when, after many years of blatant, unrepentant, and uncensored crimes against blacks, the authorities finally acknowledged responsibility and made amends to the victims.

GLADYS L. KNIGHT

See also
Anti-racism; Jim Crow Laws; Slavery

Further Reading:
Horowitz, David. *Uncivil Wars: The Controversy over Reparations for Slavery*. San Francisco: Encounter Books, 2002.
Winbush, Raymond A. *Should America Pay?: Slavery and the Raging Debate on Reparations*. New York: HarperCollins, 2001.

Reservations and Casinos

Casinos have become a pervasive part of the public image of contemporary Native Americans. Since the 1970s, casinos and other gaming operations have become a source of income and development on many Native American reservations. Common misperceptions of the nature of Indian gaming include the myth of the "rich Indian." "Indian gaming" is defined by federal law as gaming (casinos, bingo halls, and other gaming operations) conducted by an "Indian tribe" on "Indian lands," meaning a federally recognized tribal government conducting gaming operations on federal reservation lands or on trust lands. Indian casinos have also been a source of suspicion for non-Natives who do not understand why Native Americans are "allowed" to have casinos when other groups are not.

The main difference between tribal gaming and commercial gambling is that tribal gaming is conducted by tribal governments for the main purpose of benefiting tribal members. Reservations and reservation casinos are both founded on the concept of tribal sovereignty. The development of casinos and other gaming on Native American reservations was a result of legal decisions regarding the sovereignty of tribal governments. *Bryan vs. Itasca County* was the 1976 Supreme Court case in which it was decided that states did not have the authority to tax Indians living on Indian lands, neither did it have the right to regulate the activities of Indians living on Indian lands.

The U.S. Constitution states that the federal government has jurisdiction over Indian reservations, but in 1953,

Bryan v. Itasca County (1976)

Bryan v. Itasca County was the landmark 1976 Supreme Court decision that paved the way to Native American gaming on reservation lands. Russell and Helen Bryan, a Chippewa couple living on Indian land in Minnesota, received a $147 property tax bill from the county in which their land resided. Refusing to pay it, they took it to legal aid attorneys who challenged the tax in the Minnesota courts. After the case was lost at both the district and state supreme court, they submitted it for review by the U.S. Supreme Court. It was accepted for review, and Justice Brennan authored the unanimous decision that held that states do not have the authority to tax Indians on Indian reservation land. The decision, however, went beyond the issue of taxation to declare that the states do not have the authority to regulate activities by Indians on Indian reservations. It was this portion of the decision that provided the legal basis for Indian gaming.

Congress passed Public Law 280 giving criminal jurisdiction to certain states. After several other court cases over the years, the Indian Gaming Regulatory Act (IGRA) of 1988 was passed to address confusion about state and federal jurisdiction over Indian gaming. The act declared that Indian tribes have the right to regulate gaming activity on Indian lands if that gaming activity is not specifically prohibited by federal law, and if the gaming is conducted within a state which does not prohibit that gaming activity. The IGRA established the National Indian Gaming Commission (NIGC) as a regulatory body. The stated goals of the NIGC are: (1) promoting tribal economic development, self-sufficiency, and strong tribal governments; (2) maintaining the integrity of the Indian gaming industry; and (3) ensuring that tribes are the primary beneficiaries of their gaming activities. The Indian Gaming Working Group was created in 2004 by the Federal Bureau of Investigation and the NIGC to address criminal violations in Indian gaming.

According to Darian-Smith (2004), for many Native Americans gambling does not have the same moral meaning as it does in mainstream Western societies. Rather than being seen as being associated with deviance and immorality, Native American communities tend to view gaming behavior as an important way to learn lessons about winning and losing. Devoid of the moral connotations, casinos and other gaming facilities are mainly viewed as a means to an economic end. However, because of the mainstream view of gambling with its negative connotations, Indian gaming is an opportunity for some to connect general negative associations with gambling to older stereotypes of the "savage" Indian who lacks self-control and discipline. A high-profile case, the Pequot tribe of Connecticut, sealed the stereotype of the "rich casino Indian" in the imaginations of many non-Native American. This stereotype has led to depictions of the mystical but shrewd Indian casino businessman in mainstream media.

In 2000, the median household income for Native Americans was 25 percent lower than that of the entire U.S. population, and Indians living on reservation have lower income levels and higher unemployment and poverty than those who do not. For tribes that operate casinos and other gaming businesses, the revenue gambling activities generates can be a tremendous help to tribe members. Economist Robin Anderson found that Native Americans living on gaming reservations with large or medium casinos gained an average 7.4 percent increase in per capita income compared to those living on nongaming reservations, as well as a reduction in family and child poverty rates. Living on reservations with smaller casinos was not associated with improvements in well-being. Per capita income is affected by gaming in a number of ways including an increase in wages paid to individuals, employment rates, and cash transfers from the tribe to members from gaming revenue.

Despite these gains in economic well-being for members of some tribes, only about a quarter of all recognized tribes operate gaming ventures, and casinos are not universally accepted or successful among all nations. For tribes, the geographic isolation of tribal lands from metropolitan areas and potential customers has made economic success difficult if not impossible. There are also many tribal leaders and members who do not fully approve of gaming as an economic strategy, and would prefer to use the profits from gaming to develop other economic activities. As the 21st century unfolds, the fate of the well-being of Native American communities may well rest on the success of gaming and its ability to spur diverse economic development.

RENEE S. ALSTON

See also

Indian Reservations; Tribal Sovereignty. Document: *California v. Cabazon Band of Mission Indians* (1987)

Further Reading:

Anderson, Robin J., "Tribal Casino Impacts on American Indians Well-Being: Evidence from Reservation-Level Census Data." *Contemporary Economic Policy.* 2011.

Darian-Smith, Eve. *New Capitalists: Law, Politics, and Identity Surrounding Casino Gaming on Native American Land.* Belmont, CA: Wadsworth, 2004.

Light, Stephen A., and Kathryn R. L. Rand. *Indian Gaming and Tribal Sovereignty: The Casino Compromise.* Lawrence: University Press of Kansas, 2005.

National Indian Gaming Association. http://www.indiangaming .org/.

Reagan, Patricia B., and Robert. J. Gitter. "Is Gaming the Optimal Strategy? The Impact of Gaming Facilities on the Income and Employment of American Indians." *Economics Letters* 95 (2007): 428–32.

Residential Segregation

The term *residential segregation* is used to describe the creation and maintenance of separate neighborhoods for various racial and ethnic groups. Segregation can be either voluntary or involuntary. Involuntary segregation occurs when members of a minority group are forced to live in segregated neighborhoods against their will. There is a long history of racial residential segregation in the United States. Despite some modest to moderate declines in levels of segregation, racially separate neighborhoods remain quite common in the United States. African Americans, in particular, still maintain a high level of involuntary segregation partly because of various forms of housing discrimination and mainly because of the tendency of white Americans to avoid contact with them. The persistence of racial residential segregation among African Americans and other racial minority groups has some serious negative implications for the quality of their lives.

Sociologists have created the dissimilarity index to measure the level of segregation. The scores for the dissimilarity index range from 0 to 100. A score closer to 0 suggests that the two groups are almost completely integrated, while a score closer to 100 indicates that they are almost completely segregated.

A dissimilarity index of 0.5 between African Americans and whites means that one-half of the African American population should move to white neighborhoods to achieve complete residential integration between the two groups.

Most measures indicate that residential segregation has declined for African Americans in the last two decades. Even with these moderate declines, segregation levels for African Americans remain high. In 2000, the dissimilarity index for African Americans was .640, which represents a 12 percent decline since 1980. An exceptionally high level of overall segregation for African Americans is partly the function of their high concentration in major American cities, as the level of segregation is highly correlated with the level of the population concentration.

Since the 1970s, African Americans, like all Americans, have been steadily increasing their presence in the suburbs. This suburban movement has contributed to the modest declines in segregation levels for African Americans. Nevertheless, the levels of residential segregation for African Americans remain high, because even in the suburbs they remain isolated from other racial groups, especially whites. African Americans tend to reside in older suburbs that have been abandoned by whites. Even wealthier African Americans who do reside in new suburban communities tend to reside in predominantly African American communities in an effort to avoid harassment from white neighbors who may not be pleased to have them as neighbors.

Most of the indices used to measure residential segregation indicate an increase for Hispanic Americans between 1980 and 2000. The dissimilarity index for Hispanic and Latino Americans in 2000 was .509, which represents a 1.5 percent increase since 1980. This is not a large increase and mostly represents voluntary segregation among recent Hispanic immigrants who settle in ethnic enclaves that have an abundance of resources for new immigrants. Hispanics who were born in the United States and reside in medium to large cities have experienced steadily lower levels of residential segregation than blacks.

Most of the sizable concentrations of Asians and Pacific Islanders are found on the West Coast. Several measures of residential segregation indicate increases in segregation for both groups since the 1980s. The greater the percentage of the population accounted for by Asians and Pacific Islanders in a metropolitan area, the more isolated they are and the more likely they are to live together. The various segregation indices suggest that Asians are more segregated than Pacific Islanders. Based on the dissimilarity index estimate, the segregation of Asian Americans increased by 14 percent between 1980 and 2000 to .411, but it is not high, compared with African Americans and Hispanics.

These lower levels of segregation among Asian Americans are in great part due to the ability of Asian immigrants to bring enough economic resources to the United States to purchase the American dream house in the suburbs. Asian Americans have moved into the suburbs of U.S. metropolitan areas at a great rate. This high level of suburbanization for Asian Americans also reflects the low level of resistance they received from white suburban dwellers upon moving into predominantly white neighborhoods.

Levels of residential segregation for Hispanics and Asian Americans are not explained by the attitudes of whites to the same extent that segregation levels for African Americans are. Many Hispanic and Asian Americans voluntarily segregate themselves by establishing enclaves. In the enclave, they can associate with others who share a similar background and have access to the resources and commodities that they are accustomed to in their home countries. New and recent immigrants find living and working in these communities to be extremely beneficial because they are able to establish social networks, which help them to navigate their new environs.

Since the early 1980s, Native Americans have experienced an 11 percent nationwide decline in residential segregation, with midsize metropolitan areas having less residential segregation than large and small ones. The dissimilarity index for Native Americans in all metropolitan areas in 2000 was .333, which is not indicative of drastic segregation, as only 33 percent of the population would have to move to achieve complete integration.

The low levels of residential segregation for Native Americans in metropolitan areas generally reflect lower levels of prejudice toward Native Americans compared with African Americans. The rate of intermarriage between Native Americans and whites is quite high, especially in comparison to the level of intermarriage between African Americans and whites. The levels of residential segregation for Native Americans and their levels of intermarriage with white Americans suggest that Native Americans are much more accepted by

white Americans than are African Americans. The Native American population in urban areas is quite small as well, so it is easy for the population to be dispersed in metropolitan areas. The lack of concentrated Native American communities in urban areas prevents other Americans from feeling threatened by their presence.

White Prejudice and White Preference

The hierarchy of residential settlement patterns suggests that white Americans are most comfortable living in neighborhoods where they are in the majority. When nonwhite families move into their neighborhoods, they are most at ease with the presence of Asian Americans, followed by Hispanics, and are most uncomfortable with African Americans.

Attitudes toward integrated housing have changed considerably over the last several decades. Many whites cite concerns about higher levels of crime, lower property values, and a lack of respect for culture as reasons for their reluctance to live in neighborhoods with large numbers of minority members in general and African Americans in particular. Gradually, the tipping point or the percentage of African American households in a white neighborhood that would lead whites to leave, also known as "white flight," has increased over time. In 1976, 7 percent of whites said they would move if one of 15 homes in their neighborhood were occupied by African Americans, but by 1992 only 4 percent indicated this neighborhood composition would motivate them to move.

Whites' attitudes regarding neighborhood composition have changed considerably over time. In 1976, only 16 percent of whites were willing to move into a neighborhood where 53 percent of the homes were black. By 1992, 29 percent of whites were willing to move into such a neighborhood. By contrast, almost all blacks preferred to live in such a racially mixed neighborhood in the two time periods (99 percent in 1976 and 98 percent in 1992). Despite moderate changes in whites' attitudes over the years, there is still a big difference between African Americans and whites in the type of neighborhood they find most comfortable. Also notable is the decline from 1976 to 1992 in the percentage of African Americans who were willing to move into all-white neighborhoods (from 38 percent to 31 percent) and the increase in the percentage of African Americans who were willing to live in all-black neighborhoods (from 69 percent to 75 percent).

Dual Housing Markets

Dual housing markets refers to racially segmented housing markets that provide different resources and opportunities (one for whites and one for blacks in particular). The persistent racial segregation in U.S. metropolitan areas has turned many scholars' attention to the existence of a dual housing market, in which racial minorities are served by a different set of housing and real estate practices than are whites. These scholars argue that dual housing markets have reinforced and perpetuated racial segregation through the use of racial steering, block-busting, home-mortgage programs of various public and private lending institutions, and the redlining activities of mortgage lending agencies and real estate firms. Moreover, it has been found that housing prices and rents are generally higher for blacks than for whites and that conventional loans for home purchases and remodeling tend to be more available to whites, whereas blacks are often forced to buy with cash, on contract, or through federal loan programs. There is also evidence that dual housing markets have channeled blacks and whites into different types of dwellings. Blacks at every income level tend to live in lower-quality dwellings than their white counterparts. As a result, a white majority occupies the outlying areas of new construction and existing zones of superior residential amenity in metropolitan areas, while blacks and other minority groups are restricted to multifamily projects, public housing units, and deteriorating housing in inner cities.

SOOKHEE OH

Apparently, some African Americans have given up the idea of racially integrated neighborhoods, but why?

African Americans express serious concerns about moving into predominantly white communities. They fear that white neighbors may display hostile attitudes or even threaten them with physical harm. Attitudes have changed, but the change has been slow and attitudes do not always match actions. Despite more tolerance among white Americans for integrated neighborhoods and a desire among African Americans for more integrated communities, measures indicate high levels of residential segregation for African Americans. In fact, whites and African Americans are more segregated from each other than any other two groups.

Recent research indicates that the primary determinant of residential segregation is one's economic status. This literature suggests that rather than choosing where to live based on one's racial status, the financially better off isolate themselves from the economically disadvantaged regardless of race. Still, there are considerable differences in wealth between whites and racial minorities. The average net financial worth of whites is considerably more than that of African Americans and Hispanic Americans. Racial minorities are a disproportionate share of the low-income population. The economic disparity between whites and racial minorities does translate into real differences in terms of buying power when it comes to choosing a neighborhood and contributes to African Americans' and Hispanics' much lower rates of home ownership when compared to whites. So, opportunities for whites and minorities to live together are constrained due to disparities in wealth.

The economic explanation for residential segregation patterns that implies that rich whites and rich people of color will live together, while poor people regardless of race will live together has largely been discounted, because upper- and middle-class minorities, especially African Americans, have a difficult time establishing separate residential communities from poor minorities. Meanwhile, wealthy whites certainly do not often share their zip code with poor whites.

There is a long legacy of separate living communities for whites and people of color in the United States. After slavery was abolished, separate communities for whites and African Americans were established. This separation was further encouraged by housing laws and policies. Zoning laws and ordinances prevented mixed-race residential areas or subtly discouraged them by regulating the sizes of houses and lots that could be built in certain neighborhoods. Today, many communities have restrictions that prohibit the erection of multiple-dweller units, such as apartments and duplexes, which might be more economically feasible for some minority families. American housing laws have also served to limit the range of possible neighborhoods available to Asian

Exposure Index

Researchers studying racial/ethnic segregation of residential areas or school systems sometimes use an "exposure index" as a measure, either in conjunction with or as an alternative to the index of dissimilarity. For example, an exposure index can be computed to rank a city's schools in terms of how much interracial contact they provide in their classrooms. In doing this, exposure-index computations indicate, for students who are black (or for any race/ethnicity being studied), the average percentage of their classmates who are black and the average percentage that are of some other race/ethnicity. In other words, this index measures how much or little exposure the average member of one racial/ethnic group has in his or her classroom (or in a neighborhood, if one is studying residential segregation) to fellow members of the group and to members of other groups. Zero is the lowest value an exposure index can have, if a school's index measuring exposure of blacks to whites is 0, then black students in that school do not have any whites in their classes. If the black-to-white exposure index is 40 (or 0.40 if proportions are used), then the average black student is in a class in which 40 percent of his or her classmates are white; 100 (or 1.00) is the maximum value.

An interesting feature of exposure indexes is that they are "asymmetrical," unlike the index of dissimilarity and other measures of segregation. This means that exposure indexes reflect the principle that the level of contact experienced by a pair of groups can vary depending on from which group's perspective one views the situation. For example, in a school in which most classes comprise many whites and few Latinos (e.g., 28 white students and two Latino students), the white-to-Latino exposure index is low, but the Latino-to-white exposure index is high. This distinction is important in comprehending the results of research on school resegregation reported by organizations such as the Harvard University Civil Rights Project.

CHARLES JARET

Americans. Anti-immigration policies, such as the Alien Land Law, which were introduced in the western states during the 20th century, extended to housing policies, precluding Asian immigrants from settling in certain areas.

The 1934 Federal Housing Act established the Federal Housing Administration (FHA) to insure private mortgage loans and provide protection to lenders against losses on loans for residential properties. In its early years, this agency primarily worked to stabilize the housing industry, which had experienced some serious downturns after the Great Depression. The FHA also financed the development of military housing and created programs to facilitate homeownership for military veterans. In 1965, the goals of this agency shifted considerably when it was consolidated into the Department of Housing and Urban Development's (HUD) Office of Housing. Its primary responsibility continued to be providing opportunities for affordable homeownership and developing healthy and prosperous communities, but once the 1968 Fair Housing Act was enacted, HUD also assumed the responsibility for ensuring that housing-related transactions were not affected by discriminatory practices.

Federal housing laws actually condoned separate housing, if not explicitly, until the 1968 Fair Housing Act was passed. The Fair Housing Act, also known as Title VIII of the 1968 Civil Rights Act, bans discrimination when selling, renting, or financing dwellings or in conducting any housing-related transactions, based on race, color, national origins, religion, sex, family status, or disability. Subsequently, several amendments to this act have been passed to enhance the effectiveness of the policy and to promote enforcing the act.

Despite the passage of the Fair Housing Act of 1968, discrimination in the housing industry is quite prevalent. The housing choices of minorities are restricted unofficially by the practices of real estate agents, such as steering minorities to neighborhoods that are less integrated, providing poor service in the form of showing fewer properties, making minorities wait longer, asking them fewer questions about specific needs and more questions about income, making fewer positive comments and fewer follow-up calls, and giving different price quotes to racial minorities. Apartment managers have also been known to claim there are no vacant units to avoid renting to racial minorities. Local leaders and politicians in predominantly white communities may promote policies such as zoning laws and restrictive covenants that discourage or prohibit racial minorities from moving into certain neighborhoods. Racial minorities may also hesitate to move into predominantly white areas because of concerns about being harassed by white residents who would resent their presence.

Some commercial banks hinder the house-search process for minorities by establishing different standards for loan qualifications. Other factors that restrict members of minority groups, especially African Americans, in choosing housing include racially motivated site selection in public and government subsidized housing, as well as in the establishment of urban-renewal programs, the implementation of zoning and annexation laws that promote racial segregation, the attachment of restrictive covenants to housing deeds that prohibit the sale of property to certain ethnic groups, the exclusion of African American real estate agents from realty associations and multiple-listing services, and financial institution policies that discourage developers from building racially integrated housing and force African Americans to live in neighborhoods that are predominantly African American if they desire to receive loans.

Residential segregation remains a volatile topic, because of the practical implications associated with residential communities separated by race. Predominantly racial minority communities tend to have much higher levels of poverty than predominantly white or even mixed-race communities. Not only are minorities in racially segregated neighborhoods isolated from other racial groups, they also face a greater likelihood of living in concentrated poverty. Living in communities where poverty is concentrated is associated with a seemingly never-ending list of social ills, including high unemployment rates, dilapidated buildings, housing abandonment, low housing values, higher mortality rates, higher crime rates, toxic environments, poor education facilities, low educational achievement, family instability, and welfare dependency. Clearly, the consequences of racial residential segregation are considerable, and the impact is most heavily felt in the African American community.

Most African Americans continue to live in neighborhoods that are predominantly African American, closer to

---

Toxic Neighborhoods

A report issued in 1987 by the Commission for Racial Justice found that abandoned toxic waste sites and waste landfills were more likely surrounded by black than by white neighborhoods. A Government Accounting Office report in 2000 found likewise that in nine Southern states studied, all the hazardous waste landfills were in majority-black neighborhoods. There are serious consequences for those who live in these neighborhoods. The Centers for Disease Control has noted that as a result of high air-pollution levels in these neighborhoods, blacks are more likely than whites to experience blood and respiratory problems.

Toxic neighborhoods have been created by a complex combination of economic factors. Polluting industries have been induced by favorable tax treatment to locate in underdeveloped neighborhoods that governments want to build up. In many cases, environmental concerns took backstage to development goals and in some cases, environmental regulations were simply waived. The industries had little to fear from its disenfranchised and impoverished neighbors, who tended to have no political power. The choice was between jobs and pollution. These factors, combined with the discriminatory practice of redlining neighborhoods to limit access to housing funds, have left the country littered with toxic waste sites next to poor, minority neighborhoods.

The federal government became involved when President Bill Clinton signed Executive Order 12898 in 1994. The Environmental Protection Agency (EPA) developed its Environmental Justice Strategy, defining environmental justice as the "fair treatment for all people of all races, cultures, and incomes, regarding the development of environmental laws, regulations, and policies." The EPA also developed the Toxic Release Inventory, which is available in a Web-based database and contains information on toxic chemical releases in neighborhoods, organized by zip code.

BENJAMIN F. SHEARER

the central city, and have lower property values than the neighborhoods of their white counterparts who earn about the same level of income. African American neighborhoods are more likely to be in transition and are characterized by higher rates of poverty, crime, substance abuse, and mortality. Although trends suggest that segregation has declined modestly in the last two decades, African Americans are the most isolated of all ethnic minority groups in America.

African Americans tend not only to live in more isolated communities but to live in communities with a lower resource stock. The resources available in African American neighborhoods are dwarfed by those available in white or mixed neighborhoods. Schools are poorer and fewer. Roads and infrastructure are allowed to deteriorate well beyond levels of safety or repair. Grocery stores are not well stocked or conveniently located. Hospitals are understaffed and underbudgeted. All of this makes African American neighborhoods quite unattractive, so it is understandable that whites and other ethnic groups do not wish to move into these areas. Even African Americans would prefer not to move into these types of neighborhoods, but they are often prevented from moving into the types of neighborhoods they would prefer to live in, so African Americans frequently must make due with the second-class neighborhoods that are open to them.

The social ills associated with concentrated poverty due to residential segregation also serve to discourage property owners from investing in real estate in predominantly African American areas. Property owners who are already invested in these areas look for ways to divest from the community, leading to further deterioration of neighborhood buildings. More subtle social problems that emerge due to the concentration of poverty in African American neighborhoods include social disorders such as street-corner drinking, catcalling, sexual harassment, graffiti, and littering. On the surface, these disorders do not seem that harmful, but over time they lead neighbors to become distrustful of each other. To avoid these situations, many residents will withdraw from the community and opt to stay indoors when possible. This strategy may be effective for individuals or families, but for the broader community it further weakens social control in the neighborhood. Ultimately, these small social-order violations create conditions conducive to the perpetuation of more serious crimes.

It is not only low-income African Americans who are subjected to these substandard living conditions. Recent research indicates that middle-class African Americans are much more likely than middle-class whites to live in resource-poor neighborhoods. Even high-status blacks are frequently unable to settle in neighborhoods that befit their level of income, education, and social prestige. Beyond the physical and material disparities, continued levels of moderate to high residential segregation based on race diminish efforts to create racial and social harmony in the United States.

ROMNEY S. NORWOOD

See also

American Apartheid; Blockbusting; Hypersegregation; Reverse Redlining; Segregation

Further Reading:

Environmental Protection Agency. http://www.epa.gov/tri.

Farley, Reynolds, Charlotte Steeh, Maria Krysan, Tara Jackson, and Keith Reeves. "Stereotypes and Segregation: Neighborhoods in the Detroit Area." *American Journal of Sociology* 100 (1994): 750–80.

Jargowsky, Paul. "Take the Money and Run: Economic Segregation in U.S. Metropolitan Areas." *American Sociological Review* 61 (1996): 984–98.

Massey, Douglas S., and Nancy A. Denton. *American Apartheid, Segregation and the Making of the Underclass*. Cambridge, MA: Harvard University Press, 1993.

Oliver, Melvin, and Thomas Shapiro. *Black Wealth/White Wealth: A New Perspective on Racial Inequality*. New York: Routledge, 1995.

U.S. Census Bureau. "Housing Patterns." June 18, 2002. http://www.census.gov/hhes/ www/housing/resseg/.

Yinger, John. *Closed Doors, Opportunities Lost: The Continuing Costs of Housing Discrimination*. New York: Russell Sage Foundation, 1995.

Zhou, Min, and John R. Logan. "In and Out of Chinatown: Residential Mobility and Segregation of New York City's Chinese." *Social Forces* 70 (1991): 387–407.

Reverse Discrimination

Reverse discrimination is a concept that is difficult to define because people use it in widely different ways. Some argue that it refers to intentional actions that deny equal treatment to whites in education and the labor force; this is the first notion of reverse discrimination. The perpetrators of these

Allan Bakke is trailed by news and television reporters after attending his first day at the Medical School of the University of California at Davis on September 25, 1978. Bakke sued the university for reverse discrimination after his application was rejected in 1973 and 1974. (AP/Wide World Photos)

actions are said to be people of color either at the institutional or individual level. For example, a black supervisor might deny a promotion to a qualified white because of race or the government of a predominantly Hispanic city might favor Hispanic rather than white workers. These actions are clearly illegal, and most people would probably find them abhorrent.

A second definition of reverse discrimination refers to whites being hurt by affirmative action programs in education and the labor force where less qualified people of color get hired/admitted over more qualified whites. In this case, programs that are intended to level the playing field are said to discriminate against whites. This second definition is highly contested, extremely emotional, and legally fluid.

The evidence suggests that instances where whites are discriminated against by individual people of color or by institutions controlled by people of color are far less common than acts of discrimination against people of color. In 2011, for example, 28,913 blacks filed charges of race-related employment discrimination with the EEOC compared to 4,987 complaints filed by whites. This means that blacks filed almost six times more complaints than whites. When corrected for differences in population, the gap becomes even larger. Those whites who can prove they are victims of intentional discrimination are covered by the same legal procedures as people of color.

It is much more difficult to quantify the second type of reverse discrimination where whites do not receive a job, promotion, college seat or government contract due to affirmative action. Again, the evidence suggests that it is rare. The Office of Federal Contract Compliance Programs (OFCCP) of the U.S. Department of Labor has a complex set of requirements for government contractors with 50 or more employees and with contracts of $50,000 or more. Although contractors must file an affirmative action plan, in the end, they must hire the most qualified person. Favoring someone because of their race is considered to be illegal. It is unlikely that a white person would be legally discriminated against under OFCCP guidelines.

Of course, it is possible that a white person would not be hired under OFCCP guidelines but would have been hired without the guidelines. The reason for this is that the guidelines make it more difficult for an employer to practice discrimination against people of color. In other words, whites are no longer the beneficiaries of discrimination against people of color. The OFCCP guidelines try to level the playing field and reduce the privilege that whites have. This should not be called discrimination of any kind.

In other situations, people of color are given a break when it comes to employment or college admission. In employment, this is often the result of a lawsuit where people of color allege that the employer has practiced race-based discrimination for a long period of time. Some of these lawsuits are resolved by a consent decree where the employer agrees to a set of procedures which includes hiring a certain percentage of people of color over a specified period of time. Again, there are complex legal procedures here that could result in a white not being hired when they may have been hired without the procedures.

Opponents of these procedures take an ahistorical view and argue that these whites are discriminated against because they would have been hired without the procedures. Proponents, on the other hand, argue that these procedures are the only way to get the employer to stop discriminating against people of color.

In higher education, some colleges and universities have developed admissions procedures to increase the number of underrepresented minorities in their entering classes. This sometimes means that blacks and Hispanics might be admitted with somewhat lower grades and test scores than comparable whites. Critics of these policies have called this reverse discrimination and argue that it should be illegal.

Since the 1970s, the U.S. Supreme Court has ruled that colleges and universities can take race into account if it is one of many factors that are considered in the admissions process. Just as musical ability, athletic ability, type of high school, geography, and a whole host of factors are considered in addition to grades and test scores, race can also be considered. The court, however, has sharply restricted how race can be considered in college admission. While it is true that some whites might not be admitted in these new processes when they would have been admitted without them, this should not be called reverse discrimination when it is not illegal.

The first type of reverse discrimination is simple to define and is likely to be rare. The second type of reverse discrimination, on the other hand, is both hard to define and quantify. If white privilege is reduced by leveling the playing field, it is not proper to use the term *reverse discrimination*.

FRED L. PINCUS

See also

Criminal Justice System and Racial Discrimination; Cumulative Discrimination; Discrimination; Financial Institutions and Racial Discrimination; Housing Discrimination; Institutional Discrimination; Statistical Discrimination; Structural Discrimination

Further Reading:

Ditomaso, Nancy. *The American Non-Dilemma: Racial Inequality Without Racism*. New York: Russell Sage Foundation, 2013.

Pincus, Fred L. *Reverse Discrimination: Dismantling the Myth*. Boulder, CO: Lynne Rienner Publishers, 2003.

Wise, Tim J. *Affirmative Action: Racial Preference in Black and White*. New York: Routledge, 2005.

Reverse Racism

Traditionally, racism is seen as prejudiced beliefs and actions that whites wage against people of color, as whites have been at the top of the racial hierarchy while people of color occupy the bottoms strata of the racial hierarchy. Over the past 20 years, claims to reverse racism have become increasingly more common as whites argue they are the ones without the power and are the ones unfairly experiencing discrimination. As whites are still at the top with regard to household income, wealth, pay/salary, and political representation, there is much debate over whether reverse racism is a valid concept.

Charges of reverse racism are most often made in relation to Affirmative Action policies. Affirmative Action was initially mentioned in a 1961 Executive Order by President Kennedy and followed up with regulations and goals by the Nixon administration in 1970. The overall goal was to ensure antidiscrimination efforts while also taking measures to ensure equal opportunity. Affirmative Action extends to racial minorities, women, people with disabilities, and veterans although the reverse racism conversation is centered on the goals for racial minorities. The logic behind Affirmative Action is to help mitigate some of the long-term consequences of historical discrimination, particularly for African Americans whose relatives had to endure plantation slavery and Jim Crow racism. Stated another way, the purpose of Affirmative Action is not to give unjust help to and *preferences* for minorities but rather to take positive steps to increase *opportunities* in a white-dominated society. However, those who claim reverse racism argue that Affirmative Action violates the American doctrine of equal opportunity and unfairly gives jobs and college admissions to people of color when whites are equally or more qualified; thus, the policy is racist against white people. Another popular instance of reverse racism is when whites are denied the opportunity to have a race-based student organization at colleges/universities. In an effort to create a safe space and sense of solidarity, racial minority–based student organizations such as black student unions, Latino student associations, or Asian American student associations are popular on many campuses. Yet when whites try to create a white student association on campus, they have faced opposition. A recent example is Matthew Heimbach, who tried to create a white student union at Towson University as he believed the union was necessary to create a space for whites and protect the campus from crime, enacted largely by non-whites. Heimbach and white student leaders like him claim reverse racism, for, if blacks can have student groups, then why can't whites?

Charges of reverse racism have resulted in some successes on the behalf of white college students and have, at the very least, resulted in the phrase "reverse racism" becoming popular. Many schools and universities have lessened their Affirmative Action policies; most notably, in 1996

the California system banned the use of race in admission decisions. In 1996 the Texas system also banned the use of race, but after minority enrollments plummeted and the Supreme Court, in 2003, found the use of race constitutional, the Texas system reinstituted the use of race in its admission policy. Affirmative Action again came to the Supreme Court in 2012 when a white student, Abigail Fisher, stated that the University of Texas–Austin did not admit her because she is white. With strong arguments for reverse racism, Affirmative Action and other race-related policies will continue to be socially and legally challenged.

Advocates of reverse racism often make two arguments to support their stance: (1) two wrongs don't make a right; and (2) it is undemocratic and un-American to give one group of people privileges and unfair advantages over another. While these arguments of reverse racism have supporters, these claims have also come under attack for essentially being racist themselves by not paying attention to the history and the structural racism that has made rectifying policies and civil rights organizations necessary in the first place. Specifically, the first argument, two wrongs don't make a right, assumes that Affirmative Action is a "wrong," rather than understanding it as essentially a small response to 400 years of slavery, Native American genocide, and denial of full citizenship status (including the right to vote and own property) for racial minorities. The second argument, that it is undemocratic and un-American to provide privileges, again ignores the historical, structural conditions that have awarded whites privileges and advantages in the United States. In this respect, the "privileges" given to racial minorities today are attempts to make opportunities *equal*, rather than raising racial minorities *above* whites. Overall, the fallacy of reverse racism is that it makes the centuries-long systemic and systematic discrimination against people of color equal to "discrimination" against whites via help intended to ameliorate the current and past legacy of racism.

HEPHZIBAH STRMIC-PAWL

See also
Affirmative Action; Color-Blind Racism; Cultural Racism; *End of Racism, The*; Racism; Reverse Discrimination; Systemic Racism

Further Reading:
Affirmative Action. "About Affirmative Action." http://www.affirmativeaction.org/about-affirmative-action.

Fish, Stanley. "Reverse Racism or How the Pot Got to Call the Kettle Black." *Atlantic Monthly*, November 1993.

Hing, Julianne. "At Towson University, A Student Makes His Case for a White Student Union." September 19, 2012. http://colorlines.com/archives/2012/09/ at_towson_univ_a_white_student_makes_his_case_for_a_white_student_union.html.

Sacks, Mike. "Affirmative Action at Supreme Court: University of Texas Program Had a Bad Day." October 10, 2012. http://www.huffingtonpost.com/2012/10/10/ affirmative-action -supreme-court_n_1954239.html.

Reverse Redlining

Redlining was a practice that began with the National Housing Act of 1934. As part of the New Deal legislation, this act was meant to make home ownership more accessible to many Americans, especially GIs returning from World War II. However, embedded in this policy was the racist practice of redlining, which systematically denied financing for African Americans seeking mortgages.

In the vein of providing the least risky mortgages, the federal government with the help of the Home Owners' Loan Corporation mapped cities in order to determine which areas were safe investments. Parts of cities that were older and that had mostly people of color were outlined in red, which indicated that they were the highest risk in terms of lending. This practice made it impossible for people of color to get financing for homes in their neighborhoods. The highest rated areas were those that were newer and predominantly white. This policy resulted in white homeowners being able to amass wealth, and African Americans and other people of color being denied this opportunity for wealth accumulation.

Starting in the 1990s, a new kind of redlining emerged. Reverse redlining functions differently than traditional redlining. Rather than making it difficult to receive financing, reverse redlining involves predatory lending "where lenders target minority, elderly, and low-income homeowners and charge them high interest rates and fees unrelated to the credit risk posed by the borrower" (Williams, Nesiba, and McConnell 2005: 188). While on the surface it may appear that these loans made home ownership a possibility for many families who would not otherwise have had this option, it also results in people of color facing higher fees, closing costs, interest rates, and a higher risk for foreclosure. "Instead of contributing to homeownership and community development, predatory lending practices strip the equity homeowners have struggled to build and deplete the wealth of those communities for the enrichment of distant financial services firms" (Squires 2005). There is also a great deal of evidence

---

National Housing Institute and Predatory Lending Practices

This is a list provided by the National Housing Institute of various predatory lending practices used by banks that resulted in reverse redlining.

Balloon payments that require borrowers to pay off the entire balance of a loan by making a substantial payment after a period of time during which they have been making regular monthly payments;

Required single premium credit life insurance, where the borrower must pay the entire annual premium at the beginning of the policy period rather than in monthly or quarterly payments. (With this cost folded into the loan, the total costs, including interest payments, are higher throughout the life of the loan);

Homeowners insurance where the lender requires the borrower to pay for a policy selected by the lender;

High prepayment penalties that trap borrowers in the loans;

Fees for services that may or may not actually be provided;

Loans based on the value of the property with no regard for the borrower's ability to make payments;

Loan flipping, whereby lenders use deceptive and high-pressure tactics resulting in the frequent refinancing of loans with additional fees added each time;

Negatively amortized loans and loans for more than the value of the home, which result in the borrower owing more money at the end of the loan period than when they started making payments.

showing that people of color were specifically targeted for these types of loans. According to a report done by the Center for Community Change, "The national urban lending totals for all 331 metropolitan areas show racial disparities in the percentage of refinance loans that are subprime. 17.42% of the conventional refinance loans made to white borrowers in 2000 were subprime loans. The comparable figures are 49.28% for African-Americans, 30.33% for Hispanics, and 27.94% for Native Americans" (Bradford 2002: 3).

Predatory lending suggests that banks were expecting borrowers to default on their loans, so that banks could seize the home and then resell it. However, this practice is illegal. According to a *New York Times* article by Charlie Savage from 2010, "Under federal civil rights laws, a lending practice is illegal if it has a disparate impact on minority borrowers, and the Obama administration is signaling that it intends to make the enforcing of fair lending laws a signature policy push in 2010. The division has already opened 38 investigations into accusations of lending discrimination. Under federal lending laws, it can seek compensation for borrowers who were victimized by any illegal conduct, as well as changes in a lender's practices." An investigation of Wells Fargo demonstrated that the bank "had systematically singled out minority borrows for high-interest, high-fee mortgages, bypassing its own underwriting rules" (Savage 2010).

Countrywide was also investigated by the Justice Department for its predatory lending practices. Allegations included charging "200,000 minority homeowners higher interest rates and fees than white borrowers who were similarly qualified, with similar credit ratings. The complaint also alleged that Countrywide had failed to offer minority homeowners conventional mortgages for which they qualified and which they would have been offered, were they white" (Rothstein 2012). Because of these loan terms, many African American and Latino homeowners faced foreclosure, ultimately damaging their credit and stripping them of any wealth accumulation typically gained from homeownership. Though Countrywide agreed to a settlement of $335 million, homeowners only received about $2,000, clearly not enough to compensate for their losses.

These lending practices led to a global financial crisis. Additionally, there were disastrous effects for people of color caught in the reverse redlining web. The wealth gap between whites and people of color increased dramatically. It also led

Redlining

Derived from the practice of banks, which drew red lines on city maps to mark areas and neighborhoods in which they did not want to lend money, the term *redlining* describes the refusal of banks and other institutions to provide services, such as banking and insurance, to residents of certain areas. Although this practice is illegal in the United States when it is based on race, religion, gender, disability, ethnic origin, or the presence or absence of children in a family, it has been used, especially against African Americans and other racial minorities, to restrict their ability to obtain affordable housing to only certain areas or parts of a city, and thus greatly increased residential segregation in the United States in the early and mid-20th century.

The practice of redlining was given major impetus by the Housing Act of 1934, which was passed to foster the development of affordable housing for the urban poor. Despite this basic aim, the act also required cities to designate certain areas and neighborhoods for particular racial groups, a practice that effectively prevented minorities from obtaining mortgages for housing outside their designated areas. In many cities, such as Philadelphia, Boston, and Kansas City, redlining forced African Americans into certain well-defined neighborhoods and preserved the all-white composition of others. Today, the federal government requires all banks to provide a map showing the locations of recent home loans it has made in a city to assure potential customers that no redlining is taking place.

JOHN A. WAGNER

to reinforced residential segregation, higher levels of poverty for people of color, and increased homelessness.

KATHRIN A. PARKS

See also

American Apartheid; Blockbusting; Housing Covenants; Matched-Pairs Housing Audits; Segregation; Urban Renewal; U.S. Department of Housing and Urban Development

Further Reading:

Bradford, Calvin. *Risk or Race? Racial Disparities and the Subprime Refinance Market*. Washington, DC: Center for

Community Change, 2002. http://www.knowledgeplex.org/kp/report/report/relfiles/ccc_0729_risk.pdf.

Charlie Savage. "Justice Dept. Fights Bias in Lending." *New York Times*. http://www.nytimes.com/2010/01/14/us/14justice.html?_r=1&.

Kochhar, Rakesh, Richard Fry, and Paul Taylor. "Wealth Gaps Rise to Record Highs Between Whites, Blacks, and Hispanics: Twenty-to-One." Pew Research Center. July 26, 2011. http://www.pewsocialtrends.org/2011/07/26/wealth-gaps-rise-to-record-highs-between-whites-blacks-hispanics/.

Lang, William W., and Leonard I. Nakamura. "A Model of Redlining." *Journal of Urban Economics* 33, no. 2 (1993): 223–34.

Rothstein, R. "A Comment on Bank of America/Countrywide's Discriminatory Mortgage Lending and Its Implications for Racial Segregation." Economic Policy Institute. 2012. http://www.epi.org/publication/bp335-boa-countrywide-discriminatory-lending/

Schafer, Robert, and Helen F. Ladd. *Discrimination in Mortgage Lending*. Cambridge, MA: MIT Press, 1981.

Squires, G. D. "Predatory Lending: Redlining in Reverse." National Housing Institute. http://www.nhi.org/online/issues/139/redlining.html.

Tootell, Geoffrey M.B. "Redlining in Boston: Do Mortgage Lenders Discriminate against Neighborhoods?" *Quarterly Journal of Economics* 111, no. 4 (1996): 1049–1079.

Williams, R., R. Nesiba, and E.D. McConnell. "The Changing Face of Inequality in Home Mortgage Lending." *Social Problems* 52 (2005): 181–208.

Zenou, Yves, and Nicolas Boccard. "Racial Discrimination and Redlining in Cities." *Journal of Urban Economics* 48 (2000): 260–285.

Rhythm and Blues

Rhythm and Blues (R&B) is a term used to describe or designate certain types of music associated with the African American community. R&B has had a number of different meanings over the years: it was used by *Billboard* magazine as a broad category to track the sale of music produced and consumed by African Americans from the 1940s on; it also referred to a specific genre of African American music that fused blues sensibilities with danceable rhythms and beats, peaking in popularity from the late 1940s through the early 1960s; and, finally, in contemporary times, it refers to modern interpretations of soul music. The postwar genre of R&B

had the most relevance to the African American struggle against Jim Crow. This specific incarnation of R&B, with its driving backbeats, its instrumental virtuosity, and its positive energy, led to the creation of rock and roll, played a pivotal role in moving black culture into mainstream America, and channeled black aspirations for integration.

R&B in the 1940s developed out of three traditions in black music: jump blues, a dance-friendly style of blues that came out of African American urban areas; gospel music, which had its origins in all-black Christian churches; and the performances of the blues shouters, who lamented lost loves in powerful (and often racy) lyrics. Featuring smaller lineups than the big bands of the swing era, R&B groups often included four to eight members, with a lead vocalist and lead instrumentalist, a rhythm section, and a percussion section. R&B was another manifestation of the Great Migration, the decades-long movement of blacks out of the rural South and into Southern cities and Northern metropolises such as Chicago and Detroit. Featuring a more modern sound than traditional acoustic blues, R&B made use of the electric guitar and the electric bass to provide a soundtrack to blacks celebrating their improving economic standing in urban America. A number of musicians helped create R&B's distinctive sound and performance style, including Muddy Waters, who gradually shifted from a rural, rustic sound featuring slow and stilted tempos to a polished, urban style that emphasized dance-friendly backbeats. While male performers such as Waters, Big Joe Turner, and Billy Ward and the Dominoes, were central to R&B's development, black women also made major contributions to the genre. Ruth Brown and LaVern Baker, for example, each had numerous R&B hits, and both achieved some crossover success on the pop market, helping the genre overcome the racial divide.

Two significant changes in the music industry helped black R&B artists gain a wider audience for their music in the postwar period. The first major change involved radio. Although radio stations had previously ignored most music played by and for African Americans, that trend changed in the late 1940s and early 1950s. As national broadcast networks began to invest more resources in the burgeoning medium of television, radio networks scrambled to fill available airtime. As a result, programmers increasingly turned to music outside the mainstream, including black music such as R&B. These stations quickly became popular, as black audiences, eager to hear African American music, tuned in. Gradually, stations such as WDIA in Memphis, Tennessee, became exclusively devoted to black music, and R&B musicians had increased opportunities for their songs to reach a wider black audience. In the process, these stations also attracted white listeners, who appreciated the musical inventiveness they heard from black musicians.

The other major change in the music industry involved record labels. As the economy boomed in the postwar period and the cost of recording technology dropped, new "independent" labels formed, such as Chess Records and Atlantic Records. Because the major labels such as Capitol, Decca, and RCA had locked up most of the major pop stars, these independent labels turned to alternative forms of music, hoping to find market niches that had escaped the majors' attention. R&B proved to be one such opportunity, and independent label owners were delighted to see the demand for the music among black (and select white) audiences. As sales for R&B records boomed, independent labels sought out more black performers to record, hoping to cash in on the genre's popularity. Major labels followed suit, unwilling to let independents earn all of the profits. Legendary R&B musicians such as T-Bone Walker, who signed with Capitol, and Arthur Crudup, who signed with RCA, produced records directed at the black market for these major labels. While most black-oriented radio stations and record labels (including both the independents and the majors) were controlled by white owners and managers, black musicians nonetheless had more opportunities to produce their music for a consumer audience. In the process, they also reached across the color line, introducing whites to aspects of black culture of which they had been previously unaware.

Because of its increasing popularity with white audiences, R&B played a pivotal role in the development of rock and roll. White musicians and performers such as Elvis Presley, Bill Haley and His Comets, and Jerry Lee Lewis borrowed heavily from the songs and sounds of R&B as they launched their careers in the mid-1950s. Indeed, Presley's "Hound Dog" was originally by Big Mama Thornton, Haley's "Shake, Rattle, and Roll" was by Big Joe Turner, and Lewis's "Great Balls of Fire" was by Otis Blackwell—all R&B performers and composers. Although rock and roll performers often changed R&B songs, adding elements of country and

Influential rhythm and blues singer Ruth Brown, circa 1950. (Photofest)

speeding up the tempo, they were clearly indebted to black artists, and many felt that white rock and rollers appropriated—and outright stole—from R&B pioneers. The term "rock and roll," a slang expression for sexual intercourse, masked the black origins of the music—R&B—for some listeners. However, rock and roll's increasing popularity also led to demand for R&B versions of songs, and for R&B performers. Thus, Chuck Berry, "Little Richard" Penniman, and other black performers became stars with black and white audiences across the country, playing in front of integrated crowds and achieving success on both the R&B and pop charts. As more R&B songs crossed over to the pop charts, black artists had increased opportunities for financial success as musicians.

Although R&B certainly opened up opportunities for black musicians, and had some positive effects on integration, there were some negative impacts of R&B's popularity as well. Many R&B songs featured sexually explicit lyrics (usually masked by creative double entendres) that came out of the blues tradition. Expressing delight in the pursuit of sexual pleasure, and animosity at members of the opposite sex who did not come through in providing that pleasure, these songs were clearly tongue-in-cheek, part of a broader trend in African American culture that emphasized witty verbal sparring. However, while black listeners understood these songs to be one small slice of African American life, many white listeners took the themes of these songs to be representative of black culture at large, and thus used this material to bolster stereotypes of African Americans as lustful, violent, and incapable of controlling their emotions and sexual appetites. Indeed, many nervous whites lamented rock and roll's popularity among white teens precisely because they feared that their youth were being exposed to the hedonism supposedly inherent to the African American community. White fans' appreciation of black musicians did not necessarily mean that white audiences would be more receptive to black calls for civil rights; fraternities at white Southern schools such as the University of Virginia, for example, welcomed black bands to perform but wholeheartedly supported segregationist efforts well into the 1960s.

As R&B evolved in the 1950s and early 1960s, two offshoots of the genre provide insight into the hopes of black performers and many in the black community at large. The first innovation was "doo wop," which developed from urban a cappella groups. Usually featuring four members, doo wop groups often featured teenagers who hailed from specific local communities. Instead of featuring the bawdy lyrics and raucous rhythms of earlier R&B performers, these young musicians instead sang about romantic love and youthful heartbreak. Groups such as Frankie Lymon and the Teenagers rose to the top of the charts with songs like "Why Do Fools Fall in Love?" and were embraced by black and white audiences alike for their smooth vocals, their polished image, and their nonthreatening personas. Following the lead of popular groups such as the Platters, these doo wop artists actively courted an integrated audience, optimistic that the changes taking place in civil rights in the 1950s, such as the U.S. Supreme Court decision in *Brown v. Board of Education*, portended a more equitable future for black Americans.

Black pop artists of the late 1950s and early 1960s followed a similar trajectory. Smooth male balladeers such as Sam Cooke and "girl groups" such as the Shirelles and the Supremes courted an integrated youth audience by singing pop music tinged with R&B sounds and styles. Berry Gordy's founding of Motown Records in 1959 reflected similar aims. A black-owned and largely black-run organization, Motown reached out to a wide audience in its early years by creating a distinct R&B sound that was radio-friendly. By dressing his artists in glamorous attire, Gordy assured nervous whites that these performers were no threat to conventions of middle-class respectability. And by having his in-house songwriters focus on romantic love instead of sexual pleasure, these artists avoided radio censorship. Hopeful that the end of Jim Crow segregation was drawing near, and optimistic that integration would solve most of the black community's problems, these groups also tended to eschew overt political themes in their songs (although never ignoring the political, economic, and social realities of blacks' lives entirely). Singing pop standards and courting an integrated audience, these groups—male balladeers, the "girl groups," and the Motown acts of the early to mid-1960s—represented the apex of black hopes for integration.

By the mid-1960s, however, many of those hopes for integration were dashed, as the Civil Rights Act of 1964 and the Voting Rights Act of 1965 improved conditions for African Americans but largely failed to address the ongoing economic inequalities that ravaged the country. As the civil rights movement shifted to an emphasis on "black power" and black solidarity, these changes were reflected in African American music: R&B gave way first to soul music, which featured a greater emphasis on the black gospel tradition, and then to funk, which employed heavily syncopated rhythms and Afrocentric attire. Although the term *R&B* would continue to be employed in various contexts through to the present day, the trend-setting genre of the 1940s, 1950s, and early 1960s would largely be relegated to the bin of "oldies" music. However, it had a lasting impact on popular music and social movements, playing a pivotal role in the development of rock and roll, soul, funk, and present-day hip-hop, and providing an outlet for African Americans to express their hopes for black equality and uplift.

GREGORY KALISS

See also

Jazz; Music Industry, Racism in; Rap Music; Rock and Roll

Further Reading:

Altschuler, Glenn C. *All Shook Up: How Rock 'n' Roll Changed America*. New York: Oxford University Press, 2003.

George, Nelson. *The Death of Rhythm & Blues*. New York: Pantheon Books, 1988.

Guralnick, Peter. *Sweet Soul Music: Rhythm and Blues and the Southern Dream of Freedom*. New York: Harper and Row, 1986.

Ward, Brian. *Just My Soul Responding: Rhythm and Blues, Black Consciousness, and Race Relations*. Berkeley: University of California Press, 1998.

Rice, Thomas D. (1808–1860)

Thomas D. Rice was a white performer and playwright who used African American vernacular speech, song, and dance to become one of the most popular entertainers of his time. Although his most famous character—known as Jim Crow—later became synonymous with American racism and discrimination, there is no evidence that Rice himself was racist.

Rice was born on Manhattan's Lower East Side, near the bustling commercial district of the East River docks. His father may have been John Rice, a ship's rigger, and his mother may have been Eleanor Rice. Most likely the family was poor, Protestant, and of English ancestry. After some schooling, Rice apprenticed in his teens with a woodcarver named Dodge, but somehow soon found his way to the stage. By 1827, he was an itinerant actor, appearing not only as a stock player in several New York theaters but also performing on frontier stages in the Ohio River valley and the coastal South.

The actual genesis of the Jim Crow character has become lost to legend. Several sources describe how Rice happened to encounter an elderly black stableman working in one of the river towns where Rice was performing. The man—with a crooked leg and deformed shoulder, according to some accounts—was singing about Jim Crow, and punctuating each stanza with a little jump. A more likely explanation is that Rice had observed and absorbed African American traditional song and dance over many years: first while growing up in a racially integrated Manhattan neighborhood, and later while touring the Southern slave states. African folktales of trickster birds, such as crows and buzzards, may also have influenced the vernacular traditions observed by Rice.

Whatever its origins, Rice had made the Jim Crow character his signature act by 1830—dressed in rags and torn shoes, his face and hands blackened, impersonating a very nimble and irreverently witty African American field hand who sang, "Turn about and wheel about, and do just so. And every time I turn about I jump Jim Crow." There had been other blackface performers before Rice, and there were many more afterwards. But it was "Daddy Rice" who became so indelibly associated with a single character and routine.

During the years of his peak popularity, from roughly 1832 to 1844, Rice often encountered sold-out houses, with audiences demanding numerous encores. He not only performed in more than 100 plays but also created plays of his own, providing himself slight variants on the Jim Crow persona—as Cuff in *Oh, Hush!* (1833), Ginger Blue in *Virginia Mummy* (1835), and Bone Squash in *Bone Squash Diavolo* (1835). Moreover, Rice wrote and starred in *Otello* (1844), transforming Shakespeare's tragedy into a musical in which Othello and Desdemona live happily ever after; he also played the title character in *Uncle Tom's Cabin*, starting in 1854. On one of his stage tours in England, Rice married Charlotte B. Gladstone in 1837. She died in 1847, and none of their children survived infancy. As early as 1840, Rice suffered from a type of paralysis, which began to limit his speech and movements, and eventually led to his death.

Although several studies have pointed to the hostility and racism underlying much blackface minstrelsy in the late 19th and early 20th centuries, more recent scholarship—particularly by W. T. Lhamon Jr.—regards Rice as a daring interracial rebel who mocked the discriminatory stereotypes of African Americans and championed the working class by ridiculing the authority figures of the day, all of whom were white. In Rice's songs and plays, poor blacks align themselves with poor whites to express solidarity of the underclass that would subsequently find more lasting expression in the work of Karl Marx, Elvis Presley, and others.

JAMES I. DEUTSCH

See also
Minstrelsy

Further Reading:

Lhamon, W. T., Jr. *Raising Cain: Blackface Performance from Jim Crow to Hip Hop*. Cambridge, MA: Harvard University Press, 1998.

Lhamon, W. T., Jr. *Jump Jim Crow: Lost Plays, Lyrics, and Street Prose of the First Atlantic Popular Culture*. Cambridge, MA: Harvard University Press, 2003.

Lott, Eric. *Love and Theft: Blackface Minstrelsy and the American Working Class.* New York: Oxford University Press, 1993.

Robinson, Jackie (1919–1972)

Jackie Robinson was an African American athlete, activist, and businessman, most famous for his Hall of Fame pioneering career in Major League Baseball. Born in 1919 in Cairo, Georgia, Robinson moved with his mother and four older siblings to Pasadena, California, in 1920, where he grew up in a majority white neighborhood. Although involved in minor acts of vandalism and confrontations with the police as a youth, Robinson moderated his behavior under the influence of Karl Downs, a young black minister in the area. Excelling in a variety of sports in high school, Robinson chose to attend Pasadena Junior College (PJC) to be close to home and his beloved mother, Mallie. At PJC, Robinson set national marks in the broad jump and led the football team to an undefeated season in his sophomore year, earning acclaim in nearly every area newspaper for his brilliant open-field running as the team's quarterback. In February 1939, Robinson enrolled at the University of California at Los Angeles (UCLA), where he became the first athlete in the school's history to letter in four sports: baseball, track, football, and basketball. He earned the most acclaim for his performance on the football field, where, as a junior, he teamed with two other black starters, Kenny Washington and Woody Strode, to lead UCLA to a 6–0–4 record, only narrowly missing the school's first-ever invitation to the Rose Bowl.

After leaving UCLA in February 1941 to earn money to support his mother, Robinson briefly played professional football in Hawai'i before being drafted into the military in March 1943. Sent to Fort Riley, Kansas, for basic training, Robinson earned high marks in a variety of tests, thanks to his intelligence and physical aptitude, but was consistently passed over for admission into Officer Candidate School because of his race. Robinson's friendship with famed heavyweight boxer Joe Louis, also stationed at Fort Riley, helped gain him entrance into the school, where he earned the rank of second lieutenant. After being transferred to Camp Hood, Texas, Robinson faced court-martial charges after refusing to move to the back of a military bus when ordered to do so by the bus driver. Asserting his rights as an officer and an American citizen, Robinson was arrested. Eventually acquitted, Robinson was granted an honorable discharge because of an ongoing ankle ailment in November 1944. Robinson then played one year of baseball for the Kansas City Monarchs, a Negro League Baseball team.

Robinson's performance for the Monarchs attracted the attention of Branch Rickey, the president of the Brooklyn Dodgers, a Major League Baseball team. Although there were no formal rules against black players in the major leagues, an unwritten "gentleman's agreement" had kept African Americans out of the sport since the late 19th century. Robinson's athletic ability and strong character made him the ideal candidate to integrate Major League Baseball, and Rickey signed him to play that role in August 1945. The decision was announced publicly in October of that year. In 1946, Robinson played for the Dodgers' top minor league affiliate, the Montreal Royals. Although encountering bitter racism from fans, opposing players, and even some teammates and coaches, Robinson excelled and helped lead his team to a league championship. He also married his longtime girlfriend, Rachel Isum, at the conclusion of the 1946 season. The following spring, Robinson trained with the Dodgers and earned a starting spot on the team for the 1947 season.

On April 15, 1947, Robinson became the first African American player to participate in Major League Baseball in the modern era when he took the field with the Brooklyn Dodgers at the age of 28. Robinson faced racist taunting from opposing players and fans, and players often attempted to injure him by throwing pitches directly at him and deliberately "spiking" him with their cleats. African American fans turned out in droves to support him, and some white fans, particularly youths, were also enthusiastic admirers. Robinson initially received little support from his teammates, but an early series against the Philadelphia Phillies, managed by virulent racist Ben Chapman, helped unite the Dodgers. As Robinson withstood a torrent of racial abuse from the Phillies players without responding (a strategy of nonconfrontation he and Rickey had agreed upon), his teammates rallied to his support. In another key incident from that season, team shortstop Pee Wee Reese, a Southerner and one of the Dodgers' best players, silenced a hostile Boston crowd by putting his arm around Robinson and chatting with him on the field. In his nine-year career, Robinson won numerous accolades, including the National League Rookie of the Year in 1947, the National League Most Valuable Player in 1949, and a World Series championship in 1955. Following Robinson's debut, other clubs began to sign African American baseball players, and many consider Robinson's successful turn in baseball, "the national pastime," a pivotal event in the broader struggle for African American civil rights. He was awarded the Spingarn Medal in 1956 by the National Association for the Advancement of Colored People (NAACP) for his contributions to civil rights as a baseball player, the first athlete ever to receive the award.

After retiring from baseball in 1956, Robinson became a vice president for "Chock Full o' Nuts," a popular brand of coffee. He also became active in the NAACP, campaigning as a fund-raiser and supporting a variety of civil rights causes across the country. Although beloved by the black community on the whole, Robinson generated controversy in later years by campaigning for Richard Nixon in the 1960 presidential election, a decision he later regretted. He remained a supporter of the Republican Party until 1964, when the nomination of Barry Goldwater over friend Nelson Rockefeller led him to leave the party. He also resigned from the board of the NAACP in 1967 because he thought that long-time executive director Roy Wilkins had become too autocratic and was not open to new ideas and young leaders. In his last years, as he struggled with diabetes, Robinson bitterly complained in his autobiography *I Never Had It Made* about the lack of black managers in baseball and the ongoing racial inequalities that persisted across the country. One of his last major public appearances was for Major League Baseball's celebration of the 25th anniversary of his first game. He appealed to baseball owners to hire black managers and executives, but did not live to see it happen. He died in October 1972 from complications of diabetes, and was buried in Cypress Hill Cemetery in Brooklyn, New York. Posthumously, he was awarded the nation's highest civilian award, the Medal of Freedom, in 1984. Major League Baseball also retired his number, 42, in 1997, to honor the 50th anniversary of his debut with the Dodgers.

GREGORY KALISS

See also
Sports and Racism

Further Reading:
"Baseball and Jackie Robinson." Library of Congress American Memory. http://memory.loc.gov/ammem/collections/robinson/ (accessed May 29, 2008).
Rampersad, Arnold. *Jackie Robinson: A Biography*. New York: Alfred A. Knopf, 1997.
Robinson, Jack, with Alfred Duckett. *I Never Had It Made*. New York: G. P. Putnam's Sons, 1972.
Tygiel, Jules. *Baseball's Great Experiment: Jackie Robinson and His Legacy*. New York: Oxford University Press, 1983.

Rock and Roll

Rock and roll is a musical genre that first emerged in the 1950s. Heavily influenced by African American music, particularly rhythm and blues (R&B), rock and roll galvanized the nation's emerging teen culture with its pulsating beats, ecstatic vocals, and risqué lyrics. Spread predominantly through black radio stations in its early years, rock and roll became wildly popular across the color line, and many saw it, either fearfully or hopefully, as a powerful integrationist force. Generating anxiety among the elders of both races, rock and roll stirred up controversy and helped push black culture into the mainstream.

The term "rock and roll" was first used to describe this musical genre in 1951 by famed white disc jockey Alan Freed. Although originally a euphemism for sexual intercourse, Freed's term became widely accepted as the genre's name. The new moniker was accepted in part because it had none of the racial connotations of R&B, a term coined by the music industry to refer to popular African American music in general, but one that had come to define a genre in its own right. Rock and roll was closely aligned with R&B, and three musical traditions that shaped R&B in the 1940s and 1950s—jump blues, gospel music, and blues shouters' performances—deeply influenced rock and roll's evolution as well. However, many casual fans were unaware of the influence black music had on rock and roll, and some have claimed that the genre's change of name served to slight the importance of African American musicians. This was one of many criticisms of uncredited appropriation of music styles, songs, and performance elements by white musicians. Although it is quite clear that rock and roll leaned heavily on

R&B, the genre also changed as it was performed by white musicians. "Rockabilly," one subgenre of rock and roll, fused R&B with white country instrumentation and vocal styles, for example. Other white musicians, such as rock and roll pioneers Bill Haley and His Comets, sped up the tempo of R&B songs such as "Shake, Rattle, and Roll," replacing their sensuousness with a frenetic pace that appealed to young, high-energy audiences.

Rock and roll's increasing popularity owed a good deal to the changing character of radio in the late 1940s and early 1950s. The same factors that propelled R&B's increased accessibility to white audiences—national broadcast networks' decisions to invest more resources in the burgeoning medium of television, which left radio networks scrambling to fill available airtime—similarly impacted rock and roll's fortunes. As programmers increasingly turned to music outside the mainstream, up-and-coming rock and roll artists (black and white) found more opportunities to have their music reach a wider audience. Freed played a key role in this development, as his radio show for Cleveland radio station WJW (called the "Moondog Rock 'n' Roll Party") showed that the genre could attract numerous listeners, particularly teenagers. Freed then moved to New York in 1954, generating even more interest in rock and roll with radio station WINS. Even as the music reached a wider audience through radio, controversy over rock and roll's racial politics continued to dog the genre—with many white parents concerned by the fact that white teens were listening to black musicians and attending concerts with mixed-race audiences. These anxieties only increased as the music made its way into films such as 1955's *Blackboard Jungle*.

Elvis Presley's ascension to stardom as a rock and roll musician marked a particularly important moment in the genre's history, expanding rock and roll's appeal to a wide audience but also illustrating the complicated racial terrain that stars navigated. Presley, originally from Tupelo, Mississippi, was a 19-year-old truck driver, movie usher, and part-time musician, when he recorded his first record with Sam Philips at Sun Records Studio in Memphis. His first local hit was a cover of the blues song "That's All Right," originally performed in 1946 by black musician Arthur Crudup. As the record received more airtime, it became increasingly popular with black and white audiences, who admired Presley's vocals and the fusion of country and R&B styles. After releasing a number of songs in 1954 and 1955, and gaining in popularity across the South, Presley became a national sensation in January, 1956, when he released "Heartbreak Hotel." While many or Presley's early hits were covers of black artists' R&B songs, such as "Tutti Frutti" and "Hound Dog," he earned considerably more airtime and wealth than black performers, in part because of his race. Appropriating black songs and some elements of black performance styles, Presley was more palatable to mainstream audiences than black R&B performers, a fact that black artists lamented then and in later years. As Presley launched his career, however, he acknowledged his indebtedness to black artists, especially Crudup, and his covers of R&B songs also led to greater wealth and exposure for black songwriters. Unlike other unscrupulous white artists, who simply copied black songs' instrumentation and performance style, Presley also significantly changed the music when he covered the material, adding a high, tremulous vibrato to his vocals and using different instrumentation. As he rose to stardom, nervous parents lamented his hip-shaking dance moves and worried about the racial origins of his songs, but teen audiences—both black and white, initially—could not get enough, suggesting that rock and roll could reach across the color line to the nation's diverse population of youth.

Rock and roll's impact on integration remains a contested issue, although a number of examples suggest both the possibilities and the limitations of the genre to effect lasting change. On the one hand, many rock and roll shows in the 1950s were attended by interracial audiences, and while violence sometimes broke out, most attributed the behavior to the music and not to racial tensions. Indeed, performers reported that black and white teens on occasion pulled down barriers meant to segregate them at rock and roll shows in the South, and black stars delighted in their popularity with white youth culture. The black press, in general, trumpeted rock and roll's popularity, pointing to African American musicians' cultural contributions and praising the color-blind nature of the record-buying public. Spotlighting the successes of black stars such as Antoine "Fats" Domino and Chuck Berry, many in the black press saw rock and roll as proof that the color line could be permanently erased and that equality could be achieved. There were signs of this potential everywhere: the nationally popular television show *American Bandstand*, which featured teens dancing to the latest rock and roll hits of the day, integrated in 1957, for example. Although the show did not depict interracial couples—black teens danced with other black teens alone—the image of both black and white teens dancing to rock and roll must have had symbolic resonance for many across the country. However, there were significant limits to rock and roll's integrationist potential. In 1957, the same year *Bandstand* integrated, Freed's rival show *Rock 'n Roll Dance Party* was cancelled in part because of widespread outrage when black teen performer Frankie Lymon spontaneously danced with a white teen girl as the show was ending. The Ku Klux Klan also targeted rock and roll concerts and radio shows for violent protests because of the music's popularity across the color line. Releasing broadsides that indicated that rock and roll's interracial popularity would lead to miscegenation, Klan leaders played on long-held stereotypes of black male sexual predators. On the business side, white covers of black artists' songs also received disproportionately more airplay than black originals, revealing that ongoing inequalities persisted even in the supposedly color-blind realm of popular music. As a result, inferior white performers such as Pat Boone, who cultivated a lily-white image, outsold black stars such as Little Richard, and many lamented that black performing artists were not being given a fair opportunity to succeed in the music business. Chuck Berry, for example, was bilked out of royalty rights by white record executives, a common experience for black artists. African American leaders worried, too, that rock and roll's association with black culture would lead whites to equate blackness with the genre's supposedly negative traits, such as lewdness, wild behavior, and juvenile delinquency. For African Americans hoping to break into the expanding middle class, rock and roll seemed dangerous because of its association with "low" culture and its eschewal of middle-class conventions of behavior and deportment. Finally, white fan appreciation of black musicians did not necessarily mean that white audiences would be more receptive to black calls for civil rights; fraternities at white Southern

schools, for example, wholeheartedly supported segregationist efforts well into the 1960s, even as they welcomed black bands to perform.

Women performers also found restrictions on their ability to participate in the burgeoning genre. While black women such as Ruth Brown and LaVern Baker were major R&B stars who had considerable success in the early years of rock and roll, very few women participated in the latter half of the 1950s. White women were especially absent from rock and roll groups, a reflection of the dominant gender ideologies of the time, which expected women to be submissive and chaste. Because rock and roll concerts demanded that performers cut loose on stage, it was considered inappropriate for women to participate. Black women initially had greater freedom to take part in rock and roll's excessive energy and celebration, but only because they were often ignored by mainstream cultural ideals of womanhood. However, as the civil rights movement gained momentum in the late 1950s and aspirations for integration ran high in the black community, black women performers also became less conspicuous in R&B and rock and roll. "Girl groups" such as the Shirelles and the Supremes became more popular, with their stars dressing in elegant attire and singing hyperfeminine, smooth pop hits.

Three key African American performers of the 1950s, Domino, Berry, and "Little Richard" Penniman, highlight some of the avenues open to black male rock and roll artists as well as the color line's continuing importance. All three became major stars among both black and white audiences (all coincidentally releasing their first rock and roll hit songs in 1955), and cashed in on their success: Domino's "Ain't That a Shame" launched him to stardom with interracial audiences, Richard scored with "Tutti Frutti," and Berry first made it into the mainstream with "Maybellene." Each continued to produce major hit songs in the ensuing years, and headlined well-attended concerts across the country, showing the possibilities for black recording stars to reach a nationwide, biracial audience.

However, each of these three stars also faced certain limitations in their music and performances that showed the ongoing power of Jim Crow. When writing songs, each was careful to avoid explicitly addressing issues of racial injustice in their music. Although certain songs such as Berry's "Brown-Eyed Handsome Man" hinted at racial oppression, none targeted racism explicitly. Apparently fearful that they would be shunned by the industry and the general public, these recording artists shied away from the political, social, and legal issues being raised by the ongoing civil rights movement. These artists also strategically managed their public images. Domino's portly physique, jolly demeanor, and dutiful black wife, for example, allayed any fears that nervous whites may have had of him as a sexual predator; similarly, Richard's over-the-top hairstyle, outrageous makeup, and closeted, though apparent, homosexuality made him a nonthreatening figure as well. Aware of long-standing white fears of black men, these artists carefully crafted images that enabled them to succeed in mainstream America, still cautious of the Jim Crow line even as they achieved remarkable success. Berry even changed the protagonist of his 1958 hit song "Johnny B. Goode," from a "colored boy" to a "country boy," so that he would not alienate any white fans.

As rock and roll evolved into the genre of "rock" in the 1960s, issues of race continued to take center stage. When The Beatles and The Rolling Stones kicked off the so-called British Invasion in the early 1960s, both groups enthusiastically credited black R&B performers as their major influences, drawing more attention to rock and roll's history of racial crossing-over. Ironically, however, bemused British musicians often found that they had to educate white American fans who were unaware of the debt rock and roll owed to black performers of the 1940s and early 1950s. Meanwhile, as rock evolved in the 1960s, black musicians drifted away from the genre, devoting more energy and attention to music styles that seemed to fit better the changing climate of the late civil rights movement, such as soul and funk, before eventually turning to hip-hop in the 1980s. While some black performers continued to play rock music, such as the legendary guitarist Jimi Hendrix, on the whole, the genre gradually came to be dominated by white artists and white fans. The tenuous interracial coalition that had propelled rock and roll to the top of the charts in the mid to late 1950s largely dissolved. Its cultural legacies, however, in the form of crossover artists, the various subgenres that formed in its wake, and the visible signs of an integrated America, remained resonant for years to come.

GREGORY KALISS

See also
Jazz; Music Industry, Racism in; Rap Music; Rhythm and Blues

Further Reading:
Altschuler, Glenn C. *All Shook Up: How Rock 'n Roll Changed America.* New York: Oxford University Press, 2003.
Bertrand, Michael T. *Race, Rock, and Elvis.* Urbana: University of Illinois Press, 2000.
"Chuck Berry." Rock and Roll Hall of Fame and Museum. http://www.Rockhall.com/exhibitfeatured/chuck-berry/ (accessed May 29, 2008).
Szatmary, David P. *Rockin' in Time: A Social History of Rock-and-Roll.* Upper Saddle River, NJ: Pearson/Prentice Hall, 2007.
Ward, Brian. *Just My Soul Responding: Rhythm and Blues, Black Consciousness, and Race Relations.* Berkeley: University of California Press, 1998.

Rodney King Beating

The beating of Rodney King by police in Los Angeles in 1991 is often cited as a classic example of police brutality in the United States. On March 3, 1991, officers in the Los Angeles Police Department pursued Rodney King for speeding. He refused to pull over, and after a lengthy car chase through Los Angeles streets, King's vehicle was finally stopped. More than 20 officers surrounded King. At least two officers used batons or nightsticks, a stun gun, and physical force, beating King repeatedly. The others, including police supervisors, simply looked on. The officers did not stop, even though King was apparently subdued. A nearby apartment dweller caught the incident on videotape. The videotaped beating was seen over and over again on the news and in various media outlets.

There were two trials associated with the beating. In the first trial, in a California state court, the officers were acquitted by the jury. The officers claimed that they had acted appropriately in that they were responding to King's resisting arrest. All the jurors viewed the videotape and still came to that verdict for all four defendants. The not-guilty verdict led to civil disobedience in Los Angeles as riots broke out in April 1992. The police response to those riots has also been the subject of criticism in that they were very slow to react. Even before the riots, police were making fewer arrests. Some claim this was because

Brutally beaten by four white Los Angeles police officers after being pulled over while driving, Rodney King became a symbol for many of police brutality and racial prejudice. Shocked and angered by the acquittal of the officers, Los Angeles erupted into riots that lasted four days and left 54 people dead. Here, King meets with the press on April 29, 1992, in the midst of the riots, with a plea to the city: "Can't we all get along?" (AP/Wide World Photos)

of the publicity of the King case, specifically, fear of retaliation by the media or the public. Nevertheless, the officers were put on trial again, this time in federal court on civil rights charges, for which two of the officers were found guilty.

JOHN ETERNO

See also

Criminal Justice System an Racial Discrimination; Los Angeles (California) Riots of 1992; Racial Profiling

Further Reading:

Gerstenfeld, Phyllis B. *Hate Crimes: Causes, Controls and Controversies.* Los Angeles: SAGE, 2011.

Perry, Barbara. *In the Name of Hate: Understanding Hate Crimes.* New York: Routledge, 2001.

Ryan, Matt E. and Peter T. Leeson. "Hate Groups and Hate Crime." *International Review of Law and Economics* (2011).

Southern Poverty Law Center. "Active U.S. Hate Groups," http://www.splcenter.org/get-informed/hate-map (cited December 20, 2012).

Southern Poverty Law Center. "Hate Map," http://www.splcenter.org/get-informed/hate-map (cited December 20, 2012).

Roosevelt, Eleanor (1884–1962)

Eleanor Roosevelt, wife of Franklin D. Roosevelt (FDR), and first lady during the Great Depression and World War II, was the most prominent white American to work actively toward elimination of the country's Jim Crow laws.

The niece of President Theodore Roosevelt, Roosevelt was born into a wealthy family in New York City in 1884. Both her parents died during her childhood, but she grew up in a privileged household and attended a distinguished boarding school in England. FDR, a distant cousin, was part of her socially prominent circle of friends. They were engaged in 1903 and married in 1905. The couple had six children, including a son who died in infancy.

Roosevelt first acted on her concern for social activism in work with poor immigrant families at a settlement house in New York's Lower East Side during the early years of the 20th century. When FDR was stricken with polio in 1921, she cared for him devotedly and encouraged him to remain in politics. At the same time, she herself continued to work for social service agencies for the benefit of the underprivileged. When FDR was elected president in 1932, Roosevelt transformed the role of first lady, traveling the country, lecturing, holding press conferences, and writing a daily syndicated newspaper column, "My Day." By the time she began to speak on behalf of African Americans during the Great Depression, Roosevelt was already well experienced in conducting herself in the public eye and speaking out, in a moderate tone, on issues of justice and democracy.

From the start of her husband's presidency in 1933, Roosevelt was in the planning and implementation of progressive New Deal programs designed to help poor Americans. This work led her to counter Jim Crow laws. "There must be equality before the law," she wrote, "equality of education, equal opportunity to obtain a job according to one's ability and training and equality of participation in self government." But her egalitarian beliefs ran counter to the Southern social mores. An indication of the resentment Roosevelt engendered was the rumor that spread across the South of "Eleanor Clubs," which were said to have been organized among black domestics to agitate for better pay and working conditions. No evidence was ever found to substantiate the existence of any such clubs.

Eleanor Roosevelt worked with New Deal administrators to mitigate the effects of Jim Crow. In 1935, for example, she pushed Works Progress Administration officials to enact equitable policies in the administration of relief funds to black Southerners. She was also effective in involving black leaders in New Deal initiatives. For example, she brought to prominence Mary McLeod Bethune, who would become the most prominent African American in the New Deal, and the first black woman to hold an influential position in the U.S. government. Through Eleanor Roosevelt, Bethune would become a powerful influence in White House policies throughout the national crisis of the Great Depression.

Eleanor and Franklin Roosevelt worked together, in a sense, to weaken Jim Crow. FDR thought he could not himself directly attack long-standing Southern social traditions without losing necessary political support from white, Southern Democrats, but Eleanor Roosevelt felt compelled to be more outspoken on behalf of racial justice.

Her approach to Jim Crow was seen most famously in her appearance at the 1938 Southern Conference on Human Welfare (SCHW), held in Birmingham, Alabama. The high-water mark of Southern liberalism during the Great Depression, the conference brought together 1,200 black and white Southerners, labor leaders, the poor, and the dispossessed, along with political and business leaders, newspaper editors, and academics. The conference called for equal salaries for black and white teachers and endorsed federal anti-lynching laws.

Unexpectedly, the SCHW was forced to confront racism directly. Conference organizers had not planned to address the issue of segregation, but Birmingham's police chief decided to enforce an ordinance requiring segregation in the city's municipal auditorium. To avoid arrest, conference participants decided to arrange their seating with blacks on one side of the hall's central aisle and whites on the other.

Eleanor Roosevelt arrived late and quickly took a seat with the black participants. When a policeman informed her that she would have to move, the first lady moved her chair to the middle of the aisle. Asked later about her actions, Roosevelt avoided making any inflammatory remarks. "In the section of the country where I come from, it is a procedure that is not followed," she explained. "But I would not presume to tell the people of Alabama what they should do." Typical of her approach to questions of Jim Crow, Eleanor Roosevelt allowed the symbolism of her action to carry the weight of her beliefs. Conference organizers responded by vowing never again to conduct a segregated meeting.

By the time of the SCHW's 1942 meeting, Eleanor Roosevelt felt emboldened enough to claim the conference's work "is really as important as the war . . . because making the South a real part of the United States, and progressive in its racial and labor attitudes, is the finest work any one could do at the present time."

Eleanor Roosevelt actively supported a variety of initiatives aimed at ameliorating the injustice experienced by African Americans, including a controversial federal anti-lynching bill and the abolition of poll taxes. She famously resigned from the Daughters of the American Revolution when the organization refused to allow black opera singer Marian Anderson to perform in Constitution Hall in the spring of 1939. Eleanor Roosevelt's resignation was front-page news in hundreds of papers, and it turned the incident into a national event. The result was the scheduling of a groundbreaking concert in which Anderson sang to a live, nationwide radio audience from the steps of the Lincoln Memorial.

After her husband's death in 1945, Roosevelt became even more vocal in her opposition to Jim Crow. She joined the Board of Directors of the National Association for the Advancement of Colored People, in which capacity she lobbied the Truman administration to introduce low-income, federally financed housing. President Harry S. Truman's subsequent decision to integrate the military was instrumental in Roosevelt's decision to endorse his candidacy for the presidency in 1948.

During the 1950s, Roosevelt worked with Martin Luther King, Jr. and Rosa Parks to raise money for the Montgomery Bus Boycott and supported the Southern Conference Education Fund's work in desegregating hospitals. She warmly endorsed the U.S. Supreme Court's landmark 1954 decision in *Brown v. Board of Education* that called for the desegregation of nation's public schools. In her public addresses, she took aim at the hypocrisy of segregationists' simultaneous criticism of communism and support for Jim Crow. During the civil rights movement, Eleanor Roosevelt was a staunch defender of nonviolent civil disobedience. Indeed, in her elder years, before her death in 1962, Roosevelt called for a new "social revolution" to defeat the forces of segregation.

LOUIS MAZZARI

See also

Roosevelt, Franklin D.; World War II

Further Reading:

Egerton, John. *Speak Now Against the Day: The Generation Before the Civil Rights Movement in the South*. New York: Alfred A. Knopf, 1994.

"Eleanor Roosevelt and Civil Rights." Eleanor Roosevelt National Historic Site. http://www.nps.gov/archive/elro/teach-er-vk/lesson-plans/notes-er-and-civil-rights.htm (accessed May 29, 2008).

Freidel, Frank. *FDR and the South*. Baton Rouge: Louisiana State University Press, 1965.

Sitkoff, Harvard. *A New Deal for Blacks: The Emergence of Civil Rights as a National Issue*. New York: Oxford University Press, 1978.

Sullivan, Patricia. *Days of Hope: Race and Democracy in the New Deal Era*. Chapel Hill: University of North Carolina Press, 1996.

Roosevelt, Franklin D. (1882–1945)

Franklin Delano Roosevelt, who served as U.S. president from 1933 until his death in 1945, did more for racial justice in the United States than had any chief executive since Abraham Lincoln. The civil rights movement of the 1950s and 1960s had its beginning in the efforts of black and white Americans working under the auspices of the Roosevelt administration to ameliorate the most injurious effects of Jim Crow. Indeed, Roosevelt and his New Deal policies were responsible for the great majority of black Americans to shift their allegiance to the Democratic Party from their traditional base, the Republican Party of Lincoln.

Elected to lift the nation out of the Great Depression, Roosevelt's initial primary focus was resurrecting the American economy, and to do so, he needed the cooperation of the Southern Democrats in Congress. So he did not directly challenge Jim Crow, leaving the states to determine their own laws concerning race. Instead, he relied on liberals in his administration to push the South and the country toward equality and integration. In a sense, Roosevelt traded acquiescence to the South, in terms of segregation, for support for his liberalizing economic policies. In spite of his refusal to actively work toward ending Jim Crow, Roosevelt's administration was the nation's first to promote equality both in the workplace and on Main Street.

Roosevelt's focus on economic restructuring necessarily ate away at the underpinnings of Jim Crow. The New Deal's extensive programs in support of Americans' general welfare, in the areas of health, education, and housing, as well as workplace and agricultural reforms, meant the institution of greater federal planning. Inevitably, Southern states' control of their own racial policies was undermined by federal regulations that had the effect of standardizing even social policies across the nation. Federal efforts to strengthen American society in general worked to enervate local efforts to maintain white supremacy. New Deal programs themselves and the way they touched more blacks, from the use of birth certificates to the introduction of agricultural extension agencies, brought the federal government closer to the average African American and made the idea of political participation more likely.

Roosevelt's belief in the activism of the progressives he had attracted to his administration allowed him to avoid speaking directly to the inequalities of race and class in America. For example, FDR depended on the guidance of social scientists he brought to Washington—many of them from the University of North Carolina at Chapel Hill—to plumb the fallacies beneath the South's racial myths, and to turn new knowledge into practical service. Socialist leader Norman Thomas remembered a meeting with the president, in which Roosevelt refused to back Thomas's call for strong union legislation. "I know the South," Roosevelt told him, "and there is arising a new generation of leaders in the South and we've got to be patient."

Roosevelt hired for the upper echelons of New Deal agencies more than a hundred African Americans. He appointed the first black federal judge and the first black general officer in the U.S. Army. The New Deal disturbed the social, as well as economic, relations that Southern society had developed over decades. Important among the possibilities created by the New Deal was the destruction of Jim Crow laws.

Typical of Roosevelt's approach to racism and Jim Crow was his executive order integrating defense production, signed on June 25, 1941, as Europe was embroiled in World War II and the United States prepared for the possibility of entry into the conflict. Black leaders saw an opportunity to secure work in defense plants and to integrate the armed forces. A. Philip Randolph, president of the Brotherhood of Sleeping Car Porters, the nation's first black labor union, formulated the idea for a march on Washington to demonstrate African Americans' desire for their share of defense work, and the nation's black newspapers overwhelmingly supported the concept.

Roosevelt's response was characteristic. He invited Randolph and Walter White, head of the National Association for the Advancement of Colored People, to the White House and promised fairer treatment in the workplace. Randolph wanted what Roosevelt did not want to give him—a piece of legislation that conservatives could hold against him. With war imminent, the president did not intend to alter the makeup of the military, but he was willing to legislate against job discrimination once he was assured that it would not diminish war production. Randolph called off the march a week before black Americans were set to converge on Washington.

The order promulgated the rationale that the nation needed all the help it could get, "in the firm belief that the democratic way of life within the Nation can be defended successfully only with the help and support of all groups within its borders." Typically, Roosevelt couched this effort on behalf of black Americans in language that claimed no special prerogatives for minorities, but spoke instead to national security and the general welfare of all Americans. Innocuous as it seemed, the executive order set a precedent against discrimination in hiring that would be cited time and again in the coming years of the civil rights movement.

If Roosevelt thought he could not push to abolish Jim Crow laws, he was happy to be tugged along by the tide created by black leaders, including Randolph, White, and Mary McLeod Bethune, president of the National Association of Colored Women, as well as white civil rights leaders, including—most prominently—Eleanor Roosevelt, his wife.

Eleanor Roosevelt knew her husband's true feelings about civil rights. She wrote about a conversation with FDR and Walter White. "You go ahead," the president told White. "You do everything you can do. Whatever you can get done is okay with me, but I just can't do it." Afterwards, she asked, "Well, what about me? Do you mind if I say what I think?" Roosevelt answered, "No, certainly not. You can say anything you want. I can always say, 'Well, that is my wife; I can't do anything about her.'"

The initial steps taken by Roosevelt toward racial equality created an enormous influence on the subsequent generation of Democratic politicians. Among the most ardent young New Dealers came the sentiment that Roosevelt "was just like a daddy to me always." A died-in-the-wool Texan, Lyndon B. Johnson, would knowingly sacrifice the white

Southern vote to the Republicans for generations by sponsoring the most important civil rights legislation since Reconstruction, legislation that finally killed legal Jim Crow. "I don't know that I'd have ever come to Congress if it hadn't been for him," Johnson claimed. "But I do know I got my first great desire for public office because of him—and so did thousands of young men all over the country."

LOUIS MAZZARI

See also

Great Depression; New Deal; Roosevelt, Eleanor; Works Progress Administration; World War II

Further Reading:

Egerton, John. *Speak Now against the Day: The Generation before the Civil Rights Movement in the South.* New York: Alfred A. Knopf, 1994.

Freidel, Frank. *FDR and the South.* Baton Rouge: Louisiana State University Press, 1965.

Sitkoff, Harvard. *A New Deal for Blacks: The Emergence of Civil Rights as a National Issue.* New York: Oxford University Press, 1978.

Sullivan, Patricia. *Days of Hope: Race and Democracy in the New Deal Era.* Chapel Hill: University of North Carolina Press, 1996.

Woodward, C. Vann. *The Strange Career of Jim Crow.* New York: Oxford University Press, 1955.

Rope and Faggot: A Biography of Judge Lynch

Published in 1929, Walter White's *Rope and Faggot: A Biography of Judge Lynch* was praised by James Weldon Johnson as the most comprehensive and authoritative treatise on lynching to date. Building on the important work of anti-lynching crusader Ida B. Wells-Barnett, *Rope and Faggot* explores the social, political, and economic motives behind lynching. According to White, less than 30 percent of African American men lynched in the South were actually accused of sexually assaulting white women. More often than not, lynching was used as a means of intimidation, as an attempt to control black labor. *Rope and Faggot* publicized these and other harsh truths about the phenomenon of lynching.

Walter White first experienced the dark, violent side of human nature at the tender age of 13 during the Atlanta race riots (*see* Atlanta [Georgia] Riot of 1906). In his autobiography, *A Man Called White* (1948), White admits to being too naïve to fully appreciate the ramifications of the mounting racial tension that preceded the riots. He recalls reading the inflammatory headlines in the local newspapers, which fuelled the flames of racial hatred with their accounts of alleged rapes and other crimes committed by African Americans. Barricaded inside his home while an angry white mob marched through his neighborhood, White was enlightened to the fact that he belonged to a race condemned to suffering and abuse for no less a reason than the pigmentation of their skin. Yet, even as a boy, White recognized the inexplicable—that his skin was as white as the skin of those who sought to destroy him. With his blonde hair, blue eyes, and white skin, Walter White could have aligned himself with the dominant race. Instead, White chose to use his fair complexion to investigate crimes committed against members of his own race.

While working undercover for the National Association for the Advancement of Colored People (NAACP), White investigated more than 30 lynchings and eight race riots, the facts of which would later be published in *Rope and Faggot*. Within two weeks of joining the NAACP, White requested permission to investigate the lynching of an African American sharecropper in Tennessee named Jim McIlherron. The trepidation White felt as he embarked on his first planned attempt to pass as a white man was intensified by his knowledge of the severity of the penalty for such a trespass should he be caught. By feigning first ignorance of and then a lack of interest in the lynching, White successfully entrusted himself to the guilty parties. Boasting of more exciting lynchings, White was able to goad the participants into revealing the exact details of the murder. Despite the harrowing nature of this experience, White continued to pass for white in an attempt to expose the magnitude and severity of the lynching epidemic in the South. He even went so far as to infiltrate the most notorious white supremacist organization, the Ku Klux Klan (KKK). Although his deception was eventually discovered and his life threatened, White was nonetheless successful in obtaining incriminating evidence against the Klan. With the assistance of an ex-Klan member, White was able to confirm the Klan's involvement in a triple lynching in South Carolina. Ironically, when it was revealed how he obtained the pertinent information, it was White who was threatened with prosecution. The culmination of more than a decade of hands-on research, *Rope and Faggot* was the first full-length indictment of lynching of its time. Through *Rope and Faggot*, Walter White hoped to expose the barbarity of lynching and to sway public opinion against the perpetrators of such heinous crimes.

CAROL GOODMAN

See also

American Literature and Racism; Lynching; National Association for the Advancement of Colored People (NAACP)

Further Reading:

Janken, Kenneth Robert. *White: The Biography of Walter White, Mr. NAACP*. New York: New Press, 2003.
White, Walter. *A Man Called White: The Autobiography of Walter White*. New York: Viking Press, 1948.
White, Walter. *Rope and Faggot*. New York: Arno Press, 1969.

Rosewood (Florida) Riot of 1923

The town of Rosewood, Florida, which had previously seen little racial conflict, erupted in racially motivated violence in January 1923. An accusation from a white woman from a nearby town about an assault by a black man caused Rosewood to experience mob behavior, collective amnesia, and many years later produced a movie and debate over reparations to the families of the Rosewood victims.

The town, now nonexistent, was located in Levy County on the western coast of the state of Florida, 40 miles west of Gainesville, and nine miles east of Cedar Key. By 1923, Rosewood comprised approximately 120 to 150 residents, most of whom were African American. The small town consisted of approximately 30 homes, which were mostly small shanty shacks, a post office, a hotel, and a few small businesses, a school, a few churches, a Masonic lodge, a railroad depot, and a sawmill. One of the small businesses was a general store that was operated by the town's only white resident, John Wright.

The town received its name for the area's abundance of trees that were highly valued for furniture. When the trees had been exhausted, mill operations were moved from Rosewood to the predominantly white community of nearby Sumner, and many of the residents of Rosewood found work at the Sumner mill. The men who continued to work in Rosewood were primarily farmers, hunters, and trappers. The women of Rosewood often found work as domestic laborers for the white families of Sumner. According to reports, there had been a generally harmonious relationship between the blacks and whites of the area until January 1, 1923.

With the new year came an unusually cold spell of weather, causing frost to accumulate on the palmettos that covered the area. Although it was New Year's Day, the mill at Sumner continued to operate, and the mill workers from Rosewood made their normal three-mile walk to their workplace. James Taylor, a white mill worker, was on the job at the mill that day, having left his young housewife, Fannie, and their two children at home. At one point that morning, Fannie came running out of the Taylor home, crying and shrieking that she had been assaulted, perhaps sexually, by an unidentified black man. Fannie Taylor told her neighbors of the attack and produced visible bruises, such as a bleeding mouth, as a confirmation of her story and was taken to a neighbor's house when she became faint. Several of Sumner's citizens gathered outside of the house and quickly spread the word of the attack. The white community became extremely angry and set out to find the perpetrator of this act. Although the young housewife was obviously assaulted by someone, no examination was ever performed on Taylor by a physician.

The black community, however, had a different version of the story. On hearing the accounts of the alleged attack, Sarah Carrier, a housekeeper for Mrs. Taylor, and her granddaughter both claimed that an unidentified white man visited Taylor at her home that morning. They believed that she and this unknown person were secretly having a romantic affair, and that morning they got into an argument and he physically assaulted her.

A group of white men from the Sumner area embarked on a hunt for the black man they believed was responsible for the attack. Robert Elias "Rob" Walker, the Levy County sheriff, had reported that an escapee from a prison work crew named Jesse Hunter was being sought, and this person became the key suspect. The sheriff brought in tracking dogs, and the trail was followed to Rosewood.

Aaron Carrier, a black resident from Rosewood, and a veteran of World War I, was questioned and coerced into providing information about the whereabouts of Jesse Hunter, the alleged attacker. After being tied to the back of a car and dragged, Carrier stated that Sam Carter, a local blacksmith, might be responsible for hiding the assailant. Carrier was delivered to a jail in Bronson, Florida, for his protection, and was later removed from the area. The bloodhounds carried the angry mob to Sam Carter's house. The whites became convinced that Carter was guilty of hiding the fugitive from the authorities. Carter, who was not at home, was found at a relative's house and abducted. The posse strung up Carter over a tree limb to get him to tell them where he hid the culprit.

Ernest Parham, a white citizen and an employee of the general store, later claimed that he implored the mob to release Carter, which they did. The posse began to cut him with knives to force him to give information as to where the wanted man was left by Carter. Seriously wounded by the knife cuts and beatings, Carter led the group to a place where he claimed to have left Hunter. The dogs failed to pick up a scent, however, and Carter was unexpectedly shot in the face and killed by one of the members of the mob. Authorities found Carter's mutilated body the next day. From reports, it seems possible that neither Sheriff Walker nor his deputy Clarence Williams were aware of this vigilante squad.

Three days had passed since Fannie Taylor made the accusations when the Sumner residents heard that Hunter was in Rosewood, in the care of a man named Sylvester Carrier, known locally as "man." Carrier was a large man who had an intense anger toward whites in the area. A mob of white men went to Carrier's residence that night, broke into the home, and was met with gunfire from Carrier. Two of the members of the mob, C. P. Wilkerson and Henry "Boots" Andrews, were killed when they tried to enter the residence; the other members of the party retreated from the house. Gunfire resumed by both groups, however, and Sarah Carrier was killed in the gunfight. The children in the house, who had been moved upstairs for protection, retreated into the woods with adult relatives. Sylvester Carrier was reportedly killed in the exchange of gunfire; however, some reports say that the person believed to be Carrier was actually someone else, and that Carrier left that night and moved away from Rosewood. This version was believed by many, as it was claimed that Carrier sent cards and letters to Rosewood families years after the incident.

The violence increased the following day as people from other North Florida towns and cities such as Gainesville and Jacksonville, and even some people from towns in South Georgia, came to observe the situation playing out in Rosewood. It appears that they also came prepared to participate, if possible. Ailing widow Lexie Gordon was killed and her house was set ablaze, Mingo Adams was shot by an angry mob north of town, and James Carrier, who had been rescued from the swamp, was killed after being forced to dig his own grave.

Seeing the situation escalate, some whites from Sumner came to the aid of the blacks, hiding them and arranging for safe passage from the area. Two white conductors from Cedar Key, on hearing of the carnage in Rosewood, sent railcars into the area to transport blacks. Only women and children were allowed to take the train ride because hauling the male passengers would be too risky for the conductors and crew as well as the women and children. The general store owner, John Wright, also hid several of the blacks in his expansive home until they could be rescued by the train and relocated to Gainesville. Homes in Rosewood were burned to the ground, but Wright's house was passed over since he was the only white resident in the town.

After five days, the racial violence sparked by Fannie Taylor's accusations in the small town of Rosewood ended. The remaining residents eventually moved away when the sawmill in Sumner burned and relocated to Pasco County. Rosewood survivors moved to Jacksonville, Miami, or out-of-state locales.

A special grand jury was convened on January 29, 1923, in Bronson at the request of Gov. Cary Hardee to investigate the incident at Rosewood. The grand jury found no evidence of criminal activity by law enforcement officials in the handling of the situation. Charges were never brought against any of the people who were involved in the Rosewood killings, participated in arson, or were a party to the alleged assault against Taylor. There are no records of the grand jury proceedings, except for descriptions that were given in local newspapers.

Newspapers, not only in Florida but those across the nation, reported the events of the Rosewood melee. For the most part, the issue left the public eye until 1982, when a journalist named Gary Moore investigated the history of the Rosewood situation and reported on it in a local publication called *The Floridian*, a magazine supplement for the *St. Petersburg Times* newspaper. The article gained national attention and, in 1983, CBS aired a segment of its *60 Minutes* news program on the events in Rosewood in 1923.

In 1993, largely due to the work of Arnett Doctor, a descendant of Rosewood survivor Philomena Goins, the matter appeared before the Florida state legislature in an attempt to recognize the event and to consider compensation to the families of the victims. As a result of House and Senate bills, an investigation was promulgated and a research team of scholars from three state universities, the University of Florida, Florida State University, and Florida A&M, were commissioned to provide additional information about the events. Issues were raised about possible reparations to the families of the Rosewood victims, and connections were made between other complaints that ended up providing reparations, especially in the case of the evacuation and displacement of Japanese-Americans during World War II. Since both cases involved relocation without the ability to return to their homes (in the Rosewood situation, they were unable to return due to fear), the fact that law enforcement at the time did little to fully investigate the situation or arrest those responsible, and due to the failure of the legal system to investigate and prosecute the perpetrators of the violence, awards in the amount of $220 to $450,000 were given to 172 Rosewood survivors for emotional trauma. Also, funds were provided for demonstrated property loss as a result of the massacre. In addition, the Rosewood Bill required an investigation into any possible surviving perpetrators to consider criminal proceedings; this investigation occurred, and there were no survivors located. The last provision of the bill was to provide a state university scholarship for the Rosewood descendants.

In 1996, a book about the incident titled *Like Judgment Day: The Ruin and Redemption of a Town Called Rosewood* was published. It was followed by a movie version simply titled *Rosewood* that was released by Warner Brothers Motion Pictures in 1997. Many Americans who had never heard the story of a Southern town that was wiped out because of racially motivated behavior that left several dead, many traumatized, and many more displaced, were stunned to learn of the event. The lives of those involved with the so-called massacre and their descendants would forever be changed as a result of the events in Rosewood, Florida, on New Year's Day in 1923.

LEONARD A. STEVERSON

See also

Race Riots in America; Rape as Provocation for Lynching; White Mobs. Documents: The Report on the Memphis Riots of May 1866 (July 25, 1866); Account of the Riots in East St. Louis, Illinois (July 1917); The Cook County Coroner's Report Regarding the 1919 Chicago Race Riots (1919); A Southern Black Woman's Letter Regarding the Recent Riots in Chicago and Washington (November 1919); The Final Report of the Grand Jury on the Tulsa Race Riot (June 25, 1921); Testimony from *Laney v. United States* Describing Events during the Washington, D.C., Riot of July 1919 (December 3, 1923); The Governor's Commission Report on the Watts Riots (December 1965); Cyrus R. Vance's Report on the Riots in Detroit (July–August 1967); The Reports of the Oklahoma Commission to Study the Tulsa Race Riot of 1921 (2000–2001); The Draft Report of the 1898 Wilmington Race Riot Commission (December 2005)

Further Reading:

D'Orso, Michael. *Like Judgment Day: The Ruin and Redemption of a Town Called Rosewood.* New York: G. P. Putnam's Sons, 1996.

Hixson, Richard. "Special Master's Final Report." Letter to the Honorable Bo Johnson, Speaker of the House of Representatives, March 24, 1994. http://afgen.com/roswood2.html.

Jones, Daryl L. "Address to the Black Reparations & Self-Determination Conference." Washington Metropolitan A.M.E. Church, Washington, D.C., June 11, 1999. http://www.directBlackaction.com/roserep.htm.

Runaway Slave Advertisements

During the antebellum period, many slave owners placed advertisements in newspapers to alert people about escaped slaves, to provide information to identify the individuals who had run away, and to offer a reward to encourage whites to capture runaway slaves and return them to the advertisers. Details in the advertisements help 21st-century scholars learn about the attitudes of masters toward their slaves, the clothing worn by slaves, the material objects that enslaved laborers used, the skills that slaves possessed, the ties that enslaved laborers formed to family and friends, the reasons why some slaves escaped, and the ways in which slavery varied in the United States.

Slave owners wanted to regain possession of escaped laborers for several reasons. First, the act of running away was a direct challenge to the institution of slavery and the laws that whites used to control slaves. Second, masters depended on the work of the enslaved men, women, and children who tended plantation crops, practiced trades, and took care of domestic work. In addition, owners wanted to have possession of the people whom they saw as their personal property and the equivalent of cash.

Having learned of a slave's escape, an owner usually waited several weeks or even months before writing an advertisement. Masters put off the expense of placing an announcement in a newspaper because they believed that they knew where the escapees had gone and that many of these individuals would return on their own. Owners expected some runaways—described as "absentees"—to head back after they spent a few days with family members. Slave owners used the term "lying out" in reference to runaways who remained in the area of their home plantation. Some lying-out slaves left to protest harsh treatment from an overseer. While away, they demanded better treatment in the form of time off, additional food, new clothes, and amnesty for leaving the plantation. If the absentee and lying-out slaves did not return after a short time, masters began to search for them on plantations where their family members lived.

After waiting for some escapees to return and failing to locate these individuals in the local area, a number of slave owners might decide to place an advertisement in their newspaper. Masters classified this group of runaways as "fugitives." Some fugitive slaves ran short distances from their master's home; others tried to get as far away as possible from their owner's property.

Many of the advertisements began with "Ran," "Run," "Ran away," or "Run away." Often the printer set the opening in bold, capital letters to catch the eyes of the reader. Other openings included the date a slave ran away and the place from which the escape was made. Also, some advertisers used a reward to attract whites and interest them in helping to capture a runaway.

Having gained the reader's attention, the advertiser turned to pertinent details about the appearance of the escaped slave. When possible, owners included the name of the escapee, often in capital letters, the fugitive's gender, and a physical description of the individual. In some cases, the master also knew the approximate age, height, and hairstyle of the runaway. If the escapee had scars—either from ritual scarification in Africa or work-related injuries—or body piercings, the advertiser noted this information in the announcement.

In addition to details about a fugitive's appearance, owners often described the clothing that the individual wore when last seen. A runaway who wore ill-fitting clothes made of coarse osnaburg was a field slave. An escapee attired in finer, tailored clothing was a domestic slave. Some masters knew that the runaway took additional garments, sometimes pilfered from the slaveholder, when leaving and included information about these items.

After describing a runaway's appearance and attire, the advertiser turned to additional details that a white person could use to identify a fugitive. Announcements might include the master's subjective assessment of a slave's personality. Owners used a wide range of adjectives to describe escapees. Some were described as shy, surly, or bold. Others were described as self-confident, determined, resourceful, and articulate. An owner might comment on the skills of the escapee if he was a proficient agricultural worker or a trained artisan or if she was an accomplished domestic servant. If a master thought that a skilled slave carried the tools of his trade—including carpentry, joining, blacksmithing, and shoemaking—enabling him to earn money and try to pass as a free black in an urban area, it was noted in the advertisement.

Some slave owners commented on the possible destination of the fugitive. The advertisers who included these details did so because they had knowledge about the escapee's family and friends. Masters noted the location of a spouse's plantation or a runaway's previous owner if they believed that the runaway left to see relatives and others whom they knew. These destinations ranged from a few miles from the owner's residence to hundreds of miles away. The distances that a fugitive traveled increased in the 19th century. The domestic slave trade divided families and tore apart the communities slaves had created. This forced migration led to an increased number of slaves running off to visit spouses, children, and other kin. Many runaways traveled along rivers—including the Ohio, Mississippi, and Tennessee—to their previous homes. Others moved north along the Natchez Trace and then across the Appalachian Mountains to find family members.

Advertisers knew that slaves escaped for reasons other than to visit relatives and friends. Some slaves departed from their master's property because they were preachers and wanted to teach enslaved men, women, and children about their faith. Masters were aware that some escapees struck out from plantations, cities, and towns because they believed that they had a right to their freedom. During the American Revolution, thousands of slaves ran to the British to fight against their "rebel" masters and to seize their independence. In the 19th century, abolitionists helped slaves to escape and find freedom in Northern states and in Canada.

After noting a wide range of details that would help a white person to identify an escapee, some owners reminded readers that they should not assist a runaway. Many advertisers concluded their notice with information about the amount of the reward and where the captured fugitive should be taken. A few noted that a particular slave had been outlawed and could be returned dead or alive.

The odds of escaping slavery were small, and runaway slave advertisements helped many masters regain possession of enslaved laborers. In some instances, whites captured fugitives who refused to state either their name or that of their master. Local officials placed the escapee in jail until the master could be notified. Jail keepers placed advertisements in newspapers to let readers know about the slaves held in prisons. Often the notices written by jailers were shorter and had fewer details because the runaway refused to provide information. The jailer noted the gender and physical description of the escapee. The announcement concluded with an appeal to the owner to claim the slave and to pay the costs of keeping the fugitive in prison as well as a reward to the white person who found the escapee.

Details in the runaway slave advertisements and notices placed by jail keepers indicate that whites were aware of the humanity of enslaved laborers even though they considered these men, women, and children to be personal property. Taken as a whole, the particulars about 17th-, 18th-, and 19th-century fugitive slaves reveal the variety of experiences that enslaved men, women, and children had during the time that slavery was legal in Britain's North American colonies and the United States.

JULIE RICHTER

See also

Slave Trade; Slavery; Slavery in the Antebellum South

Further Reading:

Costa, Tom. "The Geography of Slavery in Virginia." http://www2.vcdh.virginia.edu/gos/.

"Enslavement: Runaways." Toolbox Library: Primary Resources in U.S. History and Literature, National Humanities Center. http://nationalhumanitiescenter.org/pds/maai/enslavement/text8/text8read.htm.

Franklin, John Hope, and Loren Schweninger. *Runaway Slaves: Rebels on the Plantation.* New York: Oxford University Press, 1999.

Greene, Lorenzo J. "The New England Negro as Seen in Advertisements for Runaway Slaves." *Journal of Negro History* 29, no. 2 (April 1944): 125–46.

Smith, Billy G., and Richard Wojtowicz. *Blacks Who Stole Themselves: Advertisements for Runaways in the Pennsylvania Gazette, 1728–1790.* Philadelphia: University of Pennsylvania Press, 1989.

Rustin, Bayard (1912–1987)

Bayard Taylor Rustin was an organizer and activist for racial equality around the world. As one of the earliest American proponents of nonviolent direct action, he brought groundbreaking protest strategies out of the pacifist movement to leaders in the civil rights movement. Rustin worked behind the scenes for many organizations, and leaders including A. Philip Randolph and Martin Luther King, Jr. considered Rustin's gifts as a strategist and theorist integral to their campaigns. As an openly gay African American man, Rustin personally faced a good deal of discrimination, even within the progressive organizations with which he worked. Of Rustin's many achievements, he is perhaps best known for serving as the chief organizer for the 1963 March on Washington for Jobs and Freedom. Throughout his life, Rustin sought to illuminate connections between racial discrimination and economic inequality and to reveal the power of nonviolence as a tool for social change.

Born on March 17, 1912, Rustin was raised by his grandparents Julia and Janifer Rustin in West Chester, Pennsylvania. Julia Rustin raised her grandson as a Quaker and taught him about nonviolence and about respecting all people as part of a human family. Julia Rustin also helped charter West Chester's National Association for the Advancement of Colored People (NAACP) chapter. The Rustin household served

Bayard Rustin was one of the most skillful organizers among the leaders of the civil rights movement. He was also influential in a range of other causes: pacifism, refugees, nuclear disarmament, Japanese American rights, and gay rights. (Library of Congress)

as a guest house for African American leaders denied service at local hotels, including W.E.B. Du Bois and James Weldon Johnson. West Chester remained segregated during Rustin's youth, but the town's small size necessitated the integration of West Chester High School. Rustin excelled athletically, academically, and socially in high school, but began to feel the sting of racism more clearly as he got older. Rustin cultivated friendships with students of many different backgrounds, but found that they could not interact freely outside of school or on school trips.

Rustin spent time at Wilberforce University in Ohio and Cheney State Teachers College in Pennsylvania from 1932 to 1936. He joined the Society of Friends (Quakers) in 1937 and soon moved to New York City. Living in Harlem in 1937,

Rustin embraced a locally thriving gay community that allowed him a good deal of personal growth, even within a larger African American culture that urged extreme discretion in matters of sexual identity.

Rustin joined the Young Communist League (YCL) at City College of New York in 1938, drawn by the Communist Party of America's commitment to peace and civil rights. Rustin left the YCL in June 1941, and began working with influential African American labor leader A. Philip Randolph. Randolph made Rustin a youth director for a planned March on Washington for Negro Americans. When President Franklin D. Roosevelt integrated the defense industry to avoid the demonstration, Randolph cancelled the march. Rustin bitterly disagreed with Randolph's decision, but their work in 1941 began a long partnership between the two leaders.

In 1941 Rustin also began working with A. J. Muste at the pacifist Fellowship of Reconciliation (FOR). As a youth secretary with the FOR, Rustin traveled throughout the South teaching about nonviolent direct action, or using techniques of peaceful protest in an organized way to agitate for social change. Rustin's work slowed in 1943, however, when the federal government sent him to prison for resisting the draft as a conscientious objector. In the Ashland, Kentucky, prison where he was held, Rustin led protests against Jim Crow eating areas within the facility. Upon his release in March 1947, Rustin returned to the FOR and worked with Muste, James Farmer, and George Houser in the affiliated Congress of Racial Equality (CORE).

Farmer, Houser, and Rustin planned the Journey of Reconciliation through the upper South to test the U.S. Supreme Court decision in *Morgan v. Virginia* (1946), which prohibited segregation on interstate transportation. The CORE plan called for interracial duos of men to travel from Washington, D.C., on public buses and nonviolently resist orders to abide by Jim Crow seating arrangements on a moral and legal basis. Authorities in Chapel Hill, North Carolina, arrested Rustin and sentenced him to 30 days on a chain gang. While the journey was only marginally successful, it marked a turning point in Rustin's work, and inspired the Freedom Rides attempted by CORE and the Student Nonviolent Coordinating Committee (SNCC) in 1961. Throughout the 1950s, Rustin worked closely under Muste and Randolph and spoke around the world. However, in January 1953, California police arrested and prosecuted Rustin for sodomy (coded as "lewd conduct"), a charge that Rustin denied. Muste then distanced himself from his protégé because of the negative publicity the arrest could bring in the intolerant political climate of the 1950s.

Rustin denied the charges and found his feet quickly as executive secretary for the War Resisters League. On a short leave of absence in 1956, Rustin traveled South to offer counsel to the new leader of the Montgomery Bus Boycott, Martin Luther King, Jr. Rustin became one of King's closest advisors and strengthened King's commitment to nonviolence in all aspects of his life and work. From New York, Rustin continued to speak with King about effective organizing techniques, and about the need for a permanent organization to build on

the success of Montgomery. At meetings in Atlanta and New Orleans, Rustin worked with Stanley Levinson and Ella Baker to draft the original documents that would form the Southern Christian Leadership Conference (SCLC) in 1957, stressing voter education and the use of nonviolent mass protest to force integration. Rustin remained in the SCLC for several years and helped coordinate plans to stage protests at the Democratic National Convention in 1960. Harlem Congressman Adam Clayton Powell Jr., upset at being excluded from planning, jealously threatened to publicize rumors centering on Rustin's sexuality. King flinched at the potential damage the threat held, and accepted Rustin's resignation from the SCLC. Distraught over yet another ousting from the inner circle of movement leadership, Rustin turned to international peace activism in Europe and Africa in the early 1960s.

Rustin's return to the national civil rights movement came again at Randolph's insistence in 1963. Randolph asked Rustin to plan a march in Washington, D.C., to decry the still unrealized promise of freedom for black Americans. Randolph and Rustin sought the involvement of a broad coalition of progressive groups, including the SCLC, the NAACP, the Urban League, CORE, the SNCC, and various labor unions. Randolph countered NAACP head Roy Wilkins's objections to Rustin's involvement by agreeing to head a committee to organize the march, and immediately naming Rustin as his deputy. Thus, Rustin controlled of all aspects of the march, delegating responsibility and orchestrating among the sponsor organization. In roughly two months, Rustin planned the March on Washington for Jobs and Freedom that took place on August 28, 1963. The march brought hundreds of thousands of people into the capital to peacefully protest continued segregation around the country and to plead for economic equality. Rustin deftly coordinated between leaders of all involved movement groups, metropolitan and police authorities, transportation and sanitation services, thousands of volunteers, celebrities and speakers, and with the U.S. government. The March on Washington proved a success, and has been judged by many to be a high point in the national civil rights movement, anchored by King's "I Have A Dream" speech. National publicity as well as face-to-face meetings between the civil rights leaders, President John F. Kennedy, and members of Congress helped garner support for the legislation that would eventually become the Civil Rights Act of 1964 and the Voting Rights Act of 1965, which invalidated Jim Crow practices around the United States. After the march, Rustin appeared with Randolph on the cover of *Life* magazine.

Rustin found himself disappointed at the inability of civil rights groups to build upon the success and consensus of the March on Washington. As factionalism grew between and within groups like the SNCC and the SCLC, Rustin also found himself becoming more distant from their leadership. Rustin served as an advisor during SNCC's Mississippi "Freedom Summer" in 1964, working to help plan the mass voter registration campaign, and training volunteers in nonviolence at the request of James Lawson. His work with the SNCC to fight Jim Crow in Mississippi that summer was among his last operations with the SNCC. Once the young radical, Rustin came to view participation in the political process, as opposed to direct action, as the next step in achieving racial equality. His influential essay, "From Protest to Politics: The Future of the Civil Rights Movement" (*Commentary*, February 1965) evinced the widening gap between Rustin and militancy and racial separatism gaining popularity among young activists. In March 1965, Rustin announced the creation of the A. Philip Randolph Institute. As head of the organization, Rustin worked to strengthen relationships between civil rights groups and labor unions in order to build coalitions that would affect social and economic equality. Rustin viewed the oppression of racial minorities and systemic poverty as closely intertwined, and saw solving both problems as a necessary and achievable goal.

Rustin continued to work for peace and civil rights throughout the 1960s, leading youth marches for integrated schools in New York and mobilizing for King's Poor People's Campaign in 1968. Rustin remained active internationally through the 1970s, speaking against the Vietnam War and bringing attention to the struggles of refugees in Southeast Asia. In the 1980s, Rustin began to speak out more publicly for gay rights, pointing out the continuities between oppression based on sexuality and race. Bayard Rustin died in August 1987 at the age of 75.

BRIAN PIPER

See also
Civil Rights Movement

Further Reading:

Anderson, Jervis. *Bayard Rustin: Troubles I've Seen*. New York: HarperCollins, 1997.

D'Emilio, John. *Lost Prophet: The Life and Times of Bayard Rustin*. New York: Free Press, 2003.

Levine, Daniel. *Bayard Rustin and the Civil Rights Movement*. New Brunswick, NJ: Rutgers University Press, 2000.

Rustin, Bayard, Devon W. Carbado, and Donald Weise, eds. *Time on Two Crosses: The Collected Writings of Bayard Rustin*. San Francisco: Cleis Press, 2003.

S

Sainte Genevieve (Missouri) Riot of 1930

The Sainte Genevieve (Missouri) Race Riot was a four-day racial disturbance occurring between October 12 and 15, 1930, during which mobs of armed white vigilantes drove nearly all of the black residents from this small Mississippi River town, including several families whose ancestors had lived there for more than a century. The mob's action irrevocably changed the racial composition of the town and almost completely destroyed its long-standing African American community. Except for the double murder that triggered the unrest, no bloodshed or property destruction actually occurred during this incident, which might be more accurately described as a "near riot" or "averted riot." Nonetheless, white mobs succeeded in using racial terrorism, intimidation, and threats of violence to decimate Sainte Genevieve's African American population and to reinforce the community's traditional racial hierarchy.

Founded around 1750, Sainte Genevieve was one of the first French colonial outposts west of the Mississippi River; today it holds the distinction of being Missouri's oldest permanent white settlement. In 1930, on the eve of the riot, Sainte Genevieve was a lime-mining and agricultural center with a population of 2,658 residents, the overwhelming majority of whom were white Roman Catholics. Many of the town's adult male residents worked for one of the four lime-mining companies in the area, one of several stone quarries,

or for the Missouri-Illinois Railroad, which maintained a roundhouse and shop just north of town. Approximately 160 African American residents also lived in the town, with an almost equal number scattered throughout the surrounding county. Race relations in Sainte Genevieve were complicated by the fact that, at the time, two distinct black communities actually existed within the town. One group consisted of approximately 70 longtime residents. Many of them were descended from Sainte Genevieve County slaves and free people of color, some of whom were of mixed French and African heritage. The other group consisted of about 90 Southern migrants, chiefly from Tennessee, Mississippi, and Arkansas, who had arrived during the mid-1920s to work in the local lime mines and rock quarries. Most of these newcomers were Protestants, owned little or no property, and lived in a shantytown called the Shacks or in mining camps on the outskirts of town. Apparently, the two black communities seldom interacted.

The trouble that precipitated the four-day Sainte Genevieve race riot began on Saturday night, October 11, 1930, when two white lime kiln workers named Harry Panchot and Paul Ritter attended a black dance at the Shacks. At around 12:50 A.M., as the dance broke up, three black migrants—a quarry worker named Lonnie Taylor, originally from Tennessee; Columbus Jennings, a Mississippi native and also a quarryman; and Vera Rogers, from nearby Crystal City,

Missouri—offered Panchot and Ritter $1.50 to drive them to a craps game at a boat landing located two miles north of town. According to Ritter, when the group arrived, the two black men drew .38-caliber revolvers, ordered them out of the automobile, and then robbed them of $45 in cash and a pocket watch.

After collecting their valuables, Taylor fatally shot Panchot in the chest at point-blank range and then fired once at Ritter, wounding him in the abdomen. The bullet lodged in Ritter's spine, paralyzing him below the waist. Taylor and Jennings then dragged the white men to the edge of the riverbank and heaved them into the Mississippi River. The frigid water revived the unconscious Ritter, and, after realizing he was still alive, Taylor and Jennings hurled rocks at the wounded man, one of which fractured his skull. Thirty minutes later, federal prohibition agents, who were guarding a confiscated bootlegger's boat nearby, heard Ritter's cries for help. They rescued him and recovered Panchot's body from the river. Ritter was rushed by ambulance to St. Anthony's Hospital in St. Louis, where he was diagnosed to be in critical condition.

Within hours of the shootings, Sainte Genevieve County Sheriff Louis Ziegler and his deputies launched an intense manhunt for the alleged murderers. They soon arrested Taylor, Jennings, and Rogers, whom several witnesses had seen leaving the dance in Ritter's automobile. Meanwhile, news of Panchot's murder and Ritter's wounding spread throughout the town and the surrounding countryside. As Sunday Mass let out at the Sainte Genevieve Catholic Church, a crowd of more than 500 people assembled at the courthouse to await news of the ongoing investigation. Inside the courthouse, after more than four hours of intense questioning, Jennings and Rogers confessed to being at the boat landing the previous night. They both denied taking part in the shooting, and claimed that Taylor was the actual triggerman. Confronted with his accomplices' signed statements, Taylor confessed to shooting the two white men, but stated that he had done so in self-defense. He had shot the men, he told authorities, during a fistfight that broke out after Ritter insulted Rogers by offering her 50¢ to have sex with him. What actually transpired will probably forever remain a mystery, but after wringing confessions from the three prisoners, Sheriff Ziegler and two deputies whisked them away to Hillsboro, Missouri, located 40 miles to the northwest, to prevent them from being lynched by the angry crowd gathered outside.

That Sunday night, armed bands of white men in automobiles visited the black districts in Sainte Genevieve and the outlying districts and warned black residents to leave town by 5:00 P.M. the next day, or else face serious reprisals. These self-appointed vigilantes, some of whom a St. Louis newspaper claimed belonged to the Knights of Columbus, made no distinction between longtime residents and recent newcomers; all African Americans, regardless of family background or social status, were banished from Sainte Genevieve. On Monday morning, October 13, the exodus began, and throughout the day, more than 200 terrified black residents fled the town and the surrounding area. Sheriff Ziegler, fearing possible mob violence, telephoned Missouri governor Henry S. Caulfield to request the assistance of the National Guard in maintaining the peace during the mass exodus. Acting on the sheriff's request, the governor dispatched Companies M and H of the 140th Infantry from the towns of Festus and DeSoto, 30 miles and 40 miles, respectively, to the northwest, to restore order in Sainte Genevieve and prevent any further disturbances. Approximately 90 national guardsmen arrived in Sainte Genevieve that evening, set up machine guns around the courthouse and on the roof of the City Hotel, and patrolled the town. By nightfall, only three black families remained in Sainte Genevieve, at least one of which sought protection with Fr. Charles Van Tourenhout, pastor of the local Catholic church.

On Tuesday afternoon, October 14, the National Guard withdrew from a quiet Sainte Genevieve. But when the second shooting victim, Paul Ritter, died at 1:15 P.M. in St. Anthony's Hospital, news of his death triggered renewed mob action in Sainte Genevieve. Around 10:30 P.M. that night, three carloads of white men armed with shotguns and rifles attempted to kidnap a mail carrier named Louis "Cap" Ribeau, one of the few black residents who had refused to leave town. After seizing Ribeau, the mob huddled on the road in front of his home to discuss what to do with him. An approaching car accidentally collided with one of the mob's parked cars and then plowed into the group, knocking down Ribeau and several others. No one was seriously injured, but in the ensuing chaos Ribeau managed to escape into the woods and find safe harbor with a neighboring white family, who hid him in their well for the night.

Notified of the attempted kidnapping, Sheriff Ziegler and several deputies arrested six white Sainte Genevieve men

(Russell Stockle, James Hurst, William Martin, J. A. Crowley, Herman Steiger, and Louis Ryan) on charges of unlawful assembly. Rumors soon circulated, however, that a mob might attempt to spring the six men from the Sainte Genevieve County Jail, and Sheriff Ziegler, fearing that he could not repel such an attack, again requested the National Guard's assistance. Companies M and H, whose members had only hours before returned to their homes, again rushed to Sainte Genevieve. When the troops arrived at 3:00 the next morning, they mounted machine guns in front of the jail and on the porch of the Ribeau home, and patrolled the streets of Sainte Genevieve.

On Wednesday morning, October 15, Cap Ribeau boarded a train for St. Louis under the armed guard of postal inspectors. According to the *St. Louis Argus* (October 17, 1930), he was in "a highly nervous state" from his traumatic encounter, and was admitted for treatment in a St. Louis sanitarium. Sainte Genevieve civic leaders and National Guard officers held a mass meeting at the courthouse that afternoon to discuss how best to end the racial disorder. Before a standing-room-only crowd, Fr. Van Tourenhout called on every citizen to cooperate in combating the racial strife that had wracked the town. That evening, the local post of the American Legion called an emergency meeting during which its members unanimously pledged to serve as sheriff's deputies in quelling any future mob outbreaks. The Legionnaires also adopted a resolution guaranteeing protection to "certain native, property owning blacks" (*Ste. Genevieve Herald*, October 18, 1930) if they wished to return to their homes. Absolutely no other African Americans would be permitted to return to Sainte Genevieve, however. By the following day, Thursday, October 16, the crisis in the community had subsided, and the National Guard troops, whose strong presence very likely prevented a full-blown race riot from erupting, returned to Festus and Desoto. Their departure marked the end of what one local newspaper called "one of the most serious situations ever experienced in Sainte Genevieve" (*Ste. Genevieve Herald*, October 18, 1930). But the aftershocks of the four-day racial disturbance reverberated in the community for decades to come.

On October 15, 1930, the six men arrested for attempting to kidnap Ribeau were tried in a Sainte Genevieve court and pled guilty. Each was fined $300 or sentenced to six months in jail, or both, but the judge stayed their sentences on promise of good behavior, and Wednesday evening the men were released. Two days later, however, U.S. postal inspectors rearrested the six men on federal warrants, charging them with conspiracy to prevent a federal employee from performing his duties, a crime punishable by a maximum sentence of six years in the penitentiary, a $5,000 fine, or both. In March 1931, all of them pled guilty in a U.S. district court in St. Louis and were paroled.

Meanwhile, Lonnie Taylor and Columbus Jennings were tried for the first-degree murders of Panchot and Ritter in circuit court in Farmington, Missouri, on a change of venue. Both men were convicted of first-degree murder and sentenced to life imprisonment in the Missouri State Penitentiary in Jefferson City. Charges against their female companion, Vera Rogers, were eventually dismissed.

In the week following the riot, Sainte Genevieve civic leaders invited some 70 longtime black residents who had fled their homes to return to the community. Eventually, almost all of them did return, but the mobs succeeded in banishing the black migrants who had been recruited by the local lime plants and stone quarries, and the town's African American population never again reached pre-riot levels. In fact, in the decades following the riot, Sainte Genevieve gained a reputation as a town hostile to African Americans. By 1940, the number of black residents living in Sainte Genevieve had dwindled to only 45. By 1960, only 16 remained. Today, Sainte Genevieve, a town dedicated to preserving and trading on its French colonial historical past, has largely forgotten this incident, which so dramatically affected its racial demographics. Indeed, the first historical account of the riot did not appear until 1999, almost 70 years after the incident. Meanwhile, Sainte Genevieve's African American population, which numbered slightly more than 120 in the 2000 census, is slowing beginning to increase.

PATRICK HUBER

See also

Race Riots in America. Documents: The Report on the Memphis Riots of May 1866 (July 25, 1866); Account of the Riots in East St. Louis, Illinois (July 1917); The Cook County Coroner's Report Regarding the 1919 Chicago Race Riots (1919); A Southern Black Woman's Letter Regarding the Recent Riots in Chicago and Washington (November 1919); The

Final Report of the Grand Jury on the Tulsa Race Riot (June 25, 1921); Testimony from *Laney v. United States* Describing Events during the Washington, D.C., Riot of July 1919 (December 3, 1923); The Governor's Commission Report on the Watts Riots (December 1965); Cyrus R. Vance's Report on the Riots in Detroit (July–August 1967); The Reports of the Oklahoma Commission to Study the Tulsa Race Riot of 1921 (2000–2001); The Draft Report of the 1898 Wilmington Race Riot Commission (December 2005)

Further Reading:

Naeger, Bill, Patti Naeger, and Mark L. Evans. *Sainte Genevieve: A Leisurely Stroll Through History*. Sainte Genevieve, MO: Merchant Street Publishing, 1999.

Sainte Genevieve Herald, October 18 and 25, 1930.

Sainte Genevieve *Fair Play*, October 18, 1930.

St. Louis Argus, October 17 and 24, 1930.

Uhlenbrock, Tom. "Sainte Genevieve's Rich History Includes Indians and Blacks, Too." *St. Louis Post-Dispatch*, April 1, 2001.

San Francisco (California) Riot of 1966

In 1966, San Francisco experienced its only race riot, the result of a police shooting in the Hunters Point area of the city. However, leading up to the riot, many conditions for African Americans had become desperate. Overcrowded and segregated neighborhoods, insufficient and poor-quality housing, police brutality, and underemployment had grown worse since the end of World War II. By 1966 racial tensions were stretched tight.

Prior to the 1960s, San Francisco had one of the most proactive stances toward race relations of any city in the United States. As early as 1942, concerned citizens formed the Bay Area Council Against Discrimination (BACAD), an organization that would become the prototype for interracial societies during that time. Functioning as a pressure group and fact-finding agency, the BACAD forced city officials, business leaders, and trade unions to implement nondiscriminatory policies. By 1944, the Council for Civic Unity formed under the direction of Edward Howden and soon became the premier interracial organization working against discrimination in San Francisco. Its aim was to end discrimination in housing, employment, health, recreation, and welfare. It scored many victories throughout the 1950s.

However, organizations that combated racial discrimination were fighting an uphill battle. For one, San Francisco's population was increasing faster than the housing market was able to accommodate. Between 1940 and 1950 the city's population increased by 22 percent and the African American population increased nearly 800 percent. Discrimination in housing was the norm, and both redlining and restrictive covenants functioned to keep African Americans segregated primarily in just two enclaves: Hunters Point and the Western Addition. Further, employment prospects were grim, especially for African American youth. Shortly after World War II, many African Americans who had migrated to San Francisco for wartime employment were laid off their jobs. The combination of fewer jobs, poor-quality housing, and ever-increasing population proved volatile, and it was under these conditions that San Francisco experienced its first race riot.

On September 27, 1966, police officer Alvin Johnson attempted to stop a car in the predominantly African American neighborhood of Hunters Point. The two teenagers who were in the vehicle fled the scene, and Johnson chased one youth, Matthew Johnson, across an empty lot. When Matthew Johnson ignored Officer Johnson's command to stop, the officer shot and killed him. Shortly thereafter, a crowd of residents gathered and demanded a meeting with Mayor John Shelley. However, by the time the mayor arrived at the Bayview Neighborhood Center, the crowd had grown both in size and discontent, and the mayor was forced to retreat as people threw bricks and a firebomb at him and the police. After the mayor's hasty departure, 200 police officers were called in to seal off a six-block area of Hunters Point. Although some youths managed to leave the area and smashed windows in other districts of the city, most of the disturbance was contained in Hunters Point.

One important aspect of the riot is that many of the leaders of the community, moderate, middle-class residents, were totally unable to assuage the anger of the lower-income, younger residents. This would foreshadow an ongoing conflict between the two groups that would only deteriorate over the next decade.

The Hunters Point riot lasted 128 hours and, in contrast to the 1965 Watts riot (*see* Los Angeles [California] Riot of 1965 entry), was characterized by only minor incidents of violence and looting, mainly directed at white- and Chinese-owned businesses. In the end, property damage was estimated around $100,000 and no one was killed; 146 people were arrested, 2 police officers were hurt, 42 African Americans were injured (10 from gunshot wounds), and many fire department vehicles and police cars were damaged.

City officials blamed the riots on unemployment among African American youth but failed to note that abysmal housing conditions in the area and ongoing tension between the police and the African American community were contributing factors as well. Following the riot, a presidential task force reported that a lack of good jobs for low-income minority youth was the primary cause of the disturbance. It urged local, state, and federal agencies to create employment opportunities for the residents of the area. After the riot, although unemployment remained high and police-community relations floundered, San Francisco's race relations remained relatively calm for the rest of the decade.

PAUL T. MILLER

See also

Police Brutality; Race Riots in America; Reverse Redlining; Segregation. Documents: The Report on the Memphis Riots of May 1866 (July 25, 1866); Account of the Riots in East St. Louis, Illinois (July 1917); The Cook County Coroner's Report Regarding the 1919 Chicago Race Riots (1919); A Southern Black Woman's Letter Regarding the Recent Riots in Chicago and Washington (November 1919); The Final Report of the Grand Jury on the Tulsa Race Riot (June 25, 1921); Testimony from *Laney v. United States* Describing Events during the Washington, D.C., Riot of July 1919 (December 3, 1923); The Governor's Commission Report on the Watts Riots (December 1965); Cyrus R. Vance's Report on the Riots in Detroit (July–August 1967); The Reports of the Oklahoma Commission to Study the Tulsa Race Riot of 1921 (2000–2001); The Draft Report of the 1898 Wilmington Race Riot Commission (December 2005)

Further Reading:

Broussard, Albert. *Black San Francisco: The Struggle for Racial Equality in the West, 1900–1954.* Topeka: University Press of Kansas, 1993.

Crowe, Daniel. *Prophets of Rage: The Black Freedom Struggle in San Francisco, 1945–1969.* New York: Garland Publishing, Inc., 2000.

Fleming, Thomas. "Violence Hits the Streets." *Sun-Reporter,* October 1, 1966, 2.

Hippler, Arthur. *Hunter's Point: A Black Ghetto.* New York: Basic Books, 1974.

Savage Inequalities

Savage Inequalities: Children in America's Schools (1991), written by Jonathan Kozol, focuses on the educational disparities present in America's urban public schools. Through observations and interviews with students, teachers, and parents in schools throughout the country, Kozol portrays the gross inequities that exist in schools composed of poor, minority students compared to schools with white students from middle- and upper-class backgrounds. In his book, the voices of those who are disadvantaged by the educational system are heard as he takes his readers on a journey concerning the challenges of attending a dilapidated, poverty-stricken school.

To document the gross atrocities that exist in poverty-stricken, racially segregated schools, Kozol visits a number of schools throughout the country. His book begins with an in-depth look at the school system in East St. Louis; however, in every community he visited, community resources were instrumental in the creation of student opportunity. Schools in Illinois, New York, New Jersey, Texas, and Washington, D.C., all had similar problems—class and racial segregation

---

Jonathan Kozol (1936–)

Jonathan Kozol was born on September 5, 1936, in Boston, Massachusetts. After graduating from Harvard in 1958 with a degree in English literature, Kozol has devoted his life to social activism and educational opportunity. His first nonfiction book, *Death at an Early Age*, was an account of his first year as a teacher in a Boston public school. Published in 1967, it won the National Book Award in Science, Philosophy, and Religion. Some of Kozol's other publications include *Rachel and Her Children: Homeless Families in America* (1989), *Savage Inequalities* (1992), *Amazing Grace: The Lives of Children and the Conscience of a Nation* (1995), *Ordinary Resurrections: Children in the Years of Hope* (2000), *Shame of the Nation* (2005), and his most recent book, *Fire in the Ashes: Twenty-Five Years Among the Poorest Children in in America* (2012). A leading advocate for educational opportunity, Kozol has spent his entire career teaching, writing, and creating organizations devoted to children in need.

Jonathon Kozol with his book *Savage Inequalities*. (AP Photo)

were prominent, and in those communities, resources for education were sparse.

A substantial amount of funding for public schools is derived from local property taxes. As depicted in Kozol's description of schools in the Chicago area, suburban school districts are located in areas where the average home is often more worth than $400,000, compared to the city, where thousands of poor people are housed in substandard housing. Thus, even though poor communities often have higher tax rates for public education, the amount of return is less, as their overall tax base is much lower. This disparity in educational funding leads to unequal outcomes, where children from poor communities attend schools with poor infrastructures, disparate resources in the classroom, and underqualified teachers and other personnel.

Throughout his book, Kozol also explores the differential learning that takes place in white and affluent schools compared to poverty-stricken, minority schools. Similar to

Oakes's (2005 [1985]) findings on tracking, students from poor communities are taught skills that prepare them for semiskilled jobs while students in affluent communities are taught skills that prepare them for white-collar jobs—jobs that often lead to social mobility. According to Kozol, the disparity in educational resources not only hurts the individual, but it devastates whole communities. If schools in poor communities have a curriculum that hinders the chances for educational, economic, and political mobility among their students, how will those same students be able to economically invest in their home communities? This is important, as it is the economic investment in homes and businesses that increase funding for public schools.

Savage Inequalities highlights how unequal funding in public schools adversely impacts individuals and whole communities. While other scholars have also highlighted the impact financial resources have on educational achievement, others contend that there is not a strong relationship between school resources and educational outcomes. For instance, in the Coleman Report (1966), which was the first nationally representative sample to explore the relationship between school funding and academic attainment, Coleman concluded that family background was more important than school resources, a surprising finding of the time. This finding had serious implications, as many educators, scholars, and political leaders started to believe that putting more financial resources in schools would not solve the problem of educational inequality. Yet, since the monumental Coleman report scholars have shown that school financial resources are important. In 2011, Konstantopoulos and Borman found that school resources do matter in regards to educational opportunity among females, minorities, and disadvantaged students. While many studies have refuted the Coleman Report and similar findings, policy makers remain adamant about not increasing federal, state, or local property taxes to fund public education.

Although many scholars and policy makers ignore the gross disparities found in Kozol's book *Savage Inequalities*, it is a great account of the extreme disparities that exist between schools in affluent and poverty-stricken communities. Kozol highlights how these disparities lead to gross educational inequalities among whites and minorities. However, since the implementation of No Child Left Behind (NCLB) in 2001, the words *accountability* and *testing* have become all too familiar. Under NCLB, if a school persistently fails to meet AYP—Adequate Yearly Progress—the school can be sanctioned in a number of ways. For instance, in failing schools parents are given the option to send their children to better performing schools, thus siphoning money away from an already failing school. Instead of giving schools the resources they need to succeed in an era of accountability, much-needed resources are taken away from schools that are already financially strained. Although one of the goals of NCLB was to narrow the gaps between minorities and their white counterparts, significant gaps remain. NCLB, other governmental policies, and the funding of America's public schools have created a divide between the rich and the poor, and in the words of Kozol, have created "Savage Inequalities."

BOBETTE OTTO

See also

Education and African Americans; Educational Achievement Gap

Further Reading:

Baker, Bruce D. "Revisiting the Age-Old Question: Does Money Matter in Education?" The Albert Shanker Institute. http://www.shankerinstitute.org/images/doesmoneymatter_final.pdf.

Coleman, James. *Equality of Educational Opportunity* (Rep. No. OE 38001). Washington, DC: National Center for Education Statistics, U.S. Department of Health, Education, and Welfare, 1966.

Hanushek, Eric A. "The Economics of Schooling: Production and Efficiency in Public Schools." *Journal of Economic Literature* 24 (1986): 1141–77.

Konstantopoulos, Spyros, and Geoffrey Borman. "Family Background and School Effects on Student Achievement: A Multilevel Analysis of the Coleman Data." *Teachers College Record* 113 (2011): 97–132.

Kozol, Jonathan. *Savage Inequalities: Children in America's Schools.* New York: Harper Collins, 1991.

Kozol, Jonathan. *Shame of the Nation: The Restoration of Apartheid Schooling in America.* New York: Three Rivers Press, 2005.

Oakes, Jeannie. *Keeping Track: How Schools Structure Inequality*, 2nd ed. New Haven, CT: Yale University Press, 2005[1985].

Rothstein, Richard. *Class and Schools: Using Social, Economic, and Educational Reform to Close the Black-White Achievement Gap.* Washington, DC: Economic Policy Institute, 2004.

Scapegoat Theory of Racial Prejudice

The scapegoat theory of racial prejudice is a psychological theory that attempts to explain individual prejudice within personality dynamics. This personality-centered explanation of prejudice links prejudice to the individual's needs to deal with frustration and express aggression against a substitute target or a "scapegoat." The theory asserts that when individuals find themselves in circumstances in which the cause of frustration is unavailable or inappropriate, a process called *displacement* might occur. In this case, the frustrated individuals find a substitute target or a "scapegoat" against whom they transfer their hostility and aggression. This theory also suggests that the level of prejudice that exists in a society will reflect the level of individual frustration. In this respect, periods of difficult socioeconomic and political conditions, such as high inflation or unemployment, are usually characterized by an increase in displaced aggression and expressions of prejudice against a subordinate group.

Most frequently, groups that have been targeted are economically or politically weak. Moreover, preexisting stereotypes against certain ethnic/racial groups supply oversimplifications about those groups and make the scapegoating process easier. For example, in many different times and countries, Jews have been held responsible for economic crises and unemployment of a society, as a whole, while in the United States, blacks have been blamed for high crime rates. Typically, by scapegoating others, the group that does the blaming fails to realize and analyze the existing social and economic realities that contribute to their misfortunes.

The scapegoat theory has been criticized for being overly simplistic. Some critics argue that aggression is not an automatic or unvarying reaction to frustration and also that the likelihood of displacement varies widely for different types of individuals. Although the scapegoat hypothesis provides some insights into one cause of prejudice, it does not adequately explain the complexity of many other possible variables and factors involved in any general explanation of prejudice.

NICHOLAS ALEXIOU

See also

Prejudice; Prejudice Theory

Further Reading:

Bobo, Lawrence and Vincent L. Hutchings. "Perceptions of Racial Group Competition: Extending Blumer's Theory of Group Position to a Multiracial Social Context." *American Sociological Review* 61.6 (1996): 951–972.

Omi, Michael and Howard Winant. *Racial Formation in the United States: From the 1960s to the 1990s.* London: Routledge, 1994.

Pettigrew, Thomas F., George M. Fredrickson, Dale T. Knobel, Nathan Glazer, and Reed Ueda. *Prejudice.* Cambridge: Belknap Press of Harvard University Press, 1982.

School Segregation

School segregation refers to the separation of students in schools by race either by government actions and law (de jure) or by individual actions (de facto). The U.S. Supreme Court's decision in the 1954 *Brown v. Board of Education* case defined school segregation as state actions that explicitly created dual systems of education based on race.

One of the earliest court decisions that dealt with de jure school segregation was the *Robert v. City of Boston* case in 1848. Five-year-old Sarah Robert was barred from the local primary school because she was black. Her father sued the city. The lawsuit was part of an organized effort by the African American community to end racially segregated schools. In 1855, Boston's black community finally reaped the rewards of their years of struggle for equal school rights when racially segregated schools were abolished by the Massachusetts State Legislature. In 1896, during the Jim Crow era, the Supreme Court, however, decided in *Plessy v. Ferguson* that separate facilities for blacks and whites were justified. Separate schools for white and colored children soon became a legitimate part of everyday life in the South for the next half century.

The 1938 Supreme Court began to change course, starting with *Missouri ex rel. Gaines v. Canada.* In this decision, the Court ruled that graduate and professional schools for blacks could not possibly be both separate and equal and that, therefore, blacks had the right to be admitted to white programs and schools. In 1954, *Brown v. Board of Education* finally ended this long history of legal school segregation by declaring school segregation unconstitutional.

San Francisco School Board Crisis of 1906

In 1906, the San Francisco School Board ordered the segregation of Japanese and Korean children in the San Francisco city school system (Chinese children already attended separate schools). At the time of this decision, there were only 93 Japanese American students attending public school in San Francisco, and they were scattered across the city's 23 schools. The decision was related to the anti-Asian movement then gaining strength in California (and across the United States), particularly among labor groups. This movement came about from the belief that Asian immigration was a threat to the entire nation and its way of life.

This resulted in a diplomatic crisis between the United States and Japan, which was outraged about how its citizens and their children were being treated. President Theodore Roosevelt convinced the school board to back down and allow Japanese children to attend school with white children, but only by promising Californians an end to Japanese immigration, the result of which was the Gentlemen's Agreement, which barred Japanese laborers from migrating to the United States. This agreement also stopped the immigration of Japanese by way of Canada, Mexico, and Hawaii.

MIKAILA MARIEL LEMONIK ARTHUR

In 1968, after the Brown ruling, the court turned its attention to the remedy for this violation of the Constitution in *Charles C. Green v. County School Board of New Kent County* and defined what it meant by desegregation. School segregation, the Court said, was reflected not only in enrollments by race, but also in the district's success in desegregating and eliminating discrimination in terms of faculty, staff, transportation, extracurricular activities, and facilities. The Court's guidelines mandated massive integration from 1968 to 1973 because the Court placed an affirmative duty on school boards to integrate.

Laws can be changed, but people's attitudes linger. De facto school segregation results not from laws but primarily from individuals' actions or residential choices. This kind of school segregation occurs when a neighborhood is racially homogeneous. De facto segregation generally stems from a variety of residential patterns, population migration, and economic and political factors.

The Supreme Court first used the term *de facto* in the 1971 *Swann* decision, when it said that de facto school segregation did not require court action. In 1973, however, after hearing the *Keyes* case in Denver, the Court found that many governmental actions (in this case, the actions of urban-development agencies) had led to de facto school segregation. So even though de facto school segregation may not be the result of explicit state or local government actions, government policies can reinforce it. For example, white flight into suburban areas combined with the Supreme Court's *Milliken v. Bradley* ruling in 1974, which prevented a multidistrict desegregation plan, increased disparities in racial composition between the city and suburban districts.

Racial integration of schools, or school desegregation, is important for three major reasons. First, the racial integration of schools is considered the most effective method to equalize educational resources across racial groups. Second and more importantly, the racial integration of schools can contribute to overall racial integration in society. White students who have attended an integrated school are more likely to accept minority members as their coworkers or neighbors than are those who have attended an all-white school. Third, there is considerable evidence that students who attend integrated schools have more access to social networks that may have both economic and social influence in the lives of young people than those who attend segregated schools.

But black students still attend highly segregated schools. A 2003 Harvard study (Frankenberg, Lee, and Orfield 2003) found that American schools have become segregated although the nation's minority student enrollment has approached 40 percent of all public school students. For example, 70 percent of black students now attend school where minority enrollment is over 50 percent. About 37 percent of Latino students go to schools where less than 10 percent of the school population is white. White students on average attend schools in which 80 percent of the students are white.

SOOKHEE OH

See also

American Apartheid; *Bolling v. Sharpe* (1954); *Brown v. Board of Education* (1954); *Brown v. Board of Education* Legal Groundwork; Busing; *Cooper v. Aaron* (1958); *Cumming v. Richmond County Board of Education* (1899); Desegregation; Education and African Americans; Gray Commission; Little Rock Nine; Oppositional Culture; *Savage Inequalities*; Segregation; Separate But Equal Doctrine. Document: *Brown v. Board of Education* (May 1954)

Further Reading:

Clotfelter, Charles. "Public School Segregation in Metropolitan Areas." Working paper 6779, National Bureau of Economic Research, 1998.

Frankenberg, Erika, Chungmei Lee, and Gary Orfield. "A Multiracial Society with Segregated Schools: Are We Losing the Dream?" The Civil Rights Project, Harvard University, 2003.

Raffel, Jeffrey. *Historical Dictionary of School Segregation and Desegregation: The American Experience*. Westport, CT: Greenwood Press, 1998.

Wollenberg, Charles. *All Deliberate Speed: Segregation and Exclusion in California Schools, 1855–1975*. Berkeley: University of California Press, 1976.

School-to-Prison Pipeline

The school-to-prison pipeline describes the situation in which school disciplinary policies have led to the criminalizing of student misbehavior and increased the chances that at-risk students will end up in jail.

In the wake of highly publicized incidents of school violence, schools across the United States have adopted zero-tolerance policies to address discipline problems. Zero-tolerance policies aimed at reducing school violence and removing children deemed to be "problems" from schools have created alarming levels of school disruption for children—disruption that begins a process moving these children from the school system into the prison system. This process, which entails the criminalizing of childhood classroom disruptions and the increase in school-based arrests, disciplinary alternative schools, and secured detention, marginalizes at-risk youth and denies them the very education that could prevent future incarceration. Put simply, it has created a "pipeline" that moves the most vulnerable of school-aged children from the school system to the prison system.

Poor children, children of color, children who lack access to medical and mental health care, and those who suffer from abuse or neglect begin their school experiences with multiple strikes against them. Government policies such those espoused under the No Child Left Behind Act, which rewards schools for academic achievement and restricts funding for underachievement, create a climate where struggling children are unwelcome.

In cases of vulnerable populations, learning differences or disabilities may not be detected until the child enters the public school system. Studies have shown that most children who end up in detention facilities have disabilities that would make them eligible for special education services, but only 37 percent of them have received any kind of services at school, either because the schools failed to identify their disabilities or due to lack of parental awareness of the child's limitations.

Emotional disturbances, which are a qualifier for special education consideration, create particular risks for students, including the worst graduation rates, the highest dropout rates, and higher arrest and pregnancy rates than those for these students' peers. Children with emotional disturbances make up seven out of every 10 children in the juvenile justice system and are three times more likely than their peers to be arrested before leaving school. Almost three-fourths of children with emotional disturbances will be arrested within five years of leaving school.

Clearly, the safety needs attached to the very real dangers of school-based violence must be addressed, and real responses are needed for legitimate threats. However, zero-tolerance disciplinary policies represent a "one size fits all" response to school based incidents that impose severe discipline on students without taking into account their individual circumstances. These policies and the resultant suspensions, expulsions, and arrests are often the first step in a child's journey though the school-to-prison pipeline.

Equally concerning are the racial disparities resulting from the enforcement of these zero-tolerance policies. Black children are four times as likely as their white peers to be incarcerated. Black children are almost five times and Latino children more than twice as likely to be incarcerated for drug offenses as white children. Black children are twice as likely as white children to be put in programs for mental retardation, twice as likely to be held back a grade, three times as likely to be suspended, and 50 percent more likely to drop out of school. In 2011, 580,000 black males were serving prison sentences in the United States, while fewer than 40,000 black males earned a bachelor's degree each year. Often, poverty is a factor in incarceration; while wealthier families can provide options such as counseling or private rehabilitation programs, drug counseling, or even military school as alternatives to detention, poor families have limited options—another factor that contributes to their disproportionate representation within the justice system.

As early as kindergarten, some children may begin to show signs for potential risk of offending. In particular, the 10 percent to 11 percent of children who enter the school system lacking the social skills that would prevent them from arguing or fighting with teachers are at a significantly higher risk for school failure, delinquency, and potential incarceration. Mandatory expulsions for offenses committed by children as young as age five, while intended to make schools safer, may create the unintended consequence of pushing children—often the most vulnerable children—into a trajectory of delinquency and incarceration.

As concerns for safety grow, a growing number of school districts have begun to rely on police officers to patrol hallways and enforce discipline. These officers often focus on using the legal system to discipline students for conduct that might otherwise be addressed by school programs, counseling, or parent education.

Behavior that historically would have been handled in the principal's office, such as schoolyard fights, is now being attended to by school-based police officers, who move students directly into the local courts and detention centers. While initial offenses such as truancy, defiant behavior, or fighting might result in a minor punishment, these offenses often begin a paper trail or "record" for the offending child; as these offenses add up over time, the courts' and school's reaction to the child's behavior tend to become harsher. Many areas do not have comprehensive rehabilitation and support programs; as a result, incarceration becomes the only option for at-risk youths.

Marginalized children, when labeled by the school system as "deviant" at a young age, may feel that they are not wanted, or valued, or smart—which puts them on a downward spiral from the beginning of their school experiences. Many begin to mentally drop out as early as the third or fourth grade, when the academic and behavioral demands of school may outstrip their earlier academic development and home-based support. Lack of mental health support and early intervention for children with severe emotional and behavioral problems and their families, issues of substance abuse, the absence of a positive home-based support system, or a combination of these factors often bring children into the juvenile justice system. The deeper a child gets into this system, the harder it is to get out. Once expelled from the school system, it is difficult for the child to return, making the risk of dropping out of high school a very real possibility. High school dropouts are 63 times more likely to be incarcerated than graduates from four-year colleges.

Addressing the harsh realities of the school-to-prison pipeline will require a shift in emphasis from punishment to support. Resources for at-risk families, including health, nutrition, mental health support, and preschool to give children a more level social and academic entry process into the school system, can contribute to fewer disparities in the classroom. School resources that address the social, developmental, and behavioral needs of the most vulnerable children can keep them in school rather than taking them out of the only known path to future success. Support for educational deficiencies, combined with a reduction of suspensions, expulsions, and arrests, can minimize disparities in achievement for all children, but especially those at highest risk. While it is important to keep schools safe for all students, implementing interventions such as mediation, counseling, and conflict resolution as first-line alternatives can contribute to keeping all children in mainstream educational environments and help them build the skills they need to realize their full potential.

DOREEN MALLER

See also
Education and African Americans; Prison-Industrial Complex; Prisons

Further Reading:
America's Cradle to Prison Pipeline. Washington, DC: Children's Defense Fund, 2007.

Finley, Laura L. *Encyclopedia of School Crime and Violence*. Santa Barbara, CA: Greenwood, 2011.

"School to Prison Pipeline: Talking Points." Washington, DC: American Civil Liberties Union, 2008.

Scott v. Sandford (1857)

In 1857, the U.S. Supreme Court ruled in the case of *Scott v. Sandford*, a decision that definitively articulated the government's position on slavery and the rights of the country's black population. In the end, the majority opinion upheld the notion that slavery was both legal and constitutional and further asserted that free black people were not entitled to the full and equal rights of citizenship.

The legal case that became known as *Scott v. Sandford* originally began in 1846, when Dred Scott sued for his freedom on the grounds that he had been illegally held in bondage in a free state. Dred Scott was born into slavery in the state of Virginia in 1799 and was the legal property of the Peter Blow family. In 1830, the Blows brought Scott to St. Louis, Missouri, where he was eventually purchased by John Emerson. Because Emerson was a military surgeon, he and Scott traveled extensively throughout Illinois and the Wisconsin Territory, where slavery had been prohibited by the Missouri Compromise (1820). During this period, both men married; Scott wed Harriet Robinson, and Emerson married Irene Sanford. In 1843, Emerson died, and three years later, in February 1846, Scott tried to purchase his freedom from Irene Emerson, but she refused. Thus, two months later, on April 6, 1846, Scott sued for his freedom, arguing that because he had lived in both a free state and a free territory, he had become legally free and could not be justifiably enslaved.

Scott's case was first brought to trial in 1847 in the St. Louis Courthouse. Scott lost the first case on a technicality, but a judge quickly ordered a second trial. Although Emerson appealed the order, the Supreme Court of Missouri ruled against her in 1848. Two years later, Scott's case was heard before a jury, which determined that he and his family should be emancipated. Again, Emerson appealed the decision to the Missouri State Supreme Court. This time, the court found in her favor and reversed the decision to grant the Scotts their freedom. This decision was particularly significant because it diverged from the court's precedents. The Missouri Supreme Court had previously ruled, rather routinely, that slaves taken into free states were automatically free.

Shortly after this decision, however, with the assistance of a new team of lawyers who were committed antislavery activists, Scott filed suit in St. Louis Federal Court in 1854 against John F. A. Sanford, Irene Emerson's brother and executor of the Emerson estate. (This was the official case that became known as *Scott v. Sandford*, due to the fact that John Sanford's name was misspelled in the official documents).

Because Sanford resided in New York, legal wrangling over jurisdiction caused the case to be brought before the federal courts. This shift in venue, however, raised a new issue. In order to bring a lawsuit in federal court, Scott had to show that he was a citizen. Sanford's attorneys countered that because blacks were not citizens in Missouri, Scott had no standing to sue, and the court lacked jurisdiction. The trial judge agreed that Scott's legal status depended on the law in Missouri, not his residence in free territory, and the jury decided in Sanford's favor.

Undeterred, Scott's lawyers next appealed to the U.S. Supreme Court, a decision that launched the Dred Scott case into the national spotlight. In fact, even president-elect James Buchanan expressed interest in the case. Concerned about the growing divide over the issue of slavery, Buchanan sent a letter to Supreme Court Justice John Catron, asking whether the U.S. Supreme Court would decide the case before his inauguration in March 1857. Buchanan hoped that the Court would issue a decisive ruling that would remove the question of slavery from political debate, thereby quieting the social and political unrest plaguing the fragile Union. Buchanan later successfully pressured Supreme Court Justice Grier, a Northerner, to join the Southern majority in the Dred Scott decision in order to avoid the implication that the decision was made along sectional lines.

Buchanan's concerns were well founded, given that the *Dred Scott* case ultimately encompassed a series of issues that were causing tremendous strife in American society, namely, the extension of slavery and the question of black citizenship. These issues were exposed during oral arguments before the Court in February 1856, when Sanford's attorneys raised an additional issue. They argued not only that Scott was a slave and not a citizen, but also that he could not have become even temporarily a freeman by residing in a free territory because the Missouri Compromise was unconstitutional. Because the constitutionality of the Missouri Compromise was a hotly contested issue in the 1850s, *Scott v. Sandford* was immediately placed at the center of a political firestorm.

On March 6, 1857, Chief Justice Roger B. Taney delivered the Supreme Court's majority opinion in the *Dred Scott* case, with each of the concurring and dissenting justices filing separate opinions. Seven justices concurred (although Samuel Nelson concurred with the ruling but not its reasoning),

and two justices, Benjamin R. Curtis and John McLean, dissented. Regardless, Taney's majority opinion unequivocally illustrated the strength and power of slavery in the United States. Taney declared that as a slave, Scott was not a citizen of the United States and therefore had no right to bring suit in the federal courts on any matter. In addition, he declared that Scott had never been free because slaves were personal property; thus, the Missouri Compromise of 1820 was unconstitutional, and the federal government had no right to prohibit slavery in the new territories.

The Supreme Court's ruling in *Scott v. Sandford* was devastating not only to the Scotts but also to antislavery activists and the entire black community. In fact, many historians have argued that the Dred Scott decision ultimately brought the United States one step closer to Civil War. Undoubtedly, in the aftermath of the decision, public opinion became increasingly polarized over the issues of slavery, governmental rights, and black citizenship. As for Scott, he and his family were eventually emancipated; the sons of Peter Blow, Scott's first owner, purchased them on May 26, 1857, and gave them their freedom. Scott, however, died of tuberculosis only 18 months later, on November 7, 1858. In the end, although the Scotts gained their freedom from bondage, their legal case served to fix, ever more strongly, the bonds of slavery and inequality upon the black population in America.

LESLIE M. ALEXANDER

See also

Racism; Reparations; Slavery; Slavery in the Antebellum South

Further Reading:

Fehrenbacher, D. E. *The Dred Scott Case*. New York: Oxford University Press, 1978.

Finkelman, Paul, ed. *Dred Scott v. Sandford: A Brief History with Documents*. New York: Palgrave Macmillan, 1997.

Graber, Mark A. *Dred Scott and the Problem of Constitutional Evil*. New York: Cambridge University Press, 2006.

Scottsboro Boys Case (1931)

In 1931, a series of court trials involving an alleged rape of two white teenage girls by nine youths in Scottsboro, Alabama, reflected the climate of racial relations in the South preceding the Great Depression. The allegations sparked

Known as the Scottsboro Boys, these nine young African American men were imprisoned in Scottsboro, Alabama, after being falsely accused of raping two white women on a train. (Bettmann-UPI/Corbis)

violent responses that almost resulted in a lynching and spawned legal actions that spanned several decades. A hotly debated issue in the 1930s and 1940s, the controversy died down until a movie about the case, titled *Judge Horton and the Scottsboro Boys*, broadcast in the 1970s, brought the issue back to the nation's attention.

The effects of the Depression were evident by the poverty-stricken people who rode freight trains during the early 1930s in search of employment. On March 25, 1931, a fight broke out between several young people on the Chattanooga to Memphis train in Tennessee. A number of black boys threw a smaller group of white boys from the train. When the injured boys caught the attention of a train stationmaster, the sheriff of Jackson County, Alabama, was contacted about the incident. Sheriff W. L. Wann ordered his deputy to deputize as many men as possible in the town

of Paint Rock and bring them to the next stop in Scottsboro. A posse was formed and met the train. After a search, they found nine black youths, one white boy, and two white girls dressed in caps and overalls. The girls were not immediately identified as females due to their dress. When Victoria Price and Ruby Bates were questioned, they stated that the black boys had raped them at knifepoint on the train. The boys were taken to jail and word of the incident quickly spread throughout the area. On March 26, a crowd gathered with the intention of lynching the nine boys, a common practice in the South at the time. Sheriff Wann was able to fend off the mob and tried to send the accused boys to another jail for their safety, even going as far as contacting the National Guard for assistance.

The nine defendants—Clarence Norris, Charlie Weems, Haywood Patterson, Olen Montgomery, Ozie Powell,

Willie Roberson, Eugene Williams, Andrew Wright, and Roy Wright—ranged in age from 12 to 20. On March 30, a grand jury indicted the youngsters for rape. On April 6, the first of a series of legal actions took place as the nine went on trial before Judge A. E. Hawkins. Eight of the nine "Scottsboro Boys" were found guilty and sentenced to death. Only Roy Wright, whose trial ended in a mistrial, escaped the death penalty. The pace of the trial process seemed to reflect the intensity of the prosecution and jury to convict the defendants.

The National Association for the Advancement of Colored People decided not to appoint an attorney to represent the boys due to the controversy over the case. The Communist Party decided to take the case and represent the youths through its legal arm, the International Labor Defense (ILD); this was seen as an opportunity to promote the party in America by connecting the issue to the oppression of workers nationwide. The trial drew not only national attention but international notice due to the details of the case, the obvious racial implications, the youthfulness of the defendants, and the swiftness of the disposition.

The case was appealed to the Alabama Supreme Court and the convictions were upheld except for that of Eugene Williams who was deemed to be a juvenile according to state law. In May 1932, the U.S. Supreme Court reviewed the case and reversed the decision due to inadequate representation of the defendants in the case.

In January 1933, Samuel S. Leibowitz was hired by the ILD as the Scottsboro Boys' defense attorney. In April of that year, a second trial again resulted in convictions and a sentence of the death penalty. The next month, there were many protests throughout the nation, including a large protest march in the nation's capital. Judge Edwin Horton Jr., the new jurist in the case, overturned the verdict and granted a new trial. Shortly afterward, jurisdiction was transferred from Judge Horton to William Callahan. Judge Horton later lost a bid for reelection, most likely due to his perceived leniency on the Scottsboro defendants, and would never return to the bench.

Over the next several years, there was a series of local court convictions followed by appeals, all the way to the U.S. Supreme Court. Even the recanting of the rape accusation by one of the victims failed to change the jury's mind about the boys' guilt. Although Governor Graves denied the parole applications in 1938, some of the defendants were later covertly granted parole in the 1940s. In 1976, Clarence Norris,

the last of the Scottsboro Boys, was given a full pardon by Alabama's governor George Wallace, ending a series of legal actions dealing specifically with the defendants in the case.

However, that was not the last of the legal activity involving the alleged victims. When a made-for-television movie about the Scottsboro case called *Judge Horton and the Scottsboro Boys* was aired by NBC in 1976, both Ruby Bates Schut and Victoria Price Street filed lawsuits for libel, slander, and invasion of privacy. Ms. Bates Schut died before her case was completed, and Ms. Price Street lost her case against the network.

LEONARD A. STEVERSON

See also
Lynching; *Powell v. Alabama* (1932); Rape as Provocation for Lynching

Further Reading:
Carter, Dan. *Scottsboro: A Tragedy of the American South.* Baton Rouge: Louisiana State University Press, 1979.

Secure Communities

Secure Communities is one of a number of ICE ACCESS (Agreements of Cooperation in Communities to Enhance Safety and Security) programs that enables state and local law enforcement agencies to assist federal immigration authorities in the identification of unauthorized immigrants. Specifically, Secure Communities expands information sharing practices between federal, state, and local law enforcement agencies to enable the interoperability of fingerprint databases maintained by the Federal Bureau of Investigation (FBI) and the Department of Homeland Security (DHS).

When an individual is arrested and booked, the local jail routinely submits his or her fingerprints and booking information to the FBI's Criminal Justice Information Services Division (CJIS) to check for outstanding warrants. The CJIS processes the biometric fingerprint information through IAFIS—the Integrated Automated Fingerprint Identification System—a national database containing fingerprint and criminal history information. This process is entirely automated.

Under Secure Communities, fingerprints submitted to IAFIS are automatically transmitted to the Automated

Biometric Identification System (IDENT), an immigration database maintained by the DHS's United States Visitor and Immigrant Status Indicator Technology Program (US-VISIT). The process of connecting the DHS's immigration database with the FBI's criminal database is referred to as IDENT/IAFIS interoperability. The purpose of such interoperability is to streamline the process of identifying the immigration and criminal status of arrestees.

Secure Communities specifically refers to IDENT/IAFIS interoperability and information sharing between local law enforcement agencies, the FBI, and the DHS. However, the interoperability made possible through Secure Communities may prompt additional involvement from immigration authorities. If the IDENT database identifies the arrestee as an immigrant—whether authorized or unauthorized—the DHS automatically notifies ICE. ICE then determines whether the arrestee is removable (deportable) due to unlawful presence or previous criminal convictions. ICE may also issue an immigration detainer—a request that the local jail detain the arrestee for ICE custody.

The Secure Communities program has proliferated rapidly since its inception. Beginning with just 14 programs in 2008, Secure Communities now functions in more than 3,000 jurisdictions, comprising 97 percent of law enforcement jurisdictions in the United States; DHS plans to activate the program in every jurisdiction by 2013. Since 2008, the Secure Communities program has processed 19.1 million submissions, resulting in more than 1 million matches in the IDENT database. Of those, more than 220,000 individuals have been removed or returned.

The Secure Communities program has faced much controversy. Initially, jurisdictions were told that they could choose to participate in the Secure Communities program. As such, several state and local governments—including Illinois, Massachusetts, New York, San Francisco, and Washington, D.C.—attempted to suspend or terminate existing programs. In 2011, however, the DHS declared that participation in Secure Communities was mandatory and that jurisdictions could not opt out of the program, an announcement that was strongly criticized by state and local policymakers.

Several high-ranking law enforcement officials have publicly condemned the program, stating that it jeopardizes the ability of local officers to adequately police their

ICE ACCESS: ICE ACCESS, or Agreements of Cooperation in Communities to Enhance Safety and Security, is the umbrella acronym given to 13 programs of Immigration and Customs Enforcement (ICE), including Secure Communities. The purpose of ICE ACCESS is to promote cooperation and collaboration between ICE and state and local law enforcement agencies. Through the ACCESS initiative, state and local law enforcement agencies are authorized to share information with ICE or execute specific functions related to immigration enforcement that ordinarily they would not be able to perform. Secure Communities is among the most well-known of these ACCESS programs; others include 287(g) delegation of immigration authority, the Criminal Alien Program (CAP), and the Border Enforcement Security Task Force (BEST).

communities. In particular, officers worry that the program undermines community trust in the police and deters individuals from reporting crimes. Thus, Salt Lake City police chief Chris Burbank argues that Secure Communities has "driven a wedge between the police and the public" (National Community Advisory Commission 2011: 7). Robert Morgenthau, the former district attorney of New York County, states, "When immigrants perceive the local police force as merely an arm of the federal immigration authority, they become reluctant to report criminal activity for fear of being turned over to federal officials" (National Community Advisory Commission 2011: 9).

Immigrant rights advocates—including the American Civil Liberties Union and the American Immigration Lawyers Association—contend that those who are identified through Secure Communities do not reflect ICE's stated enforcement priorities. In 2010, ICE director John Morton issued a memo emphasizing that ICE's limited resources should be used to target immigration offenders who pose a threat to public safety or national security. However, since Secure Communities transmits fingerprints to the DHS at the point of booking (rather than upon conviction) regardless of the cause for arrest, ICE continues to receive information about low-priority immigration offenders. ICE data on the total number of removals who were initially identified through Secure Communities indicate that many of these individuals were low-priority offenders. Of the more than 220,000 individuals who have been removed or returned after being identified through Secure Communities, only 27.8 percent met ICE's top priorities as serious criminal offenders, while nearly 30 percent were convicted of misdemeanors and 21.8 percent were convicted of no crime whatsoever.

In 2011, a task force composed of law enforcement officers, attorneys, academics, and social service workers issued a report on the operation and impact of Secure Communities. The group found widespread misperception of the program and its implementation, which it partially attributed to the confusing and often conflicting information issued by the DHS. The report also indicated that the majority of those identified through Secure Communities did not comply with ICE enforcement priorities. Finally, the report noted pervasive concerns from local communities and law enforcement regarding the program's impact on community trust in police.

Several members of the task force recommended the immediate suspension or outright termination of the program until such issues are resolved. ICE has responded that it will address these concerns. Nevertheless, many believe that Secure Communities is fundamentally flawed and remain skeptical that it can comply with enforcement priorities and preserve community trust.

MEGHAN CONLEY

See also

Immigration and Customs Enforcement (ICE); Unauthorized Immigration

---

Interoperability: Interoperability is the ability of distinct organizations to operate with one another for the purpose of promoting collaboration and efficient access to data and information. In immigration matters, interoperability refers to the practice of information sharing and interagency cooperation between Immigration and Customs Enforcement (ICE) and state and local law enforcement agencies. Under the Secure Communities program, IDENT/IAFIS interoperability refers to the routine and institutionalized sharing of biometric (fingerprint) data between local law enforcement agencies, the Federal Bureau of Investigation (FBI) and the Department of Homeland Security (DHS).

Further Reading:

National Community Advisory Commission. *Restoring Community: A National Community Advisory Report on ICE's Failed 'Secure Communities' Program.* 2011. http://bit.ly/scomm-shadow-rpt.

Department of Homeland Security. *Homeland Security Advisory Council Task Force on Secure Communities, Finding and Recommendations.* http://www.dhs.gov/xlibrary/assets/hsac-task-force-on-secure-communities.pdf.

Immigration and Customs Enforcement. *IDENT/IAFIS Interoperability Statistics.* http://www.ice.gov/doclib/foia/sc-stats/nationwide_interop_stats-fy2012-to-date.pdf.

Immigration and Customs Enforcement. *Secure Communities.* http://www.ice.gov/secure_communities/.

Sedimentation

The "sedimentation of racial inequality" is a phrase developed in Melvin L. Oliver and Thomas M. Shapiro's book *White Wealth Black Wealth* (1997), referring to the historical process of individual and institutional discrimination that led to the seemingly obdurate place at the bottom of the economic ladder that many blacks in the United States face today. Each generation's ability to access wealth is dependent on the economic position in which they were born. A person who is born into a family of wealth has a greater chance of increasing that wealth for themselves. Because, historically, blacks have had fewer opportunities to amass wealth than whites, they are much more likely to be poor and have little to no wealth. Oliver and Shapiro (1997) blame this sedimentation on the lack of access to high-quality schooling, individual and institutional discrimination, and housing segregation, which limited the ability of blacks to accumulate and increase their wealth relative to whites.

One of the most salient means of increasing assets is investing in human capital. The more education and training a person has, the higher their income will be, facilitating access to wealth. Historically, blacks were less able than whites to access human capital in the form of high-quality schooling. The *Plessy v. Ferguson* case (1896), which stated that separate facilities for whites and blacks were legal as long as the quality was equal, gave justification for segregation. Although this ruling was initially meant for train cars, it sanctioned discrimination in most areas of life, including education. Because separate never resulted in equality between blacks and whites, the *Brown v. Board of Education* case (1954) and the Civil Rights Act (1964) sought to remedy these inequities by requiring desegregation in schooling.

Although schools became less segregated in the 1970s and 1980s, increasing access to education does not tell the entire story. Educational investments today still do not have equal payoffs for blacks and whites. For example, in 2009, the annual income for blacks with a bachelor's degree was about 20 percent less than the income for whites with the same degree. The gap between white and black incomes directly affects their ability to increase wealth.

Even more important than the differences in educational payoffs is the history of institutional discrimination in the housing market. Home ownership is the primary mechanism for increasing wealth for most people. After World War II the housing market boomed in large part because of the development of the Federal Housing Administration (FHA). The Federal Housing Act of 1934 provided backing for loans and enabled citizens to buy homes with a low down payment and low interest rates. This act greatly benefitted whites because not only was homeownership available to millions of residents, but housing prices skyrocketed in the 1970s. At the same time whites were seeing their wealth increase, blacks were intentionally being left out of the market by the federal government.

In deciding who would receive a loan for suburban housing, the FHA used a racialized appraisal system that assessed the risk levels of communities. Neighborhoods that were all white were given a good credit rating, while neighborhoods that were all black or were viewed as becoming black were seen as less valuable and were "redlined." When a neighborhood was redlined, the FHA would not invest in these neighborhoods. Individuals wanting to receive loans to move into or out of these neighborhoods were at a direct disadvantage in their ability to access suburban housing.

The FHA also contributed to the sedimentation of inequality by not backing loans made in racially diverse neighborhoods, and advocating for racial restrictive covenants to be used to guarantee that neighborhoods remain homogeneous. Racial restrictive covenants are those that state that properties cannot be sold to people of specific races. Although these covenants were used to limit the purchases of

---

Radical Cartography

Cartographers use mapping to outline characteristics of neighborhoods. A new type of mapping (Radical Cartography) has been developed by Bill Rankin at Yale University. Rankin's maps use a series of dots rather than solid colors to show the heterogeneity of neighborhoods rather than solid colors which may be misleading (Radicalcartography.net). Because neighborhoods are not as homogeneous as they appear in solid color maps, if this system had been available when the FHA designed its appraisal system for home loans, lending patterns may have been different.

Chinese, Japanese, and other racial and ethnic groups, blacks were often the primary targets.

The result of housing discrimination is that the values of the properties that blacks did have access to declined, at the same time that the values of the housing available to whites was appreciating. Inner-city neighborhoods deteriorated, and the resources, such as tax money for schools, diminished along with the neighborhoods. As whites increased their wealth, they were able to pass this inheritance down to their children, resulting in differences between white and black children's life outcomes from birth. The fact that whites were able to accumulate more wealth and pass that wealth down to their children increased the wealth gap between blacks and whites.

Although discrimination in lending is illegal today, the effects can still be felt. In 2007 close to 75 percent of whites owned their homes, compared to 49 percent of blacks. Because the homes that blacks own are likely to be worth less than the homes that whites own, there are vast differences in the average net worth of blacks and whites. For example, in 2010 the median wealth of white households was 20 times that of black households, and about 15 percent of white households had zero or negative wealth compared to 35 percent of black households. The cumulative effects of institutional discrimination in housing and schooling have far-reaching effects on the wealth status of black citizens in the United States, resulting in a "sedimentation of inequality" that is not likely to be eliminated any time soon.

STEPHANIE SOUTHWORTH

Further Reading:

Anderson, Claud. *Black Labor, White Wealth: The Search for Power and Economic Justice*. Edgewood, MD: Duncan and Duncan, 1994.

Beeman, Angie, Davita Silfen Glasberg,, and Colleen Casey. "Whiteness as Property: Predatory Lending and the Reproduction of Racialized Inequality." *Critical Sociology* 37, no. 1 (2010): 27–45.

Brown v. Board of Education, 347 U.S. 483 (1954).

Carnevale, Anthony P., Stephen J. Rose, and Ban Cheah. *The College Payoff: Education, Occupation and Lifetime Earnings*. Georgetown University Center for Education and the Workforce, 2011. http://www9.georgetown.edu/grad/gppi/hpi/cew/pdfs/collegepayoff-complete.pdf (accessed December 23, 2012).

Civil Rights Act of 1964. Pub. L. 88-352, 78 Stat. 241 (1964).

Conley, Dalton. *Being Black, Living in the Red: Race, Wealth and Social Policy in America*. Berkeley: University of California Press, 1999.

Kochlar, Rakesh, Richard Fry, and Paul Taylor. *Wealth Gaps Rise to Record Highs Between Whites, Blacks, Hispanics, Twenty to One*. Pew Research Center, 2011. http://www.pewsocialtrends.org/2011/07/26/wealth-gaps-rise-to-record-highs-between-whites-blacks-hispanics/ (accessed December 12, 2012).

Rankin, Bill. http://www.radicalcartography.net.

Wolff, Edward N. *Recent Trends in Household Wealth in the United States: Rising Debt and the Middle-Class Squeeze—An Update to 2007*. Working Paper No. 589. Levy Economics Institute of Bard College, 2010.

Segmented Assimilation

Segmented assimilation is a theory of assimilation that considers not only the process, but also the outcomes of assimilation. Conceptually, assimilation is about how groups of people integrate and interact with each other into a single unified society. In the 1920s, the sociologist Robert Park put forward a model of how immigrants to the United States assimilate into the dominant American host culture. His model, called *straight line assimilation*, was the basis of assimilation theory for the next 70 years. In straight line assimilation, immigrants would arrive in this country, settle themselves, and then adapt to the dominant American culture. Left unanswered was the question of what was the dominant American culture, since the United States is not homogenous in race, religion, social class, or even geography. Later, however, Milton Gordon noted that if there was an "American" culture, it was that of the white, Anglo-Saxon, Protestant, middle class. He also noted that this is not an assimilation goal that is open to all immigrants. Gordon used a seven-stage process to describe American immigrant assimilation, where an immigrant group who went through all seven stages would be completely assimilated as Park described with straight line assimilation. However, it was possible for immigrant groups to stall at a stage and remain only partially assimilated.

Assimilation theories such as those put forth by Park and Gordon considered assimilation to be part of the process of upward mobility for immigrants, their children, and their children's children. Each generation was expected to achieve higher socioeconomic status as it became more culturally similar to the ideal American middle class. Assimilation and upward mobility were spoken of as though they were the same thing. Newer academic research suggests this may no longer be the case. Building on the work of Herbert Gans, who noted that the children of modern American immigrants could follow either upwardly or downwardly mobile paths, Alejandro Portes and Min Zhou proposed the theory of *segmented assimilation*. This theory asserts that since the United States is a stratified and essentially unequal society, there are different "segments" of society that are available for immigrants to assimilate to. Portes and Zhou discuss three possible assimilation paths for immigrants. The first is basically what is previously referred to by Park as straight line assimilation. This is marked by increasing acculturation and integration into the American middle class. The second possible path is acculturation and assimilation into the urban underclass, leading to downward mobility and increasing poverty. The third path is both the preservation of the immigrants' culture and values and their economic integration into American society. This partial acculturation is most similar to the partial assimilation noted by Gordon.

There are many factors that can lead immigrants to follow any of the paths and cause the degree of difficulty that they have following them. Some of these factors are identified by Alejandro Portes and Ruben Rumbaut in later research. They identify human capital, family structure, and how the immigrants are incorporated into the host society as the important factors that shape the experiences of the

Acculturation

Acculturation is the long-term cultural modification of a group or individual by either adapting to or borrowing traits from a separate culture that they have come in contact with. These cultural modifications can include changes in clothing or food preferences and most often include changes in language. As one group comes in contact with another culture, words are adopted or adapted from the new culture to describe aspects of that society.

initial generation of immigrants. These experiences then affect the relationship between the types of acculturation and assimilation experienced by this initial generation and the types experienced by their children. According to Portes and Rumbaut, the generational relationship between the types of acculturation experienced is important to the assimilation outcomes of the second generation.

The generational acculturation relationship can be *consonant* or *dissonant*. When the two generations acculturate at a similar speed and in similar ways, this is considered consonant acculturation. The two generations could both move smoothly into American culture, or both could remain unacculturated, or they could both agree on a middle ground of limited acculturation. In contrast, the children could acculturate more quickly or more completely than their parents. This is considered dissonant acculturation. This type of acculturation can lead to parent/child conflict and a divide between the generations. The initial generation's ability to support their children is reduced at a time when they may need increased support to adapt to a new culture. Since immigrant families tend to settle in poor, inner-city neighborhoods, immigrant children often attend underperforming and overwhelmingly minority schools. The environment the immigrant youth encounters puts them at higher risk of assimilating into a culture that can harm their chances of upward mobility and, in fact, lead downward. Under circumstances such as these, partial acculturation while maintaining the immigrant's ethnic culture can have protective effects for immigrant children, allowing the immigrant community to reinforce the behavioral norms that parents try to teach their children.

DONALD P. WOOLLEY

See also
Assimilation; Assimilation Theory; Melting Pot Theory; Pluralism

Further Reading:

Gans, Herbert J. "Second-Generation Decline: Scenarios for the Economic and Ethnic Futures of the Post-1965 American Immigrants." *Ethnic and Racial Studies* 15 (1992): 173–92.

Gordon, Milton. *Assimilation in American Life: The Role of Race Religion and National Origins.* New York: Oxford University Press, 1964.

Park, Robert E. *Race and Culture.* Ann Arbor: Free Press, 1950.

Portes, Alejandro, and Min Zhou. "The New Second Generation: Segmented Assimilation and Its Variants." *Annals of the American Academy of Political and Social Sciences* 530 (1993): 74–96.

Portes, Alejandro, and Ruben G. Rumbaut. *Legacies: The Story of the Immigrant Second Generation.* New York: Russell Sage Foundation, 2001.

Segregation

Segregation is the restriction of opportunities for different types of connections and associations between the members of one racial, religious, national or geographic origin, or linguistic group and those of other groups, which results from or is supported by the action of any official body or agency representing some branch of government. As a result of segregated activities, the groups involved do not enjoy equal social status.

Segregation was actually established and defined by legal action in the United States during the 1880s with a law prohibiting blacks from riding in the same train cars as whites. A U.S. Supreme Court ruling, *Plessy v. Ferguson*, legalized segregation in the late 1890s in the United States. Additionally, throughout the South, many states adopted segregation policies and laws that applied to public facilities such as transportation, parks, recreation facilities, water fountains, public restrooms, and other facilities.

The Supreme Court heard the issue of segregation for the first time in 1896. Homer Plessy, a light-skinned black shoemaker who claimed to be only one-eighth African American, took a seat in a white train car and refused to move to the all-black train car; he was then arrested for committing a crime. The policy was based on the Louisiana Separate Car Law, which required separate but equal railroad car facilities for blacks and whites. When Homer Plessy's case appeared before the Supreme Court, eight of the nine justices decided against Plessy and voted in favor of segregation. The Supreme Court Justices said that as long as train cars for black and white Americans were of equal quality, separating the races was legal and did not contradict the constitution. The Plessy case later became known as the "separate but equal" concept and mandated legal segregation.

The first Civil Rights Act was passed in 1875 indicating "That all persons ... shall be entitled to full and equal enjoyment of the accommodations, advantages, facilities, and privileges of inns, public conveyances on land or water, theaters, and other places of public amusement" (Hasday 2007: 11). In 1883, the Supreme Court declared this act unconstitutional and specified that the act protected social but not political rights of individuals, and the Fourteenth Amendment "prohibited the states from depriving individuals of their civil rights but did not protect the abuse of individuals' civil rights by other individuals" (Hasday 2007 12). This set the stage for Southern states and their lawmakers to develop segregation laws.

Segregation laws were heavily enforced during the era known as Jim Crow, a method of legally maintaining segregation. In *The History of Jim Crow: Creating Jim Crow*, author Ronald L. F. Davis explains:

> In general, the Jim Crow era in American history dates from the late 1890s, when southern states began systematically to codify [strengthen] in law and state constitutional provisions the subordinate position of African Americans in society. Most of these legal steps were aimed at separating the races in public spaces [public schools, parks, accommodations, and transportation] and preventing adult black males from exercising the right to vote. In every state of the former Confederacy, the system of legalized segregation and disfranchisement was fully in place by 1910. (Hasday 2007: 13)

Several historical events occurred that highlighted the extent and extremity of segregation throughout the United States. Segregated city buses and rail trains were part of daily life and blacks were humiliated with verbal and physical reminders as a way of life in all areas of living. Segregation in terms of transportation and bus services consisted of white

Jo Ann Robinson, an Alabama State College English professor and later president of the Women's Political Council, advocated for black passengers after being humiliated after she accidentally sat in the white section of a nearly empty bus. Professor Robinson wrote to the mayor, advising him that if blacks did not ride the buses, the bus company would not be able to continue operating solely on white ridership. In 1953, black residents of Baton Rouge, Louisiana, held a successful bus boycott and provided blacks with the motivation for a possible boycott in Montgomery, Alabama. Professor Robinson and the Women's Political Council developed a plan to execute a boycott, which would eventually lead to events that were significant in ending segregation.

passengers entering the front of the bus, paying their bus fare, and always sitting on the bus as long as seats were available that were not occupied by other white passengers. Black passengers entered the front of the bus only to pay the fare, immediately exited the bus, and then reentered the bus using the rear bus door. Black passengers were only allowed to sit in the area of the bus identified for blacks only, which was in the rear section. Even if seats were available in the white section of the bus, black passengers remained standing and were not allowed to sit in the whites-only section.

Segregation restricts opportunities for members of a specific group and between those of other groups, resulting in the members of the segregated group being relegated to an unequal social status. Usually the segregated group is subjected to humiliation and embarrassment at the hands of those inflicting the segregation. Segregation was considered legal in the United States and applied to every aspect of life. In cities where higher proportions of other minority groups such as Asians, Hispanics, Hispanics, Pacific Islanders, and Native Americans reside, the racial segregation of blacks appears to be decreased. However, when compared to other racial and ethnic groups, blacks are the most segregated. American census data indicates that levels of segregation increased for Asians and Hispanics during the 1980s to 2000. Additionally, patterns of segregation of Hispanics also increased over several decades, possibly due to a pattern of immigration. During the 20th and 21st centuries, segregation continues to exist and is seen primarily in the nation's largest cities. Today, because of the Civil Rights Act of 1964, segregation is illegal.

SONJA V. HARRY

See also

Plessy v. Ferguson (1896); Segregation, Rural; Segregation, Suburban; Segregation, Voluntary versus Involuntary. Document: *Plessy v. Ferguson* (1896)

Further Reading:

Clark, Kenneth B., Isidor Chein, and Stuart W. Cook. "The Effects of Segregation and the Consequences of Desegregation: A (September 1952) Social Science Statement in the *Brown v. Board of Education of Topeka* Supreme Court Case." *American Psychologist* 59, no. 6 (2004): 495–501. DOI: 10.1037/0003-066X.59.6.495.

Hasday, Judy L. *Civil Rights Act of 1964 : An End to Racial Segregation*. n.p.: Chelsea House, 2007. eBook Collection (EBSCOhost), EBSCOhost (accessed November 11, 2012).

Kutty, Nandinee K., and James H. Carr. *Segregation: The Rising Costs for America*. n.p.: Routledge, 2008. eBook Collection (EBSCOhost), EBSCOhost (accessed November 11, 2012).

McGill, Sara Ann. "Segregation in the United States." *Segregation in the United States* (2009): 1. MasterFILE Complete, EBSCOhost (accessed November 14, 2012).

Segregation, Rural

Rural Southern race relations built upon traditions forged under slavery. Masters and slaves occupied positions in a clear hierarchy, but generally not in a segregated one. They shared the space of the plantation, where whites insisted upon close physical proximity to their African American laborers in order to direct their work and prevent their escape. After Emancipation, this centralized pattern of residence was altered, as black wage laborers and tenants scattered their cabins a distance from the homes of their landlords. Yet, while this dispersal opened some space between black and white homes, it did not establish a regionwide pattern of residential segregation. Instead, rural residential segregation, or its absence, came to be shaped by the particular racial demography of each rural community.

In subregions where one race made up an overwhelming majority, de facto residential segregation resulted, and little social interaction or cultural exchange took place between the races. For example, in places like the Georgia and South Carolina coast, large parts of the Mississippi Delta, and in some communities in the Cotton Belt, most residents lived, prayed, and worked in a completely segregated, all-black world. In *Souls of Black Folk* (1903), W.E.B. Du Bois described just such a setting. On a tour of a southwest Georgia county, he traveled 10 miles past decaying antebellum mansions and saw "no white face" but only a vast and impoverished "black peasantry." Similarly the poor, sandy-soil regions, the hill country, and the mountainous regions of Appalachia, the Cumberlands, and the Ozarks never contained many African Americans. In many counties in these sections, whites drove out the few black residents in the late 19th and early 20th centuries, creating sundown towns and counties. Generally, this seems to have been an action by white tenants who resented competition with black sharecroppers. But as the census manuscripts attest, in many parts of the South, black and white farmers frequently lived on neighboring farms, whether as tenants, yeomen, or planters. Because much of the rural South remained a highly local, walking and wagon culture until World War II, a high level of interracial interaction was possible, and sometimes nearly unavoidable in such communities.

The history of segregation's origins is still debated. The historian C. Vann Woodward argued that it arose in late 19th-century legislation, beginning in trains and train stations, and then spreading and systematizing to cover most imaginable points of social contact between blacks and whites. Other critics responded by arguing that late 19th-century, legally mandated segregation merely encoded preexisting de facto segregation; or more frequently, the complete exclusion of African Americans from a wide range of privately owned restaurants, motels, and other establishments. All agree that by 1920, the South was legally segregated by a confining thicket of regulations. But most historians of the field have followed Woodward's lead in telling the story essentially from an urban and legal perspective. Meanwhile, the majority of Southerners lived in rural communities until the 1950s, and their interaction across the race lines has left little evidence and attracted the attention of few historians. For the most part, their distinctive story can be explored directly only through oral history, the classic sociological studies of the early 20th century, and rural autobiographies.

Whatever the exact origin of the practice of segregation, its elaboration into a methodical separation of space into black and white zones was a child of the Progressive movement, when expert planners sought to employ systematic solutions to the nation's problems. Historians have argued that urban elite and middle-class whites systematized segregation as a means of maintaining white supremacy in an anonymous, tumultuous social setting. Urban African Americans were achieving upward mobility and gaining new purchasing power in stores, restaurants, and trains, thereby taking for themselves the symbols of middle-class respectability that had previously been badges of white privilege. Segregation offered a "modern," uniform, scientifically approved means by which urban whites could reestablish clear marks of their superiority. In a white Progressive culture preoccupied with "racial purity" and hygiene, and that identified interracial social and sexual mixing with uncleanliness, segregation opened "sanitary" space between black and white bodies without relying on the disruptive power of private white violence for its ordinary enforcement. According to Southern Progressives, the day-to-day violence needed to defend white supremacy could be supplied by urban police forces, which were formally trained to employ legal force.

In contrast, rural elite and middle-class whites at the turn of the 20th century had less need of new methods of distinguishing their status from that of their African American neighbors. Generally, rural African Americans did not have access to the symbols of middle-class attainment. Most dressed in overalls or simple dresses and worked in the fields of white landlords. Additionally, rural people were sewn into a culture of personalism, in which each individual, and the particulars of his economic status, was well known to all others in the community. Familiarity, proximity, and black economic dependency provided rural whites with powerful tools by which to remind black neighbors of their "place," and to punish any who strayed from it. The well-dressed and apparently independent black stranger who caused such discomfort to urban whites was a rarity in the countryside. Rural whites also maintained unambiguous white supremacy through an elaborate and humiliating system of racialized social etiquette by which black and white people daily used word and gesture to demonstrate their understanding of their relative place in the social order.

In rural spaces, interracial interaction—not racial segregation—actually was the primary means of symbolizing white supremacy. And in the end, violence stood as the instrument in reserve, to threaten or make object lessons of African Americans who too directly challenged the status quo. Usually, white-on-black violence took the form of one-on-one, ostensibly legal murder; but ultimately, individual white violence was backed up by the terrifying power of the mob and the noose. As white farmers were already armed with all of these powerful sanctions, social segregation appeared as a superfluous urban innovation, ill-fitted to the actual conditions of much of the rural south. Segregation, after all, is impossible without spaces and institutions to segregate. The rural South had few restaurants, motels, libraries, parks, theaters, swimming pools, train stations, and stadiums. These existed overwhelmingly in the county seats, although towns and villages might have a restaurant or train station, frequently housed in a country store. The only segregateable spaces commonly appearing in the countryside were schools and churches, which will be examined below.

As rural white supremacy winked at all manner of white-on-black crime, in reality, African Americans had no rights that a white person was legally bound to recognize. In general, white Southerners were free to act as they wished, and demonstrated the full range of possible responses, including pathological violence, contemptuous nonrecognition, paternalistic condescension, and neighborly decency. Yet, although expression ranged widely, white supremacy remained a constant. Even the most neighborly relationships were marked by signs of the racial hierarchy. For example, blacks used "Mr." or "Ms." when addressing whites, while whites invariably called blacks by their first names.

The intimacy encouraged by the nonsegregation of most rural residential space and by the culture of personalism posed a series of problems for rural African Americans. For them, physical proximity made it easier for planters to exploit and attempt to direct their labor. It put them at more direct risk to daily insults and casual violence from whites generally. And it exposed black women, particularly those who worked in white homes as domestic servants, to the threat of sexual abuse and rape.

Without the power to demand the legal rights of citizenship, some rural African Americans sought a degree of protection from white patrons. Paternalistic white elites often were willing to consider a few individual African Americans as "exceptions" worthy of extra benefits. Sometimes they would assist a longtime tenant to landowning status, or help a black neighbor obtain government benefits. They could shield their tenants or other black individuals from mob violence and sometimes from legal action as well. Planters controlled law enforcement in their counties, and sometimes made their plantations off-limits to sheriffs and deputies, all the while retaining the right to intervene in their tenants' personal lives themselves, including the use of personal violence. These benefits of patronage were privileges. They could be abrogated at any time and thus gave white elites control—which is what they wanted after all. Ultimately, this system respected not black civil rights, but the right of the white elite to protect their favorites.

Other African Americans sought to lessen the humiliations of the Jim Crow system by withdrawing where possible from contacts with whites. The black sociologist Charles Johnson believed that this was the most common type of response of African Americans in this era. In some places, particularly in Oklahoma, African Americans built all-black towns in the decades after the Civil War. In the 1920s, Marcus Garvey tapped this separatist impulse and cultivated it through black nationalist ideology. Recent scholarship shows that the Universal Negro Improvement Association had more chapters in the rural South than it did in any other region of the United States. Particularly in counties with heavy black majorities, rural African Americans turned to Garvey's message of racial pride, economic development, self-defense, and racial separation from whites.

Some rural white individuals also tried to isolate themselves from interracial contacts. Particularly if they lived in a mostly white community, it was possible to withdraw into a more racially homogenous world. Yet, in the countryside, unlike the city, this choice was frequently not supported by community pressure or economic self-interest, much less by legal barriers. Early in the 20th century, one white movement proposed a more thoroughgoing, intentional segregation of rural space. In 1913 at the height of the movement to codify residential segregation in the urban South, Clarence Poe, the editor of the widely read *Progressive Farmer*, began a two-year campaign to extend systematic residential segregation across the countryside. Rural whites unequivocally rejected this urban solution. The idea of farming without black laborers close at hand seemed unworkable to most white landlords.

Necessity reinforced the Southern tradition of neighborliness. When a man was incapacitated, neighbors plowed his field; when a woman was unable to work, nearby families would bring plates of food and help manage the household. This was not merely a practical application of Sunday school lessons. Everyone knew that illness and injury could befall anyone. Next year, perhaps you would need neighborly assistance. Oral histories attest that neighborly assistance crossed the race lines in both directions. Other forms of premodern, noninstitutional community aid also were sought and given without respect to color. Families of poor women about to give birth would seek out the nearest midwife, regardless of color. So too, when someone fell ill with ailments beyond the skills of their family, someone would run for the nearest herb specialist or root doctor. If illness was leading to death, the neighbors would increase their support, allowing the stricken family to sleep by taking turns sitting up first with the dying person, and then for a couple of days with the body in deathwatches.

Necessity of a sort also promoted another aspect of the rural South's interracial culture. In part because of the diffuse scattering of families, rural children played with any other children who were nearby. Rural Southern autobiographies attest to the frequency of interracial play among children in many regions of the South. But as they approached adolescence and the threshold of their public adult identities, they became subject to adult rules regarding interracial relationships, particularly those governing relationships between black men and white women.

In rural counties during the Jim Crow period, there were few professionally organized entertainments, and aside from churches, the few spaces set aside for leisure were usually concentrated in the county seats. These social activities—the theater, restaurants, the circus, and the county fair—were systematically segregated. Social activity in farm country tended to be informal, and so was not subject to strict segregation. As a result, depending on the particularities of their local culture, rural individuals were often free to socialize interracially. Most entertainment centered on the famous Southern propensity for talk, which happened everywhere across race lines: fields, roads, country stores, and ginhouses. Entertainment was also found at fishing holes, which were shared or used on a first-come, first-served basis, and on hunting expeditions, which were sometimes interracial affairs. In many parts of the rural South, sporting events drew black and white people together. While athletic contests in towns were invariably segregated, outside of town, farm boys frequently did not have enough local talent to field a team, much less a league. As a result, black and white baseball players faced each other on segregated or blended teams in isolated pastures, sometimes with an audience standing in the bushes. Sometimes high school baseball or football teams set up informal games where local bragging rights could be settled. Other social activities were less pastoral. Across the South, men gathered to gamble or drink moonshine at campfires by the railroad tracks and isolated cabins in the woods. Although gambling sites tended to be predominately white or black, the players cared mostly about the color of one's money; and the moonshining profession was famously interracial.

When people live close to each other, sexual relations will occur. While interracial sexual activity had fallen well off its peak in the colonial era, Jim Crow plantation belt counties still witnessed a wide range of relationships, almost entirely between black women and white men: rape, prostitution, casual sex, concubinage, and long-term common-law marriage. How these relationships were dealt with depended entirely on the culture of race relations in a local community. Sometimes offending couples were driven from the county; sometimes they were left in peace.

Schools and churches were the central institutions in the rural South. The schools were absolutely segregated, and memoirs sometimes note bursts of interracial violence between racially segregated groups of children on their way to school. Yet during most of the era of Jim Crow, most rural people attended them for only a few years. Churches, on the other hand, drew attendees throughout their lives. Under slavery, many planters required their slaves to attend services in white churches. After Emancipation, most African Americans left these churches, and brought out into the open the secretive, all-black "brush arbor" churches that they had also been attending. This religious migration established the mostly segregated sacred spaces that persist to the present.

Yet, when examined closely, the story is more complex than it appears at first glance. A small number of black farmers continued to attend white churches, in part because as African Americans had few citizenship rights, one of their best means of obtaining legal protection in the rural South lay in cultivating the patronage of an influential white person, such as a pastor. Yet, by the 20th century, few African Americans regularly attended white churches, although some continued to make irregular visits. Some rural whites also visited black churches during the early decades of the 20th century, drawn by the music or the oratorical gifts of a minister. Usually, the visitors would sit on a separate bench, frequently at the back of white churches and the front of black churches. Then, in the 1920s, this tradition of interracial church visitation contracted. Visitors continued to come, but only during revival services or other special events. In the years following World War II, this tradition attenuated further, and only funerals would draw rural people from across the race lines and into interracial space.

A person's class powerfully shaped the context of his interaction with others across the race lines. Black farm owners usually found a white patron to assist them in difficulties, but they could otherwise retreat somewhat from the humiliations of Jim Crow on their own land. Black tenants on the other hand regularly dealt with their landlord or his agent. Similarly, white planters normally had many contacts with long-term black dependents: domestics, tenants, and wage laborers. These white elites could act as they wished toward them. They could murder recalcitrant laborers without fear of punishment, or they could maintain close relationships under the rhetorical cloak of paternalism. Poor whites did not share these privileges. Sometimes eager to validate their superior racial status, sometimes willing to extend neighborly mutual aid or exchange hospitality, they seemed an unpredictable mystery to African Americans.

What has been described is neither integration nor segregation, both of which imply intentionality. Rather, race relations in the rural South were marked by premodern haphazardness. These traditions never entirely died out, but they attenuated throughout the first half of the 20th century, and did so most steeply as the rural South depopulated and the sharecropping system of labor collapsed around World War II. In these years, federal programs and war munitions factories quickly replaced what was left of the tattered garments of paternalism. As rural neighbors moved to different parts of town, their opportunities for interaction declined, even as black opportunities for economic advancement and escape from Jim Crow's humiliations increased. Meanwhile, out-migration opened space between the homes of rural neighbors; paved roads, television, and bureaucratic systematization intervened; and much that had given shape to the distinctively intertwined lives of black and white farmers unraveled.

MARK SCHULTZ

See also

Plessy v. Ferguson (1896); Residential Segregation; Segregation, Suburban. Document: *Plessy v. Ferguson* (1896)

Further Reading:

Cell, John W. *The Highest Stage of White Supremacy*. Cambridge: Cambridge University Press, 1982.

Chafe, William H., ed. *Remembering Jim Crow*. New York: New Press, 2001.

De Jong, Greta. *A Different Day*. Chapel Hill: University of North Carolina Press, 2002.

Gilmore, Glenda Elizabeth. *Gender and Jim Crow*. Chapel Hill: University of North Carolina Press, 1996.

Hale, Grace Elizabeth. *Making Whiteness*. New York: Pantheon Books, 1998.

Kirby, Jack Temple. *Rural Worlds Lost*. Baton Rouge: Louisiana State University Press, 1987.

Litwack, Leon F. *Trouble in Mind*. New York: Knopf, 1998.

Rolinson, Mary G. *Grassroots Garveyism*. Chapel Hill: University of North Carolina Press, 2007.

Rosengarten, Theodore, comp. *All God's Dangers: The Life of Nate Shaw*. New York: Knopf, 1974.

Schultz, Mark. *The Rural Face of White Supremacy*. Urbana: University of Illinois Press, 2005.

Williamson, Joel. *The Crucible of Race*. New York: Oxford University Press, 1984.

Segregation, Suburban

Though suburbs are often imagined as primarily white and middle class, they in fact have a long history of racial and class diversity. However, that diversity has often existed within the boundaries of residential segregation. Over the first several decades of the 20th century, residential patterns became increasingly segregated as suburbanization occurred. Suburban segregation was fostered and maintained through a combination of transportation availability, restrictive covenants, zoning, real estate practices, federal policies, and white community resistance. It became the norm in not only the South, but the rest of the nation as well. Though explicitly racial restrictions declined starting around 1950, suburban segregation persisted throughout the rest of the century through indirect mechanisms.

Up through the late 19th century, the lack of affordable transportation meant that cities remained relatively small and manageable for pedestrians. For this reason, wealthy citizens with access to carriages were the first to build residences far outside the city. When railroads established routes feeding into cities, upper- and upper-middle-class residents began to build homes in communities located along the radiating spokes of rail lines. These homeowners required support staff in order to attain the contemporary ideals of domestic comfort. Thus, the working class and racial minorities followed them out of the city. Domestic help, though, no longer automatically lived under the same roof as their employer. At each rail station outside the city, a pattern of roughly concentric development appeared. Wealthier suburbanites with carriages built their estates farther away from the train station. Domestic workers, still limited to foot travel, constructed dwellings within walking distance of the rail line. For those residents remaining in the city, it was not uncommon for whites and blacks to live in the same neighborhoods.

With the advent of affordable transportation in the form of streetcars and then automobiles, suburban areas became more accessible. Beginning in the early 20th century, community builders and developers began to employ restrictive covenants and subdivision regulations to limit who could live where. Restrictive covenants had remained relatively rare in the late 19th century, but by the 1910s, they had gained popularity and were the rule in 1920s housing developments. These covenants were agreements attached to property deeds, which placed prohibitions on the use or sale of the property. Developers originally employed the covenants to protect subdivisions from nuisance businesses such as slaughterhouses and maintain a level of uniformity in the neighborhood. Soon they also prohibited sale of property to nonwhites and became primarily a mechanism of maintaining residential segregation. In 1926, the U.S. Supreme Court upheld their constitutionality in *Corrigan v. Buckley* because they were private contracts. Neighborhood property owners associations often formed to enforce the covenants. While these agreements were usually set for an initial term of approximately 20 years, they renewed automatically unless a majority of property owners voted to remove the covenants. That renewal mechanism meant that in reality, these covenants persisted indefinitely.

Though the Supreme Court eventually declared restrictive covenants unconstitutional in 1948's *Shelley v. Kraemer*, the Federal Housing Administration did not begin to heed the ruling until 1950, and still largely ignored it for years thereafter. During political campaigns in the 1950s and 1960s, many candidates faced accusations of owning property covered by racially restrictive covenants. The more general use of restrictive covenants endured throughout the 20th century. By placing limits on purchase price, occupancy, and setting strict maintenance requirements, developers and homeowners associations continued to pursue an air of exclusivity by excluding portions of the general population.

Even in their heyday, though, restrictive covenants only applied to subdivisions, were difficult to enforce fully, and could not control what happened with adjacent property. Therefore, covenants worked in tandem with zoning, which soon became another popular exclusionary mechanism. Baltimore enacted racial zoning in 1910, and other cities followed suit until the practice was declared unconstitutional in *Buchanan v. Warley* in 1917. After that, zoning typically did not use any explicitly racial classifications, but that did not curb its discriminatory effects. Rather, municipal zoning set out what areas of land could be used for which purpose. Zoning decisions had a discriminatory impact because class overlapped so heavily with race. For example, white residents were much more likely to possess the resources to afford a single-family detached dwelling. Black residents, particularly the black working class, were more likely to reside in row housing or multiunit properties such as apartment complexes. Thus, when a municipality zoned an outlying area as single-family detached residential, it served to exclude many blacks and other racial minorities. The rise of comprehensive land-use planning increased local government control over the contours of growth, and the distribution of municipal services reinforced racial and class lines. In Atlanta, for example, the city manipulated the paving of new streets and closed or disrupted old ones to separate white and black neighborhoods and traffic.

Proponents of residential segregation often argued that it would reduce conflict by preventing recurrent confrontations over housing.

Real estate practices reinforced racially restrictive covenants and zoning. Real estate had become more professionalized and consolidated in the early 20th century; a small minority of powerful real estate agents set standards for the rest of the field. Up through 1950, the Code of Ethics of the National Association of Real Estate Boards prohibited agents from changing the existing character of a neighborhood and disrupting its stability. That included introducing any racial minorities into an all-white neighborhood. Meanwhile, some independent agents practiced "blockbusting" tactics. Blockbusters would introduce one or more black families into a white neighborhood, scare the remaining white homeowners away, and buy up their properties at a discount. They would then turn around and sell the homes to black residents at inflated prices, reaping a large profit. These tactics accelerated racial turnover in outlying neighborhoods and hindered stable integration.

Beginning with the Great Depression and the resulting New Deal, federal policies began to influence suburban segregation as well. The Home Owners Loan Corporation (HOLC), established in 1933, set the precedent for long-term mortgages with low monthly payments and created a formalized appraisal system. This appraisal system rated black neighborhoods unfavorably, while giving the highest ratings to white, homogenous, outlying neighborhoods. Private lenders across the country soon adapted the HOLC system. Because they had such unfavorable ratings, it was difficult to obtain a loan to buy property in older, black, or integrated neighborhoods. At the same time, the Federal Housing Administration endorsed racially restrictive covenants as a means to maintain the racial and social homogeneity of suburban areas. Urban renewal projects controlled the expansion of black populations by destroying existing housing stock, often replacing it with more expensive units or changing the land use altogether. The federal government left planning for public housing projects at the local level, thereby allowing patterns of residential segregation to persist. Local control of federal funding for highways produced similar results. City officials sometimes planned highways to serve as racial boundaries or remove black populations from the area.

The two World Wars and increasing mechanization of the Southern cotton industry released a Great Migration of Southern blacks, first from the rural South to Southern cities, and then to the urban North and West. Black migrants moved in search of better opportunities, but often found formidable resistance to their residential dispersal in their new hometowns.

These considerable barriers, though, did not prevent blacks from moving to suburbs. The first wave to do so was predominantly working class and looked to the suburbs for some measure of economic independence in the early 20th century. They sometimes built their own houses, tended gardens, rented rooms, and raised small livestock to help make ends meet. Others lived near employment in industrial suburbs. By the 1940s and 1950s, black migration to the suburbs was more heavily middle class, as families drew upon their economic resources to leave the crowded city and claim their own piece of domestic tranquility. Some black suburbanites found the experience isolating. They had distanced themselves from the black working class, but white suburbanites did not accept them as equals. As a result, black leaders built a strong community within the bounds of segregation, where black churches and businesses remained central. By the 1960s and 1970s, blacks were moving to the suburbs in unprecedented numbers, and over one-third of the black population would live there by the end of the century.

Other black families moved into already integrated outlying neighborhoods, deemed relatively safe in comparison to all-white areas. Some went through a third party when purchasing property to limit confrontations with inhospitable whites. Black families that settled in previously all-white neighborhoods often faced dire circumstances. White neighbors harassed them at all hours, damaged their property, and, in the worst cases, inflicted bodily injury. Local law enforcement often refused to provide protection. Many of these families relied on friends, family, or occasionally groups of sympathetic, liberal-minded whites to stand vigil over their homes and loved ones. While some stuck it out, others eventually made the decision to leave and seek safer accommodations for their families.

Fair and open housing policies sought to overcome barriers to residential integration by prohibiting discrimination in the sale and rental of housing. In the decade following the 1954 *Brown v. Board of Education* decision, fair housing made headway at the local and state level. Fair housing laws had been enacted in 22 states by 1968, though none of those were in the South. In 1962, President John F. Kennedy signed an executive order that curbed discrimination in federally associated housing and loans; a federal fair housing law finally passed in 1968. These laws are difficult to enforce because aggrieved parties must report individual cases of discrimination. They are also unpopular because much of the population views housing as a private realm that should not be subject to government interference. A property rights movement began to emerge in the mid-1960s, culminating in voters' rejection of California's fair housing law. The Nixon administration soon declared that the federal government would not force subsidized low-income housing upon suburbs; subsequent administrations emulated this nonintervention policy. State policies have not necessarily been effective, either. In the 1975 and 1983 *Mount Laurel* decisions in New Jersey, the state supreme court struck a blow against exclusionary zoning, declaring that suburban communities had to provide their "fair share" of low-income housing. Politics influenced enforcement, though, and suburbs were allowed to participate in a regional credit system where they could pay other areas to build up to half their share of low-income housing.

Though the legal space for housing discrimination shrank over the course of the 20th century, residential segregation persists, with pervasive consequences. Suburban segregation has impacted the demographic profile of both outlying and city schools. Because predominantly white suburbs often draw upon a larger tax base, their public schools are better funded than their inner-city counterparts. White suburbs were also largely successful in preventing mass transit from extending into their communities, choosing instead to rely on automobiles and freeways. Their lack of accessibility has further served to limit residential diversity. Many black suburbanites still live in predominantly black neighborhoods. In addition, residents remaining in central cities are often isolated from job opportunities on the booming suburban fringe. The result has been enduring disparities along racial lines.

ALYSSA RIBEIRO

See also
Plessy v. Ferguson (1896); Segregation, Residential; Segregation, Rural. Document: *Plessy v. Ferguson* (1896)

Further Reading:

Bayor, Ronald H. *Race and the Shaping of 20th Century Atlanta.* Chapel Hill: University of North Carolina Press, 1996.

Delaney, David. *Race, Place, and the Law 1836–1948.* Austin: University of Texas Press, 1998.

Fogelson, Robert M. *Bourgeois Nightmares: Suburbia, 1870–1930.* New Haven, CT: Yale University Press, 2005.

Lamb, Charles M. *Housing Segregation in Suburban America Since 1960.* New York: Cambridge University Press, 2005.

Meyer, Stephen Grant. *As Long as They Don't Move Next Door: Segregation and Racial Conflict in American Neighborhoods.* Lanham, MD: Rowman and Littlefield, 2000.

Plotkin, Wendy. "Racial and Religious Restrictive Covenants in the U.S. and Canada." http://www.public.asu.edu/~wplotkin/DeedsWeb/index.html (accessed June 1, 2008).

Sugrue, Thomas J. *The Origins of the Urban Crisis: Race and Inequality in Postwar Detroit.* Princeton, NJ: Princeton University Press, 1996.

Wiese, Andrew. *Places of Their Own: African American Suburbanization in the Twentieth Century.* Chicago: University of Chicago Press, 2004.

Segregation, Voluntary versus Involuntary

Segregation refers to members of two or more ethnic/racial groups and/or classes maintaining separation in residential patterns, schools, and social interactions. Voluntary segregation occurs when people with a common culture or common interests group together in areas of residence, leisure, schools, and so forth. Involuntary segregation occurs when the state actively enforces policies of rigorous separation of members of a group and other people or when economic disparity and/or social stigma causes a group to be isolated.

Voluntary and involuntary segregation are often related to each other because what appears to be voluntary segregation may be caused by underlying social and economic forces imposing involuntary segregation on people. For example, though there is a notable trend of the African American middle class choosing to live in segregated suburban enclaves, it is more often the case that residential segregation among African Americans is not voluntary. Rather, it is usually caused by a lack of financial resources, as well as a history of social stigmatization that results in African

Americans not being accepted by white neighbors (e.g., "white flight"). Likewise, many immigrant groups segregate in residence and business enterprise to form immigrant enclaves initially because they may not have the language or cultural skills to maneuver through the mainstream society. However, often these immigrants voluntarily remain in these enclaves even when they have the financial resources to move into other neighborhoods. In these cases, the commonality of culture and language in these enclaves outweighs the allure of living in a traditional, largely white, middle-class environment.

In U.S. history, various types of involuntary segregation have occurred, such as the forced segregation of Native Americans and the internment of Japanese American citizens during World War II. But involuntary segregation most often refers to a systematic and historical pattern of isolation that has affected African Americans long after slavery. In the United States, post–Civil War policies of forced segregation permeated all facets of existence for freed African American slaves and their children. Even after the Jim Crow era, when official policies of involuntary segregation in schools, residences, and other venues were made illegal, African Americans in all parts of the country were forced by intimidation, violence, prejudice, and ongoing poverty to remain segregated in squalid neighborhoods with inferior public resources and schools. This legacy of isolation continues in contemporary America, where lower-income African Americans are often trapped in a form of involuntary segregation, which, while not enforced by law or legislation, is born out of a history of oppression, poverty, and social stigmatization.

Voluntary segregation, on the other hand, can be seen as a means to empowerment. For example, many immigrant communities find strength, as well as social capital, in their shared values and culture. Likewise, African Americans often voluntarily segregate themselves—in schools, college campuses, and leisure associations—for political and cultural reasons, citing the preservation of group identity as justification. Historically, the feeling of black solidarity has been the basis of black cultural expression. The history of racial oppression that perpetuated involuntary segregation between blacks and whites served to create a black culture founded on difference from, as well as defiance against, white institutions.

Class is a key factor in looking at voluntary segregation among African Americans. The middle-class African Americans who choose to segregate from whites are not representative of the kind of segregation associated with most African Americans. More often, "voluntary" segregation, especially in housing and schools, is a result of low-income African Americans' lack of economical resources, rather than their act of racial solidarity. While African Americans may justifiably prefer to live in separate racial enclaves with access to black institutions, churches, and businesses, according to scholar Charles Abrams, "The test is not whether a group is segregated but whether there are elements of compulsion which keep its members in place when they are ready, willing and able to live elsewhere."

TRACY CHU

See also
Plessy v. Ferguson (1896). Document: *Plessy v. Ferguson* (1896)

Further Reading:
Abrams, Charles. *The City Is the Frontier*. New York: Harper Colophon, 1965.
Finkenstaedt, Rose L. H. *Face-to-Face: Blacks in America: White Perceptions and Black Realities*. New York: William Morrow, 1994.
Meyer, Stephen Grant. *As Long as They Don't Move Next Door: Segregation and Racial Conflict in American Neighborhoods*. Lanham, MD: Rowman and Littlefield, 2000.
Rabinowitz, Howard N. *Race Relations in the Urban South, 1865–1890*. New York: Oxford University Press, 1978.

Sellers, Cleveland (b. 1944)

Cleveland Sellers is a civil rights organizer and activist, an advocate of Pan-Africanism, and a former Student Nonviolent Coordinating Committee (SNCC) executive board member.

Born in segregated Denmark, South Carolina, on November 8, 1944, Cleveland Sellers and his older sister Gwendolyn grew up in a working-class home. His father, a disciple of Booker T. Washington, was a farmer, restaurateur, taxi driver, and real estate owner, and his college-graduate mother was a teacher and dietician at Denmark's South Carolina Area Trade School.

Sellers became aware of class divisions in the black community when, among other things, he saw friends from the poor section of black Denmark eating out of trash cans. He had little contact with whites before his teenage years. By the late 1950s, Sellers was radicalized while following televised accounts of the Montgomery Bus Boycott, the Emmett Till murder, and integration of Little Rock High School, among other events.

Sellers graduated from Voorhees High School and Junior College, where he watched news accounts of the first sit-in, which occurred on February 1, 1960, in Greensboro, North Carolina. Two weeks later, Sellers helped plan a sit-in involving Voorhees students at a local drugstore. He expanded his protest activities to Rock Hill, North Carolina, where he met Ruby Doris Smith of the SNCC. Sellers subsequently founded a youth chapter of the National Association for the Advancement of Colored People (NAACP) in Denmark, South Carolina.

In September 1962, Sellers enrolled at Howard University, where he met Stokely Carmichael and joined the Nonviolent Action Group (NAG), a friends of SNCC affiliate. NAG assisted with logistics for the 1963 March on Washington, and Sellers went to Cambridge, Maryland, to assist Gloria Richardson and the Cambridge Nonviolent Action Committee in organizing a protest against visiting Alabama governor George Wallace. The protesters were gassed and shot at by law enforcement, and Sellers was among those who were arrested.

Sellers recruited students for the Freedom Summer (Mississippi) of 1964 and worked in the Mississippi Summer Project. He helped found the Mississippi Freedom Democratic Party, participating in the famous confrontation at the Democratic National Convention in August 1964. Sellers was named project director of SNCC Mississippi field operations, where he helped execute the Mississippi Challenge to congressional elections and helped provide SNCC logistical support for the Selma to Montgomery March of 1965.

In November 1965, Sellers was elected SNCC national program secretary, joining John Lewis (chairman) and James Forman (executive director) on the three-person Executive Committee of the SNCC, which was rapidly moving in a black consciousness and internationalist direction. The SNCC issued an anti–Vietnam War statement in January 1966. Sellers helped create the Lowndes County Freedom Organization in Alabama and was reelected as program secretary in the spring 1966 election that brought Carmichael to the chairmanship. As demonstrated by its support for James

Cleveland Sellers, second from right, program director of the Student Nonviolent Coordinating Committee (SNCC), ponders a newsman's question after he refused induction into the army at Atlanta. Second from left is SNCC chairman Stokely Carmichael (1967). (Associated Press)

Meredith's March Against Fear, the SNCC thereafter shifted to a Black Power philosophy, which Roy Wilkins and Hubert Humphrey criticized at the July 1966 NAACP National Convention.

Heavily influenced by Malcolm X, by the work of Kwame Nkrumah and Frantz Fanon, and by international liberation struggles, Sellers refused to be drafted into the U.S. Army in May 1967. The SNCC thereafter became more militant. The dismissal of white staffer Bob Zellner was followed by a series of increasingly violent confrontations with law enforcement, which culminated in the Cambridge, Maryland, shoot-out that resulted in the arrest of new SNCC Chairman H. Rap Brown. An SNCC position statement on anti-Zionism in Palestine also led to increasingly shrill criticism of the organization. In October 1967, Sellers, who with Carmichael had not stood for reelection to the SNCC executive board, moved to Orangeburg, South Carolina.

That same month, Sellers assisted the Black Awareness Coordinating Committee, a group of students from historically African American South Carolina State University, protest segregationist policies at a local bowling alley, which led to a series of increasingly violent confrontations with police. Shortly thereafter, on February 8, police, state troopers, and the South Carolina National Guard attacked the South Carolina State campus, wounding 27 (most while attempting to flee) and killing three students. Shot during this "Orangeburg Massacre," Sellers was arrested and held on $50,000 bail as the principal organizer of the student protests. In 1970, a jury convicted him of inciting a riot, and he spent seven months in jail as a consequence.

The April 1968 murder of Dr. Martin Luther King, Jr. accelerated the deterioration of the SNCC. In February 1968, Forman, Carmichael, and Brown entered into an alliance with the Black Panther Party; Sellers was jailed on a draft evasion charge (eventually dismissed) and a Louisiana weapons charge. In 1969, he took a position as lecturer in the Africana Studies Program of Cornell University, enrolling at Harvard to pursue a master's degree in education the same year.

In the following year, he declared a Pan-Africanist philosophy and expanded his activities, working with the Student Organization for Black Unity, African Liberation Day, and Malcolm X Liberation University, among other efforts. He was also affiliated with Stokely Carmichael's (Kwame Ture's) All-African People's Revolutionary Party. In subsequent years, Sellers received a doctorate in history from the University of North Carolina at Greensboro (1987) and taught at both that university and the University of North Carolina at Chapel Hill and at Shaw. He is currently director of African American Studies for the University of South Carolina. On July 20, 1993, he finally received a pardon from the Parole Board of South Carolina for his conviction in the Orangeburg incident.

GREGORY E. CARR

See also

Civil Rights Movement; Student Nonviolent Coordinating Committee (SNCC)

Further Reading:

Nelson, Jack, and Jack Bass. *The Orangeburg Massacre*. New York: World Publishing Co., 1970.

Sellers, Cleveland. *The River of No Return: The Autobiography of a Black Militant and the Life and Death of SNCC*. New York: William Morrow and Company, 1973.

University of South Carolina College of Arts and Sciences, African American Studies. "Cleveland Sellers." www.cas.sc.edu/AFRA/sellers1.html.

Sentencing Disparities

The United States is one of the most diverse, multiracial, multiethnic democracies in the world. Despite this diversity, there are vast disparities in education, housing, employment, wealth, poverty, health, and mortality among Americans divided by race, ethnicity, class, and gender. As the United States incarcerates more of its population than any other nation in the world, these disparities have a profound impact on citizens of color, as we will discuss below.

Seven million Americans—one in 32 adults—are under some form of correctional supervision—jail, prison, probation, or parole. Since 1970, the American incarcerated population has grown six-fold, with an unprecedented 2,239,800 people in jails and prisons today. Whereas in 1970, 70 percent of the incarcerated population was white, today, over 60 percent of the incarcerated population consists of people of color. While African Americans compose 13.1 percent of the United States population, they compose about 43 percent of the people behind bars. Compared to white men, African American men are eight times more likely to be incarcerated. Today, one in three African American men can expect to serve time in prison during their life. Similarly, Hispanic or Latino American men make up 16.7 percent of the American population, but are six times more likely to be incarcerated than white men. While rates of incarceration are significantly lower for women than men across all racial groups, black and Hispanic women have a much higher likelihood of incarceration than white women.

Several scholars tender that such disproportionate rates of incarceration reflect disproportionate rates of offending for both violent and nonviolent offenses, such as robbery, homicide, and drug-related crimes over the past few decades. Between 1980 and 2000, rates of nonviolent crime decreased and violent crime remained relatively stable; however, incarceration rates for African American men grew substantially and well beyond rates of offending. The American War on Drugs, which began during this time, has contributed to an imprisonment binge, longer sentences, and mandatory sentencing for women and men of all racial and ethnic groups. Yet, African Americans have been targeted and sentenced disproportionately to such harsh drug penalties. Sentencing disparities between powder and crack cocaine best illustrate this trend as African Americans are overwhelmingly more likely to be sentenced under existing crack cocaine laws despite having nearly equal rates of drug use as whites. Additionally, although the majority of illicit drug dealers and users are white, three-quarters of

Sentencing Disparities Organizations

While there are many nonprofit organizations currently dedicated to reforming sentencing disparities, state and federal governments have hardly addressed the need for reform. Organizations such as the Sentencing Project, the Equal Justice Initiative, and the American Civil Liberties Union have been collectively working toward combating mass incarceration through targeting sentencing reform and federal spending on corrections. Their efforts have yielded some commendable results, namely President Obama's passage of the Fair Sentencing Act in 2010 that changed the 100:1 ratio for crack cocaine versus powder cocaine to 18:1. Additionally, the recent amendment of Three Strikes in California eliminated a mandatory sentence of life in prison for those charged with a nonviolent felony as their third strike. Despite these advancements, over 2 million individuals remain incarcerated and over 6 million continue to be under correctional supervision. Mass incarceration was not once addressed in the 2012 presidential election, and its reform does not appear to be a main priority at the federal level despite widespread disparities.

individuals serving time for drug-related offenses are black or Latino.

Other scholars take a historical view on the role of crime and racially disparate sentencing to understand mass incarceration, arguing that the extensive segregation of black citizens in jails and prisons today is similar to slavery and Jim Crow segregation. The most blatant parallel between racialized institutions of the past and today's incarcerated population is racial composition. A trend in racialized social control, from slavery to present-day mass incarceration, reveals this connection: African Americans were first enslaved, subsequently segregated and discriminated against via Jim Crow laws, continue to occupy residential pockets of extreme poverty, and now compose the majority of the prison population. Law enforcement patrols areas of high black populations with far greater diligence than elsewhere. With greater surveillance and institutionalized racial profiling programs such as "stop and frisk," African Americans experience an increased likelihood of criminalization.

Such disparate practices have had dire consequences for communities of color. Incarceration not only removes individuals from their families and communities, but also marks them upon returning from jail or prison. Familial life is disrupted by incarceration. Children with incarcerated parents face poverty, instability, and decreased social support, and often have poorer social, educational, and economic outcomes. The removal of potential income earners, a status made worse by a criminal record, furthers familial disruption. It is legal in the United States to discriminate against individuals with criminal records, reducing their chances at finding and keeping a job or home. Additionally, millions of citizens of color have permanently lost their right to vote through felon disenfranchisement laws, calling American democratic principles into question. Lastly, studies demonstrate that concentrated incarceration in communities has a destabilizing effect that actually contributes to further crime, compounding issues of disparities.

The United States has the highest rate of incarceration in the world, explained by sentencing changes involving mandatory minimums, lengthy prison sentences, high recidivism rates, and the influx of women into jails and prisons. Some scholars seek to propose factors apart from race, such as class, to explain the disparate prison composition. Regardless of these other factors, race cannot be dismissed as an unfortunate coincidence of criminal justice sentences.

JAZMINE BRAND, EMMA ZACK, AND DANIELLE DIRKS

See also

Criminal Justice System and Racial Discrimination; Prison Gangs; Prison-Industrial Complex; Prison Riots; Prisons

Further Reading:

Alexander, Michelle. *The New Jim Crow: Mass Incarceration in the Age of Colorblindness.* New York: New Press, 2010.

Chesney-Lind, Meda, and Lisa J. Pasko. *The Female Offender: Girls, Women, and Crime.* Thousand Oaks, CA: Sage, 2012.

Mauer, Marc. *Race to Incarcerate.* New York: Sentencing Project, 2006.

Reiman, Jeffrey H. *Rich Get Richer and the Poor Get Prison: Ideology, Crime, and Criminal Justice.* Boston: Allyn & Bacon, 2006.

Russell, Katheryn K. *The Color of Crime: Racial Hoaxes, White Fear, Black Protectionism, Police Harassment, and Other Macroaggressions.* New York: New York University Press, 2001.

Tonry, Michael. *Malign Neglect: Race, Crime, and Punishment in America*. New York: Oxford University Press, 1995.

Western, Bruce. *Punishment and Inequality in America*. New York: Russell Sage, 2006.

Separate But Equal Doctrine

"Separate but equal" refers to the creation of a system in which states were allowed to provide separate facilities and accommodations for blacks and whites. These separate facilities and accommodation helped to give birth to Jim Crow segregation throughout the country. The legal precedence for separate but equal laws and policies were established in the cases of *Roberts v. the City of Boston* (1848) and *Plessy v. Ferguson* (1896). Each ruling confirmed the states' right to segregate blacks and whites as long as both groups received equal treatment and services.

Although laws required that separate, "equal" facilities be maintained, the states were largely unmonitored and left to their own implementation and devices. As a result, many African Americans, especially those located in the Southern region of the country, were exposed to grossly unequal facilities and accommodations. Separate schools for African Americans were poorly funded. The students were not provided with the necessary tools needed for learning that white students were given. Hospitals, water fountains, public restrooms, and other accommodations provided for African Americans were substandard.

Many activist groups, such as the National Association for the Advancement of Colored People (NAACP), sought recourse through the courts, but the U.S. Supreme Court refused to entertain the cases or intervene until the 1954 case of *Brown v. Board of Education*.

The *Brown* case provided the NAACP with the opportunity to challenge the legality of separate but equal policies in the public school system. The NAACP's dream team of attorneys, led by Thurgood Marshall, who would later become a U.S. Supreme Court justice, argued that segregated public schools were unequal and psychologically damaging to African American children. They reminded the Court that the Fourteenth Amendment gave the federal government the power to prohibit racially discriminatory state actions such as those that existed in the public school system. In a surprising ruling, the Supreme Court ruled in favor of the plaintiffs, outlawing segregated public education facilities for African American and white students, overturning *Plessy*'s separate but equal doctrine. Chief Justice Earl Warren handed down the verdict, noting:

> Segregation of white and colored children in public schools has a detrimental effect upon the colored children. The impact is greater when it has the sanction of the law, for the policy of separating the races is usually interpreted as denoting the inferiority of the Negro group. . . . Any language in contrary to this finding is rejected. We conclude that in the field of public education the doctrine of "separate but equal" has no place. Separate educational facilities are inherently unequal.

The Court ruling enraged many Southern whites. They turned to scare and intimidation tactics to prevent the Court's ruling from being enforced. In Arkansas, Gov. Orval Faubus vowed to maintain the state's separate school system. He respected the Court's ruling only after President Dwight D. Eisenhower sent in federal troops to enforce it.

In Mississippi, Gov. Ross Barnett attempted to block African American student James Meredith's entrance into the all-white University of Mississippi, even after a U.S. Supreme Court ruling granting him entrance was handed down. President John F. Kennedy federalized the National Guard to enforce the Court's ruling. Before the ruling was enforced, a riot ensued and two people were killed.

The *Brown* ruling also laid the foundation for the challenging of separate but equal policies in other areas. In *Bolling v. Sharpe*, separate but equal polices were outlawed at the federal level of government. In *Loving v. Virginia*, the Court deemed all race-based legal restrictions on marriage in the United States unconstitutional.

BARBARA A. PATRICK

See also

American Apartheid; *Bolling v. Sharpe* (1954); *Brown v. Board of Education* (1954); *Brown v. Board of Education* Legal Groundwork; Busing; *Cooper v. Aaron* (1958); *Cumming v. Richmond County Board of Education* (1899); Desegregation; Education; Gray Commission; Little Rock Nine; Oppositional Culture; *Plessy v. Ferguson* (1896); *Savage Inequalities*; Segregation. Document: *Brown v. Board of Education* (May 1954)

Further Reading:

Harris, John. "Education, Society, and the *Brown* Decision: Historical Principles Versus Legal Mandates." *Journal of Black Studies* 13 (1982): 141–54.

"Separate Is Not Equal: *Brown v. the Board of Education.*" Smithsonian National Museum of American History. http://americanhistory.si.edu/brown/history/5-decision/courts-decision.html (accessed July 2007).

September 11, 2001, Terrorism, Discriminatory Reactions to

On Tuesday September 11, 2001, at 8:45 A.M., a plane crashed into the North Tower of the World Trade Center in New York City. Then at 9:03 A.M., a second plane hit the South Tower. At 9:43 A.M. a third plane flew into the Pentagon in Washington, D.C. A fourth plane went down near Somerset County, Pennsylvania, near Pittsburgh, as passengers struggled with the hijackers who had commandeered United Airlines 93 toward a more strategic target. The "Attack on America" is the most heinous terrorist act ever to have occurred on U.S. soil, killing 2,819 innocent men and women. As the world watched in horror the collapse of the Twin Towers on television screens repeatedly following this tragedy, retaliatory acts of bias and discrimination escalated against Middle Eastern and South Asian Americans. This backlash was based on the news that al-Qaeda had masterminded the hijacking of these commercial U.S. planes. Individuals who looked Middle Eastern, or had Arabic- or Islamic-sounding names, became the scapegoats of citizens' anger and vengeance. Hate crimes and bias incidents skyrocketed in the weeks after 9/11. Balbir Singh Sodhi was the first murder victim of the backlash, evidently because his traditional Sikh looks—turban and unshorn hair—were confused with al-Qaeda leader Osama Bin Laden's kafieh and beard. Ironically, Sikhs are neither Arab nor Muslim—the identity of most of the al-Qaeda terrorists.

Men and women of Middle Eastern ancestry have not been immune to stereotyping and discrimination in U.S. history. However, after September 11, the exponential increase in hate crimes and bias incidents is correlated with the gravity of the terrorist attacks, the targeting of Arabs and Muslims by government initiatives, and the continued climate of insecurity in the country. Hate-motivated incidents peaked immediately after 9/11 and then declined but remained at higher rates than the pre-9/11 period. This was probably due to the cautionary appeals of public officials, including the president of the United States, who condemned all vigilante-style acts of retaliation and hate crimes as soon as the backlash started. The president visited the mosque at the Islamic Center of Washington, D.C., on September 17 and warned against confusing terrorists with all Muslims. Occasional flare-ups of violence since 9/11 have led some critics to criticize the government by arguing that it should have repeated its message of tolerance with more consistency. Yet as soon as the backlash started, the government ordered the Civil Rights division of the U.S. Department of Justice to prosecute individuals for taking the law into their hands. Indeed, the FBI has been more diligent in investigating cases of suspected hate crimes since 9/11. In areas with large numbers of Arab and Muslim residents, the local police had preexisting ties with Arab and Muslim leaders. While law enforcement officers were dispatched to protect sensitive sites, neighborhood officials and community representatives engaged in intense dialogue and negotiation. Together, they were instrumental in maintaining calm and cohesiveness among these diverse communities.

Following on the heels of the hate crimes and discrimination, the government set in motion a series of initiatives and policies that targeted the Middle Eastern and Asian communities and that profiled Arab and Muslim immigrant men in particular. Even though these directives were part of the "War on Terror" policies of the Bush Administration, they sent the reverse message. They institutionalized backlash by condoning ethnic and religious profiling of Middle Eastern or South Asian immigrant men. In other words, the series of government initiatives have become codified as formal procedures of the agencies involved in the nation's security and immigration. It is important to distinguish between two types of backlash. One consists of hate crimes and bias incidents, such as murder, arson, and acts of harassment, perpetrated by ordinary Americans against fellow citizens who are believed to be Middle Eastern. The second category encompasses various official directives, initiatives, and laws carried out by the U.S. government at the federal and/or local level, and has consequences for the Middle Eastern and South Asian American communities. The post-9/11 backlash is not one discrete event or action. The backlash is a phenomenon encompassing all these elements—that is, the hate crimes and bias incidents perpetrated by the public as well as the succession of official directives from the government.

There are conflicting reports on how many hate-motivated murders were committed as backlash in the week after the September 11 events. The FBI confirmed only four murders, though another seven cases are suspected of having been hate crimes. But in the post-9/11 era, hate-crime motivation must be ruled out in the murder investigation of any individual of Middle Eastern or South Asian origin, demonstrating the seriousness of the situation.

Overall, the toll from the hate crimes and discriminatory incidents from 9/11 was substantial. A September 19, 2001, *New York Times* article put it most succinctly: "Since the attacks, people who look Middle Eastern and South Asian, whatever their religion or nation of origin, have been singled out for harassment, threats and assaults." One organization—South Asian American Leaders of Tomorrow (SAALT)—tallied 645 incidents in just the week after September 11 from newspaper reports in cities across the United States. In its 2001 annual hate crimes report, the FBI discovered an increase of 1,600 percent in incidents against Muslim individuals, institutions, and businesses. There were 28 cases in 2000 compared with 481 in 2001. These data suffer from an undercount for a number of reasons. Some state and local law enforcement agencies do not keep records of hate crimes, do so inaccurately, or do not send them to the FBI. Moreover, ethnic origin and religious affiliation are not always reported or probed. Still, the FBI hate-crimes statistics are the most systematic for comparisons across time, if not across the country.

Hate crimes and bias incidents include hate speech, airline or airport discrimination, vandalism, assaults on individuals, employment discrimination, incidence of prejudice in public schools, and murder. Most Arab and Muslim American organizations received threatening phone calls. The American-Arab Anti-Discrimination Committee has published some of the messages that were sent to them, including, "You F****** ARABS go to hell. You will pay . . . ," "ROT IN HELL FOREVER," "The only good Arab is a dead one," and "You people are animals. . . . I feel sick to my stomach to see an Arab." Several fundamentalist Christian evangelists, such as Pat Robertson and Franklin Graham (son of Billy Graham) have, since 9/11, voiced their anti-Muslim beliefs on television and other public venues. Their rhetoric has heightened tensions and distrust in the multi-religious American society, even globally.

Airport and airline cases of discrimination were frequent after September 11, given the nature of the terrorist attacks. The costs of profiling Middle Eastern–looking individuals at airports are both psychological and monetary. In addition to being inconvenienced and humiliated in public, some individuals incurred expenses because of lost airline connections. Although careful inspections of all passengers are a legitimate procedure at airports and on airlines, singling out individuals with Arab/Muslim looks or names is unfair. These policies have been particularly harmful to members of the Sikh community. Their characteristic turban and beard have singled them out as Bin Laden look-alikes. Even a year after 9/11, a flight attendant on Delta Airlines informed Hansdip Singh Bindra, a Sikh software consultant who was traveling from Newark, New Jersy, to Dayton, Ohio, that he and his fellow Middle Easterners should keep a low profile. When he tried to explain who he was, he was told to "Shut up," "Stay seated," and "not to cause any problems." Sikh Mediawatch and Resource Task Force (SMART), and their counterparts in the Arab and Muslim American communities, have been helping victims of racial profiling to take their cases to court. More important, Sikhs have been actively educating the general public about who they are and what they believe in, while being prudent about the rights of Arabs and Muslims.

There have been numerous cases of physical assaults against Muslims and Arabs including vandalism; but women wearing the hijab (headscarf) have been particularly vulnerable to harassment. Some women who used to wear the veil before 9/11 have since removed their head covering, while others camouflaged their looks with hats and baseball caps. Veiled women were cursed, yelled at with racial slurs and death threats, spit at, hit with a stick, kicked, asked to remove the hijab in public, and prevented access to their destination. In spite of this, some Muslim women started to cover their hair with the hijab after 9/11 as an assertion of their religious identity.

Vandalism against mosques, religious schools, and Arab American community property was also common following the 9/11 attacks. The 2002 Council on American Islamic Relations (CAIR) Report includes a case in Bridgeport, Connecticut, on September 16, 2001, in which phone lines were cut and the words "You will die" were written on the mosque. There were also several cases of arson, such as the Molotov cocktail thrown at the Islamic Society of Denton, Texas, on November 17, 2001, and the suspicious fire at the Arab America Network, a social-service agency for Arab immigrants, in Chicago on December 3, 2001.

The Equal Employment Opportunity Commission (EEOC) has reported a marked increase in the number of job discrimination complaints filed by Arab and Muslim Americans since September 11, 2001, revealing another kind of fallout from the 9/11 attacks. In fiscal year 2000, there were 7,792 cases of discrimination based on national origin. This increased to 8,025 cases in 2001 and 9046 in 2002. Likewise, there was an increase in religious retaliation cases from 1,939 in 2000 to 2,127 in 2001 and 2,572 in 2002. Much of this growth is due to Arab and Muslim cases. More specifically, individuals have complained about workplace intimidation and ridicule by employers or co-workers, threats of being fired or job terminations for no valid reason, denial of hiring or promotion, and the refusal to accommodate religious requests such as prayer, fasting, and the accommodation of the veil for women and beard for men (and in the case of Sikhs, the turban). Other forms of discrimination, such as in obtaining mortgages or other bank loans, renting apartments, or seeking services of many kinds, have also increased.

The nation's public schools have been a fertile ground for perpetuating hate and bias. Students of Middle Eastern or South Asian origin were cursed, mocked, and called "terrorists" by their peers; boys named Osama or Mohammad were particularly vulnerable. They were also spat at, kicked, and beaten. Instead of sowing seeds of tolerance, even some teachers, coaches, counselors, and other school staff singled out Arab and Muslim American students in a negative way. Many parents kept their children away from school for a few days or a week after 9/11, and several Muslim schools were closed because of threats.

Within a few weeks following the September 11 attacks, the Bush administration issued a series of initiatives and directives as part of its "War on Terrorism" policy. The USA Patriot Act is perhaps the most monumental piece of

legislation to date that aims to ensure the security of the land and its citizens. It was passed on October 25, 2001, by Congress without many members reading it and with little debate or opposition, and signed into law the next day by President Bush. The USA Patriot Act, an acronym for the Uniting and Strengthening America by Providing Appropriate Tools Required to Intercept and Obstruct Terrorism Act, introduced sweeping changes in domestic law and intelligence agencies overseas, giving unprecedented powers to the government with little oversight from the courts. Due-process provisions, protections against unreasonable searches and seizures, detentions without hearings, probable cause, and denial of bail are some of the issues that have concerned constitutional scholars and civil rights activists.

Detentions and deportations were the first of a series of initiatives issued by the U.S. attorney general in the effort to apprehend terrorists. Starting on September 17, 2001, immigrants from Middle Eastern and/or Islamic countries became subject to detention. If suspected of terrorism, detainees could be kept without charge for an extended period of time; hearings could be "secure," that is, closed to the public; bond could be denied; and attorney/client communication privilege could be disregarded. According to the "Report on the September 11 Detainees," issued April 2003 by the Inspector General of the U.S. Department of Justice, 762 illegal immigrant men from Arab and/or Muslim countries were detained, some for weeks and months, but none were charged with terrorism. Most of the arrests took place between September and December 2001, though arrests continued until summer 2002. Secrecy shrouded the entire process. Estimates on the number of detainees vary from 500 to over 1,200. Even Congress did not receive an answer when it questioned the Department of Justice about the detainees. The Inspector General's report was also critical of the physical and legal treatment of the detainees. Most were housed in the Metropolitan Detention Center in Brooklyn, New York, and the Passaic County Jail, in Paterson, New Jersey. Pakistanis made up the largest number of the detainees, followed by Egyptians, Turks, and Yemenis, suggesting that both Arabs and non-Arab Muslims were targeted. The "absconder initiative" was named for the announcement made by INS commissioner James Ziglar on December 6, 2001, to publish the names of more than 300,000 aliens who were still in the United States in spite of deportation orders. This was followed on January 8, 2002, by an announcement by the Department of Justice to enter into the FBI database the names of about 6,000 male absconders, Arab and/or Muslim nationals, believed to be from al-Qaeda–harboring countries. These suspects were to be apprehended.

An important strategy in tracking terrorists is securing the nation's frontiers, since all the hijackers had managed to enter the country legally. The administration set in motion several measures to regulate the traffic of people, goods, and money across borders. The National Security Entry-Exit Registration System (NSEERS) obligates aliens from 25 predominantly Muslim countries (Afghanistan, Algeria, Bahrain, Djibouti, Egypt, Eritrea, Indonesia, Iran, Iraq, Jordan, Kuwait, Lebanon, Libya, Malaysia, Morocco, Oman, Pakistan, Qatar, Saudi Arabia, Somalia, Sudan, Syria, Tunisia, United Arab Emirates, and Yemen) to be registered, fingerprinted, and photographed upon arrival and periodically afterwards. NSEERS has been criticized for ethnic profiling, a violation of the equal-protection principle in U.S. law.

The Student and Exchange Visitor System (SEVIS) is a computer system that tracks all foreign student enrollments and as such is the only measure that is not limited to Muslim countries. Officials at institutions of higher education and U.S. embassies gather data on such details as start date of each semester, failure to enroll, full-time student status, disciplinary action by the institution, and early graduation. SEVIS became law on January 30, 2003, even though there were many glitches in the system that continued to create backlogs afterwards. Critics argue that these problems have contributed to the decrease in foreign students in U.S. colleges and universities, reversing a trend that showed a steady growth between 1948 and 2001. The dilemma is that the new restrictions imposed on foreign students may discourage from coming to the United States genuine students who are likely to become goodwill ambassadors for the United States when they return home.

Special registration is another legally problematic provision under NSEERS. Men older than age 16 who were citizens of Iran, Iraq, Libya, Sudan, and Syria, allegedly terrorist-training countries, and who had entered the United States before September 10, 2002, and planned to remain at least until December 16, 2002, were required to register with the INS before December 16, 2002. On December 16, 2002,

other countries were added to the list. Failure to report to the INS was cause for deportation. Ironically, many people who obeyed the order were deported anyway. Special registration increased the workload of an already strained INS staff. The men who complied with the orders complained of harsh treatment by INS staff and long waits without access to food or water. More seriously, the lives of many families were disrupted as husbands were detained and deported, leaving wives and children without any means of support and no opportunity to rejoin the men unless they return to his country of origin. More than 80,000 men had registered by early May 2003.

Special registration resulted in the arrest of several hundred Iranians in Los Angeles who were deemed in violation of their visas. This order created unprecedented demonstrations and protests from the Iranian American population in Los Angeles, the largest such concentration in the United States. Having designated the Islamic Republic of Iran part of the "Axis of Evil," individuals bearing Iranian passports were denied visa issuance and subjected to Special Registration, even though Iranians had nothing to do with the 9/11 attacks. In November 2003, almost coinciding with the first anniversary of the special registration, the government reversed its decision on requesting that men from a number of Arab and/or Muslim countries repeat this procedure annually, because this initiative did not lead to the apprehension of any terrorists.

The profiling of men from Arab and/or Muslim countries has been a persistent problem in many government initiatives after September 11, 2001. The supposedly voluntary interviews fall into this category. The attorney general ordered the FBI to interview some 5,000 men, ages 18 to 33, who had entered the United States between January 2000 and November 2001 from countries suspected of al-Qaeda presence or activity, once again targeting the Americans fitting the profile of the hijackers. On February 26, 2002, the Final Report on Interview Project was released. It revealed that out of the 5,000 Arab and/or Muslim men on the list, 2,261 were interviewed, but fewer than 20 were taken into custody—3 on criminal violations and the rest on immigration charges. In spite of the ineffectiveness of this policy as a means of finding terrorists, on March 19, 2002, the Department of Justice declared that it would conduct an additional 3,000 interviews. The results of this decision are not known.

In November 2002, with the war in Iraq pending, more than 10,000 individuals born in Iraq were sought for questioning. Many were naturalized U.S. citizens, an exception to the detentions and special registration policies that previously only sought foreign nationals.

The government has been tightening controls of financial transactions internationally to dry up the sources of funding for terrorist organizations. To that end, in December 2001, the government froze the assets of three large Muslim charitable organizations—the Holy Land Foundation for Relief and Development, Benevolence International Foundation, and Global Relief Foundation—accusing them of money laundering. The government claimed that these organizations were funneling monies to terrorist organizations such as Hamas, a radical Islamic organization. These actions created fear and suspicion among the Middle Eastern and South Asian Americans and slowed down charitable contributions for a time. The Internal Revenue Service (IRS) continues to scrutinize the accounts of nonprofit organizations in these ethnic and religious communities more meticulously than before. Muslim Americans have been concerned with the government's interference in their religious obligation to pay *zakat* (alms). Another manifestation of this strategy was a raid in late March 2002 by the U.S. Customs Service, the IRS, other federal agencies, and local police on 14 homes and businesses in northern Virginia alleged to be laundering money for terrorist organizations.

The "Homeland Security Act of 2002," signed into law on November 25, 2002, established the Department of Homeland Security and defined its mission and responsibilities. This new department, which employs 170,000 individuals, merged 22 federal agencies, including the USCIS, formerly known as the INS. Around the same time, President Bush also signed into law the Justice Department's Operation TIPS (Terrorism Information and Prevention System), which would enlist thousands of truck drivers, mail carriers, bus drivers, electricians, plumbers, and so on as "citizen observers." Because of heavy criticism from civil rights groups and the public, TIPS was not successful.

In the end, the government's appropriation of unprecedented powers to catch terrorists within its borders has thus far not been successful. Perhaps the closest the FBI came to arresting anyone of Middle Eastern or South Asian origin remotely related to al-Qaeda was the capture on September 14, 2002, of six U.S. citizens of Yemeni descent in Lackawanna, New York. This is not to say, however, that some of the government initiatives in the aftermath of 9/11 were unnecessary. Indeed, many immigration procedures had been lax and flawed, and stricter border controls are a requirement in this age of global terrorism. However, the targeting and profiling of a specific population was unnecessary and unjust.

As the administration's critics often noted, searching for leads to terrorist cells requires the trust and collaboration of the very ethnic and religious communities that were angered and alienated by the presumption of guilt by association. Instead of winning the hearts and minds of Middle Eastern and South Asian Americans, the government's policies of singling them out had the opposite effect. The government initiatives enflamed the suspicions and stereotypes of the general public against Arabs and Muslims and heightened the climate of fear and insecurity. Clearly, Arab and Muslim Americans as a community could challenge individual hate crimes much more effectively than the government initiatives. In fact, they have walked a fine line between displaying loyalty to the United States and diplomatically challenging profiling. To do otherwise would have been un-American.

MEHDI BOZORGMEHR AND ANNY BAKALIAN

See also

al-Qaeda; Arab/Muslim American Advocacy Organizations; Government Initiatives after the September 11, 2001, Attack on the United States; Hate Crimes in America; Muslims, Terrorist Image of

Further Reading:

Lalley, Pat. *9.11.01: Terrorists Attack the U.S.* Austin, TX: Raintree Steck-Vaughn, 2002.

National Commission on Terrorist Attacks upon the United States. *The 9/11 Commission Report: Final Report of the National Commission on Terrorist Attacks upon the United States.* New York: W. W. Norton, 2004.

Sharecropping

Sharecropping, an agricultural labor system, emerged in the Southern United States after the Civil War destroyed the slave labor economy. After Emancipation, former slaves suddenly needed to support themselves, and cash-poor planters required cheap labor to raise and harvest crops. Since planters had little capital and freed slaves had no land, equipment, or farm animals, many entered into labor agreements whereby planters furnished land and equipment and former slaves worked the fields. They split the harvest, and the Freedmen's Bureau, established in 1865 to protect the interests of former slaves, initially considered these agreements beneficial. Sharecroppers were provided between 25 and 40 acres to grow their own food and sell what was left over after they provided the planter with his half of the harvest.

Sharecroppers paid for the rental of tools, wagons, animals, and shelter with additional liens on their crop. Provisions like coffee, sugar, flour, cornmeal, and even clothing were available to them through "furnishing merchants" who also accepted liens. After renting and purchasing everything he needed, a sharecropper could find himself down to 25 percent or less of the proceeds of his harvest. Plantations, as in slave days, were closed communities, and sharecroppers were required not only to purchase their supplies and provisions from the landlord's furnishing merchant, but to market their crop through him. All debts were settled at harvest time. A few bad seasons could doom a cropper to a life of revolving debt and credit, and by 1869, the Freedmen's Bureau could no longer advocate for him. President Andrew Johnson not only disbanded the Bureau, but also returned most of the confiscated land to Southern planters. This dashed all hope of land redistribution that the Freedmen's Bureau had advocated for the former slaves.

Sharecropping was part of a three-tier system that included tenant farming, share renting, and sharecropping. In a tenant farming arrangement, the landlord provided land, a cabin, and fuel, for which the tenant paid a fixed rental rate per acre. Most tenant farmers were poor whites who had lost their land, but still had tools and farm animals. In share renting, the landlord provided the same things, and the share renter pledged to pay him one-quarter to one-third of his crop. Most share renters were also white. In sharecropping, however, the landlord provided *everything* and the cropper divided the harvest with him—less the cost of supplies and provisions purchased from the furnishing merchant. By law, tenant farmers and share renters owned the crops they produced and therefore could sell them wherever they chose.

An African American sharecropper plows a field in Alabama, ca. 1937. (Library of Congress)

The sharecropper, however, had to sell through the plantation's furnishing merchant.

Since furnishing merchants controlled the commissaries and kept all the accounts, the sharecropping system was fertile ground for abuse. If a cropper challenged the landlord's figures, he and his family could be evicted from the plantation. Sharecropper families often worked 10-hour days and were closely supervised by overseers. Women labored in the fields as well as in the home, and child labor was shamelessly exploited. Despite the U.S. Congress passing legislation in 1867 outlawing debt servitude, croppers who owed their landlords money were not permitted to leave the plantation until they worked it off. If they escaped, they were often tracked down and returned by local law enforcement officers. Many of the restrictions imposed on sharecroppers were simply extensions of the slave system.

Organizing sharecroppers into alliances to demand reform was difficult because croppers were spread out over many plantations, and landlords threatened to evict them for even associating with organizers. The Colored Farmers Alliance, an early attempt, was established in Leflore County, Mississippi, in 1888 by Oliver Cromwell to win the right to trade with stores and cooperatives outside the plantations. Black organizing terrified white planters, who tended to equate it with slave insurrection. In 1889, Cromwell was ordered to leave Leflore County. He refused, and when a group calling themselves the "Three Thousand Armed Men," organized to protect him, the governor sent in the state militia. Cromwell escaped, but 25 Alliance men were killed, and Leflore County's Colored Farmers Alliance was disbanded. By 1890, however, chapters were operating in Norfolk, Charleston, New Orleans, Mobile, and Houston.

In 1919, a group of black World War I veterans under the leadership of Ike Shaw and C. H. Smith organized the Farmers and Laborers Household Union of America in Phillips County, Arkansas. They drafted a legally binding contract with plantation owners to provide croppers with a written guarantee of their percentage of the harvest as well as a written statement of account at the end of each season. The planters refused to negotiate, but despite their almost constant intimidation, with assistance from allies in law enforcement and the Ku Klux Klan, union membership increased. On September 30, 1919, a sheriff, his deputy, and a black trustee broke up a Farmers and Laborers union meeting at a church in Hoop Spur, Arkansas. In the ensuing struggle, one of the officers was killed and the other wounded. A posse returned the following morning to arrest the union leaders, but the armed membership surrounded and protected them. Advised that a race war was imminent, the governor sent in 500 state militia troops who burned the church, killed 29 blacks, and arrested hundreds. The idea of black sharecroppers controlling their own destinies was so terrifying to white planters that they were willing to commit massacres in order to destroy the organizers and intimidate croppers into submission.

In the spring of 1931, black sharecroppers and tenant farmers in Tallapoosa County, Alabama, organized the Croppers and Farm Workers Union under the leadership of Ralph and Tommy Gray and Mack Coad, a black steelworker from Birmingham who organized industrial workers for the Communist Party. During the 1930s the Communist Party succeeded in creating bargaining units of black and white industrial workers in Birmingham and Memphis, and black sharecropper alliances in rural Alabama and Georgia. The Croppers and Farm Workers Union recruited 800 members in just two months, and in July 1931, at a meeting held in a local church, they voted to support cotton pickers in their demand for a one-dollar-a-day wage. (They were earning 50 cents.) Local sheriff Kyle Young and his deputy Jack Thompson, who had been tipped off about the meeting by a cropper and wanted to earn extra points with his landlord, broke up the gathering, killing Ralph Gray, wounding five union members, and arresting dozens more. After Young was wounded, the church was burned to the ground. Once again, the effort to unionize ended in violence and death

Tommy Gray, his daughter Eula, and black communist Al Murphy reorganized as the Share Croppers Union. By the summer of 1932, they had reclaimed 600 members. The Croppers Union revived the demand for a one-dollar-a-day cotton picker wage, and demanded payment for the cropper's share of the harvest in cash instead of merchant script, credit, or supplies. They also sought freedom to buy what they needed at any store they chose; and the right to sell their crops to whomever they chose. These demands, structured as they were to defeat the planters' monopoly, posed a threat not only to white supremacy but to the planters' cheap labor supply, and planters became determined to destroy this union as they had the Croppers and Farm Workers.

In December 1932, Sheriff Cliff Elder went to the Reeltown, Alabama, farm of black Tallapoosa County organizer Clifford James (one of the few black landowners in the county), to impound his two mules and a cow as payment for a $6 debt he owed a white grocer. Without his stock, James could not farm, and he refused to surrender the animals. A dozen armed members of the Croppers Union stood with him. Elder left, but later returned with an armed posse. The subsequent shootout left the sheriff and several deputies wounded, Clifford James dead, and many croppers injured. Thirty-two were arrested, and five were later convicted of assault with a deadly weapon. A search of the James home uncovered a Share Croppers Union membership list, and vigilantes terrorized everyone on it. Many were beaten and jailed, and hundreds subsequently left the county. Despite the ongoing violence, however, the union continued to grow. By June 1933 nearly 2,000 members were operating in 73 locales across the Deep South.

During the last decade of the 19th century and into the early years of the 20th century, a sharecropper could net $333 in a good year, a share renter $398, and a tenant farmer as much as $478. The outbreak of World War I, however, disrupted the world cotton market, and prices fell precipitously. They remained depressed throughout most of the 1920s. The end of that decade brought droughts, dust storms, boll weevil infestations, and eventually the Great Depression. Bankrupted Southern planters lost their land at twice the national average as the price of cotton fell from 20 cents a bale (500 pounds) in 1927, to less than five cents in 1932. Many croppers found themselves not only unemployed, but also homeless. In 1933, in response to Southern planters' pleas for federal assistance, the administration of President Franklin D. Roosevelt established the Agricultural Adjustment Administration (AAA). Planters who agreed to reduce their crop by 30 percent were guaranteed rental payments and the promise of an additional subsidy if their harvests did not cover their costs. It was an attempt to revive the agricultural economy by limiting supplies of cotton, corn, and soybeans and hoping that consumer demand would increase market prices. These federal agreements stipulated that tenant farmers and sharecroppers were to receive a percentage of the payments. Most never did. The New Deal's agricultural policies changed the lives of sharecroppers and tenant farmers forever. After cotton production was drastically reduced, planters no longer needed as many tenants, and croppers were turned off the plantations. The cities, plagued by a concurrent industrial depression, could not absorb them, and without income or shelter, many starved. Others became radicalized.

As mass evictions from the plantations began, the Share Croppers Union in Tallapoosa County, Alabama (which remained a black communist organization), grew to almost 8,000. At the same time, a socialist-supported interracial alliance, the Southern Tenant Farmers' Union (STFU), was organized on the Fairview Cotton Plantation near Tyronza, Arkansas, on July 11, 1934. Eleven white and seven black men met at a local schoolhouse and vowed to stop the evictions on the Fairview Plantation and to demand their fair share of AAA money. Founding members included white socialists H. L. Mitchell and Ward Rodgers and black cropper Ike Shaw, who had survived the 1919 Hoop Spur, Arkansas, massacre. Despite its name, the STFU consisted largely of black and white sharecroppers and day laborers. Interracial organizing was rare, since the sharecropping system by its very nature drove poor whites and blacks into competition. Animosity was not unusual, since black sharecropper labor was cheaper, and when times were hard, the landlord accepted fewer tenants. Plantation owners encouraged racial divisiveness because it kept agricultural workers with similar grievances against them divided. New Deal politics, however, had convinced the croppers and tenants that they shared a common misery and that there was strength in numbers. In Arkansas a large percentage of the evicted sharecroppers were white.

Late in 1934, the STFU sent a delegation to Washington, D.C., to meet with Secretary of Agriculture Henry Wallace to demand that planters stop evicting tenants and croppers and pay them their share of the rental and parity subsidies. The Roosevelt administration subsequently created the Resettlement Administration and charged it with assisting destitute landless farmers. When this agency proved bureaucratic and unresponsive, the STFU took matters into its own hands. In August 1935, just before picking season, they threatened to strike. Ultimately they won a 75-cent wage increase without resorting to the strike and grew so rapidly that by 1936, there were over 25,000 members in the South. That year the Farm Security Administration (FSA) replaced the Resettlement Administration. This agency's Tenant Purchase Program bought failed plantations and offered them for sale at low interest rates to croppers and tenants. Most sharecroppers were not in a financial position to buy land, however. Housing projects were also acquired for dispossessed farm workers, but since the program was mandated federally but administered locally, the housing projects were often segregated, and white croppers and tenants ultimately received the largest share of assistance.

Another factor that mitigated against reform was disenfranchisement. Croppers, especially black croppers, did not vote. Some were illiterate, some were too intimidated by their planters to register, and others could not afford to pay the poll tax, a common barrier in the Deep South. Poll taxes compounded every year after age 21 and were required to be paid in full before a citizen could vote. Lack of political clout cut croppers off from the help those liberal Southern politicians who might have extended them under the umbrella of New Deal reform.

By 1936, the Alabama Share Croppers Union had chapters in Louisiana and Mississippi and counted 12,000 members. It made several overtures to the STFU, whose membership was spread over Arkansas, Mississippi, Tennessee, and Missouri, to merge, but the socialist STFU leadership was not interested in joining forces with Communists. Traditional Southern racial attitudes had also infiltrated the movement by that time. Although the STFU had been established as a biracial organization, its black membership grew more quickly and ultimately constituted a majority. White croppers and tenants began to drop out and form their own splinter unions. This pleased planters, who feared the threat that interracial organizing posed to their cheap labor supply and to the entire segregated system.

By 1939, the South finally began to recover from the devastation of the Great Depression, and New Deal assistance was no longer either needed or welcome. While Franklin Roosevelt had bailed out planters with his Agricultural Adjustment Administration policies, they had no intention of allowing New Deal liberals and the activist first lady Eleanor Roosevelt to encourage union organizing or farm worker reform. The region reverted to its traditional distrust of "big government" and its determination to maintain white supremacy.

Despite strikes, protests, the support of many New Deal liberals, and winning some minor reforms, small wage increases, and benefits, the STFU and the SCU were not able to solve the fundamental problems of sharecroppers. Ultimately croppers and tenants were needed less and less, as machinery designed to plant, pick, and harvest cotton became affordable. By 1937, the Share Croppers Union had liquidated and transferred its membership to the Agricultural Workers' Union, an affiliate of the American Federation of Labor. That same year, the Southern Tenant Farmers' Union affiliated with the Congress of Industrial Organization's (CIO) agricultural workers. Two years later, however, it withdrew, and tried to establish itself once again as an independent union. But by that time, membership had fallen drastically, as thousands of sharecroppers left the South. In the end, it was not the reformers or the activists, or even the croppers themselves who ended the system that had locked them into virtual slavery, but economics. It was tractors, mechanical cotton pickers, and the shift in efficiency from tenancy to seasonal wage earners that changed the course of sharecropping.

MARY STANTON

See also

Colored Farmers' Alliance; Slavery; Southern Tenant Farmers Union (STFU)

Further Reading:

Beecher, John. "The Share Croppers' Union in Alabama." *Social Forces* 13 (October 1934).

Biegert, M. Langley. "Legacy of Resistance: Uncovering the History of Collective Action by Black Agricultural Workers in Central East Arkansas from the 1860s to the 1930s." *Journal of Social History* (Fall 1998).

Clark, Thomas D. "The Furnishing and Supply System in Southern Agriculture Since 1865." *Journal of Southern History* 12 (February 1946): 28–33.

Kelley, Robin D. G. *Hammer and Hoe: Alabama Communists during the Great Depression.* Chapel Hill: University of North Carolina Press, 1990.

McMillen, Neil R. *Dark Journey: Black Mississippians in the Age of Jim Crow.* Urbana: University of Illinois Press, 1989.

Raper, Arthur F., and Ira De A. Reid. *Sharecroppers All.* Chapel Hill: University of North Carolina Press, 1941.

Rosengarten, Theodore, comp. *All God's Dangers. The Life of Nate Shaw.* New York: Vintage Books, 1984.

Sharia Law

Sharia Law is, in brief, an Islamic moral code that guides the daily conduct of a Muslim in accordance with a certain understanding of the Koran and the sayings of the Prophet Mohammed. Sharia law is derived from four primary sources: (1) the *Koran*, which is held to be the divinely revealed word of Allah; (2) *Hadith*, or the recorded teachings of the Prophet Mohammed; (3) *'Ijma*, or scholarly consensus; (4) *Qiyas*, a deductive method of analysis or reasoning. It is one of the most widely misunderstood areas of Islamic practice and belief. In popular print media and televised news, sharia law has been linked to rigid applications of standards and harsh penalties meted out for lack of fidelity to Islamic codes of conduct. Such portrayals, however, are often exaggerated or inaccurate and reveal more of an unwillingness to explore the actual tenets of Islam with

Anti-Sharia and the Elections of 2012

The proposed amendment to the Oklahoma State constitution, aimed at officially adopting an anti-sharia stance, eventually met its demise. This was not, however, the end of the anti-sharia debate. Republican presidential candidates took up the banner against sharia. The well-known Republican Newt Gingrich, while campaigning in South Carolina, asserted that he would support a Muslim presidential candidate only if such a candidate publicly committed to renounce sharia. Rick Santorum and Michele Bachman both signed a pledge to reject sharia Islam, linking it explicitly with anti–human rights, antiwoman practices. Mitt Romney, the eventual Republican presidential candidate that ran against Barack Obama, specifically averred that sharia would have no place in American courts. Such wholehearted embrace of anti-sharia views may further magnify the differences between conservative and liberal political camps. The debate may benefit from exploring how biblical principles and Roman Catholic canon law have been treated and defended in the U.S. legal system. Courts in the United States have used biblical principles to enforce arbitration agreements and canon law to settle property matters of the Roman Catholic Church. Would not enforcing sharia for certain life matters of Muslims encourage a double standard?

actual adherents of the faith as the conversation partner. One opponent of sharia law, Frank Gaffney, has decried the application of sharia tenets to the lives of American Muslims. Gaffney, the head of the Center for Security Policy, asserted that sharia is, "a legal-political-military doctrine" that is the "preeminent totalitarian threat of our time." In 2010, Oklahoma passed the "Save Our State Amendment," becoming the first state to officially prohibit "Sharia law." Even though a federal court issued an injunction blocking the ballot measure intended to change Article 7, Section 1 of the Oklahoma State Constitution—holding that the ban violated the Establishment Clause of the U.S. Constitution—about two dozen state legislatures have since recommended parallel measures. One measure proposed in Tennessee makes any adherence to sharia a felony, punishable by up to 15 years in prison. Sharia law, moreover, has received substantial attention in Great Britain, where sharia tribunals were established in 2007 in five major cities of England. In these settings—officially considered "arbitration tribunals" under the English Arbitration Act of 1996—a Muslim legal expert takes on cases brought forth by members of an Ummah (a community of Muslims) and decides upon them in adherence to applicable Islamic standards of practice and belief. At least one political scholar has complained that British law ought to be maintained as absolute, refusing any hints of a "dual" legal system. With claims of such severity circulating in local political venues and through mainstream political media, it is no wonder

that fear and confusion seem to dictate most public discussion about standard Islamic practices. Clarification is certainly in order.

Literally translated, *sharia* simply means "road to the watering place" or "path leading to the water," or, in practical terms, "the way to the source of life." It is, in other words, not exactly a "law" as the term is popularly understood. It is more of an ethical code that aims to guide the action of Muslims on a daily basis in order to garner the mercy of Allah. In terms of dogmatic application or rigidity, *'Ijma* and *Qiyas* (number [3] and [4] above), are often cited as support for the flexibility of sharia tenets. Beyond this, concern over sharia law as a potential rival to the established body of American (or Anglo-Saxon) law is also unfounded. Many scholars have demonstrated that the sharia tenets are predominantly concerned with personal religious devotion and, in fact, were developed without any concern for formal governmental enforcement. To be more precise, legal scholar Yasir Ali helpfully summarizes thus: "nearly 70 percent of Shariah deals with the performance of religious rituals such as fasting and the giving of alms, 25 percent deals with economic, family, and dietary regulations, and only about 5 percent deals with Islamic criminal law, which would be implemented by a Muslim government." Another Islamic law scholar, Yasir Qadhi, elaborates that most American Muslims are not seeking the national legal implementation of sharia regarding criminal offenses, yet would still consider themselves "sharia adherents" because they perceive sharia as being fully consistent with the U.S. Constitution.

GABRIEL SANTOS

See also
Islamophobia; Pluralism; Stereotype Threat

Further Reading:

Ali, Yaser. "Shariah and Citizenship—How Islamophobia Is Creating a Second-Class Citizenry in America." *California Law Review* 100 (2012): 1027–68.

Bhabha, Faisal. "Between Exclusion and Assimilation: Experimentalizing Multiculturalism." *McGill Law Journal* 54 (2009): 45–90.

Edwards, Richard. "Sharia Courts Operating in England." *The Telegraph*, September 14, 2008. http://www.telegraph.co.uk/news/uknews/2957428/Sharia-law-courts-operating-in-Britain.html (accessed December 18, 2012).

Qadhi, Yasir. "A Proud, Patriotic Shariah Practicing American." *Faith in Memphis*, March 10, 2011. http://faithinmemphis.com/2011/03/10/a-proud-patriotic-shariah-practicing-american/ (accessed December 18, 2012).

Reed, Melanie D. "Western Democracy and Islamic Tradition: The Application of Sharia in a Modern World." *American University International Law Review* 19 (2004): 485–521.

Sharpton, Al (b. 1954)

Alfred (Al) Charles Sharpton Jr., was born in Brooklyn, New York, to Alfred Sharpton Sr. and Ada Richards Sharpton on October 3, 1954. Rev. Al Sharpton grew up in both Brooklyn and Hollis in Queens, New York. From the age of four, young Al began preaching in the pulpits of Pentecostal churches. From 1969 to 1971 Sharpton worked for two years with Operation Breadbasket, which was led by Rev. Jesse Jackson. Through this organization, he led protests against companies that discriminated against black people.

Reverend Sharpton later founded the Brooklyn-based National Youth Movement. Through this organization he advocated against police brutality and racial discrimination, and organized civil protest demonstrations. He attended Brooklyn College during the 1970s, but later dropped out to work with the singer James Brown. While working with James Brown, he met his wife Kathy Jordan, who was a backup singer for Brown. He married Kathy Jordan in 1983, and the couple later had two daughters, Dominique and Ashley.

Sharpton became known as a public persona during two controversial and significant cases involving two New York teenagers, Michael Griffith and Tawana Brawley. Griffith was a young African American man killed in a predominantly white area of Howard Beach in Queens in December 1986. The Howard Beach killing made national headlines and was considered one of the most significant racial hatred cases of the 1980s. Sharpton worked closely with two African American lawyers, Alton Maddox and C. Vernon Mason, to lead protest marches in Howard Beach. The leaders of the protest demanded that a special prosecutor be assigned to investigate the murder of Michael Griffith and prosecute his killers. The special prosecutor was eventually assigned in this case, and three white youths from Howard Beach were convicted of manslaughter in Griffith's death.

Tawana Brawley was an African American teenager who alleged that she was beaten and sexually assaulted by white men in Wappinger Falls, New York. According to Brawley, the attack took place in November 1987. Sharpton became involved in the case and was a leading spokesperson in support of Brawley. Sharpton and others pressured the local police department and investigators in the case primarily because the incident involved the assault of a young African American woman and white male perpetrators. The case was later dropped by the police department and the state attorney general because after an intense investigation it was concluded that Tawana Brawley and her mother had fabricated the story to protect the girl from a harsh punishment by her stepfather.

These two incidents catapulted Al Sharpton into the national limelight. He became known as a brazen and loquacious advocate for social justice. In 1990, another African American teenager was killed in the Bensonhurst section of Brooklyn, New York. Yusef Hawkins was murdered by a group of whites. A leading activist and agitator, Sharpton again became actively involved in protest demonstrations to raise awareness of the case. During one of these protests, Sharpton was stabbed by a white man. After his recovery, Sharpton began to shift his political agenda and focused on running for political office. He ran in the Democratic primary for the U.S. Senate in 1992. Although he did not win the election, he did receive tremendous support in the African American community, including two-thirds of the black vote. He again ran unsuccessfully for the U.S. Senate in 1994.

Sharpton's political and professional career has been laced with controversy. At one time, he was labeled an informant for the Federal Bureau of Investigation. He was also sued for defamation of character and came under fire for both tax and financial fraud charges against his youth organization. Sharpton was acquitted of the tax and financial fraud charges but was required to pay $65,000 in a defamation suit by a white attorney he had accused of being involved in the rape of Tawana Brawley. These controversies have contributed to the public perception of Al Sharpton as a divisive figure who sometimes engages in self-aggrandizement and promotion.

Sharpton's most important contribution to the cause of civil rights and social justice came after the brutal murder of an innocent man that took place in New York. Amadou Diallo, an unarmed African immigrant, was shot 41 times by four white policemen in February 1999 in New York. This horrific killing led Sharpton to mobilize the city and organize many civil protests against police brutality within Manhattan. This significant event led hundreds of whites and African Americans to join together in civil protest to end the continued racial profiling and brutality that many African Americans were experiencing in New York City. Sharpton, along with many of his supporters, was arrested during some of these protests. Sharpton sought nomination as the Democratic candidate for the U.S. presidency in 2004. Although he did not receive the nomination, he did stimulate the election with his forthright speeches and his challenges to those candidates who would eventually receive their party's nominations.

Sharpton is both a controversial and passionate leader who has inspired debates on issues as important as police brutality, racial bigotry, and employment discrimination. His brash style and biting intellect are juxtaposed with his outward appearance (which includes a processed hairstyle reminiscent of James Brown) and the pedantic speech of a Baptist preacher. Al Sharpton has become one of the most notorious African American activists of the early 21st century.

KIJUA SANDERS-MCMURTRY

See also

Jackson, Jesse; Jena Six

Further Reading:

Appiah, Kwame Anthony, and Henry Louis Gates Jr., eds. *Africana Civil Rights: An A–Z Reference of the Movement That Changed America*. Philadelphia: Running Press, 2004.

Howell, Ron. "Sharpton, Al." In *African American Lives*, edited by Henry Louis Gates Jr. and Evelyn Brooks Higginbotham. New York: Oxford University Press, 2004.

Shelley v. Kraemer (1948)

In 1948, the U.S. Supreme Court decided the case of *Shelley v. Kraemer*, 334 U.S. 1 (1948), in which the Court unanimously ruled that it was unconstitutional to enforce private agreements between neighbors that purported to forbid the sale of property to racial minorities. This case is significant not only because it promoted the rights of African Americans to purchase property freely and discouraged the ghettoizing of American neighborhoods, but also because it added momentum to the civil rights movement and the Supreme Court's trend of interpreting the Constitution to expand minority rights.

In 1945, the Shelley family, who were African American, bought a house in St. Louis, Missouri. When the Shelleys purchased the home, they were unaware that a prior owner had agreed along with neighbors to execute a restrictive covenant (a legal obligation written into a property's deed) that purported to prevent the sale of the home to "people of the Negro or Mongolian Race." Upon learning that the Shelleys had been sold the home in violation of the restrictive covenant, a neighbor sued the Shelleys in an attempt to prevent them from moving in. The Missouri trial court ruled in the Shelleys' favor. However, when the case was appealed by the neighbors, the Supreme Court of Missouri reversed the trial court's decision and ruled that the restrictive covenant was enforceable and that the Shelleys could not take possession of the property they had purchased. The Shelleys, with the support of civil rights organizations, appealed the Missouri Supreme Court decision to the U.S. Supreme Court.

Represented by a legal team that included National Association for the Advancement of Colored People counsel Thurgood Marshall, the Shelleys' attorneys argued to the U.S. Supreme Court that discriminatory restrictive covenants should be unenforceable under the U.S. Constitution. The Court agreed, deciding that the equal protection clause of the Constitution's Fourteenth Amendment prevented the government from using its power to enforce a private agreement that violated the constitutional requirement of the government treating the races with equality. In reaching this decision, the Court reasoned that discriminatory restrictive covenants are not themselves unconstitutional because they are merely contracts between private citizens that do not involve the government's endorsement or participation. However, a person seeking to *enforce* a discriminatory restrictive covenant would require the involvement of the courts and other government agencies to put the restriction into effect. Because the Fourteenth Amendment bans government actors from using their power to enforce unequal treatment based on one's race, the restrictive covenant in the *Shelley* case could not be enforced because doing so would require government involvement to impose it. Therefore, the Court ruled that the covenant was unenforceable and the Shelley family was entitled to live in the home they had purchased.

The *Shelley* case is a milestone in legal and civil rights history. Narrowly read, it had the effect of preventing racist landowners from refusing to allow property sales to minorities. The destruction of discriminatory restrictive covenants had the effect of promoting the rights of African Americans to freely buy, sell, and enjoy home ownership. More broadly, the success of *Shelley* encouraged the growth of the civil rights movement by signaling that the Supreme Court was inclined to promote civil rights and also served as an impetus for federal, state, and local legislatures to implement laws that clearly defined the illegality of housing discrimination.

GABRIEL H. TENINBAUM

See also

Fair Housing Act of 1968; Fair Housing Amendments Act of 1988; Fair Housing Audit; Housing Covenants; Housing Discrimination; Residential Segregation

Further Reading:

Rosen, Mark. "Was *Shelley v. Kraemer* Incorrectly Decided?" *California Law Review* 95 (2007): 451–512.

Shotgun Policy

The term "shotgun policy" refers to the violent exploits of conservative whites against blacks and Republicans to restore the Democrats to power in Mississippi in 1875. The tumultuous overthrow of Republican governments, also known as Redemption, took place throughout the South and inaugurated the ensuing years of unrestrained violence against blacks.

Prior to the Civil War, Mississippi, like other Southern states, was dominated socially, politically, and economically by white landowners. At the bottom of the hierarchy were the black slaves. Conflicts in regional interests precipitated a split between the Union of the North and the Confederacy of the South and resulted in the Civil War.

In the aftermath of the Civil War, the federal government established the policy of Reconstruction, the purpose of which was to reintegrate the Southern states into the Union, provide assistance to the newly freed slaves, and set up Republican-led state governments. Conservative Democrats were infuriated by these changes. White mobs and newly formed organizations, such as the Ku Klux Klan, attacked and murdered black and white teachers who established schools for former slaves. They also terrorized black and white Republican politicians. In response, the federal government installed troops across the South to suppress the violence.

However, Democrats conspired to regain control of their state governments. Virginia, Tennessee, and North Carolina were the first states to seize back power. To do this, they resorted to fraudulence and violent intimidation. In 1870 and 1871, the federal government attempted to restore order by creating anti-Klan laws, but the success of these laws was short-lived. In 1874, white mobs murdered black and white Republican leaders and destroyed crops and homes. Violence erupted at the polls in Louisiana between 1868 and 1876.

In 1875, white Mississippians unleashed their infamous Shotgun Policy. In the same year, whites murdered 30 teachers, church leaders, and Republican officials in Clinton. Riots broke out in Vicksburg and Yazoo City, Mississippi, as well as in other Southern states. White Mississippians also tormented and even lynched blacks to keep them from the polls. In response, politicians fled Mississippi in fear of their lives or were coerced to join the Democrats, and numerous blacks refrained from voting on election day.

Mississippi's Governor Ames appealed to President Ulysses S. Grant for assistance, but Grant was already preoccupied with problems of his own. Ames met with representatives from the Democratic Party, and they agreed to a peaceful election day in exchange for Ames's promise not to organize a black militia. Although Ames kept his bargain, the Democrats set homes on fire before election day and set up armed guards at the polls. While most blacks hid in the woods and stayed away from the polls, the Democrats celebrated their win. Following their return to power, conservative whites set about resuming their pre–Civil War life in Mississippi. Although blacks were legally free, they were bound by oppressive and discriminatory laws and practices (*see* Black Codes). Meanwhile, the violence against blacks continued unabated, and this time, the federal government did not intervene on the behalf of blacks.

Similar attacks against blacks and Republican politicians persisted throughout Redemption. In 1876, whites in South Carolina emulated Mississippi's Shotgun Policy. On the Democrat side were 600 Redshirts who beat and killed blacks to keep them from voting. Although President Grant sent federal troops, the Democrats retained power. By 1877, all of the Southern states of the Confederacy were under Democratic control.

GLADYS L. KNIGHT

See also

Hate Groups in America; Jim Crow Laws; Ku Klux Klan (KKK); White Mobs; White Nationalism

Further Reading:

Perman, Michael. *The Road to Redemption: Southern Politics, 1869–1880.* Chapel Hill: University of North Carolina Press, 1984.

Rable, George C. *But There Was No Peace: The Role of Violence in the Politics of Reconstruction.* Athens: University of Georgia Press, 1984.

Simmons, William J. (1882–1945)

William Joseph Simmons founded the second incarnation of the Ku Klux Klan in 1915. Simmons was born in 1880, to a country physician and former Klansman on a farm near Harpersfield, Alabama. He had little formal schooling. Simmons served in the Spanish-American War and attempted afterward to pursue a career in the ministry of the Methodist Episcopal Church, South. His several years of itinerant ministry in Florida and Alabama were not rewarded by a permanent church, sparking his departure from the group.

William Joseph Simmons founded the second incarnation of the Ku Klux Klan in 1915. He is pictured here in 1921. (AP Photo)

Simmons joined over a dozen various Masonic orders, including the Woodmen of the World, where he—as did all his fellow Woodmen—received the honorific title of colonel. Simmons combined fraternal membership and personal career by becoming a field representative and salesman of fraternal insurance for the group. He sought the revival of what he called the original Klan of the lost era—the period of Southern humiliation, defeat, and redemption starting with the original Klan's birth in 1866 in Pulaski, Tennessee.

According to Klan lore, Simmons swore at that time to found the Klan memorializing organization. According to Jonathan B. Frost, a fellow Woodman who joined the reborn Klan and later embezzled several thousand dollars from its beginning coffers, Simmons took the idea of restarting the Klan from a presentation he had made at a Woodmen's convention. A subsequent period of convalescence following an automobile accident led Simmons to develop detailed plans for rebuilding the Klan, an idea that had possessed him more firmly after having perhaps read of the March 1915 release of D. W. Griffith's paean to the Klan, *The Birth of a Nation*. After the film opened in December in Atlanta, Simmons persuaded the theater owner to allow him to view it free and repeatedly.

On Thanksgiving Day in 1915, Simmons and 15 others ascended Stone Mountain in Georgia, where he led them in the first initiation ceremony of a memorial organization to the original Klan, known as the Invisible Empire, Knights of the Ku Klux Klan. The ceremony followed the general format of the initial Klan ceremony nearly 50 years before—an altar held an American flag, an open Bible, a sword, and a canteen of water. One major innovation was to become the lasting symbol of the various Klan and Klan-sympathizing groups—the erection and burning of a Christian cross. This symbol could be seen from nearby Atlanta.

The next week, Simmons incorporated the organization in Fulton County, pursuing yet another departure from original Klan procedure. Simmons, unlike his predecessors, sought to have the Klan protected by legal status and situated to assume a remunerative function as well. Drawing on research on the original Klan, he completed a 54-page *Kloran*, a text of ritual, administrative rules, and coded jargon that was to serve as "the book" governing Klan business.

Simmons divided the country into eight administrative domains. Each domain was governed by a Grand Goblin, then a state (province) hierarchy, then intrastate provinces, and finally the local Klanverns. Many of these Klanverns assumed the names of preexisting or newly named organizations to avoid detection and to lend their efforts to ongoing work, such as the 100 percent Americanism movement in Colorado.

Until 1920, the Klan was confined almost exclusively to Georgia and Alabama. In 1920, however, Edward Young Clarke and Elizabeth Tyler formed the Southern Publicity Association and used it to parlay national antiblack, anti-Jewish, anti-Catholic, anti-Asian, and pro-Nativist sentiments into an explosion of Klan membership from 2,000 to 50,000 members by the time of congressional hearings on Klan activities in 1921. By 1924, 40 percent of the Klan's membership was in Indiana, Ohio, and Illinois, followed by a quarter in six southwestern states. Only 16 percent were in the southeast.

By 1923, Simmons had come into conflict with the organization by supporting Clarke and Tyler during a series of Tyler's indiscretions. Simmons's own incompetence and alcoholism led to his removal as Imperial Wizard in favor of Dallas's Hiram Wesley Evans. A series of legal battles ensued, leading to his banishment on January 5, 1924. He died in May 18, 1945, in Luverne, Alabama. The organization he restarted continues to hold sway in the popular imagination and to morph into other white supremacist organizations.

GREGORY E. CARR

See also

Ku Klux Klan (KKK)

Further Reading:

Jackson, Kenneth T. *The Ku Klux Klan in the City: 1915–1930*. New York: Oxford University Press, 1967.
Randel, William Pierce. *The Ku Klux Klan: A Century of Infamy*. Philadelphia: Chilton Books, 1965.

Sioux Outbreak of 1890

The Sioux "outbreak" in 1890 was in reality a rumor spread by ignorance and hysteria that resulted in the massacre of almost 300 Native Americans at Wounded Knee, South Dakota. By 1890, the Sioux had experienced incredible deprivations as the result of broken promises by the U.S. government. Since 1825, the government had promised to protect the Sioux, and in 1868, both parties agreed to perpetual peace. With that mutual agreement, the government promised further to hold the Sioux reservation inviolate, permit Sioux hunting in the Bighorn Mountains, and acquire reservation land only with the approval of 75 percent of adult male Sioux on the reservation.

Congress violated this agreement only nine years later when it acted unilaterally to confiscate 7.3 million acres of reservation land in the Black Hills. This deprived the Sioux of their hunting lands, so in return, Congress declared it would provide them with rations and other assistance as long as necessary. The Sioux were also placed under the protection of U.S. law. Thus, the Sioux and other Native American groups were effectively placed under the military, which tried to enforce a policy of subjugation by disarming them and making them farmers. With the buffalo gone by the mid-1880s, the Native Americans claimed that the government had failed to appropriate enough funds to feed and support them. Interior Department inspectors, military officers, and missionaries all noted the government's failure in this regard.

In 1889, Congress again acted to acquire the reservation territory for white settlement, this time another 9 million acres. Contrary to the spirit of the 1868 agreement, Sioux reservation men were coerced into voting for Congress's proposal, and a number of illegal votes were cast for it. The law was passed without the required vote and signed by President Benjamin Harrison. What was left of the reservation was divided up into six smaller reservations. Rations were cut after the law was passed, leaving Indians on the reservations desperate for food, as there were widespread crop failures and an anthrax outbreak in the previous year. In fact, one military observer noted that the government had failed to provide required land titles, the required amount of seed and farm equipment, the required number of cattle, the required ration of food, or the required amount of annuity supplies—all things required by the treaty.

The Sioux became acquainted with the Ghost Dance after several Sioux men went to meet with Wovoka, its progenitor. The Ghost Dance religion, a mixture of Christianity and shamanism, promised the end of hostility, freedom from hunger, and freedom from white oppression. The time of this mystical transformation and rebirth of the earth could be quickened by the Ghost Dance. These dances, which lasted many nights, caught the attention of whites, and were interpreted incorrectly as war dances. Unfounded fears of a Sioux outbreak spread rapidly. In November 1890, President Harrison ordered the military to contain the Sioux on their reservations and to arrest the Sioux leaders until the Ghost Dancing had ceased.

December 1890 brought a series of tragedies in quick succession. A South Dakota militia, called the Home Guard, killed and scalped 75 Ghost Dancers at the Pine Ridge Reservation. On December 15, Sitting Bull and eight of his men were killed, allegedly because Sitting Bull had resisted arrest. With Sitting Bull gone, a warrant for the arrest of Chief Big Foot, his half-brother, went out. Wishing to avoid arrest and further conflagration, Big Foot, along with 350 others, including some of Sitting Bull's followers who had fled the

Standing Rock Reservation after the chief's death, set out on the long journey through the Badlands to the Pine Ridge Reservation. Chief Red Cloud had promised them food, shelter, and horses there. On December 28, however, the 7th Cavalry, George Armstrong Custer's old regiment, had surrounded the group. In spite of flying the white flag of surrender, Big Foot's group was forced to the bank of Wounded Knee Creek. Cannons were perched above them.

A false rumor among the penned-in Indians that had them being removed to Indian Territory led to some agitation. When Colonel James Forsyth took over command with his 500 reinforcements on the evening of December 28, the natives were disarmed and interrogated without sleep, which led to further agitation. Some began singing Ghost Dance songs. In the tension of the moment, a gun was fired, injuring no one, but the soldiers immediately began to shoot the unarmed Indians with pistols, and cannon fire rained down upon them. Big Foot was killed. The few survivors of the massacre at Wounded Knee were hunted down as the soldiers sought revenge for the death of Custer and the 231 soldiers who were killed at Little Big Horn.

While this incident has in the past been cited as the end of the Native American skirmishes with whites, it was in truth not a skirmish but a slaughter, an exclamation point to the long and sordid history of Euro-Americans' dealings with Native Americans. Long before the massacre at Wounded Knee, the natives' ability to mount an effective challenge to white dominance had ended.

BENAMIN F. SHEARER

See also
American Indian Movement (AIM); Native Americans, Conquest of; Native Americans, Forced Relocation of

Further Reading:
Brown, Dee Alexander. *Bury My Heart at Wounded Knee: An Indian History of the American West*, 30th anniv. ed. New York: Henry Holt, 2001.

Lazarus, Edward. *Black Hills/White Justice: The Sioux Nation versus the United States, 1775 to the Present*. New York: HarperCollins, 1991.

Ostler, Jeffrey. *The Plains Sioux and U.S. Colonialism from Lewis and Clark to Wounded Knee*. New York: Cambridge University Press, 2004.

Viola, Herman J. *Trail to Wounded Knee: Last Stand of the Plains Indians, 1860–1890*. Washington, DC: National Geographic Society, 2003.

Sit-Ins

Sit-ins were a tactic used frequently as a means of nonviolent direct action against racial segregation. In 1960, prompted by a sit-in in Greensboro, North Carolina, a national sit-in movement developed, usually involving students. Between 1960 and 1964, sit-ins were one of the key tactics of the civil rights movement. The sit-ins established many of the philosophical positions and tactics that would underscore the movement. Many activists who would go on to play leading roles in the civil rights movement were first involved in sit-ins.

During the 1940s and 1950s, sit-ins were used sporadically as a tactic by organized labor and early civil rights organizations. Both the Fellowship of Reconciliation (FOR) and the Congress of Racial Equality (CORE) supported the use of sit-ins as a tactic during the 1940s. In Marshall, Texas, a sustained challenge to Jim Crow during the late 1940s and early 1950s saw the use of several sit-ins, which were supported by FOR and CORE. Sit-ins were used in several locations throughout the 1950s to challenge segregation. In July 1958, sit-ins helped desegregate Dockum Drugs in Wichita, Kansas, and one month later, sit-ins were held at the Katz Drug Store in Oklahoma City. Various other sit-ins took place in border states during the last years of the 1950s, often helping to achieve integration of the establishment targeted. Despite the success of these sit-ins, the tactic failed to grow into the mass movement it would become in the 1960s.

The sit-in movement was sparked by a sit-in in Greensboro, North Carolina. On February 1, 1960, four students at North Carolina Agricultural and Technical College staged a sit-in at the lunch counter of the F. W. Woolworth's department store in Greensboro. The sit-in was not a spontaneous event: the four protestors—Ezell Blair Jr., Joseph McNeill, David Richmond, and Franklin McClain—had all been members of the National Association for the Advancement of Colored People (NAACP) college or youth groups (although the sit-in was not conducted under the auspices of the NAACP), and had spent many hours discussing ways in which they could participate in the integration movement. They had also been exposed to the burgeoning civil rights movement: Greensboro had been visited by both Martin Luther King, Jr. and the African American students involved in the Little Rock, Arkansas, desegregation case. The group

intended to use the sit-in to illustrate the hypocrisy of allowing African Americans to shop in the store, but preventing them from using the lunch counter. Woolworth's was chosen specifically because it was a national chain and was vulnerable to pressure from outside the South. Having made purchases in the store, the four sat at the lunch counter and asked for service. When they were refused, they remained at the lunch counter until the store closed.

Unlike earlier sit-ins, the Greensboro protest prompted an almost instant movement. While previous sit-ins had been part of local protests and had not necessarily made connections with other local movements, news of the Greensboro sit-in spread quickly through a network of young activists, often connected to black colleges, black churches, and local civil rights groups in the South. The four protestors themselves contacted Floyd McKissick, an NAACP Youth Council leader, on the evening of the first sit-in. McKissick, along with the Reverend Douglas Moore, who was the Southern Christian Leadership Conference's (SCLC) North Carolina representative, soon arrived in Greensboro, where they helped to organize the sit-ins. Both men had protest experience: Moore in particular had been involved in direct action in Durham, North Carolina, including a sit-in in a segregated ice cream parlor. The presence of older, more experienced activists like McKissick and Moore helped to maintain the momentum created by the first sit-in and to coordinate the enthusiasm of the growing numbers of student protestors eager to participate.

The next day, the group returned to Woolworth's and again requested service at the lunch counter; once again, they were refused service. However, the group had been joined by 19 other students; by the third day of the protest, over 80 students took part in the sit-in. Over the course of the week, under the guidance of McKissick and Moore, increasing numbers of students from a variety of colleges (including some white colleges) joined the Woolworth's sit-in, and began sit-ins in different stores in downtown Greensboro. By the end of the first week of sit-ins, over 400 students were participating in sit-ins in Greensboro. By this point, white mobs were gathering to harass the protestors, and store managers, who until then had attempted to accommodate the protests, were threatening legal action. When the manager of Woolworth's closed the store at lunchtime, claiming a bomb threat had been received, the

On February 1, 1960, four young African American college students walked into the Woolworth Company, sat down at a whites-only lunch counter and triggered the civil rights movement that spread across the nation. Shown here on February 2, 1960, are (left to right) Joseph McNeil, Franklin McCain, Billy Smith, and Clarence Henderson. (Library of Congress)

protestors decided to halt the sit-ins to allow negotiations to take place. When the store opened on Monday, the lunch counter remained closed.

The Greensboro sit-ins quickly inspired similar protests elsewhere. Moore and McKissick made use of their connections to activists in other states and were pivotal in helping the sit-in movement to spread to other North Carolina cities and into other states. Within days of the first Greensboro sit-in, other protests had taken place in Durham and Raleigh, as well as other communities in North Carolina. Central to the quick spread of sit-ins was the network of civil rights activists that was spread throughout the South. Fred Shuttlesworth of the SCLC witnessed a sit-in in High Point, North Carolina, and was impressed not only by the tactic, but also by the way in which the protestors conducted themselves. Such was his enthusiasm for sit-ins that he urged King to get involved. Sit-ins moved quickly from upper South states like North Carolina, and within a week of the first Greensboro

sit-in, sit-ins had taken place in Rock Hill, South Carolina, under the auspices of an SCLC minister.

Of all the locations to which sit-ins spread, it was in Nashville, Tennessee, that the movement developed what would come to be its identifying characteristics. Nashville was fertile ground for sit-ins. A cadre of student activists, many of whom, such as Diane Nash and John Lewis, were students at Fisk University, had been searching for a way in which to challenge segregation. Many of these students had been attending nonviolent workshops run by James Lawson, a divinity student at Vanderbilt University, who had been urged to relocate to the South from Ohio by Martin Luther King, Jr. Lawson was planning to instigate several protests against segregation in downtown department stores. The Greensboro sit-ins presented themselves as the ideal way in which to do this.

Lawson organized a meeting to discuss the use of sit-ins in Nashville, at which over 500 volunteers, as well as the

75 students who had attended the nonviolent workshops, were in attendance. The volunteers' enthusiasm for sit-ins was so overwhelming that, in spite of his reservations, Lawson—who was at least a decade older than most of the students—agreed to begin sit-ins the following day. The meeting closed after Lawson had instructed the volunteers how to behave during the protests. Lawson's greater experience and links to the burgeoning civil rights movement were crucial to establishing the Nashville sit-in movement, articulating its underlying philosophy of nonviolence and organizing it so that pressure could be persistently applied to segregation. However, the enthusiasm and devotion to the cause of the student volunteers drove the movement and provided a constant stream of protestors to participate. The day after the meeting, over 500 neatly dressed protestors entered stores in downtown Nashville to politely ask for service.

For two weeks, daily sit-ins were held in downtown Nashville. As in many cities in which sit-ins were held, the authorities did not react immediately, hoping that the protests would peter out; indeed, the presence of so many students led authorities, as well as the media, to assume that sit-ins would be a short-term movement. As it became clear that the protests were organized, disciplined, and persistent, store owners became increasingly concerned that sales would be lost. The chief of police announced that, at the request of store owners, trespassing and disorderly conduct arrests would be made. This was a development for which many in the Nashville movement had prepared themselves, but it was a particular source of anxiety for the organizers of the movement, who would in effect be advocating that the protestors staged sit-ins in the knowledge that they were likely to be arrested. Sit-in protestors in Raleigh, North Carolina, had already been arrested, and few in Nashville were deterred by this possibility. Indeed, being arrested and jailed would quickly become a mark of honor for protestors; the tactic of "jail, not bail" would soon spread to other forms of direct action.

In response to the Nashville chief of police's announcement, John Lewis committed to paper a code of conduct, by which protestors should abide. These underscored the tenets by which the movement had thus far been conducted and included reminders not to strike back if struck or abused, to be friendly and courteous at all at times, and to

remember love and nonviolence. On February 27, as they took up seats at the lunch counters of chosen downtown stores, protestors were attacked by hostile whites; police arrested 77 protestors and five whites. Sixteen of the protestors, including Lewis and Diane Nash, declared that they would not accept bail, but would instead serve a jail sentence. Nash told the judge that in refusing bail, they were rejecting the practices that had led to their arrest. On hearing Nash's speech, the majority of the other protestors decided spontaneously also to refuse bail.

The jailing of the protestors sparked outrage in Nashville, but also brought the sit-ins to national attention. As the protestors were sentenced to workhouse detail, support was received from people such as Ralph Bunche, Harry Belafonte, and Eleanor Roosevelt. Further controversy was created when James Lawson was expelled from Vanderbilt's divinity school. If this was designed to distance Vanderbilt from the sit-ins, it backfired: the story made the front page of the *New York Times*, and Lawson was reinstated. In response to growing external criticism, the mayor of Nashville offered a compromise: in return for the ending of protests in the downtown, the jailed protestors would be freed, and a biracial committee to consider the desegregation of downtown would be established. Unbowed by her imprisonment, Diane Nash quickly led a protest at the lunch counter of the Greyhound bus terminal, which was not included in the compromise deal. Unexpectedly, the protestors were served, and segregation at the bus terminal ended suddenly.

The arrest of the Nashville protestors revealed a growing gap between their outlook and that of the wider black community in Nashville, as well as many older activists in the movement. The NAACP's Thurgood Marshall believed the students had made their point through the sit-ins and their arrests. He argued that such protests should now be abandoned and integration pursued through the courts. John Lewis roundly dismissed this approach and identified a fundamental philosophical difference between the protestors and older activists. To Lewis, the sit-ins had created a mass movement that was confronting Jim Crow; the strength of the sit-in movement was the energy and spontaneity of the large numbers of protestors who were willing to risk abuse, violence, and imprisonment to challenge segregation. This difference would find its expression in the formation of the

Student Nonviolent Coordinating Committee (SNCC) at a conference at Shaw University, Raleigh, in April 1960, which brought together many of the young activists involved in the sit-in movement. While King hoped that the activists would use their enthusiasm and power for the SCLC, those attending the conference resisted this, and SNCC remained independent of other organizations.

By the point at which the SNCC was formed, the sit-in movement had spread to other states. Between February and April, sit-ins were held in over 70 locations, and had reached Georgia, West Virginia, Texas, and Arkansas. As well as capturing the zeal of so many activists who were eager to challenge Jim Crow, sit-ins proved to be a successful method of ending segregation. In Greensboro, the persistence and organization of the sit-in movement offset authorities' hopes that the summer would see a dip in sit-in activity; locals and high school students had been mobilized to carry on the protests when student numbers declined during nonterm time. The pressure brought by continued sit-ins forced the authorities to negotiate. In particular, the economic effects on businesses helped sit-ins to achieve their aims. The combined effects of the sit-ins, the loss of African American business through attendant boycotts, and the loss of business from whites who were discouraged from entering stores because of the protests, meant that Woolworth's lost $200,000 in Greensboro in 1960. By the end of July, lunch counters in downtown Greensboro had been integrated.

Other success occurred elsewhere: in Nashville, the city finally conceded in the face of the unstinting pressure of the sit-ins, and downtown lunch counters were integrated in early May. In Durham, downtown businesses began to desegregate as a direct result of sit-ins, while in Virginia, two drugstore chains planned to end the segregation of lunch counters. The federal government also stepped in, and U.S. Attorney General William Rogers negotiated with the owners of chain stores in the South to end segregation. Trailways announced that it would desegregate restaurants in bus terminals throughout the South. Although these victories were achieved relatively rapidly, they came as a result of the tenacity and vigor of the protestors, whose refusal to bow to white intimidation and the more moderate approaches of older activists helped to underline the value of sit-ins.

Indeed, the early burst of the sit-in movement helped to frame the civil rights movement that was coalescing under the leadership of King. As well as sit-ins, other forms of direct action, often involving young activists, became keystones of the movement. Many young African Americans were inspired to action by seeing news coverage of sit-ins, and activists like Bob Moses and Cleveland Sellers would later credit the sit-ins as their introduction to the civil rights movement, and for many more, sit-ins were their first active involvement. By the end of 1960, over 70,000 students had participated in sit-ins or direct action inspired by the sit-ins, and more than 3,600 protestors had been arrested. Sit-ins became perhaps the most identifiable tactic of the civil rights movement and were used consistently in the first half of the 1960s.

While the Greensboro sit-ins and the protests they prompted elsewhere helped to erode some of Jim Crow's unassailability, segregation continued to exist in many forms. As the civil rights movement developed, sit-ins were held throughout the South, including those cities in which segregation had already been partly overcome. Organized sit-ins, such as that which sought to integrate the Toddle Inn restaurant chain in Atlanta, Georgia, continued to be a vital source of protest. During the winter of 1962–1963, a boycott of downtown Jackson, Mississippi, was accompanied by sit-ins. The reaction of white mobs, which shouted abuse at protestors, doused them in food, and dragged them from stools, brought to national attention the extent to which whites in that state were resisting integration. Such sit-ins continued to follow the model established by the Greensboro and Nashville movements, and nonviolence remained the underlying philosophy. Other, less prolonged, forms of sit-ins were also employed. During marches and demonstrations, protestors would often spontaneously stage a sit-in, frequently when faced with police brutality, while variants such as pray-ins at segregated churches or in the face of violence, and wade-ins at segregated beaches were also used.

After the passage of the Civil Rights Act of 1964 and the Voting Rights Act of 1965, sit-ins became less relevant as the goals of the movement shifted. Indeed, in some states, such as Mississippi, sit-ins were a relatively minor tactic, often limited to urban areas. With the passage of legislation outlawing segregation, the frequency of sit-ins declined. Although sit-ins were still used from time to time, as the focus of the movement turned from segregation to voter registration and broader economic goals, new tactics took their place. The emergence of Black Power also undermined the value of sit-ins, as the validity of nonviolence as a tactic and philosophy was increasingly questioned.

SIMON T. CUTHBERT-KERR

See also

Greensboro Four; *Plessy v. Ferguson* (1896). Document: *Plessy v. Ferguson* (1896)

Further Reading:

Branch, Taylor. *Parting the Waters: America in the King Years, 1954–63.* New York: Simon and Schuster, 1988.

Carson, Clayborne. *In Struggle: SNCC and the Black Awakening of the 1960s.* Cambridge, MA: Harvard University Press, 1981.

Chafe, William H. *Civilities and Civil Rights: Greensboro, North Carolina, and the Black Struggle for Freedom.* New York: Oxford University Press, 1980.

Lewis, John, with Michael D'Orso. *Walking with the Wind: A Memoir of the Movement.* New York: Simon and Schuster, 1998.

Moody, Anne. *Coming of Age in Mississippi.* New York: Bantam Doubleday, 1968.

Skin Lightening

Skin lightening is a process in which chemical agents are used to lighten the complexion of one's skin (Blay 2011). Also referred to as *skin whitening* or *skin bleaching*, the practice of skin lightening can be traced to ancient Egypt and Greece, and could be found amidst the European medieval aristocracy and 18th-century Japanese geishas. In modern times, skin lightening is a global, multi-billion-dollar industry that is disproportionately used among people of color both in the United States and around the world (Blay 2011; Glenn 2008). Although scholars offer a number of historical, cultural, sociopolitical, and psychological explanations for the practice of skin lightening, most agree that colonialism, slavery, and white supremacy drive this continuing trend (Blay 2011).

Justification for both colonialism and slavery were rooted in the diametric oppositions found in Christianity—Christ and Satan, good and evil, light and dark, white and black (Blay 2011). This ordering constructed a hierarchy in which whiteness is viewed as civil, rational, beautiful, and superior to savage, irrational, ugly, and inferior blackness (Blay 2011;

Hunter 2007). While colonialism and slavery had economic benefits, these institutions also created and maintained a system of dominance in which whites, by virtue of their skin color or select Anglo-Saxon heritage, received social and cultural privileges (Blay 2011).

Within this hierarchical system based on skin color, also known as "colorism," skin lightening is a method that can be used to approach or emulate the white ideal (Blay 2011). Colorism is dominant in nations that possess a history of European colonialism and African slavery (Hunter 2007). In some European colonies in Africa, a small group of "elite" light-skinned natives were used to help rule the colony. For example, during colonial rule of what is now Rwanda, German and Dutch colonialists separated the Rwandan people into two categories based on folk understandings of ethnic difference; the Tutsis (understood as descendants of invaders from the Middle East) and the Hutus (understood as indigenous Africans). This ethno-racial theory and practice served to solidify the Tutsis' social control over the Hutus.

In the United States, slave owners often used skin color to develop hierarchies on their plantations (Hunter 2007). Dark-skinned slaves were relegated to work in the fields while lighter-skinned slaves worked indoors as servants or craftsmen (Glenn 2008). Those with lighter skin held a closer approximation to whiteness, which led to a belief that they were naturally more intelligent. These beliefs often translated into resource attainment; lighter-skinned blacks were more likely than their darker-skinned counterparts to receive a basic education and to be released from slavery (Glenn 2008).

In Latin America, skin color is an important marker of social status (Glenn 2008). In Brazil, for example, the elite are overwhelmingly composed of light-skinned individuals while dark-skinned individuals are both rural and poor (Glenn 2008).

Colorism in Asia varies from country to country. In the formally colonized countries of Southeast Asia and India, the influence of the Western ideal of light skin is still evident in the predominance of a large skin-lightening market (Glenn 2008). Indian communities around the world form the largest market for skin-lightening products; market research conducted in 2004 reports that 50 percent of those surveyed in the Philippines used skin lighteners (Glenn 2008). But even prior to the influx of Western ideals, East

Asian countries practiced their own form of colorism based on class (Glenn 2008). Dark skin color was associated with the poor and working class who labored outdoors, while light skin was indicative of a life of leisure (Hunter 2007). In Japan, for instance, both upper-class men and women wore white-lead-powder makeup (Glenn 2008). Today, the continued use of skin lightening is driven by a combination of Western mass-mediated ideologies and traditional Asian cultural values (Li et al. 2008).

Many of the currently used skin-lightening products, made by multinational companies such as L'Oreal, Shiseido, and Unilever, have serious adverse health effects. Products are made with ingredients such as mercury, costeroids, and hydroquinone, which can cause neurological damage, kidney disease, ochronis, eczema, and bacterial and fungal infections (Glenn 2008). Although the use of skin-lightening products is increasing in places such as Southern Africa, efforts have been made to curtail the use of such products. Despite the negative health effects of many of these products, research shows that locations experiencing rapid rates of modernization and increased levels of Western influence witness increasingly higher demands for skin-lightening products (Glenn 2008).

Sheena Kaori Gardner and Matthew W. Hughey

Further Reading:

Blay, Yaba Amgborale. "Skin Bleaching and Global White Supremacy: By Way of Introduction." *Journal of Pan African Studies* 4 (2011): 4–46.

Glenn, Evelyn Nakano. "Transnational Circuits in the Marketing and Consumption of Skin Lighteners." *Gender & Society* 22 (2008): 281–302.

Hunter, Margaret L. "The Persistent Problem of Colorism: Kin Tone, Status, and Inequality." *Sociology Compass* 1 (2007): 237–54.

Li, Eric P., Hyun Jeong Min, Russell W. Belk, Junko Kimura, and Shalini Bahl. "Skin Lightening and Beauty in Four Asian Cultures." *Advances in Consumer Research* 35 (2008): 444–49.

Slave Codes

A key component in the complex social and political system governing slavery, slave codes emerged as part of an extensive body of law aimed at regulating the lives and activities of enslaved African Americans in the United States. Slave codes were clear in defining slaves as property without full legal status, and they made slavery a permanent condition that was usually inherited through one's mother. The reach of these codes extended beyond those enslaved, however, given that many also had provisions that regulated free blacks, their movement, their employment, and their options for housing and setting up permanent residence. The reach, breadth, and severity of individual slave codes varied, but all had a vested interest in curtailing slave resistance, policing the everyday lives of those enslaved, and protecting slave owners. Although these codes are commonly associated with Southern slave states, they could be found in their Northern counterparts as well.

All slave codes shared certain characteristics in terms of the control they attempted to wield over the personal activities of slaves and often free blacks, but individual slave states had their own codes in place that dictated their provisions and informed their court systems. Slaves had very few legal rights in a court of law; their testimony was seldom duly considered in any litigation involving whites and could be dismissed in its entirety. Trials for slaves were occasionally held in taverns or country stores and seldom resulted in parity. Codes banned slaves from owning property, marrying, or entering into contracts. They were also written to exert dominion over the language that slaves spoke and the clothes that they wore. Speaking words considered defamatory meant that one could be arrested, whipped, and/or sold at auction. Manumission, or the freeing of one's slaves, was also restricted through slave codes in many states, in an effort to secure the growth of slavery and restrict the presence of free blacks.

Because slave codes were used largely to act as a form of social control, they were always subject to reformulation if a state felt that they needed to be strengthened in order to further discourage slave rebellions or to supplement already existing laws set out to protect the property and physical well-being of slave owners. Those enslaved were not allowed to assemble freely with one another or engage in communal worship, they could not be taught to read or write or possess literature that was considered inflammatory, and they could not vacate an owner's premises without explicit permission. Codes made it illegal for slaves to own firearms, attend unlawful assemblies, and participate in riots. Thus, the codes not only operated in an attempt to inhibit any form of resistance carried out by an individual person who was enslaved, but also were developed to suppress any semblance of communal gatherings that might lead to wide-scale uprisings or rebellions.

Slave codes and their corresponding punishments made them one of the most violent aspects of slavery. Submission to these codes was enforced through various measures, most of which exerted extreme force over any enslaved person found to act against a given code. Whippings, beatings, and floggings were commonly used forms of punishment, but other codes called for branding, dismemberment, imprisonment, and for males, castration. A 1690 statue in South Carolina, for instance, stated that slaves or runaways who struck a white person would be severely whipped on the first offense, followed by slitting of the nose and burning of a part of one's face with an iron for a second offense. A third offense could include death or any other punishment. In Virginia, robbing or committing any other major offense could be met with 60 lashes, being placed in stocks, and dismemberment. Slave owners, on the other hand, who killed their slaves or other enslaved blacks were usually subject only to fines. Slave codes were frequently enforced by what were known as slave patrols, or groups of usually white men who went around various plantations ensuring slaves were inside of their quarters or otherwise not moving about freely. These patrols are sometimes seen as precursors to the Ku Klux Klan that flourished following Emancipation, given the violence that they inflicted and the presence that they had.

Slave codes were also antecedents to the black codes developed immediately after the Civil War that extended throughout the earliest waves of Reconstruction. Like their predecessors, these later codes were developed to act as an agent of social control in the interest of curbing the social, political, and economic opportunities available to African Americans, who, though legally free from bondage, were subject to an ever-increasing number of laws that in many ways attempted to reenact the restrictions and chief aims of slave codes.

Amanda Davis

See also
Slave Families; Slave Revolts and White Attacks on Black Slaves; Slave Songs; Slave Trade; Slave Women and Sexual Violence; Slavery; Slavery and American Indians; Slavery in the Antebellum South

Further Reading:
Franklin, John Hope, and Alfred A. Moss. *From Slavery to Freedom: A History of African Americans*, 8th ed. New York: Alfred A Knopf, 2000.
Horton, James Oliver, and Louis E. Horton. *Slavery and the Making of America*. New York: Oxford University Press, 2004.
Kolchin, Peter. *American Slavery: 1619–1877*, 10th anniv. ed. New York: Hill and Wang, 2003.

Slave Families

In Southern white society, the institution of the family revolved around a clear model of the ideal family type. Nuclear in structure, characterized by monogamous marriage, and bound by patriarchal privilege, this ideal was a fundamental base upon which a "civilized" patrician social order could be built. In contrast, slave families exhibited a large degree of variation in structure and composition. This diversity was partly the result of African cultural forms transplanted to the American context. However, the course and shape of black family life was also intimately bound to the exigencies of slavery itself.

Contemporary observers and slave narratives noted the presence of matrifocality (women-headed households), polygamy, single-parent households, multigenerational extended households, and fictive kinship as part of slave-family structures. This represents to some degree the extent to which slave families deviated from the norm of the nuclear family espoused by whites. Though it is clear that wide variation existed, scholars generally agree that the extended-family structure and an emphasis on matrifocality were core features of most slave families.

Why was this the case? Some scholars argue that certain aspects of black family structure during slavery, such as extended kinship, polygamy and matrifocality, can be traced to slaves' African heritage. Although this may be correct, the institution of slavery itself must also be examined. It is evident that slavery mitigated against the formation of nuclear families and monogamous marriage bonds. Slave marriages were not binding because slaves could not legally enter into

Five generations of a slave family in Beaufort, South Carolina, in 1862. (Library of Congress)

any contract. Their unions were also not recognized by the church. In addition, slaves' position as human property under the slave codes meant that husband, wife, and children could be separated and sold off with no notice at all. In practice, owners and slave traders did not balk at the prospect of separating spouses or family members. All familial obligations remained subordinate to a slave's primary obligation—that of unquestioning obedience to the owner.

The ramifications were manifold. Broken slave marriages became commonplace. Slave women were sometimes subject to sexual advances and rape from owners or members of their family. Slave children were socialized from an early age to expect their eventual separation from their parents. Children were often reared without the regular presence of their father because male slaves were frequently hired off to another work site or sold. If a father and mother belonged to different slave owners, restrictive slave codes prevented frequent visits. Furthermore, mothers and children were expected to retain their masters' surnames, which further erased the influence and identity of the father within the slave family. Childcare was the province of elderly or infirm slaves, although frequently children were left with little or no adult supervision. This left even the youngest children vulnerable to labor exploitation.

Many have pointed to these defining characteristics as evidence of the systematic and coercive breakdown of the African family during slavery. In this view, slavery perpetuated the dissolution of family life by eroding traditional marriage bonds, encouraging the rise of single-parent households, and contributing to male absenteeism within the family. Children of these broken families typically had low expectations and low self-esteem. Supporters of this view also contend that increased levels of crime, low educational attainment, and a host of other social ills today can be traced to this breakdown.

Detractors point out that certain features of slave family life, such as its matrifocality and emphasis on extended kinship networks, should not only be seen as unfortunate and deviant consequences of slavery. They should also be seen, and to some extent celebrated, as significant remnants of cultural forms brought from Africa and as successful adaptations by families to the limitations of slave existence.

REBEKAH LEE

See also

Slave Codes; Slave Revolts and White Attacks on Black Slaves; Slave Songs; Slave Trade; Slave Women and Sexual Violence; Slavery; Slavery and American Indians; Slavery in the Antebellum South

Further Reading:

Dunaway, Wilma. *The African-American Family in Slavery and Emancipation.* Cambridge: Cambridge University Press, 2003.

Gutman, Herbert. *The Black Family in Slavery and Freedom, 1750–1925.* New York: Pantheon, 1976.

Stevenson, Brenda. *Life in Black and White: Family and Community in the Slave South.* New York: Oxford University Press, 1996.

Slave Revolts and White Attacks on Black Slaves

Despite the fear that slave masters instilled in blacks to prevent rebellions and riots, slave revolts were widespread throughout the slavery era in the United States. From David Walker's appeal, which advocated the overthrow of slavery through violent means, to the Nat Turner uprising, slaves did their best to fight their masters and to resist a system that subjected human beings to the worst physical and mental degradation that existed in the modern world.

The fear of slave revolts and rebellions preoccupied the minds of slave masters throughout the South. In states and counties where slaves outnumbered whites, slaveholders enacted laws, created vigilante groups, and sought the assistance of other states to intimidate slaves from organizing any form of rebellion. Slaves began to rebel against their masters as soon as the institution became the primary mode of production in the colonies. In 1669, Virginia enacted a series of laws that made it a noncriminal act for slave owners to kill their slaves. These laws were a reaction to various attempts by slaves to rebel against their conditions. Slave riots and rebellions in the South ranged from individual acts that took place daily on plantations to organized massive resistance.

As one of the richest territories of the colonies, Virginia had a fair share of slave revolts. For example, on August 30, 1800, more than 1,000 slaves met outside Richmond and began to march on the city under the leadership of Gabriel Posser and Jack Bowler. A violent storm prevented them from reaching Richmond. As word had already circulated in Richmond that Posser and Bowler were fomenting a rebellion against their masters, scores of slaves in Richmond were arrested and 35 were summarily executed. Posser was captured a few months later and executed.

As news of slave revolts spread from one state to another, slave leaders in nearby states would organize their own rebellions. With the support of the newly black republic of Haiti, Denmark Vesey attempted to foment an insurrection against the slave masters in Charleston in 1822. When word leaked out to the slave masters, hundreds of slaves in Charleston were arrested. Several of them were killed to deter those who wanted to follow Vesey's leadership. In 1831, Nat Turner organized an insurrection against slave owners in Southhampton County, Virginia, which resulted in the death of 60 whites. The conspiracy of the slaves in Richmond, Virginia, prompted slave masters in North Carolina, Kentucky, and Louisiana to preemptively attack slaves who they suspected of rebellion. Fifteen slaves were hung in North Carolina for implication in conspiracies to foment riots after the Nat Turner rebellion. In December 1856, several slaves who were thought to be leaders of a failed rebellion were hung in Kentucky.

Murder was an act of last resort that slave owners would take against slaves who rebelled, because slaves produced wealth. By killing them, the masters would be deprived of a means to a good source of income. However, there were numerous other forms of attacks on slaves to prevent them from rioting against the system. Psychological manipulation, where masters attempted to convince slaves that they were innately inferior to whites, was one of the most effective forms of attack. The church and its theologians, schools, politicians, and the press played an important role in vulgarizing this form of attack on blacks. Humiliations, torture, branding, rape, the separation of slave families, and the frequent sale of slaves at auctions assured that bonding among members of the same family or slaves on the same plantation would never occur. Laws were enacted to regulate and restrict all conceivable activities of slaves, from public assembly to travel to possession of weapons to economic transactions. Slave masters organized militias to control and hunt runaway slaves. When all these forms of attacks could not control the slave population from rioting or rebelling, slaves were ultimately hung or summarily executed.

FRANCOIS PIERRE-LOUIS

See also

Slave Codes; Slave Families; Slave Songs; Slave Trade; Slave Women and Sexual Violence; Slavery; Slavery and American Indians; Slavery in the Antebellum South

Further Reading:

Aptheker, Herbert. *American Negro Slave Revolts*. New York: Columbia University Press, 1943.
Bracey, H. John, August Meier, and Elliott Rudwick. *American Slavery: The Question of Resistance*. Belmont, CA: Wadsworth Publishing, 1971.
Wish, Harvey. "American Slave Insurrections before 1861." In *American Slavery: The Question of Resistance*, edited by John H. Bracey Jr., August Meier, and Elliot Rudwick. Belmont, CA: Wadsworth, 1970.

Slave Songs

Many characteristic elements of African song recurred in African American slave songs. The music was typified by strong rhythms accompanied by bodily movement in which everyone participated. It was characterized by stamping, hand clapping, and other percussive devices that accented rhythm. Improvised words, frequently derisive or satiric in nature, and the ubiquitous call-and-response form also marked African, and African American, songs. Song was commonly used to regulate the rate of work in rowing, grinding grain, and in the fields. Song also held a major role in religion, public ceremonies, and other nonsecular aspects of life. Scholars disagree as to whether harmony was present, but the simultaneous sounding of more than one pitch was common. Vocal ornaments were frequently employed, and a strong, rasping voice quality was admired.

The transmission of African song, dance, and instruments to the Americas was encouraged by slaving captains who demanded that their captives sing and dance aboard ship during the Middle Passage. Slave singing first was documented by European travelers in the Caribbean and the North American mainland in the mid-17th century. Dance and work songs were most common. Throughout the antebellum period many work songs and songs that accompanied dancing shared similar words. Besides the occupations that had been known in Africa, new forms of work in the Americas—such as corn husking and engine firing—prompted slave songs.

The sacred songs of the slaves, the spirituals, whatever their African counterparts may have been, appeared after the slaves' gradual conversion to Christianity, a slow process. Some planters opposed the baptism of their slaves, believing that baptism might mean freedom or interfere with work. When planters permitted religious instruction, slaves did gradually convert. However, missionaries sent from England were too few to minister to widely separated plantations and to such a heterogeneous population. In the mid-18th century a few Presbyterian ministers led by Samuel Davies of Hanover, Virginia, made special efforts to convert African Americans.

By the late 18th century black worshipers joined whites at frontier protracted meetings, particularly during the Second Great Awakening. This practice continued throughout the antebellum period. Slaves both regularly worshiped and sang together in an atmosphere characterized as highly charged with emotion. Songs, parts of songs, and ways of singing were exchanged without the excited folk taking cognizance of derivation. The call-and-response style of singing especially suited the service of the camp meeting, where vast numbers of people required musical responses they could learn on the spot. For whites, it recalled the practice of "lining out"—in which a leader sang or read two lines of a hymn to the congregation who then repeated them. This practice was followed in churches with illiterate members and in congregations with too few books to go around. The camp meeting thus provided an introduction for both groups to the sound and style of each other's singing.

The earliest reports of African American religious song, distinct from European-style psalms and hymns, date from the early 19th century, somewhat earlier than the first organized program of missions to the slaves. These songs were not written down until after the Civil War, but contemporary accounts described musical elements that defied conventional musical notation then and now—notes outside European scales, the so-called blue notes, glissandos, growls, polyrhythms, and the overlapping of leader and chorus in the call-and-response style. All of these elements were characteristic of African musical forms and were present in the slaves' religious and secular songs.

Slave songs served various functions in the African American community. They provided comfort in time of grief and sorrow, raised low spirits, passed the time during tedious tasks, regulated the rate of work, heightened group feeling, and afforded psychological escape from poor conditions. Both sacred and secular songs could fill these functions, but slaves most valued the spirituals because of the comfort and inspiration they provided. The pervasive belief that the slaves shunned secular music and sang only hymns was derived from the strict evangelical belief that all secular music was sinful. Frontier sects expected their members to "put away the things of the world," and many of their African American members dutifully accepted this doctrine. Among religious slaves, sacred texts were used in work songs to replace secular words. Along the Atlantic seaboard—from Richmond's tobacco factories to the boats on the tidal rivers of the Sea Islands—work songs commonly contained religious words.

Reports by travelers before the Civil War regarding African American singing usually were vague, lacked musical detail, and frequently were condescending. Although the spirituals became widely known in the South, they were still largely unknown in the North until wartime conditions brought Northerners into contact with plantation slaves.

The first spiritual to be published with its music was "Go Down, Moses," under the title *The Song of the Contrabands "O Let My People Go," words and music obtained through the Rev. L. C. Lockwood, Chaplain to the Contrabands at Fortress Monroe. . . .* (1862). Newspaper and magazine articles described the songs in more detail, but the first comprehensive collection was not published until 1867. *Slave Songs of the United States*, edited by William Francis Allen, Charles Pickard Ware, and Lucy McKim Garrison, included songs collected by persons stationed in the South during the war as reporters, army officers, missionaries, teachers, or agents of freedmen's aid societies or the Freedmen's Bureau. Very few of these collectors were professional musicians, and none of them knew much about non-European music. However, they were all capable of writing melodies in musical notation, and they were aware that the music included elements that could not be transcribed in conventional notation. However, the three editors shared education and skills that made them qualified for preserving slave songs.

The American public, however, did not appreciate authentic folk music of this variety. Some reviews of *Slave Songs of the United States* were openly hostile, and even the most sympathetic critics stressed the curious aspects of the collection. The volume sank into oblivion, all but forgotten until the 1930s when the folk song revival brought it acclaim. More successful in acquainting the public with the spirituals were the Fisk Jubilee Singers (1871), the Hampton Singers (1872), and other groups that toured the U.S. North and Europe, singing versions designed for concert performance. These singers were only a few years removed from slavery, but many had already been trained in European music and its harmony. They were acclimated to the sound of European choral music and their versions of slave songs were somewhat removed from folk traditions. How much their versions diverged from the singing of slaves is still a matter of conjecture. The notated versions of their songs cannot be a reliable guide in such matters since so many elements of the performance style could not be transcribed. Moreover, the musicians who transcribed the songs varied in their experience with the folk tradition. Yet these transcriptions were the only form in which the music could be preserved until the development of sound recording. The public acceptance of these transcriptions as the equivalent of the music as it was performed contributed to the growth of the theory that slave songs were based on earlier white originals, a theory once widely accepted in academic circles. When recordings made available the performances themselves, the public finally heard African American slave music without the intermediation of transcribers and arrangers.

DENA J. EPSTEIN

See also

Slave Codes; Slave Families; Slave Revolts and White Attacks on Black Slaves; Slave Trade; Slave Women and Sexual Violence; Slavery; Slavery and American Indians; Slaves in the Antebellum South

Further Reading:

Allen, William Francis, Charles Pickard Ware, and Lucy McKim Garrison. *Slave Songs of the United States*. New York: A. Simpson & Co., 1867.

Epstein, Dena J. *Sinful Tunes and Spirituals: Black Folk Music to the Civil War*. Urbana: University of Illinois Press, 1977.

Epstein, Dena J. "A White Origin for the Black Spiritual? An Invalid Theory and How It Grew." *American Music* 1 (1983): 53–59.

Levine, Lawrence W. *Black Culture and Black Consciousness: Afro-American Folk Thought from Slavery to Freedom*. New York: Oxford University Press, 1977.

Slave Trade

Slave trade refers to the trafficking of human slaves both internationally and domestically. Of great significance to the course of slavery in the United States was the transatlantic slave trade, which spanned more than 300 years and was controlled first by the Portuguese and then by the British. Though debate lingers over the exact number of slaves involved, it has recently been estimated that more than 11 million slaves were exported from Africa during this period. Generally, slaves were obtained along the western coast of Africa and bought from African leaders and traders in exchange for goods and guns, although slaves were also taken

UNITED STATES SLAVE TRADE.
1830.

Domestic scene, ca. 1830. (Library of Congress)

as a result of capture by Europeans themselves. The overwhelming majority of slaves were taken to Brazil, to colonies of the Spanish Empire, and to the Caribbean. It is estimated that approximately half a million slaves were imported to the British colonies in North America. The major destinations were South Carolina, which received about 70,000 slaves between 1735 and 1775, and Virginia, which received about the same number between 1699 and 1775.

Initially, European slave traders attempted to kidnap Africans from their homes. This practice was met with violent resistance from Africans. Eventually, however, native Africans began a working relationship with the European shippers, developing various commercial networks for supplying slaves and moving them to the coast to trade with the Europeans for merchandise. The voyage from the African coast to the Americas was called the Middle Passage and lasted from 25 to 60 days. The slaves were shackled, overcrowded, and sometimes cruelly handled and driven to suicide. On average, 16 percent of the men, women, and children enslaved perished in transit.

In 1807, Britain abolished the slave trade within the British Empire. This affected the progression of slavery in the United States. After the abolition of the slave trade, slavery in America had to become a self-sustaining institution. In addition, the rise of the plantation economy in the late 18th century, particularly in the Deep South, necessitated the influx of a large number of slaves. To accommodate this need, a vigorous and profitable interstate slave trade developed. It is estimated that between 1790 and 1860, the Upper South exported almost 1 million slaves to the Deep South, which nearly quadrupled the slave population there. Virginia was a key exporter in this period. In addition, as new slave states were added to the west, the interstate slave trade ensured a regular flow of slaves into Arkansas, Texas, and Missouri. Slave trading represented another lucrative aspect of the institution of slavery.

REBEKAH LEE AND TRACY CHU

See also

Slavery; Slavery and American Indians; Slavery in the Antebellum South

Further Reading:

Cañizares-Esguerra, Matt D. Childs and James Sidbury. *The Black Urban Atlantic in the Age of the Slave Trade*. Philadelphia: University of Pennsylvania Press, 2013.

Green, Toby. *The Rise of the Trans-Atlantic Slave Trade in Western Africa, 1300-1589*. Cambridge, NY: Cambridge University Press, 2012.

Slave Women and Sexual Violence

Sexual violence is a general term for sexually aggressive behaviors, including rape, incest, harassment, coercion, and exploitation—all of which represent the most prominent aspect of black women's gendered experience under slavery. While both slave women and slave men were vulnerable to day-to-day racial violence, women were especially subjected to more torment from the physical and psychological abuse of sexual violence. Recollecting years of her struggle against her master's sexual harassment in *Incidents in the Life of a Slave Girl* (1861), North Carolina former slave woman Harriet Jacobs wrote that "slavery is terrible for men; but it is far more terrible for women." The issue of sexual violence against slave women, however, was not considered as such among scholars of slavery for a long time. Until the 1970s, historians saw sex between slaveholders and enslaved women as somewhat consensual by deeming it "sexual relations" or "miscegenation." But in the 1980s, black women scholars such as Deborah Gray White reconceptualized it as sexual exploitation, stating that the master-slave sexual relationship was not mutual, but forced and manipulated by the slaveholder's authority against the will of slave women. Black female scholars claimed that sexual violence against enslaved women was not accidental or random incidents; it was calculated and comprised institutionalized assaults that were performed daily to the benefit of the slaveholder.

There were several factors motivating the ubiquitous sexual violence against slave women, with the most important being the economic value of slave women both as producers and reproducers of labor. Because slaves were indispensable labor for the plantation economy in the South, slave owners endeavored to maintain and increase their property by purchasing, breeding, and fathering more slaves. After abolition of the transatlantic slave trade in 1808 made the further purchase of slaves unfeasible except through the domestic slave trade, slave breeding, and slave owners' sexual exploitation of slave women became more common practices in the slave-holding society.

Slave owners' sexual assaults upon slave women were particularly rampant because masters recognized reproduction of enslaved women as a profit-making function. Several factors worked to the slaveholders' advantage in their reproductive exploitation of slave women. First, following a 1662 Virginia statute, all colonial laws eventually stated that the conditions of children—slave or free—followed that of their mothers, thus defining all children born of slave women as slaves. With these laws, slaveholders were able to freely impregnate slave women without worrying about the status of their half-white children. Second, due to enslaved peoples' status as property, sexual abuse of black women was never considered rape. There were few legal rape cases of slave women on record because slaves were not allowed to testify against whites in court.

Finally, Southern whites, and particularly white women, believed that no unwanted sex could exist with slave women, because they internalized the idea that black women were sexually promiscuous by nature. This image of the immoral, sexually unrestrained, and licentious black women is referred to as the Jezebel stereotype. In the minds of many Southerners, contemporary notions of virtuous womanhood were reserved exclusively for white women. Furthermore, enslaved women sometimes made enemies of their jealous mistresses who just like slave husbands, accused slave women of having willful sexual relations with their husbands. Instead of blaming their own husbands for infidelity, plantation mistresses irrationally mistreated enslaved women in various ways. They often reproached slave women and even physically attacked them and their mixed-race children born of such infidelity. The wives also occasionally requested their husbands to sell off those children, thus forcing enslaved mothers into the family separation.

But slaveholders were not alone in their use and abuse of slave women as sexual outlets. Their sons, overseers, drivers, and other men, who all understood the sexual privileges attached to their positions, frequently exploited slave women for sex. Thus, the sexual abuse of slave women was legally and socially sanctioned to serve slaveholders' economic and sexual demands. Like slavery itself, sexual abuse of slave women was also institutionalized.

Slave breeding can also be considered as another institutionalized form of sexual violence. To produce "good" slaves, slaveholders often actively intervened in mating slave women with strong, healthy slave men. For example, Rose Williams, a Texas slave woman, struggled against unwanted sexual advances by partners chosen by her enslaver. And if she and other slave women refused, they had to face punishments such as whipping and/or being sold. Thus, slave women and slave men, both married and single, were sometimes forced to engage in sexual practices and sexual relationships against their will. As unwilling breeders, slave men as well as slave women can be considered victims of sexual violence. Historian Daina Ramey Berry uses the term "forced breeding" to highlight the violent characteristics of breeding in the slave quarters, and considers it as an indirect form of rape.

By legal definition, rape is an unlawful sexual act inflicted upon a woman without her consent. Some scholars are reluctant to use the term "rape" to describe sexual violence of slave women because enslaved female rape victims were excluded from legal protection, and hence, they were legally impossible to rape. However, recent studies maintain "rape" as an appropriate term by drawing on a handful of extant evidence like the testimony of the aforementioned Harriet Jacobs and Celia, which underscore the frequent occurrence of rape incidents during the period of slavery. In the case of Celia, she was purchased in 1850 at age 14 by a 60-year-old, widowed slave owner in Missouri to serve as his concubine. He raped her en route to his home, and his sexual abuse continued for five years during which Celia bore two children and decided to take action.

It is no doubt that sexual violence scarred slave women and left enormous signs of physical and psychological trauma. Similarly, this violence also had a significant impact on the slave family. For enslaved married couples, it was extremely difficult to maintain monogamous relationships, given that they had to constantly endure forced extramarital sexual relations such as breeding with other partners, concubinage, and coerced sex with masters and others. Emasculated enslaved husbands, who were deprived of the right to protect their wives from sexual transgressions, often expressed their irate frustration on their wives rather than their masters or other offenders. In such cases, slave women who were already victims of sexual violence also became the targets of domestic violence.

Although slave women were very vulnerable to the devastating reality and aftershocks of sexual violence, they were not totally powerless in some of these situations. Many historical sources shed light on the wide range of day-to-day resistance conducted by enslaved women. Harriet Jacobs and Rose Williams, for example, refused the life of a concubine and slave breeder, respectively. Celia, on the other hand, took an extraordinary method of resistance by killing her master after years of sexual abuse. Also abortion and infanticide, which were more psychologically driven means of resistance for enslaved mothers, yet significant acts to protest the reproductive exploitation and the plantation economy, proved less uncommon during slavery. While sexual violence against enslaved women persistently deprived them of control over their own bodies, some women within their limited degree of personal autonomy struggled to defend their sexuality through these various forms of resistance.

FUMIKO SAKASHITA

See also

Slave Codes; Slave Families; Slave Revolts and White Attacks on Black Slaves; Slave Songs; Slave Trade; Slavery; Slavery and American Indians; Slavery in the Antebellum South

Further Reading:

Berry, Daina Ramey. *"Swing the Sickle for the Harvest Is Ripe"*: *Gender and Slavery in Antebellum Georgia*. Urbana: University of Illinois Press, 2007.
McLaurin, Melton A. *Celia: A Slave*. Athens: University of Georgia Press, 1991.

Slavery

Slavery in the American context was a system of labor and social control whereby the enslaved people did not own the fruits of their labor, nor did they own their person. Slaves were chattel property, to be used as the owner saw fit. While the English enslaved some of the Indians as war captives during the first decades of settlement, African slaves were available through the Atlantic slave trade, and by the beginning of the 18th century, most slaves in the English colonies were Africans. The institution of slavery set race relations between blacks and whites in the United States in a pattern that would long outlast slavery. While the legacy of slavery did not lead directly to Jim Crow, in that race relations under Jim Crow were in many important ways quite different than

during slavery, slavery did establish a strong cultural acceptance of white supremacy and black inferiority, which would later find expression in Jim Crow laws.

Slavery existed in some form in most of the colonies, although in general, the North and upland farms in the South had far fewer slaves. While the popular image of the Old South is of the large plantation with dozens or even hundreds of slaves, most slaves lived on much smaller farms, with three slaves or fewer. Slave owners in the South as a group were a relatively small percentage of whites, but they held most of the economic and political power. The area that later became the United States took in a relatively small percentage of enslaved Africans, perhaps 4 or 5 percent of the total number who made the Middle Passage. Most enslaved Africans ended up in the Caribbean or in Brazil. The United States banned the importation of slaves in the early 19th century; thus slave owners had a vested interest in ensuring the reproduction of the slaves. In the United States, slave status was inherited through the mother: any children of a slave woman became the property of her master, regardless of the status of the father. While slave owners often encouraged the formation of families, in that they tended to make a slave less likely to run away, and provided the next generation of slaves, such marriages had no legal standing. The death of owners often meant the forced breakup of slave families.

In the years after the Revolution, Northern states abolished slavery either through immediate emancipation, such as in southern New England, or gradual emancipation, such as in New York, Pennsylvania, and New Jersey. The nation became increasingly divided on the slave issue. Southerners tended to desire the expansion of slavery into the Western territories, while Northerners tended to oppose the expansion of slavery. The slave states were seriously outnumbered in the House of Representatives, so they fought to keep a balance of free and slave states in the Senate to maintain the ability to block legislation deemed hostile to slavery. Southerners also pressed for a federal fugitive slave law, one that the federal government would enforce, to allow slave owners to retrieve slaves who had escaped to the North.

Despite the relative powerlessness of the slaves, white Southerners in areas with large slave populations lived in almost constant fear of slave revolts. Slave owners tended to justify the institution, claiming that their "servants" were happy, and almost like family. This contrasted sharply with

Slave Auctions

Slave auctions represented one of the most dehumanizing aspects of the institution of slavery. For a newly captured slave arriving from Africa, the slave auction was a chaotic, shaming introduction to the Americas. And for those slaves sold in the burgeoning interstate trade that developed once the international slave trade ended in the early 19th century, the auction block served to reemphasize their status as property. Slaves were chattel to be bought and sold with little regard to their humanity.

Slaves arrived at auctions in various ways. During the 17th and 18th centuries, auctions were held when slave ships arrived from the ports of West Africa or the Caribbean. In the 19th century, "professional" slave traders sought to cash in on the lucrative interstate trade market and were a regular presence at slave auctions, buying and selling large numbers of slaves. However, slaves were also sold to pay off a landowner's debt or to settle a deceased owner's estate.

Slave auctions were designed to provide prospective buyers ample opportunity to consider their purchase. Concurrently, sellers generally tried to present their slaves in the best possible light, to maximize profits. These two factors meant that slaves were generally subject to a regimented series of dehumanizing experiences. Slaves were washed thoroughly. Sometimes, slaves were provided with fresh clothing. Large lots of slaves were divided by sex and arranged by height. They were admonished to "look smart" and behave well. Often, they were made to dance, so that potential buyers could observe their physical condition. Slaves were routinely physically handled by customers: hands, arms, bodies, mouths, and teeth were inspected. Customers could demand an even closer inspection, and then a slave was stripped. Slaves were sold with little, if any, regard for family or marriage bonds. Regardless of the humiliation suffered, slaves could utter no protest, for this was indicative of a rebellious spirit that would decrease their value.

REBEKAH LEE

the large slave patrols and militias maintained in slave areas, and the savage reprisals for even the slightest hint of an uprising. Lurid stories of slave uprisings, especially from the Caribbean, were passed around, increasing the fear slaveowners felt. Such stories, which usually included white families having their throats slashed while they slept, indicate that despite their public pronouncements, slaveowners knew that their human property yearned to be free. Slavery set the pattern for whites that blacks should be feared, controlled, and kept subservient.

The existence of African slavery in the United States gave rise to a class of free blacks, often of mixed ancestry, who formed a middle group between free whites and enslaved blacks. In slave areas, they were sometimes looked at with suspicion by whites, as a people likely to lead a slave revolt; but in practice, such people often owed much of their status to the continuation of slavery. The free man, no matter what his skin color, was always the social superior of the slave. Communities of free blacks and mulattoes thrived in some areas of the South, such as Charleston, South Carolina, and around New Orleans. Some even became slave owners

themselves. With the ending of slavery in 1865 and the rise of Jim Crow, such communities lost much of their separate identity, and those who could not "pass" in to white society were forced by laws and custom into black society.

While slavery was deeply entrenched in the law, customs, and economy of the South in the early 19th century, its maintenance rested on violence or the threat of violence. Slaves were at the mercy of their owners. Punishments for running away, disobedience, or a host of other infractions ranged from humiliation to whippings to mutilations. Slave patrols ensured that slaves had only the freedom of movement granted to them by owners. Slave women were vulnerable to sexual exploitation by owners or other white males, with no legal recourse. Slave owners had little or no liability for the abuse or even killing of their slaves. The question of whether a slave could testify in court, or even initiate legal action, remained in flux in many states. While slaves in Connecticut and Massachusetts sued for their freedom during the Revolutionary era based on the new state constitutions that made no provisions for slavery, as the 19th century progressed, slaves had fewer and fewer legal rights.

The U.S. Supreme Court ruling in *Dred Scott v. Sandford* in 1857 marked the final act of stripping slaves, and even free blacks, of any civil rights. The ruling went far beyond the initial question of whether a slave became free when his master took him to free territory. The Court ruled that Congress had no authority to outlaw slavery in any territories, that no person of African descent could ever be a citizen, regardless of their status, and that slaves had no standing to bring suit in court. The ruling, which fulfilled most desires of the slaveowners, created unease among even moderates in the North that the slave owners had too much power in the nation.

As with later Jim Crow, slavery stripped enslaved people of human rights, legal rights, and basic dignity. It did not, however, create a segregated society. In general, slaves were not able to use public entertainments, but slave labor existed with white foremen, overseers, and others who interacted regularly with the black labor force. In an age without public transportation or automobiles, blacks and whites often lived in close proximity. The culture of slavery in the American South created the impression that keeping blacks powerless was the normal order of things, a situation Jim Crow would later reimpose after the end of Reconstruction in 1877.

BARRY M. STENTIFORD

See also

Slave Codes; Slave Families; Slave Revolts and White Attacks on Black Slaves; Slave Songs; Slave Trade; Slave Women and Sexual Violence; Slavery and American Indians; Slavery in the Antebellum South

Further Reading:

Genovese, Eugene D. *Roll, Jordan, Roll: The World the Slaves Made*. New York: Vintage Books, 1976.

Morgan, Edmund. *American Slavery American Freedom*. New York: W. W. Norton, 1975.

Winthrop, Jordan, *White over Black: American Attitudes Toward the Negro, 1550–1812*. New York: W. W. Norton, 1977.

Slavery and American Indians

American Indians have had a complex relationship with the institution of slavery since its introduction on the continent with the first wave of colonial settlers in the 15th and 16th centuries. American Indians have experienced slavery as both bondsman and master. Their position near, but not quite at, the bottom of the racial hierarchy during the antebellum period ensured a diverse response to slavery and to slaves themselves. Some groups of Indians actively took part in the slave trade and sought to emulate white-plantation-style agriculture, but other groups offered a safe haven for fugitive slaves and allowed escaped slaves a surprising degree of autonomy and integration into the Indian community. American Indians' historical involvement with, and resistance to, slavery necessarily challenges assumptions that slavery should be seen as relating only to the history of blacks and whites.

From the beginning of the colonial period, Indians were enslaved by Spanish, French, and British settlers. Enslavement was the by-product of colonial warfare and trade, and the result of slave-taking expeditions. For example, the Indian allies of a defeated colonial power would be vulnerable to enslavement. In addition, colonists exploited intertribal rivalries to gain more Indian captives, with the assistance of Indians themselves. By the beginning of the 18th century, American Indians made up a significant, if still minority, proportion of the slave population.

However, as plantation-style agriculture developed in the South, the need for a more coercive and racialized form of slavery arose. Indian slaves began to be seen as a liability because they could more easily escape bondage and blend into neighboring Native communities. Also, American Indians were perceived to be less adaptable to the harshness of the plantation labor regime, and their numbers declined dramatically because of exposure to epidemic diseases such as smallpox, against which they had little resistance. Slavery from the mid-18th century onward thus lost its multiracial character (though evidence indicates that, particularly in Brazil and Mexico, the oppression of indigenous people continued to be fundamental to the maintenance of the plantation economy) and increasingly became a systematic form of black bondage.

Studies have revealed a wide variety of Indian responses to black slavery. Some Indian nations took part in the slave trade and helped capture and return fugitive slaves. Also, some Indians became slave owners themselves. Black slaves were seen as a strategic as well as an economic asset. Black slaves could serve as messengers, translators, and spies and were considered mobile "property," something that became increasingly important as Indians were systematically

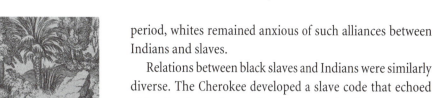

Illustration by Theodor de Bry depicts slavery at a mine in the New World under the Spanish conquistadors. From *Americae pars quinta nobilis & admiratione plena Hieronymi Bezoni*, 1595. Even though Emperor Charles V prohibited Indian slavery in the New Laws, the slavery of Africans continued because slave owners frequently ignored or contradicted Spanish law. (Jay I. Kislak Collection, Rare Book and Special Collections Division, Library of Congress)

removed from their lands in the 18th and 19th centuries. As removal devastated the Indian population and economy, owning slaves may have become an important part of rebuilding Indian life in the new settlements of the West. Some groups, such as the Cherokee, sought to emulate Southern plantation ideals and economies and generally condoned the enslavement of blacks. A prominent Creek leader was known to have possessed more than 50 slaves on his holdings.

However, there was no uniform Indian position on slavery. Even within groups such as the Creek and Cherokee, internal divisions developed between supporters and detractors of slavery. These rifts only widened with the coming of the Civil War. Some groups, such as the Seminole Indians, formed a close alliance with blacks and were seen to provide a safe haven for both fugitive slaves and freed blacks. Black involvement was fundamental to Seminole military campaigns in the 19th century. Throughout the antebellum period, whites remained anxious of such alliances between Indians and slaves.

Relations between black slaves and Indians were similarly diverse. The Cherokee developed a slave code that echoed white Southern slave codes. For example, slaves were not allowed to be taught to read or write, and free blacks who helped slaves escape were subject to punishment. The property of free blacks who had no Cherokee blood could be seized. In contrast, blacks who lived among the Seminoles were allowed to accumulate property and were granted free mobility and the use of guns. Thus, in some Indian nations the boundary between "slave" and free became blurry, and blacks were more completely integrated within Indian society. This integration was acknowledged in law in 1866, when the U.S. government made provision for the adoption of newly emancipated blacks into certain Indian nations. Under this law, the Seminoles granted blacks full and unconditional citizenship. However, groups such as the Cherokee, Creek, and Chickasaw delayed or gave only provisional citizenship with limited rights.

REBEKAH LEE

See also
Slave Codes; Slave Families; Slave Revolts and White Attacks on Black Slaves; Slave Songs; Slave Trade; Slave Women and Sexual Violence; Slavery; Slavery in the Antebellum South

Further Reading:
Brooks, James, ed. *Confounding the Color Line: The Indian-Black Experience in North America*. Lincoln: University of Nebraska Press, 2002.
Littlefield, Daniel. *Africans and Creeks from the Colonial Period to the Civil War*. Westport, CT: Greenwood Press, 1979.
Perdue, Theda. *Slavery and the Evolution of Cherokee Society, 1540–1866*. Knoxville: University of Tennessee Press, 1979.
Porter, Kenneth. *Black Seminoles: History of a Freedom-Seeking People*. Gainesville: University of Florida Press, 1996.

Slavery in the Antebellum South
The U.S. Constitution emphasizes freedom and equality for all, using the most powerful and most frequently cited clause that "all men are created equal." However, the document is also contradictory and hypocritical because it includes three clauses intended to protect slavery. Although black slavery

existed in Africa, South America, the Caribbean Islands, and parts of North America, the most rigid form of slavery was established in the antebellum South. Despite democratic and revolutionary ideals found in the Declaration of Independence and the U.S. Constitution, most of the Founding Fathers of the United States did not want to eliminate slavery from the new republic. In fact, most of them owned dozens or hundreds of black slaves. The contradictions and tensions between democratic ideals and the racial caste system have continued through the post-Emancipation segregation era to the contemporary period. The black-white racial hierarchy and boundary are still more rigid in the United States than in other multiracial societies.

Modern slavery is usually said to have begun with the Portuguese explorations along the coast of Africa in the 15th century. Although some form of human bondage had been practiced in many parts of the world since ancient times, modern slavery is almost invariably associated with African or black labor. The first Africans captured off the West Coast of Africa were sent to Europe, where they worked primarily as domestic servants and laborers in port cities. With the opening up of the Americas in 1492 and burgeoning competition among the major European nations to exploit the natural resources of the newly found lands, the transatlantic traffic in African slaves rapidly became a major enterprise in the economic development and modernization of Europe.

The Portuguese initiated what would become the transatlantic slave trade in 1444. At first they kidnapped relatively small numbers of Africans in raids during their explorations of the African coast. After they made contact with African rulers in the interior, they began purchasing enemy captives from rival ethnic groups. Although African rulers participated in the slave trade, they usually did not sell their own kin. They shipped the first captives to Portugal and Spain, but after the beginning of the 16th century, they began shipping Africans to the Caribbean, Brazil, and other parts of the Americas. Between 1452 and 1494, a series of papal decrees and treaties granted Spain dominance over the territories of the New World, gave Portugal control over India and Brazil, and recognized the Portuguese monopoly over the slave trade.

After a failed attempt to exploit indigenous people for slave labor on the island of Hispaniola (present-day Haiti and the Dominican Republic), the first shipment of African slaves was brought to the Americas in 1502. The Portuguese continued to monopolize the slave trade until the middle of the 17th century, when other European nations began to compete for a share in the lucrative trade. The route of slave ships from Europe to Africa, then to the Americas, and back to Europe is often referred to as the triangular trade. The European traders carried goods from Europe to Africa, where they purchased slaves who would be transported across the Atlantic Ocean to the Americas. The final segment of the journey was the return to Europe with raw materials and other products, such as sugar, molasses, and rum. When the ship's destination was one of the Caribbean islands, there was often another stop in the North American colonies before heading back to Europe.

Slave captives were marched in chains from the African interior to the coast, where they were examined and branded by their purchasers. They were then held in cells or dungeons until a ship was ready to transport them to the Americas. Many slaves died of injuries and disease during the long march to the coast and during their wait at the slave-trading centers. The most arduous part of their journey was the transatlantic crossing, known as the Middle Passage. The slaves were crowded into the holds of the ships, where they were chained and often packed so tightly that they could hardly move. The unsanitary, crowded conditions aboard the ships exposed the captives to numerous illnesses and diseases. Many slaves committed suicide by starving themselves to death or jumping overboard. At its worst, the difficult journey across the ocean may have resulted in mortality rates as high as 40 percent. Most of the African captives were taken from West Africa, the Congo, and Angola; some were also taken from Mozambique and Madagascar. Of the estimated 10 to 12 million Africans brought to the Americas during the transatlantic slave trade, about half a million were taken to the British colonies of North America.

Most historians of slavery in the antebellum South emphasize the gradual, complex evolution of slavery as an institution from its earliest forms during the colonial period until the mid-19th century. The first Africans brought to the North American English colonies arrived in Jamestown, Virginia, on a Dutch ship in 1619. There is some debate about the status of these first arrivals. Were they slaves or bond servants? The importance of this question lies in the fact that slavery had not yet received any legal recognition in the colonies. The early records of the period refer to Africans as "servants." Some historians believe they were indentured servants, but others point out the ambiguous use of the terms *servant* and *bond servant* in the 17th century. Bondage was common for whites brought to the colonies as debtors and convicts, and the historical records show that the status of blacks was similar to that of white indentured servants. The early colonists exploited unpaid labor wherever they could find it, whether that was among Native Americans, destitute whites, or captured Africans. Bondage was not yet synonymous with blackness, nor was it considered a permanent condition.

From the beginning, however, there were local and regional differences in how Africans brought to the colonies were treated. The greatest labor demands were in the Southern colonies, where tobacco, rice, and indigo were grown. The needs of the Mid-Atlantic and Northern colonies were met with less intensive labor. The economic activities of each region determined the need for bond servants or slaves. Differences in the relationship between slaves and slaveholders and differences in attitudes toward blacks also developed along local and regional lines. No matter how close the relationship might be, whether slave, indentured servant, or free, the black person was usually considered inferior. Whereas some argue that racial prejudice developed in direct relation to economic and historical circumstances, others maintain that Europeans were never race neutral.

The shift toward a hereditary system of slavery based on race began to develop in the middle of the 17th century. Massachusetts in 1641 and Connecticut in 1650 were the first colonies to pass legislation legalizing slavery. The New England Puritans had relatively little need for slave labor but became involved in the highly profitable slave trade, supplying slaves to the more labor-intensive, agricultural Southern colonies as well as conducting a lively trade with the West Indies. Virginia and Maryland were the first colonies to make slavery a permanent, hereditary condition determined by the status of the mother. By the middle of the 18th century, this new race-based slavery had been sanctioned by law throughout the colonies. The legal recognition of slavery was followed by increasingly restrictive statutes, or "slave codes," that limited the rights of slaves. Laws were passed forbidding intermarriage, literacy instruction, free assembly, and travel without written permission. These laws were intended to deter slave rebellions and to restrict the means by which a slave might gain freedom or participate in the daily life of the colonies. It was necessary to legalize the slave's difference from the rest of the population in every way, to such an extreme that the slave became less than fully human before the law. The idea of the innate inferiority of blacks became a necessary rationalization for the exploitation of slave labor.

As the economic and political conflicts between the colonies and England intensified, the contradictions between the revolutionary ideals espoused by the colonists and the status of blacks became ever more glaring. By the time that war broke out, the descendants of the Africans who had been arriving in ever-increasing numbers since 1619 were very much aware of the revolutionary ideas that were spreading throughout Europe, the Caribbean, and the rest of the Americas. Many of them saw the colonists' defiance of arbitrary rule as an opportunity to petition for their own freedoms. Some made appeals to local courts and colonial assemblies. Others, like Crispus Attucks, the seaman and fugitive slave who was killed by British troops in what came to be known as the Boston Massacre, gave their lives in defense of the American cause. Although blacks fought with the colonial militias in most of the early battles of the war, in late 1775, George Washington and the Continental Congress eventually decided to ban all blacks from the militias. There had always been fear of allowing blacks to bear arms and uneasiness about the inevitable demands for freedom that would come with their participation in the revolutionary struggle. Washington was forced to relax the ban and allow free blacks to enlist when the British governor of Virginia, Lord Dunmore, issued a proclamation offering freedom to any black who would fight on the side of the British. Washington, who owned some 200 slaves, lost many of them to the Loyalist troops. An estimated 5,000 free blacks served in the Continental army. But given the reluctance of the colonists to accept blacks' willingness to sacrifice their lives for the Revolutionary cause, just as many blacks decided to take their chances with the British. Slavery and the restrictions placed on free blacks were a contradiction that the leaders of the American Revolution were in no hurry to resolve. The Philadelphia Quakers formed the first abolitionist society in 1775, on the eve of the Revolutionary War.

Slavery continued to be a major inconsistency in both the Declaration of Independence (1776) and the Constitution of the United States (1787). The Declaration of Independence made no reference to slavery at all. In his original draft of the Declaration, Thomas Jefferson accused King George III of imposing the slave trade on the colonies and perpetuating an unjust system. This was an argument that had previously been made by the Virginia planters to justify levying taxes on the importation of slaves. This was not a humanitarian or antislavery measure. The planters wanted to be able to control the number of slaves coming into the colonies as a means of controlling levels of agricultural production and profits. They found themselves in the contradictory position of denouncing the inhumanity of the slave trade while at the same time insisting on their right to maintain a slave-labor system. Jefferson's reference to the slave trade in the initial draft of the Declaration was deleted when these same Southern planters objected to the strong antislavery implications of the charges made against the English king.

When the Constitutional Convention met in Philadelphia in 1787, the Northern delegates objected to any use of the word *slavery* in the laws that would govern the new nation. But since the Southern planters were determined to protect their economic interests, the Constitution refers indirectly to slaves as persons "held to service or labor." A further compromise had each slave counted as three-fifths of a person for purposes of representation and taxation in the new government. Although the earlier legislation in the same year excluded slavery from the Northwest Territory, three clauses intended to protect slavery were written into the Constitution. Existing states were given the right to continue importing slaves (i.e., those persons "held to service or labor"), and, most problematic of all for the slave population, it was made a federal offense for any individual or state to aid or harbor a runaway slave. The Declaration of Independence held out the promise of freedom and equality for all, but the Constitution closed the door to any such possibility for slaves in the Southern states. These two founding documents are written evidence of the pattern of evasion, contradiction, and compromise that would undermine the avowed democratic principles of the new nation and ultimately divide the nation.

After the American Revolution and the invention of the cotton gin in 1793, the institution of slavery underwent another major transformation. At the end of the 18th century there were nearly 700,000 slaves in the United States; by the middle of the 19th century their numbers had quadrupled,

having reached some 3,953,760. For the most part the local slave population reproduced itself and was not dependent on the direct importation of slaves from the Caribbean and Africa. Although the pattern of slave ownership and slave labor was never uniform and continued to vary from region to region and household to household, most slaves worked as agricultural laborers on tobacco, rice, and cotton plantations. It is estimated that about 400,000 slaves worked in towns and cities as servants, skilled artisans, and skilled and unskilled laborers. In both rural and urban areas, slaves were sometimes "hired out" to make money for their owners or, if they were more fortunate, to make money for themselves. Some slaves were even able to purchase their own freedom this way. With the increase in the demand for cotton in the European markets during the first half of the 19th century, more than half of the slave population of the United States became concentrated in the cotton-growing states of the lower Southern states, principally Mississippi, Alabama, Louisiana, and Georgia.

Most slave owners operated small farms and plantations with fewer than 20 slaves, but large cotton plantations usually required the labor of 30 or more slaves. These plantations were organized like rural factories with a highly regimented division of labor, which was intended to maintain high production levels. Most slave owners lived on their farms and plantations, but those who operated a large plantation usually hired an overseer to help manage their property. The overseer was often assisted by a driver, a slave chosen to keep up the work pace and help supervise the other slaves. Most slaves were field workers engaged in relentless, backbreaking labor year-round from dawn to dusk; the average field slave worked from 10 to 14 hours a day and had very little time for socializing or recreation. Unlike the individual-task system that was used in rice cultivation, the large cotton plantation used a gang system, closely supervised groups of slaves working together at specialized tasks. Overseers and drivers used coercion and fear of physical punishment to extract the maximum work from the slaves; floggings were the most common form of punishment. A smaller number of slaves worked as domestic servants and skilled laborers, such as mechanics and carpenters, who were needed for the general upkeep of the estate. All slaves, whether they were field workers or lived in the relative comfort of the house servant, were dependent on the goodwill of their owners.

By law, slave masters exercised total authority and control over their human property. Yet slaves were able to sustain themselves emotionally and spiritually with their own belief systems, stories, songs, and rituals. Although plantations were usually isolated and there was little opportunity for the rituals of courtship and marriage, slaves were able to form close relationships and family bonds. Most slave owners realized that strong family ties would ensure a more willing and reliable work force.

As the antislavery sentiment grew and abolitionist propaganda intensified, the slave owners felt compelled to protect the institution by creating ever-more-stringent laws, called "slave codes," to control the movement and activities of their slaves. These laws were intended to keep slaves isolated and dependent on their owners. Slaves were required to have written permission to travel or leave the plantation; they were not allowed to socialize with free blacks or assemble for any purpose without the presence of an authorized white person. Antiliteracy laws were passed, forbidding anyone to teach slaves how to read and write. Counties enlisted local volunteers called "patrollers" to control the movement of slaves, detect conspiracies, and put down rebellions. Even though these regulations and mechanisms for control became ever more repressive, the slaveholders continued to insist on the benevolence of the institution.

The acquisition of new territories in the first half of the 19th century as a result of the Louisiana Purchase and the Mexican-American War brought with it a debate over the expansion of slavery, which ultimately led to the crisis that almost split the new nation in two. When Missouri applied for statehood in 1819, the issue of slavery was at the center of a congressional struggle to maintain a balance in the conflicting economic and political interests of the Northern and Southern states. The irreconcilable nature of the differences between the free-labor industrial North and slave-labor agrarian South became increasingly evident in the series of failed legislative compromises that began with the Missouri Compromise of 1820. Missouri would be admitted as a state under the condition that slavery would be prohibited in the rest of the Louisiana Purchase territory north of its southern boundary.

Over the next three decades, the abolitionist campaign against slavery increased dramatically. White and black abolitionists alike became more radical and persistent in their attacks on the institution that lay at the heart of the Southern economy and way of life. The threat of slave insurrections, such as the Denmark Vesey conspiracy in Charleston, South Carolina, in 1822 and the Nat Turner rebellion in Southampton County, Virginia, in 1831, created fear among and harsh reprisals by the Southern slaveholders. Agitation by both abolitionist and proslavery forces and the acquisition of southwestern territories after the Mexican-American War resulted in the Compromise of 1850, which cobbled together a group of measures that failed to put an end to the controversy. Once again, the extension of slavery became the center of congressional debate. This compromise was far more complex than the earlier one and merely postponed the inevitable conflict over the status of slavery. Among other measures, California was admitted as a free state; Utah and New Mexico were granted legislative authority to decide for themselves, and the slave trade was prohibited in the District of Columbia. But the most contentious measure of all was the imposition of a more rigorous fugitive-slave law. Abolitionists openly defied the new fugitive slave law by organizing a rescue of slaves in the South by means of the Underground Railroad and often violent resistance to the efforts of slaveholders to force the return of slaves who found refuge in the North. Through newspapers, books, pamphlets, speeches, and continual lobbying, abolitionists kept slavery as a moral issue at the center of the power struggle between Northern and Southern states.

The Kansas-Nebraska Act of 1854 was the result of another bitter debate over the extension of slavery and in effect nullified the Missouri Compromise of 1820. Violent confrontations broke out between antislavery and proslavery factions in the new territories. The passage of this act had far-reaching consequences. The new Republican Party grew out of opposition to the bill, and the intensity of the conflict moved the nation closer to civil war. The end of all further compromise was signaled by the Dred Scott Decision in 1857, when the U.S. Supreme Court declared that the Missouri Compromise was unconstitutional and that Congress did not have the authority to ban slavery from any territories.

The national crisis reached the breaking point when the militant abolitionist John Brown led a raid on the federal arsenal at Harper's Ferry, Virginia, in 1859, and the Republican candidate, Abraham Lincoln, was elected to the presidency on an antislavery platform in 1860. After the Republican victory, seven Southern states immediately seceded, and four more joined them when Lincoln was forced to take action against the Confederate attack on Fort Sumter in Charleston, South Carolina, in 1861. Faced with the outbreak of the Civil War, Lincoln insisted on a policy of restoring national unity above all else. In an attempt to appease the four remaining slave states—Delaware, Maryland, Kentucky, and Missouri—Lincoln was exceedingly cautious about making this conflict a war against slavery. Despite his antislavery campaign, he refused to embrace the abolitionist cause.

Lincoln believed that slavery was unjust and morally wrong, but like Jefferson he had little faith in the ability of blacks to live among whites as equals. At the beginning of the war, following an all-too-familiar pattern, Lincoln prohibited blacks from participating as soldiers in the struggle against the Confederate army and vacillated about what to do with the thousands of slaves who sought refuge behind Union lines. Lincoln supported gradual, compensated emancipation, to be followed by the resettlement of as many blacks as possible in other parts of the world. He went so far as to invite a group of free blacks to the White House (the first meeting of its kind) to discuss this proposition. Some blacks were ready to leave, but most thought they had a right to stay and live as citizens in the nation they had helped build.

Since none of the Southern states, including the loyal border states, agreed to Lincoln's plan of compensated emancipation, he was forced to issue an executive order proclaiming emancipation of all slaves in rebel-controlled territories. He conceived of this limited emancipation as a "military necessity" aimed at undermining the economic viability of the Confederate states. It was no longer possible, as the black abolitionist Frederick Douglass had forewarned, "to fight slaveholders, without fighting against slavery." After the battle of Antietam, on September 22, 1862, Lincoln announced that his emancipation proclamation would go into effect on January 1, 1863. As is often observed, Lincoln's proclamation did not free a single slave, since it only applied to the rebel states. It was not until two years later, after the Confederacy lost the war, that Congress passed the Thirteenth Amendment to the Constitution, abolishing slavery in all parts of the United States. The Civil War ended slavery but did not end racial discrimination, nor did emancipation result in full citizenship rights for former slaves.

BARBARA J. WEBB

See also

Slave Codes; Slave Families; Slave Revolts and White Attacks on Black Slaves; Slave Songs; Slave Trade; Slave Women and Sexual Violence; Slavery; Slavery and American Indians

Further Reading:

Bennett, Lerone. *Before the Mayflower: A History of Black America.* New York: Penguin, 1993.

Berlin, Ira. *Many Thousands Gone: The First Two Centuries of Slavery in North America.* Cambridge, MA: Belknap Press, 1998.

Blassingame, John W. *The Slave Community: Plantation Life in the Antebellum South,* rev. and enlarged ed. New York: Oxford University Press, 1979.

Curtin, Philip D. *The Atlantic Slave Trade: A Census.* Madison: University of Wisconsin Press, 1969.

Davis, David Brion. *The Problem of Slavery in Western Culture.* Ithaca, NY: Cornell University Press, 1966.

Davis, David Brion. *The Problem of Slavery in the Age of Revolution.* Ithaca, NY: Cornell University Press, 1975.

Fields, Barbara J. "Slavery, Race and Ideology in the United States of America." *New Left Review* 181 (1990): 85–118.

Franklin, John Hope, and Alfred A. Moss Jr. *From Slavery to Freedom: A History of African Americans,* 8th ed. New York: McGraw-Hill, 1999.

Genovese, Eugene. *Roll, Jordan, Roll: The World the Slaves Made.* New York: Vintage Books, 1972.

Heuman, Gad, and James Walvin, eds. *The Slavery Reader.* New York: Routledge, 2003.

Kelley, Robin D. G., and Earl Lewis, eds. *A History of African Americans.* New York: Oxford University Press, 2000.

Kolchin, Peter. *American Slavery, 1619–1877.* New York: Hill and Wang, 1993.

Stampp, Kenneth M. *The Peculiar Institution: Slavery in the Ante-Bellum South.* New York: Vintage Books, 1989.

Thomas, Hugh. *The Slave Trade: The Story of the Atlantic Slave Trade, 1440–1870.* Cambridge: Cambridge University Press, 1992.

White, Deborah Gray. *Ar'n't I a Woman? Female Slaves in the Plantation South.* New York: Norton, 1985.

Sleepy Lagoon Case (1942)

The 1942 Sleepy Lagoon case resulted in the convictions of 17 Mexican American young men charged with the murder of fellow youth José Díaz. One of the prominent civil rights cases of the World War II era, the Sleepy Lagoon trial heightened long-simmering racial tensions between whites and minorities in Los Angeles—exacerbated by existing wartime fear and suspicion of "un-American" persons and activities—that culminated in the Zoot Suit Riots in the spring of 1943.

The events leading up to the trial began on the night of August 1, 1942, when a group of Mexican American youths—often prohibited from using the city's segregated public pools—went swimming at a reservoir dubbed Sleepy Lagoon, where they were assaulted by a rival band of Mexican American youths. After the fight, the victims returned to their 38th Street neighborhood to gather a large number of friends and returned to the reservoir to settle the score with their assailants. When they arrived at Sleepy Lagoon, they found the area deserted but followed the sounds of music to a party taking place at a ranch in the vicinity. When the 38th Street youths arrived at the party, a major brawl ensued. The next day, police discovered on a nearby road the beaten and stabbed body of 22-year-old Díaz, who died of head injuries later that day.

In accordance with the growing perception that crimes perpetrated by Mexican American youth were spiraling out of control, the Los Angeles Police Department used Diaz's murder as a call to action against Mexican American juvenile delinquency. Over the next week, police officers descended into Los Angeles neighborhoods and rounded up as many as 600 youths, mainly Mexican American "zoot suiters" whom many whites in the city associated with gang-related crime. Among those detained were Hank Leyvas and 21 others from the 38th Street group, who were charged with assault and the murder of Díaz due to their involvement in the fight at the ranch near Sleepy Lagoon.

What happened during the subsequent 12-week trial has been described as an overreaction based on anti-Mexican fears and a serious violation of the defendants' civil rights. Mainstream media coverage of the trial was sensational and racially inflammatory, effectively increasing the existing public hysteria over Mexican crime. On January 12, 1943, a jury found 17 of the defendants guilty despite lack of evidence connecting any of the 38th Street youths to the Díaz murder, as well as a biased judge, denial of counsel, and racially charged testimony, including that of one police officer who argued that criminality and violence were genetic traits inherent in Mexicans. Three of the defendants, including Leyvas, were sentenced to life in prison for first-degree

murder, while 11 others received sentences of five years to life for second-degree murder. Within a few months of the verdict, Los Angeles exploded into a week-long clash between white military servicemen and Mexican American zoot suiters.

The trial had drawn the attention of many prominent Los Angeles liberals, leftists, and social justice advocates, including journalist Carey McWilliams and civil rights activist Josefina Fierro de Bright, who formed the Sleepy Lagoon Defense Committee (SLDC) to publicize the injustice of the trial and advocate for the release of the young men. An appeal effort launched by the SLDC resulted in the unanimous reversal of the guilty verdicts by an appellate court in October 1944 on the grounds that the defendants were denied a fair trial. After spending almost two years in prison, Leyvas and the other convicted young men were finally released. Los Angeles authorities declined to retry the case, and the murder of José Díaz remains officially unsolved.

The reversal of the Sleepy Lagoon case represented one of the first major legal victories for Mexican Americans, including *Mendez v. Westminster* (1946), a precursor to *Brown v. Board of Education* (1954) that overturned racial segregation in California schools, and *Hernandez v. Texas* (1954), in which the U.S. Supreme Court decided that the equal protection clause of the Fourteenth Amendment applied to Mexican Americans and other racial groups.

ABC-CLIO

See also
Zoot Suit Riots

Further Reading:
Escobar, Edward J. *Race, Police and the Making of a Political Identity: Mexican Americans and the Los Angeles Police Department, 1900–1945*. Berkeley: University of California Press, 1999.
Mazón, Mauricio. *The Zoot-Suit Riots: The Psychology of Symbolic Annihilation*. Austin: University of Texas Press, 1984.

Social Construction of Race

A social construction, and its meaning, are bound to the specific social relations and historical context in which they are embedded. Although initially contingent on the social system in which they were created, they have the ability to be transformed throughout history and within different societies. Most sociologists agree that race is a social construct and that the *social construction of race* refers to the creation, preservation, and transformation of race through sociohistorical processes. Tracing the history of both race as a broad concept and specific racial categories reveals the socially constructed nature of race.

Race is arguably one of the most poignant examples of a social construction; race is important because people and societies have defined it as important. In fact, the contemporary concept of race did not appear before the late 17th century. While modern humans arose in Africa around 100,000 years ago, the majority of diversity we see today—represented most conspicuously in phenotypic differences—is the result of natural adaptations to geographical separation of populations for long periods of time. For instance, groups located closer to the equator have darker skin because their skin contains higher levels of melanin, which is a protector from the sun's ultraviolet rays. Humans were distinguished primarily by national or other geographical boundaries during this period; religion and language were also factors, whereas race was not.

The concept of race surfaced within the Age of Enlightenment. Among the most important developments during the Age of Enlightenment were classifications systems of all flora and fauna, which included humans. Numerous publications described four or five distinct races according to observable physical traits. Pseudoscience was used to support the categorization of humans into subspecies on the basis of geography, skin color, facial features, and bone structure. Most notably was the Linnaeus (1767) classification that claimed to use scientific discoveries to classify the human species into four distinct races according to phenotype and temperament: Native Americans who were reddish in color, easily angered, and governed by custom; Africans who were black, negligent, and governed by caprice; Asians who were yellow, haughty, and governed by opinions; and Europeans who were white, inventive, and governed by laws. According to Moya and Markus (2010), the initial creation of the races was rooted in three claims about the classification system: it is a universal scheme that can accommodate all observed human differences; it is a scientifically based system; and it is predictive of human

---

Carl Linnaeus (1707–1778)

Carl Linnaeus was a Swedish scientist known by some as the father of ecology. His work *Systema Naturae* (1767) classified the human species into four races: white Europeans, red Americans, brown Asians, and black Africans. In the 10th edition he further detailed stereotypical characteristics of the races based on the four temperaments. Johann Friedrich Blumenbach was a German scientist who is also famous for this work on human classifications. Blumenbach extended his teachings on comparative anatomy to apply to the classifications of human races. Blumenbach's (1776) classification included five races: Caucasian, Mongolian, Ethiopian, American, and Malay. Both Linneaus and Blumenbach were considered highly reputable, and their work was influential in providing scientific basic for a biological understanding of race.

---

differing capacities and characters. Therefore, the first invention of race was a biological one.

Racial distinctions became even more important for social categorization with the eminence of social Darwinism. According to the theory's founder, Charles Darwin, races had evolved into separate subspecies over time and the races that had the most power were the races better fit to be positioned in power. Social Darwinism and eugenics, or the pseudoscientific-backed promotion of higher reproduction of more desired people, were successful in imbuing a stratifying significance to race and became a significant justification of racial domination. Most notably, slavery—an institutional structure already known to most societies—transformed from a tribal conquest-and-capture system to a system based solely on race.

The biological concept of race remained prevalent through much of the 19th and 20th centuries—it was used as justification for the trans-Atlantic slave trade, plantation slavery, and Jim Crow racism in the United States. However, historical events and improvements in scientific knowledge slowly reduced the influence of the biological concept of race during the mid-1900s. For instance, the shared public contempt towards Nazi Germany and the Holocaust influenced many societies to reevaluate systems of domination. The civil rights movement in the 1960s was largely successful in ameliorating the biological notions of race that justified overt racial domination in the United States. These factors, along with refutations of pseudoscientific practices, better revealed how race was socially invented and how stratifying by race had large-scale, damaging effects.

In addition to the social construction of the concept of race, particular racial categories are also socially constructed. Tracing inclusion and exclusion of racial categories in the U.S. Census demonstrates how context can impact particular categories of race. For instance, *mulatto*, a term used in the mid-1800s to refer to black and white racially mixed children, was dropped from the census is 1920. Rampant fears of white impurity fueled the rule of hypodescent, or the one-drop rule, which reassigned anyone with any portion of black blood to be classified as black. This example shows that racial categorizes change to adapt to both population changes and sociopolitical interests. The 1960 census was significant because it dropped census enumerators and opted for self-identified race. The 2000 Census allowed respondents to choose more than one race. These changes are important because they contradicted previously held notions about race as an ascribed and mutually exclusive status to one that could represent an aspect of choice and include multiple categories. These examples are illustrative of how race has shifted from a perceived macro-level invention to a concept that individuals and groups have the agency to impact as well.

Mapping definitions and meanings of race across space is also useful for demonstrating the social construction of race. Race in Brazil is often viewed as a continuum rather than categorical. Any given survey of racial classifications could garner over 100 responses to a question about respondent's race. Furthermore, some Brazilians who identify as white or *branco* in Brazil, would be perceived to be black in the United States.

Race, as a social construction, is not a universally recognized category; racial meanings have changed throughout history, and definitions of race are not shared. Despite the fact that race has been socially invented, the importance of race in defining and stratifying people means that race has become a social fact with real consequences. Race has a significant role in social institutions and environments such as the criminal justice, education, and health systems; job markets; social networks; and even partner choices. Race is also a social status that has positive aspects in many individuals'

Race in Another America

Edward Telles's (2004) book, *Race in Another America*, comprehensively covers race in Brazil. In his chapter on racial classifications, he argues there are three competing racial classification systems in Brazil today: (1) the census system, which uses three major categories—*branco* (white), *pardo* (brown), and *preto* (black); (2) the popular system, which uses an indeterminate number of categories; and (3) the newer system, which only uses two categories—*negro* (black) and *branco* (white). Examinations of the popular system have returned more than 100 categories, including terms such as "pale," "purple," or "dark chocolate." In the popular system the racial categories range on a skin color continuum. Contrarily, the newer system originates out of the Brazilian black movement as a response to racial inequalities and focuses on clear distinctions between black and brown Brazilians who have held racially subordinate positions and the whiter, more privileged Brazilians.

lives; one's racial identity can be a significant part of the self-concept and membership within a racial category can elicit a sense of pride. For these reasons, sociologists believe that race will remain a significant feature of society and a concept that needs continual attention and reflection.

Whitney Laster

See also

Black and Non-Black Hierarchy; History of U.S. Census Racial Categorizations; Race; Racial Projects; Racial Taxonomy; Third Wave Whiteness; Tri-racialization; White Privilege

Further Reading:

Blumenbach, Johann Friedrich. *De generis Hvmani Varietate Nativa liber*. Göttingen, Germany: University of Göttingen, 1776.

Davis, F. James. *Who Is Black? One Nation's Definition*. University Park: Pennsylvania State University Press, 1991.

Hirschman, Charles. "The Origins and Demise of the Concept of Race." *Population and Development Review* 30 (2004): 385–415.

Linnaeus, Carolus. *Systema Naturae*. Stockholm: Laurentius Salvius, 1767.

Moya, Paula M. L., and Hazel R. Markus. "Doing Race." In *Doing Race: 21 Essays for the 21st Century*, edited by H. Markus and P. Moya, 1–44. New York: W. W. Norton, 2010.

Omi, Howard Winant. *Racial Formation in the United States: From the 1960s to the 1990s.* New York: Routledge, 1994.

Snipp, Mathew C. "Racial Measurement in the American Census: Past Practices and Implications for the Future." *Annual Review of Sociology* 29 (2003): 563–88.

Social Darwinism

Social theories are the product of a society. It is often perceived to serve the interests of certain groups of people and often generates both intended and unintended consequences. Social Darwinism is one of those idea systems created and used by people for different purposes. Social Darwinism is an ideology that claims that only the "fittest" in human society can survive and prosper just as in the natural world. According to its doctrine, the process of "natural" selection occurs in human societies as well as in the natural world.

It was Herbert Spencer (1820–1903) who applied natural scientist Charles Darwin's (1809–1882) theory of evolution to the human social world. Spencer, who lived in England, studied and was influenced by Darwin's work. Darwin's theory of biological evolution through the process of natural selection holds that a species changes physically over many generations as it adapts to the natural environment. Those species that adapt well to the natural environment will survive as the fittest. His theory of evolution, which was proposed in his 1859 book *The Origin of the Species*, made a significant impact upon social scientists. Social thinkers of the 19th century who were investigating the alleged superiority and inferiority of different racial groups were heavily influenced by this theory. Applying the process of natural selection to human society, they argued that superior human societies, classes, and races were the outcomes of this process of natural selection. These ideas became the basis of social Darwinism, commonly known as "survival of the fittest."

It was, in fact, Spencer, not Darwin, who coined the phrase "survival of the fittest." To Spencer, human society should ideally be modeled on nature. Thinking of a parallel natural-selection process going on in the human social world, Spencer proposed that in the human social world one should never intentionally interfere with the "natural"

English biologist and sociologist Herbert Spencer (1820–1903). (Hulton-Deutsch Collection/Corbis)

process that selects only the fittest human beings for survival, prosperity, and dominance. This idea eventually led to a variety of beliefs and practices, such as Nordic racism created by social thinkers and later used by Nazi theoreticians. In this particular version of white racism, the Nordic race was believed to be superior to the shorter "Alpines" and the darker-skinned "Mediterraneans." It also led to eugenics, in which it was understood that the unfit transmitted their undesirable characteristics, so a breeding program was developed to cultivate a better society consisting of people with more desirable characteristics.

Social Darwinism also had a significant impact on American thought. As an ideology, it has been used to justify gross inequality in the capitalistic American society by such corporate leaders as John D. Rockefeller. According to the doctrine of social Darwinism, the successful make a lot of money simply because they are innately superior to the unsuccessful. Those who are poor deserve to be poor because they are innately inferior. They are responsible for their own poverty. Government should not do anything to interfere in this process. This is the outcome of natural selection in human society.

Most important, social Darwinism profoundly affected the emergence and strengthening of white racism. In the 19th century, when white Europeans left their own societies, exploring and contacting different peoples and colonizing them, they needed to justify the subsequent inequality between the colonizers and the indigenous people. Racism as a system of ideas became a tool for dominance during the colonization period, and white racism emerged as a dominant theory explaining the racial inequality. White racists believed that white Europeans became a superior race because they had evolved much faster than other races. That is, they were chosen to dominate. Social Darwinism contributed to the emergence of such racist ideas as these and popular usage of racist ideology in the 19th century. If white Americans were the most powerful and successful, then this must be the result of innate characteristics of superiority formed through the process of natural selection in competition with other races. The belief that social achievement is essentially determined by human biological differences makes it simple and convenient to justify inequality among different groups of people who have physical differences. The idea was created and has been used to justify racial inequality in the United States and around the world.

HEON CHEOL LEE

See also
Biological Racism

Further Reading:
Bannister, Robert C. *Social Darwinism: Science and Myth in Anglo-American Social Thought*. Philadelphia: Temple University Press, 1979.

Social Distance

The concept of social distance is widely used in studies of ethnic and race relations, as well as in studies of class, gender, and status. Social distance refers to the extent to which members of a group are accepted or rejected by mainstream society. A high level of social distance between members of a group and the larger society indicates that they are not socially accepted, while a lower level of social distance indicates acceptance and closeness between the group and society.

Sociologist Emory Bogardus was the first person to create a scale measuring the concept of social distance. Developed in 1925, the Bogardus Social Distance Scale is based on willingness to allow any given group (e.g., based on race, ethnicity, or religion) within various degrees of intimacy. Respondents to the scale are asked to approve or disapprove of a range of relationships that a person from the selected group may have in relation to themselves, ranging from being a visitor to the country to being a fellow citizen, a neighbor, a close friend, a close kin by marriage, and so forth. Examples of questions from the Bogardus Social Distance Scale include, "Would you accept a [black] as a regular friend?" and "Would you accept a [black] as a speaking acquaintance?" Based on these items, scores on the Social Distance Scale run from a low of 1 (i.e., the respondent would marry a member of the group) to high of 7 (i.e., the respondent would restrict a member of that group from living in his or her country).

Results of studies using the Bogardus Social Distance Scale over the years reveal interesting trends in race relations in the United States, including how attitudes have remained fixed in regard to certain groups. Results from its original application in a 1926 national survey showed virtually no social distance (i.e., a high level of social acceptance) between respondents and those of British or Canadian descent. This finding was replicated in national studies in the 1940s, 1950s, and 1960s. In contrast, African Americans have consistently had the highest social distance score (i.e., the lowest level of acceptance). Historical analysis using the Bogardus Social Distance Scale also shows how attitudes toward certain racial or ethnic groups may be influenced by current political events and conflicts. For example, in the 1940s, there was a particularly high level of social distance between survey respondents and Japanese/Japanese American individuals, apparently in response to World War II.

Though the widespread use of the Bogardus Social Distance Scale has helped to make social distance an enduring concept in race relations, the intellectual legacy of social distance as a concept goes far beyond Bogardus. Bogardus's work is significant because he was the first to develop a scale to measure social distance. His concept of social distance was, however, based on the work of Robert Park, who in turn, had been influenced by the work of Georg Simmel. Simmel's original concept of social distance was a part of his larger work in the sociology of space, which looked at the relationship between metaphoric, or social, space and geometric, or physical, space. Simmel pointed to the way that space may be subdivided for social purposes and framed in social boundaries that are distinct from physical or natural boundaries. In contrast to natural boundaries, the social boundaries are sociological facts that are formed spatially. Thus, the social boundary can precede the spatial reality—for example, when a sense of ethnic or religious solidarity leads to the drawing of physical boundaries between disparate groups of people. It is socially acceptable to converse at a closer distance at a dinner party than it is in the workplace. Although the physical distance may be the same in both instances, only in one case is it acceptable, because the social expectation differs.

Deriving his concept of social distance from Simmel's notion of social boundaries, Park believed that it had great importance for understanding race relations because the degree of intimacy between groups and individuals indicate the influence that each has over the other. The greater the social distance between individuals and groups, the less they influence each other reciprocally. In terms of relations between dominant and subordinated races or classes, as long as the subordinate in the relationship (i.e., a servant, or a racial minority) remains mindful of his or her place or distance, the dominant person in the relationship can enjoy a certain degree of personal warmth. For example, a person of wealth may confide in and have a warm relationship with his or her servant. But this relationship is only viable as long as the servant keeps his or her "distance" from the employer; that is, as long as the servant does not step over the traditionally accepted social boundaries that predicate the relationship between servant and employer.

Tracy Chu

See also

Race Relations Cycle

Further Reading:

Bogardus, Emory S. *Social Distance*. Los Angeles: Antioch Press, 1959.

Marshall, Gordon. *A Dictionary of Sociology*. New York: Oxford University Press, 1998.

Owen, Carolyn, Howard C. Eisner, and Thomas McFaul. "A Half-Century of Social Distance Research: National Replication of the Bogardus Studies." *Sociology and Social Research* 66 (1981): 80–98.

Park, Robert E. "The Concept of Social Distance as Applied to the Study of Racial Attitudes and Racial Relations." *Journal of Applied Sociology* (later *Sociology and Social Research*) 8 (July/August 1924): 339–44.

Simmel, Georg, and Kurt H. Wolff. *The Sociology of Georg Simmel*. Glencoe, IL: Free Press, 1950.

Some Other Race (SOR)

Beginning in 2000, the U.S. Census offered the option of "some other race" as part of a series of revisions to the Office of Management and Budget (OMB) Directive No. 15. In 1977 the OMB established racial categories required of all federal agencies to use when collecting information on race and revised the categories in 1997 to include: white, black or African American, American Indian or Alaska Native, Asian, Native Hawaiian or Pacific Islander, and Hispanic or Latino. The 1997 revisions also allowed for respondents to check multiple race boxes. If a person's race was not reflected in the response categories, they could opt to check the box for Some Other Race and write in their response.

Allowing respondents to self-identify as Some Other Race and/or to check multiple race boxes represents a dismantling of a racial classification system that had its origins rooted in the concept of hypodescent or a one-drop rule that guided much of the history of racial classification in the census. Under the one-drop rule, a person with any minority blood or ancestry was considered to be of the minority race regardless of their own self-identification or the extent of their ancestry. This was viewed as an effort to assess the purity of races and to marginalize those that were not of the socially dominant race by relegating them to the minority race. Allowing people to report Some Other Race or to identify as multiracial gives saliency to the social construction of race over biological notions of race and reflects social progress in overcoming racial stratification in the United States by further moving away from rules of hypodescent.

The Some Other Race option was the third largest single race response category in the 2000 census. Almost all of those who selected this category as a single race were Hispanic or Latino, likely reflecting the movement of Latino or

Hispanic from a racial category to a separate question on Hispanic origin or ethnicity. While the 1977 Directive No. 15 mandated that Hispanic be included in the race choices, it appeared as a separate or additional question on ethnicity instead of a racial option. Approximately half of all Hispanics identified as Some Other Race, with the remainder identifying as white. The response category of Some Other Race was included in the 2010 census, but the question regarding Hispanic ethnicity was changed to allow for additional identification of nationality such as Mexican, or Mexican American, and included an open-ended category of Another Hispanic, Latino, or Spanish, where respondents could write in a Hispanic identification based on nationality, ancestry, lineage or heritage. The 2010 census reported that 6 percent of respondents that chose a single race selected the Some Other Race category and, similar to the 2000 census, it was the third largest single race classification, following white and African American, respectively.

MICHELLE PETRIE

See also

History of U.S. Census Racial Categorizations; Hypodescent (One Drop Rule)

Further Reading:

Castro, Tony. "Census Race Change for Hispanics Sparks Criticism." *Huffington Post.* http://www.huffingtonpost.com/2013/01/09/census-race-change-for-hispanics-criticism_n_2439617.html

Humes, Karen R, Nicholas A. Jones, and Roberto R. Ramirez. *Overview of Race and Hispanic Origin: 2010.* Washington, DC: U.S. Census Bureau, 2011.

Snipp, C. Matthew. "Racial Measurement in the American Census: Past Practices and Implications for the Future." *Annual Review of Sociology* 29 (2003): 563–88.

U.S. Commission on Civil Rights. *Racial Categorization in the 2010 Census: A Briefing Before the United States Commission on Civil Rights Held in Washington, DC, April 7, 2006.* Washington, DC: U.S. Commission on Civil Rights, 2009.

Sotomayor, Sonia (b. 1954)

With her appointment by Barack Obama as the 111th Justice, in 2009 Sonia Sotomayor became the first person of Hispanic descent—she is Puerto Rican—to serve on the Supreme Court of the United States. The Senate approved

Sonia Sotomayor was a federal judge on the U.S. Court of Appeals for the Second Circuit when she was nominated by President Barack Obama to replace retiring Supreme Court Justice David Souter in 2009. (White House)

her nomination by a 68 to 31 margin. Prior to her appointment to the high court, Sotomayor received an Ivy-League education. A native of the South Bronx, she graduated summa cum laude from Princeton University after writing a senior thesis on Puerto Rico's first democratically elected governor, Luis Muñoz Marín. While in college, Sotomayor was active in Puerto Rican campus organizations Acción Puertorriqueña and the Third World Center. After graduating from Princeton, she went on to Yale Law School in 1976 where she became the editor of the *Yale Law Journal.*

Upon passing the bar in 1980, Sotomayor served as an assistant district attorney in Manhattan where she prosecuted robberies, assaults, murders, police brutality, and child pornography cases. In 1984, she began working as a private attorney with the law firm Pavia & Harcourt where she specialized in litigating intellectual property cases. Sotomayor did pro bono work for agencies such as the New York City Campaign Finance Board and the Puerto Rican Legal Defense and Education Fund.

In 1992, the Senate unanimously approved President George H. W. Bush's appointment of Sotomayor to be a U.S. district judge for the Southern District of New York. She became the first Hispanic federal judge in the state of New York. At 38 years old, she was that court's youngest justice. In 1998, after being nominated by President William Clinton, she was confirmed for a seat on the Second Circuit Court of Appeals. She garnered approval from 68 out of 96 U.S. senators.

Prior to nominating Justice Sotomayor to the Supreme Court, President Obama said that empathy was an essential criterion upon which he would evaluate prospective candidates. Critics of the president claimed that the word *empathy* was meant as coded language that referred to a liberal justice who would use the bench to impose personal views that were not consistent with the law. One case that her critics in Congress and in the press pointed to as evidence of her judicial activism involved the promotion of New Haven, Connecticut, firefighters in 2008. The ruling handed down by a panel of appellate judges upheld an affirmative action policy that withheld promotion to white firefighters by disregarding the results of an exam. The ruling was based on the fact that few minorities scored well enough on it to qualify for advancement. As a result, there were few people of color who were likely to be made lieutenants or captains. A closely divided Supreme Court narrowly—five to four—overruled the appeals court and found that the white firefighters were unfairly denied promotions because of their race. The case contains several legal issues dealing with race and how the government can use it in making decisions regarding employment. Because of this decision, Justice Sotomayor's political opponents charged her with reverse discrimination and racial prejudice against white people.

Perhaps the most famous decision that Sotomayor was involved in, prior to her tenure on the Supreme Court, involved Major League Baseball. When she issued an injunction against team owners, it ended the 1995 labor strike that caused the cancellation of the World Series for the first time in 90 years. In her ruling, Sotomayor concluded that the baseball owners had tried to undermine the labor system in a way that challenged collective bargaining rights beyond professional sports.

Since being confirmed to the Supreme Court of the United States in 2009, Justice Sotomayor has provided a vocal, liberal voice on the bench, something she did not regularly do prior to her appointment to the high court. As of March 2012, Sotomayor had authored five solo dissenting opinions. As a district and appeals court justice, Sotomayor wrote 29 opinions in cases of prisoners petitioning for writs of habeas corpus. In none of those rulings did she grant the prisoners' requests. As a Supreme Court justice, however, she has proactively issued opinions that rebuff the court's rulings on the rights of inmates. In 2011 she publicly clashed with the court's decision not to hear the plea of a prisoner in Louisiana who sued because of a sentence to hard labor. The prisoner had begun to refuse medications for treating his HIV as a means of protesting the sentence. Sotomayor chose this petition out of thousands and went public with her stance.

Deeb Paul Kitchen

Memoir

In her memoir, *My Beloved World*, Justice Sotomayor defends affirmative action, without which, she says, she could not have accessed the legal profession in the ways she has. She tells her story of growing up in poverty and utilizing race-based admittance policies that put her in position to excel. Her life story is similar to one published by fellow Supreme Court Justice Clarence Thomas who also rose from poverty to a seat on the bench. The two judges reach dramatically different conclusions on the worth of affirmative action policies that they both claim to have benefited from.

See also

Obama, Barack

Further Reading:

Lewis, Neil A. "On a Supreme Court Prospect's Résumé: 'Baseball Savior.'" *New York Times*. May 14, 2009. http://www.nytimes.com/2009/05/15/us/15sotomayor.html (accessed December 6, 2012).

Sherman, Mark. "Sonia Sotomayor Memoir 'My Beloved World' Offers Personal Look At Supreme Court Justice." *Huffington Post*. December 11, 2012. http://www.huffingtonpost.com/2012/12/11/sonia-sotomayor-memoir_n_2276372.html (accessed December 11, 2012).

"Sonia Sotomayor." *Biography Channel*. 2012. http://www
  .biography.com/people/sonia-sotomayor-453906 (accessed
  December 2, 2012).
"Sonia Sotomayor." *New York Times*. March 28, 2012. http://
  topics.nytimes.com/top/reference/timestopics/people/s/
  sonia_sotomayor/index.html (accessed December 2, 2012).
Stolberg, Sheryl Gay. "Sotomayor, a Trailblazer and a
  Dreamer." *New York Times*. May 26, 2009. http://www
  .nytimes.com/2009/05/27/us/politics/27websotomayor
  .html?pagewanted=all&_r=0 (accessed December 2, 2012).

Southern Christian Leadership Conference (SCLC)

Founded as a tight coalition of spiritual leaders, the Southern Christian Leadership Conference (SCLC) emerged in the late 1950s as the leading Christian civil rights organization. It championed nonviolence, voting rights, antipoverty, and social justice in its campaign to abolish Jim Crow. Martin Luther King, Jr., Ralph Abernathy, Joseph Lowery, and Fred Shuttlesworth, all ordained ministers leading prominent congregations in Alabama and Georgia, were the original executive body of the SCLC. From its birth in 1957 to the present, the SCLC has maintained a political agenda aimed first at dismantling institutionalized racism, then addressing the emotional and economic wounds caused by Jim Crow in American communities.

The Montgomery Bus Boycott of 1955–1956 provided the greatest influence on the formation of the SCLC. The Montgomery Improvement Association invited Martin Luther King, Jr. to provide spiritual leadership for the boycott volunteers and participants. In Montgomery, King befriended Ralph Abernathy and other politically active members of the black church. The success of the boycott and the desegregation of Montgomery's bus lines motivated King, Abernathy, Lowery, Shuttlesworth, and C. K. Steele to form a faith-based organization in January 1957. The ministers settled on the name, Southern Christian Leadership Conference, as a representation of the organization's membership, congregations, churches, civic confederations, and associations of groups for social justice. The SCLC preferred not to have individuals as members; instead, it practiced collective action with nonviolent resistance as its principal philosophy.

In the first half of the civil rights movement, the SCLC emphasized desegregation of public accommodations and voting rights. In 1961, the SCLC sheltered more than 1,000 supporters of the Freedom Rides in its churches. It led voting registration campaigns in Alabama and Mississippi in 1962. In 1963, the SCLC triumphed over segregation in the nation's most segregated city, Birmingham, Alabama. The city remained a bastion of segregation, despite the *Brown v. Board of Education* decision and the growing popularity of desegregation movements across the nation. In Birmingham, segregation was absolute and complete in every part of life, including in schools, restaurants, city parks, cemeteries, and department store dressing rooms. Although blacks were about 40 percent of the population, fewer than 12 percent of blacks had registered to vote.

The SCLC embarked on a slightly different strategy from that of Montgomery—boycotting department stores and leading protest marches through downtown Birmingham. The SCLC asked for black children to join the marches and to risk jail to protest segregation. The children endured disturbing violence, in the form of attacking police dogs and high-pressure fire hoses. National outcry at the photographs and television images of children and young adults under attack had cemented public opinion against the city of Birmingham. The SCLC demanded and received an end to racist hiring practices and segregation, inaugurated by a biracial committee overseeing desegregation. The organization had similar success three years later in protesting segregation in Selma, Alabama, in 1965.

The SCLC's successful organization of Birmingham's desegregation, however, did not quell violent reactions to the group or its supporters. A few days after the announcement of a peaceful conclusion to the marches, more than 1,000 Klansmen burned crosses in a city park. Then bombs exploded in the Birmingham home of Alfred Daniel King, Martin Luther King's brother. In Jackson, Mississippi, a Klansman murdered civil rights leader Medgar Evers in his driveway in June. In September 1963, a bomb left at the Birmingham Baptist Church killed four black girls. All of the events had the effect of attracting even more support to the civil rights movement, particularly among Northern whites, who were eager to facilitate the black revolution underway. Progressive white Americans, too, faced considerable violence. For instance, in March 1965, Viola Luizzo, a white housewife from Detroit, was shot and killed by a Klansman in a passing car as she drove civil rights volunteers to voting registration drives in Alabama.

The SCLC reached its organizational highpoint with the August 1963 March on Washington for Jobs and Freedom. The march benefited from a broad base of support, including the AFL-CIO, the National Council of Churches, and the National Conference of Catholics for Interracial Justice. The appeal of King and the persuasiveness of the SCLC urged Americans to overcome their racial fears and insecurities; nonviolent protest spoke to the peaceful, political goal of full inclusion and equal rights for African Americans. With A. Philip Randolph and Bayard Rustin as the primary organizers, the March on Washington drew between 200,000 and 250,000 participants to Washington, D.C., on August 28, 1963. From its success, the SCLC was catapulted to the position as the primary civil rights organization. It brought moral pressure on President John F. Kennedy, and then President Lyndon B. Johnson to sign the Civil Rights Act of 1964 and Voting Rights Act of 1965.

Widespread and deeply rooted poverty in the 1960s, coupled with intransigent resistance to civil rights activism, challenged the SCLC to take on poverty as its next concern. The SCLC also recognized the opportunity to move beyond the notion of Jim Crow as a Southern issue. Job discrimination, unequal school funding, restrictive housing covenants, and police brutality had long troubled race relations in Northern cities and states. In 1966, at the invitation of the Chicago Freedom Movement, the SCLC set up an office in Chicago for the purpose of challenging the city to reform its housing practices. Mayor Richard Daley and the Chicago Police Department, aware of the SCLC's strategy of provoking confrontation that risked embarrassing national exposure, pledged their protection of marchers in peaceful demonstrations within the city's limit. The organization held fast to its principles of nonviolence, but its demonstrations were met with vitriolic riots in the all-white suburbs of Chicago. The Chicago campaign ended with a summit agreement between Daley and civil rights organizations to address the issue of housing segregation. Yet, failing to achieve a Birmingham-style reversal of segregation, the SCLC retreated to reexamine its tactics.

After the disappointment in Chicago, the SCLC regrouped and began planning another high-profile march, the Poor People's Campaign. Like the goals of the 1963 March on Washington, the Poor People's Campaign's guiding mission was to create awareness of poverty and its debilitating effects on Americans across the country. In 1967, the SCLC announced its plan to bring thousands of poor, unemployed, and working Americans to Washington, D.C., to demand federal programs promoting antipoverty and economic security. As the final preparations for the Poor People's Campaign were well under way, by the beginning of spring 1968, King embarked on a new direction in Memphis. Joined by Jesse Jackson and Ralph Abernathy in early April 1968, King lent the SCLC's support of the striking sanitation workers. The striking workers sought higher wages and better working conditions, demands that exemplified the new path of the SCLC. King's assassination on April 4, 1968, profoundly wounded the organization. In the short term, public sympathy and political sensitivity afforded to the SCLC immense support for the Poor People's Campaign. In the long term, the loss of a charismatic leader hurled the SCLC into a prolonged state of confusion. After six weeks of daily protest marches and continuous calls for an Economic Bill of Rights, the police dismantled "Resurrection City," the Poor People's Campaign's tent city, and evicted its 2,000 residents. The country turned its attention away from the civil rights struggle, instead focusing on the Vietnam War. The SCLC never regained its pre-1968 stature.

Without tangible goals, in the 1970s the organization drifted. In late 1971, Jesse Jackson left the organization after a falling out with Ralph Abernathy, King's successor as president. Jackson founded Operation PUSH (People United to Save Humanity), developed a high profile for his fiery rhetoric and quickly organized protest marches. Furthermore, the SCLC could no longer attract or inspire student activists. The forceful and aggressive philosophies of Malcolm X and the Black Power movement drew a younger, more militant generation of leaders away from the principles of nonviolence. A divisive battle between older religious leaders and Vietnam-era student protesters brought the SCLC to the brink of collapse in the mid-1970s. Abernathy resigned as president, and Joseph Lowery, a founding member, replaced him in 1977.

Currently, the SCLC, led by Charles Steele, maintains its commitment to voting rights, conflict resolution, and social justice. Though the organization possesses less political and religious clout in its current incarnation, the SCLC retains its place of authority in the history of the civil rights movement.

NIKKI BROWN

See also
Civil Rights Movement; King, Martin Luther, Jr.

Further Reading:
Branch, Taylor. *Parting the Waters: America During the King Years, 1954–1963.* New York: Simon and Schuster, 1988.
Branch, Taylor. *At Canaan's Edge: America During the King Years, 1965–1968.* New York: Simon and Schuster, 2006.
Fairclough, Adam. *To Redeem the Soul of America: The Southern Christian Leadership Conference and Martin Luther King, Jr.* Athens: University of Georgia Press, 1987.
Garrow, David. *Bearing the Cross: Martin Luther King and the Southern Christian Leadership Conference.* New York: Vintage, 1986.
Peake, Thomas. *Keeping the Dream Alive: A History of the Southern Christian Leadership Conference from King to the 1980s.* New York: Peter Lang, 1987.

Southern Poverty Law Center (SPLC)

The Southern Poverty Law Center (SPLC) is a nonprofit civil rights organization based in Montgomery, Alabama, the birthplace of the civil rights movement. The SPLC was founded in 1971 to combat hatred and bigotry as well as to work on behalf of the most vulnerable members of society to ensure civil liberties and justice for all.

In the late 1960s, despite newly formed civil rights legislation, blacks were still denied housing, employment, and educational opportunities, especially in the South. Morris Dee, an Alabama lawyer and businessman, recognized that few members of the poor had access to legal services to fight these injustices, and he decided to sell his successful publishing business to start a civil rights law practice for the disenfranchised, which ultimately led to the founding of the SPLC. Dee and Joe Levin, another Montgomery lawyer, started their law firm by taking pro bono cases in which victory resulted in desegregation and policy reform. In 1971, Dee and Levin formally incorporated the SPLC, named activist Julian Bond the first president, and began seeking support for their work nationwide. Since its founding, the SPLC has demolished some of the nation's most dangerous hate groups; broken

Southern Poverty Law Center in Action
One organizational success cited by the Southern Poverty Law Center is the plea agreement that was reached in 2009 with five of the black teenagers of the Jena Six initially charged with attempted murder during a fight involving a white student. Specifically, the SPLC represented Jesse Ray "Jody" Beard and helped coordinate the overall defense strategy, which resulted in the five youths pleading no contest to misdemeanor simple battery charges and avoiding jail time. SPLC board member Alan Howard not only represented Beard in a civil suit stemming from the Jena Six criminal case; he also became his legal guardian, giving Beard the opportunity to leave Jena, Louisiana, and pursue his education.

barriers to equality for blacks, women, children, and the disabled; protected immigrant workers from abuse; and helped to dismantle racism. To increase social equality, the SPLC currently focuses its resources in five areas: (1) children at risk; (2) hate and extremism; (3) immigrant justice; (4) lesbian, gay, bisexual, and transgendered (LGBT) rights; and (5) teaching tolerance.

In order to help children at risk, the SPLC places an emphasis on American youth who are pushed out of school and into the juvenile justice system, which is plagued by abuse, neglect, and overcrowding. It is the belief of the SPLC that many of these children are in their current situation because of the failing foster and mental health systems in the United States and thus warrant the SPLC's attention. Black and Latino children and adolescents are disproportionately affected by the juvenile justice system since youth of color are imprisoned at almost three times the rate of their white counterparts in the United States. The SPLC seeks to reform the juvenile justice system by using legal action, community education and mobilization, and media and legislative advocacy to protect imprisoned children and teens and simultaneously provide alternatives from incarceration, such as educational and community-based programs, to prevent school discipline practices from pushing youth out of school.

Aside from helping children at risk, the SPLC monitors hate groups throughout the United States and exposes their

...UNTIL JUSTICE ROLLS DOWN LIKE WATERS AND RIGHTEOUSNESS LIKE A MIGHTY STREAM
MARTIN LUTHER KING JR.

Family members of fallen civil rights victims view the Civil Rights Memorial at the Southern Poverty Law Center during a private family viewing, November 5, 1989, in Montgomery, Alabama. The memorial features running water over the black granite surfaces. The names of forty victims are inscribed in the round table at front. (AP Photo/Dave Martin)

activities to law enforcement, the media, and the public, as well as sues groups who have committed murder and other violent acts. The SPLC has several publications that are dedicated to revealing hate group activity, including their Hatewatch blog, Hate Map, and *Intelligence Report*, an award-winning magazine. This work is especially important because since the year 2000, the SPLC has estimated that the number of hate groups in the United States has increased by 69 percent and is expected to continue to grow as the American population becomes more and more diverse.

Not only does the SPLC seek to monitor hate and extremist groups, but it also aims to protect migrant workers who are often exploited and are increasingly targeted for hate crimes. Since 2004, the SPLC has distributed nearly $2 million in settlement money to immigrant workers who have been denied basic workplace protections. The SPLC also works to expose civil rights violations, educate the public

and media, and encourage government action concerning the mistreatment of immigrants.

Along with hate crimes against immigrants, hate crimes against the LGBT community have increased in recent years. The SPLC is specifically focusing its efforts in the Southeast region of the United States where there exist relatively few advocacy organizations for the LGBT population. The SPLC works to ensure safe schooling for LGBT youth, fair treatment for LGBT children and adolescents in juvenile and foster care facilities and LGBT seniors in nursing homes and other facilities, and parenting rights of LGBT adults.

Lastly, the SPLC fosters a Teaching Tolerance program, which is one of the nation's leading providers of antibias educational resources. The program is intended to promote school environments where equality and justice are the overarching norms, preparing a new generation for an increasingly diverse world. Some of the initiatives of Teaching

Tolerance include an award-winning magazine, multimedia teaching kits, online curricula, professional development resources, and award-winning documentary films.

Since its inception, the SPLC has combated hatred and bigotry and worked on behalf of the most vulnerable members of society to ensure civil liberties. Through its focus on children at risk, hate and extremism, immigrant justice, LGBT rights, and education, the Southern Poverty Law Center continues its success in fighting hate, teaching tolerance, and seeking justice.

ADRIENNE N. MILNER

See also

Hate Crimes in America; Hate Groups in America; Jena Six; Migrant Workers

Further Reading:

Southern Poverty Law Center. *Hate Map*. http://www.splcenter .org/get-informed/hate-map.
Southern Poverty Law Center. *'Jena Six' Teen Gets Second Chance, a New Start with SPLC Board Member*. http://www.splcenter .org/get-informed/news/jena-six-teen-gets-second-chance-a -new-start-with-splc-board-member.
Southern Poverty Law Center. *What We Do*. http://www.splcenter .org/what-we-do.
Southern Poverty Law Center. *Who We Are*. http://www.splcenter .org/who-we-are.

Southern Tenant Farmers' Union (STFU)

The Southern Tenant Farmers' Union (STFU) was a biracial labor union founded in Tyronza, Arkansas, in 1934. By 1938, the organization claimed 35,000 members, the majority of whom resided in eastern Arkansas. The STFU sought to organize the South's poorest and most vulnerable agricultural workers and managed to attract a great deal of publicity to the plight of the impoverished sharecropper. However, they were fundamentally unable to extract major concessions from Southern landowners or to halt the mechanization of agriculture, which made the South less dependent on the efforts of individual laborers.

Despite the fact that the land they farmed contained some of the richest cotton-producing soil in the United States, Arkansas tenant farmers and sharecroppers were hard pressed to eke out more than a subsistence livelihood each year.

Planters frequently kept these agricultural workers in financial subservience through unscrupulous record keeping and outright intimidation as well as by charging exorbitant interest rates on the annual loans necessary to keep the croppers afloat in a cash-poor economy.

The financial situation of this class of agricultural laborers, precarious in the best of times, only worsened with the beginning of the Great Depression. However, even before the rumblings on Wall Street impacted life in the cotton fields, Arkansas was hit with a series of natural disasters, beginning with the Mississippi River flood of 1927, followed by a series of tornadoes in the spring of 1929, and the drought of 1930–1931. These natural disasters, coupled with the chaos in the nation's financial sector, left the agricultural economy in turmoil.

In May 1933, Congress passed the Agricultural Adjustment Act, which was designed to address the agricultural crisis through an elaborate scheme of crop reduction and government subsidies. In order to reduce agricultural surpluses and thereby increase prices, the federal government paid landowners to take a portion of their acreage out of production. In addition, the government gave planters "parity payments" to subsidize the market price of cotton. In theory, owners were to spread acreage reductions across their plantations, thereby reducing each tenant's plot slightly. Planters were also supposed to share federal monies with their sharecroppers. However, more often than not, landowners neglected to equitably distribute this New Deal bounty. Furthermore, many chose to concentrate crop reductions, to eliminate some plots altogether, and then to evict the unneeded laborers.

Neither the federal government nor the Agricultural Adjustment Administration officials were willing to intervene in the planter/tenant relationship on behalf of the dispossessed croppers. Abandoned by the federal government and at the mercy of the local landowners, a group of Arkansas tenant farmers gathered in Tyronza, Arkansas, to establish the STFU. Inspired by a recent visit of socialist leader Norman Thomas, and under the leadership of H. L. Mitchell and Clay East—white, local businessmen and members of the Socialist Party—a group of disgruntled sharecroppers met at a schoolhouse on a large plantation to discuss the possibility of unionization and collective bargaining with local planters. After quickly agreeing upon the premise of the union, the first item on the agenda was to determine whether two separate segregated unions should be formed or one integrated one.

According to Mitchell, the dilemma was settled on the basis of two eloquent speeches favoring biracial class solidarity. Burt Williams, a white cropper, favored integration saying, "You know my pappy rode with the KKK, we drove the Republican officeholders out of Crittendon County some forty years ago. That time has passed, and we have to forget all that stuff." Ike Shaw, an African American who had been involved in an attempt to unionize that turned into race-based massacre in Elaine, Arkansas, in 1919, concurred, saying, "As long as we stand together black and white . . . nothing can tear [the union] down."

Shaw was right to the extent that the union was tenacious. Despite planter reprisals, STFU members continued to meet and to agitate for wage increases for day laborers and an equitable distribution of New Deal funds throughout the 1930s. The STFU managed to win some small wage increases after a cotton picker's strike in 1935. However, a similar strike in 1936 met with disastrous results when Gov. Junius Marion Futrell called out the National Guard, which forced the strikers to disperse at gunpoint.

Ultimately, the STFU did very little to directly ameliorate the economic conditions of the state's croppers. Their efforts were met with violent reprisals by the local population of landowners and their allies. However, the STFU did manage to bring the plight of the sharecropper to the attention of the national media. For example, on June 16, 1936, a group of white land owners beat two white STFU supporters, social worker Willie Sue Blagden and Presbyterian minister Claude Williams. The sensational incident of the whipping of a Southern white woman sparked something of a media frenzy, and pictures of Blagden's bruised thighs were published from coast to coast. Due in large part to negative publicity, Governor Futrell appointed a commission to study the problems inherent in farm tenancy, and violent intimidation began to abate.

However, the STFU was plagued by internal as well as external problems. Although the leadership of the organization was integrated, many locals remained segregated, and racial tensions flared from time to time. In addition, arguments arose over whether or not the union should join the Congress of Industrial Organizations (CIO), and rumors abounded about alleged communist infiltration in the STFU. These disputes led many of the group's most ardent followers to abandon the organization.

Although both the federal and the state governments were eventually pressured into conducting investigations of farm tenancy in Arkansas, these studies did not result in tangible reforms of the kind envisioned by the STFU. AAA monies allowed planters to begin to mechanize cotton production and the organization of agricultural laborers in Arkansas quickly became a moot point. It was not until 1972 that Arkansas cotton was 100 percent machine harvested; however, the need for farm workers steadily decreased after 1940 and former sharecroppers began leaving the state in large numbers. The STFU never formally disbanded, but in 1944 Mitchell migrated westward to organize migrant laborers in California and to found the organization that was to succeed the STFU, the National Farm Labor Union.

The STFU's most enduring legacy was that it modeled a nearly unprecedented degree of interracial cooperation which was not to be seen on as grand a scale again until the advent of the modern civil rights movement of the 1950s and 1960s.

JENNIFER JENSEN WALLACH

See also

Ku Klux Klan (KKK)

Further Reading:

Conrad, David Eugene. *The Forgotten Farmers: The Story of Sharecroppers in the New Deal.* Westport, CT: Greenwood Press, 1965.

Kirby, Jack Temple. *Rural Worlds Lost: The American South, 1920–1960.* Baton Rouge: Louisiana State University Press, 1987.

Wolters, Raymond. *Negroes and the Great Depression.* Westport, CT: Greenwood Press, 1970.

Spanish-American War

The United States declared war on Spain on April 25, 1898, after the sinking of the battleship *Maine* in the Havana Harbor. On the surface, it seemed that the war was fought to free Cuba, Puerto Rico, the Philippine Islands, and other islands (including Guam) from Spanish control, but an underlying

The battleship *Maine* entering Havana Harbor. (Library of Congress)

motive for the United States entering the war was U.S. imperialist expansion. The United States won the war easily within a short period of time with a few thousand American lives sacrificed. Under the terms of the Treaty of Paris, the United States acquired Puerto Rico and Guam as its colonies from Spain and was allowed to occupy Manila, while Cuba became independent.

The Spanish Empire was once a great empire of the world. Spain was the first European nation to explore and claim westward territory across the Atlantic Ocean. In its prime, the empire extended from Virginia on the eastern coast of the United States south to Tierra del Fuego at the tip of South America and westward to California and Alaska. It also included the Philippines and other islands across the Pacific. By 1825, Spain had lost most of its colonies, with only Puerto Rico, Cuba, the Philippines, and a few Pacific islands left.

The United States' interest in the war began long before the war actually started. In 1884, the price of sugar began to drop dramatically in Cuba, and the country's "sugar

nobility" began to lose the major role it had had in the island's economy and society. The United States took this opportunity to enter the Cuban sugar market. U.S. capital, machinery, and technicians helped Cuban sugar mills to remain competitive with European beet sugar. By 1894, almost 90 percent of Cuba's export went to the United States, and 38 percent of Cuba's imports came from the United States. The United States had more than $50 million invested in Cuba, and annual trade was worth twice as much as it had been 10 years earlier.

In 1895, the Cuban patriot Jose Martí began the Cuban fight for freedom that had been lost during the Ten Years' War (1868–1878), but Spain had a much greater number of troops than the Cubans. Cuban generals were forced to use guerilla warfare against the Spanish in hopes of exhausting their troops. Spain sent General Valeriano Weyler to pacify Cuba, but he began implementing a policy of reconcentration that moved the civilian population into central locations guarded by Spanish troops to deny the guerillas support in the countryside. President William McKinley, inaugurated on March 4, 1897, was anxious to become involved in the war. Two factors determined McKinley's decision to declare war. First, a letter written by Spanish foreign minister Enrique Dupuy de Lóme was published in the *New York Journal* criticizing McKinley. The second factor was the sinking of the U.S.S. *Maine* on February 15, 1898. After investigation by the U.S. Naval Court of Inquiry, it was found that a Spanish mine had blown up the ship. The Spanish government did everything to stop the war, yet less than one month after the investigation, the United States unjustifiably declared war. Martí, who had lived for many years in New York as an exile, knew about North American expansionism and that the United States always had its eye on Cuba. He feared that if the Cubans lost their fight for independence, it would lead to U.S. intervention and, ultimately, annexation of Cuba. He even believed that there was an "iniquitous plan to put pressure on the island and drive it to war [so] as to fabricate a pretext to intervene in its affairs and with the credit earned as guarantor and mediator keep it as its own."

After the declaration of war, the United States passed the Teller Amendment to emphasize that it had no intention of annexing Cuba. However, McKinley made it clear to Spain that his motive was not only to achieve independence for Cuba but the annexation of Puerto Rico and a Pacific island as well. The United States actually began fighting the war in Cuba when the marines captured Guantánamo Bay and 17,000 officers landed at Daquirí and Siboney, where Cuban revolutionaries joined them. U.S. troops attacked the San Juan Heights on July 1, 1898. Troops, including the African American 9th and 10th Cavalries and the 1st U.S. Volunteer Cavalry, commanded by Lt. Col. Theodore Roosevelt, moved up Kettle Hill while other forces led by Brig. Gen. Jacob Kent moved up San Juan Hill and pushed the Spanish forces inland, causing 1,700 deaths. On July 16, the Spanish surrendered their 23,500 soldiers around the city.

The Treaty of Paris was signed on December 10, 1898. Its contents included the independence of Cuba, transfer of Puerto Rico and Guam to the United States, and the transfer of the Philippines in return for $25 million to pay for Spanish property on the islands. To colonize the Philippines, the United States later fought a long and brutal war with the Philippines, which resulted in the killing of more than 200,000 Filipinos, mostly civilians. Although Cuba was granted independence, the Platt Amendment of 1902 limited its autonomy and created a dependent relationship with the United States. Some historians believe that the period 1895–1898 was only a transition period from Spanish Imperialism to American Imperialism. The Roosevelt Corollary of 1904 expanded on the idea of Manifest Destiny, which was the ideology claiming a God-given right to U.S. expansion across the western frontier.

TIFFANY VÉLEZ

See also
Mexican-American War

Further Reading:
Hernandez, Jose M. "Cuba Situation in 1898." Part 2. http://www.cubaheritage.com/ articles.asp?cID=1&sID=9&ssID=6&offset=133.

"The Spanish American War: A Gift from the Gods." 2000. http://www.smplanet. com/imperialism/gift.html.

Trask, David. "The World of 1898: The Spanish-American War." 2002. http://www.loc. gov/rr/hispanic/1898/trask.html.

Spatial Mismatch Theory

Spatial mismatch theory describes the economic situation of low-income, low-skilled racial and ethnic minorities who reside in a geographic location in which their skills do not match the requisites for employment. Due to the history of race relations in the United States, racial and ethnic minorities disproportionately work in low-wage, low-skill labor positions. Changes in the urban demographics and the economy have caused geographic repositioning of jobs and housing discrimination has served to further isolate these disadvantaged racial minorities from sources of eligible employment.

At the most fundamental level, a spatial mismatch occurs when there is a geographic separation of residential areas and places of employment/industry. In the context of racial inequality, this theory has mainly been used to describe how housing discrimination leads to racial inequalities in work force participation. The spatial mismatch hypothesis proposes that low-income racial minorities reside and are more heavily concentrated in spatial regions (typically urban) that are physically distant from sources of employment as a result of housing market discrimination.

John Kain (1968) is cited as the scholar who first developed the spatial mismatch hypothesis. Kain's research was seminal in explaining the marginal situation of poor, inner-city minorities. According to Kain, the spatial mismatch is a result of racial discrimination in the housing market. Blacks are restricted to housing areas in both the inner city and in the surrounding suburbs that happen to be geographically distant from thriving industry and sources of employment. This latter part is essential to the spatial mismatch hypothesis. Kain states, "The issue, as far as the spatial mismatch hypothesis is concerned, is not whether black households are segregated, but whether housing market discrimination confines them to a narrow and spatially concentrated segment of the metropolitan-area housing market" (1968: 380). Housing discrimination is a central component of the spatial mismatch hypothesis.

Kain's research was later advanced and popularized by sociologist William Julius Wilson (1996; 2009). Wilson describes the rise in the black underclass, or the perpetually poor, and asserts that spatial mismatch has also coincided with what can be considered a *skills mismatch* in postindustrial times. By the time African Americans, many of whom migrated north, were permitted to equally participate in the industrial labor force (circa 1970) there was a drastic decline in the manufacturing industry in the inner city and a sharp rise in service sector occupations in the suburbs. Wilson described the urban inner city as hosting jobs for which black residents were unqualified. The low-skill, low-wage occupations had all transformed and/or relocated. The phenomena of globalization, deindustrialization, and suburbanization left the urban inner city devoid of industry, and institutional forms of discrimination left black residents geographically isolated and ill-equipped to compete in a postindustrial workforce.

Spatial mismatch occurs in the United States and in other countries globally. Although several studies have documented the theory's validity, the policy recommendations that stem from the hypothesis are largely unsettled, mostly due to the lack of public support. However, some of these policy suggestions include: (1) providing incentives for industry to return to the low-income neighborhoods or adjacent areas, (2) opening closed-housing markets and

The Role of Technology

We can imagine how today's high-tech service sector further exacerbates this mismatch as socially marginalized racial and ethnic groups struggle to catch up to the demands of the time. First, the more complex technology used in industry often requires extensive and specialized training, which is often too expensive or too academically rigorous for undereducated and low-income minorities. Second, the companies with profit motives will frequently choose a business site in suburban industrial parks. These suburban locations are geographically and racially distant from the low-income racial and ethnic groups from the inner city. Lastly, if the "new frontier" of employment is not visible to the inner-city residents, there is less likelihood that the new jobs will be known to or desired by these urban individuals.

encouraging people of color to relocate, and (3) improving transportation between the inner city and the new suburban job locations.

Incentivizing the return of industry to a destitute area is a lofty goal, but in the last few years "urban renewal" projects have been initiated in many metropolitan areas such as Chicago, Detroit, and Washington, D.C. The second recommendation is arguably less viable. We have seen some experimentation with relocating marginalized individuals, such as Moving to Opportunity. However, these programs are often criticized for ignoring the social-psychological maladjustment that comes from uprooting families. Another integral component to understanding spatial mismatch theory is to understand the role of transportation. Workers can reside a far distance away from their places of employment if they have reliable transportation and the financial means. In this situation, the distance of the place of employment does not have a severe effect on one's earning potential or life chances. For both urban and rural residents, public transportation, to the industry-ridden suburbs for example, is inefficient or simply inexistent.

As urban development and restructuring continues, we will all have the opportunity to see which of these policy recommendations comes into fruition and which one is most effective at addressing inequality. For Kain, opening housing markets is the key to ending the spatial mismatch. That is, allowing racial minorities to live closer to job opportunities and thriving industry. For Wilson, the *skills* mismatch remains a formidable barrier to ending joblessness. The most effective policy will be one that addresses both of these concerns.

ALAN VINCENT GRIGSBY AND RASHA ALY

See also
Economic Opportunity Act of 1964

Further Reading:
Covington, Kenya. "Spatial Mismatch of the Poor: An Explanation of Recent Declines in Job Isolation." *Journal of Urban Affairs* 31, no. 5 (2009): 559–87.

Houston, Donald. "Employability, Skills Mismatch and Spatial Mismatch in Metropolitan Labour Markets." *Urban Studies* 42, no. 2 (2005): 221–43.

Kain, John. "Housing Segregation, Negro Employment, and Metropolitan Decentralization." *Quarterly Journal of Economics* 82, no. 2 (1968): 175–97.

Kain, John. "Spatial Mismatch Hypothesis: Three Decades Later." *Housing Policy Debate* 3, no. 2 (1992): 371–92.

Kain, John. "A Pioneer's Perspective on the Spatial Mismatch Literature." *Urban Studies* 41, no. 1 (2004): 7–32.

Wilson, William Julius. *When Work Disappears: The World of the New Urban Poor.* New York: Knopf, 1996.

Wilson, William Julius. *More Than Just Race: Being Black and Poor in the Inner City.* New York: W. W. Norton, 2009.

Split-Labor Market Theory

Historically, in the United States labor markets have been split along racial lines. A *split-labor market* refers to a division in the workforce based on price of labor and social group membership that leads to conflicts among groups of laborers. This is the theory of ethnic antagonism and the split-labor market first presented by Edna Bonacich (1972). Bonacich's main thesis suggests that when a workforce is split along racial lines it leads to ethnic antagonism, or conflict, between the two groups of workers. Central to the split-labor market theory is the racialized price of labor (race as a determinant), as well as the role of the employer vis-à-vis the ranking and organization of the labor groups.

A labor market that is split along ethnic or racial lines is characterized by disparate costs of labor being ascribed to workers based on their ascribed (involuntary) group affiliation. That is, the price of human capital is based on race, gender, age, etc. There are many factors that can affect the disparity in the cost of labor. However, it is important to note that the price of labor is more influenced by structural/sociopolitical forces than interpersonal discrimination. In other words, the lower wages paid to minorities are not typically the result of an employer's prejudice.

The split-labor market hypothesis specifies three main groups of actors in the labor market relationship, each unique in its goals. The first group is the owner or capitalist whose main motive is to gain profit. Then there is the high-wage laborer who is mainly concerned with securing more income. Finally, there is the low-wage labor group whose interest lies mainly in gaining and securing employment. Although these two labor group divisions can be found within one single occupation, the group conflict often leads employers to discriminate against the lower-wage group, resulting in a caste-like arrangement in which low-wage laborers are relegated to lower occupations separate from the high-wage workers.

Historically in the United States, the labor markets have been split along racial (typically black and white) lines. In this workforce organization, whites occupied the high-wage laborer position. African Americans were relegated to the low-wage positions. Capitalists, who are solely interested in gaining profit, would often use black workers as strike breakers when the newly sanctioned union-members demanded higher wages and better treatment. The high-wage labor group is still in a relative position of privilege even in the face of wage undercutting. Native-born and unionized workers have historically had access to political outlets and are able to advocate for higher wages and collectively pressure employers in ways that nonunionized workers cannot. This collective pressure can cause employers to discriminate against black workers despite it being against the employers' best interests or profit motive.

In his pivotal book *The Declining Significance of Race*, sociologist William Julius Wilson also discusses the split-labor market. In his conception, the split-labor market characterized the workforce of the "industrial era," which describes the height of the manufacturing economy in America.

During the industrial era, African Americans were used as a cheap labor force in order for employers to avoid paying rising wages to the white, working-class union members. However, according to Wilson, the workforce in postindustrial times is no longer split along racial/ethnic lines. Wilson suggests that the integration of the labor force during the end of the industrial era, along with other structural phenomena of the time, led to a new form of inequality. According to Wilson, this new disparity is where socioeconomic class (a variable of cultural competency, education, and employability or skill level) supplants race as the most reliable predictor of workforce participation.

There are several contemporary U.S. and global examples of split-labor markets. In the United States, it has been argued that racial and ethnic migrant workers occupy the low-wage labor position. Immigrant workers are even more exploitable because they lack some of the basic rights granted to native-born citizens. It is also possible to think of the global economy as including a global workforce. Many U.S. manufacturing jobs have been outsourced to developing nations which have ample supplies of low-wage workers with little-to-no political power. However, the spatial distance between the low-wage and high-wage workers in the global economy may prevent some of the antagonism present in a split-labor market where both groups of laborers work alongside one another.

ALAN VINCENT GRIGSBY

See also
Domestic Work; "Don't Buy Where You Can't Work" Campaign; Fair Employment Practices Commission (FEPC); Migrant Workers

Further Reading:
Auerhahn, Kathleen. "The Split Labor Market and the Origins of Antidrug Legislation." *Law and Social Inquiry* 24, no. 2 (1999): 411–40.
Bonacich, Edna. "A Theory of Ethnic Antagonism: The Split Labor Market." *American Sociological Review* 37, no. 5 (1972): 547–59.
Bonacich, Edna. "Advanced Capitalism and Black/White Race Relations in the United States: A Split Labor Market Interpretation." *American Sociological Review* 41, no. 1 (1976): 34–51.
Wilson, William Julius. *The Declining Significance of Race: Blacks and Changing American Institutions.* Chicago: University of Chicago Press, 1980.

Sports and Racism

The notion that blacks and whites are different athletes has existed for more than 100 years. Many coaches and athletes believe blacks are reactors and whites are thinkers. Thus, from a young age athletes are "stacked" into positions according to racial stereotypes. Whites are slotted into thinking positions like quarterback and pitchers, while coaches stack black players into reactive positions like running back, receiver, and centerfielder, in order to take advantage of the black athlete's natural abilities. Most white basketball players are stereotyped as cerebral and crafty with great outside shots, a nod to their supposed intellectual edge over their athletic black counterparts who can jump really high. Unfortunately, many people believe these stereotypes are supported by scientific data. When science cannot explain racial athlete differences, some people turn to the history of slavery. These stereotypes have created a barrier for white and black athletes.

Since the 1880s when black athletes started to participate in professional sports, Americans have been fixated on the differences between white and black athletic bodies. In boxing, writers believed that blacks had better naturally gifted bodies, but they argued blacks lacked the necessary stamina, heart, intellect, and desire to defeat the best white fighters. In 1889, for example, while discussing the potential battle between the black boxer Peter Jackson and the white heavyweight champion John L. Sullivan, a writer for the *Chicago Tribune* observed in his article "Black Men in the Ring," that: "The question has often been asked: Has the negro the grit and the staying qualities of the white pugilists? Can he stand the punishment and face the music as well and is he equal in skill?" Unfortunately, Jackson did not get to prove the racial query wrong, because Sullivan refused to battle black fighters. A black heavyweight did not get an opportunity to prove racial naysayers wrong until Jack Johnson defeated Tommy Burns in 1908. However, his victory did not dispel any racial theories about athletes.

Until the 1930s, the notion of racial athletic differences had been mere speculation among writers, fans, and athletes, but in 1936 curiosity turned into scientific research. This new scientific quest happened because Jesse Owens won four gold medals at the 1936 Berlin Olympics hosted by Adolf Hitler's Germany. For Hitler the Olympics was a test of racial

At the 1968 Summer Olympic Games in Mexico City, runners Tommie Smith and John Carlos outraged the U.S. Olympic Committee by giving a Black Power salute during the medal ceremony. (AP/Wide World Photos)

superiority. According to sports historian David Wiggin's book *Glory Bound*, after Owens's dominating performance, writers and track coaches openly speculated that blacks had different calf muscles and longer limbs that helped them run faster. Others reasoned that sprinting events perfectly suited blacks' temperament, because sprinting required little attention and stamina. Wiggins further explains that scientists also tried to explain why black athletes dominated their white counterparts. African American doctor W. Montague Cobb's study revealed that no anatomical differences existed between black athletes and white athletes, however. Instead, Cobb argued that "training and incentive" explained black dominance. Despite this important revelation, most scientists continued to argue that the different racial body type gave blacks an advantage.

After the post–World War II integration of sports the debates about racial athletic difference became more intense because Americans saw more black athletes competing against and dominating white athletes. For many, slavery became the root cause of racial athletic differences. College basketball coach Nolan Richardson, who coached the Arkansas Razorbacks to an NCAA Championship in 1994, believed that the Middle Passage—the disgusting process of moving black bodies across the Atlantic to be sold into slavery—created a superior black athlete. Richardson argued that the process created a fit and hardy race in the offspring of those that survived. Jimmy "The Greek" Snyder, a white host for the *NFL Today* in the 1980s, once controversially explained black athletic superiority by suggesting "the slave owner would breed his big black with his big woman so that he could have a big black kid." CBS fired him for his remarks.

The idea that differences exist between black and white athletes has led to a history of stacking in a number of sports. *Stacking* is the selective process of coaches assigning certain positions to athletes based on race. Coaches push black athletes into positions that require natural reactive instincts, and coaches put whites into "thinking positions." On the baseball diamond this has meant a lack of black catchers and pitchers, the two positions that supposedly require the most thinking, but an overrepresentation of black outfielders. On the gridiron, coaches select blacks as running backs, wide receivers, defensive ends, outside linebackers, and defensive backs. Whites are positioned at thinking positions like quarterback, center, kicker, and occasionally as safety and middle linebacker.

The most controversial of all positions in sports is the quarterback. For years coaches, scouts, and general managers have worried that black quarterbacks do not have the mental capacity to make good throwing decisions in the National Football League (NFL). Many blacks who played and started at quarterback in college have been asked to switch positions. Some who are not willing to switch positions go undrafted. Stacking does not exclude black quarterbacks from playing in the NFL or being high draft picks. However, teams that select blacks to lead their franchise are deemed to have made a "risky" decision. This is best exhibited in the short, but so far outstanding, career of the Carolina Panthers' Cam Newton. Despite winning the Heisman Trophy for the 2010 college season, and winning the National

Championship, many experts doubted he could succeed in the NFL. They worried about his ability to understand an NFL offense, and these pundits argued he was not worthy of a top draft pick. These doubts sounded like racism to Newton's mentor Warren Moon. Moon, the first black quarterback nominated to the NFL Hall of Fame, knew all too well about the problems of racial stacking. Even though he starred at Washington State University, Moon had to play quarterback in Canada for a number of years before an NFL team signed him. Before the 2011 NFL draft, Moon told a *USA Today* reporter "[Newton is] being held to different standards from white quarterbacks. . . . It's racism, some of it." Thankfully for Newton, the Carolina Panthers selected him first in the 2011 draft. Newton had the best rookie season of any quarterback in the history of the NFL.

The long history of racial stacking and stereotypes created self-doubt in many white athletes' minds, and they redirected themselves to other sports, or other positions that lack black athletes. In their 1997 controversial article "What Ever Happened to the White Athlete?" *Sports Illustrated* showed that 34 percent of white athletes believe that "African American players have become so dominant in sports like football and basketball that many white athletes feel they cannot compete at the same level." The piece also noted that whites "are more and more often choosing sports in which they feel they can still compete . . . thereby perpetuating a cycle. White athletes, outplayed or simply intimidated, stop playing basketball or football." According to *New York Times* sportswriter William Rhoden, racial self-doubt has had a tremendous impact on the defensive back position. In a 2011 article "Stereotypes Create Prototypes," Rhoden suggested that the lack of white defensive backs "is less about sports and more about having dreams, seeing possibility and having the courage to explore one's discomfort zone." In other words, a person should not let their race limit their potential.

Some white athletes have been known to use racial stereotypes to their advantage. These white athletes know that their black counterparts have stereotyped them as unathletic, and white athletes exploit their opponent's mental block. For example, during the 2011 NFL season the Green Bay Packers star quarterback Aaron Rodgers mentioned to *New York Times* sports columnist Pat Borzi that teams overlooked his white receiver Jordy Nelson. The article "Sneaking Up on Defenses" quoted Rodgers as saying, "When you see Jordy

out there you think, oh well, he's a white wide receiver. He won't be very athletic. But Jordy sort of breaks all those stereotypes. I'm not sure why he keeps sneaking up on guys." Teammate Jermichael Finley added "that's why you see him getting plays like that, because guys look down on him." Nelson was one of the league leaders in reception average.

The long history of race and racism has had a tremendous impact on American sports. Whereas whites are thought of as thinkers, blacks are seen as pure athletes. Because of these stereotypes, coaches and players have stacked positions based on race. Stacking has limited the opportunities blacks have had in sports, but has also led to self-doubt amongst white athletes who switch positions or sports. However, while racial stereotypes limit athletes, stereotypes are not insurmountable barriers.

Louis Moore

See also

Basketball; Football; Racism and Athletic Coaching; Sports in the Jim Crow Era; Sports Mascots

Further Reading:

Lacy, Michael G., and Ken A. Ono. *Critical Rhetorics of Race.* New York: New York University Press, 2011.

Lamb, Chris. *Conspiracy of Silence: Sportswriters and the Long Campaign to Desegregate Baseball.* Lincoln: University of Nebraska, 2012.

Rosen, David C., and Joel Nathan Rosen. *Fame to Infamy: Race, Sport, and the Fall from Grace.* Jackson: University Press of Mississippi, 2010.

Salamone, Frank A. *The Native American Identity in Sports: Creating and Preserving a Culture.* Lanham, MD: Scarecrow Press, 2013.

Thomas, Damion L. *Globetrotting: African American Athletes and Cold War Politics.* Urbana: University of Illinois Press, 2012.

Sports in the Jim Crow Era

Sports provided a key terrain for contesting the boundaries imposed by Jim Crow segregation. Although whites in the South and North consistently tried to deny African Americans the right to participate in a variety of amateur and professional sports activities, black people fought for their rights on playing fields and courts. Eventually, the supposed "level playing field" of athletics led to some opportunities, for black men in particular, to participate in integrated competition and reap some of the benefits, including professional prize money, college scholarships, Olympic glory, and a sense of personal dignity and worth. However, Southern whites were dogged opponents of integrated sports competition, and some sports, such as professional baseball, acceded to Jim Crow customs for decades. As a result, black institutions, such as Negro League baseball, developed and provided an alternate playing field on which African Americans could participate with their peers. While integrated sports competition helped break down Jim Crow barriers to some degree, many believe that sports have also perpetuated stereotypes of African Americans, as some white observers have attributed black athletic success to animalistic traits supposedly inherent to the black race.

In the years following the Civil War, African Americans had some opportunities to participate in integrated sports competition and were often very successful. Horse racing, for example, was dominated by black jockeys in the late 19th century: 14 of the 15 jockeys racing in the first Kentucky Derby, in May 1875, were African American. Even more remarkably, of the first 28 Derbys, 15 were won by black riders. Isaac Murphy, an African American from Kentucky, was perhaps the best jockey of all time, winning numerous races and earning significant prize money. The first jockey to win the Kentucky Derby three times, Murphy died of pneumonia at age 35 in 1896. Some early professional baseball leagues also permitted black players in the 1870s and 1880s, although these opportunities were rare and players sometimes passed as Latino or Indian in order to play. College football also became more popular in this time period, and scattered black players earned considerable acclaim at majority white universities in the East and Midwest. William Henry Lewis, for example, was an All-American at Harvard in 1892 before going on to a successful career as a lawyer and federal assistant attorney general under President William Howard Taft. Frederick Douglass "Fritz" Pollard also earned national acclaim at Brown University from 1916 to 1917, and Paul Robeson starred at Rutgers College from 1915 to 1919. The success of these pioneers inspired many in the black community, particularly those in the black press, who believed that athletic achievement would prove blacks' capacities in other areas of life, and would open up new opportunities for the African American community on the whole. All of these players, however, were subject to racial abuse and taunting from opposing fans, players, and coaches (and often even from members of their own teams), suggesting the limitations sports had for effecting change. Indeed, on the whole, "big-time" college football remained largely segregated, and Jim Crow customs eventually forced black jockeys out of horse racing as the sport became more popular with the general public in the 1920s.

One sport that did provide opportunities for African Americans was professional boxing. Although the sport was illegal in many states, it nonetheless became increasingly popular in the years leading up to the turn of the 20th century as Boston heavyweight boxer John L. Sullivan, an Irish-American, became a cult hero to the working class in the 1880s. Sullivan, however, steadfastly refused to fight black boxers, including Australian heavyweight champion Peter Jackson. Although black boxers in less prestigious weight classes had some opportunities to fight white boxers for championships (Joe Gans earned the lightweight title in 1902, for example), the heavyweight division remained off-limits to black participation because of its prestige. Finally, in 1908, African American boxer Jack Johnson defeated Australian Tommy Burns for the heavyweight title. Outraged whites—stunned that a black man held the title of heavyweight champion of the world—called boxer James Jeffries out of retirement to restore the championship to the white race. When Johnson defeated Jeffries on July 4, 1910, riots broke out across the country as whites violently assaulted African Americans celebrating Johnson's triumph. Johnson's victory was particularly unsettling to many whites because of his personal life; marrying white women, driving expensive cars, and wearing extravagant clothes, Johnson seemed a direct affront to notions of white male supremacy. For many blacks, on the other hand, Johnson's triumph was so inspiring precisely because it challenged long-held beliefs in white male superiority. In the months after the bout, film footage of the fight was banned in many states, a sign of the symbolic importance accorded to Johnson's triumph. Federal authorities eventually convicted Johnson of violating the Mann Act in 1913, a dubious case that was settled by an all-white jury, and Johnson fled the country. He finally lost the championship to white heavyweight Jess Willard in 1915. Because Willard refused to take on black challengers, the championship then remained in the hands of white boxers for more than 20 years.

Baseball, by far the most popular spectator sport in America in the first half of the 20th century, was strictly a segregated affair as it reached its ascendant popularity. Although scattered blacks had played professionally in the 19th century, an unwritten rule against black participation became well established in the two major professional organizations that would eventually unite to form Major League Baseball (MLB)—the National League by the late 1880s, and the American League from its inception in 1901. Because the MLB proved particularly intractable in permitting black players to participate in the game, denying blacks access to the money and prestige earned by white players, African Americans established their own barnstorming teams and eventually a variety of "negro leagues."

The first black professional baseball team was the Cuban Giants, established in 1885 in Babylon, New York, and a number of teams followed suit in the ensuing years, including the Kansas City Monarchs and the Homestead (Pennsylvania) Grays. Black professional leagues also sprung up across the country, although they seldom lasted for long and were dogged by financial difficulties. Finally, in 1920, Andrew "Rube" Foster established the Negro National League, with eight teams: Chicago American Giants, Chicago Giants, Cuban Stars, Dayton Marcos, Detroit Stars, Indianapolis ABCs, Kansas City Monarchs, and St. Louis Giants. This league was the dominant black league until it folded after the 1931 season because of the Great Depression. A second Negro National League debuted in 1933, however, and lasted until 1949. Two other leagues, the Negro Southern League and the Negro American League, were also successful and long-lasting. These leagues provided opportunities for black professional baseball players to earn a living, although their pay was never as high as their white counterparts and their traveling accommodations were never as appealing. Still, the Negro Leagues were very popular for urban African Americans in particular, who eagerly supported their hometown teams. Countless star athletes earned acclaim by playing on these teams, including legendary players such as Josh Gibson and Satchel Paige.

As the various Negro Leagues found firmer footing in the 1920s, other sports gradually opened their doors to more integrated competition. The 1930s, in particular, showed significant signs of progress. In boxing, heavyweight Joe Louis became the first African American since Johnson to hold the

heavyweight boxing crown, a title he held for 12 years, when he defeated James Braddock in 1937. Louis also earned national acclaim for his defeat of German boxer Max Schmeling in 1938, a bout many saw as a contest between American democracy and Nazi fascism. Louis's popularity with both white and black fans suggests the transcendent capability of sports, but also its limits in effecting change. While Louis was certainly popular with many white fans across the country, discrimination continued unabated in most aspects of life, and Louis was careful to avoid any behavior that would have linked him to Johnson. Meanwhile, black Olympic athletes also inspired national pride in the 1930s. Although there had been African American Olympians (and medalists) since the 1904 games, Jesse Owens's dominating performance in the 1936 Olympics in Berlin was the most nationally celebrated. Winning four gold medals at the games, the most ever won by an American track athlete, Owens visibly challenged German leader Adolf Hitler's assertions of Aryan supremacy, and Owens was celebrated as a national hero. However, advertisers also shunned Owens for endorsement opportunities because of his race when he returned to the States, and he struggled to earn a living once he concluded his amateur career. In the realm of college sports, the 1930s also saw some significant changes as more black athletes gained positions on teams in the North and West (although still in relatively small numbers), and integrated competition slowly started to take place between Southern and Northern schools. The University of North Carolina, for example, traveled north to square off against New York University and its black star Ed Williams in 1936, although games played in the South continued to require black athletes to sit out.

Perhaps the most important single event in the integration of sports in the United States occurred when Jackie Robinson took the field for the MLB Brooklyn Dodgers on April 15, 1947. Robinson, signed by Dodgers president Branch Rickey, was the perfect candidate to integrate baseball because of his athletic ability and strong character. Facing racist taunting from opposing players and fans, with players often attempting to injure him by throwing pitches directly at him and deliberately "spiking" him with their cleats, Robinson held his emotions in check, fearful that an outburst might set back the process of integration. His strong play earned him the National League Rookie of the Year Award in 1947 and inspired tens of thousands of black fans to come out to games to see him play. In his nine-year career, Robinson won numerous accolades, including the National League Rookie of the Year in 1947, the National League Most Valuable Player in 1949, and a World Series championship in 1955. Following Robinson's debut, other clubs began to sign African American baseball players: Larry Doby was the second black player in MLB history when he joined the Cleveland Indians midway through the 1947 season. Many consider Robinson's successful turn in baseball, "the national pastime," a pivotal event in the broader struggle for African American civil rights. Robinson's success in the MLB, however, also sounded the death knell for the Negro Leagues. With the best black players leaving for the higher salaries and better accommodations of the MLB, the black-run Negro Leagues could no longer complete, although the Negro American League held out until 1961. Integration of MLB teams was also painfully slow: the Philadelphia Phillies were the last National League team to integrate, in 1957; and the Boston Red Sox were the last American League team to integrate, in 1959. And it was not until 1975 that the first black manager was hired, when Frank Robinson became player-manager for the Cleveland Indians.

Jackie Robinson's debut inspired integration in a wide range of sports. The National Football League welcomed its first black players in 1946, soon after the announcement of Robinson's signing with the Dodgers organization; that year, the Los Angeles Rams signed Kenny Washington and Woody Strode, both former teammates of Robinson at UCLA. The National Basketball Association, meanwhile, saw three black players debut for the 1949–1950 season: Chuck Cooper of the Boston Celtics, Earl Lloyd of the Washington Capitals, and Nat "Sweetwater" Clifton of the New York Knicks. In the same era, colleges and universities across the country also began opening up their teams to black athletic participation, although many schools in the South opposed integration into the early 1970s. Black college stars such as Bill Russell, who won back-to-back NCAA national championships in basketball with the University of San Francisco in 1955 and 1956, and Jim Brown, who earned All-American honors in football and lacrosse at Syracuse University in 1957, symbolized the growing presence of black athletes in big-time college athletics. In the South, black schools such as Tennessee A&I and Florida A&M built their own athletic powerhouses and competed in their own all-black conferences. Black coach

John McLendon also led Tennessee A&I to the National Association of Intercollegiate Athletics (NAIA) championship in men's basketball in 1957 (the NAIA was a national organization of small colleges and universities and included both black and white schools).

Women athletes also generated publicity. Althea Gibson's stunning success in tennis in the late 1950s earned her the Female Athlete of the Year award from the Associated Press in 1957 and 1958, and Wilma Rudolph earned that same award in 1960 for winning three gold medals in that year's Olympics. Many African Americans took pride in these wide-ranging accomplishments and continued to see sports as an entry point into mainstream American culture. Most hoped that black athletic achievement would contribute to a lessening in bigotry and would continue to erode the walls of Jim Crow segregation.

Black fans' hopes for sports were met in some ways and dashed in others. Although black athletes continued to break through the walls of discrimination in a variety of sports in the second half of the 20tj century, prejudice continued to infiltrate athletics. Teams in nearly every sport were reluctant to hire black managers and executives, even as black players began to dominate rosters. High-profile positions, such as the quarterback in football and starting pitcher in baseball, were often reserved for white players. Many black activists and leaders also lamented the decline in black institutions' athletic programs, such as the professional Negro Leagues and historically black colleges and universities. Reports of exploitation of black college athletes at previously all-white schools also troubled leaders and activists, as some worried (and continue to worry) that African American student-athletes were not being prepared for a life outside of athletics. Black athletes who took public stands against government policies—such as outspoken heavyweight boxer Muhammad Ali, who refused induction into the military, and Olympic sprinters Tommie Smith and John Carlos, who raised their fists in a "black power" salute on the medal stand at the 1968 Summer Olympics—were often criticized scathingly in the white press.

It is unclear how much of an impact sports have had on broader conceptions of race and on bigotry. Although many white fans cheer for black athletes, some ascribe black success to supposedly inherited biological factors and continue to believe in stereotypes of intellectual inferiority. While, undoubtedly, sports helped to break down the walls of Jim Crow segregation, and have inspired some to abandon prejudiced beliefs, it is as yet unclear if sports have won the victory for black equality that many black leaders had hoped for.

GREGORY KALISS

See also

Basketball; Biological Racism; Football; Racism and Athletic Coaching

Further Reading:

"Baseball and Jackie Robinson." Library of Congress, American Memory. http://memory.loc.gov/ammem/collections/robinson/ (accessed May 28, 2008).

George, Nelson. *Elevating the Game: Black Men and Basketball.* Lincoln: University of Nebraska Press, 1992.

Gorn, Elliott, and Goldstein, Warren. *A Brief History of American Sports.* New York: Hill and Wang, 1993.

Grundy, Pamela. *Learning to Win: Sports, Education, and Social Change in Twentieth-Century North Carolina.* Chapel Hill: University of North Carolina Press, 2001.

Miller, Patrick B., ed. *Sporting World of the Modern South.* Urbana: University of Illinois Press, 2002.

Sammons, Jeffrey. *Beyond the Ring: The Role of Boxing in American Society.* Urbana: University of Illinois, 1988.

Tygiel, Jules. *Baseball's Great Experiment: Jackie Robinson and His Legacy.* New York: Oxford University Press, 1983.

Ward, Geoffrey C. *Unforgivable Blackness: The Rise and Fall of Jack Johnson.* New York: Knopf, 2004.

Wiggins, David K. *Glory Bound: Black Athletes in a White America.* Syracuse, NY: Syracuse University Press, 1997.

A Cleveland Indians fan shows a Chief Wahoo sign prior to game 3 of the AL Division Series at Jacobs Field in Cleveland, Saturday, October 4, 1997. (AP Photo/Tony Dejak)

Sports Mascots

Since the 1970s, American Indian activists in the American Indian Movement (AIM) and the National Coalition for Sports and Racism in the Media (NCRSM) have led a campaign to remove "Indian" mascots from collegiate and professional sports teams and replace them with something else, on the grounds that these particular mascots perpetuate racial stereotypes of American Indians. Professional sports franchises that use Indians for their names and mascots include the baseball teams the Atlanta Braves and the Cleveland Indians, and the football teams the Kansas City Chiefs and the Washington Redskins. There are also many college sports teams that use Indians for their mascots, although some schools have changed their mascots in recent years, indicating their sympathy and agreement with NCRSM that Indian mascots promote negative images of American Indians. The efforts of AIM and NCRSM have been successful in some cases, especially at the collegiate level, but professional sports teams have, for the most part, kept their Indian mascots.

According to AIM and NCSRM, the Indian mascots are as offensive to American Indians as the Sambo image was to African Americans or the "Frito Bandito" to Latino Americans. Particularly racist is the "Chief Wahoo" mascot for the Cleveland Indians. "Chief Wahoo" was designed by the team's management to have oversized buckteeth, red skin, and a big nose, exaggerated features that offend the American Indian community. For American Indians, the chief represents a position of respect, the highest and most politically powerful role in their society, but professional and collegiate sports have trivialized and degraded the image of the chief for mass entertainment. Indians have become something for sports fans to joke about. For example, in the 1998 American League playoffs between the New York Yankees and the Cleveland Indians, the *New York Post* ran a headline that read, "Take the Tribe and Scalp 'em." In Atlanta, the fans of the baseball team the Braves perform the "tomahawk chop" chant, in which fans are given styrofoam tomahawks to move up and down as they chant what is meant to represent sounds that Indians supposedly made when on the warpath. According to the American Indian community, the use of Indian sports mascots trivializes their people and their history. In short, American Indians, victims of genocide, have been reduced to objects for the entertainment of the American masses in a multibillion-dollar sports industry. In the words of NCRSM, "American Indians are a people, not mascots for other Americans' fun and games. We are human beings."

In school teams, however, progress has been made toward removing offensive sports mascots. In the 1970s, students at both Stanford University and Dartmouth College were able to pressure their administrations to change their school identities and sports mascots from Indians to other, race-neutral symbols. Stanford's team, for example, is now known as the Stanford Cardinal. In Los Angeles, California, the board of education voted to ban all images and reference to Indians in athletic and other venues at schools under their jurisdiction.

More recently, the NAACP passed a resolution in 1999 calling for an end to Native American imagery in mascots; in 2001, the U.S. Commission on Civil Rights formally advised against the use of Native American images in mascots by non-Native schools; and in 2005, the American Psychological Association made the same recommendation. Several states have banned the use of racial images in school mascots including Wisconsin (2010) and Oregon (2012). Several universities removed American Indian images and nicknames following a 2005 self-evaluation that the National Collegiate Athletic Association sent to 31 colleges asking them to evaluate their use of potentially offensive mascots. The controversy regarding the use of American Indian imagery in sports mascots continues.

MICHAEL ROBERTS

See also

Don Imus Controversy; Sports and Racism; Stereotype

Further Reading:

Berkhoffer, Robert F., Jr. *The White Man's Indian: Images of the American Indian from Columbus to the Present.* New York: Knopf, 1978.

Johnson, Bruce E. "Mascots: Honor Be Thy Name." *Native Americas* 18 (Spring 2001): 58–61.

United States Commission on Civil Rights. *Statement of the U.S. Commission on Civil Rights on the Use of Native American Images and Nicknames as Sports Symbols.* http://www.usccr .gov/nwsrel/archives/2001/041601st.htm.

Springfield (Ohio) Riot of 1904

The Springfield (Ohio) Riot of 1904 was not an aberration in early-20th-century race relations. Not since the Reconstruction era (1865–1877) had race riots swept the nation as they did in the first decade of the 20th century. The Reconstruction riots were confined to the South—New Orleans, Louisiana (1866, 1868, 1874); Memphis, Tennessee (1866); and Meridian (1870), Vicksburg (1874), and Yazoo City, Mississippi (1875). However, the turn of the 20th century saw racial violence against blacks spread north to cities where many African Americans migrated in search of economic, social, and political opportunities.

Springfield, Ohio, was one city where blacks had established a vibrant community in the section of town known as the Levee. Many of the black industrial workers and day laborers resided in this section of Springfield, which included a black business sector and informal economy (prostitution, barrooms, and gambling parlors).

On March 6, 1904, an African American resident of Springfield, Richard Dixon (also reported as Richard Dickerson), went to the Jones hotel in the Levee to retrieve his clothes from a woman, Anna (a.k.a. Mamie) Corbin, who was purported to be his mistress. Dixon requested that a police officer, Charles Collis, accompany him to Corbin's room to reclaim his clothes. Various newspaper sources reported that Dixon and Corbin quarreled until Dixon took out a gun and shot the woman. The police officer attempted to subdue Dixon, only to be shot four times by the assailant.

Dixon escaped and immediately turned himself in at police headquarters.

When news of the shooting and death of the white police officer reached the wider Springfield community, white men and boys gathered at the jail that next evening. Initially, some 300 male whites stood outside the jail demanding the release of Dixon, shouting "Lynch the nigger." At one point, the police had dispersed the crowd, but a small group of men diverted police attention so that some 250 men could storm the jail and kidnap Dixon. An estimated mob of 2,000 to 2,500 men blocked the prison gates outside, preventing the police force from protecting Dixon. The white men took Dixon away and lynched him.

When news of the lynching reached the black community, African Americans prepared to defend themselves, as rumors circulated that the mob intended to invade the Levee. Springfield's mayor G. J. Bowlus called Gov. Myron T. Herrick to send troops to subdue the potential rioters. Indeed, on March 9, some 2,000 white men shot bullets into the Levee and then set it ablaze, burning down mostly black-owned homes and businesses. Some newspaper sources numbered the mob that invaded the levee at 5,000. Springfield, Ohio, would experience another race riot in 1906.

Springfield was not the first city to experience race riots in the opening years of the new century. New Orleans and New York City both erupted in racial violence in 1900. During the same year as the second Springfield riot, "race wars" broke out in Atlanta, Georgia; Greensburg, Indiana; and Brownsville, Texas. In 1908, the Springfield, Illinois, race riot would lead to the creation of the National Association for the Advancement of Colored People (NAACP). All these riots had one element in common—white fear of a growing black presence.

JEANNETTE E. JONES

See also

Lynching; Race Riots in America; Reconstruction Era. Documents: The Report on the Memphis Riots of May 1866 (July 25, 1866); Account of the Riots in East St. Louis, Illinois (July 1917); The Cook County Coroner's Report Regarding the 1919 Chicago Race Riots (1919); A Southern Black Woman's Letter Regarding the Recent Riots in Chicago and Washington (November 1919); The Final Report of the Grand Jury on the Tulsa Race Riot (June 25, 1921); Testimony from *Laney v. United States* Describing Events during the Washington, D.C., Riot of July 1919 (December 3, 1923); The Governor's Commission Report on the Watts Riots (December 1965); Cyrus R. Vance's Report on the Riots in Detroit (July–August 1967); The Reports of the Oklahoma Commission to Study the Tulsa Race Riot of 1921 (2000–2001); The Draft Report of the 1898 Wilmington Race Riot Commission (December 2005)

Further Reading:

Capeci, Dominic J., Jr., and Jack C. Knight. "Reckoning with Violence: W.E.B. Du Bois and the 1906 Atlanta Race Riot." *Journal of Southern History* 62 (1996): 165–80.
Murray, Percy E. "Harry C. Smith-Joseph Foraker Alliance: Coalition Politics in Ohio." *Journal of Negro History* 68 (1983): 171–84.

State Apparatus

A *state apparatus* is the material collection of social relations and practices that embody "the state"—i.e., modernity's sovereign political object/actor—which is today largely responsible the world over for regulating social violence, justice, ideology, and inculcation (education). Recognizable by their flags, as well as by their state powers defined by formal state constitutions, the recent 16th century emergence and rise of the political state apparatus marks the beginnings of "modernity"; of "society"; and of all the resulting complex sociological units of contemporary group life comprising the special interests of sociologists, social-historians, demographers and economists.

Importantly, it is the state apparatus that also commands the form of officially divisive racial ideologies and racial categories appearing equally on decennial censuses and in the early U.S. and South African racial apartheid constitutions (e.g., see the opening chapters of Feagin 2000): As witnessed in South African and U.S. racial apartheids, the historical construction of racial categories and racisms in modernity, proceeds along with the experience of *centralizing social power*, i.e., those historically fewer and fewer number of political officials and institutions controlling the form and invocation of collective violence, collective justice, and collective ideology and inculcation (education).

On the one hand, these state centralizing social powers (over collective violence, justice, ideology, and inculcation), which for nation states are defined constitutionally in writing and definably as laws (governing armed forces, the courts, educational system, and patriotisms), are usually divided across judicial, executive, and legislative functions or "branches": and have the power to decide the meaning of race and who is racially enslaveable and which races may own such slaves. On the other hand, state powers are also frequently formalized as complex divisions of socially relating political offices (people) and institutions (bureaucracies, agencies, and departments): for example, the U.S. Constitution at one point required that escaped slaves, as they were property and not people, must be returned if fleeing across state lines, providing incentives for their capture and return. Together these formalizations—the rules governing the powers flowing between *office-holders* and across *social institutions*—compose what has been called the state apparatus.

Of early interest to such researchers has been the notion of the state apparatus, which was a term first written of sociologically by Marxist conflict theorists contemplating which social classes had control over which of society's *resources* (educational systems, armies, courts, laws, etc): state resources differentially constrained or made available to different social classes by those class-actors in political and ideological control of state apparatuses. As evidenced in Marx's *Communist Manifesto* and the *Eighteenth Brumaire*, Althusser (1970) writes that in the Marxist tradition, the state is explicitly conceived as a "repressive apparatus"; that is, the state is a "machine" of repression that enables the ruling classes (e.g., the 19th-century bourgeois class and the "class" of big landowners) to ensure their *domination* over the working class, domination by racial means if necessary as in American plantations, but most frequently domination occurring by way of an educational system's ability to control the dominant values and meanings at work in society. Thus in racism, the state enables the (white) former to subject the (black) latter, under racially split labor markets, to the process of surplus-value extortion (i.e., to capitalist exploitation). Marxists wrote that such was achieved "peacefully" by ideological state apparatuses and not simply through brute force: in other words, once children are taught the validity of social class and their place within that system—that blacks are slaves and whites are slave owners—they have been taught the ideological groundings of class oppression—as well as slavery.

Materially, *state apparatus* refers not only to the state applications of physical violence alone (armies, police forces, laws, and the death penalty) but also to the ruling-class interests defining the shape of society's legal practice (i.e., the police, the courts, the prisons); the ruling-class perspectives dominating the state apparatus (e.g., capitalist gaining of monetary profit by any means necessary, including racial slavery and racially split labor markets); and the distinct dominant-class interests (of maintaining class position) as represented and defended by the head of state, the government, and the administration. Importantly, *repressive state apparatus* also refers to society's army and other armed officials of state violence, which often intervene directly as a supplementary repressive force when the police and its specialized auxiliary corps are "outrun by events" such as in Kent State or the recent police forces attacking peaceful Occupy Wall Street protestors in the winter of 2011–2012. Importantly, state apparatus does not rule through violence alone, but is most effective while an ideology active in the minds and constitutions of the citizens or subjects constituting the population.

SALVATORE LABARO

See also

Du Bois, W.E.B.; Systemic Racism

Further Reading:

Althusser, Louis. *Lenin and Philosophy and Other Essays.* New York: Monthly Review Press, 2001.

Bonacich, Edna. 1972. "A Theory of Ethnic Antagonism: The Split Labor Market." *American Sociological Review* 37, no. 5 (1972): 547–59.

Feagin, Joe R. *Racist America: Roots, Current Realities, and Future Reparations.* Routledge: New York. 2000.

Statistical Discrimination

Statistical discrimination is an economics theory that proposes that the act of racial discrimination in employment is based on calculated averages and practical decision making. Statistical discrimination refers broadly to a process of decision making that uses indicators of group membership in order to calculate expected returns based on average group behavior. Group membership can include sex, race/

ethnicity, health status, physical ability, age, and other social characteristics. The literature on statistical discrimination primarily focuses on the example of employers (as decision makers) choosing to discriminate against one group of workers, irrespective of the employment field. In fact, the "decision maker" can be anyone from a mortgage banker to a school's admissions officer.

Arrow (1973) and Phelps (1972) are often cited as the first scholars to advance the theory of statistical discrimination. The proponents of statistical discrimination argue that too many theories purport to explain that inequality among whites and blacks in occupational attainment is due primarily to employer prejudice or racism, or due to ethnic tension among workers. However, theories on employer-based prejudice and group conflict are contrary to the rational choice model that prevails in economics. The rational-choice logic states that humans are rational actors who make decisions based on cost/benefit analyses, in which they seek to maximize benefits and minimize costs. According to this perspective, capital gain and racism are divergent objectives and no capitalist employer would participate in a practice that is against its best business interests.

According to the logic of statistical discrimination, decision makers in employment, in the consumer market, in lending, and in education base their decisions to discriminate based on statistical evidence that has been projected onto each member of a racial/ethnic group. For example, a white employer may not hire a black laborer because a mistaken belief that the average black employee will have a lower productivity or attendance rate than the average white employee. In the context of banking, we can think of a mortgage banker discriminating against a Latino applicant because, on average, Latinos tend to default on their payments more than whites. Based on these statistical averages, racial discrimination becomes a rational and practical choice for decision makers.

Research has focused on decision makers in various work places where statistical discrimination is utilized, i.e., in institutions of financial lending, in healthcare, and in education. Instead of focusing on interpersonal bias and racial prejudice that often lead to discrimination, statistical discrimination theory asserts that employers (or decision makers more broadly) use statistical generalizations about racial groups in order to make a rational decision in the face of uncertainty. So, hiring a white employee or giving a loan to the white applicant over the minority prospect all becomes a part of an ostensibly rational, risk-averse, and nonracist investment choice. This explains how a decision maker's cost-benefit analysis can still result in a discriminatory outcome for minorities.

In the end, discriminatory decision making results in racial disparities in income, occupational status, financial lending, healthcare, and education. In many ways, the outcomes of statistical discrimination reify the assumptions and stereotypes about different social groups. This has led some scholars to qualify the process of statistical discrimination as a type of "self-fulfilling stereotype."

ALAN VINCENT GRIGSBY AND RASHA ALY

See also

Cumulative Discrimination; Discrimination; Financial Institutions and Racial Discrimination; Institution Racism

Further Reading:

Aigner, Dennis, and Cain, Glen. "Statistical Theories of Discrimination in Labor Markets." *Industrial & Labor Relations Review* 30, no. 2 (1977): 175–87.

Arrow, Kenneth. "The Theory of Discrimination." In *Discrimination in Labor Markets*, edited by Orley Ashenfelter and Albert Rees. Princeton, NJ: Princeton University Press, 1973.

Arrow, Kenneth. "What Has Economics to Say About Racial Discrimination?" *Journal of Economic Perspectives* 12, no. 2 (1998): 91–100.

Moro, Andrea, and Norman, Peter. "A General Equilibrium Model of Statistical Discrimination." *Journal of Economic Theory* 114, no. 1 (2004): 1–30.

Norman, Peter. "Statistical Discrimination and Efficiency." *Review of Economic Studies* 70, no. 3 (2003): 615–27.

Phelps, Edmund. "The Statistical Theory of Racism and Sexism." *American Economic Review* 62, no. 4 (1972): 659–661.

Stereotype

A stereotype is a belief, usually negative, about a group of people regardless of previous interaction. In U.S. culture, stereotypes are usually negative beliefs about minority group members including, but not limited to, blacks, Asians, gays, and the poor. Stereotype research is centered in social psychology, cognitive psychology, sociology, and political science; however, many other academic fields utilize and conduct stereotype research.

Stereotypes pervade all cultures, including U.S. culture. Given the cognitive pressures of modern life (discussed below), stereotypes facilitate social interaction. Stereotypes vary from culture to culture and manifest themselves in a myriad of ways. An example of a stereotype is that black men are violent. This stereotype is both negative—violence is not socially accepted—and untrue. Based on this stereotype, many Americans alter their behavior in the presence of a black man, clutching their purse or feeling their wallet. Unfortunately, this stereotype creates systemic blockages for black men (*see* Racial Profiling).

The word "stereotype" comes from the Greek roots *stereos* and *typos*, meaning "firm impression." In print technology, a stereotype was a metal plate used to print text and images; the drawback of the stereotype print plate is that it was costly to create, and difficult to update and modify, making it less accurate than other, more dynamic, forms of printing.

According to cognitive psychology, stereotypes are tools used to avoid overstimulation. Humans have a finite amount of mental energy, and infinite mental tasks that compete for this energy. Referring to, and acting upon, a stereotype allows individuals to bypass a complex, mentally expensive thought processes and conserve mental energy.

According to social psychology, stereotypes are stored in cultural memory. Beliefs about individual groups of people vary from group to group, society to society. As a result, a stereotype in one location may be different from another location. For example, the stereotype that Asians are bad drivers may be known in the United States, but this stereotype may be unheard of in Russia.

Stereotypes fall into two categories: in-group and out-group stereotypes. In-group stereotypes regulate behavior, membership, and the identity of a group of people as dictated by its members. Out-group stereotypes protect people from people with different physical, economical, and cultural beliefs, values, and practices.

There are many types of stereotypes in U.S. culture, most of which are associated with minority groups. For example, lesbian women may be stereotyped as athletic, muscular, and aggressive. Homosexual men may be stereotyped as soft-spoken, sassy, and artistic. Low-income people may be stereotyped as lazy. Given the focus of this encyclopedia, this entry will focus on racial and ethnic stereotypes.

In colonial America (17th and 18th century), white supremacist stereotypes were utilized in order to justify African slave labor on American plantations. Stereotypes of lazy, savage, and ignorant Africans were used to justify the inhuman, unjust, and otherwise morally indefensible system of slavery in the colonies and, later, United States. Having been

---

Noble Savage

The term *noble savage* refers to a romantic view of indigenous peoples as more natural, authentic, and communal than Europeans. The "noble savage," as seen in colonial and postcolonial history, popular culture, and mythology, is a character who lives simply and in harmony with his or her natural environment. The mythology of the noble savage, closely linked to primitivism, developed during the time of European colonial expansion into Africa, the Americas, and elsewhere.

Even as colonized cultures were being destroyed with increasing brutality, Europeans and white Americans romanticized them as more ecologically sensitive, more exciting, and even more sexually pleasured. Such notions essentialize indigenous people and circulate negative stereotypes about the relative intelligence, sophistication, and sexual mores of whole groups of people who have faced colonization by Westerners. According to postcolonial scholars, the concept of the noble savage is also a nostalgic one, reflecting the West's longstanding unease with its own technological advances, ecological destruction, and cultural homogenization. For at least two centuries, Western culture generated images of noble savagery that suggest alternative, more traditionally rooted modes of living with nature that are perceived as symbolic alternatives to Western problems. In recent manifestations, primitivism is seen as a way of life, a set of values and relationships that can be experienced even within Western cultures through the appropriation of indigenous rituals, ceremonies, and spiritual and body practices.

VICTORIA PITTS

codified into U.S. culture, these stereotypes persist in U.S. culture beyond abolition and the civil rights movement (*see* White Privilege).

Although it is less researched, white supremacy affects Asian Americans. White supremacist, antimiscegenation laws kept Chinese and Filipino workers from creating families, and Executive Order 9066 relocated Japanese Americans during World War II. Native Americans are stereotyped as alcoholics, casino operators, and exotic performers. These stereotypes ignore the contributions of Indians to U.S. culture, and the fact that "American Land" is the ancestral land of the Native Americans. Latino Americans are stereotyped as undocumented workers, Catholic, and non–English speaking. These stereotypes ignore the vital labor done by Latino Americans, and create barriers to employment and social acceptance.

The field of stereotype research is extensive. Most stereotype research examines racial and sexual minorities, although other studies have branched out to include class, income, and ability status (able bodies vs. disabled) stereotypes.

Beyond the field of cognitive psychology, social psychologists, and sociologists research the ways in which stereotypes are socialized (i.e., taught) to adults and children. Sociologically, it is believed that social institutions (e.g., family, schools, media, peers, etc.) transmit stereotypes. For example, if a teenager watches a TV show where all Arabs are portrayed as terrorists, that teenager may learn the stereotype that Arabs are terrorists.

Stereotypes are characteristic of, and necessary for, all societies. The concept of a stereotype is old, but current research examines both the nature of stereotypes and how they are instilled into social members. As the United States becomes more racially and culturally diverse, outdated and racist stereotypes will become more prevalent in everyday life and racist stereotypes will need to be revisited. This revision will not be easy, but it will be necessary to function as a society.

LEIGHTON VILA

See also

Ideological Racism; Implicit Bias; Racial Essentialism; Racialized Poverty; Stereotype Threat; White Privilege

Further Reading:

Feagin, Joseph R., and Clairece B. Feagin. *Racial and Ethnic Relations.* Upper Saddle River, NJ: Prentice Hall, 2007.

McGarty, Craig, Vincent Y. Yzerbyt, and Russell Spears. *Stereotypes as Explanations: The Formation of Meaningful Beliefs About Social Groups.* Cambridge: Cambridge University Press, 2002.

Tajfel, Henri, Anees A. Sheikh, and Robert C. Gardner. "Content of Stereotypes and the Inference of Similarity between Members of Stereotyped Groups." *Acta Psychologica* 22 (1964): 191–201.

Stereotype Threat

Stereotype threat is a psychological pressure that is placed on an individual when he or she has the potential to confirm a stereotype. Most often, stereotype threat is recognized when minority group members underperform in situations that can confirm negative stereotypes about his or her self-identified minority group.

Steele and Aronson (1995) put forth the theory of stereotype threat to explain the black-white achievement gap, the empirical finding that blacks have lower standardized test scores than whites. Their study (described below) found that priming black college students with a racial cue reduces their scores on difficult verbal assignments. Since the original study, stereotype threat research has burgeoned and has been applied to female, Asian, Latino, and poor populations. While there has been criticism of the media's interpretation of Steele and Aronson's study, stereotype threat is an active area of social psychological research.

In their experiment, Steele and Aronson conducted three experiments. In the first experiment, black and white college students were given a very difficult verbal exam and primed with different instructions. Black and white students were split into two groups. The first group was told that the test examined personal factors that affect academic performance (i.e., that their scores represented how well they would perform in college). The second group was told that the test measured psychological cognition, and that their scores were not especially meaningful. At the end of the experiment, blacks' and whites' scores in both groups were compared; in the first group, blacks performed poorer than whites, but in the second group, the black scores were similar to whites. These findings suggests that there is a difference in scores according to the perceived function of the exam.

In order to better understand this finding, Steele and Aronson conducted a second experiment that examined racial attitudes under the same test conditions. This experiment asked blacks in each group to complete four- to six-letter words, each with potential positive and negative answers (e.g. D U __ __, possible answers: dunk, positive, or dumb, negative.) This experiment found that racially primed blacks in the academic performance group answered more negative words, which was interpreted as strong negative arousal.

The last experiment examined how mandatory racial identification affects test performance for black and white college students. In this experiment, half of the participants were instructed to write their race on the exam prior to its administration, and the other half were not. The black students who were instructed to write their race performed significantly worse than the black students who did not write their race. This result suggested that black students who are required to identify their race prior to an academic test perform the worse.

Based on data from their study, Steele and Aronson concluded that stereotype threat is a factor in explaining the black-white achievement gap. Later studies have suggested that reducing the importance of one's race, or reinterpreting the exam as an exercise, and not an indicator of intelligence, may ease stereotype threat. Also, it has been found that black students who place greater emphasis on academics suffer worse than blacks who do not identify with academics.

Stereotype boost, a concept that is similar to stereotype threat, occurs when a person's performance is enhanced by the potential to confirm a positive stereotype. For example, empirical studies have shown that Asians perform better when their Asian ethnicity is primed.

A criticism of stereotype threat is that the media has oversimplified and misinterpreted the implications of the study. While racial priming during test taking is a general problem, there are other structural problems that may inhibit test performance. Factors such as test preparation, access to good schools, parental attention, and family income also influence test scores.

Stereotype threat is an active area of research for social psychologists, education researchers, and other social scientists. Although stereotype threat does not completely explain the black-white education gap, it adds to our understanding of academic inequality.

LEIGHTON VILA

See also
Stereotype

Further Reading:
Armenta, Brian E. "Stereotype Boost and Stereotype Threat Effects: The Moderating Role of Ethnic Identification." *Cultural Diversity and Ethnic Minority Psychology* 16 (2010): 94–98.
Steele, Claude. "Stereotype Threat and African American Student Achievement." In *The Inequality Reader: Contemporary and Foundational Readings in Race, Class, and Gender*, edited by David Grusky and Szjona Szelényi, 252–57. Boulder, CO: Westview Press, 2006.
Steele, Claude M., and Joshua Aronson. "Stereotype Threat and the Intellectual Test Performance of African Americans." *Journal of Personality and Social Psychology* 69 (1995): 797–811.

Sterilization of Native American Women

On the phone, during long marches, occupying federal surplus property, in court fighting for treaty rights—wherever Indian activists gathered during the "Red Power" years of the 1970s, conversation inevitably turned to the number of women who had had their tubes tied or their ovaries removed by the Indian Health Service. This was, I heard one woman joke bitterly at the time, a "fringe benefit of living in a domestic, dependent nation."

Communication spurred by activism provoked a growing number of Native American women to piece together what amounted to a national eugenics policy, translated into social reality by copious federal funding. They organized WARN (Women of All Red Nations) at Rapid City, South Dakota, as Native women from more than 30 tribes and nations met and decided, among other things, that "truth and communication are among our most valuable tools in the liberation of our lands, people, and four-legged and winged creations.

WARN and other women's organizations publicized the sterilizations, which were performed after pro-forma "consent" of the women being sterilized. The "consent" sometimes was not offered in the women's language, following threats that they would die or lose their welfare benefits if they had more children. At least two 15-year-old girls were told they were having their tonsils out before their ovaries were removed.

The enormity of government-funded sterilization has been compiled by a master's student in history, Sally Torpy, at the University of Nebraska at Omaha. Her thesis, "Endangered Species: Native American Women's Struggle for Their Reproductive Rights and Racial Identity, 1970s–1990s," which was defended during the summer of 1998, places the sterilization campaign in the context of the "eugenics" movement.

"They took away our past with a sword and our land with a pen. Now they're trying to take away our future with a scalpel," one Native American woman told Arlene Eisen of the *London Guardian* (March 23, 1977: 8). She also said: "This total disregarded for the health and dignity of Native American women is the I.H.S. version of smallpox-infested blankets [and] the forced marches and massacres of Native peoples. Racism continues because it is so deeply entrenched—even enlightened professionals do not see Indian people as human. . . . They still think Indian people are in the way. They still want the land we have left, particularly our mineral resources . . . coal, oil, and uranium" (Johansen and Maestas 1979: 71).

Native Americans were far from the only victims of eugenic thinking into the 1970s. Beginning in 1929 and ending in 1978, the state of North Carolina sterilized as many as 7,600 people, "to reduce welfare costs and cleanse the gene pool" (Severson 2012: A-13). California sterilized about 20,000 people for the same purposes. In 2012, 34 years after North Carolina's program ended, the state became the first of three dozen states that had had such programs to put a price on the practice, deciding that each living survivor of the program should be paid $50,000. That figure was set by a state task force, subject to approval of the governor and legislature. The bill could reach $100 million for the 1,500 to 2,000 living victims, mostly minorities and people of limited income and low intelligence.

No one even today knows exactly how many Native American women were sterilized during the 1970s. One base for calculation is provided by the General Accounting Office, whose study covered only four of 12 IHS regions over four years (1973 through 1976). Within those limits, 3,406 Indian women were sterilized, according to the GAO.

Another estimate was provided by Lehman Brightman, who is Lakota, and who devoted much of his life to the issue, suffering a libel suit by doctors in the process. His educated guess (without exact calculations to back it up) is that 40 percent of Native women and 10 percent of Native men were sterilized during the decade. Brightman estimates that the total number of Indian women sterilized during the decade was between 60,000 and 70,000.

By 1970, anecdotal evidence of the surge in sterilization began to accumulate, according to Torpy's detailed account. For example, welfare case workers in Apollo, Pennsylvania, had removed Norma Jean Serena's daughter Lisa, three years of age, and son, Gary, age four, from her home before she underwent a tubal ligation after the birth of her son Shawn, in 1970. One day after Shawn was removed to a foster home, Serena signed consent forms for the surgery, emotionally battered by accusations of case workers that she was an unfit mother.

Three years later, with legal assistance from the Council of Three Rivers Indian Center in Pittsburgh, Serena sued Armstrong County for return of her children from foster care. She also sued a number of area hospitals for damages related to her sterilization. A jury found that the children had been taken under false pretenses from Serena, who is of mixed Creek and Shawnee ancestry.

During trial, attorneys for Serena questioned the "evidence" on which welfare case workers had decided to take her children and recommend her sterilization. The main "problem" seemed to have been the fact that black friends of Serena visited her home, as reported by anonymous tipsters in the neighborhood who asserted fear for their own children. While one caseworker described Serena's apartment as "dirty and unkempt," and her children as "undernourished and dazed," unable to walk, speak, or hold eating utensils, a doctor who examined the children shortly afterwards found them "alert and in good health." According to Torpy's account, Serena was awarded $17,000 by a jury, and her children were ordered released to her. The Armstrong County child welfare bureaucracy stalled several months before returning the children, according to Torpy's account, and did so only after officials were confronted with a contempt-of-court citation.

Parts of Serena's case were not settled until 1979, when several doctors and a male social worker were acquitted of having violated her civil rights by taking part in her sterilization. The key issue was whether she had given consent for the operation. Serena said she could not recall having signed a consent form; the attending physician said he had explained the operation to Serena and that he was convinced she understood him. A jury agreed.

At about the same time that Serena had her run-in with caseworkers, a 26-year-old Native American woman entered the office of a Los Angeles physician in 1970 seeking a "womb transplant" because she had been having trouble getting pregnant. The doctor, who never asked her name, told the woman she had been the subject of a hysterectomy, removal of her ovaries, which cannot be reversed. The operation had been performed under false pretenses. The woman, who was engaged to be married and who had hoped to raise a family was "devastated," according to Torpy.

The last vestiges of legally sanctioned eugenics played out during the 1960s, when concern about overpopulation expressed by industrial leaders in the United States (most notably by members of the Rockefeller family) became official federal policy—with massive spending to back it up—under the Nixon administration. Sterilization for the poor and minorities was officially sanctioned in 1970, just about the time students were killed at Kent and Jackson State universities as they protested expansion of the Vietnam War. Reservation populations became targets of a policy that also was being advocated nationally, especially for poor and minority women. In 1969, the American College of Obstetricians and Gynecologists also had relaxed its own restrictions on sterilizations.

In 1970, when the IHS initiated its sterilization campaign (paid 100 percent by federal funds), the Department of Health, Education, and Welfare vastly accelerated programs that paid 90 percent of the costs to sterilize non-Indian poor women, following enactment of the Family Planning Act of 1970. The rate of sterilization for women, as a whole, in the United States then jumped by 350 percent in five years, according to Torpy's research.

Before 1969, funding of sterilizations (as well as abortion) had been banned by the federal government. Between 1969 and 1974, HEW increased its family planning budget from $51 million to more than $250 million, Torpy found. HEW records reveal that between 192,000 and 548,000 women were sterilized each year between 1970 and 1977, compared to an average of 63,000 a year between 1907 and 1964, a period thay included the zenith of the eugenics movement.

Torpy reports that during 1977, Dr. R. T. Ravenholt, director of the United States Agency for International Development (office for population control), said that the United States hoped to sterilize 25 percent of the world's roughly 570 million fertile women. Ravenholt linked such control measures to the "normal operation of U.S. commercial interests around the world" (Johansen 1998a). These statements were published in a news story in the St. Louis Dispatch.

During this wave of sterilizations, no other medical structure had the captive clientele of the IHS, however. Torpy writes, "Native American women represented a unique class of victims among the larger population that faced sterilization and abuses of reproductive rights. . . . They had, and continue to have, a dependent relationship with the federal government which has put them at greater risk" (Johansen 1998a).

Within half a decade, IHS doctors were sterilizing so many reservation women that, according to Torpy, one Native American woman was being sterilized for every seven babies born. Outside of very occasional, anecdotal reports in a few major newspapers, the mainstream media generally ignored the wave of sterilizations as it was happening. The first large audience, detailed description of the sterilizations was published not in the United States, but in Germany. Torpy tapped sources of information in small, specialized (often leftist or health-related) journals of opinion that, taken together, sketch a history of the sterilization campaign. She credits Brightman and the International Indian Treaty Council and others, including Constance Redbird Pinkerton-Uri, for keeping the issue alive enough to spark the interest of Sen. James Abourezk of South Dakota, which led to a General Accounting Office report and congressional oversight hearings that eventually curbed the practice.

By 1974, some IHS doctors who were critical of the sterilizations began investigating on their own. Pinkerton-Uri, a physician and law student who is Choctaw and Cherokee, started her own inquiry after complaints were lodged by Native patients against the Claremore, Oklahoma, IHS hospital.

Taking publicity about the Serena cases and what she had found at Claremore, along with other pieces of evidence, Pinkerton-Uri began calling Senator Abourezk's office. The office also had received inquiries from Charlie McCarthy, an IHS employee in Albuquerque, regarding sterilizations of Native American women.

Torpy followed the trail of Abourezk's investigation, beginning with an intern in his office, Joan Adams, who took the initiative to investigate whether Native women were being sterilized without their consent and under duress. This preliminary investigation convinced Adams (and, later, Senator Abourezk) that further study was needed. Abourezk, using Adams' research, then called for a GAO investigation. Torpy described the findings of the GAO report, which surveyed IHS records in four of 12 Bureau of Indian Affairs regions: Albuquerque; Phoenix; Oklahoma City; and Aberdeen, South Dakota. The study covered only 46 months, between 1973 and 1976. (As of 1977, the IHS operated in 51 hospitals and 86 health centers or clinics.) Within this sample, the GAO found evidence that the IHS or its contractors had sterilized 3,406 women, 3,001 of them of child-bearing age (15–44 years).

Since the GAO study did not even begin to arrive at a total number of sterilizations, opponents of the practice looked at the data in another way, as a percentage of the women of child-bearing age in each examined area who were sterilized. In Oklahoma, using the GAO study's numbers, 1,761 of roughly 17,000 women of child-bearing age were sterilized. In Phoenix, the number was lower, 78 of 8,000; in Aberdeen, the figure was 740 of 9,000. They began to make a case that, with only 100,000 fertile Native women of child-bearing age in the United States, the sterilizations were putting a significant dent in the gene pools of many individual Native American nations. A population of 300 million (as in the United States) could support voluntary sterilization and survive, but for Native Americans it cannot be a preferred method of birth control. While other minorities might have a gene pool in Africa or Asia, Native Americans do not.

At times, the battle over sterilization became localized and quite heated. In response to Pinkerton-Uri's charges at the Claremore Hospital, physicians threatened to close the facility. In response, wrote Torpy, "an unidentified group of Native Americans pitched a tipi on the hospital lawn alongside the American Indian Movement flag" (Johansen 1998a).

By the mid-to-late 1970s, the sterilization program was well-known on the Native movement circuit. By 1974, *Akwesasne Notes* was carrying reports describing sterilizations, and Native American women's attempts to mobilize against them. By 1977, a class action suit had been initiated by three Montana Native American women. The names of the three Northern Cheyenne women who filed the class action suit were not released publicly out of fear that they would be condemned by other Cheyennes. The class-action suit never went to court, and never directly affected anyone other than the three claimants. Attorneys for the defendants approached the women's attorneys and offered a cash settlement on condition that the case remain sealed. The women accepted the settlement.

At about the same time, Marie Sanchez, the Northern Cheyennes' chief tribal judge, conducted her own informal poll, and found that at least 30 women she contacted had been sterilized between 1973 and 1976. It was Sanchez who found two 15-year-old girls who said that they had been told they were having their tonsils out, only to emerge from a local IHS hospital without their ovaries.

Torpy's account brings what became a general pattern down to a personal level. Another woman who had complained to a physician about migraine headaches was told that her condition was a female problem, and was advised that a hysterectomy would alleviate the problem. Her headaches continued, however, until she was diagnosed with a brain tumor.

Also during 1977, the American Indian Policy Review Commission found that the IHS lacked adequate policies, appropriations, delivery services, and oversight for provision of health services to Native Americans. Even in 1977, the rate of infant mortality on Indian reservations was three times that of the general population in the United States; the tuberculosis rate was still eight times as high. The average life span of a Native American living on a reservation was 47 years, compared with almost 71 years in the general population. The IHS seemed to be short of personnel and equipment to treat many things, but the agency always seemed to have enough doctors, nurses, equipment, and money to tie fallopian tubes and remove ovaries.

By the late 1970s, sterilizations continued at some IHS hospitals despite protests and suits. Brightman visited Claremore's IHS facility for six months during late 1978 and early

1979, collecting records for six months, and found evidence of 81 sterilizations. Brightman later related his findings as part of a speech on the U.S. Capitol steps, which was recorded and played for some of Claremore's nurses, who, according to Torpy, validated that sterilizations were occurring and with greater frequency.

Many Native women looked at the battle against sterilization as part of a broader, older, struggle to retain their families in a culturally appropriate context. The battle against sterilizations brought back memories of having children taken from their homes, beginning with the establishment of Carlisle School in 1879, to face a gauntlet of forced assimilation in a factory model of education. In 1977, roughly a third of reservation children were still attending the same system of boarding schools that had become a principal part of the assimilative model a century earlier. According to Torpy, in 1973, 33,672 Native American children lived in federal boarding schools rather than at home.

Many women also were reminded of the many Native children taken for foster care by non-Indians. In the mid-1970s, the proportion of Indian children placed in foster care in Western states (compared to the general population) ranged from 640 percent, in Idaho, to 2,000 percent, in North Dakota. This disparity was diminished (but not eliminated) by legislative measures beginning about 1980 that demanded that social workers appreciate Native ways of raising children instead of assuming that they were evidence of lack of parenting skills by Anglo-American, middle-class standards.

On many reservations today, Indian midwives or nurses advise women on whether sterilization is appropriate. The number of births to Indian women had risen to 45,871 in 1988, compared with 27,542 in 1975.

BRUCE JOHANSEN

See also

American Indian Movement (AIM); Native American Boarding Schools; Native Americans, Conquest of; Native Americas, Forced Relocation of; Women of All Red Nations (WARN)

Further Reading:

Johansen, Bruce E. "Sterilization of Native American Women Reviewed by Omaha Master's Student." *Ratville Times*, September, 1998a. http://www.ratical.org/ratville/sterilize.html.

Johansen, Bruce E. "Reprise: Forced Sterilizations." *Native Americas* 15, no. 4 (Winter, 1998b): 44–47.

Johansen, Bruce E. "Stolen Wombs: Indigenous Women Most at Risk." *Native Americas* 17, no. 2 (Summer 2000): 38–42.

Johansen, Bruce E., and Roberto F. Maestas. *Wasi'chu: The Continuing Indian Wars*. New York: Monthly Review Press, 1979.

Severson, Kim. "Payment Set for Those Sterilized in Program." *New York Times*, January 11, 2012, A-13.

Torpy, Sally. "Endangered Species: Native American Women's Struggle for their Reproductive Rights and Racial Identity: 1970s–1990s." MA thesis, History Dept., University of Nebraska at Omaha, 1998.

"Strange Fruit"

In 1939, Abel Meeropol presented a song to blues and jazz performer Billie Holiday that he wrote. The song was titled "Strange Fruit." Meeropol, a Jewish high school teacher and union activist from the Bronx, wrote the song to protest the lynching of black Southerners and asked Holiday to perform his piece. She agreed, and her haunting version of "Strange Fruit" became an anthem against racism that the British magazine *Q* called "one of the ten songs that changed the world" (January 2003). Jazz writer Leonard Feather deemed "Strange Fruit" "the first significant protest in words and music, the first unmuted cry against racism," while record producer Ahmet Ertegun declared it "a declaration of war" and "the beginning of the civil rights movement" (Margolick 2000: 10, 14). In short, few songs have had the impact on race relations that "Strange Fruit" continues to possess.

The "strange fruit hanging from the poplar trees" that Meeropol referred to were African Americans who hanged after their execution at the hands of a lynch mob. Although the most active period of lynching in American history had passed, the practice continued to plague the South when Meeropol, who used the pseudonym Lewis Allan, wrote "Strange Fruit" in the mid-1930s. He wanted to bring attention to this injustice, in hopes that the federal government would pass a national anti-lynching law. Meeropol's powerful prose contrasted the horrors of lynching with the gentility of the "gallant South." A "pastoral scene" of "poplar trees" could not hide "the bulging eyes and the twisted mouth" of "black bodies swinging in the Southern breeze." The song ended with the profound line, "Here is a strange and bitter crop."

Holiday first performed "Strange Fruit" at New York's only integrated nightclub, Café Society. When the song ended, Holiday later commented that "There wasn't even a patter of applause when I finished. Then a lone person began to clap nervously. Then suddenly everyone was clapping" (Margolick 2000: 9). The song proved so powerful that she closed all performances with "Strange Fruit." Word of the provocative song quickly spread throughout the city's liberal white elite, and Café Society mentioned the piece in its advertisements to attract customers. The *New York Post* reviewed Holiday's performance of "Strange Fruit" and said, "If the anger of the exploited ever mounts high enough in the South, it now has its Marseillaise" (Margolick 2000: 62).

The song was so intense, its topic so unpleasant, that white nightclub patrons sometimes assaulted Holiday for performing "Strange Fruit." Some theater owners prohibited her from including the song in her act, and the BBC and several American radio stations refused to play the record. Even Holiday's label, Columbia Records, refused to record the song. It was eventually produced and marketed by the smaller Commodore Records company.

There is little evidence that performances including "Strange Fruit" ignited racially motivated riots. But the potential for violence existed every time Holiday performed the inflammatory song because of the genuine emotions, both positive and negative, it evoked. For instance, she told one newspaper that she was chased out of Mobile, Alabama, for singing "Strange Fruit," but provided few details. Several stories also circulated of Southern jukeboxes that were demolished because the tune appeared on their playlists.

The power "Strange Fruit" possesses is evident in the numerous artists who have performed the song. Josh White, Sidney Bichet, Tori Amos, Cassandra Wilson, Pete Seeger, Ella Fitzgerald, Lou Rawls, Diana Ross, Sting, and UB-40, among others, have recorded their version of the piece. The song still evokes the horrors of late 19th- and 20th-century lynchings that took place in the United States, but it is also used to protest social injustices on a much broader scale. The fact, however, that "Strange Fruit" exposed the inhumanity of lynchings in such a troubling and intense manner made it both an anthem of the national anti-lynching movement and a timeless part of American popular culture.

J. Michael Butler

See also
American Literature and Racism; Holiday, Billie; Jazz

Further Reading:
Holiday, Billie, with William Dufty. *Lady Sings the Blues*. Garden City, NY: Doubleday & Company, 1956/1992.

Margolick, David. *Strange Fruit: Billie Holiday, Café Society, and the Early Cry for Civil Rights*. Philadelphia: Running Press, 2000.

Ward, Geoffrey C., and Ken Burns. *Jazz: A History of America's Music*. New York: Knopf, 2000.

Streetcars and Boycotts

Streetcar boycotts in the early 1900s and bus boycotts in the 1950s were significant acts of consumer protest by urban blacks. The boycotters wanted equal access to city services, and this meant overturning the Jim Crow laws of the time, laws that insisted that blacks go to the "back of the bus" or trolley. The streetcar boycotts failed to overturn the Jim Crow laws, but the bus boycotts did lead to changes in local laws in Baton Rouge and may have been helpful in influencing the 1956 federal court ruling that found bus segregation to be illegal.

These boycotts by black consumers occurred in more than 25 Southern cities from 1900 to 1906. The boycotts took place at a time of increasing hostility on the part of Southern whites and indifference on the part of Northern whites, a dual circumstance that may have encouraged acceptance of subservience as the prevailing attitude of Southern blacks.

The boycotts were initiated in response to Jim Crow streetcar laws enacted as part of the wave of segregation legislation passed in Southern states at the turn of the century. The streetcar companies generally opposed Jim Crow laws. The companies were concerned about the expense and difficulty of enforcing the laws. They also feared a loss of black customers, not a small consideration since blacks often constituted a majority of local riders.

Although, technically, the new segregation laws represented an abridgment of the consumer right to choose in that blacks were required to sit in the back of the streetcar, symbolically they represented much more—unjust acts whose effect upon blacks was that of humiliation and degradation. Many blacks responded to the boycotts called in their cities by refusing to ride on the streetcars. Moreover, all of the states of the old Confederacy were affected with the connection between the segregation laws and the boycotts being apparent to its black urban residents. Some of the boycotts lasted for several weeks, while others extended for much longer periods, with one in Augusta, Georgia, continuing for three years. But the boycotts were unable to reverse the legal tide of segregation in the South. As the only protest mechanism realistically available to blacks, however, the boycott tactic continued to be pursued even though failure was inevitable.

About 50 years later, Southern blacks once again vented their frustrations relating to the problems they experienced with urban public transportation, only this time, buses rather than streetcars had become the focus. The bus boycotts were of historic importance. The civil rights movement of the 1950s with its direct action component was an outgrowth of the bus boycott campaigns. These campaigns brought major disruptions to such state capitals as Baton Rouge and Montgomery.

Looking first at Baton Rouge, in June 1953, the city's black community initiated a boycott against the Jim Crow bus system. The boycott was led by T. J. Jemison, pastor of one of Baton Rouge's largest black churches. As a church leader, Jemison had close ties to the black people of Baton Rouge and to the city's black clergymen, and these two linkages gave the boycott its strength.

To finance the boycott, money was raised at nightly mass meetings in the churches, and it was used to pay for a "free car lift" and an internal "police force." The free car lift consisted of private cars that transported the boycotting workforce just as the buses had done prior to the boycott. The internal police department was used to patrol the black community and to provide bodyguards for the boycott leaders.

The boycott was completely effective, and a *New York Times* report found about 90 percent compliance. The boycotters had two primary demands—that blacks be permitted to fill bus seats on a first-come, first-served basis, and that no seats be reserved for whites. Within a few days of the boycott's inception, local white officials offered a compromise that largely accepted the first-come, first-served demand. The compromise was accepted at a mass meeting attended by 8,000 local blacks. The boycott, which ended officially on June 25, 1953, was a major victory against segregated busing.

The Montgomery boycott was perhaps the best-known protest action and most influential consumer boycott in American history. It marked the beginning of the civil rights movement and introduced to the world the man who would become the movement's leader, the Reverend Martin Luther King, Jr. The Montgomery bus boycott was triggered on Thursday, December 1, 1955, by the arrest of a black woman, Rosa Parks, for refusing to yield her seat on a city bus to a white man. Her action, a violation of local segregation laws, came two years after the successful Baton Rouge bus boycott.

On the night of Parks' arrest, local black leader Jo Ann Robinson, after conferring with colleagues, decided to organize a bus boycott of Montgomery for the following Monday, December 5. With two trusted aides, she distributed to local blacks a message urging them to join the boycott. The one-day boycott was a dramatic success in that fewer than 10 percent of Montgomery's blacks rode the city buses. Since most of the passengers who normally rode were black, the boycott engendered a substantial loss in bus revenues.

By Monday afternoon, local black leaders were well aware of the success of the boycott and looked for someone to lead its continuation. They had been favorably impressed with King, a newcomer to Montgomery. A local organization called the Montgomery Improvement Association (MIA) was formed to continue the boycott, and King was selected as its leader. By that Monday evening, his oratorical powers were made clear to an audience of 6,000 blacks whom he addressed at a local church.

The response to King's words bordered on pandemonium. The audience apparently felt they had found a boycott leader to confront the white power structure of Montgomery. The bus boycott continued for 382 days, from December 5, 1955, to December 21, 1956, a period far longer than its leaders could have foreseen.

The yearlong boycott was impressively executed. Not only did black riders stay off the buses on December 5, but they continued to stay away for the duration of the boycott. Their abstinence from the city buses was made possible by the creation of an alternative transportation system by the MIA. The system, which started as a crude voluntary effort, soon became far more sophisticated and reliable as the MIA secured funds from a variety of sources to establish an effective transportation service.

However, the success of the boycott campaign did not come easily, with serious signs of strain emerging in Montgomery after the first few weeks of the campaign's success. Matters intensified in late January when King's house was bombed. Moreover, just a month later a grand jury returned indictments for 90 of the leaders and supporters of the MIA, charging them with conspiring to carry out an illegal boycott.

The boycotters were defended by the National Association for the Advancement of Colored People (NAACP), which took the case to federal court. Several months later, the federal court in Montgomery declared on June 5, 1956, that bus segregation was illegal. The court's 2-to-1 decision was upheld by the U.S. Supreme Court on November 13, and a month later, Montgomery officials were notified of the ruling by federal marshals. The next day, December 21, 1956, the boycott ended and blacks resumed riding the buses.

These changes to the bus desegregation laws that came in the mid-1950s did not occur in a social vacuum. The strategies used by King were influenced by those employed by Theodore J. Jemison in the successful bus boycott campaign he led in Baton Rouge just a few years earlier. The decisions rendered by the Montgomery federal court and the U.S. Supreme Court reflected the successful court battles waged by attorneys for the NAACP, battles led by its respected special counsel, Thurgood Marshall, the man who would become the first black member of the Supreme Court. Moreover, the court decisions may also have been influenced by the national attention given to the yearlong Montgomery bus boycott campaign and the effect its eloquent and brave leader had on the American people.

MONROE FRIEDMAN

See also

Montgomery Bus Boycott; Parks, Rosa

Further Reading:

Friedman, Monroe. *Consumer Boycotts: Effecting Change through the Marketplace and the Media.* New York: Routledge, 1999.

Meier, August, and Elliott Rudwick. "The Boycott Movement against Jim Crow Streetcars in the South, 1900–1906." *Journal of American History* 55 (March 1969): 756–75.

Morris, Aldon D. *The Origins of the Civil Rights Movement.* New York: Free Press, 1984.

Structural Discrimination

Structural discrimination refers to policies of dominant-group institutions, and the behavior of the individuals who implement these policies and control these institutions, that are race-neutral in intent but that have a differential or harmful effect on subordinate groups. The key difference between institutional and structural discrimination is that the former is intentional while the latter is not. For example, college admissions policies are said to be meritocratic (i.e., based on grades and test scores): the better your grades and the higher your test scores, the more likely you are to be admitted. On the one hand, this is said to be race-neutral since anyone who makes the grades and test scores will be admitted. On the other hand, due to the history of discrimination and the poor quality of many urban public schools, blacks and Hispanics are more likely to have lower grades and test scores than whites and Asians and, therefore, are less likely to be admitted to more elite colleges. These meritocratic policies would be an example of structural discrimination because they have a disproportionate impact on blacks and Hispanics.

Some insurance company policies are also examples of structural discrimination. Homeowner, automobile, and business policies are generally more costly in areas where there are more burglaries and thefts. Since these are more likely to occur in poor communities of color, rates are higher there than in middle-class, white communities. Therefore, these insurance policies cost people of color more than whites, even without intentional racial discrimination. This makes it more difficult for people to own homes, cars, and businesses in communities of color.

Thus, structural discrimination refers to "ordinary," "rational," "good business" policies that have disproportionately negative impacts on people of color. The solution to structural discrimination does not involve appeals to universities and insurance companies to treat people in a color-blind way, since they may already being doing that. Blacks with high grades and test scores are coveted at most universities, and Hispanics living in white, middle-class neighborhoods might well get the same insurance rates as whites.

The solution is to change the so-called rational policies to have a more equal impact. In the college admissions example, the term *qualified* must be redefined and broadened. Grades and test scores are too narrow a definition of being qualified. Issues like overcoming adversity and type of high school attended should also be considered. As long as there are racial differences in school quality, neighborhood quality, family income, etc., using meritocratic standards will always be structurally discriminatory.

Insurance companies must understand the historical nature of neighborhood inequality and go beyond the profit-oriented rate setting policies. Otherwise, these policies will contribute to continuing inequality.

Not all scholars use the term *structural discrimination* as defined here. Some talk about *structural racism* rather than discrimination. Others do not differentiate between structural discrimination and institutional (intentional) discrimination and use them interchangeably. Still other scholars don't recognize structural discrimination as a valid concept because there is no negative intent involved. According to this view, meritocracy is the basis of higher education, and people of color must work hard to meet the standards. Likewise, insurance companies are profit-oriented institutions, so their rate-setting policies are rational. It is unfortunate, they say, that people of color are harmed. Generally, the courts do not recognize structural discrimination as illegal.

However, if one could magically eliminate all intentional discrimination, massive racial inequality would still exist in the United States. The concept of structural discrimination draws attention to the negative impact of so-called color-blind policies. Both intent and impact are important in understanding continuing racial inequality.

FRED L. PINCUS

See also

Cumulative Discrimination; Discrimination; Institutional Discrimination; Reverse Discrimination

Further Reading:

Bonilla-Silva, Eduardo. *Racism Without Racists: Color-Blind Racism and Racial Inequality in Contemporary America*, 3rd ed. Lanham, MD: Rowman and Littlefield, 2010.

Pincus, Fred L. "Discrimination Comes in Many Forms: Individual, Institutional and Structural." *American Behavioral Scientist*, 40 (November/December 1996): 15–21.

Student Nonviolent Coordinating Committee (SNCC)

The Student Nonviolent Coordinating Committee (SNCC) was a civil rights organization that operated during the 1960s. It was known for its radicalism and for rejecting the perceived conservatism of other organizations. The SNCC's high point was its work in Mississippi, where it sought to establish long-term movements within black communities. The SNCC later espoused Black Power, but disagreements over philosophy and direction ended the SNCC's effectiveness as a civil rights organization by 1966.

The SNCC emerged from the burgeoning student movement that had been engaged in sit-ins since the late 1950s. Many of those involved in its founding had been involved with the Nashville Student Movement. The SNCC was created at a conference of young activists held at Shaw University, Raleigh, North Carolina. Martin Luther King, Jr., who spoke at the conference, hoped that the activists would join the SCLC, but instead, urged by the SCLC's Ella Baker, who would be an important early influence on the SNCC, a separate organization was created, which would cooperate with all other civil rights organizations, but which would have formal affiliation with none (for a time, the SNCC shared the SCLC's Atlanta office, but the separation between the two organizations was clear).

From its foundation, the SNCC stood apart from other civil rights organizations. Many of those attending the conference at Shaw University were critical of the tactics that the National Association for the Advancement of Colored People (NAACP) and the SCLC tended to deploy, and were keen to adopt a more radical approach that addressed a wider range of issues. In particular, the SNCC rejected the model of charismatic leadership that other civil rights organizations followed, and emphasized the autonomy of local communities and movements, arguing that this was required to sustain local activism. At the Shaw University conference James Lawson, who had earlier been involved with the SCLC, set out much of what would become the SNCC's early philosophical standpoint. Rooted in the tenets of Christianity and Gandhian nonviolence, Lawson made clear the moral and spiritual dimension that would underpin the SNCC's direction. Along with Diane Nash, Marion Barry (the SNCC's first chairman), and John Lewis, Lawson was part of the Nashville movement that would dominate the SNCC's early period.

Stokely Carmichael, leader of the Student Nonviolent Coordinating Committee, speaks at a protest at the Capitol on January 10, 1967. (Bettmann/Corbis)

The SNCC's participation in the Freedom Rides helped establish it as an important civil rights organization. The Congress of Racial Equality (CORE) had undertaken the Freedom Rides to test compliance with the desegregation of interstate travel facilities. Following attacks on freedom riders in Alabama in May 1961, the SNCC, CORE, and the SCLC joined forces to continue the project. The Kennedy administration sought to defuse the situation and called for a cooling-off period, but the Freedom Rides continued, and hundreds of riders were arrested in Jackson, Mississippi, over the next three months. Rather than accept bail, freedom riders chose to serve their sentence, the first true example of the SNCC's "jail, not bail" philosophy.

The Freedom Rides positioned the SNCC as a more radical organization than the likes of the SCLC and NAACP. Loudly critical of white America's hypocrisy in allowing Jim Crow to go unchallenged in the South while advocating freedom and liberty across the world, the SNCC emerged as a credible challenger to the civil rights orthodoxy represented by King. The SNCC's founding spiritual and philosophical roots were soon obscured by a viewpoint founded both on the experiences of the Freedom Rides and independence from other civil rights organizations. The Freedom Rides emphasized the value of using direct action to forcefully demand the end of segregation, and the SNCC's refusal to compromise with perceived moderates became a central part of the SNCC's philosophy. For many SNCC staffers, the Freedom Rides and subsequent imprisonment were a seasoning process that helped to demarcate the line between the conservative tactics of the established civil rights leadership and their own urgency and vigor.

Although the SNCC's early orientation was toward direct action and confrontation, another early strand became arguably more important. In the summer of 1960, Bob Moses, who had originally travelled to Atlanta to work with the SCLC, travelled to Mississippi at the suggestion of Ella

Baker. In Mississippi, he met with Amzie Moore, an NAACP activist in the Delta town of Cleveland, who suggested to Moses that the SNCC should send volunteers into the state to assist with voter registration. Moses took up this idea enthusiastically, and it would become a fundamental part of the SNCC's ideology.

While Moses was enthused by the idea of working directly with black communities, others in the SNCC reacted with greater skepticism. The SNCC was marked by its tolerance of different intellectual and philosophical positions, but when voter registration was first mooted, activists who were intent on pursuing an active course of direct action were particularly scornful. This was partly a reaction to the Kennedy administration's efforts to deflect the SNCC's radicalism onto activities considered to be less controversial. After the Freedom Rides, President Kennedy encouraged the SNCC to focus its attention on voter registration in the South. Some SNCC activists argued, with justification, that Kennedy was merely trying to divert their activities from more high-profile, and arguably more effective, direct action in order to reduce the pressure on his administration to tackle the inevitable clashes and controversy that would attend direct action, as had been the case with the Freedom Rides.

While there was some truth in this charge, some SNCC staff agreed with Moses about the value of voter registration. The debate over whether to pursue direct action or voter registration marked the first real threat to the SNCC's stability, as supporters of direct action threatened to leave the organization if voter registration were pursued. The intervention and continued influence of Ella Baker helped avoid a split, and the SNCC essentially formed two wings a this point, one to engage in direct action, the other to work on voter registration. These two wings were held together by James Forman as executive secretary, but tensions over the direction and philosophical position of the SNCC would continue to cause debate and instability.

Despite the discussions over whether the SNCC should engage in voter registration, its work with black communities in Mississippi was arguably the SNCC's most enduring contribution to the civil rights movement. The establishment of a voter registration project in McComb, under the guidance of Bob Moses, in the summer of 1961 marked the start of a significant, long-term approach to challenging Jim Crow in Mississippi. In undertaking such a project, the SNCC embarked on a path that no other civil rights organization had traveled. Direct action to that point had tended to be coordinated and led by the urban middle class, and often relied on short-term confrontation. In undertaking voter registration activity, the SNCC engaged directly with the most disenfranchised communities in Mississippi. Recognizing the political impotence of such communities, and the reasons for that impotence, the SNCC endeavored to work with communities to help develop the tools required to register to vote, to make effective use of the vote, and to bring about long-term change.

The SNNC's activity in McComb set the template for future voter registration activity in Mississippi. While attempting to engage with all sectors of the black community, the SNCC was particularly keen to establish itself among young people who could both participate with the SNCC and lead future activism. The SNCC's efforts led to an almost immediate rise in the number of blacks trying to register to vote, but also to increased intimidation and violence, including the murder of Herbert Lee, a black farmer. This violence ended SNCC's McComb activities, but the lessons learned would be put to use during the summer project of 1964. Part of the SNCC's direct action wing was also active in McComb, and several protestors were jailed for their part in sit-ins. The McComb sit-ins, especially the involvement and jailing of local black youths, eroded the trust of the black community, and direct action of this sort never became a central part of the SNCC's later activity in Mississippi.

The SNCC's activities and its refusal to follow the lead of other civil rights organizations helped it gain an increasingly extreme reputation. This reputation was underlined by the SNCC's participation in the March on Washington in August 1963. The march attracted the most prominent civil rights leaders and was seen widely as an opportunity to support Kennedy's proposed civil rights legislation and bring the civil rights cause to national attention. The SNCC participated, and had been part of the delegation that President Kennedy had attempted to persuade to abandon the march, but many of its staff were unenthused and declined to take part. SNCC chairman John Lewis intended to use his speech to criticize fiercely the federal government for failing to protect blacks from police brutality. Before the march, a cadre of civil rights leaders met with Lewis to convince him to tone down the speech, but he insisted on castigating the government for its part in perpetuating the injustices of Mississippi. Most evocatively, Lewis called for a revolution to sweep the nation and to bring freedom to blacks. Lewis's speech crystallized the SNCC's radical reputation, and marked the distance between the SNCC and other civil rights organizations.

The SNCC stepped up its voter registration activity in Mississippi, and ahead of the general election of November 1963, it organized a Freedom Vote, which would allow black Mississippians to register and vote in a symbolic election that followed exactly the state procedure. More than 80,000 blacks participated, and the SNCC argued that this illustrated the frustrated demand for black electoral participation in Mississippi. Much of the registration work of the Freedom Vote was conducted by white volunteers from Northern universities. This tactic had a dual purpose of focusing attention on Mississippi and reducing incidents of violence against civil rights workers.

The success of the Freedom Vote persuaded the SNCC to embark on a larger, Mississippi-wide project, the Mississippi Summer Project (also known as Freedom Summer) during 1964. Although Freedom Summer operated officially under the auspices of the Council of Federated Organizations (COFO), an umbrella group of civil rights organizations that included CORE and the NAACP, as well as various Mississippi groups, the SNCC was at the forefront of the project and was responsible for much of its strategic and philosophical direction as well as for providing the majority of volunteers. As with the Freedom Vote, the SNCC again decided to use white students as volunteers, although this was the subject of considerable discussion within the SNCC. While some thought that such volunteers would help gain publicity for Freedom Summer, others believed that the presence of whites undermined black self-reliance and placed too much emphasis on white leadership.

These discussions reflected wider concerns within the SNCC about the role of whites in the civil rights movement. As the number of whites working with the SNCC grew (in 1964, around 20 percent of the SNCC's staff was white), some black activists feared that they would begin to dominate, even if unconsciously, and reduce the role of blacks within

the SNCC, as well as alienating the black Mississippians who were to be the focus of Freedom Summer. As a compromise, the Southern Students Organizing Committee (SSOC) was formed and was initially considered a white counterpart to the SNCC. The SSOC's relationship with the SNCC was never clear, and it gradually became more closely aligned to Students for a Democratic Society. Despite the formation of the SSOC, many Freedom Summer volunteers were white (indeed, the SNCC's efforts to recruit black volunteers had been relatively unsuccessful, and whites accounted for the majority of volunteers). Some within the SNCC were troubled by the suggestion that white volunteers should be prevented from assisting in challenging Jim Crow. The place of whites within the organization was a philosophical disagreement that would continue to trouble the SNCC.

During orientation sessions, the gap between the experience and philosophical outlook of the SNCC staff and summer project volunteers was clear to see. On several occasions, SNCC veterans clashed with volunteers. Experienced SNCC staff had well-formed intellectual positions about the purpose and aims of Freedom Summer, and many of them had firsthand experience of the extent to which Jim Crow was entrenched in Mississippi; few volunteers shared these experiences or such highly developed philosophical ideologies. Moreover, the volunteers were nervous, and SNCC staff was anxious about sending them into Mississippi. This resulted in several, often robust, debates about the meaning of Freedom Summer. Throughout the course of the summer project, differences in tactics and purpose would be a continued source of tension between SNCC staff and volunteers.

The main purpose of Freedom Summer was voter registration, but the project used a range of techniques and strategies to engage black Mississippians and help them to develop the skills and confidence to challenge Jim Crow. The SNCC viewed Freedom Summer as an opportunity for the mass mobilization of black communities throughout Mississippi. Increasingly critical of the approach of organizations like the SCLC and the NAACP, the SNCC hoped to use Freedom Summer to help develop local leadership within black communities. Rejecting the concept of imposed leadership from above, the SNCC's intention was for black communities to set their own agendas that could bloom into self-reliant, long-term initiatives.

A guiding principle for the summer project, one that Bob Moses had particularly influenced, was that black communities should make decisions for themselves. In order to help them develop the skills and knowledge to do so, freedom schools were an important part of Freedom Summer. Freedom schools were an attempt to counter the traditionally poor education offered to black children in Mississippi, but they also served to develop leadership within black communities. Eschewing traditional pedagogical approaches, freedom schools emphasized the experience and knowledge of the students and encouraged debate and challenge, placing the onus on students rather than teachers to set and define learning aims. As well as providing standard school subjects, freedom schools also held lessons on African American history and the philosophies and purposes of the civil rights movement. Students were encouraged to explore and discuss notions of democracy and to question the validity of Jim Crow.

Freedom schools were a central function of the SNCC's summer project strategy. Claiming that Mississippi institutions were fundamentally closed to black people, the SNCC argued that it was necessary not to open them, but to create new institutions; education was such an institution. The SNCC expected to reach around 1,000 11th- and 12th-grade children during Freedom Summer, but in fact, around 2,500 people of all ages attended. In encouraging students to express themselves and to understand and challenge the ideology of white supremacy, freedom schools did much to challenge the tenets of Jim Crow, as well as developing local leadership.

The Freedom Summer also saw the creation of the Mississippi Freedom Democratic Party (MFDP), established to challenge the seating of the Mississippi delegation at the Democratic national convention in August 1964. The MFDP would serve to illustrate the extent to which black people were excluded from Mississippi politics, and MFDP delegates were selected using the same method used by the state Democratic Party. The SNCC hoped that grassroots activists would dominate, but other interests within COFO ensured that around half of the delegates represented the black middle class. Although several Northern Democratic Party delegates had pledged their support for the MFDP, it failed to receive the votes required to be seated.

The MFDP was offered a compromise that would see some of the delegates seated as nonvoting special guests, but the SNCC argued that any such compromises must be rejected. Against the advice of more moderate supporters such as Martin Luther King and Bayard Rustin, as well as some MFDP delegates who were aligned more closely with the NAACP, the MFDP delegation chose to reject the compromise. Led by SNCC activists, delegates engaged in direct action protests, including a sit-in on the conference floor. These protests led to the offer of a second compromise, which was again rejected by MFDP delegates. The MFDP brought together local activists from across Mississippi, notably Fannie Lou Hamer, and would continue to be a hub for activism for several years.

Following Freedom Summer, the SNCC underwent a period of self-analysis as it sought to decide its future direction and purpose. Since 1960, the SNCC had become increasingly separate from other civil rights organizations, as well as from earlier liberal supporters. The SNCC's increasing radicalism and its criticism of organizations like the NAACP and SCLC, as well its failure to distance itself from accusations that it had links with communism, distanced it from the civil rights mainstream. In the analysis of the Freedom Summer, while the SNCC had achieved some success, the failure of many projects was clear. As the summer project came to an end, many projects were abandoned or left understaffed as volunteers returned home. The links that the Freedom Summer had helped create between the SNCC and black communities were strained, and organizations that the SNCC had helped to create, such as the MFDP, became increasingly autonomous; rather than address this, the SNCC turned inwards, as it tried to decide on its future. This marked the decline of the SNCC's influence as a civil rights organization.

The tensions that had long existed within the SNCC were brought into sharp focus after the Freedom Summer. Many felt that the failure of so many Freedom Summer projects confirmed a need for greater control and bureaucracy, while others continued to resist this argument. The SNCC's efforts in Mississippi had negative effects on its activities in Alabama, Georgia, and Arkansas, which had been denied resources and attention because of the Freedom Summer. Disagreements about the role of whites continued, and the SNCC increasingly developed projects that were staffed only by black activists, before eventually expelling whites from the organization in 1966.

After the disappointment of the Democratic National Convention in 1964, the SNCC had become increasingly disillusioned with mainstream politics, but after the Freedom Summer, the organization struggled to find a defining purpose, and it became less effective and less influential. While it achieved some success in Georgia, where Julian Bond was elected to the state House of Representatives (although the House refused to seat him because of his public criticism of the Vietnam War, a decision that the Supreme Court overturned in 1966), and in Alabama, where Stokely Carmichael helped to found the Lowndes County Freedom Organization, the SNCC lacked direction, and continued to drift further from the civil rights mainstream.

In 1966, Carmichael replaced John Lewis as chairman, dismissing the more moderate tactics of other civil rights organizations and espousing the doctrine of Black Power. In urging African Americans to unite and define their own goals, Black Power had links to the SNCC's tactics during the Freedom Summer, and Carmichael argued that the SNCC had never fought to integrate, but to challenge white supremacy. By this point, however, the SNCC had little support from other civil rights organizations, and the Black Power position essentially ended the SNCC's involvement in the civil rights movement. In 1967 H. Rap Brown replaced Carmichael as chairman, but, troubled by lack of funds and a declining membership, the SNCC had essentially ceased to function by this point.

SIMON T. CUTHBERT-KERR

See also

Civil Rights Movement; Freedom Rides; March on Washington Movement

Further Reading:

Branch, Taylor. *Parting the Waters: America in the King Years, 1954–63*. New York: Simon and Schuster, 1988.
Branch, Taylor. *Pillar of Fire: America in the King Years, 1963–65*. New York: Simon and Schuster, 1998.
Carson, Clayborne. *In Struggle: SNCC and the Black Awakening of the 1960s*. Cambridge, MA: Harvard University Press, 1981.
Dittmer, John. *Local People: The Struggle for Civil Rights in Mississippi*. Urbana: University of Illinois Press, 1995.
Lewis, John, with Michael D'Orso. *Walking with the Wind: A Memoir of the Movement*. New York: Simon and Schuster, 1998.
Mills, Kay. *This Little Light of Mine: The Life of Fannie Lou Hamer*. New York: Dutton Signet, 1994.
Zinn, Howard. *SNCC: The New Abolitionists*. New York: Beacon Press, 1965.

Sundown Towns

A sundown town is any organized jurisdiction that for decades kept African Americans or other groups from living in it and was thus "all-white" on purpose. They are so named because some marked their city limits with signs typically reading, "Nigger, Don't Let The Sun Go Down On You In ___."

These towns were not, in fact, all white. "Sundown suburbs" excepted and, to a degree, accepted black live-in servants in white households. Moreover, some communities that took pains to define themselves as sundown towns nevertheless allowed one or even two exceptional black households within their otherwise all-white populations. When Pana, for example, in central Illinois, drove out its African Americans in 1899, killing five in the process, residents did not expel the black barber and his family. With an exclusively white clientele, hence friends in the white community, no one complained about him. Pana did post sundown signs at its corporate limits, signs that remained up at least until 1960, and permitted no other African Americans to move in, so it became a sundown town. Other sundown towns have let in more temporary intruders: flood refugees, soldiers during wartime, college students, and visiting interracial athletic teams and their fans. Most sundown towns and suburbs outside the West—and some in that region—allowed Asian Americans and Mexican Americans as residents. Thus, "all-white" towns may include nonblack minorities and even a tiny number of African Americans.

Sundown towns range from hamlets like Deland, Illinois, population 500, to large cities like Appleton, Wisconsin, with 57,000 residents in 1970. Sundown suburbs could be even larger, such as Glendale, a suburb of Los Angeles, with more than 60,000; Levittown, on Long Island, more than 80,000; and Warren, a Detroit suburb with 180,000. Entire counties went sundown, usually when their county seats did.

These towns and practices date back to the Great Retreat that whites forced African Americans to make between 1890 and 1940. This period is becoming known as the "nadir of race relations," when lynchings peaked, white owners expelled black baseball players from the major (and minor) leagues, and unions drove African Americans from such occupations as railroad fireman and meat cutter. In those years, thousands of towns across the United States expelled their black populations or took steps to forbid African Americans from living in them. Independent sundown towns were soon joined by "sundown suburbs," mostly between 1900 and 1968. Many suburbs kept out not only African Americans but also Jews.

Towns that had no African American residents passed ordinances, or thought they did, forbidding blacks from remaining after dark. In California, for example, the Civilian Conservation Corps in the 1930s tried to locate a company of African American workers in a large park that bordered Burbank and Glendale. Both cities refused, each citing an old ordinance that prohibited African Americans within their city limits after sundown. Some towns believed their ordinances remained in effect long after the 1954 *Brown v. Board of Education* decision and the Civil Rights Act of 1964. The city council of New Market, Iowa, for example, suspended its sundown ordinance for one night in the mid-1980s to allow an interracial band to play at a town festival, but it went back into effect the next day. Other towns never claimed to have passed an ordinance but nevertheless kept out African Americans by city action, such as cutting off water and sewage or having police call hourly all night with reports of threats.

Sundown towns have also maintained themselves all-white by a variety of less formal measures, public and private. As far back as the 1920s, police officers routinely followed, stopped, and harassed black motorists in sundown towns. Suburbs used zoning and eminent domain to keep out black would-be residents and to take their property if they did manage to acquire it. Some towns required all residential areas to be covered by restrictive covenants—clauses in deeds that stated, like this example from Brea, California, "[N]o part of said premises shall ever be sold, conveyed, transferred, leased or rented to any person of African, Chinese or Japanese descent." After a U.S. Supreme Court 1948 decision in *Shelley v. Kraemer* rendered such covenants illegal to enforce, some suburbs relied on neighborhood associations among homeowners, allowing them to decide arbitrarily what constituted an acceptable buyer. Always, lurking under the surface, was the threat of violence, such as assaulting African American children as they tried to go to school, or milder white misbehavior, such as refusing to sell groceries or gasoline to black newcomers.

The civil rights movement left sundown towns largely untouched. Indeed, some locales in the border states forced out their black populations in response to *Brown v. Board of Education*. Sheridan, Arkansas, for example, compelled its African Americans to move to neighboring Malvern in 1954, after the school board's initial decision to comply with *Brown* prompted a firestorm of protest. Having no black populations, these towns and counties then had no African Americans to test their public accommodations. For 15 years after the 1964 Civil Rights Act, motels and restaurants in some sundown towns continued to exclude African Americans, thus having an adverse impact on black travelers who had to avoid them or endure humiliating and even dangerous conditions.

At their peak, just before 1970, the United States had perhaps 10,000 sundown towns. Illinois alone probably had at least 500, a clear majority of all incorporated places. In several other northern states—Oregon and Indiana, for example—more than half of all incorporated communities probably excluded African Americans. Whole subregions—the Ozarks, the Cumberland, a band of counties on both sides of the Iowa-Missouri border, most of the suburbs of Los Angeles—went sundown—not every town, but enough to warrant the generalization. However, except for some suburbs that became all-white mostly after 1930, sundown towns were rare in the traditional South. There, whites were appalled by the practice, not wanting their maids to leave.

The practice of exclusion was usually quite open. Hundreds of towns posted signs. The Academy Award–winning movie of 1947, *Gentleman's Agreement,* was about the method by which Darien, Connecticut, one of the most prestigious suburbs of New York City, kept out Jews, and that publicity hardly ended the practice. In the 1960s, some residents of Edina, Minnesota, the most prestigious suburb of Minneapolis, boasted that their community had, as they put it, "Not one Negro and not one Jew." Residents of Anna, Illinois, still apply the acrostic "Ain't No Niggers Allowed" to their town.

Even though proud to be all white, elite sundown suburbs have usually tried to avoid being known for it. This is the "paradox of exclusivity." Residents of towns such as Darien, Connecticut, for instance, want Darien to be known as an "exclusive" community of the social, moneyed elite rather than as an "excluding" community, especially on racial or religious grounds. So long as elite sundown suburbs like

Darien, Kenilworth (near Chicago), Edina, or La Jolla (a community within San Diego) appear to be "accidentally" all white, they avoid this difficulty.

Until 1968, new all-white suburbs were forming much more rapidly than old sundown towns, and suburbs were caving in. That year, Title VIII of the Civil Rights Act, along with the *Jones v. Mayer* Supreme Court decision barring discrimination in the rental and sale of property, caused the federal government to change sides and oppose sundown towns. Since then, citywide residential prohibitions against Jews, Asian American, Native Americans, and Hispanics/Latinos have disappeared. Even vis-à-vis African Americans, many towns and suburbs—certainly more than half—relaxed their exclusionary policies in the 1980s, 1990s, and 2000s. Hotels and restaurants, even in towns that continue to exclude black residents, are generally open. However, many towns still make it uncomfortable or unwise for African Americans to live in them.

JAMES W. LOEWEN

See also

Residential Segregation

Further Reading:

Blocker, Jack S. *A Little More Freedom: African Americans Enter the Urban Midwest, 1860–1930.* Columbus: Ohio State University Press, 2008.

Jaspin, Elliot. *Buried in the Bitter Waters.* New York: Basic Books, 2007.

Loewen, James W. *Sundown Towns.* New York: New Press, 2005.

Newman, Dorothy K., et al. *Protest, Politics, and Prosperity.* New York: Pantheon, 1978.

Pfaelzer, Jean. *Driven Out.* New York: Random House, 2007.

Pickens, William. "Arkansas—A Study in Suppression." In *These "Colored" United States: African American Essays from the 1920s,* edited by Tom Lutz and Susanna Ashton, 34–35. New Brunswick, NJ: Rutgers University Press, 1996.

Sweet, Ossian H. (1894–1960)

Dr. Ossian Sweet, a former resident of Florida, migrated to Detroit during the Great Migration of African Americans from the South to major Northern industrial cities in the United States (1910–1920s). His purchase of a home confronted racial segregation in Detroit, Michigan, and answered the question of whether an African American had the right to defend his or her property.

Most Detroit residents of apparent African American descent were forced to reside in an eastside location known as Paradise Valley. In May 1925, Dr. Ossian Sweet made arrangements to purchase 2905 Garland Street, a single home bungalow in what appeared to be an all-white eastside neighborhood. The immediate area included apartments, a grocery store, and an elementary school. Sweet made himself visible as he inspected the property and its surroundings. The home's previous owners, Ed and Marie Smith, had occupied the Garland home for two years. Ed Smith was an African American with a light complexion and apparently the neighborhood Negro haters overlooked or were ignorant of his lineage. Nevertheless, once sale of the Garland house was known, Marie Smith received a threat for selling the house and was told that the caller would get Sweet as well.

Sweet graduated from Wilberforce College, followed by Howard University School of Medicine. Raised in a politically conscious and hardworking family with at least nine siblings, Ossian Sweet's father, Henry Sweet, believed in self-sufficiency for his sons. Consequently, Ossian Sweet financed his own education. After graduating with his medical degree in 1922, Sweet married Gladys Mitchell and both traveled to North Africa and Europe—Germany, France, Austria, and England—where he received further specialized medical training. Sweet chose to practice gynecology and obstetrics at Detroit's progressive New Negro hospital, Dunbar Memorial Hospital (named after poet and writer Paul Laurence Dunbar). The Sweets had one child, Marguerite Iva Sweet, their daughter.

In 1925, the Detroit, Michigan, arm of the Ku Klux Klan (KKK) was large and active. In the 1923 Detroit mayoral election, KKK candidate Charles Bowles narrowly lost to John Smith. Commonly, during 1925, mobs of racist whites quickly formed to keep African Americans from integrating neighborhoods. On June 23, 1925, Dr. Alexander Turner, along with his wife and mother-in-law, were moving into their home on Spokane Street when they were met by the Tireman Avenue Improvement Association—hundreds of neighbors who gathered in front of them with rocks, potatoes, and garbage to throw at Turner's westside home. At gunpoint, two men forced Turner to sign his deed over to them and, with the help of the police, had the Turner family escorted from the

A Michigan historical marker is shown in the yard of the Ossian Sweet House after its dedication in Detroit, July 22, 2004. The marker commemorates a milestone in the civil rights movement and in Michigan's history, namely that a man, regardless of his race, had the right to defend his property. (AP Photo/Paul Sancya)

premises. One block away from the de facto designated Negro neighborhood, Vollington Bristol constructed and moved into his apartment building on July 7, 1925, and refused to adjust his rent and choice of who could rent an apartment. Several days of violence ensued. On June 10, 1925, John Fletcher was preparing to have dinner with his wife and two children when a mob of neighbors began attacking the house. Two shots were fired from the Fletcher home, injuring a youth. Fletcher was jailed for an evening, and the family later fled their home. Hence, Dr. Sweet knew what to expect from an angry white mob when he moved into his Garland home.

Sweet's pending move to Garland Street encouraged the formation of the Waterworks Park Improvement Association, which held at least one meeting at Howe Elementary School (named for abolitionist and composer of the *Battle Hymn of the Republic*, Julia Ward Howe), located across the street from

Sweet's home. Sweet notified the Detroit Police Department of his intention to move into his home. On September 8, 1925, Dr. Sweet and his family and friends moved in their Garland home. On their first evening, it is estimated that a group of 500 to 800 individuals, led by the Waterworks Park Improvement Association, gathered in front of the Sweet home.

On September 9, 1925, another large crowd gathered and some individuals began chucking rocks into 2905 Garland. About 8:30 P.M., fearful occupants fired shots from the upper level of the home. Leon Breiner was shot and killed, and another neighbor, Eric Houghberg, was shot in the leg. Eleven occupants were taken into custody, including Gladys Sweet, and were charged with first-degree murder.

The National Association for the Advancement of Colored People (NAACP) hired famed attorney Clarence Darrow, assisted by Arthur Garfield Hays, to defend the 11 defendants.

Judge Frank Murphy allowed Gladys Sweet to be released on bail on October 2, 1925. The other 10 defendants were Dr. Ossian Sweet, Henry Sweet, Dr. Otis Sweet, William E. Davis, John Latting, Joe Mack, Leonard Morris, Morris Murray, Charles Washington, and Hewitt Watson. On November 27, 1925, Judge Frank Murphy declared a mistrial and dismissed the jury when they were unable to reach a verdict after 46 hours of deliberation. The defendants were released on bail in December 1925.

Henry Sweet fired the gun that killed Breiner. The trial, *Michigan v. Sweet*, began on April 13, 1926. On May 13, 1926, after four hours of deliberation, Henry Sweet was found not guilty. Over a year later, in July 1927, the prosecutor dismissed all charges against the remaining defendants. The Sweet case reinforced the right of an African American to self-defense.

Tuberculosis claimed the lives of Sweet's daughter in 1926 and his wife in 1928. Dr. Sweet was unable to sell his home until 1944. He committed suicide on March 19, 1960. The Sweet home is listed in the *National Register of Historic Places*. *See also* Detroit (Michigan) Riot of 1943.

REGINA V. JONES

See also

Great Migration; Jim Crow Laws

Further Reading:

Boyle, Kevin. *Arc of Justice: A Saga of Race, Civil Rights, and Murder in the Jazz Age*. New York: Henry Holt, 2004.

Vine, Phyllis. *One Man's Castle: Clarence Darrow in Defense of the American Dream*. New York: Amistad, 2004.

Symbolic Ethnicity

Symbolic ethnicity is the expression of ethnic identity by third- and fourth-generation descendants of immigrants, for whom ethnicity no longer dictates social behaviors. The concept originated in Herbert Gans's analysis of the visibility of ethnicity among third- or fourth-generation "ethnics," whose grandparents and great-grandparents migrated to the United States from Europe.

According to Gans, the ethnic visibility among third and fourth generations (i.e., ethnic revival) does not contradict the straight-line theory of assimilation in which each new

---

Elizabeth Warren Senate Race

It is often joked that everyone in the United States makes claim to some measure of Native American heritage. The extent of the connection, however, stops at conversational claims, without exhibiting any direct connection to the culture, and often without clear documentation of ancestry. Controversy plagued Elizabeth Warren's 2012 Senate race over the legitimacy of her claims to Native American ancestry. It was discovered that, during her graduate work, she was listed in the Harvard Law School directory as a minority, and she has made reference publicly to this claim. The campaign of her opponent in the race, Scott Brown, demanded, unsuccessfully, that she release documentation proving her ancestry. The event sparked media deliberation over the looseness with which such claims are often made, in contrast to the stricter principles that typically govern official membership in Native American tribes.

---

generation of immigrants becomes increasingly assimilated to American mainstream society. The third generation and beyond—compared to the preceding generations who have actually internalized ethnic heritages and practiced ethnic cultures of their homelands in their everyday lives—emphasize concerns with identity. In order to obtain the feeling of being "ethnic," these generations resort to the use of ethnic symbols. Thus, ethnicity for them becomes symbolic rather than instrumental.

Symbolic ethnicity is characterized by a nostalgic attachment to the original culture of a homeland, a love for and a pride in a tradition that can be felt without affecting everyday behavior in American lives. One distinctive feature of symbolic ethnicity, then, is that it typically does not regulate the daily activities of those who embrace it, and also does not usually reflect a shared experience regarding lifestyle. Over time, white ethnics may activate their particular heritage as a way to manifest distinctiveness without a profound effect on social behavior. For instance, Americans with Italian roots might celebrate Columbus Day, and those of German origin may drink beer on Octoberfest to feel a sense of being "ethnic" without participating in the less public aspects of the culture. Individuals who "identify as

Irish . . . on occasions such as Saint Patrick's Day, on family holidays, or for vacations . . . do not usually belong to Irish-American organizations, live in Irish neighborhoods, work in Irish jobs, or marry other Irish people" (Hier and Bolaria 2006: 138).

In symbolic ethnicity, "the old ethnic cultures serve no useful function for third generation ethnics who lack direct and indirect ties to the old country, and neither need nor have much knowledge about it" (Gans 1979: 6). In other words, people of these generations can continue to *perceive* themselves as ethnics, while ethnic ties continue to wane for them. Mary C. Waters, in her discussion of the choice of ethnicity among Roman Catholics in the United States, argues that in their attachment to ethnic identity there is a wish for community at the same time that they want to maintain individualism. Thus, their ethnicity has a volitional dimension (Waters 1990).

Expressions of symbolic ethnicity may be manifested through participation in public festivals, visiting ethnic businesses and restaurants, or preparing ethnic dishes for holiday meals. Participation in or attendance at cultural parades also provides a mechanism for increasing symbolic attachment to ethnic groups, without typically creating strong ethnic ties. Parades have been especially crucial in the case of Irish heritage, most notably in the late 18th and early 19th centuries. Marston notes, "The parades have been seen as instrumental to the construction and maintenance of an Irish national identity in North America and to making symbolic though temporary political claims to urban space" (2002: 374). Their significant role in shaping symbolic Irish ethnicity has led to a clash over control of the events, as evidenced in the U.S. case *Hurley v. Irish-American Gay, Lesbian and Bisexual Group of Boston* (515 U.S. 557, 1995), which concerned the exclusion of LGBT groups from a public parade hosted by a private organization.

Although symbolic identity is most commonly applied to European ethnicities, the same phenomenon sheds light on other claims to ethnicity as well. In recent politics, controversy plagued Elizabeth Warren's 2012 Senate campaign over the legitimacy of her claims to Native American ancestry when it was discovered that she was listed in the Harvard Law School directory as a minority, though her appearance struck many as clearly white. The campaign of her opponent in the race, Scott Brown, demanded unsuccessfully that she release documentation proving her ancestry. The event sparked media deliberation over the looseness with which such claims are often made, in contrast to the stricter principles which typically govern official membership in Native American tribes.

As observed in Waters's work, mixed ethnic backgrounds, especially those of primarily European descent, are of the sort that one can choose whether or not to identify with them. Therefore, a person from multiple European ethnic backgrounds would have the option at any given time of identifying with any one of these ethnic identities. Due to the strength of externally imposed racial lines, however, these ethnic options are not easily available to nonwhite racial groups in the United States.

Kazuko Suzuki

See also

Ethnicity; Whiteness Studies

Further Reading:

Alba, Richard D. *Ethnic Identity: The Transformation of White America.* New Haven, CT: Yale University Press, 1999.

Gans, Herbert J. "Symbolic Ethnicity: The Future of Ethnic Groups and Cultures in America." *Ethnic and Racial Studies* 2, no. 1 (1979): 1–20.

Gans, Herbert J. "Comment: Ethnic Invention and Acculturation: A Bumpy-line Approach." *Journal of American Ethnic History* 12 (1992): 43–52.

Gans, Herbert J. "Symbolic Ethnicity and Symbolic Religiosity: Toward a Comparison of Ethnic and Religious Acculturation." *Ethnic and Racial Studies* 17, no. 4 (1994): 577–92.

Hier, Sean P., and B. S. Bolaria. *Identity and Belonging: Rethinking Race and Ethnicity in Canadian Society.* Toronto: Canadian Scholars Press, 2006.

Hurley v. Irish-American Gay, Lesbian, and Bisexual Group of Boston, 515 U.S. 557 (1995). http://www.law.cornell.edu/supct/html/94-749.ZS.html

Little, Morgan. "Brown, Warren Renew Fight over Native American Heritage Controversy." *Los Angeles Times.* September 25, 2012. http://www.latimes.com/.

Marston, Sallie A. "Making Difference: Conflict over Irish Identity in the New York City St. Patrick's Day Parade." *Political Geography* 21, no. 3 (2002): 373–92.

Siek, Stephanie. "Who's a Native American? It's Complicated." *CNN's In America.* May 14, 2012. http://inamerica.blogs.cnn.com/.

Waters, Mary C. *Ethnic Options: Choosing Identities in America.* Berkeley: University of California Press, 1990.

Symbolic Racism

Donald Kinder and David Sears first coined "symbolic racism" in 1981 in "Prejudice and Politics: Symbolic Racism Versus Racial Threats to the Good Life." Symbolic racism includes the beliefs that blacks no longer face racial discrimination, that blacks' lack of progress is due to their own inabilities, and that blacks have received more than they deserve. It is deemed "symbolic" because whites' beliefs about blacks are not rooted in tangible self-interests but rather loose ideas about the moral values of blacks, ideas that whites learn during childhood. Kinder and Sears study the origins and operations of symbolic racism as they are principally interested in how racial prejudice affects political representation and race-related policies such as affirmative action and busing.

Symbolic racism is a form of modern racism, racism that emerged after the end of the civil rights movement. Symbolic racism is a combination of whites' prejudiced attitudes against people of color and an emphasis on traditional American values. Whites come to believe early on in life that blacks violate deeply held ideologies of the United States such as individualism, hard work, and respectability; thus, whites feel that blacks violate important American ethics and develop a specific set of prejudiced attitudes against blacks. This "antiblack affect" is not a consequence of real or rational ideas about blacks, but rather a cultivated disposition towards them—hence, "symbolic." This symbolic racism has real consequences as whites then oppose race-related policies as (1) they violate whites' ideological belief in hard work and merit, and (2) whites don't believe that blacks deserve help and privileges. Whites' allegiance to symbolic racism has been tested with survey questions, which have four "themes" or sets of questions: denial of continuing discrimination, work ethic and responsibility for outcomes, excessive demands, and undeserved advantage. These questions ask whites about policies like (not exact phrasing of questions): Do you think blacks need welfare? Do blacks get more than they are entitled to? and Do you agree with busing in order to achieve racial desegregation? Results showed that whites, overwhelmingly, support the idea of equal opportunity for blacks, but they opposed racial policies like busing, racial quotas, and welfare. Moreover, this opposition to policies like busing is *not* tied to one's personal fears or "racial threats" to one's own family,

but rather is a *generalized* fear about the fate of whites should these policies take effect. Thus, proponents of symbolic racism find much support for this concept.

The theory of symbolic racism, though widely recognized and a significant contribution to the literature, has faced some scrutiny. One criticism was that by coining the concept "symbolic *racism*," Kinder and Sears were implying that whites were still (intentionally) racist. Thus, in 1996, Kinder with a new co-author, Lynn Sanders, revised the theory of symbolic racism and coined the concept of "racial resentment" in order to avoid the accusation of explicit racism. Another criticism was from Lawrence Bobo, who writes on laissez-faire racism, and who said symbolic racism is too focused on the individual and is without a thorough analysis of how individual attitudes influence group politics and political policies. Bobo (2004) and Feagin (2006) also criticize the theory for not paying sufficient attention to how whites maintain a vested interest in maintaining the racial hierarchy in their favor.

Attitudes about the necessity of racial segregation and the biological inferiority of blacks saw a quick decline after

---

Antiblack Affect

One of the hallmarks of symbolic racism is an "antiblack affect," general negative thoughts and attitudes about blacks. A recent poll by the Associated Press published in October 2012 reveals that Americans continue to have negative feelings about blacks, many of which have increased since 2010. For example, 31 percent of Americans reported liking blacks a great deal in 2010, but that number dropped to 24 percent in 2012. In 2010, 44 percent of Americans reported that "determined to succeed" described blacks moderately well, but that percentage fell to 35 percent in 2012, and 43 percent of Americans attributed "law abiding" to blacks moderately well compared to 38 percent in 2012. Furthermore, about a third believe that blacks just need to try harder in order to be as well off as whites, and a fifth believe that blacks receive more economically than they deserve. These responses to survey questions on racial attitudes reveal that an antiblack affect continues to persist in the United States.

World War II, yet attitudes about keeping an appropriate distance between blacks and whites persist. In this way, whites can support the principles of racial integration but without the desire for increased contact with blacks. Thirty years after it was first introduced, Sears and Henry (2005) defend the utility of the symbolic racism theory. They argue that the theory continues to be useful on many scales of measurement and underscores the ways whites use individualism to counter policies targeted at racial equality. They argue that though the theory has a strong focus on ideology and individual attitudes, the theory explains political consequences distinct from ideological correlations. Furthermore, they cite symbolic racism as one of the first comprehensive theories of "new racism" and as a serious challenge to post–civil rights era optimism.

HEPHZIBAH STRMIC-PAWL

See also

Affirmative Action; Color-Blind Racism; Racism; Reverse Racism

Further Reading:

Bobo, Lawrence. "Inequalities That Endure? Racial Ideology, American Politics, and the Peculiar Role of the Social Sciences." In *The Changing Terrain of Race and Ethnicity*, edited by Maria Krysan and Amanda E. Lewis, 13–42. New York: Russell Sage Foundation, 2004.

Feagin, Joe. *Systemic Racism: A Theory of Oppression*. New York: Routledge, 2006.

Kinder, Donald, and David Sears. "Prejudice and Politics: Symbolic Racism Versus Racial Threats to the Good Life." *Journal of Personality and Social Psychology* 40 (1981): 414–31.

Sears, David, and Henry, P. J. "Over Thirty Years Later: A Contemporary Look at Symbolic Racism." In *Advances in Experimental Social Psychology*, edited by M. P. Zanna, 95–150. San Diego: Academic Press, 2005.

Sniderman, Paul M., and Philip Tetlock. "Reflections on American Racism." In *Racism: Essential Readings*, edited by Ellis Cashmore and James Jennings, 217–24. Thousand Oaks: Sage, 2001.

Systemic Racism

The theory of systemic racism emphasizes how racism is infused into all of the major parts of society, hence the "system" of systemic. It also emphasizes that contemporary racism needs to be connected to the long history of oppression in the United States. This theory understands racism as a "ladder of exploitation," which has material, social, educational, and political dimensions that work together to reproduce unfair enrichment for whites. Systemic racism is developed in Joe Feagin's 2000 book *Racist America* and expanded on in his 2006 book, *Systemic Racism*.

Systemic racism analyzes the material and historical roots of racism, which contrasts with other theories of racism that (1) focus on assimilation and ethnicity, (2) focus on race and stratification, or (3) focus on the ideological constructions of race. From the standpoint of systemic racism, these other theories of race and racism ignore the historical exploitation of racial minorities that have led to current conditions and inequalities and tend to see racism as a disease or virus in an otherwise healthy society. Furthermore, these obfuscations then take the focus off (wealthy) white men who created and sustained the discriminatory institutions and who still benefit today. In order to have a more holistic analysis of race and racism, Feagin defines six aspects of systemic racism. First is the exploitation and discrimination perpetrated by whites. To "exploit" is to take advantage of another for one's own personal gain. For example, whites systematically coerced and killed Native Americans in order to acquire their land; whites also systematically bought and sold African Americans in order to grow the sugar and cotton economy. Second are the resources and power that were unjustly acquired by whites. In this case, whites unjustly gained resources and power through slavery, segregation, and Native American genocide; concurrently, the racial minorities that were oppressed by whites were unjustly impoverished. The third feature is the white-controlled ideologies and institutions that maintain unequal access to resources. In other words, the racist ideology and structures necessary to perpetuate the racial hierarchy and unequal access to resources are shared from one generation to the next. Whites have inherited wealth, power, and prestige from their ancestors while using the ideologies of hard work and merit to rationalize their contemporary positions. The fourth aspect of systemic racism is how the prejudices and stereotypes of the racist ideology maintain inequality. That is, whites have come to understand themselves as "rugged individuals," "hard workers," and "deserving" while describing blacks, on the whole, as "lazy," "criminals," and "undeserving." The fifth component is the racialized emotions that are in conjunction with prejudice and discrimination. For example, a stereotype of black men is "criminal" and the racialized emotion is "fear." Whites then act irrationally when they see a black man as they combine the image of black man, the stereotype of criminal, and the emotion of fear. The sixth aspect is the severe costs that both the oppressed and oppressors experience as a result of racism. There are many costs that are the result of consistent discrimination including economic costs, less access to resources, physical and mental health deficiencies, and loss of energy. The oppressors also experience costs as they learn a lack of compassion as ignoring the humanity in others is necessary to rationalize discrimination.

Systemic racism is particularly useful in understanding how contemporary racial inequalities are rooted in past material connections and racist ideology. For example, whites today have 20 times greater the wealth of blacks; in 2010 the median household net worth for whites was approximately $110,000 compared to $5,000 for blacks and $7,400 for Hispanics. Wealth affords access to home mortgages, cars, education, health care, and access to many other resources and institutions that afford quality of life and mobility. Wealth is accumulated intergenerationally (from parent to child), so it necessarily has a historical trajectory. Some argue that this racial wealth gap is merely a consequence of hard work and mobility, but systemic racism permits a more sophisticated analysis of the contemporary racial wealth gap. Employment segregation, denial of home mortgages, and exclusion from schools and colleges have, over time, created mass wealth for whites and denial of wealth building for blacks. As Feagin notes, "In every generation, major organizational and institutional structures protect the highly racialized enrichment and impoverishment that are central to U.S. society" (2006: 270).

Systemic racism aims to be a more holistic theory of racism by attending to historical, material, and ideological connections. The theory lends itself to both an extensive historical analysis of oppression along with a way to understand how contemporary racism persists. Furthermore, it describes how "racial framing," an organized set of ideas, emotions, notions, and inclinations, perpetuate racial inequities.

HEPHZIBAH STRMIC-PAWL

See also

Color-Blind Racism; Laissez-Faire Racism; Racism; Symbolic Racism

Further Reading:

Feagin, Joe. *Racist America: Roots, Current Realities, and Future Reparations: Remaking America with Anti-Racist Strategies*. New York: Routledge, 2000.

Feagin, Joe. "Toward an Integrated Theory of Systemic Racism." In *The Changing Terrain of Race and Ethnicity*, edited by Maria Krysan and Amanda E. Lewis, 203–23. New York: Russell Sage Foundation, 2004.

Feagin, Joe. *Systemic Racism: A Theory of Oppression*. New York: Routledge, 2006.

Luhby, Tami. "Worsening Wealth Inequality by Race." *CNN Money*. June 21, 2012. http://money.cnn.com/2012/06/21/news/economy/wealth-gap-race/index.htm.

T

Takaki, Ronald (1939–2009)

One of the nation's preeminent scholars of America's ethnic diversity and multicultural history, Ronald Takaki was a professor of Ethnic Studies at the University of California, Berkeley until his retirement in 2004. Takaki has written several award-winning books on the history of Americans, Chicanos, Native Americans, the Irish, and Jews.

In 1886, Takaki's grandfather emigrated from Japan to work in the cane fields of Hawaii. His mother was born on a Hawaiian plantation. He was born in 1939 and grew up on the island of Oahu. As a young person, he took a religion course taught by Dr. Shunji Nishi, a Japanese American with a PhD. Nishi became a mentor, and arranged for Takaki to attend the College of Wooster in Wooster, Ohio. His experiences there convinced him his fellow white students did not see him as a fellow American.

A key event in Takaki's life centered around his Caucasian wife's family's refusal to accept him because he was Asian American. He decided to dedicate his life to the cause of the acceptance of Asian Americans as Americans.

Takaki received his PhD in American history from Berkeley in 1967 and was subsequently hired by University of California, Los Angeles (UCLA) to teach that school's first black history course. He became a faculty adviser to the black students and helped them form the Black Student Union. He also helped to found the UCLA Centers for African-American, Asian-American, Chicano, and Native-American Studies.

In addition to teaching over 10,000 students, Takaki was a guest lecturer throughout the world. In 1987 and 1990, Takaki presented papers comparing race and ethnicity in the United States and the USSR and on the impact of the Cold War on racial and ethnic conflicts to the Academy of Sciences of the Soviet Union. Takaki died in 2009 after many years of suffering from multiple sclerosis.

Some of the books he has written include *A Different Mirror: A History of Multicultural America*; *Race at the End of History*; *Strangers from a Different Shore: A History of Asian Americans*; *A Pro-Slavery Crusade*; *Violence in the Black Imagination*; *Iron Cages: Race and Culture in 19th-Century America*; *Hiroshima: Why America Dropped the Atomic Bomb*; *From Different Shores: Perspectives on Race and Ethnicity in America*; and *A Larger Memory: A History of Our Diversity with Voices*.

Jo York

See also
Ethnic Studies

Further Reading:
Takaki, Ronald. *A Different Mirror: A History of Multicultural America*. Boston: Back Bay Books, 1994.
Takaki, Ronald. *A Larger Memory: A History of our Diversity, With Voices*. Boston: Back Bay Books, 1998.

Takaki, Ronald. "The Authors: Ronald Takaki." Hachette Book Group USA. http://www.twbookmark.com/authors/93/192/ (accessed July 21, 2006).

Takaki, Ronald, ed. *Debating Diversity: Clashing Perspectives on Race and Ethnicity in America*, 3rd ed. New York: Oxford University Press, 2002.

Talbert, Mary B. (1866–1923)

Mary Morris Burnett Talbert was one of the foremost African American clubwomen, civil rights activists, and educators of the early 20th century. She commanded an influential organization that aided Southern blacks who had migrated to Northern cities. Late in her life, Talbert worked tirelessly to end the lynching of blacks.

Born in Oberlin, Ohio, on September 16, 1866, Talbert spent her youth in this rural town. She graduated from Oberlin College in 1886 and moved from Ohio to Little Rock, Arkansas, where she worked as a teacher and principal of a black high school. In Arkansas, she met and married William Talbert. They relocated to Buffalo, New York, where Talbert made a life for herself as a race woman and social worker.

In Buffalo, Talbert organized community support for African Americans who settled in this industrial center of upstate New York. She was a founding member of the Phyllis Wheatley Club of Buffalo and the Empire State Federation of Colored Women. The Wheatley Club raised awareness in the Buffalo community on matters affecting African American life. The club provided social services to black residents, patronized black artistic endeavors, and promoted African American culture in the region. Talbert's stewardship of the Wheatley Club led to a high profile in the National Association of Colored Women (NACW), the governing body of black women's clubs. Talbert presided over the NACW between 1916 and 1920. Her tenure as NACW president was marked by several successful fundraising ventures, including the restoration of famed abolitionist Frederick Douglass's home in Washington, D.C., and the multimillion-dollar support of American forces during World War I.

Concurrent with her NACW duties, Talbert organized new branches for the National Association for the Advancement of Colored People (NAACP) from 1918 to 1919 and traveled to France in the spring of 1919 as an investigator for the Young Men's Christian Association. Talbert served also as vice president of the NAACP and as a keynote speaker at the International Council of Women conference in Norway in 1920. For her considerable civil rights work, Talbert was awarded the NAACP's Spingarn Medal in 1922.

In the 1920s, Talbert devoted herself to eradicating the lynching of blacks, one of the most pressing issues that drove Southern blacks northward. Talbert founded and ran the Anti-Lynching Crusaders, which focused its efforts on congressional approval of the Dyer Anti-Lynching Bill of 1922. The Dyer Bill would have mandated a jail sentence and a hefty fine for any group of three or more persons involved in a lynching. The bill met with considerable opposition from the Democratic Party, in control of much of Congress. Senate Democrats mounted a filibuster against the bill in December 1922, sinking its chances for passage. The stress of running the anti-lynching campaign proved too taxing for Talbert's already fragile health. After several months of illness following the defeat of the Dyer Bill, Talbert died on October 15, 1923 of heart failure. She is buried in Forest Lawn Cemetery in Buffalo.

NIKKI BROWN

Further Reading:

LaChiusa, Chuck. "Mary Burnett Talbert." July 2004. *Buffalo Architecture and History*. http://ah.bfn.org/h/tal/.

Salem, Dorothy. *To Better Our World: Black Women in Organized Reform, 1890–1920*. Brooklyn, NY: Carlson Publishing, 1990.

Williams, Lillian Serece. "Mary Morris Burnett Talbert." In *Notable Black American Women*, edited by Jessie Carney Smith. Detroit: Gale Research, 1992.

Talmadge, Eugene (1884–1946)

Eugene Talmadge was a dominant figure in Georgia government for 20 years (1926–1946), and for a decade after his death, the Talmadge faction that organized around him ran Georgia. Talmadge was one of the state's and the nation's most ardent supporters of Jim Crow. Two essential elements of the Talmadge political agenda were to keep African Americans out of the political system and to keep the poor whites and poor African Americans so desperate that they would work for starvation wages. V. O. Key (1949: 109) called Talmadge "Georgia's demagogue."

Talmadge ran for statewide office in every Democratic Party primary from 1926 to 1946 except one. He won seven elections and lost three. He was elected commissioner of agriculture for three two-year terms, served as governor for three two-year terms, and lost two races for the U.S. Senate and one for governor. He won the election for governor in 1948 but died before he was inaugurated. He lost elections for the U.S. Senate in 1936 and 1938 and governor in 1942.

The state Democratic Party was so dominant that nomination in its primary was in effect election in the general election. Eugene Talmadge's influence was so strong that Talmadge and anti-Talmadge factions wrestled for state elected offices.

Georgia's "county unit system," conceived in 1876 and enacted as the Neill Primary Act of 1917, allocated electoral power on the basis of county population. This winner-take-all election system gave the smallest 121 counties two votes each, the next 30 largest counties four votes, and the eight largest counties six votes. Three of the smallest counties could nullify the vote of one of the largest counties. The county unit system helped Talmadge. In his last campaign for governor, for example, he came in second in the popular vote with 44 percent, but won because the county unit system awarded him 59 percent of the county units.

The Georgia Democratic Party platform was nostalgia for the Lost Cause, brutal racism, and pretense that it represented the poor whites. In fact, Talmadge was supported by big business, especially the railroads, the oil companies, the powerful law firms, the Georgia Power Company, and the Coca-Cola Company for his ability to keep government small, oppose taxes, and leave business alone.

Talmadge often bragged that the African American boys called him "mean Lugene." Talmadge said that he liked the "n*gger" well enough in his place, and his place was at the back door, with his hat in his hand and saying, "Yes, Sir." Talmadge confessed to having flogged at least one African American. On his death bed, he told his Baptist preacher that the black race was created inferior by God. He said the white race was on top, the yellow race next, then the brown and red races, and at the very bottom, the blacks who were created to be servants to all other races.

Talmadge acted aggressively to enforce Jim Crow. His response to two federal court orders decided in 1946 illustrates his attitudes. In *Morgan v. Virginia*, the U.S. Supreme

Eugene Talmadge announces another run for governor of Georgia in 1942. (Library of Congress)

Court ruled that racial segregation on busses engaged in interstate commerce was unconstitutional. Talmadge pledged that there would be no more interstate bus travel in Georgia, only intrastate. Passengers would have to get off the bus before entering Georgia and buy a ticket good only for transit through Georgia. When they had crossed Georgia, they would get off and buy a ticket to the other state.

On March 8, 1946, the federal district court ruled in *Albright v. Texas* that political parties could no longer exclude African American voters. Admitting African Americans, about a third of the state's population would begin the end of total control of state government by Talmadge and other white supremacists. Talmadge announced plans to call a special session of the state legislature to overturn all the state's election laws. His plan was thwarted in part because eliminating all election laws would also eliminate the county unit system. Instead, he ran for governor on a platform of white supremacy.

Talmadge's 1946 inflammatory campaign speeches were credited with inspiring two notorious racial incidents. On May 9, the Ku Klux Klan held a giant cross-burning and membership recruiting rally at Stone Mountain. The national press reported that his inflammatory campaign tirades against African American-inspired white men to brutally murder four African Americans, two men and two women, in Monroe County. Talmadge received substantial support from the Klan. The hooded KKK held rallies at many rural county courthouses to intimidate any African Americans who tried to vote. Talmadge also received support from Nazi sympathizers such as the Brown Shirts. He said he believed a Julius Caesar was born in every century, and that he was the 19th century's Caesar. Talmadge opposed most of the New Deal relief programs. He opposed slum clearance, child labor laws, old age pensions, the Civilian Conservation Corps, the Works Progress Administration, and essentially all other New Deal initiatives. He said that the way to handle a relief program was like Mussolini—to line up poor people and use the troops and make them work. He opposed many New Deal programs also because they paid white and African Americans the same wages, a move that Talmadge feared would undermine Jim Crow.

Although he had promised union organizers that he would never use troops to break up a strike, in September 1934, he sent 4,000 armed Georgia National Guard soldiers to arrest thousands of striking workers and put them in temporary enclosure made with barbed wire. The militia broke the strike and brutally beat a man to death as his family watched.

Talmadge's world view was rooted in Georgia before the Civil War. Talmadge's New Jersey–born great grandfather, Tom, first arrived in Georgia while serving under Gen. Andrew Jackson in the campaign to chase Native Americans deep into Florida. Tom returned to make his fortune growing cotton on wilderness land in Monroe County, Georgia, near Forsyth.

Tom Talmadge prospered in a time when most Georgians experienced extreme economic deprivation. So did his only son, Aaron, born in 1858, and his grandson, Thomas Remalgus (T. R.) Talmadge. T. R. was educated in the best available schools and the University of Georgia. T. R.'s son graduated from the University of Georgia in 1904 with a Phi Beta Kappa, and from the law school in 1907. Eugene Talmadge's early heroes were Napoleon and the Populist Party politician Tom Watson. He bragged that he had read Adolf Hitler's manifesto, *Mein Kampf*, seven times, and was reading it again when he died.

Talmadge was a dictatorial public official. He did not recognize any court's authority to control his behavior, even when it held him in contempt. He used the Georgia National Guard to take over government offices. He declared martial law, fired state employees at will, sent safecrackers to blast open safes containing the state's money, and spent money that had not been appropriated by the legislature. Talmadge fired the dean of education at the University of Georgia who was rumored to be promoting racial integration in teacher training. His political interference cost all the state's white colleges their accreditation by the Southern Accrediting Commission on Institutions of Higher Learning.

Eugene Talmadge had two personas. He tried to be a simple hick farmer; his family had great wealth from farming and business. Both personas were resolute in his defense of Jim Crow.

JOAN C. BROWNING

See also

Jim Crow Laws; Ku Klux Klan (KKK)

Further Reading:

Anderson, William. *The Wild Man from Sugar Creek: The Political Career of Eugene Talmadge*. Baton Rouge: Louisiana State University Press, 1975.

Bass, Jack, and Walter De Vries. *The Transformation of Southern Politics: Social Change and Political Consequence Since 1945*. New York: New American Library, 1976.

Henderson, Harold Paulk. *The Georgia Encyclopedia*. 2004. http://www.georgiaencyclopedia.org/nge/Article.jsp?id=h-1393 (accessed June 1, 2008).

Key, V. O. Jr., with Alexander Heard. *Southern Politics in State and Nation*. New York: A. A. Knopf, 1949.

Talmadge, Herman, with Mark Royden Winchell. *Talmadge: A Political Legacy, a Politician's Life*. Atlanta: Peachtree Publishers, 1987.

Talmadge, Herman, with Mark Royden Winchell. "Speaking on Behalf of Eugene Talmadge." Georgia State University Government Documentation project, GSU APR 1992.3.

Watkins, Thayer. "Eugene Talmadge of Georgia." http://www.applet-magic.com/talmadge.htm (accessed June 1, 2008).

Tampa (Florida) Riots of 1987

In Tampa, Florida, the months of February to April 1987 brought several nights of violence, citizens in fear, and heightened tension between police and citizens. Between November 1986 and April 1987, four black men died at the hands of white Tampa police. These incidents heightened already strained tensions between black citizens of Tampa and local police, and served as the impetus for angry citizens to take to the streets throwing rocks and bottles. Combined, these violent outbreaks are called the Tampa Riots of 1987.

Rioting began the night of February 19, when a white police officer used a controversial chokehold technique to subdue Melvin Eugene Hair, a black man in custody. As a result, Hair died of suffocation. On the same night, local television news stations reported the outcome of a city attorney's office investigation into the arrest of Dwight Gooden, star pitcher for the New York Mets and prominent black citizen of Tampa. Gooden was arrested the previous December after having been stopped for a traffic violation that escalated into a fight. As a result, Gooden was left visibly swollen and bruised. The city attorney's report blamed Gooden for starting the fight with police.

Both of these incidents came on the heels of the death of Franklin A. Lewis, a 16-year-old who was shot by police after allegedly shooting a gun into a crowd. The official investigative report following Lewis's death exonerated the officers, reporting that they had used necessary force to subdue their suspect. However, Tampa's black citizenry was not satisfied with this account, suspicious that no gun was found on Lewis's body. Many blacks in Tampa were becoming more and more incensed, alleging that police targeted them specifically, viewing them as criminals to be subdued and controlled rather than citizens to be protected. In that vein, they charged that police took liberties with young black men especially, brutalizing them without repercussion.

The news of Hair's death, coupled with the city attorney's report that reflected unfavorably on Gooden, was incendiary. Several black youths gathered outside, discussing the incidents. As they discussed the incidents, their discontent grew, and one of them set fire to a dumpster. That drew a crowd, which then began to throw bottles and rocks. The violence continued for the next three days, causing police to cordon off a section of the city where even media were not allowed. Similar incidents continued sporadically through April of that year, sparked by continuing tensions with police. Two more black men died at the hands of white police officers, inciting the city's youth, who were already tense and angry. During waves of violence, rioters threw bottles and rocks at police, whites driving through the neighborhood, and the media.

By April, Tampa was a hotbed of anger, frustration, and tension. The waves of violence ended, leaving in their wake an unmistakable outcry from the black citizens of Tampa, who resented the treatment they were receiving from the police. Response was swift—there were several Federal Bureau of Investigation investigations into police department practices, Tampa's mayor pushed to substantially increase the number of black police officers on the force, and several task forces and city council committees were formed to look into racial tensions in the city. Both the police force and the local government pursued the reduction of police brutality and racial profiling.

Because police practices received the lion's share of attention and funding, the deeper, less visible issues received considerably less attention. By and large, the riots occurred in Tampa's College Hill and Ponce de Leon neighborhoods, two extremely impoverished sections of the city that are home to the majority of Tampa's public housing projects. In these areas, the overarching issues of extreme poverty, dwindling opportunities for social and economic growth, and insufficient housing fueled residents' unrest. For example, cuts in social programming left the housing authority grossly underfunded. While each apartment cost an average of $175 per month to maintain, the housing authority received less than $100 per month for each apartment, rendering adequate maintenance impossible. These same funding cuts resulted in decreased grant and loan programs in black communities. And those who did secure funding found it difficult to then obtain insurance. Such conditions, as outgrowths of poverty, have been shown to be predictors of high crime rates and citizen frustration.

Local authorities, however, responded with less action around the issues of poverty than around police practices. Although a summer job placement program for the community's youth was formed, and a task force was created to investigate community needs, this was considerably less programming than was set up for the Tampa Police Department. By giving less attention to the larger issues of poverty and economic growth for residents of these neighborhoods, the city was ineffective in addressing the very conditions that made it necessary for the police to be such a strong force in the affected neighborhoods. Indeed, the College Hill and

Ponce de Leon neighborhoods continue to struggle with high poverty rates, high crime rates, and tension with the police.

STEPHANIE BEARD

See also

Federal Bureau of Investigation (FBI); Police Brutality; Race Riots in America; Racialized Poverty. Documents: The Report on the Memphis Riots of May 1866 (July 25, 1866); Account of the Riots in East St. Louis, Illinois (July 1917); The Cook County Coroner's Report Regarding the 1919 Chicago Race Riots (1919); A Southern Black Woman's Letter Regarding the Recent Riots in Chicago and Washington (November 1919); The Final Report of the Grand Jury on the Tulsa Race Riot (June 25, 1921); Testimony from *Laney v. United States* Describing Events during the Washington, D.C., Riot of July 1919 (December 3, 1923); The Governor's Commission Report on the Watts Riots (December 1965); Cyrus R. Vance's Report on the Riots in Detroit (July–August 1967); The Reports of the Oklahoma Commission to Study the Tulsa Race Riot of 1921 (2000–2001); The Draft Report of the 1898 Wilmington Race Riot Commission (December 2005)

Further Reading:

Federal Emergency Management Agency and United States Fire Administration. "Report of the Joint Fire/Police Task Force on Civil Unrest: Recommendations for Organization and Operation during Civil Disturbance." Publication No. FA-142. 1994. http://www.usfa.fema.gov/downloads/pdf/publications/fa-142.pdf.

Waddington, David. *Contemporary Issues in Public Disorder: A Comparative and Historical Approach*. London: Routledge, 2001.

Tea Party

The Tea Party is an American, populist, conservative political movement. It uses the imagery of the Boston Tea Party as an iconic event in United States history to promote an agenda of strict adherence to the text of the U.S. Constitution as well as reductions to the national debt, federal spending, and budget deficits. It emerged in the wake of the 2008 electoral victories that made Barack Obama president and sent Democratic majorities to both the House of Representatives and the Senate. In early 2009, the Republican Party was seen as widely discredited when local Tea Party protests around the country began energizing white, middle-class conservatives who were trying to distance themselves from

---

Tea Party Leader's Racist Joke at an Event in Arkansas

At an event in the Ozark Mountains, a board member of an Arkansas Tea Party organization, Inge Marler, made a joke about black people being on welfare and white people being unfairly accused of racism for getting upset about it. He used a mock black dialect. There was no objection from the crowd. Supporters of the Tea Party movement have insisted that comments such as this are the views of a small number of supporters and do not represent the movement as a whole. Critics have pointed to this commentary as well as several signs that use racialized images, such as Barack Obama as a witch doctor and statements accusing the president of endorsing white slavery, to bolster findings by national surveys showing Tea Party supporters to harbor higher levels of racial prejudice.

---

the Bush-era policies and Sen. John McCain's presidential campaign. Since then, the Tea Party has continued to hold demonstrations and endorse political candidates.

The origins of the Tea Party movement trace back to multiple, unconnected, local protests. The first national Tea Party demonstrations began early in 2009. On February 19, 2009, Rick Santelli, the business news editor for the Consumer News and Business Channel (CNBC) denounced a proposal from the Obama administration to help the ailing housing market by refinancing mortgages. His statements, made on the floor of the Chicago Mercantile Exchange, included a call for capitalists to join him in a demonstration to speak out against the proposed policies. Video of the commentary became an Internet sensation and proved to be a catalyzing event for protests around the United States. Protesters dressed in clothing from the American Revolutionary era. By supporters, the protests were cast as manifestations of grassroots organizing. Critics denounced the demonstrations as Astroturf activism orchestrated by elites within the Republican Party and wealthy interest groups, not unprompted actions by ordinary civilians.

Although Santelli's criticisms were directed at the Obama administration's housing policies, the Tea Party activism that ensued coalesced around multiple policy-related grievances related to the size, scope, and cost of government that were linked to both the Democratic and Republican parties. Specific legislation included the Troubled Assets Relief Program (TARP) for insolvent banks, the American Recovery and Reinvestment Act—better known as Obama's stimulus bill—and the Patient Protection and Affordable Care Act that reformed the U.S. health insurance system (also known as Obamacare). Tea Party supporters also frequently voice opposition to gay marriage and support tighter immigration policies as well as racial profiling in airports.

Data on Tea Party support in the United States varies considerably based on the way survey questions are asked, but demographic data on Tea Party participants consistently presents them as mostly white, men, who are married, older than 45 years of age and politically conservative. Although some commentators have asserted that Tea Party supporters constitute an onset of new activists on the American political scene, research demonstrates that this group is actually composed of partisan Republicans, from the ranks of the religious right, who had been politically active prior to the Tea Party's emergence.

Accusations of racism and bigotry have consistently been leveled at the Tea Party since it took hold nationally in 2009. Proponents of such claims provide support for them with both survey research and anecdotal accounts that received media attention. In a national survey by the University of Washington Institute for the Study of Race, Ethnicity, and Sexuality, Tea Party support was found to be a good predictor of racial resentment, even after controlling for ideology and partisanship. The research found that a majority of Tea Party supporters say that blacks and Latinos are less hardworking, less intelligent, and untrustworthy. White Tea Party supporters also hold negative views towards gays and lesbians. Prominent nonwhite conservatives, such as Ward Connerly of the *National Review* and presidential candidate Herman Cain, have offered defenses of the Tea Party against accusations of racism and bigotry, claiming that they are both off-base and counterproductive.

The Tea Party's most pronounced influence came in the 2010 midterm elections that returned control of the House of Representatives to the Republican Party, reduced the size of the Democratic majority in the Senate, and gave the Republicans a majority of governorships at the state level. Research measuring the Tea Party's influence finds that endorsements

---

2012 Elections

It is unclear as to what influence the Tea Party Movement had on the 2012 election cycle that sent Barack Obama back to the White House and returned incumbent parties to control over each chamber of Congress, Republicans in the House of Representatives, Democrats in the U.S. Senate. As in 2010, the Tea Party was successful in ousting incumbent Republicans in the primaries, but their success in the general election was a mixed bag. Many of the candidates most closely affiliated with the movement either lost or narrowly won. In the Senate, Joe Donnelly beat Tea Party candidate Richard Murdock, who had unseated longtime incumbent Richard Lugar in the Republican primary. The Democrats retained the seat in Missouri held by Claire McCaskill over Todd Akin. Each race was seen as favoring Republicans.

---

by Tea Party organizations are effective electorally, particularly in elections to the House of Representatives and in primary elections. Levels of Tea Party activism have been found to influence elections as well as congressional roll call voting.

DEEB PAUL KITCHEN

See also

Birthers

Further Reading:

Bailey, Michael A., Jonathan Mummolo, and Hans Noel. "Tea Party Influence: A Story of Activists and Elites." *American Politics Research* 40, no. 5 (2012): 1–36.

Campbell, David E., and Robert D. Putnam. "Crashing the Tea Party." *New York Times*. August 16, 2011. http://www.nytimes.com/2011/08/17/opinion/crashing-the-tea-party.html (accessed October 12, 2012).

Campbell, David E., and Robert D. Putnam. "God and Caesar in America: Why Mixing Religion and Politics is Bad for Both." *Foreign Affairs*. March/April 2012. http://www.foreignaffairs.com/articles/137100/david-e-campbell-and-robert-d-putnam/god-and-caesar-in-america (accessed October 12, 2012).

Campo-Flore, Arian. "Are Tea Partiers Racist?" *Daily Beast*. April 25, 2010. http://www.thedailybeast.com/newsweek/2010/04/25/are-tea-partiers-racist.html (accessed October 26, 2012).

Celock, John. "Inge Marler, Arkansas Tea Party Leader, Makes Racist Joke at Event." *Huffington Post*. June 14, 2012. http://www.huffingtonpost.com/2012/06/14/

inge-marler-tea-party-arkansas-leader-racist
-joke_n_1597334.html (accessed October 25, 2012).

Fallin, Amanda, Rachel Grana, and Stanton A. Glantz. "'To Quarterback Behind the Scenes, Third-Party Efforts': The Tobacco Industry and The Tea Party." *Tobacco Control*, 2013.

McGrath, Ben. "The Movement: The Rise of Tea Party Activism." *New Yorker*. February 1, 2010. http://www
.newyorker.com/reporting/2010/02/01/100201fa_fact
_mcgrath?currentPage=all (accessed October 9, 2012).

Parker, Christopher S. *2010 Multi-State Survey of Race and Politics*. University of Washington Institute for the Study of Ethnicity, Race, & Sexuality, 2010.

Parker, Suzi. "Arkansas Racism, Tea-Party Style." *Washington Post*. June 15, 2012. http://www.washingtonpost.com/blogs/she
-the-people/post/arkansas-racism-tea-party-style/2012/06/15/
gJQAHQIfeV_blog.html (accessed October 25, 2012).

Reynolds, Glenn H. "Tea Parties: Real Grassroots." *New York Post*. April 13, 2009. http://www.nypost.com/p/news/opinion/
opedcolumnists/item_kjS1kZbRyFntcyNhDJFlSK (accessed October 12, 2012).

Rudin, Ken. "Who Gets the Blame for the Romney Loss? The Tea Party Has a Theory." *NPR*. November 12, 2012. http://
www.npr.org/blogs/politicaljunkie/2012/11/12/164756302/
who-gets-the-blame-for-the-romney-loss-the-tea-party-has
-a-theory?utm_source=NPR&utm_medium=facebook&utm
_campaign=20121112 (accessed November 12, 2012).

Williamson, Vanessa, Theda Skocpol, and John Coggin. "The Tea Party and the Remaking of Republican Conservatism." *Perspectives on Politics* 9, no. 1 (2011): 25–43.

Television and Racial Stereotypes

Television was one of the most influential forms of media to emerge in the 20th century. Television can serve as a reflection of the existing social norms and mores of a society. Because of its widespread accessibility and saturation in American culture, television can also act as a powerful socializing agent for both children and adults. It is an especially important socializing agent for race relations because, as a result of continued residential and school segregation, there is often very little meaningful interaction between races. Television depictions of minority members and interactions between whites and minority members can act as a vicarious racial experience for individuals who would rarely encounter minority members in everyday life. The issue of how race is portrayed on television is both a problem of large-scale exclusion of racial minorities and a problem of negative, or stereotypical, representation of those minority characters.

In terms of exclusion, top-rated shows (e.g., *Frasier*, *Friends*, and *Seinfeld*), which often take place in large metropolitan centers such as New York City, Seattle, and Los Angeles, offer only tertiary minority characters. Not only are these omissions untrue to the racial reality of the geographic location portrayed, but when minority groups are missing from the television curriculum, it implies to the viewer that they are inconsequential or unimportant. This underrepresentation of minorities, despite the reality of racially heterogeneous settings, reflects a social norm of exclusion in the consciousness of mainstream America.

With few exceptions, most of the television shows that do feature minority characters depict stereotypical representations of them. African Americans and Latino characters are limited to a set repertoire of roles, most often depicting criminals, servants, entertainers, or athletes. Latinos are often associated with criminal activity. Despite the overrepresentation of white-collar occupations on television in general, African Americans are most often depicted in menial, low class, and service jobs. Young African American men are depicted as being unintelligent, clownish, and sex-crazed. African American women are often depicted as domineering and in a position of maternal dominance, where they act as sole holders of power in a family and habitually belittle men.

Though minority characters of many different races may appear sporadically in various genres of television programming (e.g., dramas, comedies, reality programming), a limited number of television shows feature a large proportion of minority characters in their permanent cast. Most of these shows fall within the specific genre of African American situational comedies. The fact that the only television shows with large African American casts are almost exclusively comedic in nature indicates a one-dimensional or superficial interest in the depiction of African American life. Further, these comedies are almost always racially homogeneous and, in recent years, are often segregated to specific "niche" television networks, often on particular nights. This isolation further asserts a sense of racial segregation.

Given the limited portrayal of racial minorities on television, the opportunities to view intergroup interaction

Sofía Vergara's character, Gloria, on the ABC network series *Modern Family* exemplifies a stereotypical depiction of Latinas. Vergara's traditional looks—dark and curvaceous—are highlighted, along with her accent and uneven usage of the English language. Shown from left: Sofía Vergara, Ed O'Neill, Rico Rodriguez. (ABC/Photofest)

are extremely rare. When intergroup interactions are presented on television, they tend to be portrayed as neutral or positive. Minority characters tend to either appear as their "stock" stereotypical character (e.g., the criminal, the athlete, the entertainer), or they exist as "background" characters and are woven into a peer group in a public setting. Situations of racial unease or overt acts of prejudice in these interactions are rarely portrayed, thus there are few opportunities to model how to handle these types of situations.

TRACY CHU

See also

Cinema in the Jim Crow Era; Films and Racial Stereotypes; Mixed Race Relationships and the Media; Television Drama and Racism; White Savior Films

Further Reading:

Baptiste, David A. "The Image of the Black Family Portrayed by Television: A Critical Commentary." *Marriage and Family Review* 10 (April 1996): 41–63.

Graves, Sherryl Browne. "Television and Prejudice Reduction: When Does Television as a Vicarious Experience Make a Difference?" *Journal of Social Issues* 55, no. 4 (1999): 707–27.

Television Drama and Racism

The representation of black people on American television has come a long way since the days of shows like *Amos 'n' Andy* and the *Jack Benny Show*, in which blacks were portrayed in ways that reinforced white beliefs in the inherent servitude of African Americans. In the early days of television, no black characters were cast in leading roles, and most of the black characters reinforced the worst racial stereotypes prevalent in the pre–civil rights era of television. Today, however, some popular television shows not only have black characters in leading roles, but in a few cases—especially drama—TV shows depict blacks in positions of authority over whites. But serious problems remain. Despite the increasing numbers of blacks cast in leading roles, television remains a segregated medium, and for all the positive images of African Americans displayed on television today, negative stereotypes of black people continue to dominate the medium. Mass media, in short, continues to represent blacks as fundamentally different from whites, and blacks are consistently misrepresented by contradictory images on television that portray blacks disproportionately as either unusually gifted athletes or deviant drug dealers.

Media both reflect and shape the world, including the complicated network of race relations in America. In some ways, the positive images of blacks on television reflect the real-world material gains made by African Americans since the civil rights era. On the other hand, the major networks still push most of the black characters to the margins, just as in "real-world" America, blacks and whites live segregated private lives. The only place in the world of television where blacks are consistently cast in the leading roles is the nightly news, where images of chaos and crime bombard the audience each evening, saturating the mostly white audience with negative images of African Americans.

In early 2000, the National Association for the Advancement of Colored People threatened to boycott the major broadcast networks—ABC, CBS, NBC, and Fox—if they did not agree to feature more prominent black actors on primetime television. Critics pointed to the most popular shows, like *Beverly Hills 90210* on Fox, *ER* on NBC, *Friends* on NBC, *Party of Five* on Fox, and *Will & Grace* on NBC: among all these shows only two blacks, two Asians, and one Latino were cast in lead roles—as evidence that television continues to discriminate against racial and ethnic minorities.

Roots

Published in 1976, *Roots: The Saga of an American Family* was presented as the semiautobiographical history of author Alex Haley's family. The novel was written from the perspective of one of Haley's ancestors, a slave known as Kunta Kinte. Haley's epic story followed the African Kunta Kinte as he was forced to board a slave ship to America and documented his experiences in the New World, including his purchase by white slave masters, life on the plantation, and family formation patterns.

Roots received much media attention and critical acclaim, which culminated with Haley's receipt of a Pulitzer Prize in 1977. In that same year, the novel was optioned for a television film. It became an epic miniseries, which garnered for ABC what remain among the highest television ratings ever. For five nights, most American households tuned in to see the history of slavery in America dramatized. This was significant, not only because ABC had expected the movie to be a ratings bust but also because the movie brought the of slavery and its aftermath into the homes of a country that had a history of silence on the subject.

The movie gave its audience common ground and served as a starting point for conversations about the impact of slavery on America and on the black family specifically. Although initially the book and the movie were lauded as American treasures, ultimately Haley's novel became the target of skepticism due to charges of plagiarism and fabrication. In response to these charges, Haley referred to his work as "faction"—part fact, part fiction. Despite these allegations, in celebration of the 25th anniversary of the first airing of *Roots*, the miniseries was rerun in the fall of 2002.

ROMNEY S. NORWOOD

The first prime-time drama series to air on network television that had a predominantly black cast was the CBS series *City of Angels*. The show was produced by Steven Bochco, who had a string of drama series hits, including *Hill Street Blues*, *L.A. Law*, and *NYPD Blue*. Producers hoped that *City of Angels* would have crossover appeal in the white audience because Bochco's previous productions were so popular. Unfortunately for the cast of *City of Angels*, the show never made it past the first season, suggesting that a drama series with a black cast has yet to cross over to a white audience. In some ways, the increasing fragmentation of television into more and more niche markets makes it more difficult to produce a series with crossover appeal. There are a few successful crossover drama series that cast African Americans in leading roles, but none with a predominantly black cast.

For example, *ER*, a hit series consistently in the top-20 ratings for both white and black audiences, had a black lead character, Dr. Benson, played by Eriq LaSalle. Dr. Benson became one of the most popular characters on *ER*, but it took more than five seasons for the producers to build an episode around him, whereas the other principal actors had many episodes that featured their characters. But what makes *ER* stand out as a particularly sharp representation of race relations in America is the romance that developed between Dr. Benton and a white British doctor, played by actress Alex Kingston. LaSalle asked that the producers end Dr. Benson's relationship with the white doctor because he felt it sent a message that black men can only have stable relationships with white women. All of Dr. Benson's previous relationships had been with black women, and all failed. LaSalle told the *Washington Post*, "We have to take care of the message that we are sending as African Americans . . . that we have the same type of exchanges with our mates that we get to see our White counterparts have" (April 9, 1999). Fans of the show were upset that the producers ended the romance between the characters, but the producers were aware of the far-reaching implications a show as popular as theirs has in U.S. society.

The producers of television drama series are increasingly under pressure from their network bosses to present images that appeal to affluent—which in their minds means white—audiences, as a way to appease the corporate sponsors who have the power to pull the plug on "controversial"

drama series. In the words of one producer at Fox television, "I don't think anyone's crying out for integrated shows. By pursuing advertisers and demographics rather than a mass audience, the networks have declared they don't need Blacks in their audience" (quoted in Entman and Rojecki 2001: 161). If integration remains a goal of public policy in the United States, then one necessary step in that direction is to integrate television, especially popular drama series, as those shows already have black and white audiences. Perhaps in the not-so-distant future, a character like Dr. Benson on *ER* will be able to have an intimate, romantic relationship with a character not of his "race."

MICHAEL ROBERTS

See also

Cinema in the Jim Crow Era; Films and Racial Stereotypes; Mixed Race Relationships and the Media; Television and Racial Stereotypes; White Savior Films

Further Reading:

Entman, Robert M., and Andrew Rojecki. *The Black Image in the White Mind: Media and Race in America*. Chicago: University of Chicago Press, 2001.

Temporary Assistance to Needy Families (TANF)

Temporary Assistance to Needy Families (TANF) is the current version of government assistance programs commonly known collectively as "welfare." Replacing Aid to Families with Dependent Children (AFDC), the Job Opportunities and Basic Skills Training (JOBS) program, and the Emergency Assistance (EA) program, TANF was created as a result of the Personal Responsibility and Work Opportunity Reconciliation Act of 1996 (PRWORA). It is a block grant program in which the federal government gives states funds to administer benefits and services targeted to poor families. States have a great deal of flexibility in determining what benefits are available and conditions of eligibility, as long as the state programs comply with the purposes of TANF outlined in the law. The four purposes of TANF are: assisting needy families so that children can be cared for in their homes; reducing the dependency of needy parents by promoting job preparation, work, and marriage; preventing

Welfare Dependency

Before 1996, Aid to Families with Dependent Children (AFDC) was the major American welfare program. This program provided money to poor families, primarily those headed by single mothers with children. In 1996, AFDC was replaced by Temporary Assistance for Needy Families (TANF), a program that provides short-term benefits and requires that most recipients work. This change was widely known as welfare reform. While the term *welfare* has been used extensively to refer to AFDC and TANF, it can be used to refer to any number of programs. For example, in the mid-1990s, a survey found that Americans identified numerous programs, from school lunches to Medicare to Food Stamps, as constituting welfare. Some social critics also call tax breaks for corporations corporate welfare. Therefore, it is important to specify which social programs are being discussed when either welfare and welfare dependency is referred to.

Proponents of welfare reform argued that AFDC acted as a kind of narcotic, creating a destructive dependency on the state. Some critics, such as sociologist Charles Murray, argued that AFDC encouraged the formation of single-parent families and fostered socially undesirable behavior among recipients and their children. Other critics note that charges of "welfare dependency" tend to be leveled against African American women and their families more often than at white women. Feminist scholars such as Nancy Fraser and Linda Gordon further argued that dependency is, in fact, the normal human condition—everyone is in some way dependent on the labor of others. Why should dependency, then, be stigmatized for poor women?

Before the 1960s, minorities, particularly black women, were disproportionately denied welfare benefits. Through a series of court rulings and social movements, welfare eligibility became more open and black women—who are disproportionately poor—began to receive a larger share of welfare benefits. As welfare became associated with black women, public support for the program declined. By the 1980s and early 1990s, phrases such as "Welfare Queen" and "welfare dependency" carried strong racial overtones. In 1996, the entitlement to welfare was eliminated.

ROBIN ROGER-DILLON

out-of-wedlock pregnancies; and encouraging the formation and maintenance of two-parent families.

Welfare programs in the United States have undergone a number of changes since the first federal assistance programs in the New Deal era of the 1930s. The Social Security Act of 1935 provided for an entitlement to public aid, establishing Supplementary Security Income (SSI), Medicaid, and AFDC. Major overhaul in assistance programs was the result of a number of factors, which many scholars argue were based in racialized assumptions about the poor. The strategic creation of the "welfare crisis" was the impetus for welfare reform. In the 1960s, demographic changes in the welfare rolls, specifically the increase in African Americans and single mothers as barriers to access were removed through civil rights legislation, exacerbated growing backlash against the welfare state among conservatives. The main criticism was that welfare programs were creating a culture of dependency that contradicted American values like independence and self-sufficiency.

TANF and related policies are steeped with assumptions about the poor, and some research points to unfounded racialized assumptions and outcomes. *The Negro Family*, a internal U.S. Department of Labor report also known as *The Moynihan Report*, claimed that welfare dependency among single-parent black families was spiraling out of control because of a breakdown in values in black communities. Moynihan et al. suggested that the welfare participation rate for blacks was becoming "unglued" to the black male unemployment rate, indicating that the black family was becoming entrenched in intergenerational welfare dependency. That claim was later refuted, but the conclusion fit the standard narrative about poor blacks. These assumptions lead directly to welfare reform measures designed to address assumed causes of poverty. For example, some states specifically prohibit benefits for additional out of wedlock children as a disincentive to out-of-wedlock childbearing.

The specter of the "welfare queen," a characterization made popular by President Ronald Reagan during his 1976 campaign for the Republican presidential nomination, became the personification of the failures and dangers of the welfare system. The Reagan administration enacted a number of policies that significantly diminished funding for social welfare programs. While Reagan and other conservatives ramped up their attacks on the welfare system, the racialization of poverty engendered support for welfare reform among liberal whites as well. By the mid-1990s, there was widespread support for welfare reform among liberals and conservatives.

The late 1990s saw a rapid decline in welfare cases. Whether welfare reform or increased labor demand caused the drastic decline in welfare caseloads in the late 1990s is a debate in the literature that has been unresolved because analyses are typically done on a state-by-state basis and individual states implemented reforms differently. Whatever the cause, there were clear racial differences in the decline in caseloads. Research shows white TANF recipients exiting rolls at a faster rate than blacks in many states, and the proportion of white families participating in TANF decreased to 31 percent of all cases, and racial minorities accounted for over two-thirds of all cases. Pickering et al. argue that PRWORA is ignored the issues of race, class and gender and politics and economics, and that devolution has reinforced power differentials and economic inequality by transferring government resources to local elites.

Many welfare reform researchers have determined that reforms have exacerbated racial differences in welfare assistance. Differences in the administration of TANF by state and locality have lead to differential outcomes by race as a result of other racialized processes. A wide body of research has found that race is a key factor in determining TANF participants' experiences with the program and likelihood of successful transition to work. Soss et al. (2003) found that states with more black recipients have stricter policy regimes, making black families more likely to participate in TANF under the most punitive state administration of the program, which, they argue, can produce inequality in the distribution of resources and subject citizens from different social groups to systematically different treatment from the government.

RENEE S. ALSTON

See also

Culture of Poverty; Racialized Poverty; Welfare Queens

Further Reading:

Brown, M. K. "Ghettos, Fiscal Federalism, and Welfare Reform." In *Race and the Politics of Welfare Reform*, edited by Sanford F. Schram, Joe Brian Soss, and Richard Carl Fording. Ann Arbor: University of Michigan Press, 2003.

Cooke, Kristina, David Rohde, and Ryan McNeill. "The Undeserving Poor." 2012. http://www.reuters.com/subjects/income-inequality/indiana.

Moynihan, Daniel Patrick, Lee Rainwater, and William L. Yancey. *The Negro Family: The Case for National Action.* Cambridge, MA: MIT Press, 1967.

Murray, Charles. *Losing Ground: American Social Policy, 1950–1980.* New York: Basic Books, 1984.

Patterson, J. T. *America's Struggle Against Poverty, 1990–1980.* Cambridge, Massachusetts: Harvard University Press, 1981.

Pickering, Kathleen Ann, Mark H. Harvey, Gene F. Summers, and David Mushinski. *Welfare Reform in Persistent Rural Poverty: Dreams, Disenchantments, and Diversity.* Penn State University Press, 2006.

Soss, Joe., Sanford. F. Schram, Thomas. P. Vartanian, and Erin. O'Brien. "Setting the Terms of Relief: Explaining State Policy Choices in the Devolution Revolution." *American Journal of Political Science* 45 (2001): 378–403.

U.S. Congress. House. *Personal Responsibility and Work Opportunity Reconciliation Act of 1996.* H.R. 3734. 104th Cong., 2nd sess. (June 27, 1996). http://www.gpoaccess.gov/bills/index.html (accessed January 12, 2013).

Terrell, Mary Church (1863–1954)

Mary Church Terrell was a lecturer, political activist, and educator during the tumultuous Jim Crow era in the United States. As a black woman, Terrell enjoyed privileges and advantages not available to most blacks. Hers was a life that defied the constraints imposed by society on her race and gender. However, the lynching of a close friend propelled Terrell to relinquish the isolation of her immediate world and commit her life to public activism. Among the most critical issues confronted by Terrell were violence against blacks, segregation, and women's suffrage.

Mary Eliza Church was born free to former slaves on September 23, 1863, in Memphis, Tennessee, during the Civil War. On January 1, 1863, Abraham Lincoln issued the Emancipation Proclamation, which abolished slavery. While blacks were in the throes of adjusting to postslavery

Mary Church Terrell, an African American suffragist, was president of the National Association of Colored Women and a charter member of the National Association for the Advancement of Colored People. (Library of Congress)

life during Reconstruction, Mary was raised in the comfort, security, and safety of her parents' home. Mary's parents instilled in her the importance of education. Rather than send her to a segregated school, they enrolled her in the Antioch College Model School. Although she lived during this time with the Hunsters, a black family, she was the only black in her class. Two years later, she enrolled in a local public school. During this period, white Southerners were seizing back political control across the South by violently assaulting both black and white opposition and engaging in other unscrupulous tactics. By 1877, all the Southern states were under the tyrannical rule of the white Democrats. Once in power, they dismantled the rights and freedoms blacks had gained during Reconstruction. In their attempt to maintain white supremacy, whites instigated riots, and lynched, beat,

and terrorized blacks on a regular basis. The federal government did nothing to relieve or remedy the situation.

In the midst of this turmoil, Mary graduated from a public high school and, afterward, attended Oberlin College, one of the few integrated universities at that time. Few women pursued higher education in that era. The few black women who attended college generally went to the historically black colleges that had been established during Reconstruction. Women who went to college usually did not aspire to careers. More often than not, women were denied employment and were restricted to being wives and homemakers. For women, education was a symbol of status within elite society, and only a few years of college were obligatory. Mary, on the other hand, earned a bachelor's degree in classics. She then took a teaching position at Wilberforce College in Ohio, while simultaneously pursuing a master's degree. Named after the abolitionist William Wilberforce, this college was the first of its kind to be owned and operated by blacks. Her father was devastated; like most of society, Mary's father believed her place was to marry and start a family. Mary's decision caused a rift with her father that lasted several years.

While Mary's professional career peaked, conditions in the South, and in the North to a lesser degree, steadily worsened. In the absence of slavery, whites found other ways to maintain social control. White mobs hunted down blacks who were purported to have committed crimes against white women or who challenged the laws of racial etiquette. Often, no reason was needed at all. Black men of all ages were the common target, and lynching was the common method of execution. Lynching was often accompanied by burning, maiming, or castrating the victim. Whites sometimes kept body parts for souvenirs. Lynching occurred without judge, jury, or trial, whether in the privacy of the mob or before a crowd ranting its encouragement. These executions often preceded unbridled violence against unsuspecting blacks and their communities. Whites were rarely, if ever, charged and punished for their crimes.

In 1886, as violence raged in the South and in the North, and discriminatory laws were established across the nation, Mary accepted another teaching position at the Colored High School in Washington, D.C. During this period, Washington had a large community of progressive and well-to-do blacks. Although they led more privileged lives than the majority of blacks, they were, as a whole, excluded from mainstream society and confined behind the color line of segregation and discrimination. At the high school, Mary met her soon-to-be husband, Robert Heberton Terrell, a graduate of Harvard University. In 1901, Terrell was appointed justice of the peace by President Theodore Roosevelt. The following year, he was appointed to the Washington, D.C., Municipal Court, the first black to hold that position.

On earning her master's degree, Mary traveled to Europe, as was the practice of both the white and black elite. She became fluent in French, German, and Italian. Two years later, in 1891, she returned and married Robert Terrell in Memphis, Tennessee. Under her new name, Mary Church Terrell, she returned to Washington, D.C., with her husband. She willingly surrendered her career and appeared to prepare for the life that her father had once envisioned. But high-society wives who had forgone professional careers were often privately active in meaningful philanthropic societies, organizations, and activities. Terrell might well have been one of them, but prompted by a personal tragedy, she did not follow this type of quiet activism.

In 1892, Terrell was pregnant with her first child when she heard the news that her friend from Memphis, Tennessee, Tom Moss, had been lynched by whites who were jealous of the success of his grocery store. Terrell was devastated. She was again grief-stricken when her baby died a few days after birth. To come to terms with the loss of the baby, she reasoned to herself that it might have been marred by her grief and mental preoccupation with the violent death of Moss. In the same year, Terrell turned her sorrow into activism. She spearheaded a campaign against lynching and eventually collaborated with Frederick Douglass. Together, they went to Washington, D.C., to galvanize support from President Benjamin Harrison, but to no avail.

Undeterred, Terrell pursued another issue—women's suffrage. She cofounded and was the president of the Colored Women's League. In 1896, the league joined with other black women's organizations to become the National Association of Colored Women. Terrell was the founder and president of this association until 1904. In 1898, the year she gave birth to a daughter named Phyllis, Terrell was appointed honorary president for life. In 1905, she adopted a niece named Terrell Church.

The Colored Women's League went beyond working toward women's suffrage. It also established daycare centers for black children of working mothers and campaigned for improved working conditions for black women. It also fought for equal rights for blacks and the elimination of Jim Crow laws. Despite their wealth, the accolades, and degrees, the black elite suffered greatly at the expense of Jim Crow legislation. Terrell herself had once, in her youth, challenged Jim Crow. Terrell's father had purchased a first-class seat for her, although Jim Crow sent segregated blacks to the second-class seats. Nevertheless, Terrell was allowed to keep her seat when she told the conductor that her father would sue the railroad if he made her move.

From 1892 to 1954, Terrell lectured on social and racial issues in the United States and abroad. During one presentation at the International Congress of Women in Berlin, Germany, she spoke in German, French, and English. In 1895, Terrell became the first black woman to be elected to the District of Columbia Board of Education. She was a member of the board from 1895 to 1901, and again from 1906 to 1911. Terrell's clout grew quickly, as did her network of influential friends. She befriended and collaborated with giants, such as Booker T. Washington, Mary McLeod Bethune, and Susan B. Anthony. In 1901, W.E.B. Du Bois invited her to become a charter member of the National Association for the Advancement of Colored People (NAACP). She later founded the NAACP's Executive Committee and was a member of a group that investigated police harassment against blacks. She was also a member of Carter G. Woodson's Association for the Study of Negro Life and History. Terrell maintained her interests in intellectual pursuits by joining the Bethel Literary and Historical Association.

Meanwhile, as violence continued unabated across the nation, Terrell used her influence to champion the rights of the victims of violence and discrimination. She did not censor her opinions, no matter how powerful her opponents were. In 1904, Terrell wrote one of many articles to protest violence—lynching in particular—against blacks. In this article, she discussed the history of violence against blacks since the time of slavery, sparing no details. She wrote boldly that racism and lawlessness, not justice, were the real motivation behind the grievous executions of blacks. She also exposed the misconception that violence was limited to the South, proving that it was quickly intensifying across the nation.

Shortly after the Brownsville (Texas) Riot of 1906, she openly condemned President Theodore Roosevelt for dismissing three companies of black men from the Army without due process and without sufficient proof of involvement. The 167 black men were accused of having instigated a shoot-out on August 14 that injured a policeman and a resident. These men were also "barred from rejoining the military and from government employment, and were denied veterans' pensions or benefits" (Hine, Hine, and Harrold 2000: 344). Nothing was done to the whites and Mexicans who had harassed and attacked the black soldiers prior to the riot.

Terrell continued to challenge lynching, as well as other adverse conditions besetting blacks, particularly in the South, such as chain gangs, peonage, and disenfranchisement. In 1920, Terrell's responsibilities expanded to include the supervision of all campaigns among black women on the East Coast.

Despite Terrell's active schedule, she and her husband made time to indulge in the pleasantries of the black upper class. Washington, D.C., was the dwelling place of some of the most prominent elite black families. Like the white upper class, blacks enjoyed the world of culture and a lavish lifestyle. The Terrells "attended balls, concerts, and parties, traveled extensively, and belonged to Washington's most exclusive black congregation, the Lincoln Temple Congregational Church, and she was active in Delta Sigma Theta sorority" (Hine, Hine, and Harrold 2000: 372). In 1936, the Terrells were one of the first black families to move to LeDroit Park, which was originally an all-white suburb. Their house still stands today.

The 1940s and 1950s remained rigorous for Mary Church Terrell. In 1940, she wrote an autobiography titled *A Colored Woman in a White World*. In 1949, she chaired the Coordinating Committee for the Enforcement of District of Columbia Anti-Discrimination Laws. In the following year, she collaborated with a group of other blacks to challenge racial segregation. On February 28, they entered Thompson Restaurant, which was designated for whites only, to test the antidiscrimination laws that had been established in 1872 and 1873. When Terrell's group was denied service, they filed a lawsuit. The case, *District of Columbia v. John R. Thompson Co.*, went to the U.S. Supreme Court, where Terrell testified. While waiting for a decision, Terrell led and participated in several types of nonviolent protests that were commonly used in the civil rights movement, such as

boycotts, picketing, and sit-ins. On June 8, 1953, the court ruled that segregated eating places in Washington, D.C., were unconstitutional. Other victories, such as the *Brown v. Board of Education* (1954) ruling, which eradicated segregation in public schools and prompted the complete annihilation of Jim Crow legislation, marked a significant change for blacks in American society. After many long and strenuous years of activism, Terrell witnessed the dawn of a new, albeit slowly improving, world. When she died on July 24, 1954, she knew her labor had not been in vain.

Gladys L. Knight

See also

Anti-Lynching Legislation; Jim Crow Laws

Further Reading:

Hine, Darlene Clark, William C. Hine, and Stanley Harrold. *The African-American Odyssey*. New Jersey: Prentice Hall, 2000.

Jones, Beverly Washington. *Quest for Equality: The Life and Writings of Mary Church Terrell*. New York: Carlson Publishers, 1990.

Terrell, Mary Church. *A Colored Woman in a White World*. Washington, D.C.: Ransdell, 1940.

Terrorism

Terrorism is a term that applies, at a very general level, to any violent attack that intentionally targets civilians (noncombatants) and, by doing so, seeks to "terrorize" a particular group or population. The aim of instilling "terror" among members of the population of which victims are a part means that the agents carrying out the attack(s), usually referred to as "terrorists," intend to fundamentally alter the daily lives of the targeted group. This alteration to everyday life extends chiefly to economic and political matters such that the victimized population is compelled to change the way in which they promote commerce or business and make political decisions, both domestically and internationally. Terrorism, viewed from a different perspective, is an attack on the values that make a political community distinctive. With these aims in mind, it is understandable that terrorism, understood as encompassing both certain kinds of actions and the groups that carry them out, has an extraordinary range of manifestations.

Islamic Jihad

The Palestinian Islamic Jihad (PIJ) is a group of Islamist radicals based in Syria who operate primarily in Israel, the West Bank, and the Gaza Strip. Islamic Jihad is committed to the creation of an Islamic Palestinian state and to the destruction of the state of Israel. It was designated by the U.S. State Department as a "foreign terrorist organization" in October 1997. The PIJ allegedly has received funding from Iran and conducted attacks against Israeli military and civilian targets, including many suicide-bombing missions. For example, in June 2001, 21 people were killed in a suicide bombing at a Tel Aviv disco.

Since September 11, 2001, the U.S. government has more aggressively pursued possible American-based links to the organization as part of its War on Terror. In February 2003, the U.S. Justice Department indicted PIJ head Ramadan Shallah as well as other PIJ leaders for conspiring to plan, finance, and coordinate international terrorist activities using locations and facilities within the United States. Included in this group was Palestinian Sami Amin Al-Arian, 45, a professor at the University of South Florida's College of Engineering. In this indictment, it was alleged that the Tampa-based Islamic Committee for Palestine (formerly Islamic Concern Project) and the World and Islam Studies Enterprise (WISE) were used to fund militant Islamic Palestinian groups.

Muslim American advocacy groups have criticized the treatment of Al-Arian since his arrest and warn that his arrest is but one example of how Muslims in America have become increasingly and unfairly targeted due to mounting public concern over terrorism.

The Islamic Jihad has been linked to Hamas, the Palestinians' major Muslim fundamentalist movement. However, unlike Hamas, Islamic Jihad does not support any social-service activities (such as schools, hospitals, and mosques) and has no defined social or political role. Its purpose appears to be exclusively to conduct terrorist activities as part of the "holy war" against Israel and Western influence in the Middle East. *Jihad* refers to the Muslim term for a "righteous struggle" waged on behalf of Islam.

REBEKAH LEE

In the United States, terrorism became a virtually unavoidable part of national cultural, social, and political life as a result of the attacks of September 11, 2001. On this day, members of an Islamic (or "Islamicist") extremist organization named al-Qaeda boarded four planes with the intention of taking control of the aircrafts and individually directing them to previously specified targets, buildings of tremendous economic and political importance to the United States. These attacks effectively initiated the "War on Terror." The Bush administration and other lawmakers from across the political spectrum sought out a decisive response. Members of both the U.S. Senate and House of Representatives were virtually unanimous in support for some sort of military reprisal. Citizens and scholars alike earnestly sought to address the following questions: Why are we being attacked? What is being threatened? How should we respond to it? Numerous scholars weighed in on the general validity or ethical justifications regarding a military response to the attacks. Notable among these publications was *Just War Against Terror*, authored by political scientist, Jean Bethke Elshtain. In this text, Elshtain argues in support of military intervention against terrorist activity, claiming that the Islamicist leader Osama bin Laden, al-Qaeda, and any other group of similar character, should be regarded as morally equivalent to Adolf Hitler and the Nazi regime. For this reason, the United States should continue to assume a position of active involvement in international affairs to the extent that its superior military and economic power entail a responsibility to maintain right order in the world. As President Bush and other political figures (including Prime Minister Tony Blair of England) would emphasize repeatedly in the years succeeding the September 11 attacks, withdrawing from international affairs was not an option with an enemy that was construed as unable or unwilling to engage in peaceful diplomatic processes. Indeed, if organizations like al-Qaeda were popularly likened

Domestic Terrorism: Oklahoma City Federal Building Bombing

On April 19, 1995, the Alfred P. Murrah Federal Building in Oklahoma City was bombed by right-wing extremist Timothy McVeigh and his accomplice, Terry Nichols. They used a rented truck with 4,800 pounds of homemade plastic explosives (C4). The bombing killed 191 men, women, and children and injured hundreds of others. The Oklahoma City bombing is generally regarded as the most destructive terrorist act by domestic terrorists and the second most destructive terrorist incident within the United States, with the September 11, 2001, attacks being the worst.

McVeigh was apparently influenced by the domestic white supremacist movement. A page from the book *The Turner Diaries*, written by William Pierce under the pseudonym Andrew McDonald, was found on McVeigh when he was arrested for the attack. Pierce was the leader of the National Alliance (NA), a neo-Nazi hate group. The novel portrays white supremacists as exceedingly agitated over federal gun-control legislation, which leads the characters to conduct a series of terrorist attacks, including the bombing of FBI Headquarters. Pierce, who died on July 23, 2002, denied any involvement with the bombing.

Domestic terrorists, such as McVeigh and Nichols, have a familiarity with the laws, practices, and vulnerabilities in the United States that international terrorists may not have. Nevertheless, the similarities among domestic and international terrorists are striking: distorted views, overwhelming hatred of various people and the U.S. government, a total lack of respect for human life, and the unrestricted use of violence.

JOHN ETERNO

What Is Unique About Islamist Suicide Terrorism?

The suicide technique is not entirely unique to Islamist or extremist Islamic fundamentalist groups. The Tamil Tigers of Sri Lanka and the PKK (Kurdistan Worker's Party) have also employed the method. Research does suggest, however, a difference between the non-Islamic use of the technique and the strategic role that the technique has come to occupy among some violent Islamic groups. According to the findings of Ben-Dor and Pedahzur, suicide bombing by violent extremist Islamic groups is unique in terms of frequency and in terms of targeting. The suicide technique represents only 7.2 percent of the total number of attacks carried out by non-Islamic organizations since the late 1980s. Among Islamic organizations, however, the suicide technique amounts to almost a quarter of all attacks (23.9 percent). There is also a noticeable difference in the selection of targets. Non-Islamic organizations typically target politicians and governmental bodies (12.5 percent of attacks) and military and police officers (13.8 percent). Islamic organizations tend to attack passers-by (16.2 percent), citizens gathered at an entertainment venue (14.4 percent), or those using public transportation (14.4 percent).

to Hitler's National Socialist regime, then all other avenues for response seemed unreasonable. Such associations could also foreclose any serious examination about the historical causes of the attacks. Why, for instance, did Bin Laden and 120 other Saudi intellectuals claim that American foreign policy—including the presence of American soldiers in Saudi Arabia—played a direct role in the September 11 attacks? A thorough exploration of the key historical factors was bypassed in light of the immediate threat posed by this unique terrorist threat. Indeed, the key difference between this "War on Terror" and the other wars in which the United States had participated in the past was that terrorist groups traditionally did not represent a national entity or territory with a conventional army and governmental system. Rather, the terrorism that spawned the September 11 attacks seemed to thrive on covert, cell-like operations that placed agents among the population the organization intended to harm. Terrorism distrusts traditional political avenues for change—that is, it refuses to rely on national political organizations.

This key distinction, consequently, justified increased security measures (*see* Patriot Act of 2001) and counterterrorist surveillance practices that combine the resources and efforts of Federal and local law-enforcement authorities, thereby establishing a "Joint Terrorism Task Force."

"Joint Terrorism Task Forces" were established to gain "total information awareness" and led to the resurgence of racial profiling, which in turn led to the widespread arrest and imprisonment of thousands of Muslims and Arabs without warrant, trial, or release of names. Moreover, law enforcement agents detained and questioned a large number of African Americans that converted to Islam, often without any reason beyond the fact that they may have been in trouble with the law in the past and were also at the time active members of a community ("Ummah") of Muslims in a specific locale. This controversial blend of racial profiling and counterterrorism troubled minority communities and even produced deadly results. This was exemplified in the case of Imam Luqmann Ameen Abdullah, the head of a Detroit mosque who was found in a handcuffed position with 21 gunshot wounds delivered by FBI agents. An autopsy report revealed that several bullets hit the groin area and another entered through the back. Terrorism has catalyzed the use of many techniques that continue to invite complaints from residents and citizens of the United States and demand solutions that reject racist and discriminatory practices.

GABRIEL SANTOS

See also

Islamic Fundamentalism; Islamofascism; Islamophobia; Muslims, Terrorist Image of; Patriot Act of 2001; Racial Profiling; September 11, 2001, Terrorism, Discriminatory Reactions to

Further Reading:

Ben-Dor, Gabriel, and Ami Pedahzur. "The Uniqueness of Islamic Fundamentalism and the Fourth Wave of International Terrorism." In *Religious Fundamentalism and Political Extremism*, edited by Leonard Weinberg and Ami Pedahzur, 72–93. London: Frank Cass Publishers, 2004.

bin Laden, Osama. "Letter to America." *The Guardian*, November 24, 2002. http://www.guardian.co.uk/world/2002/nov/24/theobserver.

Brodie, Renee. "The Aryan New Era: Apocalyptic Realizations in The Turner Diaries." *Journal of American Culture* 21, no. 3 (1998): 13–32.

Elshtain, Jean Bethke. *Just War Against Terror*. New York: Basic Books, 2003.

Murray, Nancy. "Profiling in the Age of Total Information Awareness." *Race and Class* 52 (2010): 3–24. doi: 10.1177/0306396810377002.

Turk, Austin T. "Sociology of Terrorism." *Annual Review of Sociology* 30 (2004): 271–86.

Texas Southern University Riot of 1967

The Texas Southern University (TSU) Riot (also referred to as the TSU Riot, TSU Police Riot, or TSU Disturbance) was a violent encounter between the Houston Police Department (HPD) and students on the TSU campus on the night of May 16–17, 1967. The riot had a number of causes, but stemmed mainly from sit-ins at a garbage dump and HPD's heavy-handed tactics.

On May 8, 11-year-old Victor George fell into a garbage-filled pond and drowned at Houston's Holmes Road Dump. The city government traditionally placed landfills in segregated neighborhoods, and in 1967 most city dumps were located in black subdivisions. Beginning around May 15, students from TSU and other local universities sat down in front of the dump's entrance to stop the garbage trucks from entering the facility. The protestors hoped to convince the city to close the dump. Instead, the police responded by arresting large numbers of the students and their leaders. The students returned the following day and continued to sit-in at the dump. More arrests followed this protest. After these sit-ins, activists gathered for a number of rallies at local churches. At these rallies, militants called for battle with the police. When the police learned of this call to arms, they assumed TSU students had issued it.

Police followed the students back to TSU, used squad cars to blockade the roads leading to the campus, and shut down the school. The mostly male students fought back by throwing rocks and bottles at the officers, and by setting fire to several garbage cans. Students then barricaded themselves in the dorm rooms and exchanged gunfire with the police, who had surrounded the dormitory. Mayor Louis Welch appealed to black civic leaders to convince the students to surrender. Police escorted Rev. William Lawson, who was one of the organizers of the dump protest, to TSU with the hope that he could entreat the students to yield to the police. He found the students unorganized but unwilling to disperse. After Lawson informed HPD officials that the students would not surrender, the police opened fire, charged the dormitory, ransacked the rooms, and arrested nearly 500 students. Only a few students were injured in the melee, but two police officers were wounded. Officer Louis Kuba was the only fatality.

Houston's daily newspapers reported that the police fired between 3,000 and 5,000 rounds of ammunition at the dormitory. The papers justified police actions by fabricating accounts that the students were armed with guns and Molotov cocktails. Other papers reported that students had shared one .22-caliber pistol—a .22 was the only gun found in the dorm rooms. The district attorney charged five students with the murder of Officer Kuba. The black community vigorously supported this TSU Five. After three years of legal wrangling, the judge dismissed the charges against the TSU Five. The judge decided that evidence needed to prove the case did not exist, and that Kuba probably died from a ricocheting police bullet.

The TSU Riot stands as the most violent episode in the struggle for black rights in Houston. The only other riot to occur in the city's history was the 1917 mutiny of black soldiers stationed in Houston. A congressional investigation blamed the TSU students for the riot, but the details of the disturbance indicate that the police were largely responsible. HPD blockaded the campus and effectively shut down the school without considering how the students might react. Combined with anger over the Holmes Road Dump incident and the general mistrust and fear that many blacks felt toward police, the students' resistance seems hardly surprising.

BRIAN D. BEHNKEN

See also:

Civil Rights Movement; Long Hot Summer Riots (1965–1967); Police Brutality; Race Riots in America. Documents: The Report on the Memphis Riots of May 1866 (July 25, 1866); Account of the Riots in East St. Louis, Illinois (July 1917); The Cook County Coroner's Report Regarding the 1919 Chicago Race Riots (1919); A Southern Black Woman's Letter Regarding the Recent Riots in Chicago and Washington (November 1919); The Final Report of the Grand Jury on the Tulsa Race Riot (June 25, 1921); Testimony from *Laney v. United States* Describing Events during the Washington, D.C., Riot of July 1919 (December 3, 1923); The Governor's Commission Report on the Watts Riots (December 1965); Cyrus R. Vance's Report on the Riots in Detroit (July–August 1967); The Reports of the Oklahoma Commission to Study the Tulsa Race Riot of 1921 (2000–2001); The Draft Report of the 1898 Wilmington Race Riot Commission (December 2005)

Further Reading:

Justice, Blair. *Violence in the City*. Forth Worth: Texas Christian University Press, 1969.

Third Wave Whiteness

The 1990s ushered in a new line of research in examining the notion of "whiteness." Critical White Studies emerged as a body of scholarship committed to studying, documenting, and contesting the formation and legitimation of whiteness and the deployment of white privilege—the unearned material, political, and social advantages; psychological benefits; and positive life chances granted to persons who perform and reinforce whiteness. Whiteness, the historically and socially constructed dispositions and ideologies that generally white persons perform and embody, has been examined differently within disparate historical contexts and from diverse theoretical positions. These differences have been characterized as waves by France Winddance Twine and Charles Gallagher (2008) in a special issue of *Ethnic and Racial Studies*.

Twine and Gallagher (2008) associate the first wave of critical interrogation of whiteness with the pioneering work of W.E.B Du Bois, a prominent 20th-century African American educator, scholar, and activist. Du Bois observed that instead of establishing potentially powerful coalitions with people of color, marginalized white laborers and immigrants traded class consciousness for race privilege, gaining social advantages and psychological benefits in recompense for their complicity with white supremacy and allowing them to leverage these advantages for material and political gain. Moreover, Du Bois recognized that the invisibility of whiteness and its insidious penetration into society's major institutions established racial relations that materially, socially, and politically advantaged white people at the expense of African Americans. Because whiteness remained unseen, it served as the normative racial touchstone against which all other racial formations were pejoratively constructed and defined. Additionally, Du Bois posited that whiteness was not a monolithic racial identity: white people performed their racial identity and experienced racial privilege differently depending on geography, class, and other social and cultural constructs.

Second wave whiteness studies largely applied Du Bois's insights to highlight systemic racism and to combat common assumptions regarding race and racism that permeated public and political discourse. For instance, for much of the 20th century, race was conceptualized as biological; however, second wave whiteness conceived race as a social construction that changes over space and time. Conceiving race as a social construct reveals how persons identifying with aggrieved racial groups are differently racialized by the ideologies and discourses underpinning whiteness to maintain racial inequality. Second wave whiteness also contested the framing of racism as discrete individual acts, a framing that conveniently masks how the daily actions and attitudes of many white people and the normal operations of society's institutions surreptitiously reinforce systemic white supremacy. Fundamentally, scholarship of second wave whiteness identified and confronted how society's institutions, like the legal system, constitute and are constitutive of inequitable racial relations, particularly in how they legitimate and reinforce whiteness and enable and distribute white privilege.

Third wave whiteness extends these critical insights by not only examining the social reification of whiteness, but also exploring how whiteness and other racial formations intersect and compete with class, gender, sexual orientation, citizenship, and other social constructs, generating a deeper understanding of the mechanisms and power relations that sustain racial inequality and other forms of subordination. Also, third wave whiteness privileges empirical, interdisciplinary, and innovate methodologies that reveal and document how whiteness and white identities are locally deployed, discursively constructed, and extemporaneously reinvented to maintain structural white supremacy. Third wave whiteness, for instance, analyzes the seemingly innocuous rhetorical moves and discursive practices that white people, as well as mainstream media, employ to rationalize racial inequality, justify white privilege, and ignore complicity with systems of inequality.

Empirical, interdisciplinary, and innovative methods that raise and validate race consciousness allow third wave whiteness scholars to understand the ways in which whiteness is ideologically and discursively invented, politically and legally legitimated, and uncritically and pervasively reproduced locally, nationally, and globally. This scholarship is desperately needed as the massive expansion of global capitalism and recent demographic shifts in industrialized countries constantly blur borders and relentlessly pressure the supremacy of whiteness. Third wave whiteness scholarship studies how demographic shifts and other 21st-century social and economic contingencies compel whiteness to reinvent itself and

---

Scholarship on Whiteness

Scholarship on whiteness has increased exponentially since the 1990s, appearing in countless collections, books, editorials, dissertations, and other scholarly publications. Additionally, several academic journals from across disciplines have published special issues discussing and elaborating on scholarship in whiteness studies, a phenomenon that demonstrates the wide interest in studying whiteness, as well as the relevance of whiteness studies to a myriad of disciplines. These are just a couple of the journals that have published special issues: *borderlands e-journal* and the *Graduate Journal of Social Science*. In the fall of 2005, *Rhetoric Review* published a special symposium discussing the intersections of whiteness studies and rhetorical theory. Finally, a critical resource for anyone studying whiteness is *Towards a Bibliography of Critical Whiteness Studies* compiled by the Critical Whiteness Studies Group (2006) at the University of Illinois at Urbana–Champaign.

---

its deployment into white identities constantly to maintain racial supremacy.

As with previous scholarship, third wave whiteness interrogates constructions and dispersions of whiteness and distributions and deployments of white privilege in an attempt to deconstruct racial hierarchies and contest inequitable racial relations. However, with its emphasis on empirical studies, interdisciplinary, and innovative methodologies that allow for sophisticated, nuanced analyses of whiteness and white privilege, third wave whiteness is poised to confront the ever-changing social and historical contingencies that might "reinscribe, reconstitute, and transform" the various inflections and contours of "whiteness, white identities, and white privilege" now and in the future.

NICHOLAS N. BEHM

See also

White Privilege; Whiteness Studies

Further Reading:

Bonilla-Silva, Eduardo. *Racism Without Racists: Color-Blind Racism and the Persistence of Racial Inequality in the United States.* Lanham, MD: Rowman & Littlefield, 2006.

Critical Whiteness Studies Group. *Towards a Bibliography of Critical Whiteness Studies.* Center on Democracy in a Multiracial Society at the University of Illinois at Urbana-Champaign, 2006.

Delgado, Richard, and Jean Stefancic, eds. *Critical White Studies: Looking Behind the Mirror.* Philadelphia: Temple University Press, 1997.

Delgado, Richard, and Jean Stefancic, eds. *Critical Race Theory: An Introduction.* New York: New York University Press, 2001.

Frankenberg, Ruth. 1993. *The Social Construction of Whiteness: White Women, Race Matter.* Minneapolis: University of Minnesota Press.

Harris, Cheryl I. "Whiteness as Property." *Harvard Law Review* 106, no. 8 (1993): 1709–37.

Kennedy, Tammie M., Joyce Irene Middleton, Krista Ratcliffe, Kathleen Ethel Welch, Catherine Prendergast, Ira Shor, Thomas R. West, Ellen Cushman, Michelle Kendrick, and Lisa Albrecht. "Symposium: Whiteness Studies." *Rhetoric Review* 24, no.4 (2005): 359–402.

Lipsitz, George. *The Possessive Investment of Whiteness: How White People Profit from Identity Politics.* Philadelphia: Temple University Press, 2006.

Pedersen, Linda Lund, and Barbara Samaluk, eds. "Critical Whiteness Studies—Methodologies." special issue, *Graduate Journal of Social Science* 9, no. 1 (2012). http://gjss.org/index.php?/Volume-91-March-2012-Critical-Whiteness-Studies-Methodologies.html

Riggs, Damien W., ed. "Why Whiteness Studies?" special issue, *borderlands e-journal* 3, no. 2 (2004). http://www.borderlands.net.au/issues/vol3no2.html.

Twine France Winndance, and Charles Gallagher. "Introduction: The Future of Whiteness: A Map of the 'Third Wave.'" *Ethnic and Racial Studies* 31, no. 1 (2008): 4–24.

Thirty Years of Lynching in the United States: 1889–1918

In an effort to investigate and expose the horrors of lynching, the National Association for the Advancement of Colored People (NAACP) published a book in 1919 titled *Thirty Years of Lynching in the United States: 1889–1918*, written by Martha Gruening and Helen Boardman. The NAACP's publication of this book was indicative of the organization's numerous and strenuous efforts to eradicate lynching in the United States.

Lynching was a heinous crime instigated by racial hostility and heightened during the Jim Crow era in the United States. Lynching peaked in the years after Emancipation in the late 19th century and in the early to mid-20th century. Lynch mobs often murdered African American men and women whom they deemed guilty of a variety of crimes that could include verbally protesting mistreatment by whites or physically or verbally assaulting whites. These white mobs often did not require evidence of any crime; rather, they purposefully sought out individuals based on their status as African Americans.

The formation of the NAACP was rooted in an event that occurred in the hometown of President Abraham Lincoln. A race riot occurred in Springfield, Illinois, in 1908 and was preceded by race riots in several other cities, including Wilmington, North Carolina (1898); New Orleans, Louisiana (1900); and Atlanta, Georgia (1906). Vicious lynchings occurred in each of these cities during all of these riots and on numerous other occasions. The Springfield riots culminated in the deaths of both blacks and whites and led to such conferences as the National Negro Convention, which was considered the first official meeting of the NAACP. The NAACP was established by W.E.B. Du Bois, Mary White Ovington, and others in 1909 in the aftermath of the Springfield violence. Du Bois, a noted author, educator, and professor, was also considered one of the leaders of the black intellectual protest movement. Ovington was a descendant of New England abolitionists who had previously lived among poor African Americans in New York. These two individuals joined with others in an effort to fight social injustice and to establish an organization that would achieve this goal.

The NAACP was initially formed by an interracial group that was committed to speaking for African Americans in the United States. The organization spoke to African Americans and on behalf of African Americans, encouraging individuals and organizations to engage in activities that would advance the status and social and political conditions of African Americans in the United States. The NAACP laid the foundation for the civil rights movement, which would follow half a century later. The organization was also instrumental in obtaining civil and legal rights for African Americans well into the 20th century.

In 1918, John Shillady became executive director of the NAACP. He is credited with greatly increasing the membership and encouraging and overseeing *Thirty Years of Lynching in the United States: 1889–1918*, the first book publication of the NAACP. Under his leadership, the NAACP decided to take a stance on lynching, one of the most pressing contemporary issues concerning the safety and well-being of African Americans in the United States. The Dyer Anti-Lynching Bill, introduced by Rep. Leonidas C. Dyer, would have made participating in a lynch mob a federal crime. The NAACP publicly supported this bill and focused on pressuring the federal government to end lynching.

Since the NAACP was leading an anti-lynching movement and working to increase awareness and distaste for a practice that had become routinely tolerated, the organization determined to take an aggressive stance in the publication of a book on a 30-year period of lynching. The focus of this historic work was to examine the 3,224 recorded lynchings that had occurred during this period and identify 100 of the most heinous documented lynchings. A three-pronged approach was essential to developing a cohesive summary of each identified lynching. Each documented lynching had to meet the following three criteria: articulate in extreme detail the rationale provided for the justification of the lynching, describe the procedure followed by the lynch mob to assault its victim, and explain the related activities associated with the lynching. Great care was used to ensure that the cases described were extremely disturbing and created an unsettling image for the reader. The purpose of the book was to cause even the most hardened individuals to reconsider their complacency in addressing lynching, which was an extralegal activity that had become routine in many areas of the country.

One of the most disturbing accounts included in the book was that of Mary Turner in Valdosta, Georgia. Her husband had been wrongfully lynched when a mob was unable to locate another black man who had allegedly killed a white planter. Ms. Turner publicly protested her husband's wrongful death and was subsequently punished for her outspokenness. Her execution was especially disturbing because she was eight months' pregnant at the time. Despite this circumstance, she was lynched in a particularly violent manner, and her unborn child was murdered as well. Other lynchings provided similar gruesome details about the deaths of persons who suffered acts of brutality, and in many cases the perpetrators were never brought to justice. The narration of these atrocities contributed greatly to the NAACP's ability to challenge individuals to examine their role in the promulgation of lynching in the United States.

Nia Woods Haydel and Kijua Sanders-McMurtry

See also

Anti-Lynching Campaign; Anti-Lynching League, Anti-Lynching Legislation; Black Soldiers and Lynching; Black Women and Lynching; Lynching

Further Reading:

Berg, Manfred. *"The Ticket to Freedom": The NAACP and the Struggle for Black Political Integration*. Gainesville: University Press of Florida, 2005.

Lewis, David Levering, ed. *W.E.B. Du Bois: A Reader*. New York: Henry Holt, 1995.

Raper, Arthur. *The Tragedy of Lynching*. New York: Dover Publications, 2003 [1933].

Thomas, Clarence (b. 1948)

Clarence Thomas is the second black Supreme Court Justice in the United States, succeeding Thurgood Marshall. Serving since 1991, he has continued to exhibit conservative votes and opinions.

The second of three children, Clarence Thomas was born in Pin Point, Georgia, a small, poor community outside Savannah that was given to freed slaves after the Civil War. He was born on June 23, 1948, to Leola and M. C. Thomas. His father abandoned the family shortly after Clarence was born.

After years of living in poverty with no indoor plumbing, Thomas moved to Savannah, Georgia, to live with his maternal grandfather, Myers Anderson, a religious man and self-taught entrepreneur. According to Thomas, this move proved to be a turning point in his life. For the first time, Thomas and his brother had an adult male figure and a comfortable home, with indoor plumbing and adult supervision. His grandfather enrolled Thomas in St. Benedict the Moor, a Catholic grade school that was started to educate poor African American children. Although Thomas had difficulty adjusting, this school pushed Thomas to excel and made him believe he could achieve great things as long as he worked hard. The stern hand of his grandfather proved influential in his life, teaching him discipline, the importance of an education, and hard work.

Clarence Thomas was seated on the U.S. Supreme Court in 1991. He is the only African American Justice now serving on the Supreme Court and has generally voted conservatively in Court decisions. (U.S. Supreme Court)

Because Anderson wanted Thomas to be a priest, he enrolled his grandson in St. John Vianney Minor Seminary, a Catholic boarding school, where he experienced bigotry for the first time. After graduating the seminary, in 1967, Thomas entered Immaculate Conception Seminary in Missouri to prepare for the priesthood; however, the prejudices there almost cost Thomas his faith. He was faced with Southern bigotry from young men who were to be ordained as Catholic priests, something that troubled him. Ultimately, Thomas would enroll in Holy Cross College in Massachusetts. While at Holy Cross, Thomas worked part-time, participated in community service programs, and helped establish the Black Student Union. In 1971, he graduated with an honors degree in English and soon thereafter married Kathy Grace Ambush, who had his only child.

Thomas attended law school at Yale, where he had been accepted as part of an affirmative action program. To avoid being identified as the black student, Thomas often sat in the back of the class and avoided taking any civil rights courses. Instead, he took business classes and studied tax and property law because he did not want to be labeled a civil rights attorney. This was his first experience, as he recalls, having the "monkey on his back," being at Yale to satisfy some social goal, not because of his credentials but because of his race. It was at Yale that Thomas formulated his opinion against affirmative action programs, because they helped more middle-class African Americans and he was poor. After graduation from Yale in 1974, he accepted a position in Missouri to work in the Office of the State Attorney General John Danforth, a position that allowed him to work in the tax division. When Danforth won a seat in the U.S. Senate, Thomas became a corporate lawyer for the Monsanto Company and later went back to work as a legislative assistant for Danforth, who was now a senator.

In 1980, President Ronald Reagan gained an interest in Thomas when he attended the Fairmont Conference for black conservatives, and the *Washington Post* wrote an article about him. He was offered a job as the assistant secretary for civil rights in the U.S. Department of Education. Soon after, Reagan promoted him to chairman of the U.S. Equal Opportunity Employment Commission (EEOC), where he changed the environment of the agency. Under Thomas's leadership the EEOC stopped the use of time-tables, numeric goals, and the use of trials that relied on statistical evidence of discrimination, a move that angered many civil rights groups.

President George H. W. Bush then appointed Thomas in 1990 to the U.S. Court of Appeals in Washington, D.C. In 1991, he was picked by President Bush to be the successor to Justice Marshall, who had retired. There was widespread outcry by civil rights groups, particularly the National Association for the Advancement of Colored People and the Congressional Black Caucus, against his nomination as an associate justice because of Thomas's opposition to affirmative action. Women's rights groups also opposed his nomination because of charges of sexual harassment from Anita Hill. During Senate confirmation hearings, which were broadcast nationally, Thomas denied all allegations. The Senate Judiciary Committee recommended him to the full Senate for confirmation and Thomas was confirmed by a 52 to 48 vote in the Senate, the closest confirmation vote in history. He took the oath of office October 23, 1991, and was the youngest member of the Court at the time.

Thomas is considered a conservative justice who attracts much debate. As a black Republican, Thomas is strongly supported by conservatives and despised by black intellectuals. Yet, Thomas argues that America should not expect African Americans to speak in a monolithic voice.

ANGELA K. LEWIS

Further Reading:

Greenya, John. *Silent Justice: The Clarence Thomas Story*. Fort Lee, NJ: Barricade Books, 1997.

Mayer, Jane. *Strange Justice: The Selling of Clarence Thomas*. Boston: Houghton Mifflin, 1994.

Thomas, Andrew Peyton. *Clarence Thomas: A Biography*. San Francisco: Encounter Books, 2001.

Three Strikes Laws

Three strikes laws are criminal justice policies that mandate lengthy (or "life" sentences) for persons convicted of three or more criminal offenses, typically those considered violent or serious. Three strikes laws are one of many "tough on crime" penal policies adopted in the 1990s throughout the United States in response to growing fears about violent crime. Originally fashioned to permanently remove serious, repeat offenders from communities, in many states, individuals convicted for nonviolent or drug-related offenses receive life sentences. Below we discuss the adoption of three strikes legislation in the United States (with a focus on the state of California) and the considerations of such policies.

In 1994, the state of California passed the harshest three strikes law in the nation. In the wake of a parolee's widely publicized kidnapping and murder of 12-year-old Polly Klaas, moral panic about violent crime and repeat offenders allowed Proposition 184, a ballot initiative calling for three strikes, to be passed with overwhelming support (72 percent). Proposition 184 was adopted in record time with endorsement by both the California Correctional Peace Officers Association (the correctional officer union) and the National Rifle Association. Shortly after its passage, it became clear that the law was used primarily to give life sentences to individuals who had been charged with nonviolent or menial offenses such as the petty theft of a slice of pizza, instant coffee, or a can of beer. These notable examples demonstrated early on in California that the law was not having the intended consequence of targeting and removing repeat violent offenders from the community. After California's adoption of the 1994 three strikes law, an additional 24 states and the federal government passed three strikes legislation between 1994 and 1997. Most states that have adopted three strikes legislation have not sentenced any more than a few hundred people to life sentences in comparison to California where, in 2010 alone, approximately 41,000 individuals were serving "strike" offenses and nearly 9,000 individuals in prison as "third strikers."

While the zeal in which California applied three strikes is unique, the existence of such laws is not. Several nations, including France, England, New Zealand, Australia, Pakistan, and the United States, have some version of "habitual offender" laws that target individuals who repeatedly commit crimes. Such legislation, including three strikes, seeks to reduce or eliminate future offenses by deterring individuals from committing additional crimes, deterring the general public, and by incapacitating an individual through a life sentence in prison (typically a sentence of 25 or more years in the United States). The severity of such lengthy sentences for a third conviction are often argued to maximize the criminal justice system's ability to deter and selectively incapacitate through incarceration by targeting repeat offenders who account for a large proportion of serious crime. Supporters for three strikes legislation also argue that it is much more cost-effective to prevent future crime than allow society to pay the social and financial costs of habitual, serious, or violent crime.

To contrast, there are many arguments against three strikes legislation. First, using a wide variety of methods, scholars find very little evidence that three strikes legislation is effective in reducing violent or serious crimes in the areas it has been adopted. Second, opponents argue that the evidence for the effectiveness of selective incapacitation is mixed at best. Third, three strikes laws violate retributive principles of proportionality between an individual's crime and punishment. Fourth, opponents argue that three strikes legislation essentially gives up on the rehabilitative model of corrections,

---

The California Three Strikes Experiment

After the adoption of Proposition 184 in California, legislators and criminal justice officials hailed Three Strikes as the cause for one of the largest drops in violent and property crimes recorded in California between the 1990s and 2010. However, criminologists counter this by pointing out that crime rates were already on the decline during those years and were following a national downward trend for all types of crime. Early models of the benefits of Three Strikes predicted that sentencing roughly 85,000 individuals to life under Three Strikes by the year 2000 would provide the state the "social benefit" of billions of dollars in comparison to correctional costs to incapacitate those individuals through incarceration. In actuality, Three Strikes legislation cost the state billions of dollars and crime was not reduced as a result of its adoption. Early on, it was clear that the law was disproportionately targeting African Americans and Latinos in comparison to their rates within California's population and their rates for arrest. In 2012, California voters moved to overturn Three Strikes in Proposition 36 by a wide margin. It is estimated that ending life sentences for nonviolent crimes will save the state $100 million each year. It also allows for judges to review the sentences of individuals currently serving life to reduce their sentences.

---

and assumes that individuals cannot or will not be able to be anything but "criminals" for the remainder of their lives. Fifth, three strikes laws ignore the vast criminological literature on offending and the life-course that demonstrates that most individuals will "age out" of offending once they are no longer in their youthful "crime-prone" years. Sixth, individuals sentenced to life in prison through three strikes laws add to an increasing prison population, prison overcrowding, and an aging population that significantly contributes to prison costs. In 2010, the California State Auditor released a report detailing that, collectively, individuals sentenced under three strikes cost the state nearly $20 billion over the course of their incarceration. As detailed in additional reports, roughly a third of those costs are for health care, particularly given the needs of an aging prison population. Relatedly, persons with severe and debilitating mental illness are vastly over-represented among those serving life sentences under three strikes. Lastly, civil rights advocates point to the grossly racially disproportionate sentencing for three strikes legislation everywhere it has been adopted. For example, African American men were 13 times more likely than white men to be sentenced under the new three strikes law in California in the two years after it was adopted.

Three strikes legislation is considered a "tough on crime" penal policy, similar to mandatory minimums, life sentences without parole, and mandatory sentences adopted in the United States throughout the 1990s in response to fears about violent crime. Despite a wealth of evidence that three strikes legislation is a failed experiment rife with racial disparities, states only appear to be reconsidering such punitive sentencing guidelines out of cost considerations rather than racial concerns.

DANIELLE DIRKS AND TRAVIS LINNEMANN

See also

Crime and Race; Criminal Justice System and Racial Discrimination

Further Reading:

Ehlers, Scott, Vincent Schiraldi, and Eric Lotke. *Racial Divide: An Examination of California's Three Strikes Law on African-Americans and Latinos*. Washington, DC: Justice Policy Institute, 2004.

Shichor, David, and Dale K. Sechrest, eds. *Three Strikes And You're Out: Vengeance As Public Policy*. Thousand Oaks, CA: Sage Publications, 1996.

Tyler, Tom R., and Robert J. Boeckmann. "Three Strikes and You Are Out, but Why? The Psychology of Public Support for Punishment Rule Breakers." *Law and Society Review* 55 (1997): 237–65.

Zimring, Franklin, E., Gordon Hawkins, and Sam Kamin. *Punishment and Democracy: Three Strikes and You're Out in California*. New York: Oxford University Press, 2003.

Tijerina, Reies López (b. 1926)

In his 1969 "Letter from the Santa Fe Jail," activist Reies López Tijerina affirmed his strong commitment to Hispanic rights. He wrote: "Here in my prison I feel very content—I repeat very content and very happy because I know and understand well the cause I defend." Tijerina occupies a unique position in the Latino experience. In large measure, his leadership was based on his persuasive rhetorical skills. A fiery, compelling spellbinder, he was arguably one of the most dynamic Mexican American speakers of the 1960s. Unflagging in delivering his message, he appealed viscerally to people who lacked influence, power, and wealth. He had great resoluteness and a messianic conviction that God had singled him out to regain for Hispanos the lands they had lost.

One of 10 children, López Tijerina was born on September 21, 1926, in a tiny adobe house near Falls City, Texas, about 40 miles southeast of San Antonio. His strong-willed mother, who died when he was six years old, greatly influenced his young mind, reading her small son Bible stories and encouraging a precocious embracing of mystical experiences. His father made a precarious living as a sharecropper, and during the Great Depression the family was forced to go on the migratory harvest circuit, wintering in San Antonio. He grew up there in harsh social and economic conditions that included discrimination, extreme poverty, and at times gnawing hunger. By age seven or eight, López Tijerina was working at stoop labor in the fields alongside his father and older brothers as they followed summer harvests from Texas to Michigan.

Due to this migratory lifestyle, López Tijerina's early education was disjointed and limited. He became a serious reader of the Bible when he was 12 years old as a result of his mother's lingering influence and the gift of a New Testament from a passing Baptist minister. At age 18, he left the Catholic Church and entered an Assembly of God Bible institute at Ysleta, Texas. In this fundamentalist school, he soon became known as a fiery, inspirational speaker who was intense and sincere, but not always docile or tractable. In 1946, he was suspended for violating an institute rule against dating and left without graduating after three years of study.

A few months after leaving Ysleta, he married and began the life of a circuit preacher in the Southwest for the Assembly of God. By 1950, his disagreement with the church over tithing caused the loss of his ministerial credentials, but he continued his itinerant ministry as a nondenominational preacher. Meanwhile, he gradually moved from a purely religious concern about social justice to a more pragmatic and political consideration. In the mid-1950s, with 17 followers and their families, he founded a utopian community, La Valle de Paz, in southern Arizona midway between Tucson and Phoenix. Successful at first, the Valley of Peace soon faced severe hostility from the local community and, after harassment and violence (including arson), it was eventually abandoned.

In 1957, López Tijerina was arrested for allegedly helping one of his brothers in a jailbreak. As the result of jumping bail, he then became a fugitive from Arizona until 1962. He traveled to Mexico and then to California, where a messianic vision directed him to northern New Mexico, leading to a deep interest in the complex history of Spanish land grants. Gradually, he came to believe that all *nuevomexicanos*' problems stemmed from loss of their lands. In 1960, with a few Valle de Paz settlers, he moved to Albuquerque, where he quietly started recruiting followers. Convinced that it was his mission to regain lost grant lands, in 1963 he organized the Alianza Federal de Mercedes and began openly to recruit supporters. With evangelistic fervor, he stressed economic, political, educational, and cultural rights for his followers and all Hispanic Americans. As a result of his charisma and persuasiveness on radio and television and in the press, as well as in small meetings, the Alianza grew rapidly to 10,000 members.

To dramatize their land claims and to obtain the redress they sought, López Tijerina and his followers drew attention to Hispanos' plight by a variety of aggressive actions. They undertook a motorcade to Mexico City in a futile effort to enlist Mexican government support; filed lawsuits against both federal and state governments; marched on Santa Fe to present their demands to the governor; and took over part of the Kit Carson National Forest and proclaimed it the Republic of San Joaquín del Río Chama. A confrontation with forest rangers resulted in the arrest of López Tijerina and several *aliancistas* on federal charges.

In a running feud between the Alianza and district attorney Alfonso Sánchez, a dozen *aliancistas* were arrested in June 1967 on blank warrants and taken to the Tierra Amarilla courthouse. Fellow *aliancistas*' decision to free their comrades and make a citizen's arrest on Sánchez led to the famous courthouse raid in which two lawmen were wounded. Panic ensued. Many believed that López Tijerina was beginning "the revolution" or at least a guerrilla war. In a massive manhunt, the National Guard with tanks, artillery, and helicopters searched New Mexico's mountains for López

Tijerina and his close followers. A week later, López Tijerina was captured and charged with various state and federal offenses in connection with the raid.

Now a national front page news personality and free on bail, López Tijerina took to the lecture circuit and public forums to promote the goals of the reorganized Alianza Federal de Pueblos Libres. He spoke to young Chicanos at colleges and universities, starred in national conferences, and was an extremely vocal leader in the Poor People's March on Washington in mid-1968. Next he announced his candidacy for the governorship of New Mexico but was declared ineligible. Then, in a 1969 upsurge of militancy, he attempted a citizen's arrest on New Mexico's governor David Cargo and U.S. Supreme Court nominee Warren Burger.

Despite some acquittals in court, López Tijerina was eventually convicted on both state and federal indictments stemming from the Carson National Forest and Tierra Amarilla incidents and began serving his sentences. At the end of July 1971, he was released on parole on the condition that he hold no office in the Alianza. He told followers who greeted him on his release that he now advocated brotherhood rather than confrontation. Deprived of his leadership, the Alianza was languishing even before his release. It now split along militant and moderate lines; López Tijerina lost the support of many of his earlier enthusiastic, youthful followers.

A year later, López Tijerina spoke at the national La Raza Unida Party (LRUP) convention in El Paso, stressing brotherhood and dispensing elder statesman counsel to the young Chicano delegates. At a Tierra y Cultura congress he convened in the following October, he lost more followers after angrily sweeping from the hall upon being outvoted by youthful LRUP activists. When his parole ended in 1976, he resumed the presidency of a much diminished Alianza and devoted most of his time in the second half of the 1970s to vain efforts to persuade two Mexican presidents to champion the land grant issue at the United Nations. No longer in the media spotlight, in the mid-1980s he soft-pedaled the brotherhood theme, but continued his moderate stance, weakly supported by a much-reduced following, mostly older *nuevomexicano* land grantee descendants.

In his crusade, López Tijerina tapped into an underlying unity based on historical experience, ethnicity, and religion. Among Hispanic leaders in the 1960s, he alone seemed to answer youthful activists' calls for action, seizure of lands, and creation of a Chicano nation of Aztlán in the Southwest. Yet his legalistic approach, as well as emphasis on family and cultural traditions, also appealed to conservative rural *nuevomexicanos*. He reawakened pride in ethnic identity, language, and culture.

After a fire claimed his New Mexico house in 1994, López Tijerina moved to Uruapan, Michoacán, where he married for the third time. He presented his archival materials to the University of New Mexico on October 19, 1999. On November 5 of the same year, he met with senior staff of then Texas governor George W. Bush to discuss land issues. A translation of his memoirs, previously only available in a 1978 Spanish version published by Mexico's Fondo Cultural Economico, was published in 2000. López Tijerina currently resides in El Paso, Texas.

Matt Meier, Conchita Franco Serri, and Richard A. Garcia

See also

Chicano Movement; La Raza Unida Party

Further Reading:

Bernard, Jacqueline. *Voices from the Southwest*. New York: Scholastic Book Services, 1972.

Blawis, Patricia Bell. *Tijerina and the Land Grants*. New York: International Publishers, 1971.

Gardner, Richard. *¡Grito! Reies Tijerina and the New Mexico Land Grant War of 1967*. New York: Harper & Row, 1970.

Meier, Matt S. "'King Tiger': Reies López Tijerina" *Journal of the West* 27, no. 2 (April 1988): 60–68.

Tillman, Ben (1847–1918)

In appearance, words and deeds, Benjamin Ryan Tillman figured prominently as a grand cyclops of Jim Crow segregation. His career as a planter, terrorist, and politician was defined by a fearsome devotion to the era's racial project of white male supremacy.

Tillman was born near the town of Trenton, in the cotton plantation district of Edgefield, South Carolina. Owning over 2,500 acres and nearly 50 slaves, his family was among the wealthiest 10 percent of slaveholders in the area. The world of this slaveholding planter elite, thinly disguised by the self-comforting rhetoric of paternalism, was one in which white males sought to maintain control of the enslaved through a system of threats and the application of physical punishment. Losing an eye to illness at the age of 16, Tillman was prevented from defending slavery's racial dominion by serving in the Confederate Army. However, by the time of Reconstruction, Tillman had recovered his health and exercised his desire to restore white male mastery by joining a paramilitary rifle-club movement, which sought to topple the Palmetto state's black-majority Republican government. In this period, Tillman participated in the Hamburg Massacre of July 1876, in which five members of a black Republican militia defending an armory in the small town were coldly executed by white rifle-club members wearing improvised red shirt uniforms. During the state's gubernatorial election that same year, these "Red Shirts" used tactics of violence and intimidation towards black voters to help carry the former Confederate general and Ku Klux Klan leader Wade Hampton III to power.

During the late 1870s, Tillman enjoyed economic success as a planter, but after experiencing droughts and crop failures in the early 1880s, he took up the cause of agricultural reform and began to articulate serious political ambitions. Despite the comforts and privileges of his upbringing and lifestyle, Tillman aligned himself with the common farmers of South Carolina and railed against the elitism of the Bourbon political aristocracy, the so-called Redeemers of white rule who he claimed were failing to address the state's crisis in agriculture. Tillman's Farmer's Association movement demanded a variety of reforms, the most substantial of which was the call for a farmer's college. Elected governor of South Carolina in 1890, Tillman eventually oversaw the founding of Clemson College for white males and Winthrop College for white women, but repeatedly frustrated efforts to improve black educational opportunities.

In 1895 Tillman played a leading role in the South Carolina constitutional convention that established key elements of Jim Crow legislation: the various poll tax, literacy, education, and understanding requirements that conspired to disenfranchise black men in the state for long decades to come. That same year Tillman was elected to the U.S. Senate, in which he served until his death in 1918. Here he earned a reputation as an ill-mannered and volatile orator, as well as his nickname "Pitchfork Ben," following a speech he made on the Senate floor in 1896 in which he threatened to "poke" President Grover Cleveland "with a pitchfork." In

Ben Tillman dominated South Carolina politics for more than 20 years, serving as governor from 1890 to 1894 and senator from 1895 to 1918. (Library of Congress)

an infamous address to the Senate in March 1900, Tillman peddled an undiluted racist poison that endorsed white mob violence: "We of the South have never believed [the black man] to be the equal to the white man and we will not submit to his gratifying his lust on our wives and daughters without lynching him."

Bearing the deeply misleading legend—"friend and leader of the common people"—a Tillman monument was erected on the statehouse grounds of Columbia, South Carolina, in 1940. Standing alongside the relocated Confederate flag and on the same complex as a monument to Wade Hampton III and a statue of the Dixiecrat Strom Thurmond, Tillman's bronze figures as a central pillar in the state's pantheon of white Jim Crow rule.

Stephen C. Kenny

See also

Jim Crow Laws

Further Reading:

Edgar, Walter. *South Carolina: A History*. Columbia: University of South Carolina Press, 1998.

Kantrowitz, Stephen. *Ben Tillman and the Reconstruction of White Supremacy*. Chapel Hill: University of North Carolina Press, 2000.

Simpkins, Francis Butler. *Pitchfork Ben Tillman: South Carolinian*. Baton Rouge: Louisiana State University Press, 1944.

Toomer, Jean (1894–1967)

Jean Toomer was an African American author, born Nathan Pinchback Toomer to parents Nathan Toomer, a planter, and Nina Pinchback on December 26, 1894. Toomer's mother was the daughter of Pinckney Benton Stewart Pinchback, former governor of Louisiana, the first black governor in the nation. Because of his light complexion, Toomer could easily pass for white, a common practice during an earlier period of his life. After Nathan Toomer abandoned Toomer and his mother, they moved to Washington, D.C., to live with Nina's parents. Pinckney Pinchback began to refer to young Nathan as Eugene Pinchback Toomer, although his name was never legally changed. Toomer grew up in a racially integrated neighborhood but attended segregated schools. Nina remarried and Toomer lived briefly in New York. Upon his mother's death, Toomer returned to Washington, graduating in 1914 from the all-black Dunbar High School. After graduation, Toomer studied a wide range of disciplines, including literature, philosophy, and agriculture.

During his stint in Sparta, Georgia, Toomer's racial consciousness was roused. As the superintendent of Sparta's Industrial and Agricultural Institute, Toomer became inspired by both his racial heritage and surroundings in the rural South. The product of Toomer's combined influences was the collection *Cane*, released in 1923. Though similar in format to American writer Sherwood Anderson's *Winesburg, Ohio* (1919), *Cane* focused on the racial tensions and social structure of the segregated South and its transcendence into Northern society. Toomer's usage of natural imagery reflected the romanticized relationship between African Americans and primitivism in the South. "Blood-burning Moon," a short story about a lynching, used the figures of the moon and cane fields to demonstrate the invisible but understood boundaries between blacks and whites. The character Bob Stone, a white man, desired to see Louisa, a black woman who is the love interest of Tom Burwell, a feared black man. In order to avoid being seen, Tom and Louisa meet in cane fields, which though easy to navigate through, were sharp and painful. The moon was described as red and full, believed in Southern tradition to be the cause of hysteria and madness. The color red symbolized blood and death. It was during the blood red moon the main characters were both murdered—Bob Stone by Tom Burwell, and Tom by a white lynch mob.

The second half of *Cane* takes place in the urbanity of Washington, D.C., and Chicago. "Bona and Paul," a story about an unknowingly interracial couple's date in Chicago, ends with a dramatic explanation between a black doorman and Paul, a "passing" black man. After conversing with the doorman, Paul realizes Bona has disappeared. A reason behind Bona's disappearance was her realization of Paul's race because of his urgency to talk to the African American doorman. Bona's epiphany sheds light on the looming existence of racial separation, even in the urban North. Toomer's division of *Cane* invokes the reader to think about the role of race in society and identity, regardless of geographic location.

REGINA BARNETT

See also

American Literature and Racism

Further Reading:

O'Daniel, Therman B. *Jean Toomer: A Critical Evaluation*. Washington, DC: Howard University Press, 1988.

Toomer, Jean. *Cane*. New York: Boni and Liveright, 1923.

Trail of Broken Treaties (1972)

Conceived in South Dakota by members of the nascent American Indian Movement (AIM), the Trail of Broken Treaties strove to unite Indians from reservations all over the country in a protest "march" from the West Coast to Washington, D.C. Planned as a peaceful demonstration to confront the government with long-held Indian grievances stemming from broken treaty agreements, the protest is best remembered for its finale—the six-day occupation of the headquarters of the Bureau of Indian Affairs (BIA).

The idea of the march emerged following the annual Sun Dance on the Rosebud Reservation in August 1972 during discussions at the home of AIM's spiritual leader, Leonard Crow Dog, about the future of the movement. Robert Burnette, former two-time chairman of the Rosebud Sioux tribe, articulated the plan and suggested the demonstration be timed to coincide with the upcoming presidential election, thereby compelling presidential candidates to address issues of concern to Indian Country.

Those in attendance at Crow Dog's Paradise decided to hold a formal meeting in Denver the following month to craft a clear strategy and work out logistical details for the event. Accordingly, on September 30, AIM leaders met at the New Albany Hotel in the Colorado capital. In addition to Burnette, those in attendance included Russell Means, Dennis Banks, George Mitchell, Clyde and Vernon Bellecourt, and Reuben Snake.

Outside of AIM, representatives from National Indian Leadership Training, the National Indian Brotherhood from Canada, the National Indian Lutheran Board, the National Indian Youth Council, the Native American Rights Fund, and the National Indian Committee of Alcohol and Drug Abuse, many of whom were already in town for their annual conferences, also attended, along with members from various local activist groups. In three days, the gathering organized 11 committees and elected Burnette and Snake as cochairs of the event they chose to dub either the Trail of Broken Treaties Caravan or the less provocative Pan American Native Quest for Justice. Anita Collins and LaVonna Weller served respectively as secretary and treasurer of the group.

As envisaged in Denver, the plan called for three caravans to leave different points on the Pacific coast and travel through Indian communities in the West on their way to an October 23 rendezvous at the Twin Cities in Minnesota. Each caravan would be led by a spiritual leader carrying a sacred pipe. Drums were to be beaten day and night as a reminder to the American people of the broken treaties with Indian nations. Once in St. Paul, leaders of the march planned to craft a document outlining Indian demands of the federal government. The document would then be taken by a single caravan to Washington, D.C., and delivered to the White House. Burnette, emphasizing the need for order, self-discipline, and

sobriety on the march, stated, "The Caravan must be our finest hour."

In early October, the three caravans set out on the Trail of Broken Treaties. From Seattle, Washington, three cars and a van headed east under the direction of AIM leader Russell Means. Sid Mills, a decorated Vietnam veteran, and Hank Adams, founder and president of the Survival of American Indians Association, also provided leadership for this northernmost column. Both Mills and Adams were active in the struggle for Native American fishing rights in the Pacific Northwest. Traveling through Indian communities in Washington, Idaho, and Montana, the procession stopped often to raise money for gas and food and to attract more participants. On Columbus Day, Means and his compatriots stopped on the Crow Reservation in Montana at the site of the Battle of Little Bighorn, leaving behind a plaque honoring the warriors who fought there in 1876 against the U.S. Seventh Cavalry.

While Means, Mills, and Adams made their way across the Rockies and onto the northern Great Plains, a second caravan composed of five cars departed San Francisco, California, bound for Nevada and Utah. Led by AIM cofounder Dennis Banks, the cavalcade of vehicles slowly increased in size as it approached Salt Lake City, where Vernon Bellecourt unsuccessfully sought financial assistance from the Mormon Church. The Mormons did, however, provide aid in the form of food and gas. Then heading first toward Denver via the Ute Reservation in southern Utah, Banks ultimately led his group north through Wyoming toward the Pine Ridge Reservation in South Dakota, where he linked up with Russell Means at Wounded Knee.

The third, and last, caravan set forth from Los Angeles, California, under direction of Bill Sargent and Rod Skenandore. After a slow start, the procession traveled through the Southwest before turning north toward Minnesota. In Lawton, Oklahoma, Carter Camp, a member of AIM, made a vain attempt to take over the Fort Sill Indian School. A report of Camp's actions dismayed local and federal BIA officials and provided precisely the kind of publicity Burnette hoped to avoid. As with the other two caravans, this southernmost group depended on local support and hospitality for sustenance and shelter. On October 23, they rendezvoused with the already combined caravans under Means and Banks and merged into one procession as they entered Minneapolis.

All told, the three groups visited over 33 reservations and garnered nearly 600 participants on their way to Minnesota.

As designed, the caravan paused at the state fairgrounds in St. Paul for four days as the group's leadership, chaired by Reuben Snake, held workshops to develop position papers for collation into a final document outlining Indian demands of the federal government. Owing to his experience in treaty litigation in the Pacific Northwest, the responsibility for drafting the final manuscript fell to Hank Adams. Isolated in a motel room for almost two days, Adams created the Twenty Points—essentially a list of reforms calling for, among other things, the sovereignty of individual Indian nations, the restoration of the authority of existing treaties, the resubmission of unratified treaties to the U.S. Senate, mandatory federal injunctions against state agencies or non-Indians who contravene treaties, protection of Indian religious freedom and cultural integrity, and the abolishment of the BIA. With the Twenty Points in hand, the assembly prepared to depart for the nation's capital and dispatched Robert Burnette, George Mitchell, and Anita Collins in advance to secure accommodations for the members of the caravan and to make local arrangements for their week of planned events in the District.

With ever-increasing numbers, the Trail of Broken Treaties Caravan left St. Paul bound for Washington via Milwaukee and Indianapolis. Arriving at their destination in the late evening of November 2, five days before the presidential election, the nearly 1,000 participants in the four-mile-long procession soon sought shelter for their stay. Burnette's professed arrangements for food and housing with local churches and civil rights supporters all over the city failed to materialize (there even had been some talk of using RFK Stadium), and the tired travelers wound up in the rat-infested basement of St. Stephen and the Incarnation Church. The following morning, vowing to improve accommodations, AIM leaders took their demand for better housing to what proved to be the final stop on the Trail of Broken Treaties—the BIA.

On November 3, 1972, the caravan of cars, pickup trucks, vans, and buses that had set forth on the West Coast more than four weeks earlier pulled into parking lots and side streets around the intersection of Constitution Avenue and 19th Street in Washington, D.C. Ushered into the BIA building's auditorium to await discussion of their grievances with

officials, Indian activists found themselves growing steadily frustrated at the lack of a satisfactory resolution to their demands. As the day wore on, AIM leaders sensed duplicity in the government's intentions, and, when U.S. General Services Administration police tried to force their eviction at 5 P.M., the activists chose to take control of the building and proclaim it the Native American Embassy. The BIA occupation lasted until November 8, after White House officials agreed to create a task force within 60 days to consider the Twenty Points, to guarantee no prosecution of individuals for the seizure of a federal building, and to provide $66,650 in travel funds to help the participants return home. Before leaving, many of the occupiers (much to the chagrin of some of their leaders) expressed their personal frustration and overall dissatisfaction with the government's handling of their grievances by vandalizing the building's interior and confiscating BIA documents and files.

While at its outset a remarkable demonstration of Indian unity, the Trail of Broken Treaties failed to accomplish its goals and broke down in the end. By the beginning of November, the outcome of the presidential election was never in doubt and the caravan's presence in Washington provided no incentive for the incumbent Nixon administration to direct additional attention toward Indian concerns. The administration did, however, respond to the Twenty Points in January 1973, but only in very general terms and by highlighting the president's successful endeavors for Indian peoples during his first term. The petition for treaty reform was denied. Without a doubt, however, the Trail of Broken Treaties helped set the stage for AIM's next major confrontation with the federal government—the occupation and subsequent siege of Wounded Knee in February 1973.

BARRY M. PRITZKER

See also

American Indian Movement (AIM); Bellecourt, Clyde; Bureau of Indian Affairs; Means, Russell

Further Reading:

Banks, Dennis, and Richard Erdoes. *Ojibwa Warrior: Dennis Banks and the Rise of the American Indian Movement.* Norman: University of Oklahoma Press, 2004.

Deloria, Vine, Jr. *Behind the Trail of Broken Treaties: An Indian Declaration of Independence.* Austin: University of Texas Press, 1985.

Means, Russell, and Marvin J. Wolf. *Where White Men Fear to Tread: The Autobiography of Russell Means.* New York: St. Martin's Griffin, 1995.

Pritzker, Barry M. *Native Americans: An Encyclopedia of History, Culture and Peoples,* 2 vols. Santa Barbara, CA: ABC-CLIO, 1998.

Smith, Paul Chaat, and Robert Allen Warrior. *Like a Hurricane: The Indian Movement from Alcatraz to Wounded Knee.* New York: New Press, 1996.

Trayvon Martin Case

Trayvon Martin was 17 years old when he was shot and killed on February 26, 2012, while walking from a convenience store to a family member's home in Sanford, Florida. Martin, an African American male, was shot by George Zimmerman, a white Hispanic neighborhood watch leader of the gated community where Martin was staying. Zimmerman noticed Martin walking around the community and called the police to report Martin's activity as suspicious. At the end of the call, Martin apparently began to run and the police specifically told Zimmerman not to follow him. Although he verbally agreed to remain in his car, Zimmerman chased after Martin on foot and a violent encounter took place resulting in Zimmerman fatally shooting Martin at close range. Zimmerman alleged that Martin attacked him and that he killed him in self-defense, though Martin's girlfriend who was on the phone with Martin at the time of the attack alleges that Martin was attempting to get away from Zimmerman and never assaulted Zimmerman before he was shot. After questioning Zimmerman, police determined that there was no evidence to contradict Zimmerman's story, and he originally was not charged with any crime.

The fact that Zimmerman was released created public outrage over how an unarmed teenager could be shot and killed at close range without holding anyone responsible, especially when the assailant was known. Almost two months after the shooting, perhaps because of public pressure for his prosecution, Zimmerman was charged with second-degree murder on April 11, 2012. Under Florida law, his conviction could result in 25 years to life in prison. Zimmerman's legal team has since announced that they will rely on a self-defense explanation for his actions at trial, currently

scheduled for June 2013. This defense will be based on Florida's "Stand Your Ground" law, which gives individuals the right to use deadly force without first attempting to retreat in public places if they fear severe bodily harm.

Zimmerman and his family contend that the shooting was not racially motivated and point to the fact that Zimmerman is himself a multiracial minority who has supported the black community in the past in order to support this claim. However, race scholars explain that this general confusion about what constitutes racism is testament to the current time period and system that treats multiculturalism and multiracism as markers of equality where, in reality, someone identifying as Latino or another race is certainly not excluded from bigotry simply because they themselves are not white or have previously supported racial minorities in a different context.

Chris Serino, the Sanford Police Department's lead investigator, told the FBI that he believed that Zimmerman's actions were not race based, but rather were inspired by Martin's clothing. Martin was wearing a hoodie at the time of his death, and hoodies have since become a sign of protest against Martin's murder as well as discrimination against young black males. It is difficult to say whether Serino's comments were also subconsciously race based, as hoodies are linked with the image of the hoodlum and the gang member, and these images are still associated with young men of color. That is to say that Zimmerman would not have

---

Stand Your Ground Legislation

The murders of Trayvon Martin and Jordan Davis in Florida have created controversy surrounding the state's "Stand Your Ground" legislation. Not only have the laws been utilized to invoke self-defense strategies by Zimmerman and Dunn, which diminish these racially charged events, the laws have been criticized as applying unequally to defendants of color. For instance, Marissa Alexander, an African American woman, was sentenced to 20 years in prison after being denied the right to claim self-defense and "stand your ground" when she fired a warning shot into the celling of her garage when her abusive ex-husband threatened her and refused to leave her home.

Supporters of Trayvon Martin attend a rally in Miami, Florida, on April 1, 2012. Martin was killed on February 26, 2012, by a neighborhood watch captain, George Zimmerman, who claimed he shot the 17-year-old in self-defense. The incident has sparked controversy across the country, raising debates about racial profiling, self-defense laws, and the relationship between police and minorities. (AP/Wide World Photos)

deemed a white person, elderly person, or a woman wearing a hoodie to be suspicious and Serino would not have attributed Zimmerman's suspicions of any of these people to their attire. This argument can be located within the context of intersectionality where Martin's race, class, gender, and age all worked together simultaneously as did Zimmerman's to influence both the situation and outcome. In addition, it was raining on the night Martin was killed, thus making it logical he would be covering his head with a hoodie.

The Martin killing can be rooted within a societal context in which young black males are killed without repercussions for those responsible. Because of the implications of Florida's "Stand Your Ground Law" in the case, the death of Trayvon Martin can be explained within state sanctions that authorize and rationalize the murder of blacks by private citizens through a racial hierarchy that supports the protections of the privileged when they kill the disadvantaged. The Treyvon Martin murder can also be viewed as a restriction of blacks' basic freedoms associated with American democracy, and in this particular case, the restriction of freedom of movement where Martin was unable to move through a space, even one in which he belonged, without being labeled as suspicious and subsequently killed because of it.

The murder of Trayvon Martin has already garnered national and international attention because of the events surrounding his killing: the manner in which an unarmed black teenager was targeted as suspicious in a housing complex in which he was staying and subsequently murdered because of it, the initial failure of the police to charge Zimmerman with a crime, and Zimmerman's claim of self-defense under Florida's "Stand Your Ground" law. On July 13, 2013, Zimmerman was found not guilty on all counts by a six-person jury. The verdict continues to further incite controversy surrounding race-based violence and the American criminal justice system.

ADRIENNE N. MILNER

See also

Bernhard Goetz Case; Furtive Movement; Intersectionality

Further Reading:

Democracy Now. "'I Know He was Scared': Trayvon Martin's Girlfriend Recounts Phone Call Right Before Fatal Shooting." http://www.democracynow.org/2012/5/18/i_know_he_was _scared_trayvon.

Hanchard, Michael. "You Shall Have the Body: On Trayvon Martin's Slaughter." *Theory and Event* 15 (2012). doi: 10.1353/tae.2012.0057.

Handcock, Angie-Marie. "Trayvon Martin, Intersectionality, and the Politics of Disgust." *Theory and Event* 15 (2012). doi: 10.1353/tae.2012.0057.

Huffington Post. "Marissa Alexander Gets 20 Years for Firing Warning Shot." http://www.huffingtonpost.com/2012/05/19/ marissa-alexander-gets-20_n_1530035.html.

NBC News. "Zimmerman Investigator Blamed Black Officers for Leaks, 'Pressure' to File Charges." http://thegrio.com/2012/ 07/15/zimmerman-investigator-blamed-black-officers-for -leaks-pressure-to-file-charges/2/.

Yancy, George, and Janice Jones (eds.). *Pursuing Trayvon Martin: Historical Contexts and Contemporary Manifestations.* Lanham, MD: Lexington Books, 2012.

Tribal Sovereignty

Sovereignty is the ability of a nation to have autonomy and self-determination. Native tribes, at least those recognized by the federal government, are sovereign nations according to the United States Constitution. Native understandings of tribal sovereignty include the authority to determine membership, establish and enforce laws, provide for the welfare of members, protect traditions and culture, and interact with federal and state governments. This sovereignty is based in tribes' status as self-governing nations with legal, political, cultural, and spiritual authority. However, Light and Rand (2005) argue that tribal governments and members hold deep convictions about the meaning and immutability of tribal sovereignty that are at odds with the federal legal doctrine.

Historically, the relationship between the U.S. government and Native tribes has been one marked by the constant undermining of the tribes' sovereignty. After the

Corbell vs. Salazar (2009)

In 2009, an important court case dealing with the management of Indian trust lands reached a settlement. *Cobell vs. Salazar* is a class-action lawsuit in which Elouise Cobell and others sued the U.S. government for mismanagement of the accounts and lands. After 13 years in the courts, the parties agreed on a settlement since so many of the people being represented were in such desperate need of the money, especially those who were elderly and could not afford to wait several more years to receive compensation. The first disbursements were wired in December 2012. The settlement benefits are a distribution of $1.412 billion, plus $100 million Trust Administration. This settlement is an important step forward in holding government agencies accountable for the mismanagement of Native American interests, and will hopefully continue to pave the way toward self-determination of Native lands and assets.

majority of Native Americans had been killed or subjugated through colonial expansion, tribes were not considered to be a military threat. At that point prevailing ideology in the United States in the early centuries was that Native Americans did not possess the intelligence to successfully enact self-governance and needed the federal government as a protector. This paternalistic relationship also ensured power over tribal land, its allotment, and other tribal resources. General Allotment Act of 1887, also known as the Dawes Act, divided tribal lands among individual Indians into parcels ranging between 40 and 320 acres, breaking up ancestral lands and separating people. Some of those parcels were sold to white settlers, while others were held in trust by the United States with the promise of managing the resources and providing landholders with proceeds from the lands' production.

Light and Rand (2005) contend that in the absence of a focus on internal values, sovereignty lacks a Native perspective, and thus is only what dominant society allows. There are a variety of alternative takes on the legal concept of tribal sovereignty. For example, legal scholars Coffey and Tsosie take issue with the extent federal power Cultural sovereignty is suggested as an alternative to the legal concept of tribal sovereignty, as it is based in tribal conceptions as inherent self-determination, and not so grounded in self-governance. The purpose of the concept is to give tribes the power to use their respective values and norms to define who they are, regardless of federal policies and case law. Porter argues that the perspectives of a Native people, dominant society, and the international community must all be taken into consideration when defining tribal sovereignty.

Native American–owned and -operated casinos are a contemporary feature of Indian reservations and present an ongoing challenge to the status quo of tribal sovereignty. As a result, casinos represent the larger struggle for the economic independence and self-determination. After *Bryan vs. Itasca County*, the 1976 Supreme Court decision that held that states could not regulate the activities that occur on Indian reservations, and *California v. Cabazon Band* in 1980, in which the Supreme Court ruled that Indian gaming was to be regulated by the federal government and Congress, not state governments, Native American tribes began taking advantage of these affirmations of tribal sovereignty by establishing gaming operations. However, shortly after, the Indian Gaming Regulatory Act of 1988 (IGRA) came about as a result of the increased gaming activity on Native lands.

Some interpreted this act as a direct challenge to sovereignty, as it subjected gaming activities to regulation by a federal agency, but also mandated agreements with states for gaming in large casinos and with large jackpots.

Light and Rand (2005) refer to the relationship between tribal sovereignty and gaming as "the casino compromise" because tribes inevitably compromise sovereignty in order to generate much-needed income from gaming activities, since gaming must then be regulated by federal, and increasingly state, agencies. Referred to by pro-gaming proponents as the "New Buffalo," casinos and other gaming is a vital frontier in the economic development of Native American communities. Perhaps more importantly, it is the avenue by which many Native Americans hope to finally attain economic security, and independence from the government agencies that have controlled, contained, and in many ways suppressed, the Native American population for hundreds of years. While there are other frontiers in the struggle for sovereignty, for many, gaming remains the most promising, especially as more tribes seek to expand their operations off reservation land, thereby creating the opportunity to have both economic growth and influence outside of the confines of reservations.

RENEE S. ALSTON

National Congress of American Indians (NCAI)

The National Congress of American Indians (NCAI) was founded in 1944 as a result of the Indian New Deal, more formally known as the 1934 Indian Reorganization Act or the Wheeler-Howard Act. Most of the founders were Indians who had worked for the Bureau of Indian Affairs. With the formation of the NCAI, American Indian politics entered a new phase as leaders in the NCAI became skilled lobbyists and political advocates for Indian policies and issues at the national level.

The NCAI emphasized the need for unity and cooperation among tribal governments for the protection of their treaty and sovereign rights in response to assimilation policies that the United States forced on the tribal governments, often in contradiction of their treaty rights and status. Since 1944, the NCAI has worked to inform the public and Congress of the sovereign rights of American Indians and to serve as a forum for consensus-based policy development among its membership of more than 250 tribal governments. The NCAI has also monitored federal policies that affect tribal-government interests.

The NCAI, however, did not gain widespread support within the Native American community until the early 1950s, when it became the center of organized opposition to the termination of American Indian treaty rights. The NCAI was different from earlier Native American groups, such as the Society of American Indians, in that it maintained its focus as a national lobby and advocated for Indian issues in Washington, D.C. In the 1960s, the NCAI was often criticized by younger activists groups, such as the National Indian Youth Council and the American Indian Movement, because the NCAI's activities are limited to lobbying and advocating.

SOOKHEE OH

See also

American Indian Movement; American Indian Religious Freedom Act (1978); Native Americans, Conquest of; Native Americans, Forced Relocation of; Reservations and Casinos

Further Reading:

Darian-Smith, Eve. *New Capitalists: Law, Politics, and Identity Surrounding Casino Gaming on Native American Land.* Belmont, CA: Wadsworth, 2004.

Institute for the Study of Tribal Gaming Law and Policy. http://web.law.und.edu/npilc/gaming/

Light, Stephen A., and Kathryn R. L. Rand. *Indian Gaming and Tribal Sovereignty: The Casino Compromise.* Lawrence, Kansas: University Press of Kansas, 2005.

"Tribal and Indian Land" Office of Indian Energy and Economic Development. http://teeic.anl.gov/triballand/index.cfm

Wallace, Coffey, and Rebecca Tsosie. "Rethinking the Tribal Sovereignty Doctrine: Cultural Sovereignty and the Collective Future of Indian Nations." 12 Stanford Law & Policy Review 191 (2001):196.

Wilkinson, Charles F. *Indian tribes as sovereign governments: a sourcebook on federal-tribal history, law, and policy.* AIRI Press, 1988.

Tripping over the Color Line

In 1951 *Harper's Magazine* featured an article: "My Daughter Married a Negro." Families attempted to make arguments against intermarriage by turning to experts. Arguments were made that mixed marriages would fail. Some families made the argument that interracial marriage was a "sociological suicide." Rather than criticizing racism, families accepted that interracial couples would be stigmatized and marginalized, and few challenged the status quo. As seen in the U.S. census trends of interracial marriage, drastic changes of practices with marrying across racial lines have not dramatically changed since the 1960s. This is also reflected in popular culture representations in television. In the 1950s there were no representations of mixed race families. By 1995 5.3 percent of television shows showed mixed race families, a nominal increase over 45 years.

Sociologist Heather M. Dalmage's concept of "tripping over the color line" is useful for describing the dynamics of mixed race families. Dalmage argues how multiracial family members live so close to the color line that they are forced to contend with the changing dynamics, ambiguities, and contradictions of race. Dalmage uses the image and concept of tripping to describe the experience of race for multiracial families—to trip is a physical and emotional relationship to words and experiences about race. Multiracial families are created through interracial/interethnic marriages, but also through families who adopt children of different races.

The identity of mixed-race is visible due to policy and census data collection that began in the 1960s. Biracial babies boomed in the 1960s, reflecting the shifts in U.S. attitudes towards racial segregation. By 2000, the U.S. census released race data that referred to multiracial communities, illustrating how not only the shifts in racial composition of families, but also the language to describe such communities. "Multiracial" encompasses people who have diverse racial and ethnic ancestral origins. Some scholars argue that multiracial, mixed, and persons of mixed descent reaffirm racial distinctions. Families whose experience of race and racial difference is the norm and constantly renegotiated as family members and individuals constantly trip over racial lines confronting societal perceptions of mixed-race identities and multiracial families.

For multiracial families, the color line is experienced through border patrolling, discrimination, rebound racism, and intensified racism. The policing of borders occurs through families who disown members who marry a person of color. The racist perception of men of color as sexual predators persevered even after the end of antimiscegenation laws in the United States. The policing of such borders were witnessed in the Watsonville riots. In the film *Dollar a Day Ten Cents a Dance* (1984), the overt racist responses to Filipino men were visible in the early 1900s. Filipino male migrants worked laboriously during the day in California agricultural fields. And at night, 40,000 Filipino men dressed up and went dancing in taxi dance halls. A majority of the women that worked in the dance halls were working-class white women. And in some cases the dances led to romances between the Filipino men and white women. The men were vulnerable to violence by whites, and in January 1930 hundreds of white men roamed the streets of Watsonville armed with pistols and clubs beating Filipinos. This led to the death of Fermin Tobera, a 22-year-old Filipino. "Rebound racism" is described by Ruth Frankenberg as the growing awareness in white parents of the way their whiteness shapes their experiences and is due to larger structures of racism. Their shifting awareness enables them to become aware of the everyday racism directed at their nonwhite partners and children.

For multiracial families, tripping over the color line occurs in schools, in public spaces, and even within families. Stereotypes of multiracial individuals in the 1970s were individuals who lack culture and are destined to have social and psychological problems associated with racial identity. It is assumed, but not always the reality, that children with a white parent will identify with the parent of color. Reports of multiracial individuals show that they have similar self-esteem compared to other children, vary in racial identity, may develop a public identity that differs from their private multiracial identity, may encounter difficulties with culture should parents divorce, and are more likely to be happier when their multiple identities are embraced in the home versus those that emphasis one part of their racial identity. Mixed-race children experience overt racism from name calling to bullying, and also have varied perceptions of how they understand race.

To challenge stereotypes of multiracial people, multiracial families have developed informal communities and formal organizations and formed academic spaces to think through mixed-race experiences.

Annie Isabel Fukushima

See also

Anti-Miscegenation Laws; Domestic Violence; Down Low; Illegitimacy Rates; Lesbian, Gay, Bisexual, Transgender, Intersex, Queer, and Queer Questioning Community (LGBTQ); Miscegenation; Mixed Race Relationships and the Media

Further Reading:

Ali, Suki. *Mixed-Race, Post-Race: Gender, New Ethnicities, and Cultural Practices*. New York: Berg, 2003.

Bryant, Jennings, and J. Alison Bryant. *Television and the American Family*, 2nd ed. New Jersey: Lawrence Erlbaum Associates, 2001.

DaCosta, Kimberly McClain. *Making Multiracials: State, Family, and Market in the Redrawing of the Color Line*. Stanford, CA: Stanford University Press, 2007.

Dalmage, Heather M. *Tripping on the Color Line: Black-White Multiracial Families in a Racially Divided World*. New Brunswick, NJ: Rutgers University Press, 2000.

Harris, Henry L. "Multiracial Students: What School Counselors Need to Know." *ERIC Digest*, 2003.

Parrenas, Rhacel Salazar. "'White Trash' Meets the 'Little Brown Monkeys': Taxi Dance Hall as a Site of Interracial and Gender Alliances Between White Working Class Women and Filipino Immigrant Men in the 1920s and 30s." *Amerasia Journal* 24, no. 2 (1998): 115–34.

Romano, Renee C. *Race Mixing: Black-White Marriage in Postwar America*. Cambridge, MA: Harvard University Press, 2003.

Tri-racialization

Tri-racialization, also known as the Latin Americanization Thesis (LAT), is a theory developed primarily by sociologist Eduardo Bonilla-Silva. Bonilla-Silva proposes that the historically biracial social order (white versus black) of the United States is undergoing a profound transformation. According to LAT, the new racial order in the United States is made up of white, black, and a third category, honorary white. This third category of honorary white is made up primarily of Latin Americans and Asian Americans. Noting that increasing international migration since 1965 has dramatically changed the demography of the nation, as well as the racial structure of the global economy, Bonilla-Silva suggests that ongoing immigration from Latin America is driving the development of a complex Latin America–like racial order in the United States. According to the theory of tri-racialization, in the near future, the United States can expect to experience the social reorganization accompanying the development of another major racial category beyond just black and white.

There are two major features of the tri-racialization theory. First, the theory holds that the post-1965 U.S. social system is no longer a binary racial system of white and black social relations. Secondly, the theory contends that post-1965 U.S. social patterns are moving towards a Latin American trinary or "triracial" model of social relations. Specifically, Bonilla-Silva theorizes that the evolving U.S. racial order will have as a central feature three new racial categories: whites, honorary whites, and a category of collective black.

Bonilla-Silva's innovative but controversial theory recognizes that the racial composition of the United States since 1965 has become far more ethnically and racially diverse than the black-white biracial pattern prevalent before 1965. Just consider that between 1900 and 1960, U.S. censuses reveal that the U.S. population was primarily composed of whites

(85–89 percent) and blacks (9–12 percent) while other racial ethnic categories combined (Asian, Hispanic, and Amerindian) made up less than 2 percent of the total population. However, after increased immigration since 1965, the 2010 U.S. Census revealed a far different social make-up, with whites composing 63.7 percent of the U.S. population, blacks 12.6 percent, Hispanic multiracials 16.3 percent, and Asians around 5 percent and growing, with other groups comprising the rest.

U.S. racial and ethnic population patterns have dramatically changed under the strain of arriving Asian and Latin American immigrant generations over the past 50 years. U.S. censuses show that international, and especially Latin American, immigration has rapidly changed the racial-ethnic composition of the U.S. population over the last three decades in particular. Drawing on data from censuses and ethnographic studies of Latin American social life and racial inequality, tri-racialization theory looks specifically at Caribbean Spanish-speaking and Latin American countries in developing the triracial model. In Puerto Rico and Brazil particularly, notes Bonilla-Silva, whites stand atop the social, political, and educational hierarchy, while mixed-race people fall below them, with blacks falling at the bottom of such hierarchies. In their analysis of the developing racial hierarchy in the United States, Bonilla-Silva and other sociologists such as George Yancey see arriving Hispanic and Asian immigrants as "honorary whites," a category occupying the intermediary level between whites and blacks. According to tri-racialization theory, a third U.S. racial category is clearly emerging in a pattern similar to the racial stratification Bonilla-Silva has identified in Latin America.

However, some analysts are skeptical of LAT and have questioned whether Latin America is as racially stratified as Bonilla-Silva claims. Specifically, skeptics have wondered if there are really only three races in Latin America. Sociologist Christina Sue notes that there are many studies confirming that Brazilians and Puerto Ricans recognize, use, measure, and understand many more than just three racial categories. In addition, Sue notes there are many Latin American countries that do not share triracial patterns. For example, she points out that Mexico and Argentina barely have black populations and, therefore, do not have the black category necessary for triracial hierarchies. What is certain is that the U.S. population is increasing in complexity, in category, and in color and ethnicity, and that these increases can be understood with the triracial system proposed in Bonilla-Silva's Latin Americanization Thesis.

To strengthen the validity of Bonilla-Silva's Latin Americanization Thesis, Christina Sue suggests renaming the theory after the individual Latin American nations that most closely resemble the United States' evolving racial system. Sue suggests that Bonilla-Silva's theory would face less resistance were it renamed after the main countries (Brazil, Puerto Rico, and the Spanish-speaking Caribbean) from which he draws the empirical evidence supporting his theory. She suggests that tri-racialization or Latin Americanization be called something more akin to "Brasilianization" or "Puerto Ricanization." In any case, Bonilla-Silva brings well needed attention to the future of race-relating social theory in an era of rapid American demographic change.

SALVATORE LABARO

See also
Black and Non-Black Hierarchy; Racism; Social Construction of Race

Further Reading:
Bonilla-Silva, Eduardo. "From Bi-racial to Tri-racial: Towards a New System of Racial Stratification in the USA." *Ethnic and Racial Studies* 27, no. 6 (2004): 931–50.
Sue, Christina A. "An Assessment of the Latin Americanization Thesis." *Ethnic and Racial Studies* 32, no. 6 (2009): 1058–70.
Tienda, Marta. "Hispanicity and Educational Inequality: Risks, Opportunities and the Nation's Future," presented first at the 25th Tomás Rivera Lecture at the annual conference of the American Association of Hispanics in Higher Education (AAHHE), San Antonio, TX. (Educational Testing Service Policy Evaluation and Research Center Policy Information Center Princeton, NJ: 2009).

Trotter, William Monroe (1872–1934)

A newspaper publisher and militant civil rights activist, as well as a founder of the Niagara Movement and the National Association for the Advancement of Colored People (NAACP), William Monroe Trotter revived the black press and the tradition of organized protest as important components of the struggle for African American civil rights.

Born in Chillicothe, Ohio, on April 7, 1872, the son of a local politician and a former slave, Trotter was raised in Boston, where he graduated from Harvard University in 1895. The first African American to be elected to Phi Beta Kappa at Harvard, Trotter earned his master's degree before returning to Boston to enter the real estate field. Opening his own firm in 1899, Trotter was soon frustrated by the growing racial discrimination that he experienced in his own business and observed throughout the country, particularly the segregation, disenfranchisement, and violence that characterized race relations in the South. In 1901, Trotter and George Forbes founded the *Boston Guardian*, a crusading weekly that, under Trotter's direction, began to fearlessly and articulately demand full and immediate civil rights for African Americans.

Trotter made particular use of his newspaper to vehemently oppose the accommodationist policies of Booker T. Washington, whom Trotter believed was naively ignoring the country's worsening racial state. Through his frequent and eloquent editorials, Trotter made white Americans understand that not all black Americans adhered to Washington's conciliatory views. In July 1903, Trotter and a group of friends disrupted a speech that Washington delivered in Boston. By constantly heckling the speaker and shouting embarrassing questions, Trotter and his associates caused an uproar that came to be known as the Boston Riot. As a result of his actions, and at the insistence of Washington's supporters, Trotter was fined $50 and spent a month in jail, a punishment that Trotter later portrayed as the suffering of a martyr for the cause of civil rights.

In 1905, Trotter, W.E.B. Du Bois, and other prominent African Americans concerned with the increasing occurrence of lynching and other violence against blacks founded the Niagara movement. Although Trotter helped push Du Bois toward a greater militancy in his approach to civil rights, the two quarreled over tactics, with Trotter insisting that any national civil rights organization be led and financed entirely by African Americans. To this end, Trotter founded the all-black National Equal Rights League in 1908. In 1909, despite his disagreements with Du Bois, Trotter participated in the founding of the NAACP, although he continued to vehemently oppose white involvement in the organization.

A political independent, Trotter supported Democrat Woodrow Wilson for president in 1912. However, when Wilson supported increased segregation in federal offices, Trotter turned against the president, whom he confronted personally on the issue in the White House in November 1914. After 45 minutes of argument, Wilson declared, "Your manner offends me" (Jackson n.d.) and promptly ordered Trotter from his office.

In 1915, Trotter organized picket lines and demonstrations in an attempt to mobilize African Americans against D. W. Griffith's racist film, *The Birth of a Nation*. In one of the earliest African American protest marches in U.S. history, Trotter, who had been released from jail only two days before, led over 1,000 people in a march on the Massachusetts State House. In 1919, to Wilson's great annoyance, Trotter announced his intention to attend the Versailles Peace Conference to push for inclusion of a racial equality clause in the peace treaty ending World War I. When the U.S. government denied him a visa, Trotter took a job as ship's cook and so secured passage to France. Although he failed to obtain a hearing at Versailles, his trip and his militant editorials in the *Guardian* won worldwide publicity for his cause.

By the 1920s, Trotter was an increasingly isolated voice on the radical edge of the struggle for African American civil rights. Hit hard by the Great Depression, Trotter lost control of the *Guardian* in 1934. He died, an apparent suicide, on his 62nd birthday, April 7, 1934, when he fell from the roof of a three-story Boston building.

JOHN A. WAGNER

See also

National Association for the Advancement of Colored People (NAACP); Niagara Movement

Further Reading:

Fox, Stephen R. *The Guardian of Boston: William Monroe Trotter.* New York: Atheneum, 1970.
Jackson, Derrick Z. "About William Monroe Trotter." http://www.trottergroup.com. n.d.

Troy Davis Case (2011)

Troy Anthony Davis, 43, was executed September 2011 in Jackson, by lethal injection. The execution occurred despite widespread appeals for clemency based on serious doubts about his guilt. More than 630,000 people signed

Protesters gather outside the building where Georgia Board of Pardons and Paroles members were holding a hearing for death row inmate Troy Davis, in Atlanta, Georgia, September 19, 2011. Davis was executed for the 1989 slaying of off-duty Savannah, Georgia, police officer Mark MacPhail. (AP Photo/ David Tulis)

petitions and/or wrote personal letters to Georgia's Board of Pardons and Paroles, the body with the power to decide Troy's fate. Among Troy's supporters were Archbishop Desmond Tutu, ex-president Jimmy Carter, the Pope, 51 Congress members, and former FBI director William Sessions, usually a death penalty supporter. Troy's case was taken up by Amnesty International and the NAACP. His sister, Martina Davis-Correia, worked tirelessly on his behalf despite suffering from the breast cancer that led to her death in 2011, at age 44. At rallies around the country people wore T-shirts and carried banners proclaiming "I am Troy Davis." Such vigorous and widespread campaigns against the execution of a particular person are rare and usually occur because there is uncertainty about the condemned person's guilt and doubts over the fairness of the judicial process.

Troy Davis's life intersected with that of 27-year-old police officer Mark Allen MacPhail in the early hours of August 19, 1989. While working at his second job as a security guard, MacPhail heard a homeless man, Larry Young, screaming as he was being pistol whipped in a downtown parking lot. When the officer went to the victim's assistance he was killed with a .38 caliber pistol. His wife, Joan, became a widow and his two young children lost their father. Troy Davis, who was in the vicinity, before the killing occurred, denied shooting anyone, claiming he also was going to the victim's aid. Another man, Sylvester Coles, admitted to having the weapon shortly before the gun was fired. Coles told the police that he had seen Davis kill MacPhail. Davis, knowing he was wanted, turned himself in to the police. A week later a jury found him guilty of murder. In 1991, Savannah's district attorney Spencer Lawton Jr. asked for the death penalty, telling jurors, "Davis stopped, he turned and he shot Officer McPhail [sic]."

The pistol was never found, nor was there any other physical evidence tying Davis to the crime. However, nine alleged eyewitnesses, including Sylvester Coles, swore that Davis was the killer. After deliberating for about two hours, the jury, composed of seven African Americans and five whites, delivered a guilty verdict. Davis was imprisoned for the next 22 years. Of the nine witnesses, seven later came forward saying they had lied on the witness stand. Some met with the parole board to ask for clemency. Two claimed they had been coerced by the police. One, 16 years old at the time of the shooting, said police threatened him with prison. The other was on parole and feared a return to incarceration. Some witnesses claimed Coles, a nonrecanting prosecution witness, was the actual killer. Davis's appeals wound their way through the judicial system, with stays of execution being granted three times. Because of a U.S. Supreme Court ruling in August 2010, U.S. District Judge William Moore held hearings. Moore stated that Davis needed to have "clear and convincing evidence" that he would not have been convicted had jurors known of the recantations, which he belittled as "smoke and mirrors" (Cohen 2011; Defeo 2010). Later that year, two hours before his scheduled execution, the U.S. Supreme Court did grant a stay. In September 2011, however, Troy's lawyers made a final but unsuccessful appeal to the U.S. Supreme Court. Davis's request to the Georgia authorities, made on the day of his execution, to take a polygraph test was refused.

It is likely that race played a role in Davis's execution. Writing of the judicial system's refusal to grant clemency, the editors of *The Nation* noted, "Davis is a black man convicted of killing a white police officer—and in Southern and Northern states alike this fact alone will trump others." John Lewis, a well-known civil rights activist and a Georgia congressman since 1987, was quoted in the same editorial: "Race is everything in this case" (*The Nation* 2011). The headline on the September 24, 2011, edition of the *International Herald Tribune* read, "Racially Tinged U.S. Execution Outrages Europe."

Davis persisted in his claim of innocence. MacPhail's family came to see Troy executed. He addressed them before receiving the lethal injection: "I did not personally kill your son, father, brother. All I can ask is that you look deep into this case so you really can finally see the truth" (Severson 2011).

Summing up the feeling of death penalty opponents, a *New York Times* editorial on the day of the execution proclaimed, "A Grievous Wrong: The Davis Case in Georgia Is Further Proof of the Barbarity of the Death Penalty" (2011). Activists and organizations have renewed their efforts on this issue. On the first anniversary of Troy's death, NAACP CEO Ben Jealous joined with Amnesty International to urge a federal investigation into the justice system's misconduct during capital cases. In the aftermath of Troy Davis's death, opponents of capital punishment hope that this case will make it more likely the United States emulates other Western democracies and ends executions.

BARBARA CHASIN

Further Reading:

Cohen, Andrew. "The Death of Troy Davis." *Atlantic Monthly*. September 2011. http://www.theatlantic.com/national/archive/2011/09/the-death-oftroy-davis/245446 (accessed October 7, 2012).

Defeo, Todd. "Judge: Troy Davis 'Is Not Innocent.'" *Atlanta Examiner*. 2010. http://www.examiner.com/article/judge-troy-davis-is-not innocent (accessed Oct. 7, 2012).

Herbert, Bob. "What's the Rush?" *New York Times*. September 20, 2008, 19.

The Nation. "The Killing of Troy Davis." 2011. http://www.the nation.com/article/163522/killing-troy-davis#.

New York Times. "A Grievous Wrong: The Davis Case in Georgia Is Further Proof of the Barbarity of the Death Penalty." September 21, 2011. http://www.nytimes.com/2011/09/21/opinion/a-grievous-wrong-on-georgias-death-row.html?_r=0.

Severson, Kim. "Georgia Inmate Executed; Raised Racial issues in Death Penalty." *New York Times*, September 21, 2011, A1.

Truman, Harry S. (1884–1972)

Harry S. Truman, 33rd president of the United States, was the first chief executive in the 20th century to take substantive action in support of political and social equality for African Americans. In September 1946, a delegation of African American leaders, including National Association for the Advancement of Colored People (NAACP) executive director Walter White, met with Truman in the White House to discuss the rise of racial violence then occurring across the American South. The president was particularly shocked by the brutal attack upon an African American soldier in South Carolina.

Honorably discharged from the army in February 1946, Sergeant Isaac Woodard was traveling by bus through South Carolina when, during an unscheduled stop, he asked the white driver if he could use the restroom. The driver refused permission and cursed Woodard, who responded in kind. When the bus arrived in Batesburg, the driver informed police chief Lynwood Lanier Shull that Woodard had been unruly during the trip. Boarding the bus, the police chief arrested Woodard for disturbing the peace. When he protested that he had done nothing wrong, Shull savagely beat the discharged sergeant, blinding him in both eyes. The president, deeply troubled by this brutal act, vowed to take action. Under Truman's direction, the Justice Department prosecuted Schull for violating Woodard's civil rights, but an all-white jury found him not guilty. The beating of Sergeant Woodard and the acquittal of his assailant had a profound effect on President Truman. From that point on, he was determined to end legalized discrimination and racial violence from American life.

In December 1946, one month after Schull's acquittal, Truman issued an executive order creating the President's Committee on Civil Rights to investigate civil rights abuses and propose federal statutes that would prevent them in the future. As the committee began its work, Truman continued to call for an end to racial discrimination. On June 29, 1947, the president spoke at the annual meeting of the NAACP, the first chief executive to ever do so. Standing on the steps of the Lincoln Memorial, Truman committed the federal government to ensuring equal rights for African Americans. Four months later, the president was given the tools to make his commitment real when his civil rights committee presented him with its 178-page report on October 29, 1947. Entitled *To Secure These Rights*, the report not only catalogued egregious abuses of civil rights, but also recommended federal action to protect the constitutional liberties of all Americans.

Despite the considerable political risks, Truman sent a special message to Congress on February 2, 1948, proposing a set of laws designed to secure full equality for African Americans. The president's ambitious program included the creation of a civil rights commission and a Justice Department civil rights division to investigate and prosecute violations of civil liberties, establishment of a federal commission to prevent discrimination in the workplace and ensure fair employment practices, anti-lynching legislation, outlawing segregation in facilities servicing interstate transportation, and further protection for the right to vote.

As might be expected, Truman's message ignited a political firestorm in the American South. Bitterly opposed to his proposals, white Southern Democrats attempted to deny Truman their party's presidential nomination. When that failed, they formed the States' Rights or Dixiecrat Party, and nominated Strom Thurmond of South Carolina for president. Although 82 percent of the American people were reportedly opposed to the presidents' civil rights program, Truman defeated Thurmond and Republican Thomas E. Dewey in the November election. The Dixiecrats were unable to prevent Truman's election, but their allies in Congress did successfully block Truman's civil rights measures from becoming law. In the face of congressional inaction and the hatred of Southern reactionaries, the president remained unbowed. On July 26, 1948, Truman issued two executive orders that weakened the bonds of legalized segregation. Executive Order 9980 required all federal departments to ensure equal employment opportunities for all applicants regardless of race, color, religion, or national origin and established a Fair Employment Board to oversee compliance. The second, Executive Order 9981, was even more radical.

For decades, one of the most segregated institutions in the country was the U.S. military. Denied opportunities to advance, most black servicemen were prevented from service in combat units and were allowed only to engage in menial activities. In the Marines, for example, blacks could only enlist as kitchen personnel, while in the army, only one African American in 70 was a commissioned officer. Appalled by this, Truman ordered military commanders to integrate the armed forces. High-ranking military leaders, most notably army chief of staff General Omar Bradley, bitterly denounced the plan, but again Truman refused to back down. Before the end of his presidency in January 1953, Truman also appointed African American lawyer William Hastie to the U.S. Court of Appeals and integrated federal housing programs.

Truman was the first American chief executive to commit the power of the federal government to the elimination of legalized segregation. Although conservatives in Congress blocked most of his civil rights programs, Truman courageously ignored Southern reactionaries such as the Dixiecrats and integrated both the armed forces and federal bureaucracy. At the same time, in calling attention to the discriminatory nature of Jim Crow segregation through the creation of the Presidential Committee on Civil Rights and his address to the NAACP, Truman laid bare the plight of African Americans and emboldened their struggle to achieve social and political equality.

WAYNE DOWDY

See also

Executive Order 9808

Further Reading:

Gardner, Michael R. *Harry Truman and Civil Rights: Moral Courage and Political Risks.* Carbondale: Southern Illinois University Press, 2002.

"Harry S. Truman." In *Civil Rights in the United States*, edited by Waldo E. Martin Jr. and Patricia Sullivan, 2 vols. New York: Macmillan Reference USA, 2000.

"President's Committee on Civil Rights." In *Civil Rights in the United States*, edited by Waldo E. Martin Jr. and Patricia Sullivan, 2 vols. New York: Macmillan Reference USA, 2000.

To Secure These Rights: The Report of the President's Committee on Civil Rights. http://www.trumanlibrary.org/civilrights/srights1.htm (accessed May 31, 2007).

Tulsa (Oklahoma) Riot of 1921

The Tulsa Riot of 1921 was the last of the World War I era race riots. Like many of the other riots, from East St. Louis in 1917 to the riots of the summer of 1919 in such places as Chicago; Elaine, Arkansas; Omaha, Nebraska; and Washington, D.C., it involved an attack on an African American community. Like those other riots, the causes were both long-standing conflicts between the expectations of the white community and the increasing prosperity and self-confidence of the African American community. African American communities organized to protect themselves against racial violence.

In September 1920, following a lynching of a young African American man in Oklahoma City, the *Tulsa Star*, Tulsa's leading African American newspaper, criticized the Oklahoma City community for not doing more to prevent the lynching. The *Tulsa Star* boldly stated that Oklahoma City residents had the legal right, indeed, duty to take action to protect against lynchings. They had the right to take life if necessary to uphold the law. Leaders of Tulsa's African American section, Greenwood, frequently met in the Williams' Dreamland Theater to discuss the ideas of the Harlem Renaissance, particularly how to respond to violence and threatened lynchings. Moreover, many of those leaders were veterans of World War I.

The *Tulsa Tribune* reported on May 31, 1921, that a young African American man, Dick Rowland, had attempted to attack a young white woman, Mary Paige, the day before. That led a mob to collect at the Tulsa courthouse that evening. Simultaneously, African American men met in Greenwood to discuss how to protect Rowland. They decided to make a trip to the courthouse and offer to help protect Rowland. When several dozen African American veterans appeared at the courthouse that evening, a police officer tried to disarm them; gunfire ensued, and the riot began. Throughout the evening, the local units of the Oklahoma National Guard and the police department worked to devise a plan to disarm and arrest everyone in Greenwood. The police department hastily deputized hundreds of white men, and those who did not have guns were issued them by the police department. Meanwhile, throughout the night, there was fighting across the railroad tracks that separated white Tulsa from the Greenwood section.

The next morning, the police, their deputies, and the local units of the National Guard crossed the railroad tracks in Greenwood. Amid sometimes fierce fighting, this force methodically moved through Greenwood. Thousands of Greenwood residents were arrested and taken into custody into detention camps. Others who did not go willingly were shot. As the residents of Greenwood were taken into custody, their homes were looted and burned. By noon, units of the Oklahoma National Guard based in Oklahoma City had begun to restore order. Even as the riot itself died out, the process of restoring order remained. Thousands of Greenwood residents were held in the camps around the city until a white employer vouched for them.

Despite their release, there were few places to go given that dozens of blocks of Greenwood were destroyed. Thousands of people were left homeless and for months they lived in tents provided by the Red Cross. Many residents left Tulsa and headed for cities like Chicago, St. Louis, Kansas City, and Los Angeles. While the Red Cross provided assistance and some Tulsa leaders pledged to rebuild, Tulsa's mayor proposed a plan to relocate Greenwood farther away from downtown Tulsa and to require expensive fireproof materials in rebuilding. Some Greenwood residents attempted to sue the city and their insurance companies, which frequently denied coverage on insurance policies citing riot exclusion clauses. The lawsuits were uniformly unsuccessful. Greenwood residents who stayed rebuilt using their own resources.

As memory of the riot receded in public consciousness, decades later the Tulsa Riot would again become news. In 1982, historian Scott Ellsworth's book *Death in a Promised Land*, a study of the riot, was published. In the late 1990s, state representative Don Ross introduced a bill in the Oklahoma legislature that established a commission to study the riot. The commission's report, issued in 2001, presented the most comprehensive picture of the riot available; it also led to major controversy around the issue of whether the legislature should pay reparations to riot victims. The Oklahoma legislature issued an apology in 2001, but offered nothing in terms of payments to riot survivors.

In response, in 2003, lawyers led by Harvard Law School professor Charles Ogletree filed a lawsuit against the city and state, alleging that they were liable for much of the damage during the riot. The city and state responded that the lawsuit was filed too late. In 2004, the U.S. District Court in Tulsa dismissed the lawsuit, and the U.S. Court of Appeals upheld the dismissal. The Supreme Court refused to hear the case. In April 2007, U.S. representative John Conyers introduced a bill in the House of Representatives that would allow the lawsuit to go forward. In 2009, Conyers also introduced a bill, H.R.1843 John Hope Franklin Tulsa-Greenwood Race Riot Claims Accountability Act of 2009, which if passed, would give restitution to survivors of the riot or their descendants.

ALFRED L. BROPHY

See also

Detroit (Michigan) Riot of 1967; Race Riots in America; White Flight. Documents: Report on the Memphis Riots of May 1866 (1866); Account of the Riots in East St. Louis, Illinois (1917); A Southern Black Woman's Letter Regarding the Recent Riots in Chicago and Washington (1919); The Cook County Coroner's Report Regarding the 1919 Chicago Race Riots (1920); The Final Report of the Grand Jury on the Tulsa Race Riot (June 25, 1921); Testimony from *Laney v. United States* (1923); The Governor's Commission Report on the Watts Riots (1965); Cyrus R. Vance's Report on the Riots in Detroit (1967); The Reports of the Oklahoma Commission to Study the Tulsa Race Riot of 1921 (2000–2001); Draft Report: 1898 Wilmington Race Riot Commission (2005)

Further Reading:

Brophy, Alfred L. *Reconstructing the Dreamland: The Tulsa Riot of 1921.* New York: Oxford University Press, 2002.

Ellsworth, Scott. *Death in a Promised Land: The Tulsa Riot of 1921.* Baton Rouge: Louisiana State University Press, 1982.

Oklahoma Commission to Study the Tulsa Race Riot of 1921. "Tulsa Race Riot: A Report by the Oklahoma Commission to Study the Tulsa Race Riot of 1921." Oklahoma City: The Commission, 2001.

Turner, Henry McNeal (1834–1915)

Henry McNeal Turner was a leading proponent of black emigration to Africa as a response to the hostile conditions in the American South during the 19th century. Turner was a bishop of the African Methodist Episcopal (AME) Church, a delegate to the Georgia constitutional convention, a member of the Georgia state legislature, founder and president of Morris Brown College in Georgia, and founder of several newspapers. His life spanned a troubled period—slavery, the Civil War, Reconstruction, and the ensuing Jim Crow era. In his early years, an optimistic Turner joined the Union Army and was a member of the Freedmen's Bureau and the Republican Party. Rampant violence and racism, along with other critical events, caused Turner to launch an anti-America and pro-Africa campaign. Eventually becoming a bitter and disillusioned man, he turned to Africa as the only viable way for blacks to escape the mass violence and debilitating and racist laws in America, and to achieve dignity and self-empowerment.

Turner was born free in 1834 near Abbeville, South Carolina. In his youth, he worked in the cotton fields. After running away from home, he did janitorial work in a law office. Despite laws that forbade education for blacks, the white clerks taught him to read and write. In 1853, he received a preacher's license and evangelized throughout the

South for the white-controlled Methodist Episcopal (ME) Church, South. In 1856, he married Eliza Preacher, the first of four wives. Only four of Turner's 14 children survived into adulthood.

Exasperated by the constraints placed on him by the ME church, South, Turner joined the AME Church in 1858. He preached in St. Louis, Missouri; Baltimore, Maryland; and Washington, D.C. While on the East Coast, Turner studied Latin, Greek, Hebrew, and theology. In 1860, Turner formed the first black army troop from Washington, D.C., and was assigned by President Abraham Lincoln to be its chaplain. Turner was the first black to do so in the nation. He fought valiantly alongside his troops.

After the war, Turner, envisioning a grand future for blacks, accepted President Andrew Johnson's invitation to work with the Freedmen's Bureau in Georgia to assist the newly freed slaves. After encountering racism in the bureau, Turner resigned and spent the years from 1865 to 1867 organizing AME churches in Georgia. Turner was not discouraged, despite the escalating violence against blacks across the South during the aftermath of the Civil War. In 1866, the Ku Klux Klan (KKK), one of many formal and informal vigilante organizations, was formed. The KKK terrorized and attacked blacks accused of crimes—or for no reason at all. Also in 1866, riots erupted in New Orleans, Louisiana, and Memphis, Tennessee. In the same year, Turner gave a roseate speech at the Emancipation Day Anniversary Celebration in Augusta, Georgia, in which he explained jubilantly that their new freedom had released blacks from living in turmoil, fear, and uncertainty, and that, in due time and with honest effort, they could attain equality with whites and eliminate racism.

Despite Turner's initial optimism, life after Emancipation was precarious and brutal for blacks, and equality was as intangible as it had been during slavery. The first major event to squash Turner's faith in the future of blacks in the United States occurred in 1868 when whites refused to admit him and other black representatives into the legislature. He responded with a bold, impassioned, and eloquent speech, but to no avail. Turner was devastated. Compounding the situation was the fact that all across the South, white Democrats, abetted by private mobs, were violently seizing back political control, and the federal government was withdrawing Union troops. In 1883, the U.S. Supreme Court did away with seminal Civil Rights Act laws that forbade discrimination in hotels, trains, and other public places.

Infuriated, Turner unleashed a scathing attack on the United States, and on the heinous laws and atrocities inflicted on blacks, through numerous speeches, sermons, letters, and writings. He castigated America—and any individual, black or white—for withholding the protection, rights, and freedoms due to blacks. He lambasted white mobs for cruelly lynching blacks without due process of law. He discouraged black self-defense, since whites often outnumbered and outarmed their victims. He advocated the idea that blacks could only find peace, freedom, self-respect, and equality by establishing their own nation in Africa. He insisted that the American government should make reparations for the years blacks had toiled without pay during slavery by financing their emigration to Africa.

In 1893, Turner organized a national convention for blacks in Cincinnati, Ohio. The objective was to address the mob violence, lynchings, and other crimes against blacks, which had intensified. Turner advocated emigration, but the majority of blacks present were not interested in leaving the country to solve the problems that beset them. This was one of the major reasons that Turner's back-to-Africa strategy was not successful. Turner's Black Nationalism only interested a small number of poor farmers. It did not attract grand-scale support. Furthermore, blacks, unable to acclimate to life in Africa, often returned to the United States. Nevertheless, Turner was one of the most daring and outspoken black leaders of his time, a man who challenged the ruthless violence and injustices inflicted on blacks.

GLADYS L. KNIGHT

See also

Great Migration, The; Jim Crow Laws; Reconstruction Era; Vigilantism

Further Reading:

Redkey, Edwin S., ed. *Respect Black: Writings and Speeches of Henry M. Turner*. New York: Arno Press, 1971.

Tuskegee Experiment

The *Tuskegee Study of Syphilis in the Negro Male*, better known as the Tuskegee Syphilis Study, was one of the most reprehensible and controversial scientific studies involving human subjects ever conducted in the United States. The study was conducted from 1932–1972 in Macon County, Alabama. The blistering racial climate that characterized much of the Deep South during this period accounted for the exploitation of the 399 black men selected to participate in the study of untreated tertiary syphilis in black men. Because blacks were believed to be unkempt, unsanitary, and libidinous, the high incidences of syphilis among African Americans in Macon County was believed to have extended from these variables. The high rate of poverty and illiteracy made Macon County residents vulnerable to exploitation by the U.S. Public Health Service, which provided long-term funding for the project.

Entrenched in scientific racism, the impetus behind the Tuskegee Syphilis Study was a desire to prove that syphilis had different effects on African Americans than on whites. Whites were believed to suffer more from the neurological complications of the disease in its latent phase, whereas blacks were believed to suffer more from its cardiovascular effects. Late 19th- and early 20th-century scientific curiosities about certain physiological aspects of African Americans (for example, cranial size as a measurement of intellect), in addition to blacks' presumed susceptibility and/or resistance to certain diseases (pellagra, malaria) aided in the justification of the experiment. Thus, when the syphilis epidemic struck in the mid-1920s, it was immediately called a "black disease" as a result of the prominence of the disease among African Americans. By 1932, when the study began as an offspring of earlier syphilis studies throughout the South, the medical community was wedded to the belief that certain diseases were racially specific in regard to their effects.

The Tuskegee Study, in particular, was a continuation of the Oslo Study conducted by Dr. E. Bruusgaard, chief of the Venereal Disease Clinic in Oslo, Norway, from 1891 to 1910. The Oslo Study was designed to show the effects of untreated syphilis in whites. The primary justification for the Tuskegee Study was to observe the effects of untreated syphilis in African Americans in an effort to juxtapose scientific findings with the earlier Oslo Study.

Macon County, Alabama, was a gold mine for researchers who wanted to learn more about syphilis. In the 1920s, the U.S. Public Health Service (PHS), with help from the Rosenwald Fund, set out to perform syphilis

Herman Shaw, a Tuskegee experiment victim, smiles after receiving an official apology from President Bill Clinton on May 16, 1997, in Washington, D.C. Making amends for the shameful federal experiment, Clinton apologized to African American men whose syphilis went untreated by government doctors. (AP/Wide World Photos)

demonstrations throughout the South. The demonstrations were intended to test individuals for the disease to obtain an estimate of infected carriers. When the Great Depression struck in the 1930s, however, there was no funding to treat the subjects. Researchers did not want to completely abort their efforts, however, and started to apply their efforts toward the examination of the effects of *untreated* syphilis on black males.

When the study began in the early 1930s, there was no reliable cure for syphilis. The syphilitic subjects in the Tuskegee Study were provided some minor treatment that consisted of mercury and salvarsan, which was highly toxic and ineffective. The toxicity and unreliability of the early treatments were the basis for PHS officials denying treatment altogether. Even with the introduction of penicillin during the 1940s, the study subjects were still denied treatment. As compensation for their cooperation, the men were offered incentives such as free physical exams, transportation to and from the clinic, meals after examinations, free medical treatment for nonsyphilis-related illnesses, and the promise that burial stipends would be provided to patients' families. Many of the men were unaware of the severity of their medical condition and were merely told that they had "bad blood," a term that was applied to virtually every ailment. Eunice Rivers served as the nurse in the experiment from its inception to its collapse in 1972, when Jean Heller of the *Washington Star* published the story.

Rivers was employed by the PHS to monitor the study participants. She was in many ways a cultural mediator, "bridging the many barriers that stemmed from the educational and cultural gap between the physicians and the subjects." The study participants trusted Rivers and were unaware that she was partially responsible for their detainment. Rivers never openly contested the experiment and, to secure employment, cooperated with the PHS and doctors' orders.

Because of the Tuskegee Syphilis Study, the medical community has tightened restrictions on experiments involving human subjects. Internal review boards have been established on college campuses and elsewhere to monitor the efficacy and legitimacy of such experiments. The enforcement of certain mandates and restrictions to regulate human experimentation has proved beneficial in preventing studies similar to the Tuskegee experiment.

TALITHA L. LEFLOURIA

See also
Racism

Further Reading:
Gray, Fred D. *The Tuskegee Syphilis Study: The Real Story and Beyond*. Montgomery, AL: Black Belt Press, 1998.

Jones, James H. *Bad Blood: The Tuskegee Syphilis Experiment*. New York: Free Press, 1993.

Reverby, Susan M., ed. *Tuskegee's Truths: Rethinking the Tuskegee Syphilis Study*. Chapel Hill: University of North Carolina Press, 2000.

United States Commission on Civil Rights, Alabama Advisory Committee. *The Tuskegee Study: A Report of the Alabama Committee to the United States Commission on Civil Rights*. Washington, DC: United States Public Health Service, 1973.

U.S. Department of Health, Education, and Welfare. *Tuskegee Syphilis Study Ad Hoc Advisory Panel, Final Report*. Washington, DC: United States Public Health Service, 1973.